A SYSTEMATIC APPROACH TO BUSINESS JAPANESE

Masato Kikuchi

University Press of America,® Inc.
Lanham · New York · Oxford

Copyright © 2002 by
University Press of America,® Inc.
4720 Boston Way
Lanham, Maryland 20706
UPA Acquisitions Department (301) 459-3366

PO Box 317
Oxford
OX2 9RU, UK

All rights reserved

British Library Cataloging in Publication Information Available

Library of Congress Cataloging-in-Publication Data

Kikuchi, Masato, 1956-
A systematic approach to business Japanese / Masato Kikuchi.
p. cm
Includes indexes.
1. Japanese language—Conversation and phrase books (for business people) 2. Japanese language—Business Japanese. I. Title.

PL539 .K48 2002
495.6'83421'02465—dc21   2002026721 CIP

ISBN 978-0-7618-2370-4 (pbk.)

Contents

Acknowledgments	vii
Introduction	ix
Organization of each chapter	ix
Basic vocabulary, expressions, and grammar	x
Abbreviations used in this textbook	xix
About writing symbols	xx
Additional resources	xx
Chapter 1: Job Interview	**1**
Conversation 1A: Mr. Harris goes to a job interview. (1)	2
Conversation 1B: The reason for applying for a job (2)	3
Conversation 1C: Why work for a Japanese company? (3)	7
Conversation 1D: Extracurricular activities and hobbies (4)	10
Conversation 1E: Mr. Harris leaves the interview. (5)	12
Exercise 1	17
Chapter 2: Business Introduction	**29**
Conversation 2A: Mr. Harris meets his boss.	30
Conversation 2B: Mr. Harris' first job	33
Conversation 2C: Writing a training report	35
Conversation 2D: Introduction 1	38
Conversation 2E: Introduction 2	39

    Exercise 2   42

Chapter 3: Telephone   **50**

    Conversation 3A: Answering phone calls   51

    Conversation 3B: Transferring calls   52

    Conversation 3C: Apologizing (1)   54

    Conversation 3D: Apologies (2)   57

    Conversation 3E: Taking messages (1)   59

    Conversation 3F: Taking messages (2)   61

    Exercise 3   67

Chapter 4: Reports   **77**

    Conversation 4A: Conveying phone messages   78

    Conversation 4B: Reporting what happened (1)   82

    Conversation 4C: Reporting what happened (2)   83

    Conversation 4D: Reporting on a meeting (1)   84

    Exercise 4   90

Chapter 5: At the Bank   **101**

    Conversation 5A: Going to a bank   102

    Conversation 5B: Opening a new blank account   103

    Conversation 5C: Making an ATM card   105

    Conversation 5D: Requesting automatic fund transfer service   106

    Conversation 5E: Foreign currency exchange service   107

    Conversation 5F: Troubleshooting 1   108

    Conversation 5G: Troubleshooting 2   109

    Exercise 5   111

Chapter 6: "Work" after Work   **122**

    Conversation 6A: An invitation to a welcome party   123

    Conversation 6B: Mr. Harris goes to a second party. (1)   128

    Conversation 6C: After the welcome party   132

Exercise 6	135
Chapter 7: Appointments	**146**
Conversation 7A: Making an appointment (1)	147
Conversation 7B: Making an appointment (2)	148
Conversation 7C: Making an appointment (3)	150
Conversation 7D: Mr. Harris' friend (1)	153
Conversation 7E: Mr. Harris' friend (2)	156
Exercise 7	160
Chapter 8: Describing a Company	**170**
Conversation 8A: Mr. Harris reunites with Ms. Lewis.	171
Conversation 8B: Ms. Lewis introduces her company. (1)	172
Conversation 8C: Ms. Lewis introduces her company. (2)	175
Exercise 8	180
Chapter 9: Describing Products	**186**
Conversation 9A: Ms. Lewis demonstrates her product. (1)	187
Conversation 9B: Ms. Lewis demonstrates her product. (2)	191
Conversation 9C: Ms. Lewis demonstrates her product. (3)	193
Exercise 9	197
Chapter 10: Negotiating Prices	**205**
Conversation 10A: Ms. Lewis negotiates prices. (1)	206
Conversation 10B: Ms. Lewis negotiates prices. (2)	207
Conversation 10C: Mr. Tanaka anticipates oppositions. (1)	209
Exercise 10	213
Chapter 11: Concluding Negotiations	**218**
Conversation 11A: Price competition starts.	219
Conversation 11B: Mr. Yamada needs to fill in the details.	220
Conversation 11C: Finally, a decision is reached.	223

Exercise 11	226
Appendix A: Kanji Index	233
Appendix B: Japanese-English Glossary	244
Appendix C: English-Japanese Glossary	276
Appendix D: Grammar Index (English Headers/Alphabetical Order)	298
Appendix E: Grammar Index (English Headers/Appearance Order)	300
Appendix F: Grammar Index (Japanese Headers/あいうえお Order)	303
Appendix G: Grammar Index (Japanese Headers/Appearance Order)	305

Acknowledgments

The idea of writing this textbook was born in 1994 when we started to prepare for a summer program called "Language for Business and Technology (LBAT)" at Georgia Institute of Technology. We were expected to build three new courses simultaneously (Business Japanese, Technical and Scientific Japanese, and Japan Today) for the program, and we needed a textbook for Business Japanese. We studied available textbooks then and came to a conclusion that none of them would completely meet our requirements to provide classroom-based, structured instruction to university students in an intensive learning environment like ours. Consequently, we wrote our first textbook in 1995. This textbook has been field-tested in our program but has never been published until now. Since then, many modifications have been added to the original textbook and new online materials have been prepared on our web site. This textbook represents the results of our continuing efforts to improve the quality of language instruction for Business Japanese.

I would like to thank everyone who gave me valuable comments and recommendations regarding the content of this textbook. Especially, my gratitude goes:

to Dr. Rumiko Shinzato, my mentor and associate, who has been the driving force behind all aspects of writing this textbook including the grammar explanations and conversations;

to Ms. Atsuko Ohashi, a former banker, M.B.A. from Georgia Tech, who provided insights into the Japanese banking industry and created some of the initial conversations;

to Ms. Masako Kanno, M.A. from the Ohio State University and my associate, who has been patiently field-testing this textbook in her classes at Georgia Tech;

to Dr. Kathy Negrelli, a former associate of our program, who currently teaches at Roswell High School and Elkins Pointe Middle School while developing and coordinating the Japanese program for graduates of the model Japanese program at Mimosa Elementary School in Roswell, Georgia;

to Mr. Teruhisa Ishino, a retired business executive at one of the Japanese banks;

to the Japanese-language students, particularly in the LBAT program at Georgia Tech, whose questions and answers to the class affected the content of this book;

to all volunteers and teaching staff who helped me create additional resources for the textbook.

In addition, I am deeply grateful to my wife, Yuko, and my daughter, Yuka, who understood me, encouraged me and even put up with me during all those days when I had to devote myself to research and was unable to provide ファミリーサービス ("family service"). This book was never possible without their patience and support.

Masato Kikuchi

Introduction

This textbook is designed to help you build a good grammatical foundation, acquire business terminology, refine discourse styles and increase sensitivity to corporate culture in Japan. The intended audience of this textbook is intermediate-level learners of Japanese. Here, an "intermediate" learner is defined as someone who has completed a one-year, university-level, general-purpose Japanese program or its equivalent. If you are a beginner of Japanese, please read the summary of basic grammar and vocabulary below carefully before proceeding to the first chapter.

Language structures used in business contexts are more complex than the structures used in everyday, general-purpose Japanese. Business Japanese reflects hierarchical relationships of the business world (e.g., a subordinate worker speaking with a section chief). In addition, business Japanese reflects distinctions between in-group (うち) and out-group (そと) (e.g., a member of company X speaking with a member of another company Y). Students of business Japanese need to identify specific business relationships and to understand how they affect the choice of language in a given context (e.g., You, as marketing manager of company X, call a section manager of the sales department of company Y to make an appointment.).

The arrangement of themes and grammar

The themes of this textbook are arranged as if a story of an American college graduate hired by a Japanese corporation unfolds in Japan. Grammatical structures are systematically sequenced according to the complexity of the structures. For example, if Structure X is required to understand Structure Y, Structure X is introduced always before Structure Y is introduced. New structures in the model conversations are always explained within each chapter. Each model conversation was made as natural and authentic as possible under these constraints. The textbook also contains references to sociological factors that affect the language styles.

Organization of each chapter

Each chapter consists of the following sections. Long conversations are divided into several parts. Each conversation is followed by kanji introduction, vocabulary, and grammar explanations. An exercise section is located at the end of each chapter.

> **Priming**   This provides you with background information to facilitate the understanding of the conversations that follow.

Conversation 1A: Title of the conversation

Vocabulary 1A
This section introduces the definition of new words.

Structures 1A
Grammar explanations for the new structures introduced in the conversation are provided here.

Additional conversations (1B, 1C, 1D, etc.) will follow the first conversation. Whenever relevant, culture notes are attached in a footnote with the heading: 文化ノート. At the end of all conversations and the subsequent grammar explanations, Exercise sections will follow.

Exercise

This section provides Grammar Utilization Exercises, Reading-Writing Exercises, Communicative Exercises and Listening Comprehension. This last section provides additional dialogues to test your listening abilities. Dialogues for listening activities are available from the web site shown at the end of this section under **Additional Resources**.

Basic vocabulary, expressions, and grammar

This textbook assumes that students are familiar with the following vocabulary and grammatical structures.

1. Basic Greetings

1. おはようございます。 — Good morning!
2. こんにちは。 — Hello! Good afternoon!
3. こんばんは。 — Good evening!
4. おやすみなさい。 — Good night.
5. じゃ、また（あした）。→さようなら。 — See you again (tomorrow). → Good bye!
6. どうも。→あ、いいえ。 — Thanks. → Oh, not at all.
7. ありがとうございます。→どういたしまして。 — Thank you. →You are welcome.

Apologies are used frequently in Japan. In (10), すみません literally means "I'm sorry (for not reciprocating your kind act)." Apologies are higher forms of showing appreciation.

8. あ、どうも、すみません。→いえいえ、いいんですよ。 — Oh, I'm sorry. →No, no, that's all right.
9. しつれいしました。→いえいえ、こちらこそ。 — I'm sorry [Lit. I was rude].→No, I (was rude).
10. どうも、すみません。→どういたしまして。 — Thank you. →No, not at all.
11. しつれいします。→どうぞ。 — Excuse me (when entering a room). →Please (come in).
12. しつれいします。→おつかれさま。 — Excuse me (when leaving). →Take care.
13. ごめんください。 — Excuse me (said at the door/entrance way).
14. しつれいしました。→あ、いえいえ。 — Excuse me (for having done something rude). →Oh, not at all.
15. はい／ええ／うん — Yes (うん is casual.)
16. いいえ／いや／ううん — No (ううん is casual.)
17. はい — Here you go!/Here it is!

2. Numbers and Counters

	long	bound	flat	general	people	minutes
0	ゼロほん・れいほん ０本・０本	ゼロ・れい ０さつ・０さつ	ゼロ・れい ０まい・０まい	ゼロ・れい ０	ゼロにん・れいにん ０人・０人	ゼロふん・れいふん ０分・０分
1	いっぽん 一本	いっ 一さつ	いち 一まい	ひと 一つ	ひとり 一人	いっぷん 一分
2	に 二本	に 二さつ	に 二まい	ふた 二つ	ふたり 二人	にふん 二分
3	さんぼん 三本	さん 三さつ	さん 三まい	みっ 三つ	さんにん 三人	さんぷん 三分
4	よんほん 四本	よん 四さつ	よん 四まい	よっ 四つ	よにん 四人	よんぷん 四分
5	ごほん 五本	ご 五さつ	ご 五まい	いつ 五つ	ごにん 五人	ごふん 五分
6	ろっぽん 六本	ろく 六さつ	ろく 六まい	むっ 六つ	ろくにん 六人	ろっぷん 六分
7	しちほん・ななほん 七本・七本	しちさつ・ななさつ 七さつ・七さつ	なな 七まい	なな 七つ	しちにん・ななにん 七人・七人	しちふん・ななふん 七分・七分
8	はちほん・はっぽん 八本・八本	はちさつ・はっ 八さつ・八さつ	はち 八まい	やっ 八つ	はちにん 八人	はちふん・はっぷん 八分・八分
9	きゅうほん 九本	きゅう 九さつ	きゅう 九まい	ここの 九つ	きゅうにん・くにん 九人・九人	きゅうふん 九分

10	じゅっぽん・じっぽん 十本・十本	じゅっさつ・じっさつ 十さつ・十さつ	じゅう 十まい	とお 十	じゅうにん 十人	じゅっぷん・じっぷん 十分・十分
100	ひゃっぽん 百本	ひゃく 百さつ	ひゃく 百まい		ひゃくにん 百人	ひゃっぷん 百分
1,000	せんぼん 千本	せん 千さつ	せん 千まい		せんにん 千人	せんぷん 千分
10,000	いちまんぼん 一万本	いちまん 一万さつ	いちまん 一万まい		いちまんにん 一万人	いちまんぷん 一万分
?	なんぼん 何本？	なん 何さつ？	なん 何まい？	いくつ？	なんにん 何人？	なんぷん 何分？

3. Time Counters

Date and clock		Duration	
しょうわ 昭和	Showa Era (1926-1989)		
へいせい 平成	Heisei Era (1989-to present)		
ねん 〜年	the year	ねん かん 〜年（間）	years
がつ 〜月	the month	げつ かん 〜か月（間）	months
		しゅうかん 〜週間	weeks
にち 〜日	the day of the month	にち かん 〜日（間）	days
じ 〜時	the hour	じかん 〜時間	hours
ぷん 〜分	the minute	ぷん かん 〜分（間）	minutes
なんねん 何年？	what year?	なんねん かん 何年（間）？	how many years?
なんがつ 何月？	what month?	なん げつ かん 何か月（間）？	how many months?
なんにち 何日？	what date?	なんにち かん 何日（間）？	how many days?
なんじ 何時？	what time/hour?	なん じかん 何時間？	how many hours?
なんぷん 何分？	what time?	なんぷん かん 何分（間）？	how many minutes?

| 1999 | せんきゅうひゃくきゅうじゅうきゅうねん
千九百九十九年
or
せんきゅうひゃくきゅうじゅうきゅうねん
一九九九年 | 2000 | にせんねん
二千年
or
にせんねん
二〇〇〇年 | 2001 | にせんいちねん
二千一年
or
にせんいちねん
二〇〇一年 | 2002 | にせんにねん
二千二年
or
にせんにねん
二〇〇二年 |

4. Relative Time

Present - 2	Present - 1	Present	Present + 1	Present + 2	Every
	きょねん 去年	ことし 今年	らいねん 来年	さらいねん 再来年	まいねん／まいとし 毎年／毎年
せんせんげつ 先先月	せんげつ 先月	こんげつ 今月	らいげつ 来月	さらいげつ 再来月	まいつき 毎月
せんせんしゅう 先先週	せんしゅう 先週	こんしゅう 今週	らいしゅう 来週	さらいしゅう 再来週	まいしゅう 毎週
おととい	きのう 昨日	きょう いま 今日／今	あした 明日	あさって	まいにち 毎日

5. Calendar

Sunday	Monday	Tuesday	Wednesday	Thursday	Friday	Saturday
にちようび 日曜日	げつようび 月曜日	かようび 火曜日	すいようび 水曜日	もくようび 木曜日	きんようび 金曜日	どようび 土曜日
1 ついたち 一日	2 ふつか 二日	3 みっか 三日	4 よっか 四日	5 いつか 五日	6 むいか 六日	7 なのか 七日
8 ようか 八日	9 ここのか 九日	10 とおか 十日	11 じゅういちにち 十一日	12 じゅうににち 十二日	13 じゅうさんにち 十三日	14 じゅうよっか 十四日

15 じゅうごにち 十五日	16 じゅうろくにち 十六日	17 じゅうしちにち 十七日	18 じゅうはちにち 十八日	19 じゅうくにち 十九日	20 はつか 二十日	21 にじゅういちにち 二十一日
22 にじゅうににち 二十二日	23 にじゅうさんにち 二十三日	24 にじゅうよっか 二十四日	25 にじゅうごにち 二十五日	26 にじゅうろくにち 二十六日	27 にじゅうしちにち 二十七日	28 にじゅうはちにち 二十八日
29 にじゅうきゅうにち 二十九日	30 さんじゅうにち 三十日	31 さんじゅういちにち 三十一日				

6. Pronouns

Noun Forms		Prenominal Forms				Adverbial Forms	
これ	this one	この	this	こんな	this kind of	こう	this way
それ	that one near you	その	that	そんな	that kind of	そう	that way
あれ	that one far away	あの	that	あんな	that kind of	ああ	that way
どれ？	which one?	どの？	which?	どんな？	what kind of?	どう？	what way/how?

Noun Forms		Noun Forms	
ここ	here, this place	こちら	this side (near me)
そこ	there, that place	そちら	that side (near you)
あそこ	over there, that place	あちら	that side (over there)
どこ？	where?	どちら？	which side?

7. "Alphabetical" Order in Japanese and Verb Conjugation

The alphabetical order in Japanese is called あいうえお order. Knowing this order helps you look up words in the Japanese dictionary and predict verb conjugation forms.

		k/g	s/z/j	t/d	n	h/b/p	m	y	r	w	nn*
a	あ	か／が	さ／ざ	た／だ	な	は／ば／ぱ	ま	や	ら	わ	ん
i	い	き／ぎ	し／じ	ち／ぢ	に	ひ／び／ぴ	み		り		
u	う	く／ぐ	す／ず	つ／づ	ぬ	ふ／ぶ／ぷ	む	ゆ	る		
e	え	け／げ	せ／ぜ	て／で	ね	へ／べ／ぺ	め		れ		
o	お	こ／ご	そ／ぞ	と／ど	の	ほ／ぼ／ぽ	も	よ	ろ	を	

* The ん symbol represents a syllable by itself.

The following table is similar to the table above and contains only the sounds that occur in verb conjugation. Vowel verbs (also called る verbs) and irregular verbs are exceptions. You must be familiar with all forms but the last two rows. The last two rows will be explained in subsequent chapters.

Verb Forms	k/g	s	t	n	b	m	r	w	Examples	Exceptions
negative	か／が	さ	た	な	ば	ま	ら	わ	書かない 言わない	食べない 来ない／しない
ます	き／ぎ	し	ち	に	び	み	り	い	書きます 言います	食べます 来ます／します
dictionary	く／ぐ	す	つ	ぬ	ぶ	む	る	う	書く 言う	食べる 来る／する
provisional	け／げ	せ	て	ね	べ	め	れ	え	書けば 言えば	食べれば 来れば／すれば
volitional	こ／ご	そ	と	の	ぼ	も	ろ	を	書こう 言おう	食べよう 来よう／しよう

Introduction

Here is a rule of thumb to predict verb conjugation by using the table above. First, remove ます from the ます form (e.g., 書きます→かき). This (e.g., 書き) is called the stem of the verb.

Rule 1. If the stem ends in a "...e" sound (e.g., 食べ／ます tabe-masu), it is a vowel verb (=る verb).
add る (e.g., 食べる) to get the dictionary form (plain-affirmative).
add ない (e.g., 食べない) to create the plain-negative form.

Rule 2. If the stem ends in a "...i" sound (e.g., 書き／ます kaki-masu), it is a consonant verb (=う verb).
use the sound in Row 3 (e.g., 書く) to create the dictionary form.
use the sound in Row 1 (e.g., 書かない) to create the plain-negative form.

Exceptions to Rule 2: (1) Two irregular verbs (来ます "come" & します "do") do not follow Rule 2. (2) One-syllable verb stems (e.g., 見／ます, い／ます) behave like "...e" sound verbs (Rule 1 or vowel or る verbs). Thus, 見ます→見ない／見る and います→いない／いる.

Predict the ない form and the dictionary form of the following verbs.

		dictionary form (plain affirmative)	**ない form** (plain negative)
使います	use		
帰ります	return		
行きます	go		
話します	speak		
待ちます	wait		
急ぎます	hurry		
飲みます	drink		
呼びます	summon		
言います	say		
変えます	change		
出ます	go out		

8. Irregular Verbs

		Polite-Affirmative	Polite-Negative	Plain-Affirmative	Plain-Negative
Non-past	do	します	しません	する	しない
Past		しました	しませんでした	した	しなかった
て form				して	しなくて
Non-past	come	来ます	来ません	来る	来ない
Past		来ました	来ませんでした	来た	来なかった
て form				来て	来なくて

9. Vowel verbs (also known as る-verbs; The root ends in a vowel "e" or "i").

		Root	Polite-Affirmative	Polite-Negative	Plain-Affirmative	Plain-Negative
Non-past	eat	tabe	食べます	食べません	食べる	食べない
Past			食べました	食べませんでした	食べた	食べなかった

						食べて	食べなくて
Non-past	look, watch	mi		見ます	見ません	見る	見ない
Past				見ました	見ません	見た	見なかった
て form						見て	見なくて

10. Consonant verbs (also known as う-verbs; The root ends in a consonant.)

		Root	Polite-Affirmative	Polite-Negative	Plain-Affirmative	Plain-Negative
Non-past	call, summon	yob	呼びます	呼びません	呼ぶ	呼ばない
Past			呼びました	呼びませんでした	呼んだ	呼ばなかった
て form					呼んで	呼ばなくて
Non-past	hurry	isog	急ぎます	急ぎません	急ぐ	急がない
Past			急ぎました	急ぎませんでした	急いだ	急がなかった
て form					急いで	急がなくて
Non-past	write	kak	書きます	書きません	書かない	書かない
Past			書きました	書きませんでした	書いた	書かなかった
て form					書いて	書かなくて

* 行く (go) is a う-verb like 書く above, but its plain past form is 行った and its plain て form is 行って.

Non-past	drink	nom	飲みます	飲みません	飲む	飲まない
Past			飲みました	飲みませんでした	飲んだ	飲まなかった
て form					飲んで	飲まなくて
Non-past	understand	wakar	わかります	わかりません	わかる	わからない
Past			わかりました	わかりませんでした	わかった	わからなかった
て form					わかって	わからなくて
Non-past	speak	hanas	話します	話しません	話す	話さない
Past			話しました	話しませんでした	話した	話さなかった
て form					話して	話さなくて
Non-past	wait	mat	待ちます	待ちません	待つ	待たない
Past			待ちました	待ちませんでした	待った	待たなかった
て form					待って	待たなくて
Non-past	use	tsukaw	使います	使いません	使う	使わない
Past			使いました	使いませんでした	使った	使わなかった
て form					使って	使わなくて

11. Stating simple past, present, and future actions

	Noun	Particle	Verb
Topic	田中さん	は	来ます／来ました。
Subject	私	が	話します／話しました。
Object	本	を	読みます／読みました。
Means	車	で	行きます／行きました。
	英語	で	話します／話しました。
Pathway	道／右	を／に／へ	行きます／行きました。
	まっすぐ	(に)	歩きます／歩きました。

Joint action	田中さん	と	します／しました。
Adverbial	いっしょ	に	行きましょう。
Place of existence	あそこ	に	あります／ありました。
Place of activities	デパート	で	買います／買いました。
Destination	駅	に／へ／まで	行きます／行きました。
Relative time	去年／先月／先週／昨日		しました。
	今年／今月／今週／今日／今		します／しました。
	来年／来月／来週／明日		します。
Specific time	日曜日／5月／9時／1998年	に／から	します／しました。
Exclusive	月曜日	だけ	休みます／休みました。
Approximation	十日／1時間／3時	ほど／ぐらい	休みます／休みました。
		ごろ	帰ります／帰りました。

12. Stating simple past, present, and future states

		Noun	Pt.	い-Adjective	Copula/Endings
Affirmative	Non-past	電車	は	はやい	です。
	Past			はやかった	です。
Negative	Non-past			はやく	ないです／ありません。
	Past			はやく	なかったです／ありませんでした。

		Noun	Pt.	Noun (Pt.) な-Adjective	Copula/Endings
Affirmative	Non-past	辞書	は	3000円	です。
	Past	ニュース		6時から	です。
Negative	Non-past	お休み		二十日まで	じゃないです／じゃありません。
	Past				じゃなかったです／じゃありませんでした。

13. Noun Modification

Prenominal	Noun	
この／その／あの こんな／そんな／あんな	車	this car / the car near you / the car over there this kind of car that kind of car (known to you) that kind of car (known to both of us)
い-Adjective	Noun	
高い	辞書	an expensive dictionary
高い	の	an expensive one
同じ (special adjective)	色	the same color
Noun (+ particle) + の	Noun	
田中さんの	本	Mr. Tanaka's book
東京から／へ／までの	電車	a train from/for/as far as Tokyo
2000円から／までの	ケーキ	a cake (costing) up from/up to 2000 yen
6時から／までの	ニュース	news from six/news until six
アメリカの	車	an American car
Noun (+ particle)	の	
田中さん	の	Mr. Tanaka's (one)

東京から	の	the one from Tokyo
な-Adjective	**Noun**	
だめな	車	a no good car
きれいな	車	a pretty car
ざんねんな	こと	a regretful matter

14. Joint Nouns

Noun (+ Pt.)	Particle	Noun (+ Pt.)	Particle
ペン	と	えんぴつ	
ニューヨーク	と	アトランタ	に／で
月曜日	と	火曜日	に
電車	も	地下鉄	も
駅に	も	駅の前に	も
駅で	も	駅の前で	も
6時から	も	11時から	も

15. Adverbs

Adverbs	Predicate (Verbs, Adjective です, and Noun です)
あんまり／ぜんぜん／やっぱり	使いません。
いっしょに／先に	しませんか／行きました。
はやく／大きく	行きました／書きます。
(もう)すこし／もっと	大きいです／はやく行きましょう。
あんまり／ぜんぜん／やっぱり	おもしろくないです／おもしろくありません。
とても／ずいぶん／やっぱり	おもしろいです／おもしろい本です。

16. Question Words

	Question Words	Sentence Samples
Who?	だれ？	だれがしますか。／だれを見ましたか。 だれに言いましたか。
What?	何？／何〜？	何ですか。／何がおもしろいですか。 何を食べますか。／何で食べますか。
(About) When?	いつ(ごろ)？ 何時(ごろ)？ 何日(ごろ)？ 何年(ごろ)？	いつ行きましたか。 何時にしますか。 何日に行きますか。 何年に来ましたか。
Where?	どこ？	どこにありますか。／どこで見ましたか。 どこに／へ／まで行きますか。／どこから来ましたか。
How?	どう？	どうしましたか。
What kind of?	どんな？	どんないろがいいですか。
Which (one)?	どちら？ どっち？ どれ？ どの〜？	どちらですか／どちらの色ですか。 どれですか／どの色ですか。 どれがいいですか／どの色がいいですか。 どれを使いますか／どの色を使いますか。

Introduction   xvii

		どれに書きますか／どの紙に書きますか。
		どれで行きますか／どの色で書きますか。
How much? How long? How many? etc.	いくら？ どのぐらい？ いくつ？ 何人？ 何時間？	いくらでしたか。 どのぐらいかかりますか。 いくつありますか。 何人来ますか。 何時間しましたか。
Why?	どうして？ なぜ？	どうして行かないんですか。 なぜですか。

17. Polite vs. Plain Styles

	Polite	Plain
Verb sentences	行きます。 行きません。 行きました。 行きませんでした。	行く。 行かない。 行った。 行かなかった。
い-Adjective sentences	高いです。 高くないです／高くありません。 高かったです。 高くなかったです／高くありませんでした。	高い。 高くない。 高かった。 高くなかった。
な-Adjective or Noun sentences	英語です。 英語じゃないです／英語じゃありません。 英語でした。 英語じゃなかったです／英語じゃありませんでした。	英語（だ）。 英語じゃない。 英語だった。 英語じゃなかった。
でしょう forms	来るでしょう 高いでしょう そうでしょう。	来るだろう 高いだろう そうだろう。

18. んです Form (It's that .../... explains it.)

The んです form is used when there is something that needs an explanation, or when there is a reason why the situation at hand occurred or is occurring or will occur. The plain style sentences must come before the んです form.

	Plain	んです forms (polite)	んです forms (plain)
Verb sentences	行く。 行かない。 行った。 行かなかった。	行くんです。 行かないんです。 行ったんです。 行かなかったんです。	行くの。 行かないの。 行ったの。 行かなかったの。
い-Adjective sentences	高い。 高くない。 高かった。 高くなかった。	高いんです。 高くないんです。 高かったんです。 高くなかったんです。	高いの。 高くないの。 高かったの。 高くなかったの。
Noun sentences or な-Adjective sentences	英語（だ）。 英語じゃない。 英語だった。 英語じゃなかった。	英語なんです。 英語じゃないんです。 英語だったんです。 英語じゃなかったんです。	英語なの。 英語じゃないの。 英語だったの。 英語じゃなかったの。

19. Past Experience

	Plain Past V + ことがあります	
Experience	日本へ行ったことがあります。 おすしを食べたことがあります。	I have been to Japan. I have eaten sushi.

20. Progressive/Repeated Events/Resultant State: V ている Form

	Polite/Plain	
On-going action (present)	テレビを見ています／見ている。 1時間勉強しています／している。 毎日学校に行っています／行っている。	I am watching TV. I have been studying for 1 hour. I am going to school every day.
Resultant state (present)	日本に行っています／行っている。 大学を出ています／出ている。	He has gone to Japan. He has graduated from a university.
On-going action (past)	テレビを見ていました／見ていた。 1時間勉強していました／していた。 毎日学校に来ていました／来ていた。	I was watching TV. I had been studying for 1 hour. I was coming to school every day.
Resultant state (past)	日本に行っていました／行っていた。 大学を出ています／出ている。	He had gone to Japan. He had graduated from a university.

21. Quoting and Thinking

	Sentence (Plain Style)	Particle	Verb
Quoting	その本を読んだ 日本語はおもしろい あしたは雨だろう	と	言いました。
Thinking (I think)	その本を読んだ 日本語はおもしろい あしたは雨だ	と	思います。
Thinking (He/She thinks)	その本を読んだ 日本語はおもしろい あしたは雨だ	と	思っています。

22. Clausal Connections

	Clause 1	Clause 2	Clause 1 + Clause 2
Chronological	おちゃを飲みました。	行きました。	おちゃを飲んで行きました。
Errand	ランチを買います。	来てください。	ランチを買って来て下さい。
Causal	事故がありました。	遅くなりました。	事故があって、遅くなりました。 事故があったから、遅くなりました。
Antithesis	事故がありました。	遅れませんでした。	事故がありましたが、遅れませんでした。 事故があったけど、遅れませんでした。
Relevance	今、5時です。	帰りませんか。	今、5時ですが、帰りませんか。 今、5時ですけど、帰りませんか。
Listing	食べました。	飲みました。	食べたり、飲んだりしました。

23. Communicative functions using verbs

Affirmative statement	しきます／しきました。
Negation	しません／しませんでした。
Question	しますか／しませんか／しましたか／しませんでしたか。
Let's ... !	この店で飲んでいきましょう！
Let's ..., shall we?	しましょうか。
Invitation	しませんか。
Expressing soft agreement	しますね／しませんね／しましたね／しませんでしたね／そうですね。
Expressing strong agreement/amazement	よく／ずいぶんしましたねえ。／そうですねえ。
Seeking agreement	しますね？／しましたね？／そうですね？
Assertion	しましたよ／しませんでしたよ。／そうですよ。
Uncertainty	田中さんは来ないでしょう。／あの本は高いでしょう。 あしたは雨でしょう。／そうでしょう。
Request	して下さい。
Polite request	して下さいませんか。
Indirect request	この本を読みたいんですけど…
Hesitation	私は行きませんが／行きませんけど…／そうですが／そうですけど…
Background	すみませんが…、それ何ですか。 今、午後5時ですけど、帰りませんか。

24. Family Terms

Noun	Honorific (out-group)	Humble (in-group)	Noun	Honorific (out-group)	Humble (in-group)
wife	奥さん	家内	brother	お兄さん	兄
husband	ご主人	主人	sister	お姉さん	姉
children	お子さん	子／子ども	grandfather	おじいさん	祖父
son	息子さん	息子	grandmother	おばあさん	祖母
daughter	娘さん	娘	house	おたく	うち
father	お父さん	父	family name	田中さん	田中
mother	お母さん	母			

Abbreviations used in this textbook

い-adj	い-adjective or simply adjective (e.g., おもしろい)
な-adj	な-adjective (adjective that takes な to connect with other nouns: きれいなペン)
adv	adverb (e.g., ゆっくり)
interj	interjection (e.g., はい、いいえ、ああ、etc.)
N, n	noun
p	particle
prenom	prenominal (その、そんな)
phr	phrase
rt	root (fixed part of the verb)
S	sentence
suf	suffix (くん、さん、さま)
V, v; vt, vi	verb; vt = transitive verb (e.g., 電話をかける), vi = intransitive verb (e.g., 電話がかかる)

cv	consonant verb (verbs whose root ends with a consonant) also called "う verb" (e.g., 書く)
vv	vowel verb (verbs whose root ends with a vowel "e" or "i") also called "る verb" (e.g., 食べる)
iv	irregular verb (する and 来る verbs)
n/v	noun or verb (e.g., 電話 or 電話する)
sv	special verb (いらっしゃいます、ございます、なさいます、おっしゃいます、下さいます)
X	any expression
↓	humble forms
↑	honorific forms
●	This indicates additional vocabulary in the vocabulary list section.

About writing symbols

The Japanese writing system consists of phonetic symbols called kana and ideogram symbols called kanji. There are two types of kana ム hiragana (ひらがな) and katakana (カタカナ). This book assumes that you are completely familiar with ひらがな and カタカナ. Each kanji symbol represents ideas. In general, kanji is used to write content words (e.g., 田中先生), カタカナ to write words of foreign origin (e.g., ピザ、スパゲッティ、ビデオ、コンピュータ) and many onomatopoeia expressions (e.g., キーキー squeak-squeak, グラグラ wobbly), and ひらがな for the rest (e.g., particles, suffixes, some content words, etc.). It is assumed that you are already familiar with the following 75 kanji symbols. These kanji symbols are from the first 11 chapters of *Nakama 1* (Hatasa, Hatasa, and Makino, 1998).

山	日	田	人	上	下	中	大	小	本	学	生	先	私	川
一	二	三	四	五	六	七	八	九	十	百	千	万	円	
月	火	水	木	金	土	曜	年	時	間	週	何	分	半	今
家	族	父	母	兄	弟	姉	妹	男	女	子	目	口	耳	足	手
行	来	帰	食	飲	見	聞	読	書	話	高	校	出	会	買

It is also assumed that you already know some basic facts about kanji such as the fact that kanji typically has two or more separate readings. When a kanji character is introduced for the first time in this textbook, two types of readings are distinguished as shown below. The native Japanese readings (called 訓読み) are written in ひらがな. The Chinese readings (called 音読み) are written in カタカナ. After this initial reading help, all subsequent reading help is provided in ひらがな.

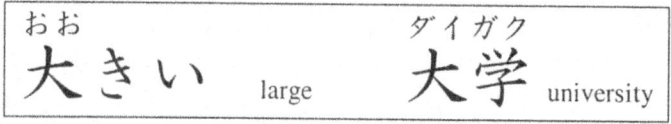

Additional resources

Free additional learning resources are available at the following web site:

http://www.iac.gatech.edu/modlangs/program-japanese.html
(or http://www.iac.gatech.edu/modlangs/Programs/Japanese/program-japanese.htm)

Chapter 1

面接(めんせつ)
Job Interview

Priming

Imagine that you are about to graduate from your university and are looking for a job in Japan. You have surveyed various companies in your field of specialty, received job application forms, and set up an appointment for a job interview. Now imagine that you have arrived in Japan and that today is your first company visit or 会社訪問(かいしゃほうもん).

- How do you greet your interviewer?
- Can you state your name, school, major, and your specialty in a succinct manner?
- How do you answer if you are asked why you have chosen the company?

A job interview provides a good opportunity to demonstrate your communication skills in Japanese. After you send your resume, a preliminary interview may be conducted over the telephone before you travel to Japan or to a local office in your country. Before you go, familiarize yourself with basic business etiquette, such as wearing a suit and tie (men) and a suit or conservative dress/skirt (women), and greeting upon entering and leaving the interview room. The interviewer will be watching your nonverbal behavior as well (e.g., bowing, posture, etc.). Interviewees are not expected to bring their own business cards or other items such as gifts. You should not be surprised if group interviews are conducted.

Structures 1A

1A.1. Humble forms (もうします／(V て) おります) ↓

Japanese verbs, adjectives, and the copula can be plain or polite. Plain forms are typically used within a sentence (e.g., きのう行ったとおもいます。 or おもしろかったでしょう？) or they can be used in casual speech among family members and friends (e.g., ピザ、食べた？→うん、おいしかった。). However, in business situations, conversations are dominated by polite forms of speech, and in-group and out group are distinguished explicitly by the use of humble vs. honorific forms. Honorific forms are used to refer to actions of members of an out-group and humble forms are used to refer to actions of our own in-group, including the speaker.[1] In this section, humble forms will be introduced.

Respect can be expressed by exalting out-group members or by lowering in-group members. The notion of lowering in-group to show respect to out-group is seen most clearly in personal address terms. When we refer to an in-group member, the title (さん) is dropped as shown below (田中は). Verbs can also be in humble forms as shown below.

Neutral	Humble ↓	
いいます (いう)	もうします	私はスミスともうします。 I am called Smith.
います (いる)	おります	田中はニューヨークにおります。 Mr. Tanaka is in New York.

The humble forms of いいます and 専攻しています are 申します↓ and 専攻しております↓, respectively. The humble form おります can also be used in the V ている construction.

Neutral	Humble ↓	
勉強しています	勉強しております	うちのたろうは英語を勉強しております。 My (son), Taro is studying English. [on-going action]
でかけています	でかけております	田中はでかけております。 Tanaka (in-group, superior) has gone out. [resultant state]

Ranking within an organization also affects the use of honorific and humble forms. In general, honorific forms are used to refer to actions of our superiors while humble forms are used to talk about the speaker. When we must refer to actions of our superiors (in-group) in the conversation involving an outsider, in-group/out-group distinction overrides the rank differences within the same organization, as in the last example shown above.

1A.2. N について

N について means "about N" or "regarding N." It is used to introduce the topic of what you will say next, or the topic of the project someone is involved in.

今、日米貿易について勉強しています。
Right now, I am studying Japan-U.S. trade.

今度のミーティングではインターネットについて話します。
We'll talk about the Internet at the next meeting.

---

[1] 文化ノート An in-group consists of all the members of the same organization as the speaker. The smallest form of an in-group is the family. Anyone outside of one's family is a member of an out-group. However, the notion of an in-group can be flexibly expanded to include members of other social organizations such as one's own class, club, school, company, or any other groups the speaker is affiliated with.

In Conversation 1B below, Mr. Harris, ハリス, honorifically refers to the company as 御社 ("your company").[2]

Conversation 1B: The reason for applying for a job (2)

1. 中：では、我が社を志望する理由は何ですか。
2. ハ：はい。御社は82年の歴史があり、また、新製品の超小型テレビ電話もたいへんすばらしいと思いました。私はその方面の研究にとても興味がありますので、御社を志望いたしました。
3. 中：ハリスさんの専門はどういった形でこちらで活かせると思いますか。
4. ハ：はい。通信ソフトの開発にたずさわりたいと思います。私の専門もその方面で活かせると思います。

1. N: Then, what is the reason why you have chosen our company?
2. H: Your company has a 82-year-long history, and I thought your brand-new ultra-small video phone is excellent. I am very much interested in that research area. That is why I have chosen your company.
3. N: How do you think you can make the most of your specialty in this company?
4. H: I would like to take part in the area of developing communication software. I think I can make the most of my specialty in that area.

思う (おも) think   電 (デン) electricity   面 (メン) surface, face, aspect

Vocabulary 1B

では (con) then [More formal than じゃ(あ)]
我が社 ↓ (n) my company or our company
志望する (n/v) to desire, choose
理由 (n) reason
御社 ↑ (n) [your] company. [御 is an honorific prefix.]
● 会社 (n) company
歴史 (n) history
また (con) furthermore, in addition
新製品 (n) new products
● 製品 (n) products
超小型 (n) ultra small [超 is a prefix meaning "super."]
● 小型 (n) small size
● 新型 (n) new model
テレビ電話 (n) video phone

たいへん (な-adj) very much, extraordinarily
すばらしい (い-adj) wonderful, terrific
方面 (n) direction, way, sphere
研究 (n) research [研究する "to research"]
興味 (n) interest [X に興味がある "be interested in X"]
志望いたしました ↓ (n/v) chose, desired
どういった (phr) what kind of (=どういう；どんな)
形 (n) shape, form [どういった形で In what concrete ways? =どういう／どんな形で]
活かせる (cv: ikas) [potential of 活かす] can make the most of
通信ソフト (n) communication software
開発 (n) development
たずさわりたい (cv: tazusawar) [たい form of たずさわる] want to take part in, handle, be concerned with

Structures 1B

1B.1. Clause modifiers

In order to describe people and things, the Japanese extensively use a structure called clause modifiers. In English,

---

[2] 文化ノート Mr. Harris responds with はい to a WH questions (what, when, who, where, and how questions). This can be translated as "OK, (I heard your question.)" This allows a momentary pause in conversation and indicates the formal nature of the conversation.

modifiers of a noun can precede or follow that noun (e.g., "an expensive book" or "a book that was expensive"). In Japanese, modifiers always precede the noun, and no relative pronouns (which, who, that, etc.) or particles are used between the modifier and the noun.

Clause(plain form)	Noun	Translation	Compare:
あんまり高くない	ホテル	the hotel that is not very expensive	あのホテルはあんまり高くない。
きのう借りた	本	the book I borrowed	きのう、その本を借りた。
病気だった	人	the person who was sick	あの人は病気だった。
私が行った	町	the city to which I went	私はその町に行った。
コーヒーがおいしい	店	the shop where coffee tastes good	その店はコーヒーがおいしい。
何という	会社	the company called what?	その会社は何というんですか。
我が社を志望する	理由	the reason for choosing our company	この会社を志望します。

Clause modifiers are typically in the plain form (e.g., 借りた). The word order of a Japanese clause modifier structure may resemble that of the English word order, but one should not be misled by superficial similarity. The phrase below does not mean "Mr. Kim made the coffee." It means "The coffee Mr. Kim made..."

キムさん	が	作った	コーヒー	the coffee Mr. Kim made
Kim	subj	made	coffee	

When you hear a verb (e.g., 作った) after a subject or object or other parts of speech, that normally signals the end of the sentence in Japanese. However, if you hear an extra noun after the verb, it signals the beginning of a new larger sentence. This is illustrated below.

    キムさんが作った…　　　　　　　　　　Kim made... [The end of the sentence?]
    キムさんが作った コーヒーは…　　　　　The coffee Kim made... [A new sentence begins.]
    キムさんが作った コーヒーは おいしい。　The coffee Kim made tastes good.

The subject within a clause modifier can be marked by の instead of が. The use of の helps the listener detect the presence of a clause modifier structure quickly.

    キムさんの作った…　　　　　　　　　　　　　　　　[This is a clause modifier. Expect a noun to follow.]
    キムさんの作った コーヒーを 田中さんが 飲んだ。　　[The expectation is confirmed.]

Sometimes, the modified noun may not immediately follow the modifier as illustrated below.

    きのう行ったレストランの料理　　　　　the food of the restaurant I went to yesterday

    きのう食べたレストランの料理　　　　　the food of the restaurant I ate at yesterday

The subject within a clause modifier is usually marked by が or の. However, the particle は may be used if は signals a contrast.

    歴史がある 会社　　　　a company that has a history
    歴史のある 会社　　　　a company that has a history
    歴史はある 会社　　　　a company that has a history (at least)

When a noun modifies another noun, the copula です/だ changes to の. If a な-adjective modifies a noun, the copula changes to な. If a い-adjective modifies a noun, the copula is simply deleted.

その車はハンドルが左です。 → ハンドルが左の車はアメリカの車です。
The car has a steering wheel on the left. The car whose steering wheel is on the left is an American car.

そのオフィスはきれいです。 → きれいなオフィス　　a beautiful office

その電話は便利です。 → 便利な電話　　a telephone that is convenient

あの人はせが高いです。 → せが高い人　　a person who is tall

1B.2. Honorific vs. humble forms (お N, なさる／いたす, 〜さん)

An honorific prefix (お、おん、or ご) can be attached to some nouns to create their honorific form. Not all nouns can be changed to their honorific forms this way. Common nouns like ごはん ("meal") and おじぎ ("bowing") are preceded by an honorific prefix ご／お, but they are such commonplace words that they are not considered honorific nouns. Humble forms of nouns are relatively rare. Some neutral nouns such as 我が社 can be considered "humble" by the fact that they are used to refer to one's in-group. In addition, it is not unusual to refer to other companies with a personal title さん as if the whole company were a person. This way of addressing is limited to out-groups (companies that are not one's own), and it shows a friendly respect to other companies.

Neutral	Honorific ↑	Humble ↓
会社	御社 (your company)	我が社 (my company)
志望	御志望	Non-existent
[family name]	田中さん (out-group)	田中 (self/self)
[company name]	ソニーさん (out-group)	うち (my company, home/self)

The verb する／します and its derived form (N する／します as in 研究する／します) also have the honorific form なさる／なさいます and the polite-humble form いたします, but not the plain-humble form.

Neutral	Honorific ↑	Humble ↓ (no plain forms used)
します (する)	なさいます (なさる)	いたします
研究します (研究する)	研究なさいます (研究なさる)	研究いたします
しています (している)	なさっています (なさっている)	しております or いたしております
研究しています (研究している)	研究なさっています (研究なさっている)	研究しております or 研究いたしております

Examples:

A: 何を専攻なさいましたか。↑　　What did you major in?
B: 私はアジア経済を専攻いたしました。↓　　I majored in Asian Economy.
A: どんな製品を開発なさっていますか。↑　　What kind of product are you developing?
B: 新しいメモリーチップを開発しております。↓　　I'm developing a new memory chip.

1B.3. Verb sentence connection (V て／V-stem)

Verb sentences can be combined by using the gerund forms of verbs (V て forms). For example, to combine verb sentences involving "eating" and "drinking" actions, we can use the following V て form:

V て ＋ Predicate	
銀座で食べて飲んだ。	I ate and drank at Ginza.

When two sentences are relatively independent of one another, verb stems (e.g., あり) are more likely to be used instead of the て-forms (e.g., あって).[3] To emphasize the separate nature of the two sentences, an additional phrase like また ("furthermore") can be inserted between the two verb sentences. This form appears more often in written texts.

V-stem + Predicate	
御社は82年の歴史があり、また、製品もすばらしいです。	Your company has an 82-year history, and, furthermore, its products are great.
午前中は雨が降り、午後は晴れるでしょう。	During the morning it will rain, and in the afternoon the sky will probably clear up.

1B.4. Expressing desires: V たい Form

The V たい form ("want to V") is created by adding the suffix たい to the stem (V ます without ます) of verbs. The particle が can be used to mark the object instead of を.

Regular Expressions	V たい Expressions
本を読む。	本を読みたい。 or 本が読みたい。
コンピュータを使う。	コンピュータを使いたい。 or コンピュータが使いたい。

When the speaker's desire is offered as the explanation for something (e.g., asking for directions or asking for a permission), the んです ending usually follows the V たい form.

ここで携帯電話[4]を使いたいんですが、いいですか。　　I would like to use a cell phone here, but is it all right?
銀座に行きたいんですが、どちらの方ですか。　　I would like to go to Ginza, but which way is it?

1B.5. Potential: VV-rareru/CV-eru[5]

The potential form of verbs referring to actions can be made according to the following rules:

Vowel verb (る verb)	root + rareru/reru	Potential	
食べる	tabe + rareru/reru =	食べられる／食べれる	can eat
見る	mi + rareru/reru =	見られる／見れる	can see/watch

Consonant verb (う verb)	root + eru	Potential	
使う	tsuka(w) + eru =	使える	can use
呼ぶ	yob + eru =	呼べる	can call/summon
行く	ik + eru =	行ける	can go
話す	hanas + eru =	話せる	can speak
待つ	mat + eru =	待てる	can wait
急ぐ	isog + eru =	急げる	can hurry
読む	yom + eru =	読める	can read
作る	tsukur + eru =	作れる	can make

---

[3] A verb stem is the polite form of verbs without the ます ending. For example, the verb stem of たべます is たべ and the verb stem of かきます is かき. This is different from the て-form such as たべて and かいて.

[4] 携帯電話 is often written in katakana as in ケータイ.

[5] Vowel verbs (also called る verbs) are verbs whose root (the semantic core of the verb) ends with a vowel "e" or "i" (e.g., いる [root = i], みる [root = mi], たべる [root = tabe]). Consonant verbs (also called う verbs) are verbs whose root ends with a consonant (e.g., かく [root = kak], まつ [root = mat], かう [root = kaw], etc.).

Irregular verbs	Potential	
する	できる	can do
来る	来られる／来れる	can come

Like the たい form of verbs, the object of the potential verb can be marked by either を or が.

日本でアメリカ車が／を買えます。　　　We can buy American cars in Japan.
日本語が／を活かせる仕事が／をしたい。 I want to do a job where I can take advantage of my Japanese.

1B.6.　S ので／N なので

To state a reason for something, the connective ので ("because"), a formal equivalent of から, is used. Unlike English, the reason always precedes the result in Japanese. The reason statement can take a polite form or a plain form. If the reason statement is a noun or な-adjective sentence, the copula だ changes to な.

Reason (Verb or い-Adjective Sentence)	ので、	Result
山川は3時からの会議に出ます (or 出る)	ので、	すぐ戻ります。
Because Yamakawa is going to attend a meeting at three, he is returning shortly.		
Reason (Noun or な-Adjective Sentence)	ので、	Result
ブラウンさんはアメリカ人です (or な)	ので、	日本語が話せない。
Ms. Brown doesn't speak Japanese because she is an American.		

The S ので clause can be embedded in a larger structure ～とはいえない ("I can't say that...") as shown below.

アメリカ人なので (or だから) 日本語が話せないとはいえない。
I can't say that she doesn't speak Japanese (just) because she is an American.

Caution: The connective から can be used at the end of a sentence to state only the reason for something (～からです "It's because..."), but ので cannot be used in the same structure.

A: どうして日本に行きたいんですか。　　Why would you like to go to Japan?
B: 日本が好きだからです。　　　　　　It's because I like Japan.
(* 日本が好きなのでです is ungrammatical.)

Mr. Nakayama is looking at Mr. Harris' resume. He uses honorific expressions when he refers to Mr. Harris' father but maintains neutral (non-honorific) expressions when he asks Mr. Harris. This is typical in a job interview situation. Note also that Mr. Harris also uses neutral expressions in his reply because he is referring to Japanese companies in general, not the specific company he is applying for.

Conversation 1C: Why work for a Japanese company? (3)

1. 中: ところで、ハリスさん、お父さんはワールドコンピュータさんにお勤めなんですね。	1. N: By the way, your father is working for World Computer, isn't he?
2. ハ: はい。	2. H: Yes.
3. 中: それで、どうして日本の企業を選んだんですか。	3. N: Then why did you choose a Japanese company?
4. ハ: はい。高性能で、小型の製品を低コストで作りだすという点で　日本の企業は世界的にもすぐれている	4. H: I believe that Japanese companies excel in the world in making high-performance and miniaturized products at low cost. I

と思います。そういった企業で私は力を出せると思います。 5. 中: ああ、なるほど。	think I can fulfill my potential in such a company. 5. N: Oh, I see.

力 (ちから) power, strength   企 (キ) scheme, plan   業 (ギョウ) profession, skill

Vocabulary 1C

ところで (phr) by the way
選んだ (cv: erab) [past of 選ぶ] chose
ワールドコンピュータ (n) [company name] World Computer
お勤めなんです (vv: tsutome) [おつとめです: honorific form of つとめる] work (for)
それで (con) given that; so; thus
● 会社員 (n) company worker
企業 (n) enterprise, company
● ハイテク産業 (n) high-tech industry
● 経済 (n) economy
高性能 (n) high performance
低コスト (n) low cost [低コストで "with low cost"]

作りだす (cv: tsukuridas) to produce, create [作る "make" + だす "put outside"]
点 (n) point, aspect, fact
～という点で (phr) with regard to the fact that...
世界的 (な-adj) world-wide; of the world [世界的に "all over the world"]
すぐれている (vv: sugure) [て-form of すぐれる "excel (at)"] is excellent
そういった (phr) that kind of [= そんな]
● こういった (phr) this kind of [= こんな]
● ああいった (phr) that kind of [= あんな]
出せる (cv: das) [potential of 出す] can take out, can bring forth [力を出す "realize one's potential"]
なるほど (phr) I see; That makes sense.

Structures 1C

1C.1.   **Place** ではたらく／**Place** につとめる

The verb はたらく is associated with a place where one works (Xではたらく), but the verb つとめる is associated with a destination of your daily commuting (to work) (Xにつとめる). When referring to the present employment, one must to use the Vている pattern.

母は銀行につとめているが、父は工場ではたらいている。
My mother works for a bank, but my father works at a factory.

It is not unusual for interviewers to ask family-related questions. Be prepared to give short "standard" answers and avoid mentioning family complications such as parental divorce. If the interviewer asks questions about family members with honorific forms, one must always reply with the humble forms when referring to one's own family members.

A blunder in interview

1C.2.   **Generic honorific form:** おVです↑

Mr. Nakayama uses an honorific form when he refers to Mr. Harris' father (out-group). Generic honorific forms of some verbs can be created by an honorific prefix お + verb stem + です. (Caution: Not all verbs work this way.)

The んです ending can be attached to the end of this form おつとめだ. In this case, the copula だ changes to な before んです as in おつとめなんです.

	Plain Honorific			Polite Honorific			Polite Honorific + んです			
	お	Verb	だ	お	Verb	です	お	Verb	な	んです
つとめます	お	つとめ	だ	お	つとめ	です	お	つとめ	な	んです
わかります	お	わかり	だ	お	わかり	です	お	わかり	な	んです
帰ります	お	帰り	だ	お	帰り	です	お	帰り	な	んです

The お V です form can refer to past, present, and future actions (on-going or one-time) without changing its ending.

Neutral	お + V-Stem + です↑
あした帰ります。	あしたお帰りです。↑
今、帰っています。	今、お帰りです。↑
きのう帰りました。	きのうお帰りです。↑

Past: A: おわかりですか。↑
B: ええ、わかりました。

Present: A: お父さんはどちらにおつとめですか。↑
B: 父はソニーにつとーております。↓

Future: A: あした、何時にお帰りですか。↑
B: 6時に帰ります。

Although 使いませんか can be a question ("Don't you use it?") or an invitation ("Would you like to use it?"), お使いじゃありませんか is a pure question and cannot function as an invitation.

使いますか／使いましたか　＝　お使いですか↑
使いませんか／使いませんでしたか　＝　お使いじゃありませんか↑

1C.3. Noun/Adjective sentence connection (N で／A くて／A く)

We can use the copula gerund で to combine a noun sentence or a な-adjective sentence with another sentence. The copula gerund can be used when two sentences are parallel (a & b below) or when the sentences are related (c & d).

N で + Sentence	
(a) 兄は会社員で、姉は大学の先生です。	My older brother is a company employee, and my older sister is a university professor.
(b) その製品は小型で、あの製品は安いです。	That product is small and that product (over there) is inexpensive.
(c) デザインが簡単で、いいです。	The design is nice and simple (Lit. "The design is simple, so it's good").
(d) 田中さんは病気で、会社を休みました。	Mr. Tanaka is sick, so he took a day off from work.

The て-form of an い-adjective (Aくて) is used to combine an い-adjective sentence with another sentence.

Aくて + Sentence	
携帯は小さくて便利です。	Cell phones are small and convenient.
このコーヒーは熱くて飲めない。	This coffee is hot, and (so) I can't drink it.

Sentences connected by て-forms are usually of a similar or related type. Compare the following.

→ 地下鉄は速くて便利です。　　　　　　　Subways are fast and convenient.
→ 地下鉄は速いですが、混んでいます。　　Subways are fast, but they are crowded.

The く form of い-adjective is used when the two items are relatively independent of one another. The A く form is used more frequently in written texts.

アメリカは広く、日本は狭い。　　　　　America is spacious while Japan is cramped.

In Conversation 1D, Mr. Nakayama is asking about more personal matters. As a job candidate, you would make a good impression if you have experiences in participating in extracurricular activities requiring team work, job flexibility, and/or enthusiasm. Occasionally, female job candidates may be asked if they intend to work after marriage. If you are asked such a question, state clearly that you wish to continue working after marriage. You may also be asked about your college life because it is often different from the typical college life in Japan. For example, internship programs and teaching or research assistantships are relatively rare in Japan.

Conversation 1D: Extracurricular activities and hobbies (4)

1. 中：それから、ええ、ハリスさんは「日本語話そう会」の会長をしていますね。それはどういう会ですか。
2. ハ：はい。月に一度、日本語を勉強している人が日本語で親睦を深める会です。
3. 中：ほう。それで日本語がお上手なんですね。
4. ハ：いえ、まだまだ勉強中です。
5. 中：ええ、それから、テニスもお得意なんですね。
6. ハ：いいえ、あまり得意ではないんですが、するのは好きです。
7. 中：なるほど。

1. N: And then, umm, you are the president of "Let's Speak Japanese Club." What kind of club is that?
2. H: It's a club through which people studying Japanese develop friendship.
3. N: I see. Is that why you are good at Japanese?
4. H: Oh, no. I'm still studying [Japanese].
5. N: Well... in addition, you are good at tennis, too, right?
6. H: No, I'm not very good at it, but I like to play [tennis].
7. N: I see.

語 language　　　好き like　　　度 times, degree

Vocabulary 1D

日本語話そう会 (n) Let's-Speak-Japanese Society
会長 (n) president, chairman
会 (n) meeting, club, society
どういう (n) what kind of
親睦 (n) friendship, good will
深める (vv: hukame) to deepen
お上手 (な-adj) skillful, is good at

得意 (な-adj) is good at (and like [it])
● 下手 (な-adj) unskilled, is poor at
● 苦手 (な-adj) is poor at (and dislike [it])
勉強中 (n) in the middle of studying
～ではない (cop) is not... [formal form of ～じゃない]
なるほど (phr) I see. That makes sense.

Structures 1D

1D.1. N が好き／V のが好き

好き "to like" and 嫌い "to dislike" are な-adjectives (also called "な nouns" in some textbooks) in Japanese. The thing/person liked or disliked is marked by the particle が.

	N + が	すき／きらい	
田中さんは	ゴルフが	好きです。	Mr. Tanaka likes golf.
私は	ビールが	嫌いです。	I don't like beer.

A clause modifier structure can be used to talk about preferences for activities. In this case, a non-past plain-form verb is followed by the nominalizer の as shown below.

	V (plain-form) + のが	すき／きらい	
田中さんは	ゴルフをするのが	好きです。	Mr. Tanaka likes to play golf.
私は	人前で歌うのが	嫌いです。	I don't like to sing in front of people.
	大きい町に住むのは	嫌いじゃありません。	I don't dislike living in a big city.

References to skills as 得意 "be good at," 上手 "be good at," and 下手／苦手 "be poor at" have the same kind of structures.

田中さんは英語で話すのが得意だ。　　Mr. Tanaka is good at speaking in English.

ブラウンさんは通訳するのが上手だ。　　Mr. Brown is skillful at interpreting.

私はスピーチが下手なんです。　　I am poor at (making) speeches.

When you refer to likes, dislikes, and skills of other people, polite expressions are used by adding the honorific prefix お.

課長はカラオケがお好きです。　　Section Manager likes karaoke.

山中さんは英語がお上手です。　　Mr. Yamanaka is good at English.

部長のお得意は演歌です。　　Division Manager is good at (singing) Japanese blues.

Since 上手 (skillful) is an expression of praise, expressions such as 私はワープロが上手です sound like you are praising yourself. If you are asked about your skills during the job interview, use 得意 instead (e.g., ワープロが得意です). The word 得意 has an additional implication that the speaker likes the object. 苦手 ("no good at") has an additional implication that the speaker dislikes the object.[6] In general, the Sの structure can be combined with other predicates besides 好き／きらい, 上手／下手, and 得意／苦手 and creates a generic expression for "V-ing" as shown below:

ワープロを使うのは簡単です。　　It's easy to use a word processor.

たばこを吸うのをやめました。　　I quit smoking.

吉田さんが来るのを待っています。　　I'm waiting for Ms. Yoshida to come here.

---

[6] 文化ノート In general, humility is considered a virtue in Japan, and Japanese typically understate their abilities. Don't underestimate their skills when they merely say 少しはできますが ("I can do that a little, but...") or とんでもない ("Heavens no!") or それほどでもありません ("I'm not that good...").

我が社を選んだのはどうしてですか。 What is the reason for having chosen our company?

カードは買い物をするのに便利です。 Cards are convenient for shopping.

1D.2. Maintaining polite speech

Your interviewer may relax a little and start to use casual speech patterns[7] after a while. However, the interviewee should stick with the polite form of speech. Use はい, not ええ, and avoid the んです sentence ending.

A: 趣味は？("What about your hobbies?")
B: ゴルフ。☠   → ゴルフです。☺

A: ご出身はテネシーなんですね。 ("Is your home state Tennessee, isn't it?")
B: ええ、そうなんです。☠   → はい、そうです。☺

At the end of the interview, the interviewee stands up, bows, and exits the room.   No handshakes will take place.

Conversation 1E: Mr. Harris leaves the interview. (5)	
1. 中: では、今日はどうもありがとうございました。 　　　本日の結果は追ってお知らせいたします。 2. ハ: どうもありがとうございました。 3. ハ: 失礼いたします。	1. N: Thank you very much [for your time], today. I will notify you later regarding today's outcome. 2. H: Thank you very much. 3. H: Excuse me (for leaving).
ケツ・ケッ 結 conclude; tie　　　　カ 　　　　　　　　　　　　果 fruit	

Vocabulary 1E

本日 (n) today
結果 (n) results, consequences

追って (phr) later, subsequently
お知らせいたします (vv: shirase) [polite-humble style of 知らせる] to notify

Structure 1E

1E.1. Humble forms - continued

In 1B.2, N いたします was introduced as the humble form of N します. Mr. Nakayama uses another rule to create humble forms of verbs. This humble form consists of the prefix お (or ご) + verb stem + します or いたします. With N します verbs, the prefix お (or ご) can also be attached to make their humble form: お (or ご) N します↓. The same can be done with the already humble verb N いたします↓ → お (or ご) N いたします↓. Verbs constructed this way refer to the action of in-group members only, and the action must benefit the out-group member (e.g., "I/We work FOR you"). If the action is not for the benefit of others, that is, if you can't add the English phrase like "for you", this humble form is inappropriate.[8]

---

[7] Casual speech includes the use of sentence fragments (e.g., ご趣味は？) and plain forms.

[8] The request verb お願いします (願う "wish for") is also derived this way. お願いします is different from other humble verbs of this type because it is said for the benefit of the speaker or in-group members.

Neutral	Humble Form (↓)		
	お／ご	V-stem／Noun	します／いたします
知らせる "notify"	お	知らせ	します／いたします
見せる "show"	お	見せ	します／いたします
書く "write"	お	書き	します／いたします
紹介する "introduce"	ご	紹介	します／いたします

Examples:

コピーをお取りいたしましょうか。　　Shall I make some copies (for you)?

ご紹介いたします。　　I will introduce [this person].

The following chart summarizes the honorific and humble forms introduced so far. Practice asking questions using honorific forms and replying in humble forms. The forms marked by a check mark (√) are used appropriately only when the action benefits an out-group member. Practice these latter forms in the phrase おVしましょうか ("Shall I V for you?").

Neutral	Honorific ↑	Humble ↓
言います	to be introduced later	申します
います	to be introduced later	おります
勤めます／ました	お勤めです	お勤めします √／お勤めいたします √
勤めています	お勤めです	勤めております
紹介します	紹介なさいます	紹介いたします／ご紹介します √／ご紹介いたします √
専攻しています	専攻なさっています	専攻しております／専攻いたしております

1E.2. Japanese resumé

You can purchase a standard resumé form at a Japanese bookstore or stationery shop. Keep in mind that Japanese resumés should be handwritten. Handwritten resumés are viewed as more trustworthy than type-written ones. Typically, the Japanese resumé has two parts: 履歴書 (Biographic Summary Form) and 身上書 (Personal Disclosure Form). Sample forms are shown on the next page.

When filling in a form like this, it is important to be concise. Frequently, the する ending of Nする verbs or the だ ending are deleted. This results in a compact style of writing.

新宿高校を卒業しました。 → 新宿高校を卒業。
(I) graduated from Shinjuku High School.

卒業見込みです。 → 卒業見込み。
(I am) expected to graduate.

モトローラ・ジャパンでアルバイトしました。 → モトローラ・ジャパンでアルバイト。
(I) worked part-time for Motorola Japan.

履歴書
Biographic Summary Form

履歴書 asks your name, date of birth, current address and phone number, educational history, and employment history (if any). You also need your recent photograph. There is a box to stamp your signature seal (if you have one) as shown below.

身上書*
Personal Disclosure Form

身上書 asks you rather personal information about your family, and your health conditions. While such questions are not allowed in the U.S., it is standard practice in Japan. Prepare generic answers for health and family-related questions. If you are not married, include information on your parents and siblings. If you are married, include information on your spouse and children. If you live in an extended family, you may include your living grandparents, step-siblings, or other dependents who share the same household and whom you are financially obliged to support (typically, your parents or in-laws).

* This form may also be called
自己紹介書 (Self-Introduction Form).

A detailed view of the form follows. Familiarize yourself with the form.

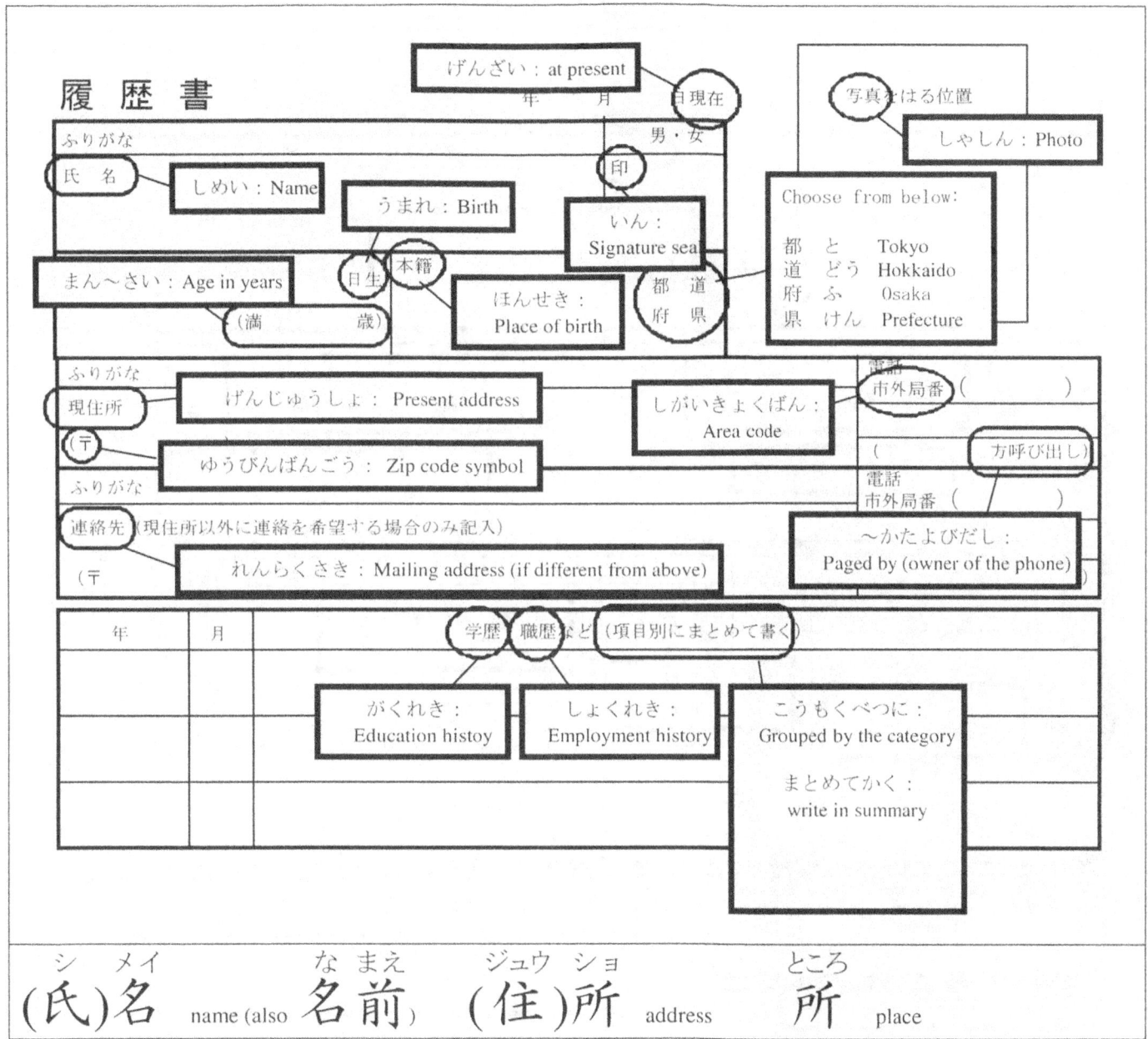

身上書

ふりがな		現住所（〒　　－　　）	電話 市外局番（　　　）
氏　名			（　　　方呼び出し）

年	月	免許・資格

免許・資格 めんきょ・しかく: Licenses and Qualifications

得意な学科 とくいな がっか: School Subjects Excelled in

趣味 しゅみ: Hobbies

スポーツ

健康状態 けんこうじょうたい: Health Conditioins

志願の動機 しぼうの どうき: Reasons for your choice

	氏　名	続柄	生年月日	氏　名	性別	生年月日
家族			．　．			．　．
			．　．			．　．
			．　．			．　．
			．　．			．　．

家族 かぞく: Family Members

続柄 つづきがら: Relationship

生年月日 せいねんがっぴ: Date of Birth

本人希望記入欄（特に給料・職種・勤務時間・勤務地その他について希望があれば記入）

ほんにん きぼう きにゅうらん: Your preferences for salary, type of job, work hours, place of work, etc.

保護者（本人が未成年の場合のみ記入）

ふりがな			電話 市外局番（　　　）
氏　名			（　　　方呼び出し）

ほごしゃ: Enter only if the applicant is under 20.

採用者側の記入欄（志願者は記入しないこと）

さいようしゃがわの きにゅうらん: Employer's Box: Do not write here.

エイゴ　　　　　　セイネンガッピ
英語 English　　**生年月日** date of birth

Exercise 1

Grammar Utilization 1   Name:_____ Sec:_____ #:____

G1. Use the humble form of the verb (お V します、お N します、(V て)おります、N いたします or special humble forms if any) and reply to A's question. Change the verb form if necessary and make sure to maintain the appropriate politeness level. (Note that Mr. Tanaka below is an in-group member of the company.)

1. A: お名前は？
   B: 私はブラウンと_____。(言う)

2. A: 大学では何を専攻なさいましたか。
   B: 経済学を_____。(専攻する)

3. A: お住まい (home) はどちらですか。
   B: 東京に_____。(住んでいる)

4. A: 田中さんはどちらですか。
   B: 田中は今、出かけて_____。(いる)

5. A: お父さんはどちらにお勤めですか。
   B: 父はワールドテックに_____。(勤めている)

6. A: 御社はどんな会社ですか。
   B: 我が社はメモリーチップを_____。(作っている)

7. A: アメリカの大学では何を研究なさいましたか。
   B: データコンプレッションを研究_____。(研究しました)

8. A: 山田さんに電話なさいましたか。
   B: ええ、電話_____。(電話しました)

   私は、山田さんにあした来ると_____。(言いました)

9. A: スミスさんはどの人ですか。
   B: ああ、あの背が高い人です。私が_____。(紹介しましょう)
   A: ありがとうございます。

10. A: 失礼ですが、メールアドレスを教えて下さいませんか。
    B: いいですよ。あ、私が_____。(書きましょうか)
    A: あ、どうも。お願いします。(A hands over a pen and paper.)

G2. You (A) are speaking to a person (B) below. A superior/outsider is marked by a triangle (▲). Rephrase your original question if necessary by using the honorific form of the verb お V です or お／ご N です or (N)なさる.

18   A Systematic Approach to Business Japanese

	You	Listener	
1.	A:	B: ▲	A: 課長はコーヒーを(飲みますか)＿＿＿＿＿＿＿＿＿＿＿＿＿＿＿＿＿＿。 B: うん、よく飲むよ。
2.	A:	B: ▲	A: 課長、紅茶を(入れましょうか)＿＿＿＿＿＿＿＿＿＿＿＿＿＿＿＿＿＿。 B: ああ、お願いするよ。
3.	A: ▲	B:	A: ブラウンさん、(どうしましたか)＿＿＿＿＿＿＿＿＿＿＿＿＿＿＿＿＿＿。 B: ちょっと気分が悪いんです。
4.	A:	B: ▲	A: 部長、私が(タイプしましょうか)＿＿＿＿＿＿＿＿＿＿＿＿＿＿＿＿＿＿。 B: あ、じゃ、お願い。
5.	A:	B:	A: ミラーさんは何時に(帰りますか)＿＿＿＿＿＿＿＿＿＿＿＿＿＿＿＿＿＿。 B: 6時に帰ります。
6.	A:	B: ▲	A: 田中さんはどちらに(勤めていますか)＿＿＿＿＿＿＿＿＿＿＿＿＿＿＿＿＿＿。 B: 銀行に勤めております。
7.	A: ▲	B:	A: 大学ではどういった研究を(していますか)＿＿＿＿＿＿＿＿＿＿＿＿＿＿＿＿＿＿。 B: 日本の歴史について研究しております。
8.	A:	B:	A: 田中先生がロビーで(待っています)＿＿＿＿＿＿＿＿＿＿＿＿＿＿＿＿＿＿。 B: わかりました。今、すぐ行きますから。
9.	A:	B: ▲	A: 今日は5時で失礼するけど。 B: あ、(急ぐんですか)＿＿＿＿＿＿＿＿＿＿＿＿＿＿＿んですか。
10.	A:	B: ▲	A: その本(読みましたか)＿＿＿＿＿＿＿＿＿＿＿＿＿＿＿＿＿＿。 B: ああ、読んだよ。
11.	A: ▲	B: ▲	A: どのコンピュータを(使っていますか)＿＿＿＿＿＿＿＿＿＿＿＿＿＿＿＿＿＿。 B: A社のコンピュータを使っています。
12.	A:	B:	A: お兄さんは何を(専攻していましたか)＿＿＿＿＿＿＿＿＿＿＿＿＿＿＿＿＿＿。 B: 兄は国際関係論 (international relations)を専攻しておりました。

G3. What are the potential forms of the following verbs?

		Potential			Potential
いる	is located/stay		書く	write	
言う	say		飲む	drink	

Chapter 1: Job Interview

教える	teach/inform		思う	think	
買う	buy		なる	become	
止める	stop something		帰る	return/leave	

G4. Respond to the following questions posed by the speaker (X). Use potential verbs in your response (Y).

A. Your colleague wants to confirm the rumor that you are not coming tomorrow. You will come the day after tomorrow.

   X: あした来ませんね？

   Y: ええ、＿＿＿＿＿＿＿＿＿＿＿＿が、あさっては＿＿＿＿＿＿＿＿＿＿＿＿。

B. Your colleague is asking if you are good at [speaking] Spanish.

   X: スペイン語はどうですか。

   Y: スペイン語はあまり＿＿＿＿＿＿＿＿＿＿＿が、フランス語は＿＿＿＿＿＿＿＿＿＿＿。

C. In a job interview, your interviewer is asking why you have chosen the company.

   X: どうして我が社を ご志望なんですか。

   Y: 私の大学の専攻が＿＿＿＿＿＿＿＿＿＿＿＿＿＿＿からです。(make use of...)

D. Your colleague is concerned about your smoking habit.

   X: たばこを やめたいんでしょう？

   Y: やめたいんですけど、＿＿＿＿＿＿＿＿＿＿＿＿＿＿＿んです。

E. Your colleague is asking if you would wait until five (before leaving).

   X: 5時まで待ちますか。

   Y: いや、5時までは＿＿＿＿＿＿＿＿＿＿＿から、今日は帰ります。

F. Your colleague is asking if you can see him on Wednesday. Tell him that can't meet him on Wednesday, but you can meet him on Thursday.

   X: 水曜日にお時間がありますか。

   Y: 水曜日には＿＿＿＿＿＿＿＿＿＿＿＿が、

   木曜日には＿＿＿＿＿＿＿＿＿＿＿。

G. Your colleague has asked if you can work until six. Tell him you can't work until six, but you can work until five-thirty.

   X: 6時まで、仕事ができますか。

   Y: ＿＿＿＿＿＿＿＿＿＿＿＿＿＿＿。

H. Your colleague has just entered the room and asked if she can use a computer. Tell her that Mr. Tanaka is using that one, but she can use this one.

   X: このコンピュータ、ちょっといいですか。

   Y: それは田中さんが お使いですよ。でも、こっちのは

   今＿＿＿＿＿＿＿＿＿＿＿＿＿＿＿。

20 *A Systematic Approach to Business Japanese*

I. Section Chief Tanaka confirms if Mr. Yamada is good at Chinese. Tell him that Mr. Yamada can speak not only Chinese but also English as well.

  X: 山田君は中国語が得意って聞いたけど。

  Y: 山田さんは_____も_____も_____。

J. Section Chief Tanaka asks how the conference went yesterday. You reply that you weren't able to attend the conference yesterday because...

  X: きのうの会議に出ましたか？

  Y: 病気_____ので、_____。

G5. Fill in the blanks based on the sentence in the boxes below.

> 1. おととい 私は デパートで ミラーさんと バレンタインの プレゼントを 買いました。
>   The day before yesterday, I bought a Valentine's gift with Ms. Miller at the department store.

  a. 私_____買ったのはバレンタインのプレゼントです。

  b. 私とバレンタインのプレゼントを_____はミラーさんです。

  c. おととい私がミラーさんとバレンタインのプレゼントを買ったのは_____です。

  d. 私がミラーさんとデパートでバレンタインのプレゼントを買ったのは_____です。

> 2. 田中さんは新聞を読んでいますが、山田さんはコーヒーを飲んでいます。
>   Ms. Tanaka is reading a newspaper, but Mr. Yamada is drinking coffee.

  a. 新聞を_____人は田中さんで、_____人は山田さんです。

> 3. 先月、ハリスさんは飛行機で奥さんと北海道へ行きました。
>   Last month, Mr. Harris went to Hokkaido with his wife by plane.

  a. ハリスさん_____奥さんと行ったのは北海道です。

  b. 奥さんと北海道へ_____はハリスさんです。

  c. 先月、ハリスさんが奥さんと飛行機で行ったのは_____です。

  d. 先月、ハリスさんが奥さんと北海道へ行ったのは_____です。

> 4. 田中さんは手で書いていますが、ハリスさんはワープロを使っています。
>   Mr. Tanaka is writing [it] by hand, but Ms. Harris is using a word processor.

  a. 手で_____人は田中さんで、_____人はハリスさんです。

> 5. 田中さんはドイツ車が好きですが、ハリスさんは日本車が好きです。
>   Mr. Tanaka likes German cars, but Ms. Harris likes Japanese cars.

  a. ドイツ車_____人は田中さんで、_____人はハリスさんです。

Chapter 1: Job Interview

G6. Fill in the blanks in the following conversation with the combinations of verbs and adjectives (e.g., 安(やす)くて便(べん)利(り) "It's cheap and convenient."; 疲(つか)れて休(やす)んだ "I became tired, so I took a rest.").

A. X: シントミホテルは新宿駅(しんじゅくえき)から遠(とお)いんですか。

   Y: いいえ、＿＿＿＿＿＿＿＿＿＿15分です。＿＿＿＿＿＿＿＿＿＿ビルです。

   A: Is Shintomi Hotel far from the Shinjuku Station?
   B: No. It's 15 min. on foot (lit. "walk and 15 min."). It's a new and tall building.

B. X: 買いましたね、新しいプリンター。

   Y: ええ、このプリンターは＿＿＿＿＿＿＿＿＿＿＿＿＿＿＿＿＿＿＿＿。

   A: You bought it --- a new printer!
   B: Yes. This printer is quiet and prints fast.

C. X: 「なかじま」って、いいレストランなんですか。

   Y: ええ、あそこは＿＿＿＿＿＿＿＿＿＿＿＿から、若者(わかもの)に人気(にんき)があるんです。

   A: Is Nakajima a good restaurant?
   B: Yes. That place is cheap and tasty, so it is popular among young people.

D. X: 新幹線(しんかんせん)で行くんです。

   Y: いいですね。新幹線は＿＿＿＿＿＿＿＿＿＿＿＿＿＿＿＿＿＿＿＿。

   A: I'm going by bullet train.
   B: That's good. Bullet trains are nice and comfortable (lit. "comfortable and good").

E. X: わかりますか。

   Y: このコピーは字(じ)が＿＿＿＿＿＿＿＿＿＿、＿＿＿＿＿＿＿＿＿＿＿＿＿＿＿＿。

   A: Do you understand?
   B: This copy is small and I can't read it

F. X: どうしたんですか。

   Y: ゆうべ11時まで＿＿＿＿＿＿＿＿＿＿、きょうは頭(あたま)が＿＿＿＿＿＿＿＿＿＿＿＿＿＿。

   A: What happened?
   B: Last night, I drank beer till 11 and I have a headache today.

G. X: ご両親(りょうしん)のお仕事(しごと)は？

   Y: 父はIBMに＿＿＿＿＿＿＿＿＿＿、母は図書館(としょかん)で＿＿＿＿＿＿＿＿＿＿＿＿おります。

   A: What's the jobs of your parents?
   B: My father works for IBM, and my mother is working at a library.

H. X: どうして我(わ)が社(しゃ)をご志望(しぼう)なんですか。

   Y: 御社(おんしゃ)は高性能(こうせいのう)ロボット＿＿＿＿＿＿＿＿、歴史(れきし)も＿＿＿＿＿＿、私はこういった企業(きぎょう)で働(はたら)きたいと思ったんです。

   A: Why did you choose our company?
   B: You are the company that makes high-performance robots, and it has a (long) history, so I thought I would like to work for such a company.

G7. By following the examples, create sentences using sentence modifiers.

Example: A. 田中さんは電子メールを出すのが好き(or きらい／得意／苦手)です。

B. 吉田さんは_____

C. 菊池さんは_____

D. 山中さんは_____

E. 西さんは_____

F. スミスさんは_____

G. 木村さんは_____

H. 鈴木さんは_____

I. ジョンソンさんは_____

J. 田村さんは_____

K. 石井さんは_____

L. ブラウンさんは_____

Chapter 1: Job Interview   23

Example: メールを出すのが好きなのは田中さんです。

1. _____が得意(とくい)なのは_____さんです。
2. _____が苦手(にがて)なのは_____さんです。
3. _____が好きなのは_____さんです。
4. _____が上手(じょうず)なのは_____さんです。
5. _____が下手(へた)なのは_____さんです。

G8. Combine the sentences with ので or から so that one sentence states the reason for the other.   Caution: The sentences are not necessarily in the order of reason-result below.

1. ラケットボールをしたいです。体育館(たいいくかん)に行きます。
   _____。

2. 用事(ようじ) (errand) があります。先(さき)に帰ります。
   _____。

3. 銀行(ぎんこう)に行きます。キャッシュがありません。
   _____。

4. 昼(ひる)ごはんを食べられませんでした。会議(かいぎ)は11時から2時までありました。
   _____。

5. めがねがありません。新聞(しんぶん)が読めません。
   _____。

6. 5時です。帰ります。
   _____。

7. ウォールストリートジャーナル (WSJ)が読めます。田中さんは英語(えいご)が得意(とくい)です。
   _____。

8. あまりよくわかりませんでした。むずかしかったです。
   _____。

9. 駅(えき)から遠(とお)くて不便(ふべん)です。家賃(やちん)は高いです。(家賃:rent)
   _____。

10. 横浜銀行(よこはまぎんこう)の副社長(ふくしゃちょう)を存(ぞん)じております。ご紹介(しょうかい)いたしましょうか。
    _____。

A Systematic Approach to Business Japanese

11. 日本語がまだ下手です。日本に一年います。

    _____。

12. 会社に遅れました。電車の事故がありました。(遅れる: be late; 事故: accident)

    _____。

Reading & Writing 1

Study Ms. Yamada by using her resume (Section 1E.2) and answer the questions below. The glossary is provided.

履歴書 (Resume)
   a. Find her date of birth and present address.
   b. Find the place she has written her educational history. Has she graduated from a university?
   c. Find the place she has written her employment history. How many jobs did she have so far?

平成	(n) Heisei Era (1989-)	工科大学	(n) Institute of Technology
昭和	(n) Showa Era (1925-1989)	電気工学科	(n) Electrical Engineering Division
東京都	(n) Tokyo Capital	卒業見込	(n) Expected to graduate
大田区上田	(n) Ota Ward, Ueda (part of the ward)	現在まで	(phr) Up to now
東京都立	(n) Tokyo Municipal	アルバイト	(n) part-time work
新宿高校	(n) Shinjuku High School	賞罰なし	(phr) awards and charges: none
卒業	(n) graduated	以上	(n) The above is all.

身上書 (Personal Disclosure Form)
   a. Find the place she has written her licenses and qualifications.
   b. What are her favorite school subjects and hobbies? What sports does she enjoy?
   c. What is her reason for choosing this company?
   d. Find about her family members.
   e. What are her desired job areas if she is hired?

アマチュア無線	(n) ham/amateur radio	良好	(n) good
一級、二級	(n) first class, second class	山田太郎	(n) Taro Yamada
免許	(n) license	春子、夏男	(n) Haruko, Natsuo
情報処理	(n) information processing	ハードウェア関係	(n) related to hardware
技術	(n) skills; technology	仕事	(n) work
英語、スペイン語	(n) English, Spanish	希望(する)	(v) prefer
数学	(n) mathematics	電気工学	(n) electrical engineering

Reading & Writing 2

Name:_____ Sec:_____ #:___

Create your own resume using the two-part form below.

履　歴　書			年　　月　　日現在	写真をはる位置
ふりがな			男・女	
氏　名			印	

年　　　月　　　日生 （満　　歳）	本籍	都道府県

ふりがな	電話 市外局番（　　　　）
現住所 （〒　　－　　　）	（　　　　方呼び出し）
ふりがな	電話 市外局番（　　　　）
連絡先（現住所以外に連絡を希望する場合のみ記入） （〒　　－　　　）	（　　　　方呼び出し）

年	月	学歴・職歴など（項目別にまとめて書く）

身上書

ふりがな	現住所（〒　　－　　）	電話 市外局番（　　）
氏　名		（　　　　方呼び出し）

年	月	免　許・資　格

得意な学科 趣　味 スポーツ	健康状態 志願の動機

家族	氏　名	性別	生年月日	氏　名	性別	生年月日
			． ．			． ．
			． ．			． ．
			． ．			． ．
			． ．			． ．

本人希望記入欄（特に給料・職種・勤務時間・勤務地その他について希望があれば記入）

保護者（本人が未成年の場合のみ記入） ふりがな		電話 市外局番（　　）
氏　名	現住所（〒　　－　　）	（　　　　方呼び出し）

採用者側の記入欄（志願者は記入しないこと）

Communicative Exercise 1   Name:_____ Sec:_____ #:____

C1. You are in a job interview.   Person A is interviewing you. Complete the conversation with appropriate phrases.

A: スミスさんの専攻は？
B: 大学ではコンピュータサイエンスを_____。
A: そうですか。我が社を志望する理由は何ですか。
B: _____は長い歴史が_____、すばらしい製品を_____ですから。
それから、私は日本語が(can speak)から、日本語が(make use of)仕事をしたいんです。
A: なるほど。お父さんのお仕事は？
B: _____はワールドテレコムに勤めて_____。
A: スミスさんはスポーツがお得意なんですね？
B: _____、あまり_____が、テニス____ゴルフ_____好きです。

C2. Find a partner and ask the following questions.

a. 名前 (name)
b. ご両親の住所 (parents' address)
c. transportation to school
d. major or specialty
e. length of studying Japanese
f. skills, hobbies, sports, likes and dislikes, etc.

C3. Based on what you learned above, introduce him/her to the rest of the class.

C4. Based on the activities in C3, answer the following questions.
a. ご両親の家が大学に近い (near)人はいますか。
b. 大学へ車で来る人はだれですか。
c. エンジニアリングが専攻の学生がいますか。マネジメントを勉強している学生はどうですか。
d. 日本語を一年間だけ勉強している学生がいますか。
e. コンピュータが使える人はいますか。
f. スポーツをする人はだれですか。
g. 映画が好きな人はいますか。
f. 和食(= 日本料理)がきらいな人はいますか。

The role playing activities below are more effectively performed after finishing the Reading & Writing activities.

C5. Find a partner.   You will become the interviewer and your partner will be a job applicant.   Ask the applicant (1) the name of the school he/she graduated from, (2) his/her major, (3) his/her date of birth, (4) his/her current address, and (5) his/her prior job experiences.

C6. After the previous role playing, switch the roles.   Ask the applicant about (1) his/her licenses and other qualifications, (2) hobbies, favorite subjects, sports, and (3) the reason why he/she is applying for the company.   In addition, ask about (4) his/her family and (5) the specific job she would like to perform.

Listening Comprehension 1 Name:_____ Sec:_____ #:____

Listen to the conversation on the accompanying media. Write down what you hear and answer the questions below.

1. <u>Voc: やまばと宅急便(たっきゅうびん): (n) Yamabato Parcel Delivery Service</u>
   やまばと宅急便がいいのはどうしてですか。

2. <u>Voc: 通勤(つうきん): (n) commuting; 喜ぶ(よろこ): (cv: yoroko) feel glad; 入る(はい): (cv: hair) enter</u>
   Bさんはどうして東京(とうきょう)にある会社に入(はい)りたいんですか。

3. <u>Voc: 朝日電気(あさひでんき):(n) Asahi Electric; 製品(せいひん):(n) product</u>
   Aさんが話しているのはどんなコンピュータですか。

4. <u>Voc: 有名(ゆうめい):(な-adj) famous; 簡単(かんたん):(な-adj) simple</u>
   Bさんがきのう行った会社はどんなところですか。

5. <u>Voc: ドイツ: (n) Germany; 封筒(ふうとう): (n) envelope; 探す(さが):(cv: sagas) look for</u>
   Aさんの探しているのは何ですか。

6. <u>Voc: 国際会議(こくさいかいぎ):(n) international conference; 通訳(つうやく): (n) interpreting; 経験(けいけん): (n) experiences</u>
   BさんがAさんの会社を選(えら)んだのはどうしてですか。

7. <u>Voc: 国際関係論(こくさいかんけいろん): (n) international relations; アジア: (n) Asia; 経済(けいざい): (n) economy</u>
   スミスさんは大学で何を勉強(べんきょう)しましたか。

8. <u>Voc: 音楽(おんがく): (n) music; カラオケ: (n) sing-along bar, karaoke bar</u>
   Bさんは_____は苦手(にがて)ですが、_____は好きです。

9. <u>Voc: セントオーガスティン:(n) St. Augustine; フロリダ: (n) Florida</u>
   ブラウンさんと、彼女(かのじょ)のご家族がいるところはどこですか。

Chapter 2

ビジネスでの
紹介(しょうかい)
Business Introduction

Priming

Newly hired college graduates (called 研修社員(けんしゅうしゃいん)) typically go through an intensive training period during which they will learn the general history, values, and attitudes appropriate for the company, and be socialized into the company community. They may attend lectures, visit local factories, and have computer training during this time. During this period, they are also taught company dress codes, greetings and general demeanor when interacting with clients and customers. After the initial training, technical graduates may be initially posted at a local factory and learn to do manual work on the floor before moving on to their own field of expertise. Managerial graduates may also be initially assigned to non-managerial work before moving on to a lower managerial position.

When trainees arrive at their post for the first time, they must introduce themselves properly to their superiors and colleagues as part of their initiation rituals. First impressions are important. When members of the same in-group meet, hierarchical relationships among them will determine the use of polite language. As a member of the company, you need to use honorific expressions to refer to your superiors and humble forms to refer to yourself. However, when you meet someone from an out-group, in-group vs. out-group distinction takes precedence over the hierarchical distinction among the in-group members. As a result, when you are speaking with an outsider, you have to use honorific expressions to refer to outsiders, and use humble forms to refer to insiders including your superiors.

Ms. Aoki has brought Mr. Harris, a company trainee, to Section Manager Tanaka. In this conversation, Mr. Tanaka uses plain form speech while Mr. Harris maintains polite form speech with both Mr. Tanaka and Ms. Aoki.

Conversation 2A: Mr. Harris meets his boss.

1. 青木: 課長、研修社員のハリス君です。
2. 田中: お！君がハリス君か。私がここの課長の田中だ。
3. ハリス: トーマス・ハリスです。今日からお世話になります。
4. 田: まあ、わからないことがあったら、まわりの先輩に聞いて。そうだな、なれるまで青木君について。
5. ハ: はい、わかりました。青木さん、よろしくお願いします。
6. 青: こちらこそよろしく。

1. A: Section Manager. This is our trainee, Mr. Harris.
2. T: Oh! You're Mr. Harris! I'm Tanaka, Section Manager here.
3. H: I am Thomas Harris ready to begin work today.
4. T: OK, if there's anything you don't understand, ask senior colleagues here. Well, why don't you follow Ms. Aoki till you get used to (this place).
5. H: Yes, sir. Ms. Aoki, I'll be asking for your help.
6. A: Gladly. (Lit. "The same here.")

課 [カ] section, lesson　　員 [イン] member　　君 [クン] title for peers/subordinates　　君 [きみ] you [peers/subordinates]

Vocabulary 2A

- 上司 (じょうし) (n) one's superior
- 部下 (ぶか) (n) one's subordinate
- 同僚 (どうりょう) (n) colleague
- 青木 (あおき) (n) Aoki [family name]
- 課長 (かちょう) (n) section manager [cf. 部長 (ぶちょう) (n) division manager]
- 研修社員 (けんしゅうしゃいん) (n) company trainee
- 研修 (けんしゅう) (n) training
- 社員／会社員 (しゃいん／かいしゃいん) (n) company employee
- 係長 (かかりちょう) (n) subsection manager
- はじめまして (phr) How do you do?
- お世話になる (おせわになる) (phr) receive someone's care [お is an honorific prefix]

こと (n) fact, thing
あったら (cv: ar) [conditional of ある] if ... exists, if one has [something]
まわり (n) surrounding
先輩 (せんぱい) (n) one's senior [colleagues, students]
- 後輩 (こうはい) (n) one's junior [colleagues, students]
な (sp) [blunt confirmation]
そうだな (phr) well; let's see [blunt]
なれる (vv: nare) become accustomed to
ついて (cv: tsuk) [て-form of つく] be attached; be assigned; accompany
こちらこそ (phr) It's this side that...; The same here.
こそ (p) [emphasis]

Structures 2A

2A.1. Personal References

Like the suffix 〜さん, 〜君 can be added to names (family names or given names) and is used to refer to a peer (typically a male) or someone younger than the speaker. For example, a student may call his/her male classmates with 〜君. In business settings, 君 is typically used by a superior to refer to his/her subordinates ム male or female. When you refer to your colleagues (同僚) or senior colleagues (先輩), you should use 〜さん instead of 〜君. To refer to your superiors, you should use their title (e.g., 係長 "subsection manager"). To refer to an outsider, you should add an honorific suffix 〜様 (さま) to his/her family name such as 田中様. If you don't know the family name, you can refer to that person by his/her company name (e.g., ワールドコンピュータ様). If you know neither his/her family name nor company name, you can refer to that person as お宅様 or by the role term such as お客様.

	In-group	Out-group (name known)	Out-group (name unknown)
Lower ranks	[family-name]君／さん	[family-name]さん／様	[company-name] 様 or お宅様
Colleagues	[family-name] さん		
Superiors	[family-name] + title, or title by itself	[family-name] + title, or title by itself (さん／様)	

When you refer to your own company, you should use 我が社, or 私ども ("we"), or 私どもの会社 ("our company"). ども is a humble plural suffix.

2A.2. Conditionals: たら

One of the most productive structures in Japanese is a conditional structure "If/When S1, S2." The conditional form consists of a past form + ら (often called "たら form"). Conditional forms may look like past tense predicates, but they can refer to past, present, or future events and states. In every day use, the plain conditional forms (e.g., できたら) are used more often than the polite conditional forms (e.g., できましたら). In business settings, the polite conditional forms are not uncommon. Conditional い-adjective forms are limited to the plain form.

	S1	S2
	V たら／V ましたら、	
ご質問が	あったら／ありましたら、	聞いてください。
	If you have any questions, please ask.	
	N だったら／N でしたら、	
	な-Adj だったら／な-Adj でしたら、	
あした	お休みだったら／でしたら、	来ませんか。
	暇だったら／でしたら、	
	If you are free tomorrow, would you like to come?	
	い-Adj かったら、	
今	お忙しかったら、	あとでお願いします。
	If you are busy now, please do it later.	

Note 1: Affirmative たら form can be interpreted as conditional ("if...") or non-conditional ("when...") depending on whether or not S1 is presupposed to happen or have happened. This distinction is not obvious from the surface form. Negative forms (V なかったら) can only be interpreted as conditional.

全部できたら、行きます。	If I finish everything, I will go. (S1 is not presupposed.)
全部できたら、行きます。[non-conditional]	When I finish everything, I will go. (S1 is presupposed.)
全部できなかったら、いいですよ。	If you can't finish everything, it's all right.

Note 2: The event referred to in S1 must be realized before the event in S2 happens. If S1 and S2 happen at the same time or S2 happens before S1, the たら form cannot be used. The first sentence marked by ＊ below is ungrammatical because S1 ("going to Japan") and S2 ("taking a camera") occur at the same time.

＊日本に行ったら、カメラを持っていきます。	If I go to Japan, I'm going to take a camera.
日本に行ったら、カメラを買います。	If I go to Japan, I'm going to buy a camera.

Note 3: When the sentence refers to a past event ("When S1 happened, S2 happened"), S2 must be an event the subject of S1 had no control over. The first sentence below is unacceptable because the subject of S1 (i.e., "I") has

control over the action in S2 (= "used the computer"). The second sentence is acceptable because the event in S2 (the phone call from Mr. Tanaka) is not controlled by the subject of S1 ("I").

*会社に行ったら、コンピュータを使った。	When I went to the company, I used the computer.
会社に行ったら、田中さんから電話があった。	When I went to the company, I had a call from Mr. Tanaka.

Note 4: The sentence can also refer to a counterfactual event in the past (i.e., "If S1 had happened, S2 would/could have happened [but, in reality, S1 did not happen, so S2 did not happen]").

コンピュータを使ったら、速くできたでしょう。	If I had used a computer, I could have done it quickly.

The V たらどうですか (or いかがですか) structure is often used to make suggestions ("How about...?" or "Why don't you...?"). V たらいいです can also be used to make suggestions ("It would be good if you ...").

電話したら、いかがですか。	Why don't you call them? (Lit., What if you call them?)
病院に行ったら、どうですか。	Why don't you go to hospital?
病院に行ったら？	Why don't you go to hospital? (casual style)
田中さんにたのんだらいいですよ。	It would be good if you ask Mr. Tanaka (to do it).

More たら form examples follow.

 何て言ったら、いいですか。 How shall I say it? (Lit. "If I say what, would it be good?")
 私でしたら、コーヒーにします。 If I were you, I would choose coffee.
 使ったら、洗ってください。 If you have used it, please wash it.
 よかったら、お一つどうぞ。 If it suits you, please take one.

2A.3. V まで

The particle まで marks the endpoint of coming and going actions as in アトランタまで行った。 ("I went as far as Atlanta") or marks an endpoint of an activity as in 十時まで仕事をしました。 ("I worked until 10 o'clock"). More examples follow:

田中さんを駅まで送りました。
I escorted Ms. Tanaka as far as the station.

今日、勉強したところまで、テストに出ますよ。
There will be a test on what we have covered up to today.
(Lit. "The point where we have studied up to today will emerge in the test.")

Instead of a time noun, a plain-form verb can precede まで. This verb refers to an event that terminates an on-going activity ("until an event happens, an activity continues"). The verb preceding まで must be a non-past, affirmative verb regardless of the overall of tense of the sentence as shown below. The last sentence marked by ＊ is ungrammatical.

 会議が終わるまで、待ちました。 I waited until the meeting was over.
 8時になるまで、働きました。 I worked until it became eight o'clock.
 ＊8時になったまで、働きました。 [ungrammatical]

2A.4. おじぎ (Bowing)

Like speaking with honorific-humble forms, bowing in Japan has elaborate rules. As a form of greeting, you bow with your entire upper body when you meet your superiors or important visitors. (Some department stores train their new recruits using a special bowing machine to measure bowing angles.) You gaze down naturally by following the angle of your upper torso. (Keep your back straight!) You bow lower and longer to higher-ranking people. You often greet them (e.g., おはようございます、失礼します) as you bow. When bowing, men should keep their hands straight down to the sides with the fingers extended. Women should clasp their hands lightly in front as they bow. If you pass by someone for the second time later on the same day, you can just do a short head bow.

In a large Japanese company, frequently there is a distinction between "career post" (総合職, lit. "comprehensive profession") employees and "clerical post" (一般職, lit. "general profession") employees. Those hired as career-post employees have a career track and are promoted accordingly, while those hired as clerical-post employees (frequently female graduates of a two-year college or high school) are limited to clerical work including typing, copying, mail delivery, and even tea-serving to visitors and co-workers. Newly-hired career-post employees may also be asked to do such chores. In the next conversation, Mr. Harris encounters this strange custom and ends up serving tea to everyone in the office.

Conversation 2B: Mr. Harris' first job

1. 青: じゃ、さっそくだけど、ここがハリス君の机で、コンピュータはそこのを使って。それと、電話はわからなかったら、私に回してね。
2. ハ: はい。
3. 青: あ、それから、お茶出しは新入社員の仕事だから、お願いね。
4. ハ: え？ お茶出し？
5. 青: ええ、毎日10時と3時にお茶を出すの。コーヒーとか紅茶なんかが好きな人もいるから、みんなに聞いてね。

1. A: Well then, let's get started. This is your desk, and as for your computer, use that one there. And, if you don't know how to answer phone calls, forward them to me.
2. H: OK.
3. A: Oh, in addition, serving tea is the job of the newly-hired, so it's your job.
4. H: What? Serving tea?
5. A: Yes, you serve tea at ten and at three everyday. Some people prefer coffee or black tea, so please ask everyone.

使う use　仕事 work,　事 thing, matter　毎日 everyday,　毎 every

Vocabulary 2B

さっそく (n) immediate, without delay
机 (n) desk
わからなかったら (cv) [conditional form of わからない] if you don't understand
回して (cv: mawas) [て-form of まわす, Vt] re-route, rotate, pass, spin

●回る (cv: mawar) [Vi] to go around
それから (phr) and then
お茶出し (n) serving tea
新入社員 (n) newly-hired employee
仕事 (n) work, job

お願いね (phr) [short form of お願いしますね]
とか (p) and/or [A とか B "A and B and the like"]
紅茶 (n) black tea

なんか (suf) [informal form of など] and so on, and the like

Structures 2B

2B.1. Listing (X など／X なんか／X とか／X や)

X など and X なんか both mean "X, and the like," "X, and so forth," or "X, for one." なんか is more colloquial than など. The particles は, が and を are often dropped after なんか (or など).

休みの日にはよくゴルフなんか(を)します。　　On my days off, I play golf, etc.
コーヒーなど(は)いかがですか。　　How about coffee or something?
私なんか(は)、ぜんぜんわかりません。　　I, for one, don't understand it at all.

We know that the particle と is used to list nouns as in 本と雑誌. The particle とか can also be used to list nouns, and it means "and as such." Unlike と, however, とか can be used to list nouns as well as verbs. なんか can be added after the listing.

日本のサラリーマンはゴルフとかカラオケが好きなんです。
= 日本のサラリーマンはゴルフとかカラオケなんか(が)好きなんです。
Japanese salaried workers like golf and karaoke, and so on.

はじめはコピーするとか、お茶を出すとか、そんな雑用が多いです。
In the beginning, copying and serving tea, and the like --- there are a lot of chores like that.

Another particle for listings is や. Like the particle と, the particle や can be used to list only nouns However, the expression A と B implies "A and B (and nothing else)", the expression A や B implies "A and B (and things like that)." なんか can be added after the listing.

休みの日にはマージャンやパチンコをします。　　On my days off, I play mahjong, and pachinko, etc.
ケーキやパイはいかがですか。　　How about a cake and pie (and things like that)?
= ケーキやパイなんかいかがですか。

Compare the last sentences above with the と／も listings below. Note that なんか cannot follow と／も.

コーヒーとケーキはいかがですか。　　How about a coffee and cake (that's all I have)?
＊コーヒーと紅茶なんかいかがですか。　　(Ungrammatical)

課長も係長も同じ部屋で仕事をしています。
Both section manager and subsection manager work in the same room.[9]

---

[9] 文化ノート A typical company office in Japan is a large room shared by many workers within each section including lower-post managers. Desks are packed together without partitions. This room arrangement blurs rank distinctions and facilitates communication among the workers, but privacy is practically non-existent. This work ethic emphasizing group cooperation in a large, partitionless room is called 大部屋主義 ("large-room-ism").

Some company trainees are required to submit a training report, a kind of "graduation paper," for the completion of their initial training.   Mr. Harris below is working on such a report and needs help.

Conversation 2C: Writing a training report

1. ハ: 青木さん、ちょっとお願いがあるんですが…	1. H: Ms. Aoki, I have a little favor to ask.
2. 青: え、何？	2. A: Oh, what is it?
3. ハ: 今、研修レポートを書いているんですが、日本語で何て言ったらいいかわからないところが二、三か所、あって。ちょっと教えて下さいませんか。	3. H: I'm writing a training report, but there are a few places where I don't know how to say it in Japanese. Could you help me a little?
4. 青: いいわよ。いつ提出するの？	4. A: Sure. When are you going to turn it in?
5. ハ: 30日までに出すつもりだったんですけど、ちょっとその日までには、まにあわないだろうと思うんです。	5. H: I intended to turn it in by the 30th, but I'm afraid I won't make it by then.
6. 青: ハリスさんだったら、だいじょうぶよ。	6. A: If it's Mr. Harris [in charge], it'll be alright.

言う say   提出 submission   出す (Vt) submit, take out   出る (Vi) go out; leave

Vocabulary 2C

お願い (n) request, wish
レポート (n) report.
● 論文 (n) paper, thesis
言ったら (cv: iw) [conditional of 言う] if (I) say
ところ (n) place
二、三か所 (n) two or three places [かしょ is the counter for places or parts of a larger area]
わ (sp) [feminine] [いいわよ "Sure."]
提出する (n/v) submit, turn in

までに (p) by
出す (cv: das) turn in, submit, serve, take out.
つもり (n) intention
まにあわない (phr) [negative of まにあう] not make it on time
だろう (cop) [plain style of でしょう, the tentative form of です] probably, I guess
だったら (cop) [conditional of だ]

Structures 2C

2C.1. Embedded Questions

When we are unable to answer a yes-no question (e.g., "Is it X?"), we can respond by saying "I don't know whether or not X." This kind of structure is called "embedded questions" since a question is "embedded" in the statement "I don't know [...]." Note that the verb inside an embedded question must be in the plain form.

Embedded Questions (plain)	Main Verb
Xか どうか	わかります／わかりません

Main verbs can be other verbs such as 知っている, 覚えている, 忘れる, 教える, 聞く, etc.

あしたまでに提出できるかどうか聞きました。
I asked whether or not he/she can submit it by tomorrow.

Alternatively, embedded questions can take the following forms.

Embedded Questions (plain)	Main Verb
Xか X(じゃ)ないか Xか Yか	わかります／わかりません

あした、会議があるかないか知っていますか。
Do you know whether or not there is a meeting tomorrow?

会議は一時からだったか、二時からだったか忘れました。
I forgot whether the meeting was from one o'clock or from two o'clock.

When the answer to an information question (i.e., wh-question) is unknown, forgotten, etc., the question can also be embedded within a sentence. In this case, the phrase どうか is deleted. The response marked by an asterisk (*) below is ungrammatical.

あした、だれが来ますか？ → さあ、だれが来るか覚えていません。
　　　　　　　　　　　　　　I don't know who is coming tomorrow.

あした、どこへ行きますか？ → どこへ行くか忘れました。
　　　　　　　　　　　　　　＊どこへ行くかどうか忘れました。
　　　　　　　　　　　　　　I forgot where we will go tomorrow.

何をつくりますか。 ＝ 何をつくるか教えてください。
　　　　　　　　　　Tell me what you are going to make.

いつ来ますか。 ＝ いつ来るか聞きました。
　　　　　　　　　I asked when he/she is coming.

空港までどのぐらいかかりますか。 ＝ 空港までどのぐらいかかるか知っていますか。
　　　　　　　　　　　　　　　　　　Do you know how long it will take (to go) to the airport?

2C.2. S つもりだ ("I intend to...")

S つもりだ expresses the intention of the speaker. This structure takes a clause modifier structure. A negative intention (i.e., an intention not to V) is expressed by a negative clause before つもりだ.

Clause (plain form)	つもりだ	
日本に行って何をする	つもりですか。	What do you intend to do after going to Japan?
日本に行って働く	つもりです。	I intend to go to Japan and work [there].

| 日本語の勉強はやめない | つもりです。 | I don't intend to quit studying Japanese. |

If you would like to deny the existence of an intention itself, use つもりはない (instead of つもりじゃない).

Clause (plain form)	つもりはない	
日本語の勉強をやめる	つもりはありません。	I have no intention of quitting my Japanese studies.

When a past form appears before つもりだ, it expresses the notion of attempted (and often failed) intention ("I tried my best to...") or the notion of private conviction ("I am convinced that.../pretend as if...").

急いで行ったつもりですが、遅れました。　　　I tried my best to get there quickly, but I was late.
きれいに書いたつもりですが、読めませんか。　I tried my best to write it neatly, but you can't read it?

2C.3.　だろう（と思う）

だろう is the plain tentative form of the copula だ. Its polite form is でしょう. Both だろう and でしょう express uncertainty ("probably" or "I guess"). Caution: The plain form だろう ending sounds rather blunt if it is used by itself at the end of the sentence.

Plain S or N だろう／でしょう	
ファーストクラスは楽だろう／でしょう。	First Class is probably comfortable.
10分は遅れるだろう／でしょう。	I guess (it) will be 10-minutes late.
「ことぶき」のお寿司はおいしいだろう／でしょう。	Sushi at Kotobuki is probably delicious.

だろう can be combined with と思う "I think" and create additional uncertain statement. でしょう cannot be used for this structure. No blunt connotation exists for this structure.

Plain S or N だろう ＋ と思う	
ファーストクラスは楽だろうと思います。	I think that First Class is probably comfortable.
レポートはまにあうだろうと思います。	I think that the report will probably be ready in time.
その仕事は厳しいだろうと思います。	I think that the job will probably be hard.

2C.4.　V までに

The particle までに marks the endpoint of time during which an event takes place completely ([time] までに: "by/before [time]") as in 8時までに ("by eight o'clock").

来週までにこの本を読んで来て下さい。　　　Please come back having read this book by next week.
cf. 来週までこの本を借りていてもいいですか。　May I borrow this book until next week.

Instead of a time noun, a verb can precede までに. The verb preceding までに must be a non-past, affirmative verb regardless of the overall tense of the sentence as shown below. The last sentence marked by ＊ is ungrammatical.

会議が終わるまでに、これをコピーして下さい。　Please copy this by the time the meeting is over.
飛行機の中で日本に着くまでに、映画を二本見た。　I watched two movies on the plane before I arrived in Japan.
＊日本に着いたまでに、映画を二本見た。　　　　[ungrammatical]

Compare this with the V まで construction we learned earlier.

日本に着くまで、眠っていましたから、映画は見ませんでした。
I didn't watch the movies because I was sleeping until I arrived in Japan.

Conversation 2D depicts a typical business introduction. When you introduce yourself to members of other companies, you state your (1) company name, (2) division name, and (3) your name in that order while you hand over your business card (with both hands if possible), and bow and greet at the same.

Conversation 2D: Introduction 1

1. 小林： あ、どうも、どうも。どうぞ、おかけ下さい。	1. K: Thanks (for coming). Please have a seat.
2. 田中： 失礼します。私、日本エレクトロニクスの営業課長をしております田中と申します。どうぞ、よろしくお願いします。それと、これはうちの課のハリスです。	2. T: Thank you. I am Tanaka, Sec. Mgr. of Sales at Japan Electronics. Nice to see you. (T. gives K. his business card.) And this is Harris in my section.
3. ハリス： よろしくお願いいたします。	3. H: Nice to meet you. (H. gives K. his business card.)
4. 小林： あ、おそれいります。私、海外営業課長の小林と申します。こちらこそ、よろしくお願いいたします。	4. K: Oh, thank you. I'm Kobayashi, Section Manager of Overseas Sales. Nice to meet you, too. (K. gives T. & K. his cards.)

営む (いとな) conduct　　営業 (エイギョウ) business, sales　　海 (カイ／うみ) sea, ocean　　外 (ガイ／そと) outside

Vocabulary 2D

小林 (n) Kobayashi [family name]
おかけ下さい (vv: kake) [honorific request (お + V-stem + 下さい) of かける] Please have a seat.
日本エレクトロニクス (n) Japan Electronics
しております (phr) [polite humble of している]
営業 (n) sales, business
● 販売 or セールス (n) sales
● 企画 (n) planning
それと (con) in addition

うち (n) my company (in-group)
課 (n) section
● 部 (n) division
● 名刺 (n) business card
おそれいります (cv: osoreir) [polite of おそれいる] feel terribly sorry; feel thankful
海外 (n) overseas
● 国内 (n) domestic, national

Structures 2D

2D.1. Generic honorific request form: お V 下さい

The neutral request form is V て下さい ("Please V") as in 使って下さい. However, in business, when you request an out-group member to do something, an honorific request form is used instead. This consists of an honorific prefix お + verb stem + 下さい.

Generic Honorific Request ↑				
	お	Verb Stem	下さい	
かけます	お	かけ	下さい。	Please sit down.
使います	お	使い	下さい。	Please use it.
帰ります	お	帰り	下さい。	Please go home.

Not all verbs are converted into this generic honorific request form. Some verbs like 来る and 行く have special honorific forms (to be introduced later) instead of the general honorific form shown above.

2D.2. Exchanging business cards (名刺)

Business cards are an essential business tool in Japan. Always carry some extra ones and be ready to produce them on demand. When you do not have one on hand, you should apologize (e.g., すみません。今、名刺をきらしております。"Sorry, I'm out of my business cards right now."). You look less than professional if you have to search for your cards. When you receive a business card, you should pay close attention to the person's job title because his/her job title in comparison with yours will determine what polite language to use. Do not fold it up, or write something down on the card. Show some interest in it, and do not put it quickly into your pocket.

When exchanging business cards, a lower-ranking person should offer his/her card first. When you offer your card to someone or receive one from others, always use both hands. When both parties exchange business cards at the same time, you can use one hand to give your card and the other to receive the other's card. When giving your cards to several people, they should be given individually. Do not deal them on a table during a business meeting.

2D.3. Role をしている

X をしている means "to play the role of X" or "to work as X" where X is a job title such as 営業部長 (Sales Division Manager). The humble polite expression is X をしております。

    私の父は大学の先生をしております。
    My father is a college professor (lit. "is acting as a college professor").

Mr. Harris is seeing Mr. Sakurai of Tamura Electric. Both speakers use polite-humble expressions. Personal names are very difficult to catch when you hear them for the first time. Frequently, you may have to ask how the names are pronounced. It is not improper to ask the pronunciation of names, but it should be done politely. Mr. Harris apologizes before confirming the pronunciation of Mr. Sakurai's name.

Conversation 2E: Introduction 2

1. ハ: 私、日本エレクトロニクス営業部のハリスと申します。どうぞ、よろしくお願いいたします。	1. H: My name is Harris of the Sales Division of Japan Electronics. Nice to meet you.
2. 桜: あ、どうも。ええ、私、田村電気、営業部の桜井と申します。どうぞよろしくお願いいたします。	2. S: Oh, thank you. My name is Sakurai of the Sales Division of Tamura Electric. Nice to meet you, too.
3. ハ: あ、おそれいります。あの、失礼ですが、「さくらい」様とお読みするんですか。	3. H: I'm terribly sorry, but shall I read [this as] Mr. Sakurai?
4. 桜: はい、そうです。	4. S: That's right.

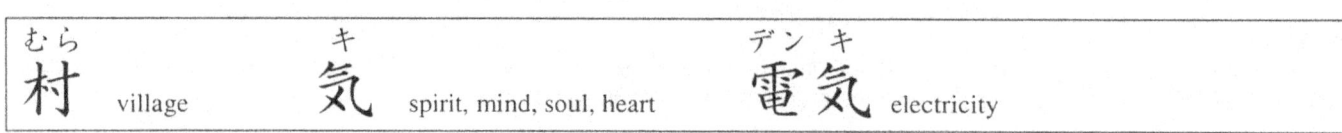

Vocabulary 2E

営業部 (n) Sales Division
田村電気 (n) Tamura Electric
● おっしゃる (sv: osshar) to say [honorific of 言う]
失礼ですが (phr) Forgive me; Excuse me.
● 恐縮です (phr) I feel obliged. I'm terribly sorry. I'm extremely grateful.

桜井 (n) Sakurai [family name]
様 (suf) Mr./Ms. [honorific title].
お読みする (cv: yom) [humble of 読む] read, pronounce.

Structures 2E

2E.1.　Xとお読みする↓

Xとお読みするんですか is a common way of asking the pronunciation of people's names. The verb お読みする (1E.1: お+V-stem+する) is the humble form of 読む ("to read/pronounce"). Don't confuse this with お読みになる, honorific of 読む.

　　A:　「みたらい」様とお読みするんですか。　　　Shall I read/pronounce [your name] Mr. "Mitarai"?
　　B:　ええ、そう読みます。　　　　　　　　　　　Yes, I will read it so.

　　A:　何とお読みするんですか。　　　　　　　　How shall I read/pronounce [your name]?
　　B:　「みたらい」と読みます。　　　　　　　　　I read it as "Mitarai."

It is possible to use the verb おっしゃいます (an honorific form of the verb 言う "to say/pronounce") to ask someone's name. For example:

　　A:　あの方は「みたらい」様とおっしゃるんですか。　Is that person called Mr. "Mitarai"?
　　B:　ええ、そうおっしゃいます。　　　　　　　　　Yes, he is.

When you are asked what your name is, you should use the verb 申します (the humble form of the verb 言う).

　　A:　お名前は何とおっしゃるんですか。[10]　　　How do you say/pronounce your name?
　　B:　「みたらい」と申します。　　　　　　　　　I say/pronounce [it] "Mitarai."

The following is the summary of the verb 言う.

"say"	Plain	Polite
Honorific (↑): Out-group	おっしゃる↑	おっしゃいます↑
Neutral: In/Out-group	言う	言います
Humble (↓): In-group	Does not exist.	申します↓

Explain why the following questions are inappropriate.[11]

　　1.　?「みたらい」とおっしゃるんですか。

---

[10] Some Japanese feel that the verb おっしゃいます is too direct if it is used to ask the listener's name.

[11] #1 does not use an honorific title 様 after the family name. #2 does not use the honorific form of the verb 言います. #3 uses the humble form of 言う (i.e., 申します) rather than its honorific form (e.g., おっしゃいます).

2. ?「みたらい」様と言うんですか。
3. ?「みたらい」様と申しますか。

Explain why B's replies below are unacceptable.[12]

1. A: 何とお読みするんですか。
   ? B: 「みたらい」とお読みします。

2. A: 「みたらい」様とおっしゃるんですか。
   ? B: はい、「みたらい」とおっしゃいます。

3. A: 「みたらい」様とおっしゃるんですか。
   ? B: はい、「みたらい」様と申します。

---

[12] In #1, because B is pronouncing his own name, お読みする↓ sounds too pompous due to the implication that B's act is for the benefit of the listener. B should respond with a humble form with no such implication (申します↓). In #2, B is using an honorific form (おっしゃいます) to speak of his own name. In #3, B uses an honorific title 様 for his own name.

Exercise 2

Grammar Utilization 2　　　　Name:_____　Sec:_____　#:____

G1. Complete the following sentences according to the English cues.

　　Example: 会議が終わったら、<u>コーヒーを飲みましょう</u>。 (Let's drink coffee.)

　a. 日本に行ったら、_____ (I want to...)

　b. 新入社員は10時と3時になったら、_____
　　 (Newly-hired employees will serve tea when it (= the time) has become 10 and 3.)

　c. 日本に一年住んだら、_____ (I will become skillful in...)

　d. お金がたくさんあったら、_____ (I would...)

　e. コーヒーがおいしくなかったら、_____ (I won't...)

　f. 私が有名なスターだったら、_____ (I would...)

　g. 研修レポートを30日までに出せなかったら、_____
　　　　　　　　　　　　　　　　　　　　(I can't go to Tokyo.)

　h. 何で読むか_____、私に聞いて下さい。
　　 (If you don't know...)

　i. 部長に何て_____いいですか。
　　 (If I say what to Division Manager, would it be good? = What should I say to Division Manager?)

G2. Make a gentle suggestion (using a conditional form V たらどう… "Why don't you V?") based on the example.

　　Example: 何時に来ましょうか。 →3時に<u>来たらどうですか</u>。

　a. だれに聞きましょうか。 → じゃあ、ミラーさん_____

　b. 何で行きましょうか。 →タクシー_____

　c. この本はむずかしいですね。辞書はありませんか。
　　　→ 私はもっていませんけど、田中さん_____
　　　　　　　(How will it be if you ask whether or not he has one?)

　d. きょうは疲れましたよ。
　　　→ じゃあ、あしたは_____ (rest)

　e. 手紙を書いたんですけど、返事 (reply) が来ないんです。
　　　→じゃあ、メール (email) を_____

G3. Fill in the blanks with either まで ("until") or までに ("by") whichever is appropriate in the context.

　a. A: 何時に来ますか。
　　 B: 3時_____来るつもりです。

b. A: 田中は今、会議に行っております。
   B: じゃあ、会議が終わる_____ロビーでお待ちしますから。

c. A: 飛行機で日本まで13時間ぐらいですか。
   B: ええ、飛行機が日本につく_____、映画が三本見られますよ。

d. A: この本、いつ_____借りられますか。(借りる:borrow)
   B: そうですね。私がアメリカに行く_____だったら、いいですよ。

G4. Make a polite request to the following people using the honorific request form.

Example: 田中部長(このペンを使う) ＝ 田中部長、このペンをお使い下さい。

a. 山田課長 (先に入る)＝ _____

b. スミスさん(この椅子にかける) ＝ _____

c. 吉田部長 (営業部に帰る) ＝ _____

d. ハリス君(このマニュアルを読む) ＝ _____

G5. Respond using the embedded question S か／N か + V. Note that some answers may require どうか.

a. A: 何時ごろ、戻りますか。 (戻る:to return, go back)
   B: 何時に_____わかりません。

b. A: 今度の週末にゴルフをしますか。
   B: ゴルフ_____わかりません。

c. A: どちらのレストランが_____教えて下さい。
   B: そうですね。はまレストランがおいしいだろうと思います。

d. A: 英語の新聞をどこで買ったら_____お聞きしましょうか。
   B: ありがとうございます。お願いします。

e. A: 田中部長は魚料理が_____聞いて下さいませんか。
   B: ああ、部長は魚が大好きだとおっしゃっていましたよ。

G6. Respond with some degree of uncertainty using だろうと思います.

a. A: 日本の夏は暑いですか。
   B: そうですね。_____

b. A: 会議は何時ごろ終わりますか。
   B: そうですね。3時ごろ_____

c. A: 飛行機の中でコンピュータを使えますか。

B: そうですね。＿＿＿＿＿＿＿＿＿＿＿＿＿＿＿＿＿＿＿＿＿＿＿＿＿

d. A: 田中さんはお酒(さけ)を飲むでしょうか。

B: そうですね。あんまり＿＿＿＿＿＿＿＿＿＿＿＿＿＿＿＿＿＿＿＿＿

e. A: マイコンソフトのスミスさんはあしたのセミナーに出ますか。

B: そうですね。忙(いそが)しいから、スミスさんは＿＿＿＿＿＿＿＿＿＿＿＿＿＿＿

G7. According to the example below, create sentences that express an intention based on some cue words.

Example: 週末(しゅうまつ)／田中さん／テニス → 週末に田中さんとテニスをするつもりです。

A. 今晩(こんばん)／田中さん／おすし

→ ＿＿＿＿＿＿＿＿＿＿＿＿＿＿＿＿＿＿＿＿＿＿＿＿＿＿＿＿＿＿＿＿

B. 7月／オーストラリア／会議(かいぎ)

→ ＿＿＿＿＿＿＿＿＿＿＿＿＿＿＿＿＿＿＿＿＿＿＿＿＿＿＿＿＿＿＿＿

C. 土曜日／山田部長(ぶちょう)／ゴルフ

→ ＿＿＿＿＿＿＿＿＿＿＿＿＿＿＿＿＿＿＿＿＿＿＿＿＿＿＿＿＿＿＿＿

D. 東京(とうきょう)／携帯(けいたい)電話

→ ＿＿＿＿＿＿＿＿＿＿＿＿＿＿＿＿＿＿＿＿＿＿＿＿＿＿＿＿＿＿＿＿

E. うち／お風呂(ふろ)

→ ＿＿＿＿＿＿＿＿＿＿＿＿＿＿＿＿＿＿＿＿＿＿＿＿＿＿＿＿＿＿＿＿

東京商事(とうきょうしょうじ)／山田さん

→ ＿＿＿＿＿＿＿＿＿＿＿＿＿＿＿＿＿＿＿＿＿＿＿＿＿＿＿＿＿＿＿＿

今日から／たばこ

→ ＿＿＿＿＿＿＿＿＿＿＿＿＿＿＿＿＿＿＿＿＿＿＿＿＿＿＿＿＿＿＿＿

H. 明日から／車／会社

→ _____

G8. Fill in the blanks below based on the picture (if any) by using listing particle (と／など／なんか／とか／や).

A.　　　　　　　　　　B.　　　　　　　　　　C.　　　　　　　　　　D.

A. 飛行中は_____使えません。（飛行中: during the flight）

B. _____見せて下さい。

C. 週末には_____します。

D. _____を押して、ペーストします。（押す: to push）

E. コンサートの切符が四枚ありますから、田中さん_____山田さんのご両親と_____スミスさんを招待します。
（切符: ticket; 招待します: to invite）

Reading and Writing 2   Name:_____ Sec:_____ #:____

R1. Create your own business card and practice business introduction with your partner. In your introduction, confirm your partner's name, telephone number(s), title, type of work he/she does, etc.

Typical Japanese business cards have the following information in this order.
1. company name
2. division/section and/or job title
3. person's name
4. address & phone number(s)

Can you locate these elements in the following business cards?

日本エレクトロニクス株式会社
営業部営業一課

ジョージ・ハン

〒103-1209
東京都港区大沢 3 − 10 − 2
電話：（03） 894 − 7327

ExperData
Japanese Business Translation Services

Patricia Amano
President

2526 Dawson Ave.
Pittsburgh, PA 15230
Phone: 412-345-9870   Fax: 412-354-5009

_{えいぎょうぶ}
営業部: Sales Division

_{えいぎょうだいいっか}
営業第一課: Sales Section 1

日本ハイテク貿易会社
社長
山田 真理子
東京都文京区本郷七丁目
電話 〇三三―八二一―七七六〇

日本タイムス社 通信員
ベス・山田友子
郵便番号 一〇三―七四五六
東京都港区三田 一―三
電話 〇三―二五八九―四四六二
電子メール yamada(at)NipoonTimes.net.jp

ハイテク: High Technology
_{ぼうえきがいしゃ}
貿易会社: Trading Company
_{しゃちょう}
社長: President

_{つうしんいん}
通信員: Reporter
_{ゆうびんばんごう}
郵便番号: zip code
_{でんし}
電子メール: email

Chapter 2: Business Introduction

Communicative Exercise 2

C1. You are Mr. Robert Norton of U.S. Business System. You just exchanged business cards with Ms. Akiko Yamaguchi of MiconSoft at a business convention. The following are your business cards. Fill in the blanks in the conversation below and complete the conversation.

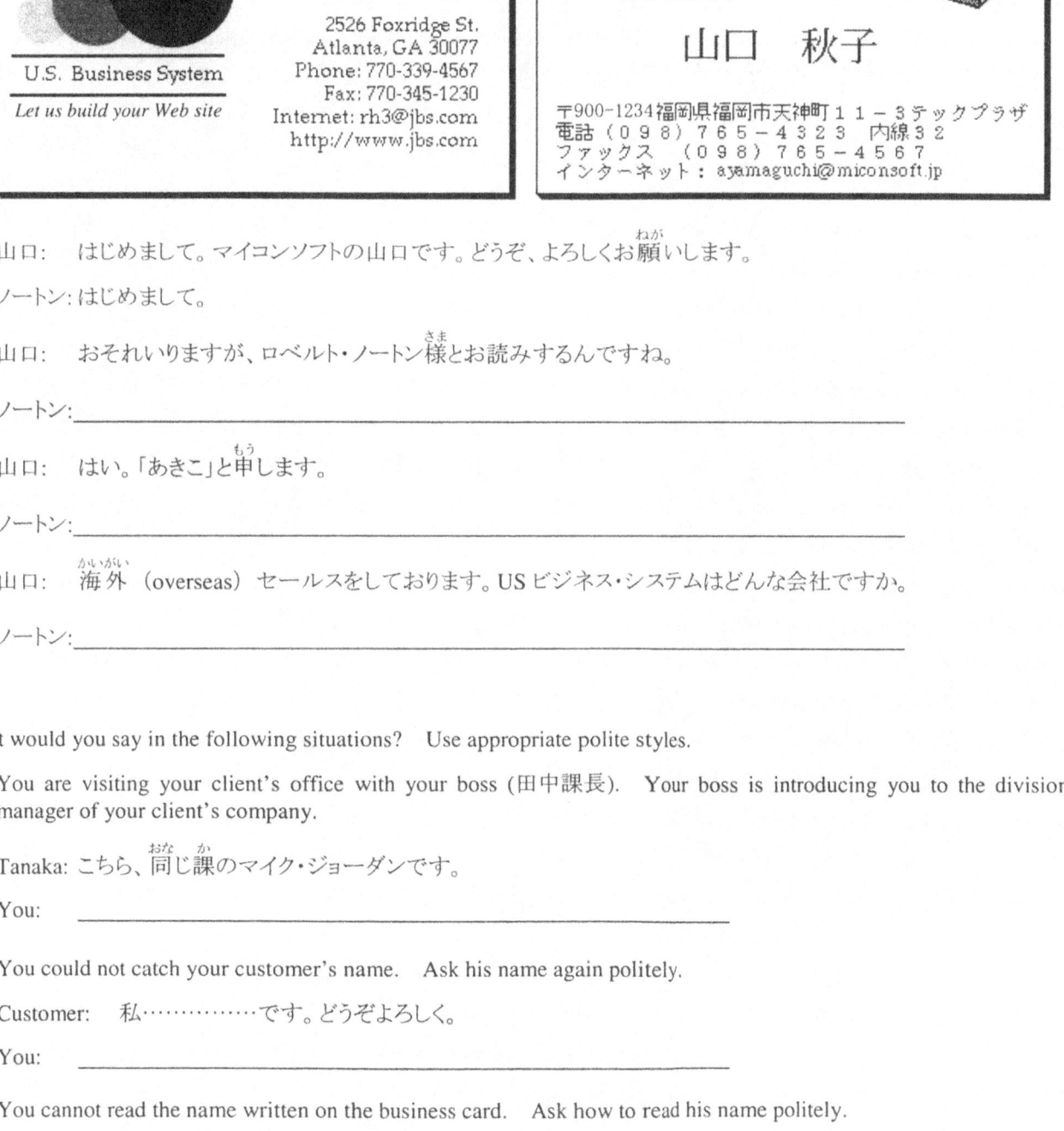

山口：　はじめまして。マイコンソフトの山口です。どうぞ、よろしくお願（ねが）いします。

ノートン：はじめまして。

山口：　おそれいりますが、ロベルト・ノートン様（さま）とお読みするんですね。

ノートン：＿＿＿＿＿＿＿＿＿＿＿＿＿＿＿＿＿＿＿＿＿＿＿＿＿＿＿＿＿＿＿＿＿＿＿＿＿

山口：　はい。「あきこ」と申（もう）します。

ノートン：＿＿＿＿＿＿＿＿＿＿＿＿＿＿＿＿＿＿＿＿＿＿＿＿＿＿＿＿＿＿＿＿＿＿＿＿＿

山口：　海外（かいがい）（overseas）セールスをしております。USビジネス・システムはどんな会社ですか。

ノートン：＿＿＿＿＿＿＿＿＿＿＿＿＿＿＿＿＿＿＿＿＿＿＿＿＿＿＿＿＿＿＿＿＿＿＿＿＿

C2. What would you say in the following situations? Use appropriate polite styles.

1. You are visiting your client's office with your boss (田中課長). Your boss is introducing you to the division manager of your client's company.

   Tanaka: こちら、同（おな）じ課（か）のマイク・ジョーダンです。

   You: ＿＿＿＿＿＿＿＿＿＿＿＿＿＿＿＿＿＿＿＿＿＿＿＿＿＿＿＿＿＿＿＿＿＿＿

2. You could not catch your customer's name. Ask his name again politely.

   Customer: 私……………です。どうぞよろしく。

   You: ＿＿＿＿＿＿＿＿＿＿＿＿＿＿＿＿＿＿＿＿＿＿＿＿＿＿＿＿＿＿＿＿＿＿＿

3. You cannot read the name written on the business card. Ask how to read his name politely.

   Customer: どうぞよろしく。(Hands over his business card.)

   You: ＿＿＿＿＿＿＿＿＿＿＿＿＿＿＿＿＿＿＿＿＿＿＿＿＿＿＿＿＿＿＿＿＿＿＿

4. You are introducing your colleague, Ms. Yoshida, to your client. Ms. Yoshida belongs to the Sales Division.

   You: _____

   Client: 私、山田と申します。よろしくお願いします。

5. You are introducing yourself to your colleagues. Ask for guidance humbly since you are new to this organization and you do not understand various things.

   Colleague: ハンさんですね？ よろしくお願いします。

   You: _____

6. You have just finished introducing yourself to your colleagues. State your resolution that you intend to work hard and ask for their assistance down the road.

   Colleague: わかりました。

   You: _____

Listening Comprehension 2   Name:_____ Sec:_____ #:____

Listen to the conversation on the accompanying media.   Write down what you hear and answer the questions below.   (A is the first speaker.   B is the second speaker.   C is the third speaker.)

1. Voc: 出身(しゅっしん)：a place of origin, a place where one comes from

    だれと だれが はじめて 会いましたか。

    ブラウンさんの出た大学は何ていう大学ですか。

2. Voc: お客(きゃく)さん： guest;　空港(くうこう)： airport;　翻訳(ほんやく)： translation

    Aさん(First speaker) はどうして困(こま)っているんですか。

    ブラウンさんはいつ帰るつもりですか。

3. Voc: さっき： a while ago

    ブラウンさんはこれから何をするつもりですか。

4. Voc: 入社(にゅうしゃ)する： enter a company;　ミラー： Ms. Miller;　はじめまして：How do you do?
    はじめて： first time;　いろいろ： various;　いっしょけんめい： one's best

    ミラーさんはどんな人ですか。
    a. 部長
    b. 新入社員(newly hired employee)
    c. お客(visitor)

5. Voc: 海外(かいがい)： overseas;　マーティン： Martin

    本田さんとマーティンさんの会社の名前(なまえ)は何ですか。

    マーティンさんはどんな仕事をしていますか。

Chapter 3

でんわ
電 話
Telephone

Priming

When answering in-coming phone calls, you are representing your company. It is important to establish quickly the identity of the calling party in order to determine the proper styles of language to be used on the phone. In this chapter, Mr. Harris answers several phone calls with standard phrases that identify his subdivision within his company. Callers in this chapter are mostly members of out-groups. Note how Mr. Harris and others maintain proper business relationships.

"Hello" on the phone is もしもし. However, in business, もしもし is not used unless the connection is bad. In general, the answering party uses the organizational name and/or division or section name and does not provide his/her own name (e.g., 日本マルチメディア営業部でございます). Individual companies have different rules for answering phone calls. It is best to ask your せんぱい about specific rules. Mr. Harris is observing how Ms. Mori is answering an in-coming call. After she recognizes the caller, Ms. Mori initiates a standard greeting (e.g., an apology) that refers to their previous encounter. That is enough for the caller (Mr. Kimura) to recognize her voice. Frequently, both parties on the phone are bowing to each other (unconsciously) even though they cannot see one another.

先日はどうも失礼いたしました。 means "Excuse my rudeness the other day." This phrase does not mean that the speaker was rude that day. Ordinarily, the opposite is true. Apologies like this function to bridge the initial greeting and the subsequent business matters.

Conversation 3A: Answering phone calls

1. 山田: はい。日本エレクトロニクス営業部でございます。	1. M: Yes. (This is) Sales Division of Japan Electronics.
2. 北川: 私、経済新聞の北川と申しますが、山田部長、おられますか。	2. K: I am Kitagawa of Keizai Shinbun. Is Division Manager Yamada there?
3. 山: ああ、北川さんですか。山田でございます。先日はどうも失礼いたしました。	3. M: Oh. Is that you, Mr. Kitamura? This is Yamada. Please excuse my rudeness the other day.
4. 北: あ、いえいえ、こちらこそ。	4. K: Oh. Not at all. WE owe YOU an apology.

部 division, part　長 chief, captain　長い long　新聞 newspaper;　新しい new

Vocabulary 3A

経済新聞 (n) Keizai Shinbun (経済 = economy)
北川 (n) Kitagawa [family name]
部長 (n) division manager
テレコム (n) telecommunication
おられます↑ (cv) [polite of おられる↑] be located. [honorific]
先日 (n) the other day

失礼いたしました↓ (n/v) [humble of 失礼する] Please excuse my rudeness
● 電話する = 電話をかける (n/v) make a phone call; call. [X に電話する "call X"]
● 電話に出る (phr) answer a phone call
● 電話に出られない (phr) cannot come to the phone
● 電話をとる (phr) pick up the phone

Structures 3A

3A.1. おられます↑ and いらっしゃいます↑

The verb います ("[someone] is located") has special honorific and humble forms. Its humble form is おります↓ ("[insider] is located") and its honorific form is いらっしゃいます↑ ("[outsider] is located."). However, the derived form of おります↓, おられます↑ ("[outsider] is located"), is widely used as the honorific form of います in Japan and this is seen in the conversation above.[13] The following table summarizes all forms of the verb いる.

---

[13] おられます↑ is used more often by male speakers.

"be located/stay/there is"	Plain	Polite
Honorific (↑): Out-group	いらっしゃる↑ おられる↑	いらっしゃいます↑ おられます↑
Neutral: In/Out-group	いる	います
Humble (↓): In-group	Non-existent	おります↓

3A.2. Common company names

Many company names end with common labels as shown below:

～株式会社 (かぶしきがいしゃ)	[company name], Inc.
～商事会社 (しょうじがいしゃ)	trading company
～商事 (しょうじ)	trading (company)
～証券会社 (しょうけんがいしゃ)	securities company
～証券 (しょうけん)	securities (company)
～工業 (こうぎょう)	manufacturing industry
～産業 (さんぎょう)	general industry
～電気工業(会社) (でんきこうぎょうがいしゃ)	electric equipment (company)
～電気産業(会社) (でんきさんぎょう)	electric equipment (company)
～電子工業(会社) (でんしこうぎょう)	electronic equipment (company)
～電子産業(会社) (でんしさんぎょう)	electronic equipment (company)
～製薬会社 (せいやくがいしゃ)	pharmaceutical company
～製薬 (せいやく)	pharmaceutical (company)
～自動車工業 (じどうしゃこうぎょう)	automobile company
～自動車 (じどうしゃ)	automobile (company)

In the following conversation, Mr. Harris is answering an in-coming call from Mr. Kimura. Because Mr. Kimura is asking for Mr. Tanaka, Mr. Harris needs to transfer the call to him.

Conversation 3B: Transferring calls

1. ハリス: はい。営業一課でございます。
2. 木村: 田中課長、お願いしたいんですが。
3. ハ: おそれいりますが、どちら様でいらっしゃいますか。
4. 木: 私、東京テレコムの木村と申します。
5. ハ: はい。少々お待ち下さい。
6. 田中: お電話、かわりました。田中です。

1. H: Hello. Sales Section 1.
2. K: May I speak with Section Manager Tanaka.
3. H: I'm terribly sorry, but may I ask who this is?
4. K: I'm Kimura of Tokyo Telecom.
5. H: Thank you. Please hold on for a moment.
6. T: Tanaka speaking. [Lit. I have switched the phone.]

様 (さま) honorific suffix　　申します (もう) say, is called　　少々 (ショウショウ) [々: repetition of the preceding]

Vocabulary 3B

どちら様↑ (n) [honorific of どちら "which one"] who

でいらっしゃいます↑ (cop) [honorific of the copula です] to be

少々 (n) a little. [More formal than ちょっと]

お待ち下さい (cv: mat) [honorific request form of 待って下さい: お+V-stem+下さい] Please wait

かわりました (cv: kawar) [plain past of かわる] changed, switched

- お電話です (phr) You have a phone call. (電話があります is NOT used for this meaning.)
- 電話が入っている (phr) You have a phone call. [Xから電話が入っている: have a call from X]
- 電話があった (phr) You had a phone call. [Xから電話があった: had a call from X]. (電話しました and 電話でした are NOT used to report an in-coming phone call.)
- 電話をかりる (phr) use [someone's] telephone

Structures 3B

3B.1. でいらっしゃいます↑／でございます

The polite form of the copula です is でございます. The polite form can be used to refer to anyone regardless of in-group or out-group distinction (私は田中でございます／あの方は田中さんでございます). The honorific form of the copula です is でいらっしゃいます↑. In general, honorific forms are used to refer to the states and actions of out-group members. Note that the honorific copula でいらっしゃいます↑ is different from the honorific verb いらっしゃいます↑ ("[someone] is located") introduced in 3A.1. This distinction becomes very obvious if the same sentences are spoken using neutral forms.

Honorific forms:
田中課長でいらっしゃいますか。   Are you/Is it Section Manager Tanaka? (identity)
田中課長はいらっしゃいますか。   Is Section Manager Tanaka there? (location)

Neutral forms:
田中課長ですか。   Are you/Is it Section Manager Tanaka?
田中課長はいますか。   Is Section Manager Tanaka there?

The following summarizes the various forms of the copula です.

copula	Plain	Polite
Honorific (↑): Out-group	でいらっしゃる↑	でいらっしゃいます↑
Polite	Non-existent	でございます
Neutral	だ	です

If you were not able to catch the caller's name, first politely ask おそれいりますが、もう一度お名前をお願いいたします ("I'm terribly sorry, but may I have your name again?") and follow up by saying "[company] の [name] 様でいらっしゃいますね？" (e.g., "You are Mr./Ms. Harris of Japan Electronics, am I correct?") before transferring the call.

Just like いらっしゃいます ("[someone] is located"), the use of でいらっしゃいます is limited to a reference to people. This limitation makes sentences 2a and 3a below ungrammatical.[14] In contrast, でございます works for both animate and inanimate objects.

---

[14] This limitation does not apply if the sentence is about something inalienable (inseparable) from the subject as in: (1) 木村さんのお宅はアトランタでいらっしゃいます ("Mr. Kimura's house is in Atlanta"), and (2) 木村さんの専攻は電気工学でいらっしゃいます ("Mr. Kimura's major is Electrical Engineering").

1. Is he/she Mr. Kimura's child?

   a. 木村さんのお子さんでいらっしゃいますか。
   b. 木村さんのお子さんでございますか。

2. Is it Mr. Kimura's car?

   a. ＊木村さんの車でいらっしゃいますか。 [Ungrammatical]
   b. 木村さんの車でございますか。

3. It's from Mr. Yamada. (Referring to a phone call)

   a. ＊山田さんからでいらっしゃいます。 [Ungrammatical]
   b. 山田さんからでございます。

3B.2.   かわる

There are two types of Japanese verbs: **transitive** verbs and **intransitive** verbs. Transitive verbs refer to action in which "someone directly acts upon an object" (e.g., 車をとめる "stop a car"). In contrast, intransitive verbs refer to a situation in which "something just happens on its own" (e.g., 車がとまる "a car comes to a stop"). In English, the same verb can be transitive or intransitive, but in Japanese, the same verb cannot usually be both transitive and intransitive. However, the verb かわる is one of a limited number of exceptional verbs that function as an intransitive verb ("[something] changes/is switched") as well as a transitive verb ("to switch/change [something]").[15] Study example sentences below.

仕事がかわった。	My jobs changed. (involuntary change of jobs)
仕事をかわった。	I switched jobs. (voluntary change of jobs)
来月から会社がかわる。	Starting next month, the company will change.
来月から会社をかわる。	Starting next month, I will switch to another company.
制服が夏服にかわる。	The uniform will switch to the summer uniform.
田中さんと電話をかわった。	I put Ms. Tanaka on the phone.
田中さんと席をかわった。	I switched seats with Ms. Tanaka.

Transitive and intransitive verbs will be discussed more fully in Chapter 6A.

In the following conversation, Mr. Harris receives a phone call from Ms. Yamamoto (an outsider) who asks for Mr. Tanaka, but Mr. Tanaka has left the company for today. Note how Mr. Harris apologizes to Ms. Yamamoto. When one receives a call from an outsider, one must refer to a member of one's own company without his/her title. This is why Mr. Harris refers to his boss as 田中は (instead of 田中さんは or 田中課長は). In-group/out-group distinction takes precedence over hierarchical distinctions within an in-group.

Conversation 3C: Apologizing (1)

1. ハリス: はい。営業一課でございます。
2. 山本: 私、朝日工業の山本と申しますが、田中課長、いらっしゃいますか。

1. H: Yes.   This is Sales Subdivision
2. Y: I'm Yamamoto of Asahi Manufacturing Industry. Is

---

[15] There is a transitive verb かえる ("to change or switch something") that implies more active involvement of the speaker in the decision to change something: 仕事をかえた ("I switched jobs").

3. ハ: たいへん申しわけございません。田中は先ほど帰りましたが…	3. H: I'm sorry. Tanaka has gone home a while ago.
4. 山: そうですか。じゃ、またあしたお電話いたしますので。失礼します。	4. K: Is that right? Then, I will call again tomorrow. Good bye.
5. ハ: 失礼いたします。	5. H: Good bye.

朝 morning　　工業 manufacturing industry　　失礼 rudeness, loss of courtesy

Vocabulary 3C

朝日 (n) [family name] Asahi; morning sun
工業 (n) manufacturing industry
山本 (n) [family name] Yamamoto
申しわけ (n) excuse, reason. [申しわけございません。 "There is no excuse." More formal than すみません]

先ほど (n) a while ago. [More formal than さっき]
また (n) again [じゃあまた。 "See you again."]
お電話いたします↓ (n/v) [Polite humble form of 電話する] call
● 電話をかけなおす (phr) call again
● 電話をかえす (phr) return the phone call

Structures 3C

3C.1. More Honorific Forms: お V になります↑

In Conversation 3C-a below, Mr. Harris receives a call from Mr. Nishi, who outranks both Mr. Harris and Mr. Tanaka, Mr. Harris' boss. (The title 君 Mr. Nishi uses to refer to Mr. Tanaka is the title for peers and subordinates.) Since Mr. Harris in Conversation 3C-a is talking among in-group members, only the hierarchical distinction within the company becomes prominent. This is why Mr. Harris refers to his boss with a title ("田中課長").

Conversation 3C-a

1. ハ: 営業一課です。	1. H: Sales Section 1.
2. 西: あ、西だが、田中君、いる？	2. N: This is Nishi. Is Mr. Tanaka there?
3. ハ: 田中課長はさきほど<u>お帰りになりました</u>。	3. H: Sec. Mgr. Tanaka left a while ago.
4. 西: そうか。じゃ、いいよ。	4. N: I see. Then, never mind.
5. ハ: 失礼しました。	5. H: I'm sorry.

Note the following differences between the Conversations 3C and 3C-a.

Conversation 3C

Ms. Yamamoto is an outsider. Mr. Tanaka is Harris' superior. Harris has no title. Harris does not use a title nor the honorific form to refer to Mr. Tanaka, his boss.

Conversation 3C-a

Mr. Nishi is the division manager who outranks Mr. Tanaka, the section manager. Harris has no title. Mr. Nishi uses the plain form without a job title. Harris uses a title and the honorific form to refer to Mr. Tanaka.

In Conversation 3C-a, Mr. Harris uses another honorific expression お帰りになりました↑ to refer to the action of his superior. This phrase is the generic honorific form of 帰りました. It consists of /お + V-stem + になる/.

	Generic Honorific Form ↑			
	お	V-Stem	に	なります
使います	お	使い	に	なりませんか。	Would you like to use it?
帰ります	お	帰り	に	なりました。	[Someone] went home.
待ちます	お	待ち	に	なって下さい。	Could you wait [for someone]?

Compare this honorific form to お + V-Stem + します↓ (1E.1), a generic humble form meaning "I will V (for you)."

    A: お待ちになって下さいませんか。↑   Could you wait for me, please?
    B: はい、お待ちします。↓   Yes, I will wait for you.

More examples of /お + V-stem + になる/ follow:

    林さん、部長がお待ちになっています。   Mr. Hayashi, Division Manager is waiting for you.
    部長が西様とお話しになっています。   Division Manager is talking with Mr. Nishi.
    部長、西様とお会いになりましたか。   Division Manager, have you met Mr. Nishi?

Not all verbs will work in this generic honorific form. If there is a special honorific form of the verb (e.g., ご存知です↑, a special honorific form of 知っています "to know"), use the special form rather than the generic form.

    山田部長はご存知ですか。   Do you know [it], Div. Mgr. Yamada?
    (Never ＊部長はお知りになっていますか。)

In Conversation 3C-b below, Mrs. Nishi is on the phone asking for her husband. Even though Mr. Nishi is Mr. Harris' in-group member, Mr. Harris quickly realizes that Mr. and Mrs. Nishi belong to a closer in-group (i.e., the Nishi family) to which Mr. Harris is an outsider. As a result, Mr. Harris correctly uses an honorific form to refer to Mr. Nishi even though Mrs. Nishi is an outsider to him. Mrs. Nishi uses other linguistic clues to indicate her close relationship to Mr. Nishi (e.g., うち↓ is a humble form of 家; もの↓ (lit. "thing") is the humble form of 人. おりますか is a humble form question of いますか, which can only be used by someone referring to a member of his/her own in-group.).

Conversation 3C-b

1.	ハ:	営業一課でございます。	1. H: Sales Section 1.
2.	西:	西と申しますが、うちの者はおりますか。	2. K: This is Nishi. Is my husband there?
3.	ハ:	西課長はさきほどお帰りになりました。	3. H: Sec. Mgr. Nishi left a while ago.
4.	西:	あ、じゃ、けっこうです。ごめん下さい。	4. K: Oh, then, never mind. Good-bye.
5.	ハ:	失礼します。	5. H: Good-bye.

In 3C-b, けっこうです is a formal form of いいです。 ごめんください, often used by women, is a polite apology gentler than 失礼します.

3C.2.   どちらの ～様でしょうか

When the caller gives his name and company, you may not always be successful in hearing the name of the company the caller is affiliated with. In such a case, you should apologize and ask as follows. If the caller is Mr. Murata, you ask: たいへん申しわけございませんが、どちらの村田様でしょうか。 ("I'm terribly sorry, but that is Mr. Murata of which company?").

In Conversation 3D, Mr. Kimura, an outsider, is asking for Subsection Manager Kawada, who is away from her desk. Mr. Harris uses a humble expression to refer to his superior, Ms. Kawada. Also, note how Ms. Kawada announces her arrival.

Conversation 3D: Apologies (2)

1. ハリス: はい。営業一課でございます。
2. 木村: 私、東京テレコムの木村と申しますが、川田係長、いらっしゃいますか。
3. ハ: 申しわけございませんが、川田はただ今、会議中で席をはずしております。お急ぎでございますか。
4. 木: ええ。ご迷惑でなければ、お願いしたいんですが。
5. ハ: 承知いたしました。少々お待ち下さい。
6. 川田: お待たせいたしました。川田です。
7. 木: お忙しいところ、申しわけございません。

1. H: Sales Section 1.
2. Ki: I'm Kimura of Tokyo Telecom. Is Subsection Manager Kawada there?
3. H: I'm sorry, but she is away from her seat right now due to a meeting. Is this urgent?
4. Ki: Yes. If it is not too much trouble, please.
5. H: Certainly. One moment, please.
6. Ka: Sorry I kept you waiting. Kawada speaking.
7. Ki: I'm sorry (to call you) when you are busy.

係長 (カカリチョウ) subsection manager 議 (ギ) consultation, deliberation 席 (セキ) seat お急ぎ (いそ) urgent

Vocabulary 3D

川田 (n) Kawada [family name]
係長 (n) subsection manager
ただ今 (n) right now
会議中 (phr) in the middle of a meeting
はずして (cv: hazus) [て-form of はずす] remove
    [席をはずす "be away from one's seat"]
お急ぎ↑ (n) urgent [お急ぎだ↑ (= 急ぐ "to hurry")]
でございます (cop) [polite of です]
ご迷惑↑ (な-adj) nuisance, annoyance. [ご is an honorific prefix]
でなければ (a) [provisional of で(は)ない]. [X でなければ "provided that it is not X"]

承知いたしました↓ (phr) Certainly.
お待たせいたしました↓ (phr) Sorry I kept you waiting.
お忙しい↑ (い-adj) busy. [honorific-polite]
ところ (n) place; point in time/space. [お忙しいところ means "when you are busy." This usage of ところ as a temporal conjunct will be explained later.]
● 話し中 (phr) The line is busy
● 留守中 (phr) while you were away
● 電話中 (phr) in the middle of a phone call
● 仕事中 (phr) in the middle of work
● 接客中 (phr) in the middle of meeting a client

Structures 3D

3D.1. Honorific Questions: お急ぎでございますか

In 1C.2, we learned a generic honorific verb form (お+V-stem+です↑). This form can be made more polite by changing the です ending to either でございます or でいらっしゃいます.

Neutral	急ぎますか。 "Are you in a hurry?"
1. お + V-stem + です↑	お急ぎですか。↑
2. お + V-stem + でございます↑	お急ぎでございますか。↑ (polite)
3. お + V-stem + でいらっしゃいます↑	お急ぎでいらっしゃいますか。↑ (very polite)

Compare this honorific form with the honorific お+V-stem+になる↑ form introduced in 3C.1. Since the お+V-stem+です↑ form cannot be a request form, the お+V-stem+下さい↑ form is shown instead.

Neutral	お + V-stem + です↑ お + V-stem + でございます↑ お + V-stem + でいらっしゃいます↑	お + V-stem + になります↑
あした帰ります。 (future)	あしたお帰りです。 あしたお帰りでございます。 あしたお帰りでいらっしゃいます。	あしたお帰りになります。
今、帰っています。 (resultant state or on-going action)	今、お帰りです。 今、お帰りでございます。 今、お帰りでいらっしゃいます。	今、お帰りになっています。
きのう帰りました。(past)	きのうお帰りです。 きのうお帰りでございます。 きのうお帰りでいらっしゃいます。	きのうお帰りになりました。
帰って下さい。(request)	お帰り下さい。	お帰りになって下さい。

3D.2. ご迷惑でなければ↑

ご迷惑でなければ↑ means "provided that it is not an intrusion/nuisance" and this phrase makes your upcoming request less imposing and more polite.

Provisional form *			Request [Please help me]	
ご迷惑	で	なければ	お願いしたいんですが。	If it is not an intrusion, I would like to request it.
nuisance	copula	provisional of ない		

The provisional forms will be discussed in detail in Chapter 7.

3D.3. お忙しいところ↑

When Ms. Kawada finally answers the phone in Conversation 3D, Mr. Kimura responds with an apology (お忙しいところ、申しわけございません。"I'm very sorry [to call you] while you are busy"). Apologies like this are readily offered when making a request. Adjectives, nouns, or V-stems can precede ところ as shown below:

お + い-Adj + ところ	Apology	
お忙しいところ	申しわけございません	I'm sorry [to trouble you] while you are busy.
お + N + のところ	Apology	
お仕事中のところ	申しわけございません	I'm sorry [to trouble you] while you are working.
お + V-stem + のところ	Apology	
お疲れのところ	申しわけございません	I'm sorry [to trouble you] while you are tired.
お急ぎのところ	申しわけございません	I'm sorry [to trouble you] while you are in a hurry.

3D.4. Transferring & Reporting Phone Calls

When you transfer phone calls, you relay the information by using the particle から. Other particles like が or は do not work here. Alternatively, you can use the verb 入っています ("has come in") to report an incoming call.

南プロダクションの黒沢様からお電話です／でございます。
It's a phone call from Mr. Kurosawa of Minami Production.

? 南プロダクションの黒沢様が／はお電話です／でございます。[Unacceptable]

南プロダクションの黒沢様からお電話が入っています。
A phone call has come in from Mr. Kurosawa of Minami Production.

When you report phone calls, you also refer to the caller by using the particle から ("from").

南プロダクションの黒沢様からお電話がございました。(= お電話がありました)
There was a phone call from Mr. Kurosawa of Minami Production.

Xが電話しました ("X called.") is a perfectly good sentence as an objective statement of facts, but it is not used in reporting phone calls.

? 南プロダクションの黒沢様が電話しました。[Unacceptable]

When the caller does not identify himself or herself, it is possible that the caller is a high-ranking executive within the company who needs no self introduction. Often, blunt language is a clue: ハリス君、いるかね？ ("Is Mr. Harris there, I wonder?"). Learn to recognize their voice as quickly as possible. Instead of responding with a standard question おそれいりますが、どちら様でいらっしゃいますか, you should transfer the call immediately.

In the following conversation, Division Manager Tanaka is not at his desk when Ms. Yamamoto, an outsider, calls. Mr. Harris apologizes and offers to ask Mr. Tanaka to return his phone call later.

Conversation 3E: Taking messages (1)

1. ハリス: はい。営業一課でございます。
2. 山本: 私、先ほどお電話しました朝日工業の山本と申しますが、田中課長、もうお戻りでしょうか。
3. ハ: 申しわけございません。まだ戻っておりませんので、戻りましたら、田中の方からご連絡するよう申し伝えますが。
4. 山: そうですか。じゃ、すみませんが、よろしくお願いいたします。こちらの電話番号は894-7327です。
5. ハ: 朝日工業の山本様、お電話番号は894-7327でございますね。承知いたしました。では、失礼いたします。

1. H: Yes. This is Sales Subdivision 1.
2. Y: I'm Yamamoto of Asahi Manufacturing Industry who called earlier. Has Sec. Mgr. Tanaka returned?
3. H: I'm sorry. He has not returned yet. When he returns, I will ask him to call you back.
4. Y: Is that right? Sorry (to bother you), but please do so. My phone number is 894-7327.
5. H: Mr. Yamamoto of Asahi Manufacturing Industry. Your phone number is 894-7327. I will certainly pass it on. Good bye.

番 (バン) number, duty 号 (ゴウ) number, item, title 伝える (つた) to communicate 伝言 (デンゴン) message

Vocabulary 3E

先ほど (n) a while ago
もう (adv) already
お戻りでしょう↑ (phr) [polite-tentative form of お戻りだ↑; 戻る (cv: modor) to return] is/has returned
まだ (adv) (not) yet
戻って (cv: modor) [て-form of 戻る] return, go/come back
〜の方から (phr) from the direction of ...

よう (n) way. [V-plain-present + よう(に)言う "tell (someone) to V"]
申し伝えます (vv: moushitsutae) [polite humble of 言い伝える; polite of 申し伝える] to communicate, tell
電話番号 (n) telephone number
さしあげる (vv: sashiage) [honorific of あげる] to give (to an out-group person)
 メッセージ／おことづけ／伝言 (n) message

- 電子メールを送る (cv: okur) ～を出す (cv: das) to send email
- 留守番電話 (n) answering machine [留守電 is its short form]
- ピーという音 (n) beep
- 発信音 (n) dial tone
- 留守電にメッセージを残す (cv: nokos) to leave, retain
- ファックスを送る (cv: okur) to send a fax

Structures 3E

3E.1. もう／まだ

もう expresses the notion that a state which existed some time ago <u>no longer exists</u>. That is, an anticipated change has occurred. In contrast, まだ expresses the notion that a state which existed some time ago <u>still remains</u>. That is, an anticipated change has not occurred. These expressions are typically translated as follows:

	Patterns	Translation
A:	もう + affirmative (e.g., もうVます／Vました／Vています)	"already" is already going to V / has already V-ed / is already V-ing
B:	もう + negative (e.g., もうVません／Vていません)	"no longer" is not going to V any more / is not V-ing any more
C:	まだ + affirmative (e.g., まだVます／Vています)	"still" is still going to V / is still V-ing
D:	まだ + negative (e.g., まだVません／Vていません)	"still not" or "not yet" is still not going to V / has not V-ed yet

The following illustrates the usage in conversation. In the question-answer exchange, if the answer is negative, the proper sequences are: Patterns A→D and Patterns C→B. Especially note in Example 2 below that the proper negative response to もうVましたか is いいえ、まだVていません (or まだVません), NOT まだVませんでした.

1. Pattern A: もうお帰りになりますか？　　　　　　Are you leaving already?
   Pattern D: いいえ、まだ帰りませんが。　　　　　No, I'm not leaving yet...

2. Pattern A: もうお帰りになりましたか？　　　　　Has he returned home already?
   Pattern D: いいえ、<u>まだ帰っていませんが</u>。　　No, he hasn't returned home yet...
   (= いいえ、<u>まだ帰りませんが</u>。)
   ? いいえ、まだ帰りませんでしたが。　[Unacceptable]

3. Pattern C: この電話、まだ使いますか？　　　　　Are you still going to use this phone?
   Pattern B: いいえ、もう使いませんから、どうぞ。No. I won't use it any more, so go ahead.

4. Pattern C: このコンピュータまだ使っていますか？　Are you still using this computer?
   Pattern B: いいえ、もう使っていません。　　　　No. I'm not using it any more.

5. Pattern D: あのレポート、まだできていないの？　You haven't finished that letter yet?
   Pattern A: いいえ、もうできました。　　　　　　(Yes,) I've already finished it.

6. Pattern D: あの手紙、まだ出してないでしょう？　You still haven't sent out that letter, right?
   Pattern A: いいえ、もう出しましたけど。　　　　(Yes,) I've already sent it out...

3E.2. Vよう(に) 言う／伝える／申し伝える↓

The following pattern is used to communicate a request to do something (e.g., "tell X to come"). The agent who executes the request is marked by the particle に. The verb before ように must be in the plain non-past form. に in ように can be deleted, but よう cannot be deleted.

Agent	Action	よう(に)	Verb	
部長に	電話なさる↑	よう(に)	申します↓	I will tell Division Chief to call X.
ハリス君に	レポートを出す	よう(に)	申し伝える↓	I will tell Mr. Harris to submit a report.
ハリス君に	休む	よう(に)	話す	I will talk to Mr. Harris that he takes a day off.

申し伝える↓ is a humble style 伝える meaning "communicate." The alternative humble style of 伝える is お伝えする↓. More examples follow:

後ほど、こちらからお電話するよう申し伝えます。
Later, I'll tell him to give you a call.

ハリスさんにも会議に出るように言いましょうか。
Shall I tell Mr. Harris to attend the meeting?

ハリスさんにあの書類をコピーするようお伝えしましたが。
I told Mr. Harris to copy that document...

Ms. Otani in Conversation 3F is a member of an out-group, identifies herself and asks for Section Manager Tanaka. Mr. Harris once again drops a title to refer to Mr. Tanaka and uses the humble forms to refer to his own action.

Conversation 3F: Taking messages (2)

1. ハリス: はい。営業一課でございます。
2. 大谷: 私、中島製作所の大谷と申しますが、田中課長、お願いいたします。
3. ハ: 申しわけございません。田中はただ今、会議中でして。四時ごろ、終わる予定でございます。もし、おさしつかえなければ、私がご用件をうけたまわりますが。
4. 大: そうですか。じゃ、至急、ご連絡いただきたいとお伝え下さい。こちらの電話番号は 853-9509 です。
5. ハ: はい、かしこまりました。中島製作所の大谷様、お電話番号は 853-9509 でございますね。では、後ほど、お電話さし上げるよう田中に申し伝えます。私、同じ課のハリスと申します。どうも失礼いたしました。

1. H: This is Sales Subsection 1.
2. O: I'm Otani of Nakajima Manufacturing. Section Manager Tanaka please.
3. H: I am sorry. He is in a meeting now, and it is scheduled to be over at around four. If it is OK with you, may I take your message?
4. O: I see. Well, could you ask him to call me as soon as possible? My number is 853-9509.
5. H: Certainly. Ms. Otani of Nakajima Manufacturing. Your number is 853-9509. Then, I will ask Tanaka to call you back later. I'm Harris of the same section. Sorry [for his absence].

ヨウ 用 business, work, function　　ケン 件 matter, case, item　　おな 同じ same

Vocabulary 3F

中島製作所 (n) Nakajima Manufacturing Co.　　　終わる (cv: owar) end; is finished; is over

予定 (n) schedule, plan
おさしつかえなければ↑ (phr) provided that it is OK with you
ご用件 (n) business, (telephone) message
うけたまわります↓ (cv: uketamawar) receive, take, listen. [humble]
至急 (n) urgently, immediately
● 大至急 (n) most urgently
ご連絡 (n) contact, communication

いただきたい↓ (cv: itadak) たい-form of いただく; polite humble of もらう] receive
お伝え下さい↑ (vv: tsutae) honorific request form of つたえる] Please tell. [お+ V-stem + 下さい "Please V"]
かしこまりました (cv: kashikomar) polite past of かしこまる] obey respectfully; certainly
後ほど (n) later
同じ (n) section

Structure 3F

3F.1. 〜でして／Vまして

〜でして and 〜まして are the て-form forms of 〜です and Vます, respectively. These forms are used in formal situations. They often precede an apology.

毎週、火曜日は定休日でして。　　　Every Tuesday is a regular store close day.

ただ今、接客中でございまして。　　He/She is having a visitor right now.

3F.2. おさしつかえなければ↑

おさしつかえなければ means "provided that it is all right with you" and it softens the upcoming offer to help. This is similar to ご迷惑じゃなければ (Conversation 3D). The difference is that おさしつかえなければ is followed by an offer to help, while ご迷惑でなければ is followed by a request.

Provisional form *	Offer to help [Shall I help you?]	
おさしつかえ　なければ nuisance　　provisional of　ない	私がいたしましょうか。	Provided that it is all right with you, shall I do it for you?
Provisional form *	**Ask for help [Please help me.]**	
ご迷惑　　でなければ nuisance　 provisional of　で(は)ない	お願いいたします。	Provided that it is all right with you, could you do it for me?

* The provisional forms will be discussed in detail in Chapter 7.

3F.3. S予定だ

四時ごろ終わる is a sentence modifier that modifies the noun 予定 ("schedule" or "plan"). The subject within the sentence modifier is understood (i.e., 会議). This sentence literally means "It is the plan that the meeting will end at about four." 終わる here is an intransitive verb ("X comes to an end"). (終わる is also a transitive verb "end X.") 予定 can be preceded by a noun phrase N の.

Sentence or N の	予定	Copula	
会議は 3時から 始まる	予定	です。	The meeting is scheduled to begin at three.
会議は 3時から の	予定	です。	The meeting is scheduled to be at three.

3F.4. Verbs of Giving: さし上げる↓ vs. 下さる↑

Japanese has two distinct polite verbs of giving, さし上げる↓ and 下さる↑, in contrast with one English verb, "give." The concept of in-group vs. out-group plays a significant role in the choice of these verbs. The giver is marked by the particles は／が and the recipient is marked by the particle に.

さし上げる↓ is used when the speaker (or an insider) gives some-thing to someone (an outsider or a high-ranking person). The kanji 上 ("up, above") in さし上げる reflects a notion that the speaker gives something "upward" to the recipient who outranks the giver. Since this verb refers to the speaker's (or in-group member's) action, it is a humble verb.

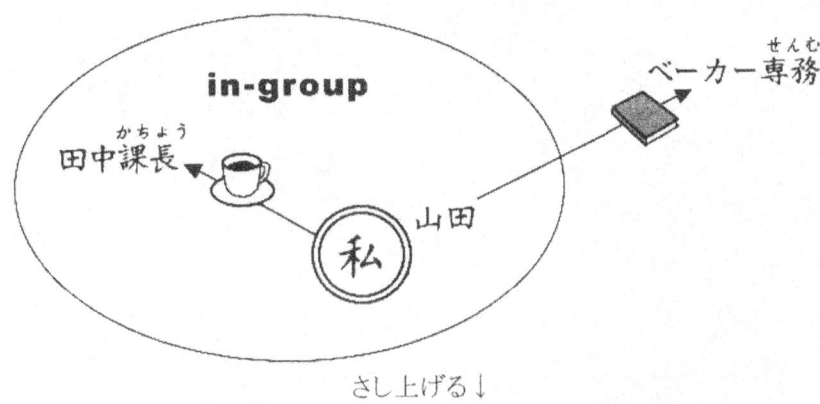

さし上げる↓

Giver (Insider)	は／が	Recipient (Outsider/Higher Rank)	に	Object	を	"give [to others]"
山田さん	は	ソニーのベーカー専務	に	本	を	さし上げた。↓
私	は	田中課長	に	コーヒー	を	さし上げた。↓

下さる↑ is used when an outsider or a higher-ranking person gives something to the speaker (or to an insider). The kanji 下 ("down, below") in 下さる reflects a notion that the giver, who outranks the recipient, gives something "downward" to the receiver (speaker). Since this verb refers to the other's action, it is an honorific verb.

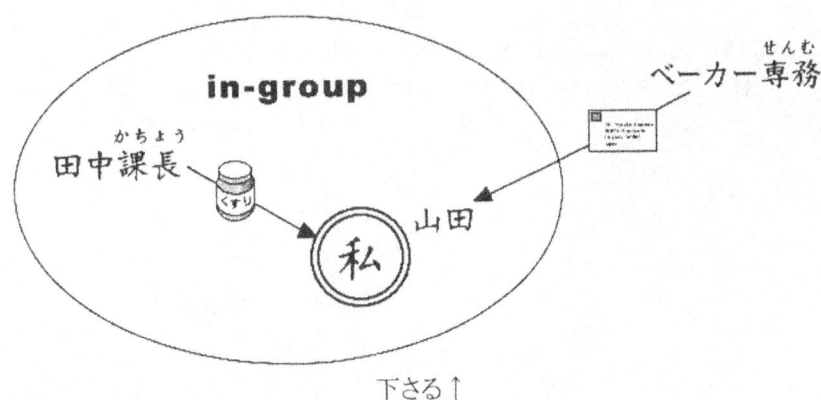

下さる↑

Giver (Outsider/Higher Rank)	は／が	Recipient (Insider)	に	Object	を	"give [to め me/us]"
ソニーのベーカー専務	は	山田さん	に	手紙	を	下さった。↑
田中課長	は	私	に	薬	を	下さった。↑

As long as you choose the correct particles, the giver, the recipient, and the object can be scrambled without changing the basic meaning of who gives what to whom.

A: ハリス君、そのバッジ、買ったの？	Mr. Harris, did you buy that badge?
B: いえ、社長が下さったんです。	The president gave it to me.
A: ハリス君、あの書類、どうした？	Mr. Harris, what happened to that document?
B: もう、木村さんにさし上げましたけど…	I already gave it to Ms. Kimura.

These giving verbs (さし上げる and 下さる) may follow a verb gerund (V て). The implication of V てさし上げる／V て下さる is that the giver does a favor to the recipient by V-ing.

Giver	は／が	Recipient	に	Object	を	V て	"give"
田中課長	は	私	に	薬	を	買って	下さった。↑
		田中課長	に	コーヒー	を	入れて	さし上げて↓ 下さい↑。

Caution: Avoid V てさし上げる (as well as さし上げる) when you are offering your service to a superior or to an outsider.[16]

    コーヒーを入れてさし上げましょうか。　[inappropriate when this is spoken to a superior]

In this case, the following expressions are more appropriate.

    コーヒーをお入れしましょうか。
    コーヒーはいかがですか。

The V てさしあげる can be safely used to make a request in which you ask someone to do something for a third party (a superior/outsider).

    ハリス君、部長にコーヒーを入れてさし上げて下さい。[appropriate]
    Mr. Harris, please make a coffee for Division Manager.

3F.5.　Verbs of Receiving: いただく↓

いただく↓ means "to receive (from an outsider)." This verb is used when the speaker or an insider receives something from others. The recipient is marked by the particles は／が and the giver is marked by the particles に／から. This verb refers to the speaker's (or in-group member's) action, and it is a humble verb.

---

[16] The act of "giving" causes the recipient to feel in debt to the giver, and in some cases, it is better to avoid causing such a feeling. This is especially true when you do something for your superior or for outsiders.

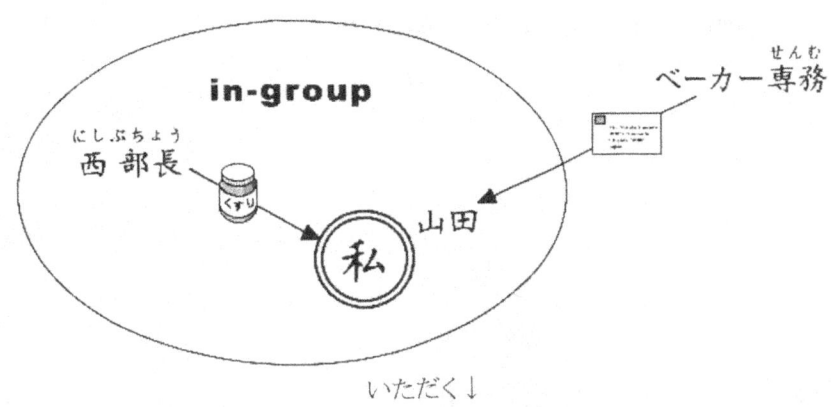

いただく↓

Recipient (Insider)	は/が	Giver (Outsider/Higher Rank)	に/から	Object	を	"receive"
山田さん	は	ソニーのベーカー専務	に	手紙	を	いただいた。↓
田中課長	は	西部長	に	薬	を	いただいた。↓

Example sentences follow:

卒業の時、私は先生にこの本をいただきました。
At the time of the graduation, I received this book from my teacher.

このパンフレットをいただきたいんですが、よろしいですか。
I would like to have these brochures. Is it all right?

ソニーの山田さんにお昼をごちそうしていただきました。
I was treated for lunch by Mr. Yamada of Sony.

Like the verbs of giving (i.e., さし上げる↓ and 下さる↑), いただく↓ can be preceded by a V て form and express a sense of "receiving a favor of V-ing from someone." In this construction, only the particle に can be used to mark the giver.

Recipient	は/が	Giver	に	Object	を	V て	"receive"
私	は	田中課長	に	カタログ	を	見せて	いただいた。↓

Section Manager Tanaka showed me the catalogue.
(Lit. "I received the favor from Sec. Mgr. Tanaka of his showing me the catalogue.")

More examples:

たくさんの方にうちの商品をテストしていただいております。
Many people are testing our products (for us).   (Lit., We are receiving many people's testing our products.)

きょうはあまり仕事がないので、早く帰っていただきました。
Because there is nothing much to do today, I asked (them) to go home early.

西さんにファックスを送っていただいた。
Mr. Nishi sent me a fax.   (Lit., I received Mr. Nishi's sending me a fax.) Or,
Mr. Nishi sent someone a fax for me.   (Lit., I received Mr. Nishi's sending someone a fax.)[17]

---

[17] It is possible to interpret this as "Someone sent Mr. Tsuji a fax for me. (Lit., I received someone's sending a fax to Mr. Tsuji.)."

Now, convert the following sentences with the verb いただく ↓.[18]

(1) 部長が田中さんに紹介状を書いて下さった。　Division Manager wrote Mr. Tanaka a reference letter.
　→

(2) パルコの西さんがカタログを見せて下さった。　Mr. Nishi of Parco kindly showed me a catalogue.
　→

You can combine verbs of giving and receiving with the S ところ／N のところ expressions learned in 3D.3.　無理を申します below is a humble expression that means to "make an unreasonable request" (lit. "say the impossible").

お Adj ところ お N のところ	V て V て下さって V ていただいて	Thanks or Apology	
お急ぎのところ	無理を申しまして "asked for the impossible"	申しわけ ございません。	I'm sorry to make an unreasonable request while you are in a hurry.
お疲れのところ	いらして下さって	ありがとう ございます。	Thank you for coming over when you are fatigued.
お休みのところ	出てきていただいて	おそれいります。	Thank you for coming over on your day off.

---

[18] (1) 田中さんが部長に紹介状を書いていただいた。　(2) パルコの西さんにカタログを見せていただいた。

Exercise 3

Grammar Utilization 3   Name:_____ Sec:_____ #:____

G1. Circle the most appropriate phrases below.

1. A: 山田君、あの手紙(もう／まだ)出した？
    B: すみません、(もう／まだ)出してないんですが。

2. A: 森さん、(もう／まだ)見えた？ (見える: come; arrive [honorific])
    B: いえ、(もう／まだ)お見えになっていらっしゃいませんが。

3. A: ハンさん、日本語がお上手になりましたね。
    B: そうですか。(もう／まだ)毎日、辞書を使っているんですよ。

4. A: ハンさん、日本に来たのはいつですか。
    B: 去年の三月です。(もう／まだ)一年になりました。

5. A: ハンさん、(もう／まだ)お昼食べた？
    B: いえ、まだ(食べませんでした／食べていません)けど。

6. A: 大阪銀行の山中部長にお会いになりましたか。
    B: いえ、(もう／まだ)お会いしていません。

7. A: 山田部長はまだ英語を勉強していらっしゃるんですか。
    B: いやあ、忙しくて、(もう／まだ)勉強はやめたんだよ。

8. A: 山田部長はもう英語を勉強していらっしゃらないんですか。
    B: いや、忙しいけど、(もう／まだ)勉強はしているよ。

G2. Circle the most appropriate phrases below.

1. A: ハンさん、きのうのプレゼンテーション、どうだった？
    B: みなさんがいろいろ教えて(下さった／さし上げた／いただいた)ので、なんとか… (なんとか: somehow)

2. A: ファックスですか？ はい、(下さって／いただいて)おります。
    B: もう、目を通して(いただきました／いただけました)でしょうか？

3. A: ハン君、アメリカの消費者ガイド、もってる？   (消費者ガイド: consumer guide)
    B: いいえ。じゃあ、リーさんに送って(さし上げ／下さい／いただき)ましょうか？

4. A: 今日、はじめてのボーナスを(さし上げた／いただいた)んですけど、あまり仕事をしてないので、申しわけなくて。
    B: ハンさんは本当に人がいいね。 (人がいい: good-natured, too trusting, naive)

5. 田中さんにミラー様に電話をかける(と／ように)言いました。
    I told Mr. Tanaka to call Mr. Miller.

6. 東京テレコムのミラー様(が／から／に)電話(がありました／しました)。
    There was a telephone call from Mr. Miller of Tokyo Telecom.

7. 電話に（でた／した／かけた）人。　　電話を（でた／かけた）人。
　　the person who answered the phone.　　the person who called.

G3. Complete the conversations by using the giving (さしあげる；くださる) and receiving verbs (いただく).　(A superior is marked by ▲ below.)

a. ●: 西山課長。あした、3時にお客さんがいらっしゃるので、3時からの打ち合わせを
　　　少し遅くして＿＿＿＿＿＿＿＿＿＿＿＿でしょうか。（打ち合わせ: preliminary consultation）
　　▲: そうか。じゃあ、4時にしよう。

b. ▲: さっき、青木部長がワープロが使えなくて、困ってるっておっしゃってたよ。
　　　すまないけど、君がワープロで打って＿＿＿＿＿＿＿＿＿＿＿＿。（打つ: type）
　　●: かしこまりました。

c. ▲: あれ？　ブラウン君、きみ、空港へミラーさんを迎えに行くんじゃなかったの？
　　　（迎えに行く: go to meet）
　　●: ああ、急ぎの用事ができたので、吉田さんに行って＿＿＿＿＿＿＿＿＿＿んです。
　　　（急ぎの用事: urgent business）

d. ▲: 大阪でのホテルはどうなった？
　　●: 吉田さんが予約して＿＿＿＿＿＿＿＿＿＿ので、助かりました。
　　　（予約する: make a reservation; 助かる: I am rescued; I am grateful.）

e. ●: 前に西山課長に紹介して＿＿＿＿＿＿＿＿＿＿ホテルは何ていうホテルでしたか。
　　　（紹介する: introduce）
　　▲: あれは「やしろ」というんだけど、ホテルじゃなくて、旅館だよ。

G4. Complete the conversations by using the /V ように + communication V/ pattern.

1. A: あした、電話して下さいませんか。
　　B: わかりました。あした、＿＿＿＿＿＿＿＿＿＿申し伝えます。

2. A: 3時までにファックスを送っていただけませんか。
　　B: わかりました。あした、＿＿＿＿＿＿＿＿＿＿申し伝えます。

3. A: 来週までに決めていただきたいのですが。（決める: decide）
　　B: わかりました。月曜日までに決められると思います。
　　(later)
　　C: 何て、おっしゃってた？
　　B: 来週までに＿＿＿＿＿＿＿＿＿＿おっしゃっていました。

4. A: 来週までに答えを出せますか。（答え: answer）
　　B: わかりました。ではそのように申します。失礼いたします。
　　(later)
　　C: むこうは何て、おっしゃってた？
　　B: 来週までに＿＿＿＿＿＿＿＿＿＿おっしゃっていました。

Chapter 3: Telephone   69

5. A: 伊藤君に飛行機の切符は通路側をとること、言った？（通路側：isle side）
    B: ええ。通路側の席を＿＿＿＿＿＿＿＿＿＿＿＿＿＿申しました。

6. A: (At the seminar)アジア経済は大きく成長しています。これからはアジアへの輸出も考えた方がいいでしょう。（アジア経済：Asian economy; 成長する：grow; 輸出：export）
    (later)
    B: セミナーでは何て言ってた？
    C: これからはアジアへ＿＿＿＿＿＿＿＿＿＿＿＿＿＿＿＿＿＿＿＿＿おっしゃっていました。

G5. You are speaking to a person shown below. Rephrase each statement if necessary using the appropriate honorific or humble expressions.

	You	Listener	Your original statement
A.	田中部長	スミス	スミスさん、いいフランス料理の店を知っていますか。 →
B.	スミス	田中部長	ええ、知っています。 →
C.	よしだ	山田社長	山田さん、東大の西本先生を知っていますか。 →
D.	よしだ	山田社長	いいえ、知りません。 →

G6. Change the underlined part of the sentence to the honorific expressions (お V になります or お V でございます or お V でいらっしゃいます or お V 下さい).

a. A: 田中部長は何時ごろ帰りますか。→＿＿＿＿＿＿＿＿＿＿＿＿＿＿
    B: 3時までには帰ると思います。

b. A: このペン、ちょっとよろしいですか。
    B: ああ、どうぞ。どうぞ。使って下さい。→＿＿＿＿＿＿＿＿＿＿＿＿＿＿

c. A: このCD、ちょっと聞きたいんですが。
    B: いいですよ。聞いて下さい。→＿＿＿＿＿＿＿＿＿＿＿＿＿＿

d. A: おもしろい本があるんですが、読みませんか。→＿＿＿＿＿＿＿＿＿＿＿＿＿＿
    B: あ、どうも。

e. A: スミスさんは日本語がわかるでしょうか。
    B: いいえ、わからないだろうと思います。→＿＿＿＿＿＿＿＿＿＿＿＿＿＿

f. A: 部長は英語がお上手ですね。
    B: ええ、部長は毎週、英会話レッスンをとっているんですよ。→ _____

G7. Fill in the blanks using the appropriate polite expressions.

a. A: 田中部長、_____か。
    B: ただ今、外出しております。(He is out.)
    A: 何時ごろ_____ご予定ですか。
    B: 3時に帰る予定です。

b. A: 失礼ですが、これはスミスさんのペン_____か。
    B: はい。私のです。
    A: おさしつかえなければ、ちょっとお借りしてもいいですか。(May I borrow it?)

c. A: あ、ハリスさんで_____か。
    B: はい、そうです。ハリスとも申します。

d. A: どちらに_____ですか。
    B: 私はソニーに勤めております。

e. A: 田中課長、IBMのスミスさまからお電話_____。
    B: 今、ちょっと接客中だから、出られないんだ。(接客中: having a visitor)
    A: わかりました。
       (to the caller) 申しわけありませんが、課長は今、席を_____。

Communicative Exercise 3

Leaving Messages on Answering Machines

When leaving your message on an answering machine, be sure to include your name, position, company name and your telephone number in addition to the message content. If there are more than one person who can reply to the phone call, you can say 私か〜(の方)まで電話をおねがいします 。 ("Please call me or [the direction of] ...").

C1. Reorder the following telephone conversation so that it follows the natural sequence. (There are three people: A, B, & C.) Also, answer the questions below based on the conversation.

___1___ A: マイコンソフト、営業一課でございます。

_____ A: 少々お待ちください。

_____ C: そうか。ちょっと今、企画会議なんだ。かわりに話を聞いておいて。＊

_____ A: かしこまりました。日本インターテックのフォード様、お電話番号は770-345-0549でございますね。私、山田と申します。

_____ A: 申しわけございません。木村はただいま、会議中でございます。おさしつかえなければ、私がご用件をうけたまわりましょうか。

_____ B: 私、日本インターテック販売部のフォードと申しますが、木村課長いらっしゃいますか。＊＊

_____ A: わかりました。

_____ A: どうも失礼いたしました。

_____ B: それではお願いします。あしたの会議の打ち合わせをしたいので、そうお伝えください。こちらの電話番号は770-345-0549です。＊＊＊

___4___ A: 課長、日本インターテックのフォードさんという方からお電話が入っております。

_____ B: 3時までここにおりますから、よろしくお願いします。失礼いたします。

　　＊　　話を聞いておく＝listen to what [he/she] says [for future use]
　＊＊　　販売部 = same as 営業部 (Sales Division)
＊＊＊　　打ち合わせ = rehearsal, preplanning

a. だれから だれに 電話が ありましたか。

_____(company)の_____(division)の_____(name)から

_____(company)の_____(section)の_____(name)に

電話がありました。電話に出たのは_____(section)の_____(name)です。

用件は_____
ということです。

A Systematic Approach to Business Japanese

C2. Based on the proper business protocol in answering a phone call, provide the appropriate expression in the following situations. Your own business card is shown below for your reference.

a. You could not answer the phone promptly.

b. Give your name and section and greet the caller by thanking him for his continued patronage to your company.

```
マイコンソフト
営業部
メアリー・キム
〒123-4567
東京都品川区川島１１番地
TEL (033) 123-4567
Email: mkim12@mikonsoft.com
```

c. The caller has said the following. Before you transfer the call, confirm the caller's name and affiliation and the person you are transferring the call to. Add the proper phrase at the end (e.g., "Please hold on for a moment.").

Caller: 私、東京工業の木村と申しますが、営業部の田中部長、お願いします。

You: _____

d. Mr. Tanaka is unavailable to take the call for the following reasons. Fill in the blank accordingly. あいにく below means "unfortunately."

あいにく (Tanaka is on the phone) _____

あいにく (Tanaka is seeing another client) _____

あいにく (Tanaka is in a meeting) _____

あいにく (Tanaka is away from his desk) _____

あいにく (Tanaka is out) _____

あいにく (Tanaka is on a business trip) _____

e. The person requested won't be available for a while. Identify yourself (e.g., "I am ... of the sales subdivision") and say that you would like to offer to take a message.

You: あいにく、田中は外出中で四時まで戻りません。

私、_____

f. In concluding the phone call, what would you say?

Caller: それでは、よろしくお願いいたします。

You: では、そのように申し伝えます。_____

Chapter 3: Telephone 73

C3. (Role Playing)　Find a partner and do the following role playing exercise.

Student 1:

You are working for 日本エレクトロニクス. You belong to 営業部 (えいぎょうぶ) (Sales Division), 営業二課 (えいぎょうにか) (Section 2). Call the people below at Yokohama Trading Company below. If the person is not available, leave him/her the message below.

Person to talk to	Message	Glossary
Sec. Manager Tanaka	Tomorrow's meeting will be postponed until next Monday. Please bring samples of the product then.	product sample: 製品(せいひん)サンプル
Subsec. Mgr. Yoshida	The time of the meeting on Wednesday has been changed from three o'clock to four o'clock.	
Div. Mgr. Yamanaka	We are waiting for you at the exhibition of new products next week. Our booth number is 3451.	exhibition: 展示会(てんじかい) booth: ブース

Student 2:

You are working for a trading company called 横浜商事 (よこはましょうじ). You are in 販売部 (はんばいぶ) (Sales Division), 北米課 (ほくべいか) (North American Section). Answer phone calls and respond appropriately. If the person whom the caller wants to speak with is not available, offer to take a message. Right now, the following people work in your section.

Sec. Manager Tanaka	He is away from his desk.
Subsec. Mgr. Yoshida	She is in a meeting. She will be back in one hour.
Div. Mgr. Yamanaka	He is on a business trip. He will be back on Monday.

Reading and Writing 3   Name:_____ Sec:_____ #:____

1. During Exercise C3, write down the message in Japanese using the message pad below.

```
┌─────────────────────────────────────┐
│          伝言メモ                    │
│      様            受               │
│        月   日   時   分            │
│                                     │
│  _____ 様から           │
│                                     │
│  □ 電話がありました                 │
│  □ 電話があったことを伝えて下さい   │
│  □ 電話をいただきたい TEL(    )  ─  │
│  □ もう一度電話します(  日  時  分ごろに) │
│                                     │
│  □ 用件は下記の通りです             │
│                                     │
└─────────────────────────────────────┘
```

伝言 (n) message
メモ (n) memo
様 (suf) honorific title
受 (suf) received by
伝えて下さい (phr) please tell
用件 (n) business; message content
下記の通り (phr) as follows

2. The following is a message taken by Mr. Harris. Answer the questions below.

```
┌─────────────────────────────────┐
│ 4月12日                          │
│                                 │
│ 田中課長殿                       │
│                                 │
│ 東京テレコムの木村課長から10時25分に電話。│
│ DSL敷設工事の件について電話がほしいとのこと。│
│ 15時から外出するので、15時以降は携帯に電話して│
│ ほしいとのことでした。             │
│                                 │
│ 東京テレコム 03-3425-7749        │
│ 携帯 010-12-345-8830             │
│                                 │
│         10時25分 トーマス・ハリス │
└─────────────────────────────────┘
```

殿 (suf) honorific title
敷設工事 (n) installation construction
〜の件について (phr) about the matter of...
ほしい (い-adj) want; need
〜とのこと (phr) said that...
外出する (v) to go out
以降 (n) after [time]
携帯 (n) cell phone
電話してほしい (v) want [someone] to call

a. Fill in the blanks below based on the message above.

_____課長から_____課長に電話がありました。

電話に出た人は_____さんです。今、3時30分です。田中課長が

かける電話番号は_____です。

Listening Comprehension 3   Name:_____ Sec:_____ #:____

A is the first speaker.   B is the second speaker.

1. Voc: 終わる:end

   会議はもう終わりましたか。

2. Bさんの言ったことはどちらですか。

   a. Mr. Han has not yet come today.
   b. Mr. Han is no longer coming today.

3. Aさんの言ったことはどちらですか。

   a. Are you still going to wait for Mr. Han?
   b. Are you already waiting for Mr. Han?

4. Voc: 外務省: Ministry of Foreign Affairs

   電話をかけてきた人はだれですか。

   その人はだれと話したいんですか。

5. Voc: 工業: manufacturing

   (日本エレクトロニクス／横浜工業)の(菊池／春日)さんから(菊池／春日)さんに電話がありました。

6. Voc: 技術開発部: Research & Development Division; つないで (V て form of つなぐ: connect)

   電話をかけてきた人はだれですか。

   辻さんは電話に出られますか。どうしてですか。

   電話をかけてきた人はあとで何をしますか。

7. Voc: 関係: Relationship

   辻係長とブラウンさんの関係は何ですか。

8. <u>Voc:</u> 呼んで: Gerund of 呼ぶ ("call, summon"); まいりましょう: come, go, stay

   ミラーさんは今、何をしていますか。

   電話に出た人はこれから何をしますか。

9. <u>Voc:</u> なるべく早く: as quickly as possible

   山田部長はどこに勤めていますか。

   ミラーさんのメッセージは何ですか。

   電話に出た人の名前とその人が働いている部は何ですか。

Chapter 4

報告
ほう こく
Reports

Priming

While you interact with someone in the absence of your direct supervisors, it is important to remember significant developments to report back later. "Significant developments" may include not only what took place in meetings, but also things like being treated for lunch by someone from another company. This will help your superiors acknowledge kindness of the other party during the next meeting (e.g., 先日はうちの者がお世話になりまして… "Thank you for your kindness toward our employees the other day"). Failing to express simple gratitude when it is clearly due is deeply embarrassing in business.

Depending on whom you report your work to, the style/level of polite expressions are different. At least, two factors influence your politeness expressions: (1) in-group and out-group distinction and (2) hierarchy within your own in-group. Your superiors may speak in plain/casual forms. This is not an automatic invitation for you to switch to plain/casual forms also. Quite the contrary, your superiors expect you to maintain politeness levels.

Before the following conversation takes place, imagine that Mr. Harris had a call from Dr. Kaneko who said that 来週、田中課長にぜひお目にかかりたい。↓ ("I want to see Sec. Mgr. Tanaka by all means next week"). お目にかかる is a humble verb "to see [someone]." Mr. Harris correctly conveys her message by paraphrasing it using an honorific verb お見えになる↑ ("come [into view]") below.

Conversation 4A: Conveying phone messages

1. ハ: あ、田中課長。午前中に大阪大学の金子様からお電話がございまして、来週、お見えになりたいとのことでした。	1. H: Oh, Sec. Mgr. Tanaka! In the morning, there was a call from Dr. Kaneko of Osaka Univ., and she said she wants to come [here] next week.
2. 田: あ、そう。じゃ、これから会議だから、その前に電話しておこうか。電話番号はもらった？	2. T: I see. I have a meeting from now, so I guess I'll call her before that. Did you get her phone number?
3. ハ: あ、いいえ。聞いておりません。	3. H: Oh, no. I haven't asked.
4. 田: 困るじゃないか。そんな時は、一応、番号を聞いておくのが常識だろう。	4. T: That's no good. In such a situation, it would be a common sense to ask for the number just in case.
5. ハ: はい、すみません。気をつけます。	5. H: Yes. I'm sorry. I will be careful.

前 (まえ) front, previous, before   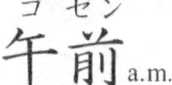 午前 (ゴゼン) a.m.   中 (チュウ) the middle   時 (とき) time; when

Vocabulary 4A

午前 (ごぜん) (n) a.m., morning [Precedes the clock time]
中 (ちゅう) (suf) during, in the middle of
大阪 (おおさか) (n) Osaka [city name]
金子 (かねこ) (n) Kaneko [family name]
ございまして (cv: ar) [て-form of ございます = polite form of あります] [inanimate object] there is
お見えになりたい (phr) [honorific of 見える "to come (into view), to see, is visible"] want to come
これから (n) from now on [=今から]
会議 (かいぎ) (n) meeting, conference

～ておこうか (phr) Shall I ... in advance? [Talking to oneself [blunt]; おこう is the volitional of おく]
もらった (cv: moraw) [past of もらう] receive. [Vてもらう "receive a favor of V-ing"]
困る (こま) (cv: komar) to be annoyed, to be in trouble
じゃないか (phr) isn't it?; don't you see? [blunt]
一応 (いちおう) (adv) just in case
聞いておく (phr) ask in advance [V ておく "do something in advance for later use"]
常識 (じょうしき) (n) common sense; norm
気をつける (き) (phr) pay attention, be careful

Structures 4A

4A.1. Reporting Messages: S とのこと／S ということ

When conveying a message, the phrase, S とのことでした, is often used. This is a simplified form of S ということでした "The fact was that [they] said that S."[19] There are two aspects of messages that need to be changed:

1. The reported message (S) is usually in the plain form because it is quoted speech. (Some verbs do not have plain forms (e.g., まいります, もうします, おります, ございます, いたします).)

---

[19] Two commonly used expressions, ～さんが電話しました ("[someone] called") and ～と言いました ("[someone] said that ..."), are NOT used for conveying someone's message.

2. Humble expressions (e.g., まいります), if they refer to the speaker's actions, should be rephrased by using honorific expressions (e.g., いらっしゃる).

The following illustrates these changes. The verb まいります ("to go/come") is the humble form of 来る／行く and the verb いらっしゃる[20] ("to go/come") is the honorific form of 来る or 行く.

> A: 明日まいりますので、Cさんにそうお伝えいただけませんか？
> "I'm going over [to your place] tomorrow, so could you inform Mr. C of that?"
>
> B: かしこまりました。 "Certainly."
> (later)
> B to C: Aさんが明日いらっしゃるとのことでした／ということでした。
> "Ms. A said that she would come over tomorrow."

original message (polite-humble)	reported message (plain-honorific)
まいりますので...	いらっしゃるということでした／とのことでした。
まいりませんので...	いらっしゃらないということでした／とのことでした。
お待ちいたしますので..	お待ちになるということでした／とのことでした。

4A.2. Plain Volitional: CV-ou/VV+you (よう)

The polite volitional verb V ましょう is used to express "Let's V" or "I/We shall V." Only the verbs of self-controllable actions (e.g., 行く, 言う, 作る) can be made into the volitional form. The plain volitional verbs are generated by the following rules:

a. Vowel verbs (る-verbs): Add "you" (よう) to the root form.

Polite volitional	root + ru → root + you (よう)	Plain volitional	
食べましょう	tabe + ru → tabe + you	食べよう	Let's eat it.
見ましょう	mi + ru → mi + you	見よう	Let's watch it.
考えましょう	kangae + ru → kangaeyou	考えよう	Let's think.
いましょう	i + ru → iyou	いよう	Let's stay here.

b. Consonant verbs (う-verbs): Add "ou" (pronounced as "oo") to the root. (Drop "w" if the root ends in "w.")

Polite volitional	root + u → root + ou	Plain volitional	
送りましょう	okur + u → okur + ou	送ろう	Let's send it.
買いましょう	ka(w) + u → ka(w) + ou	買おう	Let's buy it.
飲みましょう	nom + u → nom + ou	飲もう	Let's drink it.
書きましょう	kak + u → kak + ou	書こう	Let's write it.

c. Irregular verbs:

> する → しよう "Let's do it."
> 来る → 来よう "Let's come here."

Plain forms are used in casual conversation among in-group members (e.g., family, friends, classmates, etc.). In a business context, these forms can also be used by a superior toward his/her subordinates. In the following, plain volitional forms are used by Speaker B, who is a superior of Speaker A.

---

[20] いらっしゃる is also the honorific form of いる ("to stay/be located").

A: もう行きましょうか？　　　　　Shall we go now?
B: いや、あと十分待とう。　　　　Well, let's wait 10 more minutes.

A: いつお会いしましょうか？　　　When shall we meet [an outsider]?
B: 3時に会おう。　　　　　　　　Let's meet at 3 o'clock.

Plain volitional forms are also used in quoted speech patterns (e.g., V-volitional と言った).

田中課長はエキスポに我が社の製品を出そうとおっしゃいました。
Section Manager Tanaka said that we would exhibit our products at the exposition.

4A.3. Verbs of Receiving: もらう/V てもらう

もらう is a regular [i.e., non-humble] form of the humble verb いただく ("to receive"). Just like the verb いただく, the recipient of the もらう action is marked by the particles は／が and the giver is marked by the particles に／から. In the V てもらう construction, only the particle に can be used to mark the giver of action.

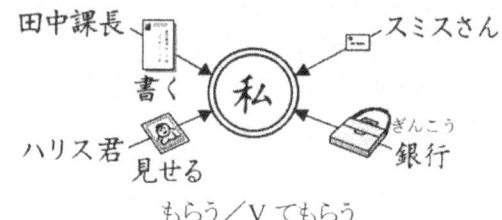

もらう/V てもらう

Recipient	は／が	Giver	に／から	Object	を		"receive"
私	は	スミスさん	に／から	名刺	を		もらった
Recipient	**は／が**	**Giver**	**に**	**Object**	**を**	**V て**	**"receive"**
ハリス君	は	田中課長	に	手紙	を	書いて	もらった

Compare the expressions below and explain why the verb もらう is used in sentences 1a and 2a and the verb いただく is used for sentences 1b and 2b.

1a. このかばんは銀行でもらったんです。
I received this bag at the bank.

1b. このかばんは課長の奥様にいただいたんです。
I received this bag from Mrs. Tanaka (lit. "Division Manager Tanaka's wife").

2a. ハリス君、君にこの手紙を翻訳してもらいたいんだけど。
Harris, I'd like you to translate this letter for me.

2b. 部長にもぜひいらしていただきたいんです。[21]
I'd like you to come [to my place] by all means.
(Lit. "I'd like to receive ↓ the favor of your coming ↑ [to my place].")

4A.4. V ておく

The verb おく literally means "to put something down [and leave it]." The verb おく can follow the て form of an action verb and creates a sense of intentionally doing something in advance for subsequent use or doing something for the time being.

来週、大阪へ出張するので、飛行機の切符を予約しておく。
I'll go to Osaka next week for business, so I'll reserve a plane ticket for then.

---

[21] いらして is a short form of いらっしゃって. いらしていただきたい consists of the honorific verb いらっしゃる ("to come") and the humble verb いただく ("to receive"). The subject of いらっしゃる is the addressee ("you [come]"), and the subject of いただく is the speaker ("I [receive]").

名刺がもうすぐなくなるので、一応、作っておきます。
Because I'll run out of my business cards pretty soon, I'll make more (just in case).

明日は忙しくなるので、その書類は今日書いておこうか。
I'll be busy tomorrow, so I wonder if I should write that document today (for the future use).

Because the V ておく pattern refers to an intentional action, it is often used in making requests as ホテルを予約しておいて下さい ("Please make a hotel reservation in advance."). In conversation, the V ておく pattern if often shortened to V とく.

明日までに、これを500枚コピーしといてくれる？
Would you make me 500 copies of this by tomorrow?

言っときますけど、私は帰るつもりなんかありませんよ。
I'll tell you (so you'll know), but I have no intention of coming back [or anything like that].

なくなる前に、買っとかない？
Shall we buy them in advance before they are gone?

4A.5. Stern advice

The expression ～するのが常識だ ("V-ing is common sense") points out the expected behavior as a member of a society. The verb can be in the negative form: ～しないのが常識だ ("Not V-ing is common sense"). Both forms function as stern advice. Other expressions with a similar function are:

お礼の手紙を出すのがあたりまえです。	Sending a thank-you letter is the obvious thing to do.
そんなことは聞かないのが普通です。	Not asking such a thing is the norm.
そんな時は電話しておくものです。	It's the (natural) thing to call in advance in such a case.

The expression V た方がいい ("It's better to V" or "You had better V") also functions as advice. The verb is usually in the past tense (e.g., 行った方がいい). This form is gentler than the expressions above but not as gentle as the suggestions based on the conditional form "V たら(どうですか)."

stern advice	電話するのが常識です。	Calling is a common-sense thing (to do).
	電話するのが普通です。	Calling is the norm.
	電話するのがあたりまえです。	Calling is the natural thing (to do).
advice	電話した方がいいですよ。	You had better/should call.
suggestion	電話したらどうですか。	Why don't you call?

Conversation 4B, Mr. Tanaka came back to his desk after a meeting. Mr. Harris greets[22] him and reports what happened while his superior was away. He expresses his thoughts succinctly.

---

[22] Both おつかれさま and ごくろうさま are said to thank for someone's hard work. These can also be used as a form of greeting. お and ご are honorific prefixes. つかれ means "fatigue" and くろう means "hardships." ごくろうさま can be used only by a superior toward his/her subordinates to thank for their hard work. おつかれさま can be used toward one's superiors, peers, or subordinates. Mr. Harris can say おつかれさま to Mr. Tanaka, but only Mr. Tanaka can say ごくろうさま to Mr. Harris in Conversation 4B.

Conversation 4B: Reporting what happened (1)

1. 田中:ただいま！
2. ハリス: お疲れ様でした。お留守の間に、森課長が決算報告書をお持ちになりました。明日の会議までに目を通して下さいとのことです。
3. 田: あ、そう。
4. ハ: あと、これは東京テレコムの注文の見積書なんですが、できたところまで見ていただきたいんですが。
5. 田: わかった。

1. T: I'm back!
2. H: Thank you for your hard work. While you were away, Sec. Mgr. Mori brought a balance sheet. He asked us to look it over by tomorrow's meeting.
3. T: Is that so?
4. H: ...and, this is the estimate of the order for Tokyo Telecom. I would like you to take a look at it as far as it is completed.
5. T: OK.

持つ hold　通す pass [through]　決める／決 decide, settle　間 while

Vocabulary 4B

ただいま！ (phr) right now; I'm home!; I'm back!

お疲れ様 (phr) Thanks for your work!; Good bye! [said to someone who is leaving after work]

お留守 (n) the time while one is away [お is an honorific prefix.]

間 (n) while; the time during

決算 (n) financial settlement

報告書 (n) report (document)

お持ち (cv: mot) [持つ] hold [お is an honorific prefix.]

通して (cv: toos) [て-form of 通す] pass [something] through; show, usher in; thread; let in [目を通す "look over"]

あと (n) the place following (something); the remainder; besides

注文 (n) order

見積書 (n) estimate (document)

できた (vv: deki) [past of できる] completed [できたところ: a place where I completed]

いただきたい (cv: itadak) [-tai form of いただく] want to receive [Vていただきたい "would like to receive a favor of V-ing"]

Structures 4B

4B.1. Nの間(に)／Vている間(に)、S

The structure /Nの間に、S/ expresses the notion that "During Event A, Event B happens." If the particle に does not follow 間, another Event B takes place continuously throughout Event A. If the particle に follows 間, Event B does not take place continuously, but rather becomes completed within that time period (Event A). Often, an adverb ずっと ("continuously") is used with the second structure.

During Event A,			Event B happens.
N	の	間(に)	電話がありました。 (there was a phone call)
お留守	の	間	ずっとお待ちしておりました。(I was waiting the whole time)

A plain-form verb (e.g., Vている) can also precede 間 as in インターネットを使っている間 ("while I was using the Internet").

While Event A is happening,		Event B happens.
Vている	間(に)	

インターネットを使っている	間に	日本テレコムからファックスが来ました。 (there was a fax from Japan Telecom)
インターネットを使っている	間	ずっと話し中でした。 (the line was busy the whole time)

The conversation continues in 4C. Mr. Tanaka wonders why the balance sheet is required for the meeting tomorrow.

Conversation 4C: *Reporting what happened (2)*

5. 田: でも、どうして決算書が要るのかな。	5. T: But I wonder why the balance sheet is necessary.
6. ハ: 来週、例のプロジェクトの取り引き条件を決めるのに必要だとおっしゃっていました。	6. H: He said that it was necessary because we were going to decide the transaction terms of that project next week.
7. 田: そうか。じゃ先に、森さんに電話して、見積りの方はあとで見るよ。ごくろうさん。	7. T: I see. I will call Mr. Mori now, and I will look at the estimate later. Good work!

取り引き　transaction; business　　先　ahead　　方　direction; side　　方　person [honorific]

Vocabulary 4C

でも　(n) however　[More casual than しかし]
どうして　(qw) why?　how come?
決算書　(n) balance sheet
要る　(cv: ir) is necessary; need
かな　(sp) I wonder. [かな is similar to かしら, but less gentle and feminine]
例の　(ph) that [known to both of us], so-called
プロジェクト　(n) project
取り引き　(n) business dealing/transaction
条件　(n) condition; terms; requirement, qualification

決める　(vv: kime) decide
必要　(な-adj) necessary
おっしゃって　(cv: osshar) [て-form of おっしゃる; honorific-polite] say, tell, is called [ます form is おっしゃいます]
見積り　(n) an estimate
ご苦労さん　(phr) Thanks for your work! [Usually said to one's subordinates. Also, there is ご苦労さま (more polite than ご苦労さん).]

Structures 4C

4C.1　～とおっしゃいます

In 2E.1, the phrase (何と)おっしゃるんですか is introduced as a way of asking for the pronunciation of other's names. The verb おっしゃいます is the honorific-polite form of 言う ("to say") and can be used to report other's message. The humble-polite form is 申します. In the following exchange, Speaker B reports what Speaker A (outsider) said. The quoted sentences are usually in the plain-form.

　　A: 5%の割り引きが必要です。　　　　　　　We need a 5% discount.
　　(Later)
　　B: 5%の割り引きが必要だとおっしゃいました。↑　[A] said that they need a 5% discount.
　　vs.
　　A: 5%の割り引きが必要だと申しました。↓　　I said that we need a 5% discount.

4C.2. V-plain-present ために／のに

ために can express either a purpose or a reason for some action or state. If an adjective is used before ために, it expresses a reason. If a noun is used before ために, it expresses either a reason or a purpose. If ために expresses a reason, the particle に can be optionally deleted.

体が弱いため(に)、健康に注意する必要がある。　Because my body is weak, I need to be careful with my health.
　(＝弱いので／弱いから)
明日の会議のために、決算書が要る。[23]　I need the balance sheet for tomorrow's meeting.
台風のため(に)、看板がこわれた。　Due to the typhoon, the billboard broke.

If the plain <u>present</u> form of a verb precedes ために (or のに), it expresses a purpose for something. A negative verb can be used with ために, but not with のに. In order for this structure to work, the main clause that follows it must refer to a self-controllable action.

V-plain-present	ため or の	に	Main clause (self-controllable)
インターネットにつなぐ	ため or の	に	モデムを買った。
In order to connect with the Internet, I bought a modem.			
きれいにプリントする	ため or の	に	レーザープリンタを使っています。
In order to print neatly, we are using a laser printer.			
病気にならない	ため (not の)	に	健康に注意して下さい。
In order not to get sick, we need to be careful with your health.			

If the plain <u>past</u> form of a verb precedes ために, it only expresses the reason/cause for something.

事故があったため(に)、電車が1時間おくれました。
Due to the fact that there was an accident, the train became one hour late.

In Conversation 4D, Mr. Harris summarizes the meeting he attended. To cut to the chase, he provides the conclusion first and awaits further instruction from Mr. Tanaka. Prior to making business decisions that affect the company, it is often the case that all parties involved must be thoroughly informed and consulted. All issues must be resolved before concluding a business deal. This process is called 根回し (root-binding). It is a time-consuming process, but it must be done in a Japanese corporation.

Conversation 4D: Reporting on a meeting (1)

1. ハ: 東京テレコムとの販売交渉の件なんですが、少々お時間よろしいでしょうか。	1. H: It's about the matter of sales negotiation with Tokyo Telecom, but may I have some time (with you)?
2. 田: いいよ。	2. T: Sure.
3. ハ: 結論から申しますと、相手側はもっと値引きしてもらいたいということです。でも、私の一存では決められないので、即答はしませんでした。どういたしましょうか。	3. H: In a nutshell (lit. Starting from the conclusion), it's that they would like us to reduce prices. I can't decide on my own, so I did not answer immediately. What shall I do?

---

[23] Note that what is needed in the 必要だ／必要がある and 要る expressions is marked by the particle が, not を. 現代のビジネスではコンピュータが必要だ。"Computers are necessary in modern-day business."

結論 conclusion　　相手 companion　　値引き price reduction

Vocabulary 4D

販売 (n) sales
交渉 (n) negotiation
件 (n) matter, incident
よろしい (a) good, all right [formal form of いい]
結論 (n) conclusion
と (cp) if/when. [結論から申しますと "(Lit.) If I may start from the conclusion (first)"]. [The S と pattern will be formally introduced in a later chapter.]
相手側 (n) the other party/person; partner
もっと (n) more

値引きして (n/v) [て-form of 値引きする =値段を引く] lower/reduce the price
もらいたい (cv: moraw) [たい form of もらう] want to receive. [Vてもらいたい "want to receive the favor of V-ing"]
一存 (n) one's own decision
決められない (vv: kime) [neg. pot. of 決める] can't decide
即答 (n) immediate answer. [即答する "answer immediately"]

Structures 4D

4D.1. Nominalization of N する verb phrases

N する verb phrases can be nominalized by changing N する to its noun form (N) and inserting the particle の after the particle as shown below. The object marker を is replaced by the particle の. The destination marker に cannot be used in the nominal form (＊ below is ungrammatical).

Verb Phrase			→	Noun Phrase			
Noun	Particle	N する		Noun	Part. + の	N	
東京テレコム	と	提携する	→	東京テレコム	との	提携	について話す。
to tie up with Tokyo Telecom				I talked about the tie-up with Tokyo Telecom.			
インターネット	で	販売する	→	インターネット	での	販売	をはじめた。
to sell via the Internet				We began the sales via the Internet.			
日本	へ or に	輸出する	→	日本	への ＊にの	輸出	がふえた。
to export to Japan				The export to Japan increased.			
車	を	輸入する	→	車	の	輸入	がへった。
to import cars				The import of cars decreased.			

A similar nominalization can be performed for the phrase N について ("about N") as shown below.[24]

レーザーについて研究する　→　レーザーについての研究がさかんだ。
to research lasers　　　　　　The research on lasers is flourishing.

4D.2. S こと

In Chapter 1, the sentence modifier pattern S の was introduced as in (1) below. The function of の here is to turn the sentence 大学で勉強した into a nominal. Accordingly, の is called a "nominalizer."

---

[24] Compare these forms to 日本からの手紙 ("a letter from Japan") and 東京までの電車 ("a train bound for Tokyo").

(1) 大学で勉強したのはコンピュータ回路です。
    The subject/one I studied at the university is computer circuit.

こと is yet another nominalizer, which turns the preceding sentence into a noun phrase as (2) below:

(2) 大学で勉強したことを活かしたいんです。
    I want to utilize what I studied at the university.

The difference between の and こと is that の captures a concrete aspect of one's experience while こと captures an abstract concept. In (1) above, の points to a specific subject matter the speaker studied, while こと in (2) points to an abstract study in general, ranging from the subject the speaker studied to "how to survive" tactics. Naturally, information we acquire through our direct experience (i.e., seeing, hearing, touching, etc.) is more concrete than information we acquire by thinking, inferring, etc. Therefore, the nominalizer の is used with the former group of verbs (perceptual verbs), and the nominalizer こと is used with the latter group of verbs (conceptual verbs). Which nominalizer below is more appropriate?

1. ハリスさんがきのう秋葉原でコンピュータを買っている(の／こと)を見ました。
   I saw Harris buying a computer at Akihabara.

2. 先生がお話しになる(の／こと)を聞きましたが、すばらしかったです。
   I heard [in person] Prof. Ono talk, and it was wonderful.

   先生がお話しになる(の／こと)を聞きましたが、それはいつですか。
   I heard [from someone] that Mr. Ono is going to talk, but when is that?

3. コンピュータのメモリーを大きくする(の／こと)を考えています。
   I am thinking of making the computer memory bigger.

The conversation continues in 4E below. In order to have successful 根回し, Mr. Tanaka knows that he needs close cooperation among all parties involved. He gathers necessary information and calls a meeting to discuss it.

Conversation 4E: Reporting on a meeting (2)

1. 田: あそことの契約はぜひとりたいから、あす、川田係長と君と私で相談しよう。それまでに経理課から売り上げ集計表と原価計算の書類をもらって、川田君にも送ってあげて。
2. ハ: はい。明日は何時に集まりますか。
3. 田: 11時はどう？
4. ハ: はい、11時ですね。
5. 田: その時、川田君にも来てもらいたいと言っておいてくれないか。
6. ハ: はい、わかりました。

1. T: I really want to get their contract, so let's discuss it among Subsec. Mgr. Kawada, you, and me tomorrow. By then, please get the sales journal and the cost account-ing documents from the accounting dept. and send them to her, too?
2. H: Yes, sir.   What time shall we meet tomorrow?
3. T: How about 11?
4. H: Yes, 11 o'clock.
5. T: Won't you tell Ms. Kawada that I would like her to come, too, at that time?
6. H: Yes, certainly.

相談 (ソウダン) consultation　集計 (シュウケイ) total　集まる (あつ) gather　表 (ヒョウ) table　計算 (ケイサン) calculation

Chapter 4: Reports

Vocabulary 4E

<ruby>契約<rt>けいやく</rt></ruby> (n) contract
とりたい (cv: tor) [たい-form of とる] want to take, get
<ruby>君<rt>きみ</rt></ruby> (n) you [君 is used to refer to one's junior.]
<ruby>相談<rt>そうだん</rt></ruby>しよう (n/v) [volitional of 相談する] consult, discuss
それまでに (phr) by that time
<ruby>経理課<rt>けいりか</rt></ruby> (n) accounting section
<ruby>売り上げ<rt>うりあげ</rt></ruby> (n) [the amount of] sales
<ruby>集計表<rt>しゅうけいひょう</rt></ruby> (n) table of totals sum; total. [表 "table"]

<ruby>原価<rt>げんか</rt></ruby> (n) original price; production cost
<ruby>計算<rt>けいさん</rt></ruby> (n) calculation
<ruby>書類<rt>しょるい</rt></ruby> (n) document
<ruby>送って<rt>おく</rt></ruby> (cv: okur) [て-form of おくる] send
<ruby>集まります<rt>あつ</rt></ruby> (cv: atsumar) to gather, assemble, meet
言っておいて (cv: iw) [て-form of 言う + て-form of おく] say it in advance
くれない (vv: kure) [neg. of くれる] not give me/us. [V てくれる "give me a favor of V-ing"]

Structures 4E

4E.1. Verbs of Giving: 上げる/V て上げる vs. くれる/V てくれる

The giving verbs, 上げる and くれる, are the plain-form counterparts of the polite verbs, さし上げる↓ and 下さる↑, respectively. The verb 上げる ("give [to others]") is used when the speaker (or an in-group person) gives something to others. In contrast, the verb くれる ("give [to me]") is used when someone gives something to the speaker (or to an in-group person). The giver is marked by the particles は/が and the recipient is marked by the particle に.

上げる／V て上げる

The verbs, 上げる and くれる, are more likely to be used among in-group members of equal or lower ranks. These verbs can also be used when the speaker does not feel it is necessary to be polite to the giver (of くれる) or to the recipient (of 上げる) as in the case of an impersonal giver as in 銀行がくれた ("The bank gave it to me").

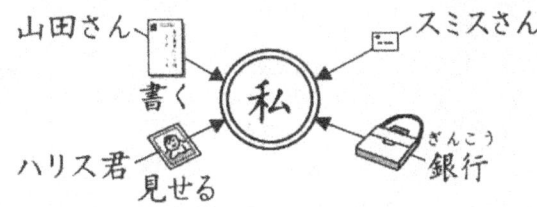

くれる／V てくれる

There is a special verb やる ("give") that can only be used when the speaker is giving something to one's own in-group members of lower ranks (typically, one's own children, pets, and plants) as in <ruby>娘<rt>むすめ</rt></ruby>にやった ("I gave [it] to my daughter") and 犬にごはんをやった ("I fed the dog"), and 花に水をやった ("I watered the flower").

Giver	は/が	Recipient	に	Object	を	"give [to others]"
私	は	スミスさん	に	本	を	上げた。
私	は	ハリス君	に	ペン	を	上げた。

Giver	は／が	Recipient	に	Object	を	"give [to me]"
スミスさん	は	私	に	名刺	を	くれた。
銀行	は	私	に	かばん	を	くれた。

These giving verbs can also be combined with a verb gerund (V て): V てあげる／V てくれる:

Giver	は／が	Recipient	に	Object	を	V て	"give [to others]"
私	は	山田さん	に	コーヒー	を	入れて	上げた。
私	は	娘	に	CD	を	買って	やった。

Giver	は／が	Recipient	に	Object	を	V て	"give [to me]"
山田さん	は	私	に	手紙	を	書いて	くれた。
ハリス君	は	私	に	写真	を	見せて	くれた。

Conversations using giving and receiving verbs follow:

1. Mr. Harris asks the Section Manager to give the Division Manager the form.

　ハリス：　課長、この書類を部長にさし上げて下さい。

　課長：　ああ、いいよ。

2. The Section Manager gives Mr. Harris' form to the Division Manager.

　課長：　ハリス君に書いてもらった書類を見ていただきたいんですが…

　田中：　うん、わかった。

The Section Manager tells Mr. Harris that he gave it to the Division Manager.

　課長：　君が書いてくれた書類を部長にさし上げたよ。
　ハリス：　どうも、すみません。

3. The Division Manager finishes the form and returns it to the Section Manager. The Section Manager then returns the form back to Mr. Harris.

　課長：　ハリス君、部長に見ていただいたよ。はい、これ。

　ハリス：　あ、もう、見て下さったんですか。どうも。

Like the verb さし上げる, the verb 上げる also expresses a sense of doing someone a favor. When you refer to your own action for your superior, it is better to avoid this verb. Instead, use expressions that sound less patronizing.

コーヒーを入れて上げましょうか。	[inappropriate to a superior]
コーヒーをお入れしましょうか。	[appropriate]
コーヒーはいかがですか。	[appropriate]

4E.2. Typical division names within a company

製造部	Production Division	経理部 or 会計部	Accounting Division
営業部 or 販売部	Sales Division	総務部	General Affairs Division
購買部	Purchase Division	人事部	Human Resources/Personnel Division
財務部	Finance Division	研究開発部	Research and Development Division

4E.3. Job titles within a large company

Members of a large company can be grouped into 役員 and 社員. 役員 are classified as "employers." Typical 役員 titles are:

会長	Chairman	専務取締役	Senior Managing Director
社長	President	常務取締役	Managing Director
代表取締役	Chief Executive Officer	取締役	Director
副社長	Vice President	部長	Division Manager/General Manager

社員 are classified as "employees." Typical 社員 titles are:

課長	Section Chief
係長	Chief (or Subsection Manager)
班長	Foreman (at factory)

Additionally, a prefix, 副〜 (Assistant/Vice...) or suffixes, 〜補佐 (Deputy) or 〜代理 (Deputy) can be attached to the titles above. Those without titles are colloquially called 平社員, a plain "employee."

Exercise 4

Grammar Utilization 4   Name:_____   Sec:_____ #:____

G1. Select the correct particles according to the English cues.

a. 部長（が／に）見積りを出してさし上げて下さい。   Please give the estimate to the Division Chief.
b. 部長（が／に）見積りを出して下さいました。   The Division Chief kindly gave the estimate to me.
c. 部長（が／に）見積りを出していただきました。   The Division Chief gave the estimate to me. (I received...)
d. ミラーさん（が／に）見積りを出してあげて下さい。   Please give the estimate to Ms. Miller.
e. ミラーさん（が／に）見積りを出してもらいました。 Ms. Miller gave the estimate to me. (I received...)
f. ミラーさん（が／に）見積りを出してくれました。   Ms. Miller kindly gave the estimate to me.

G2 Express Kimura or Tanaka's action according to the situations below using the verbs of giving and receiving. A superior (if any) is marked by a triangle (▲) below. The beginning part of each sentence is shown.

a. Ask Ms. Kimura to write a report for Section Manager Tanaka. (You are Ms. Kimura's colleague.)

　木村さん、_____？

b. Ms. Oki wrote a report for Mr. Tanaka. (You are a colleague of Mr. Tanaka.)

　大木さんが_____。
　or
　大木さんに_____。

c. Ms. Oki read a report for Mr. Tanaka. (You are Mr. Tanaka.)

　大木課長が_____。
　or
　大木課長に_____。

d. Ms. Kimura read a report for Mr. Tanaka. (You are Mr. Tanaka's superior.)

　木村君が _____。
　or
　木村君に_____。

e. Mr. Tanaka wrote a report for Ms. Oki. (You are Ms. Oki.)

　田中君が_____。
　or
　田中君に_____。

Chapter 4: Reports

f. Mr. Tanaka wrote a report for Ms. Kimura. (You are Ms. Kimura.)

田中部長が_____。
or
田中部長に_____。

G3. Complete the conversations by using the verbs of giving and receiving.　A superior is marked by ▲.

a. ブラウン：　今日はお客さんが多かったので、報告書がまだできていないんです。5時までには
　　　　　　　できると思いますが。
　　▲西山：　そうか。じゃあ、5時までに書いて_____。

b. ▲西山：　ブラウン君、あの見積書、明日までに必要なんだ。悪いけど、今日
　　　　　　　残業して_____。（残業する：work overtime）
　　ブラウン：　わかりました。

c. ブラウン：　課長さんに前に教えて_____寿司屋の名前は何でしたか。
　　　　　　　　　　　　　　　　(a sushi restaurant you told me about)
　　▲西山：　ああ、あれは「ことぶき」というんだよ。

d. ▲西山：　今、受付に外人のお客さんが来ているんだけど、英語が通じなくて困っている
　　　　　　　んだ。君が行って通訳して_____。（英語が通じる：make
　　　　　　　oneself understood in English；通訳する：interpret）
　　ブラウン：　わかりました。行ってまいります。("I will go and come back.")

e. ブラウン：　その消費者ガイド、お買いになったんですか。
　　▲西山：　いや、田中君が送って_____。

f. ブラウン：　あの電話の件ですけど、西山課長の方から青木部長に頼んで_____
　　　　　　　たいんですが。（…の件ですけど：It's about the case of …）
　　▲西山：　わかった。それは私がやろう。（やる：[colloquial form of する] to do）

G4. Choose the appropriate nominalizers.

a. 明日お会いする(の／こと)は横浜製作所の田中課長です。
b. 大学で勉強した(の／こと)を活かしたいんです。
c. 仕事を下請けに出す(の／こと)はいつですか。（下請けに出す：submit to a subcontractor）
d. 仕事を下請けに出す(の／こと)についてはどうお考えですか。
e. この話はなかった(の／こと)にして下さい。"Please consider it such that this plan never existed."
f. 先生が新しい研究についてお話しになる(の／こと)を聞きましたが、すばらしかったですよ。
g. 先生が新しい研究についてお話しになる(の／こと)を聞きましたが、本当ですか。
h. 川田係長と山田さんが二人で何か相談している(の／こと)を見ましたよ。
i. 無理な(の／こと)を申して、どうも申しわけございませんでした。

G2. You are speaking to a person shown below. Rephrase your original statement if necessary using the appropriate level of honorific or humble expressions. (Note that you may not need to change some expressions.)

	You	Listener	Your original statement
A.	平社員	同僚	石田さん、はまレストランに行きませんか。 →
B.	平社員	課長	山田課長、私が行ってきましょうか。 →

G5. Respond according to the English cues using the appropriate volitional form. A superior is marked by ▲.

a. A：30分待ちましたから、もうまいりましょうか。(We've waited for 30 min., so shall we go?)
    ▲ B：いや、もう少し＿＿＿＿＿＿＿＿＿＿。(Let's wait a little more. B is a superior to A.)

b. A：明日、何時ごろいらっしゃいますか。(What time are you coming tomorrow?)
    ▲ B：8時までに＿＿＿＿＿＿＿＿＿＿と思っているんだが… (I'm thinking of coming by 8 o'clock.)

c. A：あ、部長、まだいらっしゃったんですか。(Oh, you are still here!)
    ▲ B：うん、君といっしょに＿＿＿＿＿＿＿＿＿＿と思ってね。 (I thought I would leave with you.)

d. A：課長は私の話を聞いて下さるでしょうか。(I wonder if Sec. Manager would listen to me.)
    B：田中さんの話はいつでも＿＿＿＿＿＿＿＿＿＿とおっしゃってましたよ。
       (He was saying that he will listen to you any time.)

e. A：ブラウンさんにいつお会いになる予定ですか。(When are you scheduled to meet Mr. Brown?)
    ▲ B：来週＿＿＿＿＿＿＿＿＿＿と思っているんだ。(I'm thinking about meeting...)

G6. Fill in the blanks with various forms of V ておく ("V in advance, for later use") below.

a. A：日本に行く飛行機の切符は、いつ買ったらいいですか。(夏：summer)
    B：夏は高くなりますから、早めに＿＿＿＿＿＿＿＿＿＿下さい。(早めに：early)

b. A：この部屋は涼しいですねえ。(涼しい：cool)
    B：ええ、出かける時にエアコンを＿＿＿＿＿＿＿＿＿＿から。(つける：turn on)

c. A：日本にカメラを持って行くんでしょう？
    B：ええ、新しいフィルムをたくさん＿＿＿＿＿＿＿＿＿＿と思います。(フィルム：film)

d. A：もう英語の勉強をしているんですか。オーストラリアに行くのは来年でしょう？
    B：ええ、でも、今から勉強して＿＿＿＿＿＿＿＿＿＿たら、オーストラリアに行った時、
       困りますから。(困る：be in trouble)

Chapter 4: Reports   93

e. A: 来週の会議までにその報告書によく_____ようにおっしゃって下さい。
    B: 承知しました。そう申し伝えます。

G7. Fill in the blanks with either 間 or 間に. Don't forget other particles if necessary.

   a. お留守_____、ハリスさんから連絡がありました。

   b. 私はモデムを使っているから、インターネットをしている_____、電話が話し中になります。

   c. 学生がテストを受けている_____、静かにして下さい。(テストを受ける: take an exam)

   d. 映画を見ている_____、3度トイレに行った。

   e. お休み_____、ずっとうちで寝ていました。

   f. 日本へ行く飛行機に11時間、乗っている_____、本を読んだり、CDを聞いたりするつもりです。

G8. If possible, change the underlined verbs into the honorific or humble forms of 行く, 来る, いる, and 言う. (Caution: Plain-humble forms of some of these verbs do not exist.)

   a. A: ニューヨークでの会議に行きますか。→_____
      B: ええ、20日に行きます。→_____

   b. A: タクシーで行きましょうか。→_____
      B: そうですね。

   c. A: きのう何時までオフィスにいましたか。→_____
      B: 8時ごろまでいました。→_____

   d. A: こちらには何で来るつもりですか。→_____
      B: 新幹線で行くつもりです。→_____

   e. A: ニューヨークには何日ぐらいいる予定ですか。→_____
      B: 一週間いる予定です。→_____

   f. A: 課長にそのことを言いますか。→_____
      B: いいえ、私は言いません。→_____

   g. A: 課長、そのことを言いましたか。→_____
      B: いいえ、言ってませんよ。→_____

G9. Change the verb phrase into the corresponding noun phrase. If necessary, use appropriate particles. Also, select the meaning of the resulting noun phrase from the list below.

Example: 東京テレコムと提携する → 東京テレコムとの提携 (1)

a. インターネットで販売する →_____ ( )

b. 日本へ輸出する →_____ ( )

c. 車を販売する →_____ ( )

d. 部長と相談する →_____ ( )

e. 会議について報告する →_____ ( )

f. 東京テレコムに即答する →_____ ( )

g. 日本から輸入する →_____ ( )

h. コンピュータで計算する →_____ ( )

i. 売り上げを集計する →_____ ( )

j. 東京テレコムと契約する →_____ ( )

1. the tie-up with Tokyo Telecom	7. the sum of sales
2. the contract with Tokyo Telecom	8. the import from Japan
3. the immediate reply to Tokyo Telecom	9. the export to Japan
4. the consultation with the Division Manager	10. the sale via Internet
5. the calculation by a computer	11. the report on the conference
6. the sale of cars	

G10. Complete the following sentences according to English cues.

Example: 外国へ行くためには／外国へ行くのには　パスポートが必要だ。
外国へ行くためには／外国へ行くのには　パスポートが要る。

a. インターネットを使うためには_____。
In order to use the Internet, we need a computer.

b. _____日本語のマニュアルが要る。
In order to export our products to Japan, we need the manual in Japanese.

c. 結論を出すのには_____。
In order to come to a conclusion, we need the groundwork.

d. _____値引きが必要だ。
In order to get the orders, we need price reduction.

e. _____アメリカの企業との提携が必要だ。
In order to sell our products in America, we need cooperation with an American company.

f. _____ファックスが必要だ。

Chapter 4: Reports 95

In order to send the letter quickly, we need a fax machine.

g. Eメールを送るには_____。
In order to send email, we need...

h. _____。
In order to start a new project, it is necessary to find (見つける) good ideas ahead of others (人より先に).

i. 新しい製品を作り出すには_____。
In order to create new products, we need...

j. _____、先に電話しておく必要がある。
In order to...,　　　　　　　　　　　we need to call ahead of the time.

k. _____、健康に気をつける必要がある。
In order to...,　　　　　　　　　　　we need to be careful about our health.

G11. Reprimand Mr. Harris gently in each of the following situations.

a. Mr. Harris did not take the phone number down.

　　A:_____
　　B:はい、これからは気をつけます。

b. Mr. Harris did not return the phone call from the client.

　　A:_____
　　B:はい、これからは気をつけます。

c. Mr. Harris came to the meeting 10 minutes late. Remind him that one should not be late for a meeting.

　　A:_____
　　B:はい、これからは気をつけます。

d. Mr. Harris went home exactly at 5 p.m. when everyone else was still busy. Remind him that in Japan one should ask before leaving in such a situation.

　　A:_____
　　B:はい、これからは気をつけます。

Reading and Writing 4   Name:_____ Sec:_____ #:____

R1. Match business vocabulary on the left with the English equivalent on the right.

a. 注文をとる_____   1. my own will, decision

b. 価格の引下げ_____   2. to decide transaction terms

c. 結論を出す_____   3. sales cooperation/tie up

d. 即答する_____   4. sales negotiation

e. 根回しする_____   5. to reply immediately

f. 取り引き条件を決める_____   6. to import

g. 見積書_____   7. to export

h. 決算報告書_____   8. the other side, group

i. 売り上げ集計表_____   9. to reduce price

j. 販売交渉_____   10. to take an order

k. 販売提携_____   11. cost accounting

l. 輸入する_____   12. balance sheet

m. 輸出する_____   13. sales journal

n. 原価計算_____   14. to lay the groundwork

o. 書類_____   15. to conclude

p. 相手側_____   16. estimate

k. 私の一存_____   17. document

R2. Read the following email message and answer the questions below.

```
宛先:      kinoshita@nelectronics.co.jp
送信者:    harris@nelectronics.co.jp
日付:      2001年11月5日　13時04分
題:        販売会議
```

会議のお知らせです。

明日、11時より田中課長と東京テレコムへのソフト販売価格の引下げを検討します。

新しい見積り書を作成するため、売り上げ集計表と原価計算書が必要になりますので、持って来て下さいとのことです。

以上

宛先: To
送信者: From (Lit. "sender")
日付: date
題: subject
販売会議: sales meeting
お知らせ: notice
より: from [= から]
販売価格: sales price
引下げ: reduction

検討する: to examine, investigate
見積り書: estimate
作成する: to make, create
ため: in order to
売上げ集計表: sales journal
原価計算書: cost accounting document
必要: necessary
以上: That's all.

1. このメールはだれが、だれに書きましたか。

2. 会議では何について相談しますか。

3. 会議にはだれが出ますか。

4. 会議には何を持って行く必要がありますか。

Communicative Exercise 4

C1. Role Playing

Student #1: You are 伊藤課長, Ms. Brown's superior. You just received e-mail below from Ms. Brown. Tell her in person that you need to meet to discuss this matter with Subsection Manager Kawada (川田係長) of the Accounting Section (経理課) tomorrow. Also, ask Ms. Brown to tell Mr. Kawada to bring the cost accounting document (原価計算書).

Student #2: You are ブラウン. You came back from a meeting and sent 伊藤課長 the message below. Report orally to Mr. Ito what you have written. Tell him that you do not feel that a price reduction over 5% (5%以上の値引き) is possible.

宛先:	ito@nelectronics.co.jp
送信者:	brown@nelectronics.co.jp
日付:	2001年11月4日　15時35分
題:	東京テレコムとの取引

本日、東京テレコムとの販売交渉があり、相手側は販売価格の10％の引下げを検討してもらいたいとのことでした。返事は来週までお待ちいただくようにお願いしました。

以上

取引: business dealings
本日: today
販売交渉: sales negotiation
相手側: the other side; they
販売交渉: sales prices
引下げ: reduction
検討する: examine; investigate
返事: reply
Vようにお願いする: ask to V

Listening Comprehension 4   Name:_____ Sec:____ #:____

A is the first speaker.   B is the second speaker.

1. Voc: 場所(ばしょ): place; 再来週(さらいしゅう): a week after next

   だれが会議(かいぎ)の場所を決めますか。

   会議はいつですか。

2. Voc: 取(と)り引(ひ)き条件(じょうけん): conditions of business transaction; 上司(じょうし): superior; 部下(ぶか): subordinate

   菊池課長(きくちかちょう)はAさんの(上司(じょうし)／部下(ぶか))です。

   だれが取り引き条件を決めましたか。
      a. Aさん
      b. Bさん
      c. 菊池課長

3. Voc: お先(さき)に: early, ahead

   だれとだれが同じ in-group (同じ部／課で働(はたら)いている同僚(どうりょう))ですか。
      a. Aさんと田中さん
      b. Bさんと田中さん

4. BさんはAさんに何が悪(わる)いと言っていますか。
      a. Aさんが田中さんを待(ま)つこと
      b. Aさんが先に帰ること

5. Voc: 製作所(せいさくしょ): manufacturer; お目(め)にかかりたい↓: want to see you [humble]
        経理課(けいりか): accounting section; 決算報告書(けっさんほうこくしょ): balance sheet

   先(さき)ほど電話をかけてきたのはだれですか。

   メッセージは何ですか。

   Bさんは今から何をしますか。

6. Voc: 契約(けいやく): contract; 報告書(ほうこくしょ): report

   AさんとBさんは何について話していますか。

   契約書(けいやくしょ)はもうできましたか。

7. Voc: 書類：document; 目を通す：look over; ファックス：fax

   Aさんは何を探しているんですか。(探す：look for)

   Aさんが探している物はどこにありますか。どうしてそこにあるんですか。

   Bさんは今から何をしますか。

8. Voc: 見積り書：estimate; 計算：calculation; 違っている：be in error

   田中さんはこの会話 (conversation) の前に何をしましたか。

   田中さんはどうして困っているんですか。

9. Voc: 値引き：price reduction; 無理：impossible

   会議の結論は何ですか。

   どうして田中部長は値引きすることにしたんですか。

Chapter 5

銀行で
At the Bank
_{ぎん こう}

Priming

Japanese banks do not offer personal checking accounts. Typically, one creates a so-called "passbook" savings account with no means of writing checks. In Japan, personal checks are non-existent, and traveler's checks are rarely used.[25] One has to use either cash or credit cards to pay. It is not uncommon for Japanese people to carry a large amount of cash to cover their daily expenses such as lunch money, transportation fees, or grocery shopping. Casual restaurants and small shops accept only cash. The third option for paying is to use a "pre-paid card" designed for certain trains and subway systems, public phones, and department stores. You buy pre-paid cards typically through vending machines. Each time you use the card, the machine records the remaining value on the card.

One of the first things you need to do in order to establish everyday life in Japan is to open your own bank account. Imagine that you are in a local bank in Japan and are trying to open your new account. Without a doubt, you will encounter many new terms related to banking. Do you remember the first time you went to the bank in your home country to open your own account? Some of the questions you might be asked will be similar. Others may be different. This chapter deals with those similarities and differences.

---

[25] Only those who run businesses own checking accounts (当座預金: current checking account). 定期預金 (fixed-term account) is a time deposit account.

Conversation 5A: Going to a bank

1. 鈴木: いらっしゃいませ。	1. S: Welcome!
2. ハリス: あのう、口座を開きたいんですが…。	2. H: Umm, I would like to open an account...
3. 鈴: あ、ご新規でございますね。あちらで番号札をお取りになってお待ち下さい。	3. S: Oh, (is it) a new account? Please take a number over there and wait.
4. ハ: すみません、「ごしんき」って何のことですか。	4. H: Excuse me. What is "goshinki"?
5. 鈴: 新しく口座をお作りになることです。5番の窓口です。	5. S: It means to create a new account. (It's) Window 5.
6. ハ: あ、そうですか。どうも。	6. H: Oh, I see. Thanks.

座 seat, account　　待つ wait　　窓 window

Vocabulary 5A

いらっしゃいませ　Welcome!
口座 (n) account
開きたい (cv: hirak) [たい-form of 開く] want to open
ご新規 (n) new account [honorific-polite]
番号札 (n) number tag, card [ふだ card]

お取り (cv: tor) [honorific-polite V-stem of 取る] take. [お取りになる "take" (honorific)]
って (qt) quotation marker. [More casual than と]
●意味 (n) meaning
窓口 (n) (teller) window
お作りになる (cv: tsukur) make (honorific)

Structures 5A

5A.1.　X と(いうの) は

X というのは consists of a clause-modifier structure X というの ("the thing that we call X") followed by the topic marker は. In a casual conversation, X っていうのは is also used. If this phrase is followed by such questions as 何ですか, it is used to ask the definition of a word as shown below.

Clause modifier			N	は	question	
X	と／って	V	の			
「送金」	と／って	いう	の	は	何(のこと)ですか。	What is the thing called "soukin"?
「送金」	と／って	いう	の	は	どういう意味ですか。	What does the thing called "soukin" mean?

X というのは can be shortened to X とは as in X とは何ですか。 (or more casual X って何ですか。) ("What is so-called X?"). In reply to these questions, you need to phrase the definition by using a clause modifier structure S (という) こと or N のこと as shown below. S ということ can also be S という意味.

A: 「送金」って何ですか。　　What is this so-called "soukin"?
B: お金を送る(っていう)ことです。　　It means to "send money."

A: 「小切手」というのは何のことですか。　　What does "kogitte" mean?
B: チェックのことです。　　It means "checks."

A: 「解約」っていうのはどういう意味ですか。 　　What does "kaiyaku" mean?
B: 口座を閉じるっていう意味です。 　　It means "to close the account."

The noun の can be substituted with more specific category nouns such as 人, 食べ物, ところ, 店, etc.

マイケルジョーダンという人を知っていますか。 　　Do you know the person named Michael Jordan?
「ことぶき」というお店に行ったことがありますか。 　　Have you been to a shop named "Kotobuki"?

After taking his number (#97), Mr. Harris sits on one of the chairs in the waiting area and waits for his turn. After a while, his number is called. He goes to the teller and opens 普通預金 (regular savings account).

Conversation 5B: Opening a new blank account

1. 金井: 97番のお客様。 　　K: Customer number 97, please.
2. ハリス: はい。あの、口座を作りたいんですが。 　　H: Here. Umm... I would like to create an account, but...
3. 金: 普通預金でございますか。 　　K: Is it a regular account?
4. ハ: はい。 　　H: Yes.
5. 金: かしこまりました。こちらの用紙にご記入をお願いいたします。 　　K: Certainly. Would you fill out this form?
6. ハ: ここはひらがなで書いてもいいですか。 　　H: May I write in hiragana here?
7. 金: あ、そこは書かなくてもいいですよ。 　　K: Oh, you don't have to write there.
8. ハ: 印鑑を持ってないので、サインでもいいですか。 　　H: Since I don't have my signature-seal, is it OK to write my signature?
9. 金: はい、けっこうです。 　　K: Yes, of course.

客 (きゃく) guest, customer, client　　作る (つく) make　　紙 (かみ/シ) paper　　記 (キ) writing, narrative

Vocabulary 5B

金井 (かない) (n) Kanai [family name]
お客様 (きゃくさま) (n) customer, guest, client. [お is an honorific prefix. 様 is an honorific title]
あの (also あのう) "Umm..." is a hesitation noise directed toward someone other than the speaker.
普通 (ふつう) (n) ordinary, normal, regular
預金 (よきん) (n) money in a bank account
用紙 (ようし) (n) form

ご記入 (きにゅう) (n) write-in [honorific; 記入する "write down/fill in"]
書いても (cv: kak) [て-form of 書く + も] even if I write. [書いてもいい。"It's all right if I write"]
書かなくて (cv: kak) [negative-て-form of 書く] not write. [書かなくて(も)いい。"It's all right (even) if you don't write" or "You don't have to write"]
印鑑 (いんかん) (n) signature-seal. Also called はんこ

Structures 5B

5B.1. X てもいい／X なくてもいい

The pattern V て + も ("even") + いい expresses permission ("V-ing is permissible," "It is all right even if you V," or "You may V"). In a question form, this pattern is often translated as "May I V?" or "Is it all right (even) if I V" (も

can be dropped if the speaker believes that V-ing is readily permissible). よろしい, the polite equivalent of いい, is often used in a question form. The humble equivalent けっこう can also be used in an affirmative statement.

		Vて	も	いい (よろしい, けっこう)	
	お電話	借りて	も	よろしいですか。	Is it all right (even) if I use the phone?
はい、				けっこうです。	Yes, certainly.

    A: このコピー機、使ってもよろしいですか？   May I use this copy machine?
    B: どうぞ。   Yes. You may.

    A: その書類、ちょっと見てもよろしいですか？   May I take a look at that document?
    B: これは、まだちょっと…   This is still a bit (not ready)...

て-forms of い-adjectives, な-adjectives and nouns (い-Adj くて, な-Adj で and N で) also occur in the same pattern:

Aくて／Nで	も	いい (よろしい, けっこう)	
おそくて	も	いいです。	It's all right even if it is late.
手書きで	も	いいです。	It's all right even if it is hand-written.

    A: 今度のセミナーでインターネット商法のについて話してくれないか。   In the next seminar, will you talk about the Internet commerce?
    B: わかりました。短くてもよろしいですか？   OK. Is it all right even if it's short?
    A: ああ。5分ぐらいでどう？   Sure. How about 5 minutes or so?
    B: はい。英語でもよろしいですか。   Certainly. Is it all right if it's in English?
    A: いや、日本語でお願いするよ。   No. In Japanese, please.

て-forms may also take negative forms. Negative て-forms are formed by changing the plain negative ～ない ending into ～なくて. In its negative form, X なくてもいい yields the meaning that "it is OK even if...not...," or "do not have to V," or "do not have to be A/N."

	X なくて	も	いい (よろしい, けっこう)	
全部	しなくて	も	けっこうです。	It is all right even if you don't do all of it. (You don't have to do it all.)
見た目が	よくなくて	も	いいですよ。	It is all right even if the appearance is not good. (It doesn't have to look good.)
場所は	ここじゃなくて	も	よろしいですか。	Is it all right (even) if the location is not here?

Additional examples:

    A: 次は部長のはんこをいただくんですね。   Next, I'll get the seal from Div. Chief?
    B: それは、いただかなくてもいいですよ。   You don't have to get his seal.

    A: 普通預金は利子が高くないんですが…   The interest of the saving account is not high.
    B: 高くなくても けっこうです。   It's OK even if it is not high.

    A: 印鑑を持ってないんですが…   I don't have a seal.
    B: 印鑑じゃなくてもいいですよ。   It's OK even if it is not a seal.

Japan is a cash society, and people do not write checks to make purchases. Instead, people carry ATM cards to withdraw cash, and use cash (or cash equivalent such as prepaid cards) to pay for goods and services.

Conversation 5C: Making an ATM card

1. 金井: キャッシュカードはお作りになりますか。	1. K: Would you like to make a cash card (i.e., ATM card)?
2. ハリス: はい。	2. H: Yes.
3. 金: では、暗証番号を四桁の数字でお決めになって、この欄にお書き下さい。	3. K: Then, please decide your PIN using a four-digit number and write it in this box [of the form].
4. ハ: はい。	4. H: OK.
5. ハ: 暗証番号はこれにします。	5. H: (I) will choose this (number). [Lit. I will make it this.]
6. 金: はい、けっこうです。では、しばらくおかけになってお待ち下さい。	6. K: All right. Then, please have a seat and wait.

池 pond, lake　　数 or 数 number　　字 character, letter

Vocabulary 5C

キャッシュカード (n) ATM card
暗証番号 (n) personal identification number [Lit. "hidden verification number"]
四桁 (n) four digits
数字 (n) number, digit

欄 (n) column or box (to fill in)
しばらく (n) a while
おかけになって (vv: kake) [honorific て-form of (いすに) かける] have a seat
お決めになって (vv: kime) [honorific て-form of 決める] decide

Structures 5C

5C.1. XをYにする／なさる **vs.** XがYになる

XをYにする means cause X to be Y, or actively decide on Y as X.

　　会議の日を十日にしました。　　We decided on the 10th as the date for the meeting.
　　口座を普通預金にしました。　　I decided on my account to be a regular savings account.

In contrast, the parallel pattern, XがYになる, means X becomes Y, or Y is decided on as X. This pattern does not involve a sense of active causality as shown below.

　　会議の日が十日になりました。　　The date for the meeting was decided to be the 10th.
　　一ドルが 115円になりました。　　One dollar became ¥115.

The honorific-polite counterparts of する and します are なさる and なさいます, respectively. Be careful not to mix up these verbs with the verb なる ("become").

Also, do not confuse the structure of XをYにする／なる with the い-Adjective+くする／なる pattern.

　　OPECが石油の輸出をおさえているので、ガソリンが高くなっています。
　　Since OPEC is holding down the export of oil, gasoline has become cheaper.

　　この部屋は暑いですね。エアコンを入れて、涼しくして下さい。
　　This room is hot. Please turn on the air conditioner and cool it down.

Most people choose automatic fund transfer service for paying utility bills. It is not unusual to receive a small token of appreciation (e.g., a box of soap, a towel, or other small items) for opening a new account at a bank.

Conversation 5D: Requesting automatic fund transfer service

1. 金井: 公共料金の自動引きおとしはございますか。
2. ハ: 「自動引きおとし」ってどういう意味ですか。
3. 金: 私どもがお客様に代わって、電気、ガス、水道、電話代などの公共料金を毎月お客様の口座から自動的にお支払いすることです。
4. ハ: それは便利ですね。どうやるんですか。
5. 金: どうもありがとうございました。これ、どうぞ。
6. ハ: あ、どうも。それから、アメリカにお金を送りたいんですが、どちらの窓口ですか。
7. 金: 二階の外国為替の窓口です。

1. K: Is there automatic deduction of your public utilities bills?
2. H: What does it mean [when you say] "automatic deduction"?
3. K: Instead of you, we will automatically pay the electricity, gas, water, telephone bills, etc. every month out of your account.
4. H: That is convenient. How shall I set it up?
5. K: Thank you. This is for you.
6. H: Oh, thanks. In addition, I would like to send money to America. Which window is it?
7. K: It's the foreign currency exchange window on the second floor.

意味 meaning　　代わる substitute;　代 bill, fee　　便利 convenient

Vocabulary 5D

公共料金 (n) public utility fees

自動引きおとし (n) automatic deduction. [引きおとし is the V-stem of 引きおとす (cv: hikiotos) "deduct, withdraw"]

私ども↓ (n) we [ども is a humble-plural suffix for people]

代わって (cv: kawar) [て-form of 代わる] replace, substitute. [Xに代わって "in substitute of X"].

ガス (n) (natural) gas

水道 (n) water (line)

電話代. telephone charge [代 is a suffix for "fee"].

自動的に (adv) automatically

お支払い (cv: shiharaw) [honorific V-stem of 支払う "pay"] pay; payment. [お支払いする↓ "pay" (humble); お支払いになる↑ "pay" (honorific)]

やる (cv: yar) [colloquial form of する] to do

お金 (n) money [honorific]

送りたい (cv: okur) [たい-form of 送る] want to send

外国為替 (n) foreign currency exchange

Structures 5D

5D.1. X的(な)／X的に

The 的 is a suffix that converts certain nouns (including some unconventional ones) into な-adjectives ("X-like"). な can be optionally deleted.

Adjectival usage				
N	的	(な)	N	
日本人	的	(な)	発音	a Japanese-like pronunciation
科学	的	(な)	考え	scientific thinking
機械	的	(な)	仕事	a mechanical job

When the particle に follows X 的, it creates an adverbial form ("X-ly", "in X way"). (Caution: Not all 的な-adjectives function as 的に-adverbs.)

Adverbial usage			
N	的	に	N
日本人	的	に	発音する — pronounce [it] in a Japanese way
科学	的	に	考える — think scientifically
機械	的	に	仕事する — work like machines

After creating his account, Mr. Harris now deals with foreign currency exchange.[26]

Conversation 5E: Foreign currency exchange service

1. ハ: あのう、すみません。アメリカに五百ドル送りたいんですが、為替レートはいくらですか。
2. 阿部: 一ドル、118円です。
3. ハ: 時間はどのぐらいかかりますか。
4. 阿: 電信扱いでしたら、三日から四日かかりますが、手数料が四千五百円かかります。普通扱いでは、一週間から十日かかりますが、手数料は四千円です。
5. ハ: じゃあ、普通扱いでお願いします。

1. H: Umm, excuse me. I would like to send $500 to America. What is the exchange rate?
2. A: One dollar is 118 yen.
3. H: How long will it take?
4. A: If electronic transfer is used, it will take 3 to 4 days, but the handling fee will cost ¥4500. With regular handling, it will take from one week to 10 days, but the fee is ¥4000.
5. H: Then, regular handling, please.

リョウ 料 fee, bill   くに／コク 国 nation, country   シン 信 trust, confidence

Vocabulary 5E

為替レート (n) exchange rate
かかります (cv: kakar) [polite of かかる] take [time, money, etc.]
電信 (n) electronic transfer

扱い (n) handling, treatment. [扱う (cv: atsukaw) "treat, handle"]
手数料 (n) handling charge

Structures 5E

5E.1. N (or V-plain の) に X が かかる

In Chapter 4C.2, we introduced the structure, V-plain のに X が 必要だ／いる ("X is necessary in order to V"). The present structure N (or V-plain の)に X がかかる is similar to this structure. It means "It takes X for N (or V-ing)." The verb かかる means "takes/costs/is charged." X can be followed by a quantity expression. The X が part can be deleted if it is obvious, or it can be treated as a topic as in 手数料は ("as for the handling fee").

---

[26] 文化ノート At the end of World War II, the currency exchange rate was fixed at 360 yen per dollar for about 25 years. In 1970, the world abandoned the fixed-rate foreign exchange system in favor of the floating rate system. Since then, the yen has appreciated against dollar. In 1980, the exchange rate hit 200 yen to the dollar, and the rate fluctuated between 200 and 250 yen to the dollar until 1985, when the yen started to surge again due to increasing trade imbalance between the U.S. and Japan. In 1993, the yen rose to a record of less than 90 yen per dollar. The yen has stayed around 120 yen to the dollar during the late 1990's to the early years of the 21st century.

N V-plain の	に	X	が	Qty	かかる	"It takes/costs Quantity for N/V-ing." "X (of Quantity) is charged for N/V-ing."
送金	に	手数料	が	四千円	かかる。	A fee of 4000 yen is charged for money transfer.
送金するの	に	手数料	が	四千円	かかる。	A fee of 4000 yen is charged for transferring money.
タイプ	に	時間	が	一日	かかる。	It takes a day for typing.
タイプするの	に	時間	が	一日	かかる。	It takes a day to type [it].

Mr. Harris would like to deposit money at an ATM, but he needs help.

Conversation 5F: Troubleshooting 1

(連絡用の電話で)
1. ハリス: 振込をしたいんですが、この機械の使い方がよくわからないんです。見ていただけますか。
2. 久保田: はい、係りの者が今うかがいます。

(Through an intercom)
H: I would like to make a deposit, but I don't know how to use this machine well. Could I have you look at it?
K: Certainly. The person in charge will be there right now.

機 machine　械 instrument　者 person (↓)

Vocabulary 5F

連絡用　(n) for the purpose of communication
振込　(n) deposit (= 入金);　fund transfer
機械　(n) machine
使い方　(n) use, usage, method
よく　(a) [く-form of よい／いい] good, well.　[よくわからない "do not understand well"]

いただけます　(cv: itadak) [polite-potential of いただく; humble-polite potential of もらう] can receive.　[Xをいただけますか "Can I receive X?"]
係りの者　(phr) person in charge (者↓ = 人)
うかがいます　(cv: ukagaw) [polite of うかがう; humble-polite of 聞く] visit; ask

Structures 5F

5F.1.　Verb stem + 方

The /V-stem + 方/ pattern means the way of V-ing, or how to V.　Study the following phrases:

書き方　　the way of writing, how to write
話し方　　the way of speaking, how to speak
見方　　　the way of seeing, how to see

A common mistake students make is that they use the particle を in expressing the phrase, the way of writing a report, as in レポートを書き方.　The correct form is: レポートの書き方.　How do you say the following by using 方?　(See the answers in Footnote [27] below.)

the way of using ATM:
the way of seeing things:
the way of eating sushi:

---

[27] The answers are: ATMの使い方、物の見方、すしの食べ方

Exercise 5

Grammar Utilization 5   Name:_____ Sec:_____ #:____

G1. The bank teller has used the following words that you do not understand (underlined). Respond by asking for their meanings.

　　Example: ご新規の前でお待ちください。→すみません、「ごしんき」ってどういう意味ですか。

　　a. 普通預金の窓口は3番でございます。→

　　b. 公共料金はどうなさいますか。→

　　c. 暗証番号をお書きになってください。→

　　d. 印鑑をお持ちではございませんか。→

G2. Define the following terms by using the pattern: Xというのは…という意味／ことです。

　　Example: ご新規というのは新しく口座をお作りになることです。

　　a. 送金

　　b. 印鑑

　　c. 振り込み

　　d. 暗証番号

G3. You are a receptionist. Reply to the questions below using the conditional form X たら as shown in the example. (Use the proper styles of politeness.)

　　Example: 外国為替はどこですか。→(二階の窓口)外国為替でしたら、二階の窓口でございます。

　　a. 振り込みをしたいんですが。→(5番の窓口)

　　b. この辺に食事ができるところありませんか。→(地下)

　　c. この手紙を出したいんですが。→(ビルの前の郵便局)

　　d. 田中部長はいらっしゃいますか。→(三階の会議室)

G4. Ask a question to seek permission ("Is it all right if ...?" or "Is it all right even if ...(not)...").

Example:

Seek permission to park your car here. →すみません、ここに車を止めてもいいですか。

a. Seek permission to reply (返事をする) by tomorrow.

→_____

b. Seek permission to speak in a meeting (発言する).

→_____

c. Seek permission to ask the Division Manager's opinions (意見) first.

→_____

d. Seek permission to consult your superior (上司).

→_____

e. Ask if it is all right NOT to write in kanji.

→_____

f. Ask if it is all right NOT to receive Division Manager Aoki's signature (サイン).

→_____

g. Ask if it is all right NOT to make copies before you submit the report.

→_____

G5. Respond by giving permission based on the cue if any. Study the examples below.

Examples:
印鑑がないんですけど… → (signature) サインでもけっこうですよ。
あした来られないんですけど… →(the day after tomorrow) あさって来てもいいですよ。
あしたの朝早くうかがいたいんですが… → 早くてもけっこうですよ。

a. 黒いボールペンは持ってないんですけど…

→ (a blue pen) _____

b. プリンタがこわれて、プリントできないんですけど…

→ (write by hand) _____

c. 急ぎの用事が入って、報告書を今すぐ出せないんですが…。
(急ぎの用事：urgent business; 報告書を出す：submit the report)

→ (become late) _____

Chapter 5: At the Bank　　113

　　d. 月曜日はちょっとこちらの都合が悪いんですけど…
　　　　（都合が悪い：The schedule is full and cannot be rearranged.）

　　　　→ (Tuesday) _____

　　e. 時間は30分もらったんですけど、私のスピーチは短いんです。

　　　　→ _____

　　f. 一度、帰りまして、もう一度検討したいのですが。（検討する：examine）

　　　　→ _____

G6. You have been asked whether or not some condition still holds.　Reply negatively and inform the questioner of the changes as shown in the example.

　　Example:
　　　A：会議は三日でしょう？
　　　B：いいえ、四日になりました。

　a. A：あの喫茶店のコーヒー、一杯200円だったでしょう？

　　　B：いえ、_____。
　　　A：やっぱりインフレ（inflation）なんですね。

　b. A：あしたの会議は4時からでしょう？
　　　B：あ、ご存じありませんでしたか？　会議は_____。

　c. A：ハードディスクの空きスペース(free space)はまだ200MBぐらいありますか。

　　　B：いいえ、もう_____。
　　　A：こまりましたね。今度のシステムソフトは空きスペースが100MBほどいるんですよ。

　d. A：名古屋での会議は金曜日からですね。
　　　B：いや、予定が変わって_____。
　　　　（予定が変わった：The plan has changed.）
　　　A：じゃあ、急いで新幹線の切符を予約したほうがいいですね。

G7. For (a) through (c), you are asked to decide on something.　Respond with your decision.　For (d) through (f), ask the question that elicits each reply.

　a. A：暗証番号は何になさいますか。4桁の数字でお決めになって下さい。

　　　B：_____。

　b. A：この三つのカバー（"cover"）の中でどれになさいますか。（赤、青、黒）

　　　B：_____。

　c. A：お飲物は何になさいますか。

　　　B：_____。

d. A:＿＿。
   B:私は10時からのセクション (section) にいたします。

e. A:＿＿。
   B:田中さんはビーフで、私はチキンにします。

f. A:＿＿。
   B:エコノミークラスにしてください。

G8. Fill in the blanks with 的 and appropriate particles based on English cues.

Example: 自動的な支払い "automatic payment"; 自動的に支払う "pay (it) automatically"

a. 科学＿＿＿＿考え "scientific thinking"

b. アメリカ＿＿＿＿言い方 "American way of speaking"

c. 日本＿＿＿＿言います "say (it) in the Japanese way"

d. 英語＿＿＿＿話し方 "the English(-language) way of speaking"

e. 機械＿＿＿＿歩き方 "machine-like/mechanical way of walking"

f. 機械＿＿＿＿話したら、よくわかりません。 "You are not intelligible if you speak like a machine."

g. 90年代のバブル経済は歴史＿＿＿＿意味がある。 "90's bubble economy is historically significant."

G9. Complete the blanks with the words supplied in parentheses (if any) by following the example.

Example: A:アメリカにお金を送るのには手数料がどのぐらいかかるでしょうか。
         B:(電信扱い／4500円) 電信扱いでしたら、4500円かかります。

         A:アメリカに電信で送金するのには何日かかりますか。
         B:24時間かかります。

a. A:日本で手紙を送るのにはいくらぐらいかかるでしょうか。
   B:(郵便／80円)＿＿＿＿＿＿＿＿＿＿＿＿＿＿＿＿＿＿＿＿＿＿＿＿＿＿＿＿＿＿＿＿＿。

b. A:空港からこの荷物を家まで送るのにはいくらぐらいかかるでしょうか。
   B:(宅急便／4000円)＿＿＿＿＿＿＿＿＿＿＿＿＿＿＿＿＿＿＿＿＿＿＿＿＿＿＿＿＿。

c. A:面接会話(interview dialogues)をタイプするのには何時間ぐらいかかるでしょうか。
   B:(全部／4時間)＿＿＿＿＿＿＿＿＿＿＿＿＿＿＿＿＿＿＿＿＿＿＿＿＿＿＿＿＿＿＿。

d. A:＿＿＿＿＿＿＿＿＿＿＿＿＿＿＿＿＿＿＿＿＿いくらぐらいかかりますか。
   B:35セントかかります。

e. A:＿＿＿＿＿＿＿＿＿＿＿＿＿＿＿＿＿＿＿＿＿何日ぐらいかかりますか。
   B:三日ぐらいかかると思います。

Chapter 5: At the Bank

f.　A:＿＿＿＿＿＿＿＿＿＿＿＿＿＿＿＿＿＿＿＿＿＿＿どのぐらいかかりますか。
　　B:車でしたら、6時間ぐらいかかるでしょう。

g.　A:＿＿＿＿＿＿＿＿＿＿＿＿＿＿＿＿＿＿＿＿＿＿＿どのぐらいかかりますか。
　　B:1年ぐらいかかると思います。

G10.　You are asking how to do something below. Complete your part (B) by using N の V-stem 方 form.

a.　A:このコンピュータを使っていただけませんか。
　　B:じゃあ、＿＿＿＿＿＿＿＿＿＿＿＿＿＿＿＿＿＿を教えて下さい。

b.　A:この用紙に書いていただけませんか。
　　B:じゃあ、＿＿＿＿＿＿＿＿＿＿＿＿＿＿＿＿＿＿を教えて下さい。

c.　A:田中さんが面接していただけませんか。
　　B:わかりました。じゃあ、面接＿＿＿＿＿＿＿＿＿＿＿＿＿＿＿を教えて下さい。

d.　A:大至急、送って下さい。
　　B:じゃあ、Eメールで送りますから、＿＿＿＿＿＿＿＿＿＿＿＿＿＿＿＿＿を教えて下さい。

e.　A:このアプリケーションを使ったことがありますか。
　　B:始め方は知っているんですが、＿＿＿＿＿＿＿＿＿＿＿＿＿＿＿＿＿は忘れました。

G11.　Complete the conversations using the V てしまう ("have V-ed completely" or "have V-ed [unintentionally]").

Example:　A:ピザはまだ、少し残っていますか。 ("Is a small amount of pizza still remaining?")
　　　　　B:いいえ、もう全部食べてしまいました。 ("No, I ate it all.")

a.　A:暗証番号は何番ですか。("What is your PIN?")
　　B:あ、何番だったか＿＿＿＿＿＿＿＿＿＿＿＿＿＿＿＿＿＿＿！
　　("Oh, I forgot what number it was!")

b.　A:この用紙に印鑑をお願いします。 ("Please put your signature seal on this form.")
　　B:あ、印鑑を家に＿＿＿＿＿＿＿＿＿＿＿＿＿＿＿＿＿＿＿！
　　("Oh, I left it at home!" (Lit. "I came here laying it down [at home]." おく: lay something down)

c.　A:そのファイルのコピーを送って下さい。 ("Please send me a copy of that file.")
　　B:あ、そのファイルは＿＿＿＿＿＿＿＿＿＿＿＿＿＿＿！ ("Oh, I deleted the file completely!")
　　(消す: delete [files])

d.　A:この本はもう＿＿＿＿＿＿＿＿＿＿＿＿＿、どうぞ。 ("I read this book completely, so...")
　　B:どうも、来週中に返しますから。 ("Thank you. I will return it within next week.")

e.　A:ここにあった手紙、どうした？ ("What did you do with the letter that was lying here?")
　　B:あ、もう＿＿＿＿＿＿＿＿＿＿＿＿＿＿＿＿けど。 ("Oh, I already mailed it.")

A Systematic Approach to Business Japanese

G12. You are on the left. Make a request to the people on the right using the appropriate form of the verb いただく／もらう. Superiors are marked by ▲.

a. _____
(You are asking him to look over (目を通す) the report (報告書).) ▲

b. _____
▲ (You are asking him to meet Mr. Nishi of Tokyo Telecom.)

c. _____
▲ (You are asking her to translate (翻訳する) the report.)

d. _____
(You are asking him to form a conclusion (結論を出す) on the matter. ▲

e. _____
(You are asking your colleague to show you the report.)

f. _____
▲ (You are asking her to show you the report.)

g. _____
(You are asking him to introduce Mr. Nishi to you.) ▲

h. _____
(You are asking him to have a few minutes (お時間) with him.)

Chapter 5: At the Bank   117

Reading and Writing 5   Name:_____ Sec:_____ #:____

R1. Look at the bank form below and answer the questions.

[Bank form image with handwritten entries: 東京都大田区本町2-34, 山田 花子様, 東京テレコム, etc.]

普通預金申込書 兼 入金伝票 (ふつうよきんもうしこみしょ けん にゅうきんでんぴょう): application for an ordinary account, also deposit slip
おところ: (current) address
ご連絡(可(通 不要/通 要)/否): notification (OK: (not needed/needed)/ No)
通帳種類(普通/総合): passbook type (ordinary/general)
通帳デザイン(一般/キャラクター): passbook design (general/character)
カード種類(一般/キャラクター): ATM card type (general/character)

ご自宅電話: phone telephone number
性別(男/女): sex (male/female)
生年月日(明治・大正・昭和・平成): D.O.B. (Meiji, Taisho, Showa, & Heisei)
お勤め先(ご職業): employer name (profession name)
金額: amount of money
お届け出印: registered signature seal

You are Ms. Hanako Yamada. Today, you are opening a new bank account with an initial deposit of 35000 yen. Complete the form above based on the following information.

1. Home address: Zip 130-7654 東京都大田区本町 2-34, Home phone: 03-3234-5679

2. DOB: June 15, 1980 (昭和 65 年)

3. You want to be notified (when the card is ready).

4. You want to receive your passbook and ATM card by mail.

5. Your PIN for the ATM card: 4589

6. You work for Tokyo Telecom. Work phone: 03-3765-0014

Communicative Exercise 5

C1. Reply to each of the questions below. Your answer must have two parts: "If you do A, then X.   If you do B, then Y."

Example: アメリカに送金（そうきん）したいんですが、どのぐらいかかりますか。

| A: | electronic handling | X: | 3 days |
| B: | regular handling | Y: | 1 week to 10 days |

→電信扱（でんしんあつか）いでしたら、三日かかりますが、
普通扱（ふつうあつか）いでしたら、一週間から十日かかります。

a: 東京（とうきょう）へ手紙（てがみ）を出したいんですが、どのぐらいかかりますか。

| A: | express mail (速達（そくたつ）) | X: | 1 day |
| B: | | Y: | |

b: これをコピーしたいんですが、料金（りょうきん）はいくらですか。

| A: | color (カラー) | X: | ¥50/sheet |
| B: | black-and-white (白黒（しろくろ）) | Y: | ¥30/sheet |

c: 空港（くうこう）に行くのに、時間はどのぐらいかかりますか。

| A: | Limousine Bus | X: | 70 minutes |
| B: | Train | Y: | 60 minutes |

d: ロスアンジェルスまでの飛行機（ひこうき）の往復運賃（おうふくうんちん） (round trip fare) はいくらですか。

| A: | First Class | X: | ¥240,000 |
| B: | Economy | Y: | ¥120,000 |

e: アトランタまで飛行機（ひこうき）の予約（よやく）をしたいんですけど、往復運賃（おうふくうんちん）はいくらですか。

| A: | By May 31 | X: | ¥120,000 |
| B: | Economy | Y: | ¥120,000 |

C2. Complete the conversation between A and B. A must ask B to make a choice. B must choose one. Think about the relationship between A and B and use the proper style of politeness.

a.	[1/25 ? 1/26 Today Tomorrow]	A: ハン君（くん）の歓迎（かんげい）パーティーは明日とあさってとどちらがいいですか。(歓迎パーティー: welcoming party) B: そうだなあ。あしたは忙（いそが）しいから_____ _____
b.	[~~1/25~~ 1/26 Today Tomorrow]	A: _____ _____ B: いや、あしたにするよ。今日はお客さんが来るから。 あした、11時に来てくれないか。
c.		A: ゴルフツアーは月曜からと火曜からとどちらがいいですか。

Chapter 5: At the Bank

	Mon	Tue	Wed	B: そうだなあ。＿＿＿＿＿＿＿＿＿＿＿＿＿＿＿＿＿＿
Plan A		●	→	月曜日にはまだ計算書（けいさんしょ）ができていないだろう？
P̶l̶a̶n̶ B		●	→	
d. coffee ? black tea				A: コーヒーと紅茶とどちらになさいますか。 B: ＿＿＿＿＿＿＿＿＿＿＿＿＿＿＿＿＿＿＿＿＿＿ このごろ、コーヒー飲みすぎているから。（V すぎる：V excessively）

C3. [Role Playing]   In each of the following, try to make a request using the V てもらえない／いただけない？ pattern. Use the proper politeness styles.

a.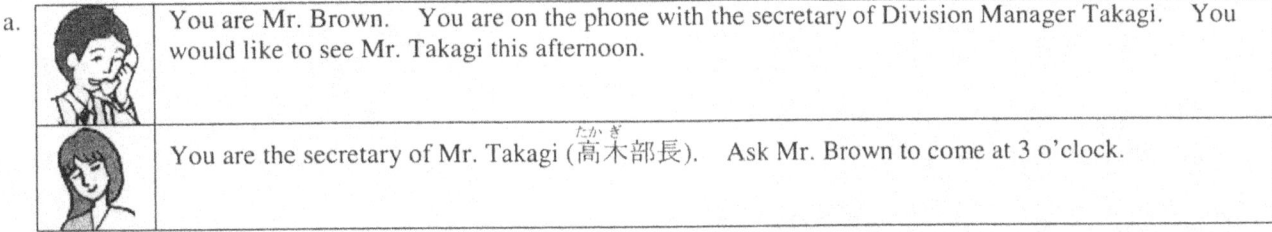

| You are Mr. Brown. You are on the phone with the secretary of Division Manager Takagi. You would like to see Mr. Takagi this afternoon. |
| You are the secretary of Mr. Takagi (高木部長). Ask Mr. Brown to come at 3 o'clock. |

b.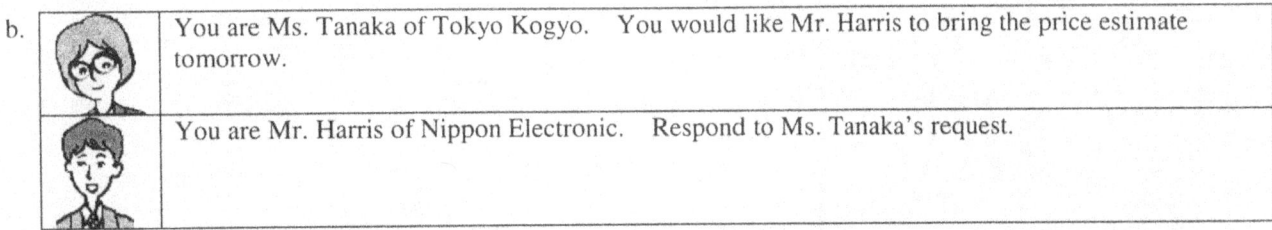

| You are Ms. Tanaka of Tokyo Kogyo. You would like Mr. Harris to bring the price estimate tomorrow. |
| You are Mr. Harris of Nippon Electronic. Respond to Ms. Tanaka's request. |

c.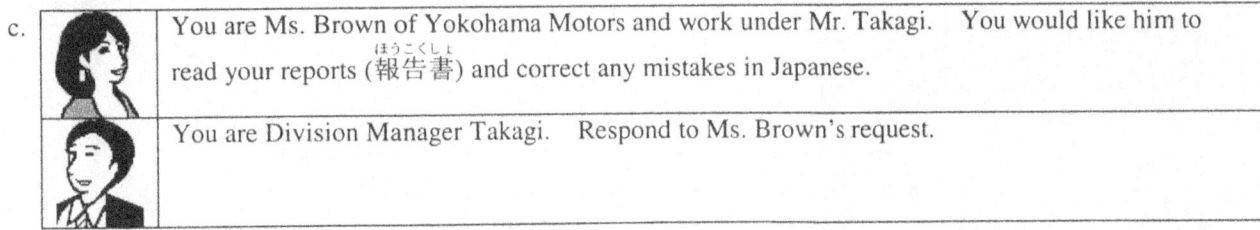

| You are Ms. Brown of Yokohama Motors and work under Mr. Takagi. You would like him to read your reports (報告書) and correct any mistakes in Japanese. |
| You are Division Manager Takagi. Respond to Ms. Brown's request. |

d.

| You are Mr. Yamamoto. Ms. Han works for you. Ask her to call Mr. Miller of American TV and confirm tomorrow's appointment at 2:00. |
| You are Division Manager Takagi. Respond to Ms. Brown's request. You are Ms. Han. Respond to Mr. Yamamoto's request. |

e.

| You are Mr. Smith of Noda Trading Company (野田商事). You would like your boss, Ms. Tanaka, to read your reports and you would like to get her approval (i.e., her signature seal). |
| You are Ms. Tanaka. Respond to Mr. Han's request. |

Listening Comprehension 5   Name:_____ Sec:_____ #:____

1. Voc: 預金する: deposit; 利子: interest; 普通預金: ordinary savings account; 定期預金: certificate of deposit

    Aさんは何をしようと思っていますか。

    普通預金の利子:いくらですか。

    Aさんは何をすることにしましたか。

2. Voc: 用紙: form 記入する: fill in

    AさんはBさんに何をしてもらいますか。

    Aさんが書いた用紙はどちらですか。

Picture 1

Picture 2

3. Voc: 勤務先: a place of work

    Aさんが使っている用紙はどちらですか。

Picture 1   Picture 2

Chapter 5: At the Bank

4. <u>Voc</u>: はんこ: signature seal (= 印鑑)

   Aさんが書いた用紙はどちらですか。

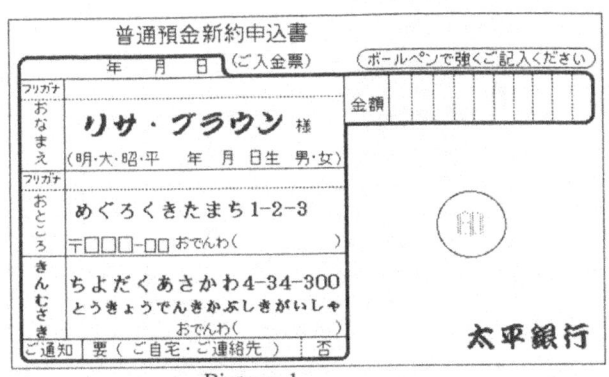 

   Picture 1   Picture 2

5. <u>Voc</u>: 両替え: exchange of money;　額: amount of money;　髪: hair

   Aさんは何について話していますか。
   a. もらったお金の額が違うこと
   b. 両替えできないこと
   c. 印鑑がないこと

   席をはずしている銀行員はどの人ですか。

   1.　　　2.　　　3.　　　4.

6. <u>Voc</u>: 自動引き落とし機: cash machine;　彼: he, that person

   Bさんはどうして山田さんに電話するんですか。

7. <u>Voc</u>: トラベラーズチェック: traveler's checks;　交換レート: exchange rate;　弱い: weak

   トラベラーズチェックで千ドル作る時、円でいくらかかりますか。

   トラベラーズチェックで千ユーロ作る時、円でいくらかかりますか。

8. <u>Voc</u>: 機械: machine;　係りの者: person in charge

   Aさんはどうして係りの人を呼んだんですか。

Chapter 6

おつきあい
"Work"
after Work

Priming

In addition to company training, おつきあい (Lit. "going along with") is an important process of socialization through which one develops a sense of self identity as a member of the company. The word おつきあい is a noun derived from the verb つきあう that refers to an act of going along with the expectation of others (and also to "go steady with" 〜とつきあっている). At work, when someone is working overtime, it is not uncommon to see others remain in the office just for おつきあい even if they have no work to do. After work, おつきあい often means going to a restaurant to eat and drink together and socialize to develop a sense of camaraderie. Even if you are from a culture where work and private life are clearly separated, occasional おつきあい may even be advisable.

Newcomers are often welcomed by an informal welcome party or reception. To go along with such an invitation after five is not part of your job specification, but it is the beginning of a long relationship you cannot avoid. This morning, a senior colleague, Ms. Yamada, has approached you with a smile. Find out how she invites you to the party.

Conversation 6A: An invitation to a welcome party

1. 山: ハリス君。今週の金曜日の晩、あいてる？
2. ハ: ええ。別に予定は何も入っていませんけど、何か？
3. 山: 実はね。みんなでハリスさんの歓迎会をしようと思ってるんで、あけといてもらえる？
4. ハ: 私のですか。すみません。みなさん、お忙しいのに。
5. 山: そんな、おおげさなものじゃないのよ。六時に「寿」を予約しておくから、来てね。
6. ハ: わかりました。
7. 山: あ！ それから、二次会もあるわよ。
8. ハ: え？「二次会」って何ですか。
9. 山: 夕食を食べてから、そのあと飲みに行くのよ。新しくできたカラオケバーにみんなが行きたがってるの。

1. Y: Mr. Harris. Is this Friday evening open?
2. H: Yes, I don't have any particular plans. What (is it)?
3. Y: Actually, we are thinking of giving you a welcome party, so can you keep it open?
4. H: For me? Thank you. But you are all so busy.
5. Y: It's not a big deal. We'll make a reservation at Kotobuki at six, so please come.
6. H: Certainly.
7. Y: Oh! In addition, there will be a second party.
8. H: Huh? What is a "second party"?
9. Y: After eating dinner, we'll go out drinking. Everyone wants to go to the karaoke bar that has newly opened.

予 (ヨ) advance, pre-　定 (テイ) fixed　入る (はい) enter　入社 (ニュウシャ) enter a company (to be employed)

Vocabulary 6A

 おつきあい (n) going along; socializing
晩 (ばん) evening
あいて (cv: ak) [て-form of あく] (something) opens; is empty
べつに (adv) [べつに～ない: not particularly...]
入って (cv: hair) [て-form of 入る] enter, go in. [予定が入る "(something) comes (into) schedule"]
何か (n) something
実は (adv) truthfully; actually; to tell you the truth
歓迎会 (n) welcome party, reception
あけといて (vv: ake) [Contraction of あけておいて. [て-form of あける + て-form of おく] keep (something) open; open in advance
～のに (con) despite that
おおげさ (な-adj) exaggeration, a big deal
予約しておく (phr) [て-form of 予約する+おく] to reserve (a seat/hotel) in advance
● 残業 (n) overtime work
二次会 (n) second party
夕食 (n) supper, dinner
食べてから (phr) after eating [V てから "after V-ing"]
飲みに (phr) [V-stem of のむ + にいく "go to drink"]
カラオケバー (n) karaoke (bar)
行きたがって (phr) [て-form of 行きたがる] [行きたい + suffix がる "show signs of"] wants to go

Structures 6A

6A.1. Transitive verbs vs. intransitive verbs

In English, we say:

(1a)　I opened the window.
(2a)　The window opened.

The English verb "open" above expresses two different notions. In (1a), "open" means "someone intentionally opens something," while in (2a), "open" means "something opens (without regard to someone's intention)." In Japanese, two separate verbs are used to express these notions. Sentence (1b) below says that someone opened the window, and that someone is Mr. Tanaka. 田中さん is the subject and 窓 is the direct object of his action. On the other hand, Sentence (2b) says that 窓 opened on its own without help from anyone. Here, 窓 is the subject and there is no object. We have seen similar distinctions in Chapter 2B (i.e., 回す (Vt: "turn [something] around") vs. 回る (Vi: "go around")) and in Chapter 3B (i.e., とめる "someone stops something" vs. とまる "something stops on its own").

Subject	が	Object	を	Vt	
(1b) 田中さん	が	窓	を	あけました。	Mr. Tanaka opened the window.
Subject	が			Vi	
(2b) 窓	が			あきました。	The window opened

The former type (1a/1b) of verbs are called **transitive** verbs (Vt), and the focus is on <u>who</u> does the action. The latter type (2a/2b) of verbs are called **intransitive** verbs (Vi), and the focus is on <u>what</u> happens. Generally, transitive verbs refer to action in which "someone directly acts upon an object." This object is referred to as a direct object and it is marked by the particle を. In contrast, intransitive verbs do not take an object, and they refer to a situation in which "something just happens on its own" without referring to who/what did it.

Transitive verbs and intransitive verbs express different situations when their respective て-forms are followed by the auxiliary verb いる. The /Vt ている/ construction expresses that "someone or something is in the process of V-ing." In contrast, the /Vi ている/ construction expresses that "someone or something is in a state resulting from V-ing." Thus, in Sentence (5) below, an on-going or routine action of Mr. Tanaka's opening the windows is mentioned, while in Sentence (6), a resultant state that the window is open (without reference to how it came to be open) is mentioned.

(5) 田中さんが窓をあけています。　　Mr. Tanaka is opening the window.
(6) 窓があいています。　　The window is open.

A similar distinction drawn above can apply to other verbs that do not have corresponding transitive or intransitive pairs. For instance, a transitive verb 食べる "eat X" does not have its intransitive counterpart, but it still expresses an on-going activity in its V ている form as in Sentence (7). Likewise, an intransitive verb 行く "X goes" refers to a resultant state as in Sentence (8) regardless of the lack of its transitive counterpart.

(7) 山田さんはおすしを食べている。　　Mr. Yamada is eating sushi.
(8) 山田さんは今、銀行に行っている。　　Mr. Yamada has gone to the bank [He is not here].

In its non-past form, transitive and intransitive verbs to "open" express the following meanings.

(9) 田中さんがドアをあけます。　　Mr. Tanaka will open the door.
(10) ドアがあきます。　　The door will open/The door opens (i.e., can be opened).

Additional pairs of transitive / intransitive verbs are shown below. Complete the chart.

	Transitive		Intransitive	
Transitive / Intransitive	**non-past**	**past**	**non-past**	**past**
Someone closes the window./ The window closes.	窓をしめる	窓をしめた	窓が_____	窓がしまった
Someone produces new products./ New products come out.	新製品を出す	新製品を_____	新製品が出る	新製品が出た
Someone turns the light on./ The light comes on.	電気をつける	電気をつけた	電気がつく	電気が_____
Someone turns off the light./ The light is turned off.	電気を消す	電気を_____ ファイルを_____	電気が消える	電気が消えた ファイルが消えた

Chapter 6: "Work" after Work

Someone deletes the file./ The file disappears.	ファイルを消す		ファイルが消える	
Someone stops the car./ The car stops.	車を____	車を止めた	車が止まる	車が止まった
Someone makes a call./ A call comes in.	電話を____	電話をかけた	電話がかかった	電話がかかった

Can you supply the subject and object for each of the verbs below?

	Transitive		Intransitive	
Transitive / Intransitive	non-past	past	non-past	past
Someone wakes up others./ Someone wakes up.	〜を起こす		〜が起きる	
Someone puts X into.../ X enters...	〜を入れる		〜が入る	
Someone decides X./ X is decided.	〜を決める		〜が決まる	
Someone repairs X./ X is repaired.	〜を直す		〜が直る	
Someone passes X through./ X passes through.	〜を通す		〜が通る	

6A.2. しようと思う／思っている

By adding と思う ("I think that...") after a plain volitional verb, the speaker expresses that he/she has not completely decided on the course of action. The question particle か adds further uncertainty to the phrase と思う.

/V-volitional + と思う/   I'm thinking of V-ing.
/V-volitional + かと思う/   I'm thinking whether to V. [more uncertain]

A：あしたは 来ないんでしょう？   You are not coming tomorrow, are you?
B：いや、来ようと思っているけど…   Well, I'm thinking of coming, but...

Typically, both しようと思う and しようと思っている can express the speaker's own intention ("I think I'll do it") while しようと思っている can additionally express the intention of someone other than the speaker.

課長に相談しようと思います。   I think I will consult with Section Chief.
課長に相談しようと思っています。   I'm thinking of consulting with Section Chief.
田中さんは課長に相談しようと思っています。   Mr. Tanaka is thinking of consulting with Sec. Chief.

Note that しようと思う is not interchangeable with すると思う. Normally, すると思う is not an acceptable sentence to express the speaker's own intention. Instead, すると思う is used to express speaker's inference on someone else's intention (＝するでしょう).

<u>Intention</u>
あしたまでに書こうと思います。   I think I will write it by tomorrow.
あしたまでに書こうと思っています。   I'm thinking of writing it by tomorrow.
（＝あしたまでに書くつもりです。）   I intend to write it by tomorrow.

田中さんはあしたまでに書こうと思っています。   Mr. Tanaka is thinking of writing it by tomorrow.
＊田中さんはあしたまでに書こうと思います。   (Ungrammatical)

<u>Inference</u>
あしたまでに書くと思います。   I guess someone will write it by tomorrow.

```
        *あしたまでに書くと思っています。                  (Ungrammatical in the sense above)
        田中さんはあしたまでに書くと思います。[29]           I guess Mr. Tanaka will write it by tomorrow.
        (＝田中さんはあしたまでに書くでしょう。)
```

6A.3. Wh + か and Wh + も

The pattern /wh + か/ is used to form indefinite nouns such as something, someone, somewhere, etc.

何か	something	いつか	some time; some day
だれか	someone	どうか	somehow
いくらか	some amount (of things)	どれか	whichever one (of many)
どこか	somewhere	どちらか	whichever one (of the two)

The following forms have slightly different interpretations.

    いくらか   how much
    どのぐらいか   how much/how long

The subject particle が or the object particle を is often deleted after these indefinite phrases:

    だれか(が)来ましたよ。   Someone came.
    何か(を)食べましょう。   Let's eat something.

However, other particles have to be retained, as shown below:

    だれかと見ました。   S/he saw it with someone.
    どこかへ行きたいですね。   I'd like to go somewhere.
    どこかで休みたいですね。   I'd like to rest somewhere.

These indefinite phrases can be used with a clause-modifier as shown below. Unlike the English counterparts, the Japanese expressions must always end with a generic noun like 物、時、人、ところ, etc.

Wh	か	Clause modifier	N	
何	か	冷たい	物	something (that is) cold
いつ	か	お暇な	時	some time (when you are) not busy
だれ	か	英語ができる	人	someone who can speak English
どこ	か	スキーができる	ところ	somewhere I can ski

The /Wh+か/ pattern can be followed by a perception/communication verb to express an embedded information question as shown below. In the following, お礼 means "thanks" (お礼を言う "Say thank-you").

    いついらっしゃるか聞いております。   I haven't heard when he/she is coming.
    どの写真を使うか決めてください。   Please decide on which photographs to use.
    何とお礼を言っていいかわかりません。   I don't know how to thank you.
    そのことをだれに聞いたか覚えていますか。   Do you remember whom you heard it from?

---

[29] Note that the verb 思います refers to the speaker's thoughts, and it cannot be used to refer to Mr. Tanaka's thoughts. To refer to Mr. Tanaka's thoughts, one should say 田中さんはあしたまでに書こうと思っています。 "Mr. Tanaka thinks/is thinking that he will write it by tomorrow."

The wh-word can also be followed by the particle も. The /Wh+も/ pattern has either inclusive ("all/every") meaning or exclusive ("nothing") meaning, depending on how the sentence ends as shown below. Caution: 何, だれ／どなた, and どう must always be followed by a negative predicate.

Wh (+ p)	も	affirmative ／ negative	
何	も	＊する／しない	[Ungrammatical] / do nothing
いつ	も	する／しない	do [it] all the time / never do [it]
だれ／どなた	も	＊する／しない	[Ungrammatical] / no one does it
どこ	も	きれい／きれいじゃない	every place is pretty / no place is pretty
どこに	も	行く／行かない いる／いない (or ある／ない)	go everywhere / go nowhere is located everywhere/is not located anywhere
どこへ	も	行く／行かない	go everywhere / go nowhere
どちら	も	いい／よくない	both are good / neither is good
どう	も	＊する／しない	[Ungrammatical] / do nothing in any way

Examples:

きのうの会議には、どなたもいらっしゃいませんでした。
No one came to yesterday's meeting.

今朝は忙しくて、何も食べられませんでした。
I was so busy this morning that I ate nothing.

東京はどこも人が多いですね。
There are many people everywhere in Tokyo.

＊きのうの会議には、どなたもいらっしゃいました。 [Ungrammatical]
＊今朝は忙しかったけど、何も食べました。 [Ungrammatical]

Having studied these patterns involving the wh-words, you should be able to distinguish the different meanings among the following sentences.

いつ　行きますか。 vs. いつか　行きますか。
いつも　行きますか。 vs. いつも　行きませんか。

6A.4. V てから

The /V1 てから、V2/ structure expresses an intentional sequence of actions ("After/Since V1-ing, V2"). The particle から "from" signals a temporal origin (V1) from which an action (V2) follows. Because the V1 て form is tenseless, the final verb (V2) determines the overall tense of the sentence. No causal relationship is implied between V1 and V2. Compare the following sentences:

(1) 風邪をひいて、病院に行きました。　　I caught a cold, so I went to the hospital.
(2) 風邪をひいてから、病院に行きました。　After I caught a cold, I went to the hospital.

In Sentence 1, "catching a cold" is the reason for "going to the hospital." However, in Sentence 2, "catching a cold (V1)" may be nothing to do with "going to the hospital (V2)." Note the following usage constraints for this structure:

1. V2 must happen immediately after V1. Sentence 3 violates this constraint.

(3) ?6時に家に帰ってから、7時に電話しました。　After I came home at 6:00, I called at 7.
(4) 6時に家に帰ってから、ずっと勉強しています。　I've been studying since I came home at 6.

2. This structure must express an intentional sequence of actions. Sentence 6 violates this constraint.

(5) 新聞を読んでから、電話をかけました。 After reading the newspaper, I called.
(6) ？新聞を読んでから、電話がありました。 After reading the newspaper, there was a phone call.

6A.5. V-stem に + 行く

The /V-stem に + 行く/ structure expresses the purpose of going: "go [somewhere] in order to V." In general, the last verb is a verb of coming and going as shown below.

V-stem	に	Verb of motion	
飲み	に	来る	come to drink
買い	に	行く	go shopping
とり	に	帰る	return home to get it

お昼を食べに「かもがわ」に行ってきます。
I'll go to "Kamogawa" to have lunch.

ハリスさんも新製品を見に来ますか。
Is Mr. Harris coming (with me) to see the new products?

ちょっと空港に迎えに来てもらえない？
Could you come to pick me up at the airport?

6A.6. V たがっている

We have learned how to say "want to V" using the V たい form. The V たい form refers to desires of the speaker. In order to state others' feelings and desires, since the speaker cannot directly experience them, he/she must use a different form. This form consists of V-stem + たがっている ("show signs of wanting to V"). V たがる itself is a consonant (う) verb ([V-tagar/u]). The direct object (if any) of the V たい form can be marked by either が or を, but the direct object (if any) of the V たがる form must be marked by the particle を as shown below.

彼は新しいラップトップを使いたがっているんです。
He apparently wants to use a new laptop [computer].

木村君もそのプレゼンテーションを聞きたがっているんですけど、連れて行ってもいいですか。
Apparently Mr. Kimura wants to listen to the presentation. May I bring him over?

横浜工業は値下げしてもらいたがっているんですが、どうしましょうか。
Yokohama Kogyo apparently wants to have it discounted. What should we do?

When people drink and socialize, it sometimes can get loud and disorderly. Some superiors may even encourage the occasion to be "no-law" (無礼講) where disrespectful words under the influence of alcohol will be overlooked and forgotten. In such a case, you are allowed to express your true feelings and frustration to some extent. Just make sure that you come to office on time the next morning. Mr. Harris is at the second party. Section Manager Tanaka is now singing at the karaoke machine. Everyone is getting louder.

Conversation 6B: Mr. Harris goes to a second party. (1)

1. 鈴木： 課長、しぶい！ 1. S: Section Manager! (That's) cool! (lit. "tastefully subdued")
2. ハリス： あんなに大声でしゃべってたら、課長さんが気を悪く 2. H: Won't Sec. Mgr. get upset if we

しませんか。 3. 山田: いいのよ。お酒の席だから、かたいこと言わなくても。 　　　課長のあと、ハリスさんも歌ってみる？ 4. ハ: え、ぼくですか。ぼく、歌は得意じゃないんです。 5. 山: 心配しないで。カラオケじゃ、みんな上手に聞こえるように 　　　なってるから。 6. ハ: そうですか。 7. 山: 速く速く！ 8. 鈴: 待ってましたー、ハリスさん！	are so loud? 3. Y: That's all right. This is a festive occasion, so you can loosen up. (Lit., "Don't need to say righteous things") Would you like to sing after him? 4. H: What? Me? I'm not good at singing. 5. Y: Don't worry. In karaoke, (the machine) makes everyone sound good. 6. H: Is that right? 7: Y: Quickly, quickly! 8. S: We've been waiting for this, Mr. Harris!

悪い bad　　心配 worry　　上手/下手 skillful/unskilled　　速い quick

Vocabulary 6B

しぶい (a) bitter, sober, quiet, subdued, tasteful
あんなに (phr) that (much); that way
大声 (n) loud voice, shout
しゃべってたら (cv: shaber) [て-form of しゃべる ("chat") + (い)たら] if/when one is chatting
気を悪くする (phr) become upset, feels bad
お酒 (n) rice wine; alcohol [酒の席 "festive occasion"]
かたい (a) rigid, stiff, bookish, hard, straight
言わなくても (phr) even if you don't say it [言わなくてもいい "not have to say it"].

歌ってみる (cv: utaw) [て-form of 歌う ("sing") + みる] sing and see [what it's like]
歌 (n) song
心配しないで (n/v) [negative て-form of 心配する] don't worry
カラオケ (n) karaoke [空 ("empty") + オーケストラ: orchestra music without words]
じゃ (phr) [カラオケじゃ = カラオケでは "in karaoke"]
みんな (n) everybody [colloquial form of みなさん].
聞こえる (vv: kikoe) can hear, can be heard.
よう (n) way, manner. [Xようになっている "is made in such a way that X"]

Structures 6B

6B.1. N のあと(で)／V たあと(で)

The N のあと pattern means "after N." A past-tense verb can also precede あと (V たあと) as in 会議に出たあと meaning "after attending the meeting." If the second event occurs some time after the first event, the particle で is required as in N のあとで／V たあとで.

　　会議のあと(で)、飲みに行った。　　　　(Some time) after the meeting, I went out drinking.
　　会議に出たあと(で)、飲みに行った。　　(Some time) after attending the meeting, I went out drinking.

The verb preceding あと must always in the past form even if you refer to a future event.

　　電話をかけたあと(で)、出かけます。　　I'm going to leave (some time) after I have called.
　＊電話をかけるあと(で)、出かけます。　　[Ungrammatical]

This structure is inappropriate when referring to a state (V2) that has held true ever since the first event (V1) took place. For this reason, Sentence 1 below is strange. The /V1 てから、V2/ structure introduced in 6A.4 is better suited to express this notion.

(1) ？アメリカに来たあと、もう三年になります。　　[Unacceptable]
(2) アメリカに来てから、もう三年になります。　　Since I came to the U.S., it's three years already.

6B.2.　Vて ＋ みる

The V てみる pattern means "V and see (what it's like V-ing)" or "try to V." Like the V ておく pattern, the V てみる pattern implies a deliberate intention on the part of the subject of the sentence, so only transitive verbs can be used in this form.

A: 北海道(ほっかいどう)はすばらしかったってハリス君が言っていましたけど…　　Mr. Harris said that Hokkaido was wonderful.
B: そうか。ぼくも行ってみたいね。　　Is that so? I want to go there and see, too.

A: この英語の手紙(てがみ)、読めますか。　　Can you read this English letter?
B: むずかしいね。ハリス君に聞いてみて。　　It's difficult. Try asking Harris.

Note that V てみる implies the completion (or at least the beginning) of the action, so the sentence like "I tried to eat it, but couldn't" cannot be said using V てみる.

食べてみましたが、おいしくありませんでした。　　I ate it (to see what it's like), but it wasn't tasty.
食べてみましたが、食べられませんでした。　　[incoherent]

6B.3.　V1 ように V2

This pattern means "V2 in the manner of V1," or "V2 so that V1," or "V2 in such a way that V1." V ようにする ("try to V") is a variation of this pattern. Its negative form is V ないようにする ("try not to V").[30]

カラオケはみんな上手(じょうず)に聞こえるようになっている。
Karaoke has been devised in such a way that everyone sounds good.

このコンピュータは日本語のワードプロセシングができるようになっている。
This computer has been devised so that one can wordprocess Japanese.

すみません、ここから見えるように大きくお書きになって下さい。
Excuse me, but would you write bigger so that we can see from here?

赤(あか)ちゃんが寝(ね)ていますから、起(お)こさないようにして下さい。
Because the baby is sleeping, please so try not to wake her up.

メールをもらったら、すぐに返事(へんじ)を出すようにして下さい。
If/When you receive email, try to send a reply immediately.

6B.4.　Negative request: V ないで(下さい)

The negative request form is made by adding で to the plain negative form of a verb: V ない ＋ で ("Please don't V"). The V ないで form is typically used in situations in which not V-ing benefits the person addressed.

---

[30] V ように言う (3.e.2: "tell someone to V") is also a variation of this pattern.

この道は通らないで下さい。今、工事中ですから。
Please don't take this road.　It's under construction.

ハリスさん、あまり上手に歌わないで下さいね。私がとても下手に聞こえますから。
Harris, please don't sing too well.　Because my singing will sound awful.

A: ハリス君、もう一杯どう？　　　　　Harris, how about one more glassful?
B: いえ、もうけっこうです。　　　　　No.　I'm fine.
A: そんなこと、言わないで。　　　　　Don't say such a thing.

遠慮しないで下さい。　　Don't hold back.　(遠慮する: act in a reserved manner)

無理しないで下さい。　　Don't strain yourself.　(無理する: over-exert)

If the V ないで structure is followed by a verb phrase other than 下さい, it means "do something without V-ing" as shown below.

毎週、金曜日は男の人はネクタイをしないで出社してもいいそうです。
Every Friday, it is said that men are allowed to come to office without wearing a tie.

Survival Phrases

忘年会を楽しみにしています。　　　　I'm looking forward to the year-end party.
ごゆっくりお楽しみください。　　　　Relax and enjoy.
乾杯！　　　　　　　　　　　　　　　Cheers!
酒はだめなんです／強くないんです。　I'm not good at [drinking] alcohol.
じゃあ、そろそろお開きにしましょう。[31]　Well then, (slowly) let's end [this party].
二日酔いで、ふらふらするんです。[32]　I have a hangover and feel dizzy.

---

[31] お開きにする is an euphemistic expression for 終わりにする ("to end").
[32] ふらふらする is an onomatopoeia expression ("to feel dizzy").　ふらふら ("dizzy") can be a noun.

The style of speech is extremely important in the business world. The subordinate employee uses honorific-polite expressions to refer to his/her superior's matters, while he/she uses humble-polite forms to refer to himself/herself (or an in-group member, including colleagues, friends, classmates, etc). The speaker in the superior position can soften his/her order/request to the subordinate by beginning with "I wonder if." In the conversation below, find such polite speech techniques.

Conversation 6C: After the welcome party

1. 田：ハリス君、君があんなに歌がうまいとは思わなかったよ。	1. T: Mr. Harris, I didn't know you were that good at singing.
2. ハ：いえいえ、とんでもないですよ。	2. H: No, no! Heavens no!
3. 田：いや、なかなかのものだったよ。ところで、今週末にアメリカからお客さんがお見えになるんで、ぼくが接待することになっているんだ。それで、君にも同行してもらえないかと思ってね。	3. T: I mean it. That was something! By the way, a visitor from America will come here this weekend, and I am supposed to entertain him. So, I was wondering if you can accompany us.
4. ハ：かしこまりました。どちらへいらっしゃるんですか。	4. H: Certainly! Where are you going?
5. 田：昼間はゴルフをいっしょにして、夜は料亭へお連れしようと思っているんだ。	5. T: I am thinking of playing golf together during the day, and then taking him to a Japanese restaurant at night.
6. ハ：じゃ、私がホテルまでお迎えにまいりましょうか。	6. H: Then, shall I go to the hotel to pick him up?
7. 田：いや、それは青木君に頼んであるから。	7. T: No, because I have already requested that Ms. Aoki (do it).

お連れする accompany   接待 entertainment of clients   頼む ask, request

Vocabulary 6C

うまい (a) skillful, tasty
とんでもない (phr) Heavens no!
なかなかのもの (phr) a pretty good thing
今週末 (n) this weekend
接待する (n/v) to receive a guest, entertain
～ことになっている (phr) is supposed that S
同行して (n/v) [て-form of 同行する] accompany
もらえない (vv) [negative potential of もらう] cannot receive
昼間 (n) daytime

いっしょに (adv) together. [いっしょにする "do together"]
料亭 (n) Japanese-style restaurant
お連れする (vv: tsure) [お+連れ+する↓] "take/bring (someone) to (somewhere)"]
お迎え (vv: mukae) [お+迎え+に行く "go to greet, meet"] meet, greet, welcome
まいりましょう (cv: mair) [humble polite-volitional of 来る] [I shall] come
頼む (cv: tanom) to ask, request

Structures 6C

6C.1. S ことになる

This pattern introduces S as something decided outside the speaker's control. It is translated as "it happens to be that" or "it turns out" or "it comes out." Because of the preference among the Japanese to refer to a situation as a natural consequence of events (rather than attributing it directly to someone's action), this pattern is frequently used even when there is an active involvement by the speaker as shown below.

私たち、結婚することになりました。
It turns out that we'll get married.

ぼくは今日、ブラウン氏を迎えに空港まで行くことになりました。
It turns out that I'll go to the airport to pick up Mr. Brown.

お宅様との契約はもう少し待つことになりましたので…
It turns out that we will wait for a little while (to sign) the contract with your company.

結局、山田さんが課長に話すことになりました。
After all, it is decided that Mr. Yamada should talk to Section Manager.

6C.2. S かと思う／考える

This pattern means "I wonder if" or "I think it is probably the case." S here has similar restrictions to those of sentence modifiers. Note that the quotation marker と cannot be deleted before 思う, but と can be deleted before 考える (more deliberate thinking than 思う).

1) A plain-style predicate must be used.

田中課長もいらっしゃるかと思います。
I think it's probably the case that Mr. Tanaka is coming.

カタログをお送りいただけないかと思いまして…
I wonder if I could have you send me the catalog.

私に何かできることがないか（と）考えています。
I've been pondering if there isn't something I can do.

2) The copula だ must always be deleted.

会場は梅園かと思っていましたが、違ったんですね。
I thought that the meeting place was Umezono, but I was wrong.

6C.3. More about しようと思う

しようと思う consists of the plain volitional + 思う, whereas するだろうと思う consists of the tentative + 思う. Only the verbs of self-controllable actions (e.g., 行く、言う、作る) can be made into a volitional form. Therefore, しようと思う typically expresses the speaker's own plan ("I think I'll do it"). On the other hand, するだろうと思う typically indicates the speaker's conjecture as to the likelihood of some event ("I think X will probably happen") or of the third person's future action ("I think he/she will probably do it."). Thus:

株はもっと上がるだろうと思いますけど…　I think the stocks will probably go up further.
課長に相談しようと思うんです。　I think I'll consult with Section Chief.
課長に相談するだろうと思うんです。　I think he/she will probably consult with Section Chief.

As a variation of this form, there is a しようとする pattern. This means "try to V" without necessarily implying that the action has been completed. Compare the following:

食べてみたら、おいしかった。　When I ate it, it was tasty.
食べようとしたが、食べられなかった。　I tried to eat it, but I couldn't.

食べるようにした。 　　　　　　　　　I tried to eat it as much as possible.

6C.4.　V て ＋ ある

The V てある pattern means someone has done something for some purpose and implies the readiness of the state resulting from that action.　It is often translated as "X has been V-ed."　If the action involves a direct object, it can be marked with either が or を.　Transitive verbs are used more often with this pattern.

鍵がかけてある！	It's locked!　(Someone locked it deliberately.)
vs. 鍵がかかっている！	It's locked!　(No attribution of deliberate intention)
案内状はもう出してあります。	The invitation letters have been sent already.
vs. 案内状はもう出しておきました。	I already sent the invitation letters (for later use).
企画案を提出してあります。	The project plan is submitted.
	I have submitted the project plan (deliberately).
vs. 企画案を提出しておきました。	I submitted a project plan (in advance).
vs. 企画案を提出しておきます。	I will submit a project plan (for future use).

Note 1: The V てある pattern (present tense) is somewhat similar to V ておいた pattern (past tense).　The distinction is that V てある refers to a current state while V ておいた refers to a past action intended for some subsequent use. Compare the following:

電気がついている。 (current state)	The light is on.
電気がつけてある。 (current state)	The light has been deliberately turned on for some purpose (and is still on).
電気をつけておいた。 (past action)	I turned on the light for some purpose (but it may or may not be still on).

Note 2: Since V ておく refers to an action and V てある to a state, the former can be used as a request, but not the latter.

ドアに鍵をかけておいて下さい。	Please lock the door in advance.
＊ドアに鍵をかけてあって下さい。	[ungrammatical]

Chapter 6: "Work" after Work   135

Exercise 6

Grammar Utilization 6   Name:_____ Sec:_____ #:____

G1. Select the appropriate transitive or intransitive verb that completes the conversation.

1. A: ハリス君、そのコンピュータ、(つけて／ついて)いる？
    B: いいえ、(消して／消えて)いますけど、(つけ／つき)ましょうか？

2. A: 例の横浜工業の見積りなんだけど、総額 (sum of money) はいくらになっている？
    B: 今、見積書のファイルを(あけて／あいて)みますので、少々お待ちください。

3. A: 部長は名古屋の会議にお(出／出し)になるんですか。
    B: うん、10日から3日間、行ってくるよ。

4. A: 横浜工業の森本さんが　お待ちになっていらっしゃいますが、お飲み物を(お出し／お出に)しましょうか？
    B: じゃ、コーヒーを(入れて／入って)くれる？

5. A: あ、なくなってる！
    B: ハリスさん、どうしたの？
    A: きのう作ったファイルが(消して／消えて)しまったんです。

6. A: 田中さんの車、もう(直して／直って)もらった？
    B: ええ、もう(直して／直って)います。
    A: よかったですね。

7. A: すみません。ここに車を(止めて／止まって)もいいですか。
    B: いいえ、ここには(止めないで／止まらないで)ください。

G2. Fill in the blank with the appropriate verb (one of ある、いる、おく) and complete the conversation.

1. A: ハリス君、ホテルはもう予約して_____ね？
    B: 申しわけございません。まだして_____。
    A: Mr. Harris.   The hotel has been already reserved, right?
    B: I'm sorry.   I haven't done it yet.

2. A: 会議録ですが、コピーは何枚作って_____？
    B: あ、それはもうやって_____から、君がやらなくてもいいよ。
    A: Regarding the meeting log, how many copies shall I make (for future use)?
    B: Oh, copying has already been done, so you don't have to do it.

3. A: ほかに翻訳する物、ありますか？
    B: じゃ、これを今週中に翻訳して_____くれないか？
    A: Is there anything else to translate?
    B: OK. Will you   translate this for me (in advance) by the end of this week?

4. A: ファイルがあけて＿＿＿＿＿＿んですが、このコンピュータ、まだだれかが使って＿＿＿＿＿＿んでしょうか？
   B: 太田(おおた)さんじゃありませんか。さっき、そこで何かしてましたよ。
   A: A file has been opened, but I wonder if someone is still using this computer.
   B: Could it be Ms. Ohta? She was doing something there a while ago.

5. A: ハリス君、今度(こんど)の新製品(しんせいひん)の展示会(てんじかい)、いっしょに行かないか。(展示会：exhibition)
   B: 残念(ざんねん)なんですけど、予定(よてい)が入(はい)って＿＿＿＿＿＿＿＿ので…
   A: Mr. Harris. Would you like to go to the upcoming new product exhibition together?
   B: Unfortunately, I have something else to do), so…

G3. Fill in the blanks using the Vないで form and complete the conversation.

1. A: このコンピュータを使いたいんですけど、いいですか。
   B: それは今、太田(おおた)さんが使っているので、＿＿＿＿＿＿＿＿ください。
   A: I would like to use this computer. Is it all right?
   B: Ms. Ohta is using that one, so please don't use it.

2. A: あ、そこはローマ字(じ)で＿＿＿＿＿＿＿＿、漢字(かんじ)でお願(ねが)いします。
   B: わかりました。
   A: Oh, don't write in Romaji there, please [use] kanji.
   B: All right.

3. A: こんな大事(だいじ)なメッセージが来ていることを私に＿＿＿＿＿＿＿＿、君(きみ)は何をしていたんだ？
   B: 申しわけございません。
   A: What have you been doing without telling me that there is such an important message for me.
   B: I'm sorry.

4. A: 明日のプレゼンテーションのこと、心配(しんぱい)なんです。
   B: ＿＿＿＿＿＿＿＿＿＿(心配する：worry)
   A: I'm worried about my presentation tomorrow.
   B: Don't worry.

5. A: もうたくさんいただきましたので…
   B: まあ＿＿＿＿＿＿＿＿＿＿(遠慮(えんりょ)する：hold back)
   A: I already have had enough.
   B: Don't hold back.

6. A: ハリス君、あまり＿＿＿＿＿＿(無理(むり)する：work too hard, strain oneself)
   B: ええ。でも、これだけ、してしまいたいんです。
   A: Mr. Harris. Please don't work too hard.
   B: I know, but I would like to finish at least this one.

7. A: ぼくは歌(うた)が苦手(にがて)で…
   B: そんなこと＿＿＿＿＿＿＿＿＿＿歌ってくださいよ。(worry：気にする)
   A: I'm not good at singing.
   B: Please sing without worrying about such a thing.

Chapter 6: "Work" after Work   137

G4. Using the V たあと or V てから pattern, complete the conversation by stating two activities in one sentence.

1. A would like to know if B reads the newspaper everyday.

    A: 毎日、新聞を読みますか。

    B: ええ、新聞を＿＿＿＿＿＿＿＿＿＿、会社に行きます。

2. A is worried that Mr. Yamada of Japan Electronics may be too busy to see him. B gives his advice.

    A: 日本エレクトロニクスの山田部長にアポイントをとらないで、会うのはむずかしいでしょうねえ。

    B: そうですね。＿＿＿＿＿＿＿＿＿＿＿＿＿方がいいでしょうねえ。
    (It's better to get an appointment and go.)

3. A is asking how B motivates workers in his company.

    A: スミタ工業さんはどんなことをしていますか。

    B: うちではみんな＿＿＿＿＿＿＿＿＿＿＿＿＿＿＿

    ＿＿＿＿＿＿＿＿＿＿＿＿＿＿＿＿＿いるんです。

    体操をする: do calisthenics
    社訓を読む: read company mottos

4. A is asking how long it would take until the merchandise arrives after ordering it.

    A: 品物を＿＿＿＿＿＿＿それが＿＿＿＿＿＿＿＿までにどのぐらいかかりますか？

    B: 一週間ぐらいかかると思います。
    品物: merchandise; 注文する: order

5. A is complimenting how good B is at making a good impression on people.

    A: 私はあいさつがどうも下手で…。田村さんはお上手ですね。

    B: いえいえ。私は＿＿＿＿＿＿＿＿＿＿＿＿＿＿＿

    ＿＿＿＿＿＿＿＿＿ことにしています。

    挨拶を練習する: practice greetings; 人に会う: meet people;
    ～ことにする: make it a rule to

G5. Complete the following conversations using the V たがっている pattern.

1. A: ハリス君、今度、うちへ食事にでも来てくれないか。実は家内が君に＿＿＿＿＿＿＿んだよ。
    B: お誘いいただいて、恐縮です。(誘う: invite, 恐縮だ: feel terribly honored)
    A: 家内は学生の時アメリカにいたので、いろいろ話を＿＿＿＿＿＿＿＿んだよ。

2. A: ハリス君、先週君が貸してくれたビデオね、林さんも_____んだよ。貸してあげてもいい？
   B: もちろんです。どうぞ。

3. A: 今度、吉田君がアメリカに行くことになったから、君に英語を教えて_____んだ。
   B: 私は英語を教えたことはないんですけど、やってみます。

G6. Complete the following conversation using /QW+か/ or /QW+も+negative/ pattern.

   a. A: もう何か食べましたか。
      B: いいえ、まだ_____食べていません。

   b. A: 青いペンか、赤いペンか、_____ありますか。
      B: どちらもありません。

   c. A: 東京テレコムとのビジネス提携の件、どなたかにお話しなさいましたか。
      B: いいえ、まだ_____話しておりません。

   d. A: 今度、_____おひまな時に、いらっしゃってください。
      B: どうもありがとうございます。その時はよろしくお願いいたします。

   e. A: どれをお買いになりましたか。
      B: どれを買おうか考えたんだけど、結局 (in the end)、_____買わなかったよ。

   f. A: コンファレンスはどうでしたか。_____にお会いになりましたか。
      B: うん、ソニーの山田さんに会ったよ。

   g. A: お休みのあいだに、どこかにいらっしゃいましたか。
      B: いいえ、_____まいりませんでした。

   h. A: 暑いですね。_____冷たい物いかがですか。
      B: それは、どうもありがとうございます。

G7. Fill in the blanks with volitional expressions "I'm thinking of V-ing..." or "I wonder if I should V").

   a. A: 来週、歓迎会を_____んだけど、いいところ知らない？
      B: そうですね。新しくできた「ことぶき」はどうですか。

   b. A: 昼間はいっしょにゴルフをして、夜はカラオケで歌を_____。
      B: それはいいですね。

   c. A: 今度のお休みは何をなさるおつもりですか。
      B: 北海道へスキーをしに_____。

d. A: コンピュータが古くなったので、新しいのを_____。
   B: それだったら、ラップトップがいいですよ。

e. A: 来学期は英語のクラスをおとりになりますか。
   B: うん、中級英語のクラスを_____。

G8. Change the verb into "V and see" or "try to V" form.

a. A: ハリスさんも、ちょっと、(歌う)_____?
   B: いいえ、私はけっこうです。

b. A: 新しいビデオ(見る)_____?
   B: あ、いいですね。見せて下さい。

c. A: 私の作ったコーヒーでよかったら、(飲む)_____?
   B: はい、いただきます。

d. A: 新しいコンピュータ買ったんですね。
   B: そうなんです。ハリスさんも(使う)_____?

e. A: 今度の会議に私が出ることになったんですが、どうしたらいいかわからないんです。
   B: じゃあ、部長に(話す)_____たらどうですか。

G9. Fill in the blanks according to the English cues using ように.

a. ここからでも_____大きい声(voice)で話して下さい。
   Please speak in loud voice so we can hear from here.

b. 毎日、テープを聞いて練習したので、英語が_____なりました。
   Because I practiced listening to the tapes every day, I became able to understand English.

c. 取り引き条件を_____川田経理課長と相談した。
   I consulted with Accounting Section Manager Kawada so we can decide on the terms of transaction.

d. 質問に_____よく勉強しておいて下さい。
   Please study hard so you can answer (答える) the questions.

e. 寒いですから、_____して下さい。
   It's cold, so try not to catch a cold (風邪をひく).

f. _____よく練習した方がいいですよ。
   It's better to practice well so you won't forget it.

g. 目が_____明るい所で読んで下さい。
   Please read it in the bright place so you won't get nearsighted (get nearsighted: 目が悪くなる).

G10. Fill in the blanks according to the English cues using ことになる。

a. 私の一存では決められなかったので、来週もう一度＿＿＿＿＿＿＿＿＿＿＿＿＿＿＿＿＿＿＿＿＿。
Since I couldn't decide on my own, it turned out that we will have a meeting again next week.

b. 鈴木さんは結婚するので、会社を＿＿＿＿＿＿＿＿＿＿＿＿＿＿＿＿＿＿＿＿＿＿＿＿。
Because Miss Suzuki is going to get married, it turned out that she is going to quit (やめる) the company.

c. 東京テレコムと＿＿＿＿＿＿＿＿＿＿＿＿＿＿＿＿＿＿＿＿＿＿＿＿＿＿＿＿＿＿＿。
It turned out that we will not cooperate (提携する) with Tokyo Telecom.

e. ハリスさんの歓迎会を「ことぶき」で＿＿＿＿＿＿＿＿＿＿＿＿＿＿＿＿＿＿＿＿＿。
It turned out that we will have Mr. Harris' welcome party at Kotobuki.

d. 来週、また＿＿＿＿＿＿＿＿＿＿＿＿＿＿＿＿＿＿＿＿＿＿＿＿＿＿＿＿＿＿＿＿＿＿。
It turned out that we will meet again next week.

f. カラーコピーは高いので、＿＿＿＿＿＿＿＿＿＿＿＿＿＿＿＿＿＿＿＿＿＿＿＿＿＿。
Color copies are expensive, so it turned out that we will not use them.

Reading and Writing 6   Name:_____ Sec:_____ #:____

R1. Read the following poster and answer the questions below.

忘年会のお知らせ

恒例の忘年会を以下のとおり行ないますので、お誘い合わせの上、おいで下さい。

日時：１２月２０日（金）６時～
場所：夢庵（ゆめあん）、日本ホテル地下１Ｆ
会費：男性５０００円、女性４０００円

ビール、お酒飲みほうだい
カラオケバーあり

参加希望者は17日までに、田中（753-4009/mtanaka@jelect.co.jp）まで連絡して下さい。

忘年会: year-end party (lit. "year-forgetting party")
お知らせ: notice
恒例の: traditional; annual; usual
以下のとおり: as follows
行ないます ＝ します
お誘い合わせの上 ＝ いっしょに
おいで下さい ＝ いらして下さい
日時: date & time   場所: place   地下: basement
会費: party fee
男性／女性: male, man / female, woman
お酒飲みほうだい: drinking is unlimited
参加希望者: those who wish to participate
連絡する: to contact

1. 忘年会はいつ、どこでしますか。

2. 会費はいくらですか。

3. 忘年会に出たい人は何をすることになっていますか。

4. あなたは忘年会の幹事 (organizer) をすることになりました。忘年会のためのポスターを作ってください。

Communicative Exercise 6

C1. Fill in the blanks with appropriate phrases based on the pictures below. In each of the situations, you are encouraging your colleague to try out something.

	A: 私、てんぷら、食べたことないんです。 B: じゃあ、_____
	A: このコンピュータ、ぜひ_____ B: わかりました。
	A: 京都で環境会議があるということですね。 B: ええ、田中さんも_____どうですか？ 環境会議：environmental conference
	A: あちらは新製品のこと、もっと知りたいと言っています。 B: じゃあ、カタログを_____ 　　どうですか。(Why don't you send them catalogues?) あちら：the other party, 新製品：new products
	A: 今、インターネットのことを勉強しているんですが、よくわからないんです。 B: 吉田部長はそのことをよくご存じだから、一度 _____どう？

C2. Express your plan to do something as indicated below and complete the conversation.

　　田中：　ハリスさん、今度の休みどうするの？

　　ハリス：＿＿＿＿＿＿＿＿＿＿＿＿＿＿＿＿＿と思っているんです。
　　　　　　"I'm thinking of going to Kyoto."

　　田中：　一人で？

　　ハリス：　いいえ、アメリカから両親が来ているので

　　　　　　＿＿＿＿＿＿＿＿＿＿＿＿＿＿＿＿＿と思っているんです。
　　　　　　"I'm thinking of taking them there."

Chapter 6: "Work" after Work   143

田中: それはいいね。それでどこを見るの？

ハリス: _____と思っているんです。
"I'm thinking of seeing Ryouanji and Kiyomizu."

田中: 京都でホテルとかに泊まるの？

ハン: 実は_____と思っているんです。
"I'm thinking of going to Nara without staying over at Kyoto."

C3. Study the following conversational exchange and make your own using the underlined patterns.

　　A: だれかスミスさんを空港まで迎えに行ける人はいないかな。(Wh + ka)
　　B: さあ、だれもいないだろうと思いますけど… (Wh + mo)

1. A: どこか_____
   B: _____

2. A: _____
   B: なにも_____

3. A: どれか_____
   B: _____

C4. Role Playing

#1: In each of the situations below, you (A) would like to invite your colleague (B) to go somewhere in order to do something. However, B has a previous engagement and tells you what's already been decided and declines your invitation politely. For example:

　　A: ブラウンさん、今度できた料亭、なかなかいいですよ。今晩、飲みに行きませんか？
　　　（料亭：Japanese restaurant）
　　B: 行きたいんですけど、実は残業でこの仕事をすることになっているんです。
　　　部長さんがあしたまでにやってくれないかとおっしゃいまして…（残業：overtime work）
　　A: ああ、そうですか。残念ですねえ。じゃあ、また、今度行きましょう。
　　B: 申し訳ありません。

　a. A invites B to come to his/her house on Saturday to have dinner together. B has a plan to go to play golf with a business client from JETRO.

　b. A invites B to go to Makuhari to see the new products exhibition (展示会) tomorrow. B has a plan to go on a business trip to Osaka tomorrow.

　c. A invites B to go to listen to a business seminar at three o'clock. B has a plan to see Mr. Hayashi of JEC until four o'clock.

　d. Today is Friday. A invites B to go drinking tonight. B has a plan to go home early this evening. (B promised to take his/her child to a musical show at Shibuya.)

#2: You (A) notice that your colleague (B) has a hangover. Ask him/her what happened last night. Make sure to express sympathy and advise him/her not to drink too much.

Your colleague (A) is asking what happened last night. You went out drinking after work with Division Manager Ishii. It was Mr. Ishii who asked you to go drinking, and you couldn't refuse. (Mr. Ishii is your boss, and you owe him a favor making it impossible for you to refuse.)

#3: Discuss your plans for the up-coming "Golden Week" holidays with your colleague. State what you intend to do and give at least two reasons why you would like to do so (e.g., My children want to go there.).

#4: Your boss (B) has come up to you (A) with a smile and has showed you a photograph of a handsome man/beautiful woman, and has explained to you that this man/woman in the photograph would be a wonderful person for you to go out with. Politely give at least two reasons why you can't date (with the consideration of marriage) him/her at this time.

You (B) are trying to help your subordinate (A) find a prospective spouse. Today, you have brought a photograph of a good candidate for your subordinate. Encourage him/her to go out with this person in the photograph and give him/her at least two reasons why this person is good for him/her.

Listening Comprehension 6   Name:_____ Sec:_____ #:____

1. Voc: 東京経済新聞：Tokyo Economy Newspaper; 新製品：(n) new products; サンプル：(n) sample
   その経済新聞の人は何を知りたがっているんですか。

   Aさんはどうしようと思っているんですか。

2. Voc: ゴルフクラブ：golf club
   Bさんはきのう何をしようと思ったんですか。

   来週、何をすることになりましたか。

3. Voc: 今度：(n) this time; バイト：(n) part-time job; まじめ：(n) earnest, serious, hard-working;
       もし：(n) if, suppose
   新しいアルバイトの学生はどんな人ですか。

   Aさんはその学生に何て言ったらいいですか。

4. Voc: 出す：(v) mail (out); 急ぐ：(v) hurry; …かもしれない：(phr) may ...
   Aさんはその英語の手紙をどうするつもりだったんですか。

5. Voc: 二次会：second party; カラオケバー：karaoke bar; 何にも：(not) at all; even whatever
   ハンさんは二次会で何をすることになっていますか。

   Bさんはどんなアドバイスをしてくれましたか。

6. Voc: 企画書：(n) plan/project paper; お昼：(n) lunch; てんそば：(n) tempura noodle
       部：(ct) counter for printouts, copies, etc.
   あしたの会議には何人来ることになっていますか。

   Aさんが明日までにすることを二つ言って下さい。

Chapter 7

面会(めんかい)の約束(やくそく)
Appointments

Priming

You are a sales manager of a U.S. company. Your company manufactures high-tech office products and is exploring the possibility of exporting them to Japan. One of the quickest ways to sell to Japan is to form a joint venture with a Japanese company which already has its own sales network. Imagine you are about to make the first contact to the sales division of a Japanese company which specializes in the type of products you are trying to market.

いつもお世話になっております。("Thank you for your regular business." [Lit. "always under your care"]) --- This greeting makes the caller feel at ease as used by Ms. Miki below. It can be used even if one has never met the caller before. It promotes a hospitable and courteous relationship in society reflecting the Japanese value of interdependence. A typical response to this greeting is いえいえ、こちらこそお世話になっております。("Not at all. Thank you for your business" [Lit. "Not at all. It's we that are under your care."]).

Conversation 7A: Making an appointment (1)

1. 三木: はい。日本エレクトロニクス営業部でございます。
2. ルイス: 私、アメリカのデジタルマシンのルイスと申しますが…
3. 三: あ、いつもお世話になっております。
4. ル: いえいえ。実は私どもの会社ではオフィス機器の製造販売をしておりますが、ジェトロの小川課長にご相談しましたところ、そちらの石野部長をご紹介いただいた次第です。おそれいりますが、石野部長とお話しできますでしょうか。
5. 三: 私、石野の秘書の三木と申します。ご用件は私がうかがいますが。

1. M: This is Sales Division of Japan Electronics.
2. L: This is Lewis of Digital Machines in America.
3. M: Oh, thank you for your regular business.
4. L: Not at all. We manufacture and sell office equipment. While I consulted with Sec. Mgr. Ogawa of JETRO, he referred me to Div. Mgr. Ishino at your company. I'm sorry to bother you, but may I speak with Mr. Ishino?
5. M: I am Miki, his secretary. May I ask the purpose of your call? (Lit. "I will ask your business.")

セイ	ゾウ／つく	セ／セイ	セ　ワ
製 make, manufacture	造／造る create	世 generation	世話 care

Vocabulary 7A

- ● 面会 (n) face-to-face meeting
- ● 約束 (n) promise, appointment
- デジタルマシン (n) Digital Machine
- ルイス (n) Lewis [family name]
- 機器 (n) machine equipment
- 製造 (n) manufacturing
- ジェトロ (n) JETRO (Japan External Trade Organization)
- 小川 (n) Ogawa [family name]
- ご相談しました↓ (n/v) consulted
- ところ (n) place; point in time/space. [S1 ところ S2 "When S1, S2"]
- 次第 (n) a turn of events
- できますでしょうか (phr) [softer expression of できますか: "I wonder if I could..."]
- 秘書 (n) secretary

Structures 7A

7A.1. S1…ところ、S2 …次第です

The /S1…ところ、S2 …次第です/ structure is a formulaic way of explaining a turn of events that led to a certain outcome. Typically, two events are stated: S1 and S2: "when S1, (this led to) S2." Usually, both S1 and S2 are in the past form.

山田先生にうかがったところ、木村様のことをご紹介いただいた次第です。
When I asked Dr. Yamada, he introduced me to Mr. Kimura, and that is how it came about.

ところ can be used without 次第です as shown below.

今日はお忙しいところ、お邪魔しまして、申し訳ありませんでした。
While you are busy, I'm sorry to have bothered you.

お休みのところ、申し訳ありませんが、こちらへいらして下さいませんか。
While you are taking a day off, I'm sorry but could you come here?

7A.2. V-stem + 次第

The expression ～次第 has a second usage. /V-stem+次第/ is a subordinate clause structure that means "as soon as V." Study the following examples.

岡田さんが帰り次第、連絡して下さい。	Please contact me as soon as Ms. Okada has returned.
予定が決まり次第、予約して下さい。	As soon as the plan is decided, please make a reservation.
会議が終わり次第、おいで下さい。	Please come as soon as the meeting is over.

7A.3. お話しできますでしょうか↓

You can soften the directness of your question or request by adding the polite tentative ending でしょうか to a polite verb sentence (e.g., ～ますでしょうか or ～ませんでしょうか, etc.). This is especially important when there is a possibility that your request might be an imposition on the other party.

木村部長とお話しできますでしょうか。
Is it possible for me to talk with Division Manager Kimura?

この件につきまして、ご検討願えませんでしょうか。
Is it not possible to make a request to investigate this matter.

先日お送りした資料は、ご覧になりましたでしょうか。
I wonder if you have seen the materials we sent the other day.

In the following, Division Manager Ishino is on the phone with his secretary Itoh. Note that the speech style of Mr. Ishino is completely different from that of Ms. Itoh. Mr. Ishino uses many blunt expressions while Ms. Itoh maintains her politeness level.

Conversation 7B: Making an appointment (2)

1. ル: 私どもでは、現在、日本への市場拡張を考えております。つきましてはその件で、石野部長にお会いできたらと思いまして。	1. L: We're currently considering the expansion of our business into the Japanese market. With that regard, I wonder if I could see him.
2. 伊: さようでございますか。それでは少々お待ち下さいませ。	2. Ito: I see. Then, could you hold on for a moment?
3. 伊: 石野部長、デジタルマシンのルイス様とおっしゃる方からお電話でございます。日本への市場拡張の件で部長にお目にかかりたいそうです。	3. Ito: Div. Mgr. Ishino. Ms. Lewis of Digital Machine is on the phone. She says she would like to see you regarding the matter of their market expansion to Japan.

4. 石: ルイスさん？ だれかからの紹介なの？	4. Ishino: Ms. Lewis? Does she have a reference from someone?
5. 伊: はい。ジェトロの小川部長からのご紹介だそうです。	5. Ito: Yes. She says that the reference is from Div. Mgr. Ogawa of JETRO.
6. 石: そうか、わかった。じゃ、会ってみようか。	6. Ishino: All right, then, I guess I should meet her and see.
………………………………………………………	………………………………
7. 伊: どうも、お待たせいたしました。石野もぜひお会いしたいと申しておりますので、近いうちにご来社いただけませんでしょうか。	7. Itoh: Sorry to have kept you waiting. Ishino says he would like to see you by all means, so could we have you come here in the near future?

市場 (シジョウ) market　　拡張 (カクチョウ) expansion　　考える (かんが) consider

Vocabulary 7B

現在 (n) at present
市場 (n) market
拡張 (n) expansion [日本への市場拡張 "market expansion into Japan"]
考えて (vv: kangae) [て-form of 考える] consider.
つきましては (phr) with that regard
さようでございますか (phr) [formal expression of そうですか] Is that so?

お待ち下さいませ↑ (v: mat) [imperative of お待ち下さいませんか] Could you please wait?
お目にかかりたい↓ (phr) [たい form of お目にかかる "see [someone]". humble form of 会う] want to see
お待たせ (cv: mat) [polite causative V-stem of 待つ] keep (someone) waiting. [お待たせいたしました↓ humble-polite of 待たせる "keep (someone) waiting"]
近いうちに (phr) in the near future
ご来社↑ (n) coming to our company [honorific]

Structures 7B

7B.1. Conditional + （いい）と思う

We have already learned how to say "if/when" using conditional forms: Vたら／Aかったら／Nだったら. As an extension of this expression, it is possible to express one's wish "(I think) it would be nice if..." This takes the following structures: Vたら／Aかったら／Nだったら いい(と思う).

山田部長に会えたらいいと思います。
I think it would be nice if I could see Division Manager Yamada.

In conversations, いい can be dropped, and this makes the expression more indirect.

日本へも市場を拡張できたらと思うんですが…
I think it would be [nice] if we could expand our business to Japan.

日本はもっと物価が安かったらいいのに…
I wish the prices were cheaper in Japan.

7B.2. Wh + か（へ）の + N

We know that Wh + か structure can express such meanings as "someone," "somewhere," etc. You can combine this structure with a noun by using the particle の:

どなたかのご紹介	an introduction by someone
だれかからの手紙	a letter from someone
どこかへの電車	a train to somewhere
cf. 日本への市場拡張	a market expansion into Japan

The particle に cannot be used in the last structure above. That is, どこかにの電車 and 日本にの市場拡張 are both ungrammatical.

7B.3.　S + そうだ

The /S + そうだ/ pattern expresses hearsay: "I heard that S" or "It is said that S." The sentence before そうだ must be a complete plain-form sentence. For example,

あのプログラムをインストールしたら、50メガバイトは取るそうです。
They say that if you install that program it takes (as much as) 50 megabytes.

今夜のカラオケパーティーでは部長が英語の歌を歌うそうですよ。
I heard that our Division Manager will sing a song in English at tonight's karaoke party.

実は課長はゴルフがとても上手なんだそうです。
Actually, I heard that (it's the case that) the Section Manager is very good at golf.

ハリス君が日本の歌を一曲ぜひ覚えたいそうです。
I heard that Mr. Harris wants to memorize a Japanese song, by all means.

The negative form of this is made by negating the sentence before そうだ. That is, /...ないそうだ/ rather than /S そうじゃない/.

隣がうるさくて、寝られないそうです。
I heard that her neighbor is so noisy, she cannot sleep.

In the following, note that Ms. Itoh refers to her own boss by his last name only (石野) without his title. This is the appropriate way of referring to your superior when you are speaking to a member of an out-group.

Conversation 7C: Making an appointment (3)

1. ル: はい、そうお願いできると、ありがたいです。いつごろがよろしいでしょうか。	1. L: I'd be grateful if I can get your help. When would be good (for him)?
2. 伊: そうですね。では、来週の月曜日の一時半はいかがでしょうか。	2. I: Let me see. Well, how about one thirty on Monday next week?
3. ル: それでけっこうです。それでは来週、月曜日の一時半にお伺いいたしますので、どうぞよろしくお願いいたします。	3. L: That will be fine. Then, I will come and see him at one thirty on Monday next week. Thank you kindly. [Lit. I will ask for your kindness.].
4. 伊: かしこまりました。ルイス様、それではご来社のさいに、小川様の紹介状をお持ちいただければと思いますが…。	4. I: Not at all. Ms. Lewis, I think it would be nice if you can bring a reference letter from Mr. Ogawa when you come next week.
5. ル: はい、わかりました。	5. L: Yes, I understand.

| 願う ねが wish, hope, request | 紹介状 ショウカイジョウ letter of introduction |

Vocabulary 7C

お願いできると (phr) [If/When I could make a request, wish]
ありがたい (a) grateful
お伺いいたします (cv: ukagaw) [humble polite of 行く] ask, visit
さい (n) occasion, time [ご来社のさい "when you come to our company"].

紹介状 (n) a reference letter, a letter of introduction
お持ち (cv: mot) [polite stem of 持つ] have; own; possess; bring
いただければ (cv: itadak) [potential of いただく + provisional ば] provided that I could have (a favor)

Structures 7C

7C.1. Non-past-S1 と、S2 (If/When S1, S2)

This pattern means that S2 happens as a natural consequence of S1: "If/When S1, S2." /S1 と、S2/ often appears in written texts. The predicate before と must be non-past, regardless of the fact that the sentence refers to a past event (e.g., 会議が終わると6時だった。 "When the meeting was over, it was six o'clock").

使ってみると、このゴルフクラブの良さがよくわかる。
If you use it and see, you would understand the good quality of this golf club.

普通、円が高いと、輸出が難しい。	Normally, when the yen is strong, it is difficult to export.
景気がいいと、ボーナスもよくなる。	Normally, when the economy is good, bonuses will increase.
電信扱いだと三日で着きます。	If it's electronic transfer, (the money) will reach there in 3 days.
新橋ですと、ここから30分かかります。	If it's Shinbashi, it'll take 30 minutes from here.

It should also be noted that S2 in the /S1 と、S2/ pattern is limited to an event that is <u>not in the control of</u> by the subject of S1, unless the sentence refers to laws of nature or routine events. In addition, S2 can never express a command, request, invitation, offer, etc. Thus, the following sentences marked by an asterisk "*" are ungrammatical. Each can be corrected, as in the sentences marked by an arrow (→).

When I went abroad on business, I bought duty-free items at the airport.

*外国に出張すると、空港で免税品を買った。	S2 is controlled by the subject of S1.
→外国に出張したとき、空港で免税品を買った。	
→外国に出張すると、いつも空港で免税品を買う。	(Acceptable because this refers to routine events.)

When the work is over, why don't we go for a drink?

*仕事が終わると、飲みに行きませんか。	S2 is an invitation.
→仕事が終わったら、飲みに行きませんか。	

7C.2. Provisionals

Earlier, we learned conditional statements: /S1 たら、S2/ "if/when S1 has happened, S2 happens." In this chapter we will learn a similar connective expression called provisionals. Provisionals are formed by the following rule:

a. VV (る verb) + reba:

    tabe + reba　食べれば　　　if/provided X eats
    deki + reba　できれば　　　if/provided X is possible

b. CV (う verb) + eba:

    wakar + eba　わかれば　　　if/provided X understands
    ik + eba　行けば　　　if/provided X goes
    mat + eba　待てば　　　if/provided X waits
    yob + eba　呼べば　　　if/provided X summons (someone)
    isog + eba　急げば　　　if/provided X hurries
    hanas + eba　話せば　　　if/provided X talks
    omow + eba　思えば　　　if/provided X thinks (that...)　Note: /w/ is dropped.

c. Irregular verbs:

    来る　→　来れば　　　if/provided X comes
    する　→　すれば　　　if/provided X does

d. い-Adj-root + ければ:

    高い　　　→　高ければ　　　if/provided it is expensive
    むずかしい　→　むずかしければ　　if/provided it is difficult

e. な-Adj/Noun + なら:

    きれい　→　きれいなら　　　if/provided it is pretty
    日本語だ　→　日本語なら　　　if/provided it is Japanese

Corresponding negative forms are:

    VV-root + なければ:　食べなければ　　if/provided that you don't eat
    CV-root + ana + ければ:　作らなければ　　if/provided that you don't make (something)
    い-Adj + くなければ:　寒くなければ　　if/provided that it is not cold
    な-Adj + じゃなければ:　きれいじゃなければ　　if/provided it is not pretty
    Noun + じゃなければ:　日本語じゃなければ　　if/provided it is not Japanese

In many cases, provisionals and conditionals are interchangeable.　However, there are differences in their uses.

1. In general, the provisional structure /S1-(r)eba, S2/ expresses a close cause-effect relationship between S1 and S2. Thus, this pattern is often used as an answer to the question "What does it take for S2 to happen? --- It takes S1 for S2 to happen."　In contrast, the conditional structure expresses that one of the results of S1's happening is S2 ("If S1 happens, what happens next? --- It's S2!").　Compare the following conversations.

    A:　明日のゴルフ大会、出たくないんです。　　I don't want to attend tomorrow's golf tournament.
    B:　雨がふれば、ゴルフ大会はありませんよ。　If it rains (tomorrow), there will be no tournament.
    　　new information

    A:　明日、雨がふるそうですよ。　　They say it's going to rain tomorrow.
    B:　じゃあ、ゴルフ大会はどうなるんですか。　Then, what will happen to the tournament?
    A:　雨がふったら、ゴルフ大会はありませんよ。　If it rains (tomorrow), there will be no tournament.
    　　　　　　　new information

2. Unlike the conditional structure, the provisional structure does not have the notion of completion of S1.　Thus, the first sentence below can be used if the speaker is going at the same time as Ms. Tanaka goes, while the second sentence below can only be used if the speaker is going after Ms. Tanaka has departed.

田中さんが行けば、私も行きます。　　　　If Ms. Tanaka goes, I will go, too.
田中さんが行ったら、私も行きます。　　　If Ms. Tanaka goes (i.e., has gone), I will go, too.

3. S2 in the provisional structure frequently expresses a "desirable" outcome. This fact makes it difficult to use the provisional as a warning. Thus, the first sentence below is a good warning, but the second one is ungrammatical.

それを飲んだら、お腹が痛くなりますよ。　　If you drink it, you will have a stomachache.
＊それを飲めば、お腹が痛くなりますよ。　　[Ungrammatical]
それを飲んだら、よくなりますよ。　　　　　If you drink it, you will be fine.
それを飲めば、よくなりますよ。　　　　　　If you drink it, you will be fine.

4. Since the provisional structure does not express the notion of when, it cannot be used to refer to a past event that actually happened.

きのう、会社に来たら、アメリカから手紙が来ていた。
When I came to the company yesterday, there was a letter from America. (Lit. "a letter had come from ...")

＊きのう、会社に来れば、アメリカから手紙が来ていた。[Ungrammatical]

Mr. Harris learned that a friend from his university is coming to visit his company next week. When he mentioned her name, Mr. Tanaka initially didn't think of her as a woman but soon realizes his mistake.

Conversation 7D: Mr. Harris' friend (1)

1. 田: いやあ、今日も暑くなりそうだね。
2. ハ: 本当に。少し涼しくなってほしいですね。実は課長、大学の友人でデジタルマシンにつとめているルイスという者がいるんですが…。
3. 田: ルイスさん？
4. ハ: はい。彼女、来週、社用で来日するそうなんです。
5. 田: あ、その方は女性の方なんだね？
6. ハ: はい、そうです。それで、できれば課長にもぜひお目にかかりたいということなんです。

1. T: Well, it seems to be getting hot today, too.
2. H: Yes. I wish it would get cooler. By the way, Section Manager, among my college friends, I have a person named Ms. Lewis who is working for Digital Machines.
3. T: Mr./Ms. Lewis?
4. H: Yes. I heard she is coming to Japan next week on business.
5. T: Is that person a woman?
6. H: Yes, she is, and she really wants to meet you, if possible.

女性 (ジョセイ) female, woman　　男性 (ダンセイ) male, man　　彼女 (かのジョ) she　　彼 (かれ) he

Vocabulary 7D

いやあ (interj) Well; Oh; Wow
暑く (a) [く-form of 暑い] hot [of weather]
なりそう (cv: nar) [stem of なる + そう "show signs of/look as if"] [暑くなりそう "it looks as if it would become hot"]
涼しく (a) [く-form of 涼しい] cool
ほしい (a) want. [V てほしい, "want to have it V-ed."
　e.g., なってほしい "I want X to become"].

友人 (ゆうじん) (n) friend [= 友だち]
彼女 (かのじょ) (pro) she; ●彼 (かれ) (pro) he
社用 (しゃよう) (n) company business
来日する (らいにち) (n/v) come to Japan
女性 (じょせい) (n) female [女性の方 (polite) woman]
●男性 (だんせい) (n) male [男性の方 (polite) man]
できれば (vv: deki) [provisional of できる] if possible

Structures 7D

7D.1.　V-stem + そうだ

The /V-stem + そうだ/ pattern is used when there are some visible clues that indicate the truthfulness of the state/event expressed by the V: "X appears to V" or "X almost V." If a verb is used, it is more natural to use a non-action verb. Action verbs tend to be used in the potential form: "X appears V-able."

V-stem + そうだ	X appears to V.
わかりそうだ	It appears to be comprehensible.
でられそうだ	It appears that I can go out.
V-stem + そうにない	X does not appear to V.
わかりそうにない	It does not appear to be comprehensible.
でられそうにない	It does not appear that I can go out.

Imagine that you are in a meeting and it appears that it takes time to reach a decision. You can say:

　　結論が出るまでにはもっと時間がかかりそうだ。 It appears that it would take more time to reach a conclusion.

Imagine that your meeting is almost over. Your colleague from another section wants to know if you would like to leave now. You can respond:

　　もう少しで終わりそうだから、待っていてくれる？
　　It appears [it] will end soon, so would you wait for me?

　　五時までには終わりそうにありませんから、先に帰って下さい。
　　It does not appear that it will finish by five o'clock, so please leave ahead of me.

Can you explain the difference between the following sentences?[33]

　　(1) 10時までに　できそうです。
　　(2) 10時までに　できるそうです。
　　(3) 10時までに　できそうでした。
　　(4) 10時までに　できたそうです。
　　(5) 10時までに　できそうにないです／できそうにありません。
　　(6) 10時までに　できないそうです。

Can you give the Japanese equivalents of the following expressions?[34]

　　(1) It doesn't look like it's going to rain.
　　(2) They say that it won't rain.
　　(3) It didn't look like it was going to rain.
　　(4) They say that it didn't rain.

---

[33]　(1) = appearance, (2) = hearsay, (3) = appearance ("looked like it was going to be completed"), (4) = hearsay ("they say it was completed") (5) = appearance ("doesn't look like it is going to be..."), (6) = hearsay ("they say it won't be...")

[34]　(1) 雨はふらなさそうだ／ふりそうにない。(2) 雨はふらないそうだ。(3) 雨はふらなさそうだった／ふりそうになかった。(4) 雨はふらなかったそうだ。

7D.2. Vて + ほしい

The pattern /Vて + ほしい/ means "X wants someone else to V." In terms of meaning, this structure is similar to /Vて + もらいたい/. The person who performs the actual action (V) is marked by the particle に. Thus, "I would like for you to attend the meeting with that company, by all means." can be said in two ways:

ハン君、あそことの会議にはぜひ君に出てほしいんだ。
ハン君、あそことの会議にはぜひ君に出てもらいたいんだ。

ほしい is an い-adjective and can be used by itself. Xがほしい means "want X." This expresses a concrete desire. The subject of this sentence is usually the speaker in a statement ("I want...") or the addressee in a question ("Do you want..."). The particle が is used to mark the object of ほしい.

何か冷たい物がほしいんですけど…　　　　　I want something cold.
部長の許可がほしいんです。　　　　　　　　I want the Division Manager's permission.

Don't equate Vてほしい and Vたい. Vたい refers to a desire that <u>the speaker himself/herself</u> does something. Vてほしい refers to a desire that <u>someone other than the speaker</u> does something. That is, Vてほしい can be rephrased by using Vてもらいたい. Just like Vてもらいたい, the person who performs the action "V" is marked by the particle に. Note the difference between the following expressions.

木村さんと<u>会いたいんです</u>。　　　　　　　I want to meet Mr. Kimura.
　　　　vs.
田中さんに木村さんと<u>会ってほしいんです</u>。　I want Mr. Tanaka to meet Mr. Kimura.
(＝田中さんに木村さんと<u>会ってもらいたいんです</u>。)

In summary, all of the following patterns express some type of desire.

Vたい　　　　　　　　　I want to V/Do you want to V?
Vたがっている　　　　　He/She/They want(s) to V.
Vたそうだ　　　　　　　It appears that he/she/they want(s) to V.
Vたいそうだ　　　　　　I hear that he/she/they want(s) to V.
Vてほしい／Vてもらいたい　　I want you/him/her/them to V.
Vてほしいそうだ／Vてもらいたいそうだ　　I hear that he/she/they want(s) X to V.

All of the following sentences are about someone's desire to publish an article about foreigners working in Japan. Explain the differences between the following sentences.[35]

(1) 日本で働く外国人について記事を<u>出したいんです</u>。
(2) 日本で働く外国人について記事を<u>出したがっています</u>。
(3) 日本で働く外国人について記事を<u>出したいそうです</u>。
(4) 日本で働く外国人について記事を<u>出してほしいんです</u>。
(5) 日本で働く外国人について記事を<u>出してほしいそうです</u>。
(6) 日本で働く外国人について記事を<u>出してもらいたいんです</u>。
(7) 日本で働く外国人について記事を<u>出してもらいたいそうです</u>。

Because ほしい and もらいたい are in the plain form, they sound too forward when you are stating your desires to your superiors. To avoid such impressions, you should use more polite forms as shown below.

許可がほしいんですが…　→　許可をいただきたいんですが…
"I want your permission."　　"I would like your permission."

---

[35] (1) speaker's desire, (2) other's desire, (3) hearsay about someone's desire, (4) speaker's desire, (5) hearsay about someone's desire, (6) speaker's desire, (7) hearsay about someone's desire

早めにご返事をもらいたいんですが… → 早めにご返事をいただきたいんですが…
"I want your reply soon."　　　　　　　　"I would like your reply soon."

In polite conversations, ほしい and もらいたい are rarely used to ask others' desires. Instead, alternative expressions as shown below are preferred.

もう一杯ほしいですか。　→　もう一杯いかがですか。
"Do you want another cup?"　　"How about another cup?"

コーヒーが飲みたいですか。　→　コーヒーをお飲みになりませんか。
"Do you want to drink coffee?"　　"Would you like to have coffee?"

手伝ってほしいですか。　→　お手伝いいたしましょうか。
"Do you want me to help?"　　"Shall I help you?"

説明してもらいたいですか。　→　ご説明いたしましょうか。
"Do you want me to explain?"　　"Shall I explain?"

Mr. Harris asks Mr. Tanaka to meet Ms. Lewis. Mr. Tanaka agrees.

Conversation 7E: Mr. Harris' friend (2)

1. 田：その人はハリス君が大学の時、一緒だったの？
2. ハ：はあ、経済学が専門ですが、もとは工学系の出身なので、新製品の技術的な面もよく知っているようです。
3. 田：新製品についての資料をいろいろ持ってきてもらえるんだね？
4. ハ：ええ。お時間作っていただけますでしょうか。
5. 田：まあ、ハリス君の友達なら、会ってみようかね。
6. ハ：ありがとうございます。

1. T: Was she with you in college?
2. H: Yes, she specializes in economics, but, originally, her background is engineering, so she seems to know the technological aspects of new products well.
3. T: She can bring various materials about the new products, can't she?
4. H: Yes. Could you please make time for her?
5. T: Well, if she is your friend, I guess I should meet her.
6. H: Thank you.

経済 economy　門 gate　専門 specialty　系 system, lineage, group

Vocabulary 7E

一緒 (n) together
はあ (interj) Yes
経済学 (n) economics
もと (n) origin
工学系 (n) engineering field
出身 (n) place of one's upbringing, background

技術的 (な-adj) technological
面 (n) aspect, face
資料 (n) information materials
なら (cop) [provisional of だ] provided that X is the case
会ってみようかね Shall I see her and see (what she's like), I wonder.

Structures 7E

7E.1. Sようだ／Nのようだ／な-**Adj**.なようだ

Earlier, we learned to say X ように ("in such a manner that X"): ここから見えるように大きく書いて下さい。 ("Please write it big so we can see it from here"). The nominalizer よう can be followed by the copula だ. The ようだ pattern implies that the X preceding よう is acquired by reasoning or inference: "It seems that S." The sentence before ようだ must be a plain-form sentence. Unlike the /V-stem or Adj-stem そうだ/ pattern, Sようだ does not require visible clues to indicate that "X appears to V" or "X appears A."

横浜電気は来月、新製品を出すようだ。
It seems that Yokohama Electric is going to bring out new products next month.

田中さんは話し中のようだ。
It seems that Ms. Tanaka is busy (i.e., on the phone).

課長は一日中、お客様を接待してお疲れになったようです。
The Section Manager entertained the guest all day and seems to have gotten tired.

The /Nのようだ/ pattern can also be translated as "X is like N."[36]

今日は日曜日のようだ。	Today is like Sunday.
今日は春のように暖かい。	Today is warm like spring.

If the nominalizer よう is followed by the な form of the copula, it can modify a noun.

今日は日曜日のような日だ。	Today is a day like Sunday.
今日の温度は春のような温度だ。	Today's temperature is like the temperature in spring.
説明してもわからないような人だ。	He is like a person who doesn't understand even if you explain.

7E.2. NについてのN

We already know that Nについて means "about N." If this structure is followed by a noun, の is required.

大型企画について話しました。	→	大型企画についての話を聞きました。
I spoke about the large project.		I heard the story about the large project.
アメリカ市場について報告しました。	→	アメリカ市場についての報告書を読みました。
I reported on the American market.		I read a report on the American market.
Cf. コピー機を正しく使います。	→	コピー機の正しい使い方
[I] use a copier correctly.		the correct way of using a copier
英語で説明します。	→	英語での説明
[I'll] explain in English.		the explanation in English
外国企業と協力します。	→	外国企業との協力
[We] cooperate with foreign corporations.		cooperation with foreign corporations

---

[36] The structure /な-Adj. + なようだ/ is possible but is not used as often. あそこも、なかなか大変なようだよ。 ("They seem to be struggling quite a bit over there.").

7E.3.　S1 なら、S2

In 7C.2, we learned that the provisional form of だ is なら．なら can follow a noun or な-adjective (e.g., 先生なら／きれいなら).

N＋なら な-Adj＋．なら	部長さんなら、もうお帰りになりましたよ。 If it's Division Manager (you are talking about), he already went home. 元気なら、仕事をしてください。 If you are healthy (or feel energetic), please work.

なら can also follow a complete sentence (past or non-past): /S1 なら、S2/ ("if it's that S1, S2"). In this case, ん or more formal の can be optionally inserted as shown below.

い-Adj.＋なら	A：暑いんです。 B：暑い（ん／の）なら、エアコンをつけましょうか。 　　If it's that you are hot, shall I turn on the air conditioner? 　＝暑ければ、エアコンをつけましょうか。 　＝暑かったら、エアコンをつけましょうか。 　　If you are hot, shall I turn on the air conditioner? A：暑かったんです。 B：暑かった（ん／の）なら、エアコンをつけたでしょう。 　　If it's that it was hot, he/she would have turned on the air conditioner. 　＝暑かったら、エアコンをつけたでしょう。 　　If it were hot, he/she probably turned on the air conditioner.
V＋なら	A：日本に行くんです。 B：日本に行く（ん／の）なら、カメラを買って来て下さい。 　　If it's that you go to Japan, please buy a camera for me (and come back). 　＝日本に行ったら、カメラを買って来て下さい。 　　If you go to Japan, please buy a camera for me (and come back). A：日本に行ったんです。 B：日本に行った（ん／の）なら、日本語ができるようになったでしょう。 　　If it's that you went to Japan, you would have become able to understand Japanese. 　＝日本に行ったら、日本語ができるようになったでしょう。 　　If you went to Japan, you would have become able to understand Japanese.
S-Neg.＋なら	明日いらっしゃらない（ん／の）なら、そうおっしゃって下さい。 If it's that you are not coming tomorrow, please say so. 忙しくない（ん／の）なら、手伝っていただけませんか。 If it's that you are not busy, could you help me? 来月、出張じゃないなら、飛行機の予約はまだしなくてもいい。 If the business trip is not next month, you don't need to make a plane reservation yet.

If S1 in the past tense, だったら is more commonly used than なら．Note that the second sentence below can be interpreted as a regular if-statement or as a counterfactual statement.

ハリスさんなら、英語がわかるだろう。
If it is Mr. Harris, he probably understands English.

ハリスさんだったら、英語がわかっただろう。
If it was Mr. Harris (in fact, it was Mr. Harris), he probably understood English.
If it were Mr. Harris (in fact, it was not Mr. Harris), he would have understood English. [Counterfactual]

Earlier, we learned that the /S1 たら、S2/ structure requires that S1 is completed before S2. This constraint makes the following statement ungrammatical because "going to Japan" and "taking a camera to Japan" occur at the same time.

＊日本に行ったら、カメラを持って行きます。[Ungrammatical]
If I go to Japan, I would take my camera.

The same statement can be said grammatically by using なら as shown below.

日本に行く(ん／の)なら、カメラを持って行きます。
If it's that I go to Japan, I would take my camera.

Exercise 7

Grammar Utilization 7 Name:_____ Sec:_____ #:____

G1. Combine the antecedent and the consequence with a provisional form (V ば, A ければ, N なら) as shown in the example below. For questions 4 through 6, supply your own antecedent or consequence.

Example: 経済(けいざい)がよくなります。 ＋ ボーナスが上(あ)がります。(上がる：increase)
 → 経済がよくなれば、ボーナスが上がります。
   Provided that the economy improves, [the amount of] the bonus will increase.

1. プレゼンテーションの練習(れんしゅう)します。   ＋   上手(じょうず)になります。
   You practice your presentation.   You will be good at [it].
   →

2. 会議室(かいぎしつ)を使(つか)いたいです。   ＋   前の日までに予約(よやく)して下さい。
   You would like to use the conference room.   Please reserve [the room] by the day before.
   →

3. 品質(ひんしつ) (product quality)がいいです。   ＋   よく売(う)れます。
   The quality of the product is good.   [The product] will sell well.
   →

4. ご覧(らん)になります。(=honorific of 見る) ＋   わかると思います。
   You look at it.   I think you will understand.
   →

5. 空港(くうこう)までタクシーで行きます。   ＋   _____
   We go to the airport by taxi.
   →

6.   ＋   仕事(しごと)が速(はや)くできます。
   →_____   You can do your work quickly.

G2. Complete the expressions that follow ぜひ ("by all means").

1. お疲(つか)れの時(とき)は、ぜひこの栄養(えいよう)ドリンクを_____みて下さい。
                               (take this nutritional drink)

2. 今、部長にぜひ_____という人が受付(うけつけ)に来ているんですが、
              (want to meet [humble]: お目にかかる)
   いかがいたしましょうか。

3. よろしければ、ぜひうちの_____いただけませんでしょうか。
                        (use our new products [honorific])

4. 毎日、5時まで 営業しておりますから、ぜひ_____下さい。
                                        (come [honorific])

Chapter 7: Appointments

G3. Complete the conversation by using the ～そうだ patterns appropriately as in the example.

Example:
A: 今日は晴れそうですね。
B: いや、天気予報によると、午後から雨が降るそうですよ。

A: It looks like it will be fair today.
B: Not quite. According to the weather forecast, they say it will rain starting this afternoon.

1. A: 岡本さん、今日は_____そうね。
   B: あれ、全部、今日中に_____そうです。

   A: Mr. Okamoto appears so busy today.
   B: They say he intends to finish it completely today.

2. A: 横浜電気との交渉は長く_____そうですよ。
   B: ええ、早くても今週いっぱいは_____そうですよ。
   （つづく：to continue; last）

   A: The negotiations with Yokohama Electric appears to last long.
   B: I know. They say it will continue throughout this week at the earliest.

3. A: 例の件、もうすぐ結論が_____そうですか？
   B: ええ、岡田部長も賛成_____そうですから。
   （賛成する：to agree）

   A: About that matter, does it appear that the conclusion will be reached soon?
   B: Yes, because I heard that Div. Manager Okada also is in agreement.

4. A: 会議はまだ_____ないですね。 B: ええ、6時までは_____そうですよ。
   （おわる：[something] comes to an end）

   A: It doesn't look like the meeting will be over yet.
   B: That's right. They say it will not be over until six o'clock at least.

5. A: 課長はわかってくれたんですか。
   B: いいえ、_____ないですよ。

   A: Has the section manager understood (our position)?
   B: No, he doesn't appear to understand us.

G4. Translate the underlined parts into English.

1. A: ハリスさん、ABC商事に就職するのはなかなかむずかしかったでしょう？
   B: 実は、大学の先輩がそこに就職していて、その人に聞いたところ、私を押してくれた次第なんです。
   （商事：trading [company]； 先輩：one's seniors； [person]を押す：push, support [person]）

2. A: いつから始めましょうか。
   B: 会議で結論が出次第、お願いするよ。(結論：conclusion)

3. A: ハリスさん、課長さんにおみやげをいただいたんですか。
   B: ええ、いつもお世話になっているのに、おみやげまでいただいて恐縮している次第です。
   （のに： in spite that； おみやげ：souvenir； 恐縮する：feel obliged）

4. A: ABC商事でございます。
   B: 実は、田中部長よりお電話いただいたとのことで、おりかえしお電話している次第です。
   (おりかえし：immediately in response)

5. A: ユーエス・リースからのファックスが来次第、こちらからの返事を出してくれないか。
   B: かしこまりました。

6. A: ハン君、横浜工業との交渉は進んでいる？
   B: 実は、こちらがもう値下げできないと言ったら、むこうは考え直したいという次第で、対応に困っているんです。
   (交渉：negotiation; 進む：make progress; 値下げする：reduce the price; 考え直す：reconsider; 対応：coping, matching)

G5. Fill in the blanks by using a ようだ or そうだ expression and complete the conversation.

1. A: 円はどうなるでしょうかね。
   B: _____
   It appears that the yen will get stronger.

2. A: 横浜工業との契約はどうなったんでしょうね。
   B: _____
   It appears that we were unable to make the contract. (契約にこぎつける：make a contract)

3. A: 来週、北海道へ行くんですが、気候はどうでしょうかね。
   B: _____
   It seems that the weather is still cold.

4. A: ハン君はおすしは好きでしょうね？
   B: _____
   It seems that he would like it a lot.

5. A: 明日のセミナー、あるかな？
   B: _____
   It appears that there won't be any seminar.

G6. Change the underlined part of S1 and connect it with S2 using one of the following structures: /S1 と、S2/ or /S1 たら、S2/ or /S1 ば、S2/ or /S1 なら、S2/. If more than one structure is possible, write all possible connections.

   Example: 値引きしてくれます。いいですね。
            値引きしてくれると／くれたら／くれれば／くれるなら、いいですね。

1. 値段が安いです。全部買いましょう。

値段が_____、全部買いましょう。
If the prices are cheap, we will buy everything.

2. 田中さんから電話があります。私に連絡して下さい。

   田中さんから電話が_____、私に連絡して下さい。
   If there is a call from Mr. Tanaka, please inform me.

3. きのう、新宿に行きました。スミスさんに会いました。

   きのう、新宿に_____、スミスさんに会いました。
   When I went to Shinjuku yesterday, I met Ms. Smith.

4. 無理をします。病気になってしまいますよ。

   無理を_____、病気になってしまいますよ。
   If work too hard, you will end up sick.

5. うちとは協力できません。そう言ってほしいですね。

   うちとは協力_____、そう言ってほしいですね。
   If they can't cooperate with us, I want them to say so.

6. 公園まで行きます。歩いて行きましょう。

   公園まで_____、歩いて行きましょう。
   If we are going to the park, let's walk there.

G7. Match the Japanese phrases on the left with the English equivalent on the right.

   a. だれかの手紙   _____   1. a letter to someone
   b. どこかの会社   _____   2. someone's company
   c. だれかへの手紙   _____   3. someone's letter
   d. どこかからの電車 _____   4. a train from somewhere
   e. どなたかの会社   _____   5. a company somewhere

G8. Rephrase the underlined part of the requests/questions according to the cues below.

1. The fax from your business partner stopped in mid-transmission. You are asking the other party to fax it again. Be very polite.
   ファックスが途中で ("in mid-operation")とまってしまいました。たいへん申し訳ございませんが、もう一度、送っていただけませんか。

   _____

2. You are calling someone who is a high-ranking member of another company. Be very polite.
   私、ソニーの山田と申しますが、森田部長いらっしゃいますか。

   _____

3. You would like to have an appointment with someone who is a high-ranking member of another company. Be very polite.

私、ソニーの山田と申しますが、来週、森田(もりた)部長に会えませんか。("Couldn't I possibly meet...")

_____

G9. You are talking to a newly-hired employee. Match the sentences and the translations. (Some translations can be used more than once.)

1. コーヒーを入れてほしいんです。　　_____　　a. Shall we have someone make us coffee?
2. コーヒーを入れてもらって下さい。　_____　　b. I want you to make me coffee.
3. コーヒーを入れてもらいたいんです。_____　　c. Could you make me coffee?
4. コーヒーを入れてもらいませんか。　_____　　d. Please have someone make you coffee.
5. コーヒーを入れてもらえませんか。　_____

G10. Go to the following Web site (http://jin.jcic.or.jp/nipponia/index.html), choose three articles and state what the articles (記事(きじ)) are about. Go to the back numbers (bottom of the screen) if necessary. In your answers below, use the structure /についての N/.

Example:
記事(きじ)の URL: http://jin.jcic.or.jp/nipponia/nipponia16/live.html
これは日本の旅館(りょかん)を経営(けいえい)するアメリカ人についての記事です。

1. 記事の URL:_____

   _____

2. 記事の URL:_____

   _____

3. 記事の URL:_____

   _____

Chapter 7: Appointments

Reading and Writing 7

Name:_____ Sec:_____ #:____

R1. Read the following introduction letter (紹介状) and answer the questions below.

石野　光一様

拝啓　初夏の候　貴社ますますご清栄のこととお慶び申し上げます。平素は格別のお引立てを賜り、厚く御礼申し上げます。

さて、突然のお願いで誠に恐縮ですが、デジタルマシン株式会社のアン・ルイス営業課長をご紹介申し上げたく存じます。

同社は、近年、アメリカのコンピュータ業界の激しい競争の中、ノートパソコン部門においてその優れた製品を持ち、市場占有率を伸ばしつつある企業です。ジェトロといたしましても、その経営ぶりを高く評価している次第でございます。

拝啓 (n) an opening greeting in a letter
初夏の候 (phr) early summer season
貴社↑ (n) your company
ますます (adv) increasingly, more and more
ご清栄のこととお慶び申し上げます↓ (phr) I/we congratulate your prosperity
平素 (n) usual; routine
格別のお引立て↑ (n) special/exceptional favor
賜り↓ (v) receive; is granted
厚く (adv) deeply
御礼申し上げます↓ (phr) I express our gratitude
さて (phr) incidentally [used before the body of a letter]
突然 (n) sudden
誠に恐縮です (phr) feel truly sorry
株式会社 (n) company incorporated [co. inc.]
申し上げたく存じます↓ (phr) I would like to say
同社 (n) this company; aforementioned company
近年 (n) in recent years
業界 (n) industry
激しい (a) severe; violent; heated
競争 (n) competition
ノートパソコン部門 (n) notebook PC sector
において (phr) in, at
優れた (phr) excellent
市場占有率 (n) percentage of market share
伸ばしつつある (phr) is expanding
といたしましても↓ (phr) as for [= としても]
経営ぶり (n) the way of business, management
評価している (v) is evaluating

The letter continues to the next page.

このたび、日本への輸出業務拡大に伴い、ぜひとも御社とのお取引をお願いしたいとのご希望がありました。ここに会社概要を同封の上、ご紹介申し上げます。 　ご多用中誠に恐縮ですが、なにとぞご引見の上、ご高配賜りますよう、よろしくお願い申し上げます。 　　　　　　　　　　　　　　敬具 平成14年6月25日 　　　　　　　　　　　　小川　洋	このたび (n) at this time; on this occasion 輸出業務 (n) export business, operation 拡大 (n) expansion に伴い (phr) along with; accompanying ぜひとも (adv) by all means; please お取引↑ (n) business (transaction) ご希望↑ (n) hope, wish, request 会社概要 (n) company brochure 同封の上 (n) enclosed ご多用中↑ (n) while you are so busy なにとぞ (phr) please ご引見の上↑ (n) by taking in something to look ご高配賜ります↑ (phr) give a kind consideration 敬具 (n) a closing remark in a letter

1. Identify the sender and the receiver of this letter and mark them "Sender" and "Receiver," respectively.
2. Identify the season's greeting and mark it "Greeting."
3. Identify the part that states the purpose of this letter and mark it "Purpose."
4. Identify the part that states Ms. Lewis' company, and mark it "Company."
5. Identify the part that states Ms. Lewis' request and mark it "Request 1."
6. Identify the part that states the sender's final request and mark it "Request 2."
7. Match the written expressions on the left with more conversational expressions on the right.

a. ___ 初夏の候
b. ___ 貴社ますますご清栄のこととお慶び申し上げます
c. ___ 平素は格別のお引立てを賜り、厚く御礼申し上げます
d. ___ 突然のお願いで誠に恐縮ですが
e. ___ ご紹介申し上げたく存じます
f. ___ 市場占有率を伸ばしつつある企業です
g. ___ ご多用中誠に恐縮ですが
h. ___ なにとぞご引見の上
i. ___ ご高配賜りますよう、よろしくお願い申し上げます

1. ご紹介したいと思います 2. 急なお願いで、本当にすみませんが 3. いつも、とてもよくして下さいまして、本当にありがとうございます 4. 市場占有率を伸ばしている企業です 5. 配慮していただくようにお願いします 6. 夏が来ましたね 7. お忙しいところ本当に申しわけありませんが 8. 御社の発展をうれしく思います 9. どうぞご覧になって

急な: sudden　　配慮する: be considerate　　発展: expansion, growth　　ご覧になる: look at

Communicative Exercise 7

C1. Role Playing

#1: You are speculating the possible reasons why your colleague, Ms. Yamamoto, is going to quit her job. Offer your own guesses to Mr. Okada, your colleague. Remember you are dealing with hearsays, possibilities, and appearances, not facts. (Possible reasons: health problems, family reasons, a job transfer, marriage, etc.).

Example:
Okada: 山本さんが会社をやめる<u>そう</u>ですねえ。
You: ええ、病気なんだ<u>そう</u>ですよ。このごろ疲れていらっしゃる<u>よう</u>だったから。

#2: You are discussing with your colleague, Ms. Brown, how much nicer life in Japan would be if the following came true.

    a. if commuter trains (通勤電車) were less crowded

    b. if the company adopted "flex-time" (フレックスタイム) working conditions

    c. if prices were cheap

    d. if the weather was nice (less rain, less heat, etc.)

    e. if the bonuses this year were good

    f. if the Japanese economy (経済) improved

    g. if the trade frictions (貿易摩擦) were gone

A sample conversation based on (a) above:

Brown: 日本はどうして、こんなに電車がこんでいるんでしょう。
You: そうですねえ。通勤電車がこんでいなかったら、日本はもっとよくなるのにねえ。

Listening Comprehension 7   Name:_____ Sec:____ #:____

Speaker A is the first speaker.   Speaker B is the second speaker.

1. Voc: エーアイテック：(n) AI Tech (name of a company); グリーン：(n) Green (last name)
   どこのだれが西本部長に電話してきましたか。

2. Voc: ミシェル：(n) Michelle (first name); 翻訳ソフト：(n) translation software;
   マーケティング：(n) marketing; コンピュータショー：(n) computer show
   グリーンさんの用件は何でしたか。

   グリーンさんはだれの紹介で西本部長のことを知ったんですか。

3. Voc: お手伝いたします：(n) humble form of 手伝う "assist, help"
   グリーンさんは西本部長に何をしてほしいんですか。

   グリーンさんと西本部長は来週、何をしますか。

4. Voc: ミーティング：(n) meeting; ソフト：(n) software; デモ：(n) demonstration
   1時からのミーティングではだれが、何をすることになっていますか。

   西本部長はいつそのミーティングに来られるそうですか。

5. Voc: 伝言：(n) message
   Aさんは何をしておくんですか。

6. Voc: 例の：(n) the so-called; what is known as; お急ぎ：(n) polite verb-stem of 急ぐ "hurry"
   グリーンさんからの伝言は何でしたか。

Bさん(部長)は電話しなくてもいいんですか。

7. Voc: お礼(れい)：(n) thanks; 拝見(はいけん)する：(v) humble of 見る "look, watch";
今後(こんご)とも：(n) both the present and the future; こちらこそ：(n) this side [emphatic]; the same here

Aさん(グリーン)は今、何をしたところですか。

Aさんは ミーティングの間(あいだ)に何をしたようですか。

Chapter 8

会社の説明 (かいしゃ の せつめい)
Describing a Company

Priming

Doing business in Japan is more than just buying and selling products and services. To form a new business relationship, one has to be able to trust the representatives and the whole company behind them. Gaining trust of a potential business partner is more important than good products and services your company sells.

After setting up an appointment, Ms. Lewis prepares information about her company. On the day of the presentation, she meets Mr. Ishino, Division Manager of 日本エレクトロニクス. After the meeting, Ms. Lewis gets down to business with Mr. Tanaka, the Manager of the Sales Section of the Japanese company. She is not just selling her products. She needs to convince her potential business partner of the merits of forming a long-term relationship with her company.

For Section Manager Tanaka, it is the first time to see his female counterpart from the U.S., and he is a little nervous. Luckily, Ms. Lewis and Mr. Harris happen to be friends from college days.

Chapter 8: Describing a Company

Conversation 8A: Mr. Harris reunites with Ms. Lewis.

1. ル: 今日はお忙しいところ、お時間をさいていただきまして、ありがとうございます。
2. 田: いやいや。ルイスさんはうちのハリスをご存知だそうですね。
5. ル: ええ、大学のとき、いっしょの研究室でした。
6. ハ: しばらく。
7. ル: お久しぶり。元気そうね。

1. L: I really appreciate (you) for (giving me) your time though you are busy today.
2. T: Not at all. Ms. Lewis, I heard you know our Harris.
5. L: Yes. We were working in the same research lab in college.
6. H: Long time no see.
7. L: The same here. You look great.

忙しい busy　　研究室 research laboratory　　元気 energetic, healthy

Vocabulary 8A

さいて (cv: sak) [て-form of さく] spare (time)
いやいや (phr) No, no. Not at all
いっしょの (phr) the same/together
研究室 (n) research laboratory

しばらく (n) a while [Also, "Long time, no see!"]
お久しぶり (n) Long time, no see. [お is an honorific prefix.]
元気そう (n) [元気 + そう: "appear great/fine"]

Structures 8A

8A.1. い-Adj-stem そうだ/な-Adj そうだ

In Chapter 7, we learned the /V-stem + そうだ/ structure which expresses "It appears V" as in つかえそうだ "It looks like I can use it." You can use an adjective stem in place of a verb stem and express "It appears [Adj]." Note that the negative form requires an extra sound さ before そうだ.

い-Adj-stem + そうだ	
やさしそうです。	It looks easy.
やさしそうでした。	It looked easy.
い-Adj く + な + さ + そうだ	
やさしくなさそうです。	It looks like it's not easy.
やさしくなさそうでした。	It looked like it was not easy.

Suppose you are at a bookstore looking over a few books. One of the books appears to be very expensive. You can say to your friend who is with you at the time:

　　この本はとても高そうだね。　　This book appears to be very expensive, doesn't it?

Note that いいです becomes よさそうです and ないです becomes なさそうです as shown below.

　　A: もう入ってもよさそうですか。　　Does it look like it's OK even if we enter now?
　　B: いいえ、まだよくなさそうですよ。　　No, it appears it's not OK. [Apparently, ...]

Given this, the earlier structure /V-stem + そうにない/ can be said using the following negative pattern.

　　10時までにできそうにありません。　　It doesn't look like it can be done by 10.
　　10時までにできなさそうです。　　It looks like it can't be done by 10.

Since V-たい form is an adjectival form, it can also be used in this pattern.

話したそうです。	S/he appears to want to talk.
話したくなさそうです。	S/he appears not to want to talk.

More examples follow:

今日も暑そうですね。	It looks like it's hot today.
おいしそう！	It looks delicious!
この本はむずかしくなさそうだ。	This book appears not so difficult.

Some な-adjectives can be used in this pattern as well. Again, note the extra sound さ in the negative form.

な-Adj + そうだ	
元気そうだ。	You look healthy.
な-Adj or N じゃ + な + さそうだ	
元気じゃなさそうだ。	You look like you are not healthy.

Compare this structure with the hearsay pattern /S + そうだ/ "I heard that S."

	Appearance		Hearsay
元気そうだ。	S/he looks healthy.	元気だそうだ。	They say that s/he is healthy.
元気そうだった。	S/he looked healthy.	元気だったそうだ。	They say that s/he was healthy.
高そうだ。	It look expensive.	高いそうだ。	They say that it is expensive.
高そうだった。	It looked expensive.	高かったそうだ。	They say that it was expensive.
できそうだ。	It looks like it can be done.	できるそうだ。	They say that they can do it.
できそうだった。	It looked like it could be done.	できたそうだ。	They say that they were able to do it.

Sentence (1) means "I heard that s/he wants to leave soon" while (2) means "It appears that s/he wants to leave soon."

(1) 早く帰ったそうです。　　vs.　　(2) 早く帰りたいそうです。

With past-tense vowel verbs, the appearance and hearsay patterns happen to be identical although intonation contour is different as shown below.

　　見たそうです。　　　見たそうです。
　　I heard that he/she saw it.　　It appears that he/she wants to see it.

After the introduction, Ms. Lewis starts her presentation.

Conversation 8B: Ms. Lewis introduces her company. (1)

1. 田: ルイスさんの会社は主にどのような製品を扱ってるんですか。	1. Tanaka: What kind of products is your company dealing with?
2. ル: 私どもはオフィス機器の製造販売をしておりまして、正直なところ、日本エレクトロニクスさんほど歴史も知名度もございません。しかし、私どもの商品の評価は決して悪くございません。ちなみにこの消費者ガイドをご覧下さい。	2. Lewis: We are manufacturing and selling office equipment. To be honest, we do not have as (long) a history nor name recognition as Japan Electronics. However, the evaluation of our products is not bad at all. On this regard, please look at this consumers' guidebook.

3. 田: あ、これはどうも。 4. ル: 手前味噌ですが、私どものマイクロスター800が品質、機能ともに高く評価されていることがおわかりいただけるかと思います。	3. T: Oh, thanks. 4. L: I am not bragging, but I hope you will understand that our product, Microstar 800, is highly ranked in terms of both quality and functions.

品 (ヒン／しな) goods, items　　器 (キ) container, instrument, apparatus　　販売 (ハンバイ) sales　　売る (う) to sell

Vocabulary 8B

おもに (adv) primarily, mainly

扱っている (cv: atsukaw) [て-form of 扱う + いる] is dealing with. [V てる = V ている]

おりまして (vv: or) [て-form of おります] be

正直 (な-adj) honest [正直なところ "to tell you the truth"]

ほど (p) as much as, about, approximately

知名度 (n) name recognition

しかし (con) but

商品 (n) merchandise

評価 (n) evaluation, rating

決して (adv) never, not at all. [always followed by a negative predicate]

悪く (a) [connective-form of 悪い] bad

ちなみに (con) in this connection; in that regard

消費者ガイド (n) consumer guide

ご覧 (n) seeing (honorific). [ご覧下さい "Please take a look."]

手前味噌 (n) home-made miso (Japanese bean paste) [手前味噌ですが (idiom) "I don't mean to brag, but..."]

マイクロスター (n) Microstar [name of a product]

品質 (n) product quality

機能 (n) function

ともに (adv) both, together

評価されて (n/v) [passive-て-form of 評価する] is evaluated/ranked

いただける (cv: itadak) [potential of いただく] can receive

Structures 8B

8B.1. Passives

A familiar "active" transitive sentence takes the following pattern, and it means "X does/did V to Y."

X (Subj)	が／は	Y (Obj)	を	Vt	
たくさんの人	が	その新聞	を	読んでいる。	Many people are reading the newspaper.

In its "passive" counterpart, the original object becomes the grammatical subject of a "passive" sentence. The passive sentence takes the following pattern:

Y (Subj)	が／は	X	に	Vt-passive	
その雑誌	は	たくさんの人	に	読まれている。	The magazine is being read by many people.

This pattern means "Y is V-ed by X." The particle に (or によって) marks the agent (X) that affects the subject (Y) of the passive sentence. The phrase, X に(よって) can be omitted if it is unknown. If the agent (X) is not a person (e.g., a natural force), it is often marked by the particle で.

Y (Subj)	が／は	X	で	Vt-passive	
看板	が	風	で	こわされた。	The billboard was damaged by the wind.

The passive of the vowel verbs are formed by adding -rareru to the root. Note that the passive form of vowel verbs are identical to the potential form of vowel verbs (e.g., oshie-rareru: "can teach/is taught"). The only way to distinguish them is by context.

	VV	Root	rareru	Passive	Potential
see	見る	mi	rareru	見られる	見られる (or 見れる)
eat	食べる	tabe	rareru	食べられる	食べられる (or 食べれる)
teach, tell	教える	oshie	rareru	教えられる	教えられる (or 教えれる)

The passive of the consonant verbs are formed by adding -areru to the root:

	CV	Root	areru	Passive	Potential
use	使う	tsukaw	areru	使われる	使える
say	言う	iw	areru	言われる	言える
drink	飲む	nom	areru	飲まれる	飲める
read	読む	yom	areru	読まれる	読める
wait	待つ	mat	areru	待たれる	待てる
have, hold	持つ	mot	areru	持たれる	持てる
speak	話す	hanas	areru	話される	話せる
make use of	活かす	ikas	areru	活かされる	活かせる
call, summon	呼ぶ	yob	areru	呼ばれる	呼べる
play	遊ぶ	asob	areru	遊ばれる	遊べる
go	行く	ik	areru	行かれる	行ける
write	書く	kak	areru	書かれる	書かれる
make	作る	tsukur	areru	作られる	作れる
take	とる	tor	areru	とられる	とれる
hurry	急ぐ	isog	areru	急がれる	急げる
swim	泳ぐ	oyog	areru	泳がれる	泳げる

The passive forms of the irregular verb, 来る, is 来られる and the passive of する is される. Additional examples:

IBMは日本でも（日本の消費者に）よく知られている。
IBM is well-known in Japan (by Japanese consumers), too.

この製品は日本の消費者によって高く評価されている。
This product has been ranked high by Japanese consumers.

産業用ロボットは危ないところでよく使われる。
Industrial Robots are often used in places of danger.

出る釘は打たれる。
The nail that sticks out gets hammered down. (proverb)

Now change the following sentences into passive sentences. If the agent who acts upon something/someone is the speaker himself/herself, you don't need to say 私に(よって).

(1) 母が私に「早く帰ってきて」と言った。
    →

(2) ハリスさんはルイスさんを歓迎会に呼んだ。(呼ぶ (cv: yob): call, summon)
    →

Chapter 8: Describing a Company   175

(3) 日本のサラリーマンはよく「日本経済新聞」を読む。
    →

(4) 韓国の会社はカラーのLCDスクリーンを作っている。
    →

(5) 横河アメリカはJITシステム[37]を活かしている。
    →

(6) だれかが田中さんにファックスを送ってきた。
    →

(7) 台風がうちの窓をこわした。(台風: typhoon; こわす (cv: kowas): break)[38]
    →

Ms. Lewis continues her presentation.

Conversation 8C: Ms. Lewis introduces her company. (2)

1. 田: そうですね。そのうえ、他社の製品より値段が安いですね。これは大量生産によるコストダウンですか。
2. ル: いいえ。大量生産によるコストダウンというより、高額な宣伝費をけずったからなんです。
3. 田: とおっしゃいますと？
4. ル: わが社は「製品の質で勝負する」という経営方針で、わが社の製品を使ってみて、いいと思った消費者が自発的に口コミで宣伝してくれているんです。
5. 田: じゃ、ここまで市場を開拓するのにずいぶん時間がかかったでしょう？
6. ル: おっしゃるとおりです。でも、この「地に足がついた」経営方針を貫いてよかったと今では社員一同、自負しております。

1. T: Right. Your product price is lower than the prices of other companies. Is the cost reduction [achieved] by mass production?
2. L: No. It is because we curtail enormous advertising costs rather than lower prices by mass production.
3. T: What do you mean by that?
4. L: Our company has a business directive to compete with product quality, so consumers who think our products are good after using them voluntarily advertise our products by word-of-mouth.
5. T: Then, it must have taken a long time to develop the market?
6. L: Absolutely. But, now we are proud that this "conservative" business policy has worked for us. [Lit. "We are glad to have kept this conservative business policy."]

やす 安い cheap	タイリョウ 大量 large volume, mass	セイサン 生産 production	ヒ 費 cost, fee

---

[37] J.I.T. システム stands for the "Just-in-time" system of inventory management in manufacturing plants.
[38] (1) 私は母に「早く帰ってきて」と言われた。(2) ルイスさんはハリスさんに歓迎会に呼ばれた。(3) 日本経済新聞は日本のサラリーマンによく読まれている。(4) カラーのLCDスクリーンは韓国の会社に作られている。(5) JITシステムは横河アメリカに活かされている。(6) ファックスが田中さんに送られてきた。(7) うちの窓は台風でこわされた。

Vocabulary 8C

そのうえ (con) on top of that; furthermore
他社 (n) other company
より (p) than. [used in comparison of two items. XはYより高い。 "X is more expensive than Y."]
値段 (n) cost, price
大量生産 (n) mass production
による (phr) by [XによるY "Y due to/thanks to X"; よる (cv: yor) "depend; is due to"]
コストダウン (n) cost reduction ["cost down"]
高額 (n) large sum of money
宣伝費 (n) advertising cost
けずった (cv: kezur) [past of けずる] reduced; shaved off
質 (n) quality. [= 品質]
勝負する (n/v) compete; fight; victory or defeat
経営 (n) management
方針 (n) policy, principle

自発的 (な-adj) voluntary. [自発的に means voluntarily]
口コミ (n) word of mouth [コミ = short form of "communication"]
宣伝して (n/v) [て-form of 宣伝する] promote
開拓する (n/v) pioneer, develop
ずいぶん (adv) very; very much; a lot [followed by an affirmative predicate]
とおり (n) way, accordance with. [おっしゃるとおりです。 "It's just as you said."]
地 (n) ground, earth
ついた (cv: tsuk) [past of つく] was put, was attached; arrive, reach [adjectival usage]
貫いて (cv: tsuranuk) [て-form of 貫く] stick with; hold onto (idea or policy); penetrate
今では (phr) by now
社員一同 (n) everyone in the company
自負して (n/v) [て-form of 自負する] take a pride

Structures 8C

8C.1. 〜によって vs. 〜による

Just like the passive phrase 〜によって, the phrase 〜による also means by. They are different as to what they modify. The former is an adverbial phrase which modifies a verb, whereas the latter is a phrase that modifies a noun. Observe the sentences below. In sentence (1), 〜によって modifies the verb 評価する, while in (2), 〜による modifies the noun 評価.

(1) この製品は日本の消費者によって高く評価されている。
This product is ranked high by Japanese consumers.

(2) この製品の日本の消費者による高い評価
high ranking of this product by Japanese consumers

Note that the phrase particle は in (1) is changed to の in (2). This is because 製品は評価 is not a permissible way of connecting two nouns. By the same token, 高く評価 is not acceptable because when an adjective modifies a noun, it has to be in its plain form (高く→高い). This is because most of Sentence (1) is now reorganized as modifiers of 評価 in Sentence (2). For instance, この製品は in (1) modifies 評価, and therefore, it has to become この製品の. By the same token, によって and 高く are necessitated to change to による and 高い, respectively.

8C.2. 〜する(の)には

This pattern means "for the purpose of V-ing/in order to V/in the process of V-ing." In the previous chapter, we learned a sentence structure expressing the purpose of going somewhere: /stem + に/. In contrast to the /stem + に/

pattern, which always has to be followed by a verb of motion (e.g., 飲みに行く), this present pattern does not have such restrictions.

このコピー機を使うのにはどうしたらいいですか？
To use this copy machine, what should I do?

このソフトの開発にはずいぶん時間がかかりました。
It took a long time to develop this software.

空港へいらっしゃるのには地下鉄が便利だと思います。
In order to go to the airport, I think the subway is probably convenient.

The particle の can be optionally dropped: 上司の許可をもらうのには ＝ 上司の許可をもらうには "to receive your superior's permission." Now, compare the following. The particle の in the second sentence cannot be dropped.

空港へ行く(の)には どうしたらいいですか。　　In order to go to the airport, what should I do?
空港へ行くのは だれですか。　　Who is the one that goes to the airport?

8C.3. Comparatives

A comparison of two items takes the following structural patterns: (1) "X is more ... than Y [by quantity]" and (2) "X does ... more ...ly than Y (does) [by quantity]." The quantity expression is optional.

1.	X	は	Y	より	(Quantity)	Predicate
	B社のパソコン	は	A社の	より	150%	速い。
	Company A's PC is faster than Company B's by 150%.					
2.	X	は	Y	より	(Quantity)	Predicate
	アメリカ人	は	日本人	より		クレジットカードをよく使う。
	Americans use credit cards more often than Japanese (do).					

When the sentence ends with a negative predicate, ほど(は) is used instead of より.

3.	X	は	Y	ほど(は)	Neg. Predicate
	B社のパソコン	は	A社の	ほど	速くない。
	Company B's PC is not as fast as Company A's.				
4.	X	は	Y	ほど	Neg. Predicate
	日本人	は	アメリカ人	ほど	クレジットカードを使わない。
	Japanese do not use credit cards as often as Americans (do).				

The pattern (5) below is used in a question comparing two items. The /X の方/ stands of "the side of X," of which の方 can be deleted. A reply to this question takes the pattern (6).

5.	XとY(と)	では	どちら(の方)	が	Predicate
	電車とバス	では	どちら(の方)	が	速いですか。
	Between trains and buses,	which one is faster?			
6.			X／Y(の方)	が	Predicate
			電車(の方)	が	速いです。
			Trains are faster.		

More examples follow:

Q: メッセージを送るのには、電子メールとファックスとどちらの方が便利ですか。
　　To send a message, which is more convenient, e-mail or fax?

A: 電子メールの方がファックスより便利です。
E-mail is more convenient (than fax).

Actions can be compared by using the pattern /V + 方/. In the reply pattern, the first 方 is often deleted.

Q: 日本語は、話す方と書く方とどちら(の方)がむずかしいですか。[39]
As for Japanese, which one is more difficult 山 speaking or writing?

A: 話す(方)より書く方がむずかしいですね。
Writing is more difficult than speaking.

How do you say the following?[40]

(1) Better late than never.
(2) Employing people is better than being employed by people.
(3) Seeing is believing (Seeing it once is better than hearing it 100 times).

8C.4. ～というより vs. ～というと

These two phrases are structurally similar in that both take the particle と and a verb いう. As a result, it is easy to confuse their usage. The comparative phrase ～というより means "rather than saying that."

A: ハン君はゴルフが上手だね。   Mr. Han, you are good at golf, aren't you?
B: というより、今日はついていたんですよ。   Rather, (I should say) I was lucky today.

A: アイコー電気にこの仕事を頼みたいけど、   I would like to ask Aiko Electric to do this
あそこは仕事がおそいからねえ。   job, but their work is slow.
B: というより、あそこは仕事がていねいなんです。   Rather, their work is very meticulous.

In contrast, ～というと？ or its polite counterpart ～とおっしゃると？ is a short-hand expression of ～というと、どういう意味ですか that means "[What do you mean] if you say that?"

A: 例のホテルの予約、キャンセルしてくれません？   Will you cancel my reservation at that hotel?
B: とおっしゃると？   What do you mean?
A: 出張に行かないことになったんです。   It turned out that I won't go on a business trip.

A: やっぱりアメリカに行くことになったよ。   It turned out that I'm going to the U.S. after all.
B: とおっしゃると？   What do you mean?
A: アメリカの子会社から、うちで働かないか   I'm being asked to work for the subsidiary
って言われているんだよ。   company in the U.S.

8C.5. Honorific Passives

The passive forms we learned in this chapter can function as honorific forms of verbs. When the verbs are used honorifically, they lose the passive sense completely.

A: 山田社長が来られたら、すぐお通しして。   When Pres. Yamada has come, send him in immediately.
B: 承知しました。   Certainly.

---

[39] This can be said by using the nominalizer の as in 日本語は、話すのと書くのとどちら(の方)がむずかしいですか。
[40] (1) おそくなっても、しないよりする方がいい。 (Lit. "Doing is preferable to not doing even if you are late.") (2) 人に使われるより人を使う方がいい。 (3) 百回聞くより、一回見る方がいい。 (based on the proverb 百聞は一見にしかず)

A: 忘年会は何時からだった？	What time is the year-end party?
B: 5時からです。部長は何時ごろ行かれますか。	It's at five o'clock. What time are you going?
A: 6時までには行けると思うよ。	I think I can go there at least by six o'clock.
A: 山田課長、おられますか。	Is Section Manager Yamada in?
B: 山田はただ今、会議中でございます。	She is in a meeting right now.

The last form おられます above is an honorific expression, not a humble expression, even though おられる comes from おる (the humble form of いる). (Caution: Don't confuse おられます with the humble form おります.) The honorific forms of the following verbs are typically in the passive honorific form:

いただく → いただかれる↑	どなたにそのペンをいただかれたんですか。[41] From whom did you receive it?
開く → 開かれる↑	パーティを開かれたそうですね。 I heard you had a party, right?

8C.6. Women in corporate Japan

Since the passage of Equal Gender Opportunity Employment Act in 1986, women's status in Japanese companies has been climbing, but they are still behind men in terms of wages. On the average, women earned 65% of that of men in 1996 (Chiezo, 1998, Asahi Shinbun), and men in managerial positions far outnumber women in the same positions (3.9% in 1995, according to the Ministry of Labor's statistics). Opinion polls gathered by Asahi Shinbun reflect the disadvantages felt by women. In 1996, 68% felt women were discriminated against at work (Japan Public Opinion Location Library, or JPOLL[42]). Women also had more difficulty in finding jobs. The primary reason for this is the perception that many women work only until they get married (50%) (1996, JPOLL originally collected by Yomiuri Shinbun). There also is a persistent cultural orientation that approves of women who put priority on their family life (75%) over women who put priority on their work (8%) (1994, JPOLL, originally collected by Asahi Shinbun). The majority of Japanese (64%) feel that some discrimination against women is unavoidable when hiring and promoting employees (1994, JPOLL, originally collected by Jiji Press). On the other hand, a great majority (85%) of respondents believe that there should be more female managers and executives in Corporate Japan. According to the statistics of the Ministry of Health, Labor and Welfare, in 2000, women comprised only 2.2% of all directors (head of a group comprised of more than 20 employees or more than 2 departments) and 4% of all section managers (head of a group comprised of more than 10 employees or more than 2 sections).[43]

---

[41] The passive honorific form of もらう (もらわれる↑) is usually avoided.
[42] Source: http://www.ropercenter.uconn.edu/jpoll/JPOLL.html
[43] Source: Japan Information Network, Statistics (http://jin.jcic.or.jp/stat/index.html)

Exercise 8

Grammar Utilization 8   Name:_____ Sec:_____ #:___

G1. Complete the following chart.

Verb (root)	Passive	Potential	Provisional
使う (tsukaw-): use	使われる	使える	使えば
作る (tsukur-): make			
話す (hanas-): speak			
見る (mi-): look			
書く (kak-): write			
呼ぶ (yob-): call, summon			
待つ (mat-): wait			
泳ぐ (oyog-): swim			
飲む (nom-): drink			

G2. Rewrite the following sentences using a passive verb as shown in the example.

　　　Example:　　メキシコではスペイン語を話している。　→メキシコではスペイン語が話されている。

　　a. 日本ではたくさんの人が読売新聞を読んでいます。
　　　　→

　　b. この会社ではアイビーエムのコンピュータを使っています。
　　　　→

　　c. 日本人はニューヨークをよく知っています。
　　　　→

　　d. ここにあった書類をだれかが捨てました。
　　　　→

　　e. きのうの会議の報告書を新しく書きなおしました。
　　　　→

　　f. あの製品は田中商事が売っています。　(売る: (cv: ur) sell)
　　　　→

G3. Expand the sentences as shown in the example.　Note how the original sentence is changed to a noun phrase.
　　Example:
　　この製品は消費者によって高く評価されている。　(This product is evaluated highly by the consumers.)
　　→この製品の消費者による高い評価について話した。(I spoke about this product's high evaluation by ...)

　　a. 大量生産によってこの製品がコストダウンした。　(This product's prices were lowered by mass production.)
　　　→ _____について話した。
　　　I spoke about the cost reduction of this product by mass production.

Chapter 8: Describing a Company   181

b. エーアイテックによって 新しいソフトが開発された。 (A new software was developed by AI Tech.)

→ _____は遅れている。
The development of the new software by AI Tech is behind the schedule.

c. 宣伝によって市場が拡張された。 (The market was expanded by advertisement.)

→ _____で売り上げが伸びている。
Due to the expansion of this product's market by advertisement, the amount of sales is increasing.

d. 日本ではタムラ商事によってうちの製品が販売されている。 (In Japan, the products are being sold by T.)

→ _____を続けたい。
We would like to continue the sales of our products in Japan by Tamura Trading Company.

G4. Fill in the blanks with appropriate comparative expressions and complete the conversations.

a. A: バスと電車とどちらの方が速く空港に行けますか。

B: 電車_____バス_____速く空港に行けますよ。

b. A: _____便利ですか。
B: いいえ、ファックスより電子メールの方が便利だと思います。

c. A: 定期預金 (certificate of deposit) より普通預金の方が利子 (interest) が高いでしょう？

B: いいえ、普通預金は_____高くありません。

d. A: タクシーで行く方が地下鉄で行くより速いんでしょう？
B: そんなことありませんよ。昼間 (during the day) だったら_____速いですよ。

e. A: アメリカで生産するのと日本で生産する (manufacture) のとどちらが安くできるでしょうか。

B: 円が高ければ、_____でしょう。

f. A: このことは岡田課長に連絡しておかなくてもいいですか。

B: そうですねえ。_____がいいと思いますよ。
... it's better to contact him than not contact him.

G5. Select the best phrase for each conversation.

a. A: いやあ、今朝は困ったよ。
B: (とおっしゃると／とおっしゃるより) 何かあったんですか？
A: 事故で電車が遅れてね。

b. A: 東京工業は仕事が遅いですねえ。
B: (というと／というより) あそこは仕事がていねいですから…
A: ああ、そうなんですか。

c. A: あしたの会議でも結論が出ないそうですね。
   B: (というと／というより)もうあそことの契約は無理のようですよ。
   A: やっぱりね。

d. A: あしたの会議に君は出なくていいよ。
   B: (とおっしゃると／とおっしゃるより)？
   A: 営業部の山田さんが君の代わりに出ることになったそうだから。(Xの代わりに = instead of X)

G6. Complete the following conversations based on the English cues (if given).

a. A: _____どのぐらい時間がかかりましたか。
   In order to write this program
   B: そうですね。毎日、8時間、3人で仕事して3か月ぐらいでしょうか。

b. A: プログラムを_____どちらが速くできるでしょうか。
   Between making the program in house or asking other companies to do it
   B: うちで作る方が速いと思います。

c. A: アメリカにお金を_____どうしたらいいですか。
   B: 電信 (electronic transfer)で送ればいいと思います。

G7. In the following, complete the conversations by paying attention to the politeness levels appropriate for the relationship between A (subordinate) and B (superior). Use the verb in the parenthesis, and change it if necessary.

a. A: 英会話の練習を(はじめる)_____そうですね。
   B: 来月、アメリカに出張することになったから、少しはできるようになっておこうと思ってね。

b. A: 木村部長に支持 (support) して(もらう)_____というのは本当でございますか。
   B: うん。今度の企画案 (plan) については前もって (beforehand) よく説明しておいたからね。

c. A: 会議ではインターネットを使った宣伝 (advertisement) について(説明する)_____んですか？
   B: うん。賛成意見 (opinions in favor) が出て、なかなか (considerably) うまく行ったよ。

d. A: 来年、国際シンポジウムを(開く)_____とお聞きしましたが。
   B: そうなんだ。だから、忙しくなりそうだよ。
   (国際シンポジウムをひらく: hold an international symposium)

e. A: 課長さん、今度の祝賀会で祝辞を(述べる)_____ことになったそうですね。
   (祝賀会:celebration party; 祝辞を述べる:offer one's congratulations)
   B: いやあ、私はスピーチが下手だから、困っているんだよ。

G8. Complete the conversation based on English cues.

Example. A: 元気そうですね。   You look great!
          B: ええ、おかげさまで。   Thank you.

a. A: 今日は_____。   It looks like it's hot today.
   B: いやですねえ、梅雨は。   I don't like the rainy season.

b. A: そのラップトップなかなか_____。   That laptop looks pretty convenient.

    B: _____でしょう？   It looks good, doesn't it?

    A: _____けど、いくらだったの？   It looks expensive, but how much was it?

    B: 17万ぐらいでした。   It was about 170,000 yen.

    A: 私もほしいけど、_____。   I want one, too, but it looks like I can't afford (i.e., buy) it.

c. A: そのお弁当_____。   That box lunch looks delicious!

    B: そうですか。きのうの残り物なんですよ。   Really? It's a leftover from yesterday.

d. A: ハリス君、今日は早く_____。   Mr. Harris looks he wants to leave early today.

    B: ええ、今日、アメリカから御両親がいらっしゃるんだそうです。   Yes, I heard his parents are coming from America today.

e. A: こんなファックスが来ていたよ。いつ来たんだろう。   This fax was here. I wonder when it came.

    B: それ、紙が黄色くなっていて、あんまり_____
_____。   The paper is yellow and doesn't look very new.

f. A: うちの新製品、売れてないようですね。   It seems the new product from our company is not selling well.

    B: ええ、あんまり人気が_____。
（人気：popularity）   Right. It doesn't look very popular. (Lit. "It appears popularity does not exist.")

Reading and Writing 8　　　Name:_____　Sec:_____　#:____

R1. You just met a businessman at a trade show and gave him your business card. He is asking for more information about your company. Create your own company brochure that include information shown below and describe your company. (Before doing this activity, you can look at home pages of some Japanese companies by using a WWW browser, and see how they introduce their own companies in Japanese.)

　　しゃめい
　社名　(company name)

　　そうりつ
　創立　(year established)

　　し ほんきん
　資本金　(capital)

　　うりあげだか
　売上高　(annual sales total)

　　ほんしゃ
　本社　(headquarters)

　　しゅようせいひん
　主要製品　(main products)

Communicative Exercise 8

C1. Role Playing

You are working for a U.S. company as a sales representative. You have just met Mr. Ishii, an executive of a trading company located in Japan. Your ultimate mission is to find out if you can set up a joint venture with Mr. Ishii's company to sell your products in Japan. Today, however, you are simply expected to describe your company to Mr. Ishii. Prepare a 5-minute presentation which includes the following information:

　　　1. Your company's mission (products)
　　　2. Your company's history
　　　3. The reputation of your products in the U.S. and how you achieved that reputation

Your instructor will play the role of Mr. Ishii.

Listening Comprehension 8

Speaker A is the first speaker.   Speaker B is the second speaker.

1. Voc: 第二会議室(だいにかいぎしつ): the second conference room; 第三会議室(だいさんかいぎしつ): the third conference room
   お通(とお)しする: humble form of 通(とお)す "lead someone/something to"

   リーさんとの会議(かいぎ)は どこでしますか。

   どうして そこで するんですか。

2. Voc: エーアイソフト: AI Soft (product name); インテリソフト: Intellisoft (product name)
   文書(ぶんしょ): documents; テクニカル: technical

   ビデオによると、エーアイソフトは普通(ふつう)1時間でどのぐらい翻訳(ほんやく)できますか。

   翻訳(ほんやく)のスピードはどの文書(ぶんしょ)でも同(おな)じですか。

   どんな文書(ぶんしょ)が一番速(はや)く翻訳(ほんやく)できますか。

3. Voc: メリット: (n) merit; エラー: (n) errors

   エーアイソフトが インテリソフトより いいのはどんなところですか。

4. Voc: 消費者(しょうひしゃ)ガイド: consumer guide; 機能(きのう): functions, capabilities; 評価(ひょうか)されている: is evaluated

   エーアイソフトのソフトウェアは消費者ガイドにどのように言われていますか。

5. Voc: 今度(こんど): (n) this time; 電子(でんし)メール: (n) e-mail

   エーアイソフトを使うと、どんなことができるそうですか。

Chapter 9

製品の説明
Describing Products

Priming

Recent trends in new products are to incorporate "high technology" into appliances and goods for family use. Since living quarters are limited in Japan, saving space by combining separate appliances (e.g., TVs and computers) into one light, thin, short, and small (軽薄短小) appliances have always been one of the main goals of consumer electronics companies. Another major trend is toward digitalization of information processing represented by such products as TVs to receive digital broadcast via communication satellites, DVD (digital video disc), virtual pets, and digital camcorders. High technology is also being applied in social welfare. This includes development of housework robots for the physically challenged. Another important trend that reflects the concern among the Japanese include the development of sterilizing and deodorizing goods (e.g., carpets, curtain, bedding, car seats, stuffed animals, etc.). Biotechnology is also impacting Japanese life with its creation of new vegetables (e.g., gene-recombinant soy beans, tomatoes, corn, etc.). With such social trends and concerns in mind, how do you approach Japanese consumers?

Ms. Lewis starts her demonstration of her products.

Conversation 9A: Ms. Lewis demonstrates her product. (1)

1. ル: それでは私どもの新製品、マイクロスター800をご説明させていただきます。
2. 田: ああ、これは立派ですね。
3. ル: これにはアルトロン社で開発されたマイクロプロセッサが搭載してあり、従来のコンピュータの中では処理速度が一番速くなっております。
4. 田: ちょっとためしてみてもいいですか。
5. ル: どうぞ。
....
6. 田: なるほど速いですね。

L: Now, let me explain our new product, Microstar 800.
T: Oh, this looks great.
L: This machine is installed with the microprocessor developed at Ultron, and among the existing computers, it is made in such a way that it has the fastest processing speed.
T: May I give it a try?
L: Please go ahead.
....
T: It certainly is fast!

説明 explanation   明るい bright   開発 development   速度 speed

Vocabulary 9A

ご説明 (n) explanation [honorific]
させて (iv) [causative of する] make/let (someone) do (something. [ご説明させていただきます。↓ "let me explain"]
アルトロン (n) Ultron [name of a company]
開発された (n/v) [passive past of 開発する] was developed
マイクロプロセッサ (n) microprocessor
搭載して (n/v) [て-form of 搭載する "be loaded with

あり (cv: ar) [verb stem of ある] [搭載してある "be deliberately loaded with"]
従来 (n) existing, past
処理速度 (n) processing speed
一番 (n) number one, the most
ためして (cv: tames) [て-form of ためす] try, attempt
みて (vv) [て-form of みる] try (and see)
も (p) also, as well, too   [Vてもいい "may V/is allowed to V"]

Structures 9A

9A.1. Causatives: V-(s)aseru

In this chapter, we will learn causative sentences. This structure expresses the idea that someone causes someone / something to do something. Causative verbs are formed by the following rules:

	VV	Root	saseru	Causative	
see	見る	mi	saseru	見させる	make/let X see
eat	食べる	tabe	saseru	食べさせる	make/let X eat
check	調べる	shirabe	saseru	調べさせる	make/let X check

	CV	Root	aseru	Causative	
use	思う	omow	aseru	思わせる	make/let X think
say	言う	iw	aseru	言わせる	make/let X say
drink	飲む	nom	aseru	飲ませる	make/let X drink
read	読む	yom	aseru	読ませる	make/let X read
wait	待つ	mat	aseru	待たせる	make/let X wait

have, hold	持つ	mot	aseru	持たせる	make/let X hold
speak	話す	hanas	aseru	話させる	make/let X speak
take out; submit	出す	das	aseru	出させる	make/let X take out/submit
call, summon	呼ぶ	yob	aseru	呼ばせる	make/let X call
play	遊ぶ	asob	aseru	遊ばせる	make/let X play
go	行く	ik	aseru	行かせる	make/let X go
write	書く	kak	aseru	書かせる	make/let X
make	作る	tsukur	aseru	作らせる	make/let X make/cook
take	とる	tor	aseru	とらせる	make/let X take
hurry	急ぐ	isog	aseru	急がせる	make/let X hurry
swim	泳ぐ	oyog	aseru	泳がせる	make/let X swim

Irregular V: する → させる   make/let X do
来る → 来させる   make/let X come

In English, we can say "My teacher made me speak Japanese" or "My teacher let me speak Japanese." In the former sense, the person who performs the actual activity is ordered or forced even if he/she may not want to do it. In the latter sense, the person who performs the activity is permitted or allowed because he/she wants to do it. In Japanese, these notions are distinguished by the particles に or を for intransitive verbs (Vi). For transitive verbs (Vt), the distinction must be distinguished from the context because only one particle (に) is used to mark the causee.

Causer	が/は	Causee	に/を			Vi-(a)seru	
私	は	子供	に	(外	で)	遊ばせた。	I let my child play outside.
私	は	子供	を	(外	で)	遊ばせた。	I made my child play outside.
Causer	が/は	Causee	に	Obj	を	Vt-(a)seru	
先生	が	学生	に	本	を	読ませた。	Teacher made/let students read the book.

Study the following sentences:

A: お茶でもいかがですか？   How about some tea?
B: 運転手を待たせているので、またこの次に。   I'm having my driver wait, so maybe next time.

うちでは新入社員に一年間、海外勤務させています。
In our company, we are making our newly-hired employees work overseas for a year.

今、うちの者に英文の見積り書を書かせていますので、もうしばらくお待ちいただけますか？
I'm having my staff write an English contract now, so would you please wait a little while?

The above sentences are all transitive sentences (i.e., the verb takes an object を). When an intransitive verb is used (e.g., natural phenomena), the causee (= agent who performs the action) is marked with either に or を. に implies the sense of "let someone do...," or "grant someone to do...," while を implies the sense of "make someone do." In the following sentences, when に is used, it is probably the case that the causee wanted to do it. In contrast, when を is used, it is not necessarily the case. Thus, "Harris wanted to go, so I had him go for the negotiation." can be said in either of the following:

ハリス君が行きたがっていたから、その交渉はハリス君に行かせた。
ハリス君が行きたがっていたから、その交渉はハリス君を行かせた。

However, "Harris didn't want to go, but I made him go to the negotiation." can be said more naturally with the particle を.

ハリス君は行きたくなさそうでしたが、その交渉はハリス君を行かせた。
？ハリス君は行きたくなさそうでしたが、その交渉はハリス君に行かせた。

9A.2. Causative V + giving and receiving verbs

When a causative is followed by a verb of receiving もらう or いただく, it literally means "I/We receive someone's granting me/us to V." It roughly corresponds to the more natural English expressions of "I'll take the liberty of V-ing" or "I'll be honored to V" or "Let me V." In this case, the sense of coercion is lost, and only the sense of permission remains. Thus, when you are accepting a request or you are volunteering for some action, you can use V(さ)せていただきます.

    それでは私どもの製品をご説明させてください。   Then, let me explain our products.
    それでは私どもの製品をご説明させていただきます。   Then, I'll take the liberty of explaining our products.

    A: 君にこの仕事をしてもらいたいんだがね…   A: I want you to do this job.
    B: 私でできるかどうかわかりませんが、   B: I don't know if I can do it, but I am happy
       よろこんでやらせていただきます。   and honored to do it.

    A: お宅の新製品を送っていただけませんか。   A: Could you send me your new products?
    B: はい、すぐに送らせていただきます。   B: Of course. Let me send it to you right away.

In addition, we can create very polite request forms by combining causative verbs and the verbs of receiving as well as giving. Two typical request patterns are:

    a. 私にV(さ)せていただけませんか。   Can't I/we receive your letting me V?
    b. 私にV(さ)せて下さいませんか。   Won't you give me/us your letting me V?

Note that いただけません is the negative potential form of the receiving verb いただく. In both patterns, the speaker is simultaneously the recipient of the favor and the causee (= agent who performs the action) and the addressee is the giver of the favor as well as the causer. The difference is that in Pattern (a), the implicit subject of the sentence is the recipient ("Can't I/we receive...?") while in Pattern (b), the implicit subject of the sentence is the giver ("Won't you...?"). Note also that in both patterns, the particle following 私 is に, not が.

    私に考えさせて下さい。
    Please let me think about it.

Now, let's see if you are able to distinguish the meanings between the following pairs of sentences:[44]

    (1) 資料を送って下さい。
    (2) 資料を送らせて下さい。

    (3) 資料を送っていただきたいんですが…
    (4) 資料を送らせていただきたいんですが…

    (5) 資料を送っていただけませんか。
    (6) 資料を送らせていただけませんか。

---

[44] (1) Please send us the materials. (2) Please let us send you the materials. (3) I would like you to send us the materials. (4) I would like you to let us send you the materials. (5) Could you send us the materials? (6) Could we have the honor of send you the materials?

9A.3. 〜の中で／のうちで 一番〜

In Chapter 8, we learned to compare two items as in 電子メール(の方)がファックスより便利です。("The side of) e-mail is more convenient than fax.") The following is a typical pattern to compare three or more items (e.g., X is the most... among X, Y, Z, etc.):[45]

Q.	XとYとZ...	(のうち)で (の中)で	どれ	が	一番	Predicate
	電車とバスとタクシー	のうちで	どれ	が	一番	速いですか。
	Among trains, buses, and taxis, which one is the fastest?					
A.			X	が	一番	Predicate
			電車	が	一番	速いです。
	Trains are the fastest.					

Instead of listing specific items, a cover term such as 日本の車の中で, 銀行の中で, etc. may also be used. Question words can be どの N or 何. (どちら cannot be used.) More examples follow.

A: 朝日新聞と毎日新聞と日本経済新聞の中でどれが一番よく読まれていますか？
B: 朝日新聞が一番よく読まれていると思います。
    A: Among Asahi, Mainichi and Nihon Keizai Shinbun, which one is read most widely?
    B: I think Asahi Shinbun is read most widely.

A: 電子メールとファックスと電話のうちでどれが一番便利ですか。
B: 電子メールが一番便利です。
    A: Among e-mail, fax, and telephone, which one is the most convenient?
    B: E-mail is the most convenient.

A: 半導体を作っている会社の中でどの会社が一番マーケットシェアが大きいですか。
B: インテルでしょうね。
    A: Among the companies which make semiconductors, which one has the most market shares?
    B: Probably Intel.

A: この三人の中でどなたが一番話しやすいですか？
B: 一番話しやすいのはXさんで、一番話しにくいのはYさんでしょうね。
    A: Among these three people, who is the easiest person to talk to?
    B: The one who is the easiest to talk to is X and the one who is most difficult to talk to is Y.

Note that (1) Xの方 ("the side of X") cannot be used in this pattern; (2) The phrase particle following the question word is typically one of が, を, or に but not は.

---

[45] 文化ノート Competitive advertisements that compare products made by one company with those of another are commonplace in the U.S., but, in Japan, they were banned until Fair Trade Commission legalized them in the late 1990s. Comparison advertisements are slowly beginning to appear to sell soft drinks, automobiles, and computers, etc. Lately, some advertisers have started to claim their products to be the "number one" product in the industry or within a product category. This new trend emerged as a countermeasure by national-class manufacturers to price-cutting wars waged by discount stores selling private-brand products.

Conversation 9B: Ms. Lewis demonstrates her product. (2)

1. 田： ところで、日本語表示も可能ですか。
2. ル： もちろんです。日本のJIS規格に合わせてありますから、どの日本の人気ソフトでも走らせることができます。
3. 田： インターネットへの接続は？
4. ル： ユーザーが簡単な質問に答えるだけで、あとは自動的に設定されるようになっております。

1. T: By the way, can it also display Japanese?
2. L: Of course. It is made to be compatible with the Japanese JIS standard, so you can run any popular Japanese software.
3. T: How about the connection to Internet?
4. L: Only by the user's answering simple questions, it is made in such a way that the rest is automatically configured.

合う match　自動的 automatic　動く move, transport　答える answer

Vocabulary 9B

表示 (n) display
可能 (な-adj) possible
もちろん (n) of course
JIS (n) Japan Industrial Standard
規格 (n) (industrial) standard, rule, gauge
合わせて (vv: aw) [て-form of causative of 合う] match [something]. [X にあわせる "match X"]
人気 (n) popularity

走らせる (cv: hashir) [causative of 走る] make (something/someone) run or operate
V ことができる (phr) be able to V
接続 (n) connection
質問 (n) questions
答える (vv: kotae) answer, reply
だけ (p) only, just
設定される (n/v) [passive of 設定する] is configured, is set up

Structures 9B

9B.1 S だけ／な-Adj だけ

We learned the use of particle だけ ("only" or "just") following a noun as in 5分だけ待ってください。 "Please wait just five minutes." だけ can also follow a plain-style sentence and means "All X does is..." or "X is just/nothing but..." as shown below:[46]

ミラーさんは見ているだけで、何もしてくれない。　All Mr. Miller does is watch, and he does nothing for me.

A: ハリスさんは日本の歴史についての本をたくさん持っているんですねえ。
B: いや、買っただけで、まだぜんぜん読んでないんです。

Mr. Harris, you have a lot of books on Japanese history.
Oh, all I did was buy them, and I haven't read them at all yet.

A: そのレストランはどうでしたか。
B: あそこは高いだけで、おいしくなかったよ。

How was that restaurant?
That place is just expensive, and it does not taste good.

With a な-adjective sentence /な-adj だ/, the copula だ changes to な.

46　できるだけ〜 is an idiomatic expression meaning "as ... as possible." This is similar to なるべく.

A: お子さん、お元気でいらっしゃいますねえ。　　Your child is very energetic.
B: いや、元気なだけで、ちっとも勉強しないんだ。　That's all she is, and she doesn't study at all.

9B.2.　Alternative potential: 〜することができる

There is an alternative to the potential verb forms we learned in Chapter 1. This one consists of a plain-style non-past verb followed by ことができる.

話すことができる　=　話せる
乗ることができる　=　乗れる
使うことができる　=　使える

ハリスさんは 中国語も話すことができます。
Harris can speak Chinese also.

この機械では一日何台ぐらいの DVD プレーヤーを生産することができますか。
How many DVD players per day can this machine produce?

この製品が JIS をパスすることができるでしょうか？
I wonder if this product can pass the JIS.

The S ことができる structure allows you to combine more than one action that you can do in one statement.

読むことも書くこともできます。 I can both read and write.
(cf. 読めて、書けます。)

9B.3　S ようになっている

The structure /S ようになっている/ expresses the notion "It's made in such a way that S" as in:

他のソフトで書かれたファイルも読めるようになっている。
It's made such that (it) can read files written by other software.

cf. 毎年2回ボーナスがでることになっている。
It's the rule that bonuses will be given twice a year.

The sentence in front of ようになっている can be a passive statement.

このごろのゲーム機はインターネットに自動的に接続されるようになっている。
Game machines these days are made in such a way that they are automatically connect to the Internet.

Conversation 9C: Ms. Lewis demonstrates her product. (3)

1. 田: ええと、これによると、アメリカでは故障した場合の無料電話サービスなどがあるようですが、日本ではどうなっていますか。
2. ル: 日本市場にはまだ進出したばかりで、アフターサービスに関しましてはまだ不十分かと思います。しかし、我が社は「消費者第一」がモットーですので、アフターサービスの方も早急に充実をはかっているところです。

1. T: Well, according to this, in case it breaks down, you have toll-free service, etc. in America, but how is it done in Japan?
2. L: We have just started to make inroads into the Japanese market, so I guess we are still inadequate as far as customer services are concerned. Yet, our company's motto is "consumers first", so we are in the process of completing the area of customer services.

場合 case, situation　無 non- [prefix]　消費者 consumer　消す erase

Vocabulary 9C

～によると (phr) according to
故障した (n/v) [past of 故障する] break down
場合 (n) case, time, occasion
無料 (n) no charge, free
サービス (n) service
進出した (n/v) [past of 進出する] made inroads; advanced
ばかり (n) just, only
アフターサービス (n) customer service; after care [after + service; a phrase coined by Japanese]

関しまして (n/v) [polite て-form of 関する] [X に関しまして "regarding, concerning X"]
不十分 (な-adj) insufficient
第一 (n) the first place
モットー (n) motto, slogan
早急 (な-adj) immediate [早急に "immediately"] 早急 is often mispronounced as そうきゅう.
充実 (n) substantiality, fullness, completion
はかる (cv: hakar) plan, scheme [充実をはかる "plan to complete"]
はかっているところ (phr) in the middle of planning

Structures 9C

9C.1.　S場合

S 場合 means "In case of..." or "In case that..." Plain past or non-past verbs or adjectives may occur before 場合. If a noun precedes 場合, the particle の (or な for な-adjectives) is required.

大丈夫だとは思うけど遅くなる場合は先に会議を始めておいて下さい。
I think I'll be OK, but in case I'm late, please go ahead and start the meeting.

あちらが値引きしてくれない場合はこちらも様子を見た方がいいね。
In case they don't give us a discount, we should also wait and see.

パートの人が残業する場合は残業手当がつきます。
In case part-timers work overtime, they will get overtime pay.

必要な場合は書類は経理に出して下さい。
In case you need it, please submit the document to the payroll department.

9C.2. N ばかり／V てばかり／Non-Past-V ばかり: "N/V for the most part/most of the time"

The N ばかり structure means "mostly N." This is similar to N だけ which means "exclusively N."

テレビゲームばかりしていると、目が悪くなりますよ。
If you play video games most of the time, your eyesight will become bad.

テレビゲームだけしていると、目が悪くなりますよ。
If you only play video games, your eyesight will become bad.

The particle ばかり can also be used after a verb て-form and expresses the excessive nature of the activity referred to by the verb. The V てばかり structure can be followed by です or います.

| V て | ばかり | です／います | X only V; All X does is V. |
| 飲んで | ばかり | です／います | All I do is drink. |

このごろ仕事が終わってから、同僚と飲みに行ってばかりだ (or 行ってばかりいる)。
These days, after work, all I do is go out drinking with my colleagues.

いつもお世話になってばかりで (or なってばかりいて)、申しわけございません。
All I do is receive your help, and I can't thank you enough.

テレビゲームしてばかりいる (or してばかりだ) と、目が悪くなりますよ。
If you keep playing video games all the time, your eyesight will become bad.

The /non-past V ばかり/ pattern is similar in meanings to V てばかり, but it can only be followed by です.

| non-past V | ばかり | です | All X does is V. Or, All that is left to do is V. |
| 飲む | ばかり | です | All I do is drink. |

いくら聞いても、あちらはもう少し待ってほしいと言うばかりなんです。
No matter how much I ask, all they say is that they would like for us to wait for a little more.

準備は全部、終わりましたから、あとは社長の承認を待つばかりです。
The preparations were completed, so all that is left to do is for us to wait for the president's approval.

すぐすると言うばかりで、本当はするつもりはなさそうです。
He keeps saying he's going to do it immediately, but actually he appears to have no intention of doing it.

9C.3. Past-V ばかり: "Just V-ed"

Although the past-V ばかり pattern has a similar structure to the V てばかり pattern explained above, the past-V ばかり pattern has an entirely different meaning. It means "(Someone/Something) just V-ed." This is similar to the past-V ところ pattern explained in the next section.

| Past V | ばかり | です | have just done... |
| 飲んだ | ばかり | です | I have just drunk it. |

A: どうもお待たせいたしました。
B: いえいえ、私達も今、着いたばかりですから。
   A: Sorry to have kept you waiting.
   B: Oh, no, we have just arrived, too.

A: あのコンピュータ、どう思う？
B: はあ。さっきちょっと使ったばかりなので、まだはっきりは申し上げられないんです。
　A: What do you think about that computer?
　B: Well, I just used it a while ago, so I can't speak definitely about it.

A: ハンさん、お昼食べに行かない？
B: あ、今、食べてきたばかりなんです。
　A: Would you like to go have lunch?
　B: Oh, I just had lunch.

9C.4. Non-Past V ところ／Past V ところ／V ているところ

The expression S ところです can refer to a point in time when something is about to happen, or is happening, or has just happened. This expression can also be used to describe a scene shown in photos, videos, etc.

Non-Past V	ところ	be about to V
Past V	ところ	have just V-ed
V ている	ところ	be in the middle of V-ing

Compare the following statements.

今、電話をかけるところです。　　　　Right now, [it's the time when] I'm about to make a phone call.
今、電話をかけたところです。　　　　Right now, [it's the time when] I've just made a phone call.
今、電話をかけているところです。　Right now, [it's the time when] I'm making a phone call.

These expressions are often used when someone talks about developing stories.

A: 今朝のニュース、ご覧になりましたか？　　　A: Did you see this morning's news?
B: それを今、新聞で読んでいるところなんだけど、　B: I'm reading it right now in the newspaper.
　これはちょっとひどいね。　　　　　　　　　　　This is terrible.

A: ロボティックスジャパンの新製品、おもしろいですね。　A: Robotics Japan's new product is interesting.
B: ぼくもさっきウェブで見たところなんだけど、　　　　B: I just saw it on the Web a while ago,
　あれはヒットするだろうね。　　　　　　　　　　　　but it'll probably be a hit.

The S ところを見る structure expresses that someone witnesses the scene in which S is about to happen, or S is happening, or S has just happened.

　田中さんがお客さんと会っているところを見ました。　I saw Ms. Tanaka meeting a client.

The /S ところに来る/ structure expresses the notion that someone arrives just when S is about to happen, is happening, or has happened.

電話をしているところに、田中さんが来ました。
When I was on the phone, ...

電話をしたところに、田中さんが来ました。
When I just finished a phone call, ...

電話をしようとしているところに、田中さんが来ました。
When I was about to make a phone call, ...

The last expression 電話をしようとしているところ above consists of 電話をしよう (volitional V) + と + している + ところ meaning "to be about to make a phone call" or "to try to make a phone call."

Chapter 9: Describing Products   197

Exercise 9

Grammar Utilization 9   Name:_____ Sec:_____ #:____

G1. Fill in the blanks by using the appropriate ところ expression.   (#9 & #10 have no pictures.)

1. 田中さんは_____です。

2. 田中さんは今_____です。

3. 田中さんは_____です。

4. ブラウンさんは今_____です。

5. ブラウンさんは今_____です。

6. ブラウンさん は_____ところです。

7. ブラウンさんが_____ところを_____。

8. 部長と課長_____ところにブラウンさんは_____。

9. A: これからお昼(ひる)ごはんを_____ですから、いっしょに食べませんか？
   B: ああ、ごいっしょしてもいいんですか。
   A: どうぞ。

10. A: お待たせしました。ずっと待っていらっしゃったんですか。
    B: いいえ、ぼくも今_____。 (I just got here.)

G2. Change the verbs below into the causative form.

a. 見る _____ g. 遊ぶ _____
b. する _____ h. 飲む _____
c. 買う _____ i. 行く _____
d. 作る _____ j. 話す _____
e. 聞く _____ k. 来る _____
f. 帰る _____ l. やめる _____

G3. Fill in the blanks using the appropriate causative verb and complete the conversations. In some cases, you need to combine the causative verb with a verb of giving or receiving and change the form appropriately.

a. A: お急ぎなら、今すぐタイプいたしますが。 B: いや、君はほかにやることがあるだろう。だれかほかの ＿＿＿＿＿＿＿＿に＿＿＿＿＿＿＿＿方がいいんじゃないか。	A: If you are in a hurry, I'll type it right now. B: No, you probably have other things to do. It's better to let someone else do it for you.
b. A: 私の意見 (opinion) を＿＿＿＿＿＿＿＿下さいませんか。 B: もちろんだよ。	A: May I ask you to allow me to say my opinion? B: Of course.
c. A: 田中さん、お昼をごいっしょしませんか。 B: せっかくですけど、タクシーを＿＿＿＿＿＿おりますので、また (again, next time) にさせて下さい。	A: Mr. Tanaka, won't you join us for lunch? B: Thank you, but I'm keeping the taxi waiting, so allow me to take a rain check.
d. A: この件について、＿＿＿＿＿＿＿＿たいんですが、よろしいでしょうか。 B: どうぞ、どうぞ。	A: I would like you to let us consult with you on this matter. Is it all right? B: Yes, of course.
e. A: 会議室を＿＿＿＿＿＿＿＿てもよろしいでしょうか。 B: 申しわけございませんが、今、会議中なので…	A: Is it all right if I ask you to allow us to use the conference room? B: I'm sorry, but there's a meeting going on right now, so...
f. A: 3時までにこれを＿＿＿＿＿＿＿＿ない？ B: わかりました。	A: Will you finish (lit. "make it end") this by three o'clock? B: Certainly.
g. A: 明日は、2時半に＿＿＿＿＿＿＿＿ないでしょうか。 B: いいですけど、どうしてですか。 A: 実は、弟の結婚式に呼ばれてまして…	A: Could I ask you to let me leave at 2:30 tomorrow? B: Of course, but why? A: The fact of the matter is I'm invited to my younger brother's wedding.

Chapter 9: Describing Products   199

G4. Fill in the blank with appropriate phrases of comparison and complete the conversations.

a. A: 日本語____英語____中国語_____話すことができますか。
    B: その三つだったら、英語でしょうかねえ。

b. A: お酒_____ビール_____よく飲まれていますか。

    B: 夏はお酒_____ビールほど_____でしょうね。(夏: summer)

c. A: Eメールとファックスと電話のうちでどれが一番便利ですか。

    B: Eメール_____ファックスや電話_____便利です。

d. A: 「根回し」というのはしても、しなくてもいいものですか。(根回し: groundwork to get support)

    B: いや、_____より_____がいいですよ。

e. A: タクシーで_____レンタカーで_____バスで_____一番安いですか。

    B: _____一番安いでしょうね。

G5. Select the appropriate phrases for the blanks from the box below.   Some phrases may be used more than once.

a. A: あの新しいソフト使ってみた？

    B: さっきインストールした (installed)_____だから、まだ使ってないんです。

b. A: この製品のアフターサービスは？

    B: 故障した_____は、無料電話サービスがございます。

c. A: 明日の朝の9時までにこの資料を150部コピーする_____ができますか。
    B: やってみましょう。

d. A: 例の見積書はできた？

    B: 今、プリントしている_____ですから、少々、お待ち下さい。

e. A: 今朝の新聞_____、新しい日本の首相 ("prime minister") が決まったそうですね。

    B: その記事 ("newspaper article")、私も今、読んだ_____です。

f. A: どうもお待たせいたしまして、申し訳ございません。

    B: いえいえ、私も今、終わった_____ですから。

g. A: あのアルバイトの学生はタイプするのが速いですねえ。

    B: そうですけど、速い_____で、間違い (errors) が多いんですよ。

h.　A: どうもお急ぎ ("in a hurry") の＿＿＿＿＿＿＿＿＿＿＿＿＿＿＿、すみません。
　　B: いえいえ、今日はひまですから。

i.　A: デジタルカメラってどうしてフィルムがなくても写真がとれるんですか。
　　B: 写真をJPEGファイルにしてメモリーチップに入れておける＿＿＿＿＿＿なっているからです。

j.　A: あちらが値引きしてくれない＿＿＿＿＿＿＿＿＿＿＿は、契約はとれませんねえ。
　　B: そうならなければ、いいですねえ。

k.　A: 新しいVTRの使い方、覚えましたか。(覚える: memorize)
　　B: ええ、でも説明書 ("manual") 一回読んだ＿＿＿＿＿＿＿＿じゃ、覚えられませんね。

| ばかり　ところ　ばあい　だけ　ように　によると　こと |

Reading and Writing 9

Name:_____ Sec:_____ #:____

R1. Read the following letter and answer the questions below.

Letter	Vocabulary
平成14年8月10日 ご担当者各位 　　　　新製品マイクロスター商品説明会のお知らせ 拝啓　時下ますますご清栄のこととお慶び申し上げます。 　さて、このたび弊社では新製品マイクロスターを来る11月1日より発売する運びとなりました。本製品はまったく新しいOSと超高速のマイクロプロセッサーを搭載した画期的な商品でございます。 　つきましては、それに先立ちまして、下記の通り商品説明会を実施いたしますので、ぜひご参加下さいますよう、ご案内申し上げます。 　なお、新製品マイクロスターのカタログを同封させていただきましたので、ご高覧下さい。 　　　　　　　　　　　　　　　　　　　　　　　敬具 　　　　　　　　　　　記 　日時　平成14年9月15日（金）午後1時〜5時 　会場　エキスポプラザ3Fショールーム 　　　（添付資料新製品マイクロスターカタログ一式） 　　　　　　　　　　　　　　　　　　　　　　　以上	ご担当者↑ (n) person(s) in charge 各位 (n) title for everyone 商品説明会 (n) product introduction expo. 時下 (n) at this time of the year ご清栄のこととお慶び申し上げます↓ (phr) I congratulate your prosperity 弊社↓ (n) our company 来る (phr) this coming より (p) from [= から] 発売する (v) start selling 運びとなりました (phr) we are planning to... 本製品 (n) this product まったく (adv) completely; utterly 超高速 (n) super fast 画期的な (な-adj) epoch-making つきましては (con) thus; and so 先立ちまして (phr) prior to 下記の通り (phr) as shown below 実施いたします↓ (v) to carry out, enforce ぜひ (adv) by all means ご参加下さい↑ (v) please participate ご案内 (n) invitation, notice, guide なお (con) in addition カタログ (n) catalogue 同封させていただきました (v) I have enclosed ご高覧下さい↑ (v) please look (at) 記 (n) notes 日時 (n) date and time 会場 (n) place of the meeting (i.e., expo) エキスポプラザ (n) Expo Plaza ショールーム (n) showroom 添付 (n) attachment [添付する: to attach] 一式 (n) a complete set

1. Identify the title of the upcoming event and mark it "Event."

2. Identify the brief product introduction and mark it "Product."

3. Identify two parts that refer to the attachment and mark them "Attachment."

4. Identify the time and location of the event and mark them "Time & Location."

5. Match the written expressions on the left with more conversational expressions on the right.

a._____ 時下(じか)

b._____ このたび

c._____ ご担当者各位(たんとうしゃかくい)

d._____ 発売(はつばい)する運(はこ)びとなりました

e._____ つきましては

f._____ ご高覧(こうらん)下さい

g._____ 下記(かき)の通(とお)り

h._____ なお

1. それについて

2. それから

3. ご覧(らん)下さい

4. 下の方(ほう)に書いてありますように

5. 発売(はつばい)することになりました

6. 今度(こんど)

7. この季節(きせつ) (season)

8. ご担当(たんとう)の皆様(みなさま)

Communicative Exercise 9

C1. Role Playing

#1: You are working for a U.S. company as a sales representative. Today, you have visited Mr. Ishii's company to demonstrate your product. Present at least three advantages of your product (performance, quality, price, service, etc.) as compared with products sold by other companies. Use visual aids if necessary. Your instructor will play the role of Mr. Ishii.

#2: Create a 3-minute TV commercial ("informercial") about an existing (or highly conceivable) product or service in which you demonstrate your knowledge and skills in Japanese based on the structures and vocabulary learned so far. You can optionally team up with a classmate and create a conversation that demonstrates the virtues of your product or service.

You will be evaluated on the basis of clarity and accuracy of your messages, NOT on the basis of complexity or novelty of your product or service. You are NOT allowed to read transcripts during your presentation. Choose your product or service carefully. Can you describe it by using the words that you have already learned in this textbook? If it requires a large number of new words, it may be the wrong product.

In your presentation, you must have a BEFORE-and-AFTER comparison. First, describe a problem, then the solution (i.e., your product or service), followed by the results of using your product or service. For example:

BEFORE: The first minute shows a housewife answering a phone call. It is a sales call promoting a product that she does not need.

PRODUCT/SERVICE: The next two minutes describe an anti-solicitation device. "Are you bothered by too many of these phone calls? If so, this is the telephone for you. If you push this button, you will hear a door chime. If you push this button, you will hear clicks that sound like an in-coming call. If you push this button, you will hear a man's voice saying 'Cut it out!'."

AFTER: The last minute shows the same wife answering another sales phone call. This time, she successfully avoids the solicitation call.

Prepare appropriate visual aids that accompany your presentation. Submit a rough draft of the presentation prior to your presentation and get feedback. Also, prepare a vocabulary list showing new words that you use in the presentation. When ready, also prepare 5 questions (in English) about your presentation to be answered by your audience on the day of your presentation.

Listening Comprehension 9   Name:_____ Sec:_____ #:____

Speaker A is the first speaker.   Speaker B is the second speaker.

1. Voc: プリントする: (v) to print
   Aさんは何をさせてもらいたいんですか。

2. Voc: 会話(かいわ): conversation
   　　a. Bさんは今、お昼ご飯を食べたばかりです。
   　　b. Bさんはまだ、仕事をしているところです。
   　　c. Bさんはこれから、会議に行くところです。
   　　d. Bさんは今、仕事が終わったところです。
   Aさんは、この会話の前に何をしたんですか。

3. Voc: 案内(あんない)する: (v) to guide
   ブラウンさん(A)は何をさせてもらいたいんですか。どうしてですか。

4. Voc: タイプする: (v) to type
   Bさんは今から何をするところですか。

   田中さん(A)はいつ帰りますか。

5. Voc: アクション: (n) action
   Aさんの奥(おく)さんは何をしているところですか。

   Bさんはどんなビデオがいいと言いましたか。どうしてそれがいいんですか。

6. Voc: 以内(いない): (n) within, inside; 部品代(ぶひんだい): (n) the cost of parts
   消費者(しょうひしゃ)がプリンタを買ったあと、どんなアフターサービスがありますか。

7. Voc: モデム: modem; つないでいる: have connected; ケーブル: cable; 始(はじ)めた: began
   ウェブページ: Web pages; 気持(きも)ちがいい: feels good
   Aさんは今、何を使ってインターネットにつないでいますか。

   Bさんは今、何を始(はじ)めたところですか。それはどうですか。

Chapter 10

価格(かかく)の交渉(こうしょう)
Negotiating Prices

Priming

You have just described your products. The Japanese business counterpart appears to be interested in marketing them. Now, it is time to negotiate the prices for the deal. You probably have some flexibility on the pricing structure depending on the size of the order.

Conversation 10A: Ms. Lewis negotiates prices. (1)

1. 田: ところで、価格の方はどうなんですか。
2. ル: はい、アメリカの方では一台1500ドルの卸値で取り引きいたしておりますが。
3. 田: それはモニターつきの値段ですか。
4. ル: いいえ、それは別になっておりまして、モニターをつけますと、全部で1800ドルでございます。
5. 田: 注文する台数によって値引きは可能ですか。
6. ル: はい。100台ですと、10%値引きさせていただいておりますし、1000台ですと、20%の値引きになります。

1. T: By the way, what is the price of this product?
2. L: Well, in the U.S., we sell each unit for $1,500 wholesale.
3. T: Does that price include the monitor?
4. L: No, the monitor is excluded, so if you include it, it would be $1,800 in total.
5. T: Can you give us a discount depending on the number of units we order?
6. L: Of course. If you order 100 units, we will give you a 10% discount [Lit., "we will receive the honor of giving you..."], and if 1,000 units (are ordered), a 20% discount will be applied.

価格 (カカク) price　台 (ダイ) counter for machines　別 (ベツ) separate　全部 (ゼンブ) all, everything

Vocabulary 10A

ところで (con) by the way
価格 (n) price
台 (unit) [counter for machines, cars, etc.]
卸値 (n) whole sale price
モニターつき (n) with a monitor [つき is V-stem of Vi つく "(something) is attached" or "is switched on"]
別 (n) being separated; excluded; apart from. [べつに + negative 'not particularly']

つけます (vv: tsuke) to attach, switch on
注文する (n/v) place an order
台数 (n) quantity of objects counted by this unit
によって (phr) depending on
値引き (n) price reduction, discount
値引きさせて (n/v) [causative of 値引きして] let us discount
し (con) and (furthermore)

Structures 10A

10A.1.　N つき

つき is the stem of the verb つきます meaning "is attached." The /Noun + つき/ structure means "with N" or "including N." See other examples of N つき:

このアパートはバス・トイレつきです。　This apartment is equipped with a bathroom and a toilet.
電話つきのスポーツカーがほしい。　I want a sports car with a car phone.

A: あのユースホステルは一泊八千円です。　That youth hostel costs ¥8000 per night.
B: それは食事つきですか。　Is that with a meal?

10A.2.　N によって

The phrase N によって means "depending on N."

人によって、好きなものがちがいます。
Depending on the person, his/her favorite things are different.

ものによって、値引きできるものとできないものがございます。
Depending on the item, we can give you a discount.   For some items we can't offer a discount.

あのプロジェクトは 新聞に（よって）高く評価されている。
That project is evaluated highly by newspapers.

Do not confuse this structure with similar structures N によって ("by N" in the passive construction) or N によると ("according to N").

あの公共事業は新聞によって評価が違います。
Depending on the newspapers, the evaluation of that public works is different.

朝日新聞によると、あのプロジェクトは人々に（よって）高く評価されている。
According to Asahi Newspaper, that project is evaluated highly by the people.

10A.3.　S1 し、S2

The connective し means "and further more." This connective combines two (or more) sentences together. The sentences combined by し must be of similar type (e.g., both good or both bad, etc.). The sentences can be plain or polite. As long as the sentences are of similar type, the connected sentences do not have any sequential implication.

国内での販売は青木君が担当だし、海外での販売はミラー君が担当です。
Mr. Aoki is in charge of domestic sales, and Mr. Miller is in charge of overseas sales.

ハン君は英語もできますし、中国語もできます。
Han can speak English and, what's more, he speaks Chinese.

ハン君、大蔵商事との契約もとれたし、どこか飲みに行きませんか？
Mr. Han, we were able to get a contract from Okura Shoji, so shall we go have a drink?

白石ホテルは駅に近いし、部屋が安いから、よく泊まります。
Shiraishi Hotel is close to the station, and its rooms are cheap, so I stay there very often.

Compare the previous sentence with the sentence below.

大山ホテルは駅に近いけれど、部屋が高いから、あまり泊まりません。
Oyama Hotel is close to the station, but its rooms are expensive, so I don't stay there very often.

As Ms. Lewis continues her presentation, she encounters Mr. Tanaka's remark そうですね. This phrase literally means "Yes" or "That's right." However, she knows from her experience that it can also mean a simple hesitation "Well..." In negotiation situations, one must watch out for various indirect expressions such as 検討します ("We will discuss the matter") or 善処します ("We will do our best"). Japanese use these uncommitted expressions to avoid outright rejection. These expressions often signal a continued need for negotiation, not a statement of acceptance.

Conversation 10B: Ms. Lewis negotiates prices. (2)

1. 田: そうですか。ざっと5％のディスカウントとして計算すると、卸値が1710ドル、うちのマージンを2割として、2052ドルですね。それに宣伝費を省くわけにもいかないですから、小売値がこのぐらいになりますね。	1. T: I see. When I calculate roughly with the assumption of a 5% discount, the wholesale price would be around $1710. By setting our margin at 20%, it will be $2052. Besides, we can't really omit the advertising costs, so the retail price would be like this.

(Tanaka shows Lewis his figures.)

2. ル: そうですね。いかがなものでしょうか。
3. 田: そうですね。
4. ル: あのう、何でしたら、もう少し安くできるかどうか本社に問い合わせてみましょうか。
5. 田: ええ、いくらの値引きになるか知りたいんで、見積書をお願いします。
6. ル: かしこまりました。
7. 田: それでは、ちょっと休憩ということにしましょうか。

(At the end of the day's negotiation)

8. ル: 今日はお忙しいところ、どうもありがとうございました。
9. 田: いや、わざわざどうも。

(Tanaka shows Lewis his figures.)

2. L: Right. What do you think? (Lit. "How is it?")
3. T: Well...
4. L: Ummm... if you would like me to, shall I ask headquarters and see if we can give you more discount?
5. T: Yes, please. I would like to know how much of a discount (I could receive), so could you give me an estimate?
6. L: Certainly.
7. T: Then let's take a little break.

(At the end of the day's negotiation)

8. L: I appreciate (your time) while you are busy today.
9. T: You are more than welcome.

少し a little   問う inquire   知る get to know   割 10%

Vocabulary 10B

ざっと (adv) roughly
ディスカウント (n) discount
として (p) as, for
計算する (n/v) to calculate
マージン (n) margin
2割 (num) 20%. [1割 = 10%]
それに (con) furthermore, on top of that
省く (cv: habuk) to omit, save, curtail, economize
わけ (n) reason, sense, situation, case. [V わけにもいかない "can't really even V"]
小売値 (n) retail price
このぐらい (phr) this much
いかがなもの (phr) What kind of things? How about it?

何でしたら (phr) [でしたら is the polite form of だったら.] If it's what (you may call it)
かどうか (phr) [embedded Yes-No question: 〜かどうか "whether or not..."]
本社 (n) main office; headquarter
問い合わせて (vv: toiawase) [て-form of といあわせる] inquire; ask
知りたい (cv: sir) [たい form of しる] want to know
んで (con) [=ので] so, therefore
休憩 (n) break, rest
〜ということにしましょう (phr) Let's decide on what you call ...
わざわざ (adv) intentionally

Structures 10B

10B.1. N として

The phrase N として means "as N" or "in the capacity of N."

ハリスさんはセールスマンとして働いています。   Mr. Harris works as a salesman.

宣伝費としてこのくらいとっておきましょう。   Let's set aside this much as advertising costs.

このコンピュータはワープロとして使っています。   I am using this computer as a word processor.

10B.2. 〜わけにはいかない／〜わけにもいかない **"Can't really (even) V"**

The phrase 〜わけにはいかない is used to offer one's submission to the circumstances that do not allow him/her to choose certain course of actions. For example, one might say 会社をやめたくても、やめるわけにはいかない。 ("Even if I would like to quit the company, I can't really quit.") when one would like to quit the company, but the circumstance does not allow him/her to do so.

A: まだ、帰らないんですか。   You are not leaving yet?
B: ええ、田中部長から頼まれた仕事が終わるまでは、   Right. I can't really leave until I finish the work
　　帰るわけにはいかないんです。   I was asked to do by Division Manager Tanaka.

The phrase 〜わけにもいかない refers to even fewer choices of actions. For example、やめるわけにもいかない。 ("I can't really even quit.") is used when the circumstances do not even allow one to quit, in addition to not allowing other alternatives. Additional examples follow.

A: ゆうべ、鈴木さんと飲みに行ったそうですね。   I heard you went out drinking with Mr. S. last night.
B: ええ、一杯飲みに行こうって言われて、   Yes. I was asked to go for a drink,
　　断るわけにもいかなくて…   and I couldn't really even refuse...

Conversation 10C: Mr. Tanaka anticipates oppositions. (1)

1. 田: ハリス君、マイクロスター800、どう思うかね？
2. ハ: スピードが速いし、使い方も簡単なので、ヒット商品になるでしょうね。あとは価格の問題ですね。
3. 田: うん、そうなんだ。今回の件に関しては石野財務部長が価格に対して悲観的だからねえ。
4. ハ: 私から、直接ルイスさんに、価格次第ではこちらも契約に乗り気だというふうに伝えておきましょうか。
5. 田: うん、それを文書で送ってくれないか。
6. ハ: わかりました。

1. T: Mr. Harris, what do you think of the computer from Digital Machine?
2. H: It's fast and the operation is simple, so I think it will be a hit product. The rest is the problem of their prices.
3. T: Right. In relation to this matter, Finance Div. Mgr. Ishino is pessimistic about their price.
4. H: Shall I directly tell Ms. Lewis that we are willing to approve the contract depending on the prices?
5. T: Yes, will you send it in writing?
6. H: Certainly.

直接 (チョクセツ) directly　商品 (ショウヒン) merchandise　問題 (モンダイ) problem　乗る (の) ride　文書 (ブンショ) writing, text

---

Vocabulary 10C

かね (p) [blunt informal question; spoken by a superior to his/her subordinate prompting for a frank answer; どう思うかね "What do you think?"]
ヒット商品 (n) hit commercial product
問題 (n) problem
今回 (n) this time. [今回の件 "this matter"]
関して (n/v) is related to; with regard to [Xに関して "with regard to X"]

石野 (n) Ishino [family name]
財務部長 (n) finance division manager
対して (n/v) [て-form of 対する] oppose, against [Xに対して "toward X" or "against X"]
悲観的 (な-adj) pessimistic
● 楽観的 (な-adj) optimistic
直接 (n) direct

次第 (n) dependence [X しだい "is up to X; depending on X"]
乗り気 (n) willingness
というふうに (phr) in such a way that..., to the effect that...

伝えて (vv: tsutae) [て-form of 伝える "communicate"]
文書 (n) writing, text

Structures 10C

10C.1. N に関して／N に対して

The N に関して ("with regard to N") structure is interchangeable with N について ("about N").

ルイスさんの提案に関して、どう思いますか。　＝ルイスさんの提案について、どう思いますか。
What do you think about Ms. Lewis' proposal?

The N に対して ("toward N") structure is often used in opinion polling or voting.

ルイスさんの提案に対して、賛成の方は手を上げて下さい。
Toward Ms. Lewis' proposal, those who agree, please raise your hand.

ルイスさんの提案に対して、反対の方はいませんか。
Toward Ms. Lewis' proposal, is there anyone who opposes?

10C.2. N次第

The structure N次第 means "(is) up to N" or "entirely depending on N." Do not confuse this with other 次第 structures such as V-past 次第 (a turn of events) and V-stem 次第 ("as soon as V-ing").

(1) (be) up to N/entirely depending on N: [N次第]

価格次第で注文するかどうかを決めます。
We will decide whether or not we will order them entirely depending on the price.

Compare this to によって:

価格によって注文台数が違います。
The number of (units) in an order will vary depending on the price.

(2) The way it turns out: [V-plain 次第]

大事故があったと聞いて、急いで来た次第です。
I heard that there was a big accident, so this led me to come here quickly.

(3) As soon as: [V-stem 次第]

田中が帰り次第、お電話します。
I will call you as soon as Tanaka returns.

10C.3. X に乗り気だ

The structure X に乗り気だ expresses one's willingness toward X. There are numerous expressions similar to X に乗り気だ. One of them is X に積極的だ ("have a positive attitude to X"). Both 乗り気 and 積極的 structures use the same particle に or its longer equivalent X に対して ("toward X") or X について ("about X").

うちは代理店契約に（対して／ついて）乗り気です。
We have a willingness toward the sales agency contract.

うちは代理店契約に（対して／ついて）積極的です。
We have a positive attitude to the sales agency contract.

我が社は日本の会社と手を結ぶことに乗り気だ。
Our company is willing to cooperate with a Japanese company.

Milder form of this expressions include 前向きに検討する ("discuss [the matter] with a positive attitude") and 興味がある ("is interested in X") as shown below:

この件に（ついて）前向きに検討させていただきます。
Let us discuss this matter.

うちは代理店契約に（ついて）興味があります。
We are interested in the sales agency contract.

アメリカの大学に留学することに（ついて）興味があります。
I'm interested in studying abroad at a university in the U.S.

10C.4. N ふうの N／X ふうに V／X というふうに

The word ふう literally represents "air" or "wind," and it is a な-adjective that expresses likelihood of something. Neither ふう nor よう can be used by itself. It requires a modifier. ふう can directly follow a noun while よう requires the particle の. When ふう follows a noun, it forms a compound noun. (N ふう is a noun, not a な-adjective.)

日本人ふうの人	a person who is likely to be a Japanese
日本人のような人	a person who seems like a Japanese
日本ふうのレストラン	a restaurant likely to be a Japanese restaurant
vs.	
日本のレストラン	a Japanese restaurant

If ふう follows こんな-series of demonstrative adjective, it behaves like a な-adjective.

こんなふうなペン、ありますか。	Do you have this kind of pen?
＝こんなペン、ありますか。	
＝このようなペン、ありますか。	[more formal]
そんなふうに言って下さい。	Please say it like that.
＝そのように言って下さい。	[more formal]

あんなふうになりたい。　　　　　I want to become like that.
= あのようになりたい　　　　　　[more formal]

The colloquial expression /X というふうに/ can be used when one would like to be vague about something.

もっと安くできないかというふうにお願いした。
I asked them to the effect that whether they can lower the prices.

cf. もっと安くできないかとお願いした。
I asked them whether they can lower the prices.

Unlike the phrase ように, the phrase ふうに cannot follow a regular verb expression.

* 契約書に書いてあるふうに、払い戻しはできません。　　[Ungrammatical]
　契約書に書いてあるように、払い戻しはできません。
　As written in the contract, we cannot refund it.

Chapter 10: Negotiating Prices   213

Exercise 10

Grammar Utilization 10   Name:_____ Sec:_____ #:____

G1. Select the best phrase for each of the blanks from the box below.

a. ブラウンさんは保険のセールスマン_____10年間働いています。(保険: insurance)

b. LCDモニターとキーボード_____の値段は一台2500ドルです。

c. 注文の台数_____では、20％以上の値引きが可能です。(以上: equal to or more than)

d. デジタルマシンと販売提携すること_____反対意見がでた。
 (販売提携: sales cooperation; 反対意見: opposing opinions)

e. うちのマージンを10％_____もう一度計算してみてください。

f. この電池は使い方_____で、1年でも2年でも使えます。(電池: battery)

g. 川田課長は商品の価格_____あまり楽観的じゃありません。(楽観的: optimistic)

h. 日本への石油の輸入量は年_____違います。(石油: oil; 輸入量: amount of import)

i. この問題_____は、ハリスさんに聞いて下さい。

| によって | として | にかんして | にたいして | つき | しだい |

G2. The following is a conversation between Ms. Miller and Mr. Yamamoto. Fill in the blanks below by selecting the appropriate connective expressions in the box.

ミラー： 部長、今度のゴールデンウィークはどうなさるんですか？
山本： 家族みんなで、グアムに行こうかと思っているんだよ。

ミラー： 家族サービスというわけですね。
山本： うん。せっかくの休みだ_____、いつもは子供と遊ぶひまがない_____、たまには(occasionally)
 いいと思ってね。ミラー君は？
ミラー： 私は5月7日からロスの国際会議に出る_____、休みの間にそのためのペーパーを
 書い_____、旅行 (travel) のための買物をし_____するつもりです。
山本： せっかくの休み_____、たいへんだねえ。
ミラー： そうですけど、ペーパーが早めにでき_____、私もどこかへ行くつもりです。

| ので | しだい | し | から | なのに | たり |

G3. Complete the following statements by using わけにはいかない or わけにもいかない.

1. 宣伝をするとお金がかかりますが、しないと、売れませんから、_____

 _____。(売れません: can't sell)

2. 今、みんな忙しいですから、少しぐらい疲れたからと言って、自分だけ＿＿＿＿＿＿＿＿＿＿＿＿＿＿
   ＿＿＿＿＿＿＿＿＿＿＿＿＿＿＿＿＿＿＿＿。(疲れた: got tired; 自分: I, oneself)

3. 仕事がきついとか、おもしろくないとか言って、＿＿＿＿＿＿＿＿＿＿＿＿＿＿＿＿＿＿＿＿＿＿＿
   ＿＿＿＿＿＿＿＿＿＿＿＿＿＿＿＿＿＿＿。(きつい: hard)

4. ていねいに仕事をすると、時間がかかりますし、＿＿＿＿＿＿＿＿＿＿＿＿＿＿＿＿＿＿＿＿＿＿＿し、
   どうしたらいいでしょうか。(ていねいに: carefully)

5. 5時になっても、ほかの同僚が働いていれば、帰りたくても＿＿＿＿＿＿＿＿＿＿＿＿＿＿＿＿＿＿
   ＿＿＿＿＿＿＿＿＿＿＿＿＿＿＿＿＿＿＿＿＿＿＿＿＿。(ほかの: other; 同僚: colleagues)

6. 日本でコンピュータを売ることにいくら乗り気でも、日本語のユーザーマニュアルがなければ
   ＿＿＿＿＿＿＿＿＿＿＿＿＿＿＿＿＿＿＿＿＿＿＿＿＿＿＿＿。(ユーザーマニュアル: user's manual)

7. 部長に飲みに行こうって言われたら、お酒が好きじゃなくても、おつきあいがあるから、
   ＿＿＿＿＿＿＿＿＿＿＿＿＿＿＿＿＿＿＿＿＿＿＿＿＿＿＿＿＿＿＿＿。

G4. Complete B's responses below by using the structures (こんなふうな N or X ふうに V or X というふうに or N1 ふうの N2) according to the English cues.

1. A: 「お好み焼き」ってどんな食べ物ですか。
   B: 一言で言うと、＿＿＿＿＿＿＿＿＿＿＿＿＿＿＿＿作ったキーシュでしょうね。
   To say it in short, it's a quiche made in the Japanese style.

2. A: ジョブズさんは何ておっしゃっていましたか。
   B: だれでも簡単に使えるソフトを作りたい＿＿＿＿＿＿＿＿＿＿＿＿＿＿＿おっしゃっていました。
   He was saying to the effect that he would like to make software that anyone can use with ease.

3. A: どんな家に住みたいですか。
   B: 私は＿＿＿＿＿＿＿＿＿＿＿家より＿＿＿＿＿＿＿＿＿＿＿家に住みたいですね。
   I would like to live in a house with a rural (田舎) touch rather than in a house with an urban (都会) touch.

4. A: 音楽を作曲していらっしゃるそうですね。どんな音楽なんですか。(作曲する: compose [music])
   B: シンセサイザーを使ったニューエージ＿＿＿＿＿＿＿＿＿＿＿＿＿音楽を作曲しています。
   I am composing New Age-like music in which I use a synthesizer.

5. A: どんなヘアスタイルにいたしましょうか。(ヘアスタイル: hair style)
   B: ＿＿＿＿＿＿＿＿＿＿＿＿＿＿＿＿＿＿＿＿＿＿＿＿＿して下さい。
   [B points to a picture on the wall in the hair salon.] Please do it like that.

6. A: 油絵をやっていらっしゃるそうですね。どんな絵をおかきになるんですか。(油絵: oil painting)
   B: モネ＿＿＿＿＿＿＿＿＿＿＿＿＿＿＿絵をかこうと思うんですが、むずかしいですね。
   I try to paint like Monet, but it's difficult.

Reading and Writing 10

Name:_____ Sec:_____ #:____

R1. Read the following letter and answer the questions below.

平成14年10月15日

デジタルマシン株式会社
販売ご担当者様

「マイクロスター800」卸値について

拝啓　初秋の候　貴社ますますご隆盛のこととお慶び申し上げます。

　さて、前回御社ご提示のマイクロスターの卸値につきまして再度検討いたしましたところ、年末商戦を目前にひかえ競争激化が予想されるため、当初のご提示価格による買い入れは困難であるとの結論にいたりました。

　つきましては、誠に恐縮ながら当初ご提示価格の3％引下げをご検討願いたく存じます。

　なにとぞ、弊社の状況をご理解賜りますよう、心よりお願い申し上げます。

敬具

以上

担当　田中和夫
電話　03-123-4569

初秋の候 (phr) early fall (time)
ますますご隆盛のこととお慶び申し上げます↓ (phr) I/we congratulate your increasing prosperity
前回 (phr) previous time
御社ご提示の↑ (phr) proposed by your company
〜につきまして (phr) [polite of 〜について] about
再度 (n) one more time; again
検討いたしました↓ (v) considered; discussed
年末商戦 (n) year-end sales competition
目前にひかえ (phr) facing
競争激化 (n) increased competition
予想される (v) [passive of 予想する] to predict
当初 (n) initial
ご提示価格↑ (n) the proposed price
買入れ (n) purchase
困難である (phr) is difficult
結論にいたりました↓ (phr) reached a conclusion
つきましては (con) based on the above; therefore
誠に恐縮ながら (phr) feel truly sorry, but
引下げ (n) reduction
ご検討願いたく存じます (phr) we would like to request your consideration
なにとぞ (phr) somehow, please
状況 (n) situation
御理解賜ります↑ (phr) We hope you understand (Lit. "give us your understanding")
心より (phr) sincerely [lit. "from the heart"]

1. What is the main purpose of this letter?

2. Underline one sentence that refers to the essential point of this letter.

3. What is the reason for the request?

4. Match the written expressions on the left with more conversational expressions on the right.

a. _____ 前回 御社ご提示の
b. _____ 卸値につきまして
c. _____ 再度検討いたしましたところ
d. _____ 年末商戦を目前にひかえ
e. _____ 競争激化が予想されるため
f. _____ 買い入れは困難である
g. _____ との結論にいたりました
h. _____ 誠に恐縮ながら
i. _____ 当初ご提示価格
j. _____ 引き下げをご検討願いたく存じます
k. _____ なにとぞ
l. _____ 弊社の状況をご理解賜りますよう

1. という結論がでました
2. はじめにおっしゃった価格
3. 安くすることを考えていただければと思います
4. 前に御社がおっしゃった
5. どうか
6. 卸値について
7. 買うのはむずかしいです
8. 競争がもっと激しくなると思いますので
9. 我が社のことをわかって下さるよう
10. もう一度話し合ってみたら
11. 年末商戦がもうすぐなので
12. 本当にすみませんが

Communicative Exercise 10

C1. Role Playing

#1: It is five o'clock and you (A) have just finished your work and are about to leave the office. As you walk out of the room, you notice your colleague (B) still working on something. Ask if he/she is going to work overtime (残業). Ask him/her why he can't leave the office.

You (B) are asked by your colleague (A) why you can't leave at five o'clock. Give two reasons why you can't really go home just yet (e.g., "Your boss asked you to finish a report." "This project is urgent.").

#2: You are working for a U.S. company as a sales representative. Today, you have visited Mr. Ishii's company to demonstrate your product. Present at least three advantages of your product (performance, quality, price, service, etc.) as compared with products sold by your competitors. Use visual aids if necessary.

You are Mr. Ishii. Ask the visiting sales agent about the following as she gives her presentation.

a. consumer evaluation (消費者の評価)

b. customer service (アフターサービス)

c. prices per order size (注文の台数による価格)

Listening Comprehension 10   Name:_____ Sec:_____ #:____

1. Voc: 付属品(ふぞくひん): (n) optional items/devices
    Aさんは何をしようと思っているんですか。

    Aさんの思っていることをすると、いくらぐらいかかりますか。

2. Voc: 海外(かいがい): (n) overseas; 事業部(じぎょうぶ): (n) business division
    来月、だれが来るんですか。その人は日本語も話せそうですか。

    Bさんはだれに聞いてみますか。どうしてその人に聞いてみるんですか。

3. Voc: 出張(しゅっちょう): (n) business trip
    BさんはAさんに何を頼(たの)まれていましたか。

    部長さんは来月、何をする予定(よてい)ですか。

    Bさんはこれから、何をするんですか。

4. Voc: いや: (な-adj) dislike; uncomfortable
    山田さん(Bさん)は毎日何をしているんですか。

    山田さんはどうしてまだ帰れませんか。

5. Voc: マージン: (n) (profit) margin; 計算(けいさん)する: (v) calculate
    AさんはBさんに何をしてほしいんですか。

    BさんはAさんに何を頼(たの)みましたか。

Chapter 11

交渉成立 (こうしょうせいりつ)
Concluding Negotiations

Priming

A great many people participate in the decision making processes in a Japanese company. Those who are affected by the decision will discuss the details of the decision and try to gain support from others until a consensus is reached.

This process, often referred to as 根回し (ねまわ) (lit. ground work or root binding work before a large tree is transplanted), is a time-consuming process, but once a consensus is reached, the implementation of the decision goes efficiently.

A group decision form (稟議書 りんぎしょ) is used to formalize this process.

After Ms. Lewis had left, there were many more follow-up questions and additional meetings. Rumor says that the competitors are going to lower the prices of their products anticipating increased competition from foreign companies. Ms. Lewis is going to send a new price quote to the Japanese company. She is confident that this last proposal will get the attention of 日本エレクトロニクス.

Conversation 11A: Price competition starts.

1. ハ: 部長！今、デジタルマシン社からファックスが届きました。卸し値を1300ドルまで下げてもいいと言っています。
2. 田: やっぱりそう言ってきたか。1300ドルなら、今週、ヤマト電子が出したばかりのコンピュータより安くなりそうだな。
3. ハ: そうですね。
4. 田: これは価格競争になるかもしれないぞ。よし、大至急翻訳して、今度の企画会議にかけよう。
5. ハ: わかりました。
6. 田: 山田君、稟議書は君が書いてくれないか。
7. 山: はい、わかりました。

1. H: Division Manager! We just got a fax from Digital Machine. They are saying that they can lower the whole sale price to $1300.
2. T: I thought they would. If it's $1300, it appears it'll be cheaper than the new computers Yamato Electronic has just introduced.
3. H: That's right.
4. T: This might lead to a price competition. All right, let's translate it immediately and present it at the next planning meeting.
5. H: Certainly.
6. T: Ms. Yamada. Will you write the proposal?
7. Y: Yes, certainly.

届く   reach, is sent   下げる   lower   電子   electron, electronic

Vocabulary 11A

届きました (cv: todok) [polite past of 届く] sent, reached, arrived
下げて (vv: sage) [て-form of 下げる] lower
やっぱり (adv) after all, as expected
言ってきた (phr) [て-form of いう + きた] came over saying; spoke [from a distant place] やっぱりそう言ってきたか [Mr. Tanaka is talking to himself.]
ヤマト電子 (n) Yamato Electronic [company name]
出したばかり (phr) has just put/introduced [to the market]

競争 (n) competition
かもしれない (phr) possibly
ぞ (sp) [expression of a strong resolve]
よし (phr) All right.
翻訳して (n/v) [て-form of 翻訳する] translate
企画会議 (n) planning meeting; project meeting
かけよう (vv: kake) [volitional of かける "attach, hang"] [会議にかける "present at a meeting"]
稟議書 (n) group decision form

Structures 11A

11A.1. V てくる

An action directed towards the speaker may be expressed more naturally by adding the verb くる to the て-form of a verb as in V てくる ("V [all the way] toward me"). For example, when someone sends a message that originates in a distant place, it is more natural to say おくってくる.[47] Frequently, the くる ("come") part of the pattern is not translated into English.

電話がかかってきた。   A phone call came in.
ファックスを送ってきた。   They sent in a fax.

---

[47] Another meaning of V てくる is "[something/someone] begins to V" (わかってきた: "I began to understand").

値段を安くすると言ってきた。　　　　They told me that they are going to reduce the price.

11A.2. V たばかりの N

The phrase V たばかり ("has just V-ed") can function as noun modifier with the particle の and expresses "N that has just V-ed."

V-past	ばかり	の	Noun	
ソニーが出した	ばかり	の	製品	a product that Sony has just introduced
アメリカから送ってきた	ばかり	の	ファックス	a fax that (someone) has just sent from the U.S.

Caution: V たところ ("has just V-ed," 9C.4) does not occur in this modifier pattern. Thus, ソニーが出したところの製品 is ungrammatical. However, the following combination (V たばかりの + ところ) is acceptable, and it emphasizes the abruptness of the event.

お仕事からお帰りになったばかりのところにお電話いたしまして、たいへん申し訳ございません。
I'm so sorry to call you when you have just returned from work.

11A.3. X かもしれない: possibly X

The structure X かもしれない is used when the possibilities of X's happening is rather low. The following statements are listed in the order of high to low possibilities.

ヤマト電子は値段を下げます。　　　　Yamato Electronics will lower the prices. [certainty]
ヤマト電子は値段を下げるでしょう。　　Yamato Electronics will probably lower the prices.
ヤマト電子は値段を下げるかもしれない。　Yamato Electronics may lower the prices.

かもしれない can directly follow an adjective, a noun, or the particles から／まで.

決裁がでるのは明日かもしれない。
The time when the approval is given may be tomorrow.

活字だけよりアニメがあった方がおもしろいかもしれない。
It may be more interesting to have animation than to have just text.

あのコンビニは午後9時までかもしれない。
That convenience store might be [open] until 9:00 p.m.

Mr. Yamada needs to fill in the details of their plan. He is now on the phone with Ms. Lewis of Digital Machine.

Conversation 11B: Mr. Yamada needs to fill in the details.

1. 山: 例の見積書の件で、二三、質問があるんですが。
2. ル: はい、何でしょう。
3. 山: 一つは支払い方法です。円建てにしてもよいものでしょうか。
4. ル: うちは円建てでも、ドル建てでも、どちらでもけっこうです。
5. 山: わかりました。では円建てでお願いいたします。運賃は

1. Y: I have some questions regarding the last estimate.
2. L: OK. What might they be?
3. Y: One is about the payment method. Is it acceptable even if we make [the payment] in terms of yen?
4. L: It does not matter to us whether it's in terms of yen or dollar.
5. Y: I see. Then, we'll choose the

エフオービーですね。	yen-based payment. Freight is FOB (Free On Board), right?
6. ル: はい。支払い条件としては100％エルシー一覧払いをお願いできればと思いますが。	6. L: Yes. As for payment terms, I would like to request L/C (Letter of Credit) at sight.
7. 山: わかりました。では、その方向で検討してみますので。	7. Y: O.K. Then, we will try to discuss the matter along these lines, so...

シツモン 質問 question	ホウホウ 方法 method	ホウコウ 方向 direction

Vocabulary 11B

支払い (n) payment
方法 (n) method
円建て (n) yen-based (payment)
よい (a) good [formal variation of いい "good"]
もの (n) a matter (of natural consequence) [よいものでしょうか "Is it OK, I wonder?"]
かどうか (phr) whether or not...
ドル建て (n) dollar-based (payment)
どちらでも (phr) either way, whichever

運賃 (n) freight fee
エフオービー (n) FOB (free on board)
エルシー (n) L/C (letter of credit)
一覧払い (n) payment at sight
お願いできれば (n/v) [provisional of お願いできる]
 [お願いできれば "if I could make a request"]
方向 (n) direction
検討して (n/v) [て-form of 検討する] discuss, study, examine

Structures 11B

11B.1. Approximate numbers

A sequence of two consecutive numbers, followed by an appropriate classifier, expresses an approximate number, which comes in a range described by the two numbers. In some combinations involving 四 and 七 as underlined below, 四 is pronounced as し and 七 is pronounced as しち, respectively, rather than as よん and なな.

一、二枚	one or two sheets	六、七本	six or seven long objects
二、三本	two or three long objects	七、八枚	seven or eight sheets
三、四人	three or four people	八、九冊	eight or nine books
四、五冊	four or five books	[九、十 non-existent]	
五、六日	five or six days	二十四、五人	twenty four or five people
		二、三百台	two or three hundred computers

11B.2. Wh-word + て-form + も

This pattern means "no matter what/when/who/..." etc. or "whatever/whenever/whoever/..." etc. as shown below:

Wh-word + V て／A くて／N で	も	
だれが して	も	No matter who does it, / Whoever does it
なにを して	も	No matter what I do, / Whatever I do
どう して	も	No matter how I do it, / However I do it
いくら 高くて	も	No matter how expensive
どんな 人で	も	No matter what kind of person he/she is

Study the following examples:

あそこはいつ電話をかけても話し中なんです。
No matter when I call them, their line is always busy.

どこへお連れしてもいいんですが、日本食がいいんじゃないですか？
It's fine no matter where we take him, but wouldn't a Japanese restaurant be good?

Adjectives and nouns have the following ても forms:

いくら高くても質のいい品物の方がいいですよ。
No matter how expensive it is, it is better (to get) items of good quality.

どんなに丈夫でもあまり無理しない方がいいですよ。
No matter how strong you are, don't strain yourself too much.

A wh-word + でも can be used as shown below:

カラオケは誰でも上手に聞こえるようになっているんです。
Karaoke is devised so that anyone (lit, whoever it is) can sound (lit. "be heard") well.

ハンさんは何でも召し上がって下さるので、ホストとして嬉しいですよ。
Mr. Han, you eat anything (lit. whatever it is) we serve, so we are very happy as hosts.

Now guess the meaning of the following phrases:

どこで食べても、おいしいです。
いつ来ても、忙しそうです。
いくら聞いても、わかりません。

11B.3. Provisionals of potential verbs

A phrase 〜できればと思う should be understood as a short form of 〜できればいいと思う in which a provisional is followed by いいと思う. It means "I would be happy if I could." Note that できれば is derived from the potential verb できる. Other examples of the potential provisional forms follow:

明日中にお電話いただければと思います。
I would be happy if I could get a call from you tomorrow.

私も明日行ければと思いますが、ちょっと無理なようなので…
I would be happy if I could go tomorrow, but it seems it's a bit difficult.

外国の人気ソフトでも、日本語が表示できなければ、意味がありません。
Even if it is a popular foreign software, unless it can display Japanese characters, it is meaningless.

Note that provisional forms are typically used to refer to future actions leading to desirable outcomes ("Provided that X happens, something good will follow"). Likewise, provisional forms can be used to refer to an absence of actions leading to undesirable outcomes ("If X does not happen, something bad will follow"). In the following, Ms. Yamada is working on a proposal that involves the use of the Internet for advertisement. She is doing the ground work by trying to obtain support for the plan from Mr. Tanaka.

山田： これからはインターネットを使えなければ、他社との競争に負けると思います。
田中： そうだね。海外に対するわが社の宣伝にもなるしね。
山田： おっしゃるとおりです。部長に支持していただければ、心強いです。

Y: From now on, if we can't use the Internet, I think we will lose the competition against other companies.
T: I agree. This is also a chance to advertise our [company] to overseas.
Y: What you say is exactly right. If we have your support, we will feel very encouraged.

A month passed and no final decision was reached. Ms. Lewis began to feel that this process would go forever. Finally, she received a phone call from Mr. Tanaka.

Conversation 11C: Finally, a decision is reached.

1. 田: ルイスさん、私の海外出張のせいで遅れましたが、本日、やっと企画会議で決裁が出て、御社の製品を購入することになりました。
2. ル: 本当ですか。ありがとうございます。これも田中課長にご尽力いただいたおかげです。
3. 田: いやいや。
4. ル: 何とお礼を申し上げてよいかわかりません。
5. 田: いや、どうもどうも。じゃ、そういうことでよろしく。
6. ル: こちらこそよろしくお願いいたします。

1. T: Ms. Lewis, we were delayed due to my overseas business trip, but finally today, we reached a decision at the planning meeting, and it's been decided that we are going to purchase your products.
2. R: Really? Thank you very much. This owes to your great efforts.
3. T: Don't mention it.
4. R: I don't know how to express my thanks.
5. T: You're welcome. Well then, let's keep in touch.
6. R: Thank YOU. [Lit. I ask for your kindness.]

企画 planning   遅れる be delayed   遅い late   決裁 decision

Vocabulary 11C

出張 (n) business trip
せいで (phr) [S せいで "due to the fact that S"; N のせいで "due to N"]
遅れました (vv: okur) past of 遅れる] be late for, be delayed
本日 (n) today [more formal than 今日]
やっと (adv) finally, at long last
● とうとう (adv) finally
企画 (n) planning

決裁 (n) decision, approval
購入する (n/v) purchase
ご尽力 (n) help, effort
おかげで (phr) [S おかげで "thanks to the fact that S"; N のおかげで "thanks to N"]
お礼 (n) expression of appreciation; thanks
申し上げて↓ (vv: moos) [stem of 申す + て-form of 上げて "give"] say (it) humbly
そういうことで (phr) being that kind of thing [＝そんなこと

Structures 11C

11C.1. おかげで vs. せいで

These two phrases both indicate the reason or cause for an event. The difference between them is that おかげで is used when the reason or cause is favorable to the speaker, whereas せいで is used in opposite situations. おかげで is often translated into English as "thanks to" while せいで is translated as "due to." Both phrases can take a verb, an adjective or a noun before it.

社長がバックアップして下さったおかげで決裁が早く出ました。

Thanks to the president's back up, the decision was made quickly.

社長のバックアップが大きかったおかげで決裁が早く出ました。
Thanks to the president's strong back up, the decision was made quickly.

社長のおかげでABC商事との契約がとれました。
Thanks to the president, I could get a contract with ABC Company.

11C.2. やっと vs. とうとう

Both of these mean "finally," but these words have different implications. やっと is used when the speaker thinks that the outcome is favorable to him/her, while とうとう has no such implication.

やっと契約にこぎつけることができました。 We were finally able to make a contract.

Thus, (1) is a strange sentence because やっと implies that the speaker is relieved to know that X fell ill. In contrast, とうとう does not have this implication.

(1) ？毎日、おそくまで働いていたので、ハリスさんはやっと病気になりました。
(2) 毎日、おそくまで働いていたので、ハリスさんはとうとう病気になりました。

If the speaker is welcoming the rise of the yen, guess which one should be used.

円が（やっと／とうとう）上がったね。

やっと also implies that the speaker regards the process leading to the consequence as unnecessarily long and involving a great effort. Thus, the speaker can exclaim about his/her own accomplishment as in (3) with either やっと or とうとう. However, when he/she comments on other's accomplishment (4 & 5), やっと sounds rather sarcastic.

(3) （やっと／とうとう）できた！　　It's finally finished!
(4) とうとう　できたね。　　　　It's finally finished!　(Congratulations!)
(5) やっと　できたね。　　　　　It's finally finished!　(What took you so long?)

Guess which expression is more appropriate.

(6) （やっと／とうとう）日本語の新聞が読めるようになりました。
(7) 山田さんは（やっと／とうとう）部長になられましたね。

11C.3. 稟議書 (Group decision form)

The 稟議書 refers to a written proposal form used for a variety of decision-making ranging from purchasing office supplies to starting a new business project. The 稟議書 form consists of the document number (稟議番号), the date of proposal (起案日), the name of the originator of the proposal (起案者), his/her division, title, the proposal content, and attachments (添付書類), if any. Before you write this form, it is necessary to inform all parties involved, explain what benefits it will bring, discuss responsibilities of each party in carrying out the decision, and clarify all questions. The final decision on the proposal is called 決裁. Different companies have different 稟議書 forms. Some forms may include boxes for approval seals and approval date. A sample form written by Mr. Harris is shown below.

平成14年　8月13日
稟議番号第3号

営業部本部長
田中　秀雄様

営業部営業一課
トム・ハリス　㊇

デジタルマシン社のマイクロスター800の販売について

年末のデスクトップコンピュータ商戦に向けて、デジタルマシン社のマイクロスター800(Microstar 800)を販売する計画が進行中です。つきましては来る11月から注文受付、発送業務が開始されます。その作業消化のためパートタイマー15名を臨時雇用を申請いたします。

記

1　要員　パートタイマー15名
　　　　年齢20歳から40歳の男女を問わない。
2　職種　マイクロスター800　注文受付、発送業務
3　期間　2001年　11月　1日から
　　　　2001年　12月　31日まで
4　給与　時間給　1500円
　　　　ほかに交通費　300円

以上

稟議番号　(n) group decision number
第3号　(n) number 3
本部長　(n) (main) division manager
田中秀雄　(n) Hideo Tanaka
年末　(n) year end
商戦　(n) business war; sales competition
向けて　(n) toward
計画　(n) plan
進行中　(n) is in progress
来る　(n) upcoming
注文受付　(n) order taking
発送業務　(n) shipping work
開始されます　(n) will be started
作業消化　(n) completion of work
男女　(n) men and women

問わない　(n) will not be asked
職種　(n) job type
期間　(n) period
給与　(n) wage
時間給　(n) hourly wage
ほかに　(n) besides
交通費　(n) commuting cost
パートタイマー　(n) part-timer workers
15名　(n) 15 people [名 is a formal counter for people.]
臨時雇用　(n) temporary hiring
申請いたします　(n) to propose, apply (for)
記　(n) As follows.
要員　(n) needed personnel
年齢　(n) age
以上　(n) That's all.

Exercise 11

Grammar Utilization 11   Name:_____ Sec:____ #:____

G1. Based on the situations pictured below, complete the sentences below by using one of the appropriate connectives among the conditional (...たら), the provisional (...ば), and S と.

a. 円が_____、アメリカでは日本のメモリーチップが高くなる。
   The higher the yen becomes, the more expensive the Japanese memory chips will be in America.

b. 田中商事との契約が_____、どこかへ飲みに行きませんか。
   If we can get the contract with Tanaka Trading Co., why don't we go for drinks somewhere?

c. 会議から_____、留守番電話に田中さんからのメッセージが入っていた。
   When I returned from the meeting, a message from Mr. Tanaka was on the answering machine.

d. 付属品 (peripherals) の値段_____、全部で2500ドルです。
   If we include the prices of the peripherals, the total price will be $2500.

e. 届いたサンプルを_____、一個こわれていた。
   When we opened the samples, one of them was broken.

f. 製品が10日までに_____、サービスセンターに連絡して下さい。
   If the product does not arrive by 10th, please contact the service center.

G2. Reply to the following questions by stating "No matter what/when/how/who/etc."
   Example:
   a. A: だれかに聞きましたか。
      B: ええ、<u>でも、だれに聞いても</u>わからないんです。

   b. A: プレゼンテーションはできましたか。
      B: いいえ、_____うまく書けないんです。

Chapter 11: Concluding Negotiations   227

　c.　A: ブラウンさんをどこかへお連れしましたか。
　　　B: ええ、＿＿＿＿＿＿＿＿＿＿＿＿＿＿＿＿＿＿＿＿＿＿＿＿＿日本はおもしろいようです。

　d.　A: 日本エレクトロニクスに電話した？
　　　B: ええ、でも、＿＿＿＿＿＿＿＿＿＿＿＿＿＿＿＿＿＿＿＿＿＿＿話し中なんです。

　e.　A: あの会社のコンピュータは性能 (capabilities) はいいですけど、高いですよ。
　　　B: ええ、でも、＿＿＿＿＿＿＿＿＿＿＿＿＿＿＿＿＿＿＿＿＿＿＿買いたいんです。

G3. Select the best phrases below.

　a.　A: 入学試験に合格したそうですね。(入学試験: entrance exam; 合格する: pass)
　　　B: ありがとうございます。先生が教えて下さった (おかげ／せい) です。

　b.　A: 試験はだめだったそうですね。残念でしたね。
　　　B: ええ、あまり勉強しなかった (おかげ／せい) です。

　c.　A: やっと御社の製品を購入できることになりました。
　　　B: ああ、リーさんのプレゼンテーションの (おかげ／せい) ですよ。

　d.　A: 今年の夏は涼しかった (おかげ／せい) で、エアコンがあまり売れなかったそうです。
　　　B: エアコン会社としては残念ですねえ。

G4. Fill in the blanks with phrases which naturally follow the phrase とうとう or やっと.

　a.　A: 毎日、英語の勉強を続けたので、やっと＿＿＿＿＿＿＿＿＿＿＿＿＿＿＿＿＿＿＿＿
　　　B: よかったですねえ。

　b.　A: よく故障するので、あの車はとうとう＿＿＿＿＿＿＿＿＿＿＿＿＿＿＿＿＿＿＿＿
　　　B: そうですか。

　c.　A: 二、三百台も欠陥品 (defective products) を出したので、あの会社はとうとう＿＿＿＿＿＿＿
　　　B: やっぱりねえ。

　d.　A: きのうの企画会議でやっと御社の製品を＿＿＿＿＿＿＿＿＿＿＿＿＿＿＿なりました！
　　　B: ありがとうございます。

　e.　A: 病気だった父がやっと＿＿＿＿＿＿＿＿＿＿＿＿＿＿＿＿＿＿＿。
　　　B: そうですか。

　f.　A: 病気だった父がとうとう＿＿＿＿＿＿＿＿＿＿＿＿＿＿＿＿＿＿＿。
　　　B: そうですか。

G4. Fill in the blanks with appropriate phrases according to the English cues.

　a.　今年の終わりまでに、エイズ患者は＿＿＿＿＿＿＿＿＿＿＿＿＿＿＿＿＿＿と言われています。
　　　By the end of this year, AID patients might increase (ふえる) by four to five hundred people.

b. 先週＿＿＿＿＿＿＿＿＿＿＿＿＿＿＿＿＿＿＿＿＿カメラがもうこわれた。
The camera I just bought last week broke already.

c. 吉田専務は体の調子が悪くなったので、会社を＿＿＿＿＿＿＿＿＿＿＿＿＿＿＿＿＿＿＿＿＿ね。
Senior Managing Director Yoshida might quit the company since his health has deteriorated. [Be polite.]

d. ラップトップの値段は、毎年、下がって＿＿＿＿＿＿＿＿＿＿＿＿＿＿＿＿から、私でも買えるようになりそうです。
Since the price of laptop computers has been coming down every year, it appears even a person like me is going to be able to afford one.

e. 日本の建設業会の談合制度について＿＿＿＿＿＿＿＿＿＿＿＿＿＿＿＿＿＿＿＿、と思いますが。
I would appreciate it if you could talk about the bid-rigging convention in the construction industry in Japan.

f. これからはインターネットで商品を＿＿＿＿＿＿＿＿＿＿＿＿＿＿＿＿＿＿、競争にまけると思います。
From now on, if we can't sell out merchandises through the Internet, we will lose the competition.

Reading and Writing 11

Name:_____ Sec:_____ #:____

R1. Read the following letter and answer the questions below.

平成14年11月1日 デジタルマシン株式会社 販売ご担当者 各位 　　　「マイクロスター800」の注文について 拝啓　貴社ますますご清祥のこととお慶び申し上げます。 　さてこのたびは、卸値引下げの件、早速ご快諾いただき誠にありがとうございました。 　つきましては、下記の通り注文いたしますので、至急ご手配をお願いいたします。また、支払い条件を念のため付記しております。ご高覧下さい。 　　　　　　　　　　　　　　　　　　　　　敬具 　　　　　　　　　記 1. 注文品名 Microstar 800 （商品No. 789358） 2. 数量・単価　　500台 @ 162,500円 3. 納期12月1日必着 4. 納入方法・場所当社（貴社ご配送） 5. 支払い条件100% L/C 一覧払い 6. 特記事項　納期 必ず厳守のこと。 　　納期遅延の場合、注文を取り消す場合がございます。ご了承下さい。 　　　　　　　　　　　　　　　　　　　　　以上 　　　　　　　　　　　　　　　担当　田中和夫 　　　　　　　　　　　　　　電話 03-123-4569	ますますご清祥のこととお慶び申し上げます (phr) I congratulate your increasing prosperity. さてこのたびは (phr) as we discussed [lit. "well, this time"] ご快諾↑ (n) (prompt) approval ご手配↑ (n) delivery 念のため (n) to make sure 付記しております (phr) attached a note ご高覧下さい↑ (phr) Please look at... 記 (n) notes 注文品名 (n) name of product to order 商品 (n) commercial product 数量 (n) quantity 単価 (n) price per unit 納期 (n) delivery date 必着 (n) must arrive 納入方法 (n) shipping method 当社 (n) our company ご配送↑ (n) delivery 特記事項 (n) special remarks 必ず厳守のこと (phr) must be adhered to [必ず absolutely] 納期遅延 (n) delay in delivery date 取り消す (v) to cancel ご了承下さい↑ (phr) Please understand.

1. What is the main purpose of this letter?

2. Identify the specific content of the order.

3. Under what circumstances may the order be canceled?

4. Match the written expressions on the left with more conversational expressions on the right.

a. _____ 早速ご快諾いただき	1. 急いでご手配をお願いします
b. _____ 誠にありがとうございました	2. メモをつけました
c. _____ 至急ご手配をお願いいたします	3. 納期は絶対に守って下さい
d. _____ 付記しております	4. わかって下さい
e. _____ ご高覧下さい	5. 本当にありがとうございました
f. _____ 納期必ず厳守のこと	6. すぐ受け入れていただき
g. _____ 納期遅延の場合	7. ご覧下さい
h. _____ ご了承下さい	8. 納期が遅れた場合

Communicative Exercise 11

C1. Role Playing

#1: You (A) are discussing with your colleague (B) various consequences of doing or not doing something. Based on the list below, discuss the actions (non-actions) and its possible consequences.

	Actions		Outcomes
1.	We don't explain the plans to Division Manger Aoki.	→	_____
2.	We can get the support of Mr. Aoki.	→	_____
3.	We cannot get the support of Mr. Aoki.	→	_____
4.	_____	→	Our firm will be able to expand the market overseas.
5.	_____	→	Our firm will lose customers to Japan Electronics.

#2: You are working for the Sales Division of a very traditional Japanese company named Sakura Seika which sells Japanese candies. Sakura Seika has never dealt with advanced technology before. Lately, orders to your company are dwindling. You have heard that your competitors are snapping up your customers. In fact, they are getting purchase orders from all over the world! What's going on? It is time for your company to get on the Internet to survive the increasing competition. You must advertise Sakura Seika and your products through the Internet. Since no one in your company has any expertise in this field, it is a good idea to hire some outside contractors. However, first, you must convince your superiors including the president and the executives using the consensus building processes. After all, this is a very traditional organization.

You (A) are at an advertisement planning meeting. Make a five-minute presentation describing how your plans will work as follows:

1. Describe the recent decline of the orders.
2. State the reasons for the decline.
3. Explain your plan. Include the following:
   a. the goals
   b. the benefits of advertisement using the internet
   c. the consequences of not implementing your plan
   d. the cost of your plan

Listening Comprehension 11

Listen to the conversation on the accompanying media. Write down what you hear and answer the questions below.

1. Voc: 調(しら)べる: (v) to check, examine

   AさんはBさんに何をしてもらいたいんですか。

   Bさんによると、Aさんの書いたものはどうですか。

   Aさんによると、それはAさんが一人で書いたものですか。

2. Voc: オリエンタル貿易(ぼうえき): (n) Oriental Trading (name of a company); 交渉(こうしょう)する: (v) to negotiate
   円高(えんだか): (n) high yen; appreciation of the yen (against the dollar)

   Aさんはオリエンタル貿易の人と何について交渉することになっていますか。

   円建てだと、どうして問題(もんだい)になるんですか。

   川田係長(かかりちょう)の話によると、Aさんの会社の製品(せいひん)はどうなりそうですか。

3. Voc: 都合(つごう): (n) schedule; 自分(じぶん): (n) self

   今度(こんど)の企画会議(きかくかいぎ)はいつになりそうですか。

   企画会議の時間はAさんが自分で決(き)められますか。

4. Voc: 辞令(じれい): (n) company order; マンション: (n) condominium; 仕方(しかた)がない: can't help it
   単身赴任(たんしんふにん): (n) one-person relocation (transfer to a distant work place)
   お淋(さび)しい: (n) lonely [お is an honorific marker.]

   Aさんは来月、何をすることになってしまったんですか。

   Aさんは どうして大阪(おおさか)に行きたくないんですか。

   Aさんは家族みんなで大阪に行くつもりですか。

5. Voc:　　5階: (n) fifth floor; 直って: (v) is repaired; 田中商事: (n) Tanaka Trading Company;
　　　　　〜しかありません: (phr) There is no other way but...

Aさんはどうして困っているんですか。

Bさんはどうしたらいいって言っていますか。

Aさんは田中商事の人に聞かれたら、何て説明するでしょうか。

6. Voc:　　かまわない: (phr) doesn't mind; プロジェクト: (n) project; やる: (v) do, perform [colloquial]

Bさんはハンさんに何をさせようと思っているんですか。

Aさんはどうしてハンさんにそれを頼むわけにはいかないと言っているんですか。

Bさんによると、ハンさんが来てから、どうなったそうですか。

Appendix A: Kanji Index

Kanji assumed to be known prior to using this textbook

★ marks the reading of kanji that is assumed to be known prior to using this book.

	Kanji	訓読み Japanese reading	音読み Chinese reading	Examples
1	山	★やま	サン	山田 (やまだ)
2	日	★ひ／★び	★ニチ／★ニ ★カ	日、日本、十日、日曜日 (ヒ、ニホン、とおカ、ニチヨウび)
3	田	★た	デン	田中 (たなか)
4	人	★ひと	★ニン ★ジン	人、五人、外人 (ひと、ゴニン、ガイジン)
5	上	★うえ あ(げる) のぼ(る)	ジョウ	本の上 (ホンのうえ)
6	下	★した さ(げる) ★くだ(さい)	カ ゲ	本の下、下さい (ホンのした、くだ さい)
7	中	★なか	チュウ	へやの中、中国 (なか、チュウゴク)
8	大	★おお(きい)	★ダイ	大きい、大学 (おお、ダイガク)
9	小	★ちい(さい)	★ショウ	小さい、小学校 (ちい、ショウガッコウ)
10	本	★もと	★ホン	日本、山本 (ニホン、やまもと)
11	学	まな(ぶ)	★ガク	学生 (ガクセイ)
12	生	い(きる)	★セイ	大学生 (ダイガクセイ)
13	先	さき	★セン	先生 (センセイ)
14	私	★わたし	シ	私の本 (わたしのホン)
15	川	★かわ	セン	大きい川 (おおきいかわ)
16	一	★ひと(つ)	★イチ	一時、一人 (イチジ、ひとり)
17	二	★ふた(つ)	★ニ	二時、二人 (ニジ、ふたり)
18	三	★みっ(つ)	★サン	三時、三人 (サンジ、サンニン)
19	四	★よっ(つ)	★ヨン／★ヨ ★シ	四時、四人 (ヨジ、ヨニン)

20	五	★いつ(つ)	★ゴ	ゴジ ゴニン 五時、五人
21	六	★むっ(つ)	★ロク	ロクジ ロクニン 六時、六人
22	七	★なな(つ)	★シチ	シチジ シチニン 七時、七人
23	八	★やっ(つ)	★ハチ	ハチジ ハチニン 八時、八人
24	九	★ここの(つ)	★ク ★キュウ	クジ キュウニン 九時、九人
25	十	★とお	★ジュウ	ジュウジ ジュウニン 十時、十人
26	百		★ヒャク	ヒャクニン 百人
27	千		★セン	センニン 千人
28	万		★マン	イチマンニン 一万人
29	円		★エン	ヒャクマンエン 百万円
30	月	つき	★ゲツ ★ガツ	ゲツヨウび イチガツ イッ ゲツ 月曜日、一月／一か月
31	火	ひ	★カ	カヨウび 火曜日
32	水	みず	★スイ	スイヨウび 水曜日
33	木	き	★モク	モクヨウび 木曜日
34	金	かね	★キン	キンヨウび 金曜日
35	土	つち	★ド	ドヨウび 土曜日
36	曜		★ヨウ	ナンヨウび 何曜日
37	年	とし	★ネン	イチネン 一年
38	時	とき	★ジ	イチジ 一時
39	間	あいだ	★カン	ジ カン 時間
40	週		★シュウ	イッシュウカン 一週間
41	何	★なに／なん		ナンニチ 何日
42	分	わ(かる)	★フン／ブン／プン	ゴフン 五分
43	半	なか(ば)	★ハン	ハンブン 半分
44	今	★いま	★コン／コ	いま コンシュウ ことし 今、今週、今年
45	家	いえ ★うち	★カ ケ	いえ なか 家の中
46	族		★ゾク	カゾク 家族

47	父	★ちち ★とう	フ	父、お父さん
48	母	★はは	ホ／ボ	母、お母さん
49	兄	★あに	ケイ ★キョウ	兄、兄弟
50	弟	★おとうと	テイ ★ダイ	弟、兄弟
51	姉	★あね	シ	姉
52	妹	★いもうと	マイ	妹
53	男	★おとこ	ダン／ナン	男の人、男の子
54	女	★おんな	ジョ／ニョ	女の人、女の子
55	子	★こ	シ	子ども
56	目	★め	モク	目がいたい
57	口	★くち	コウ	口が大きい
58	耳	★みみ	ジ	耳がわるい
59	足	★あし	ソク	足がながい
60	手	★て	シュ	手が小さい
61	行	★い(く)	★コウ ギョウ	銀行に行く
62	来	★く(る)	★ライ	来月来る
63	帰	★かえ(る)	キ	家に帰る
64	食	★た(べる)	ショク	ごはんを食べる
65	飲	★の(む)	イン	水を飲む
66	見	★み(る)	ケン	ビデオを見る
67	聞	★き(く)	ブン	CDを聞く、新聞
68	読	★よ(む)	ドク	本を読む
69	書	★か(く)	ショ	メールを書く
70	話	★はな(す)	★ワ	電話で話す
71	高	★たか(い)	★コウ	高い、高校生
72	校		★コウ	中学校
73	出	★で(る)★だ(す)	シュツ	大学を出る、手紙を出す

| 74 | 会 | ★あ(う) | ★カイ | 会社(カイシャ)で会(あ)う |
| 75 | 買 | ★か(う) | バイ | 本(ホン)を買(か)う |

Kanji introduced in this book

★ marks the reading of kanji that is introduced in this book.

	Kanji	Chapter	訓読(くんよ)み Japanese reading	音読(おんよ)み Chinese reading	Examples
76	専	1A	もっぱ(ら)	★セン	専門(センモン)
77	攻	1A	せ(める)	★コウ	専攻(センコウ)する
78	社	1A		★シャ	会社(カイシャ)、社会(シャカイ)、御社(おんシャ)、我(わ)が社(シャ)
79	思	1B	★おも(う)	シ	思(おも)う
80	電	1B		★デン	電話(デンワ)をかける
81	面	1B	つら	★メン	面接(メンセツ)に行(い)く、方面(ホウメン)
82	力	1C	★ちから	リョク リキ	力(ちから)、水力(スイリョク)、火力(カリョク)、電力(デンリョク)、力学(リキガク)
83	企	1C	たくら(む)	★キ	企業(キギョウ)、企画(キカク)する
84	業	1C	わざ	★ギョウ	業績(ギョウセキ)、業務(ギョウム)、職業(ショクギョウ)
85	語	1D		★ゴ	日本語(ニホンゴ)、語学(ゴガク)、言語(ゲンゴ)
86	好	1D	★す(き)	コウ	好(す)き
87	度	1D	たび	★ド	一度(イチド)、今度(コンド)、この度(たび)
88	結	1E	むす(ぶ)	★ケツ	結論(ケツロン)を出(だ)す
89	名	1E	★な	★メイ	名前(なまえ)、有名(ユウメイ)
90	所	1E	★ところ	★ショ	住所(ジュウショ)
91	果	1E		★カ	結果(ケッカ)、効果(コウカ)がある
92	英	1E		★エイ	英語(エイゴ)を話(はな)す
93	日	1E	ひ/び/★ぴ	ニチ/ニ カ	生年月日(セイネンガッピ)を書(か)く
94	課	2A		★カ	課長(カチョウ)、営業一課(エイギョウイッカ)、課目(カモク)
95	員	2A		★イン	会社員(カイシャイン)、全員(ゼンイン)
96	君	2A	★きみ	★クン	ハリス君(クン)、君(きみ)
97	使	2B	★つか(う)	シ	使(つか)う、使用(シヨウ)する
98	仕	2B	つか(える)	★シ	仕事(シごと)をする
99	事	2B	こと/★ごと	ジ	事実(ジジツ)がわかる

100	毎	2B	ごと	★まい	マイニチ チャ ジ だ 毎日、お茶を3時に出す
101	言	2C	★い(う)	ゲン ゴン	イ ゲンゴ 言う、言語
102	提	2C		★テイ	テイシュツ 提出する
73	出	2C	だ(す)で(る)	★シュツ	チャだ シュツリョク シュッシン お茶出し、出力、出身
103	営	2D	★いとな(む)	★エイ	いとな エイギョウ ジエイ 営む、営業、自営
104	海	2D	★うみ	★カイ	うみ カイガイ 海、海外
105	外	2D	そと	★ガイ	そと ガイコク 外、外国
106	村	2E	★むら	ソン	むら たむら きむら 村、田村さん、木村さん
107	気	2E		★キ	デンキ 電気をつける
108	部	3A		★ブ ヘ	ブチョウ エイギョウブ へや 部長、営業部、部屋
109	長	3A	★なが(い)	★チョウ	カチョウ シャチョウ 課長、社長
110	新	3A	★あたら(しい)	★シン	あたら シンニュウシャイン 新しい、新入社員
111	聞	3A	き(く)	★ブン	シンブン 新聞
112	様	3B	★さま	ヨウ	やまださま 山田様
113	申	3B	★もう(します)	シン	もう シンセイ 申します、申請する
114	少	3B	すく(ない)	★ショウ	すく タショウ 少ない、多少
115	々	3B	repetition symbol		ショウショウ 少々
116	朝	3C	★あさ	チョウ	あさひ チョウレイ 朝日、朝礼
117	工	3C		★コウ	コウギョウ コウガクブ 工業、工学部
118	失	3C	うしな(う)	★シツ	シツレイ 失礼する
119	礼	3C		★レイ	レイ い お礼を言う
120	係	3D	★かか(り)	ケイ	かかりチョウ 係長
121	議	3D		★ギ	カイギ ギチョウ 会議、議長
122	席	3D		★セキ	セキ シュッセキ 席、出席する
123	急	3D	★いそ(ぐ)	キュウ	いそ キュウコウデンシャ 急ぐ、急行電車
124	番	3E		★バン	サンバン コウバン 三番、交番
125	号	3E		★ゴウ	バンゴウ 番号
126	伝	3E	★つた(える)	★デン	もう つた デンゴン 申し伝える、伝言
101	言	3E	い(う)	★ゴン	デンゴン 伝言をのこす
127	用	3F	もち(いる)	★ヨウ	ヨウケン ヨウジ シヨウ 用件、用事、使用する
128	件	3F		★ケン	ケン はな その件について話す
129	同	3F	★おな(じ)	ドウ	おな ドウジ ドウコウ 同じ、同時、同行する

#	漢字	課	訓	音	例
130	午	4A		★ゴ	午後
131	前	4A	★まえ	★ゼン	午前、前
7	中	4A	なか	★チュウ	中、中国
38	時	4A	★とき	ジ	時、時々、三時
132	持	4B	★も(つ)	ジ	かばんを持つ、気持ちがいい
133	通	4B	★とお(す)	ツウ	目を通す、通知する
134	決	4B	★き(める)	★ケツ	決める、決算報告書
39	間	4B	★あいだ	カン	お留守の間、時間
135	取	4C	★と(る)	シュ	取る、取得する
136	引	4C	★ひ(く)	イン	取り引き、値引き、引力
13	先	4C	★さき	セン	先に帰る、先生
137	方	4C	★かた	★ホウ/ポウ	右の方、女の方、先方
138	論	4D		★ロン	結論を出す
139	相	4D	★あい	★ソウ	相手に言う
140	値	4D	★ね	チ	値引きする、価値がある
141	談	4E		★ダン	部長に相談する
142	集	4E	★あつ(まる)	★シュウ	集計する、集まる
143	計	4E	はか(る)	★ケイ	時計、計る、合計
144	表	4E	おもて	★ヒョウ	表を作る、表に書く
145	算	4E		★サン	計算する、算数
146	座	5A		★ザ	口座を作る、座席にすわる
147	待	5A	★ま(つ)	タイ	待つ
148	窓	5A	★まど	ソウ	窓をあける、同窓会
149	客	5B		★キャク / カク	お客
150	作	5B	★つく(る)	サク / サ	作る、工作、動作
151	記	5B	しる(す)	★キ	記入する、記号
152	紙	5B	★かみ	★シ	紙に書く、用紙をもらう
153	池	5C	★いけ	チ	池田、電池を入れる
154	数	5C	かず	★スウ	数、数学を専攻する
155	字	5C		★ジ	数字、文字、ローマ字
156	意	5D		★イ	意見を聞く、同意する
157	味	5D	あじ	★ミ	意味がない、味がいい

#	Kanji	Code	Kun	On	Examples
158	代	5D	★か(わる)	★ダイ	代わる、ガス代を払う
159	便	5D		★ベン ビン	便利、郵便
160	利	5D		★リ	利子、利用する
161	料	5E		★リョウ	手数料、料金が安い
162	国	5E	★くに	★コク	外国に行く、国
163	信	5E		★シン	電信、信号、信用する
164	機	5F		★キ	計算機、飛行機、オフィス機器
165	械	5F		★カイ	機械を使う
166	者	5F	★もの	シャ	係りの者、新聞記者になる
167	忘	5G	★わす(れる)	ボウ	忘れる、忘却
168	暗	5G	★くら(い)	★アン	暗い部屋、暗号
169	証	5G	あか(し)	★ショウ	暗証、証明する
170	予	6A	あらかじ(め)	★ヨ	ホテルを予約する
171	定	6A	さだ(める)	★テイ	予定、決定、定める
172	入	6A	★はい(る) い(れる)	★ニュウ	入る、入れる、入社する
173	悪	6B	★わる(い)	アク	悪い、悪人、悪事
174	心	6B	こころ	★シン	心、安心する
175	配	6B	くば(る)	ハイ／★パイ	配る、心配する
5	上	6B	うえ あ(げる) のぼ(る)	★ジョウ	以上
60	手	6B	て	シュ	★上手 (idiomatic reading)
6	下	6B	した さ(げる) くだ(さい)	カゲ	★下手 (idiomatic reading)
176	速	6B	★はや(い)	ソク	足が速い、車の速度
177	連	6C	★つ(れる) つら(なる)	レン	連れて行く、連行する
178	接	6C		★セツ	直接言う
179	待	6C	ま(つ)	★タイ	接待する
180	頼	6C	★たの(む)	ライ	タクシーを頼む
181	製	7A		★セイ	新製品、日本製の車
182	造	7A	★つく(る)	★ゾウ	製造する
183	世	7A	よ	★セ★セイ	お世話、世界、二世

#	漢字	Lesson	訓	音	例
184	市	7B	いち	★シ	市場／市場 (シジョウ／いちば)
185	場	7B	ば	★ジョウ	工場で生産する (コウジョウ、セイサン)
186	拡	7B	ひろ(げる)	★カク	拡大する (カクダイ)
187	張	7B	は(る)	★チョウ	拡張する、出張 (カクチョウ、シュッチョウ)
188	考	7B	★かんが(える)	コウ	考える (かんが)
189	願	7C	★ねが(う)	ガン	お願いします、願望 (ねが、ガンボウ)
190	紹	7C		★ショウ	紹介する (ショウカイ)
191	介	7C		★カイ	ご紹介します (ショウカイ)
192	状	7C		★ジョウ	紹介状 (ショウカイジョウ)
53	男	7D	おとこ	★ダン	男性 (ダンセイ)
54	女	7D	おんな	★ジョ	女性、男女 (ジョセイ、ダンジョ)
193	性	7D		★セイ	性質を調べる (セイシツ、しら)
194	彼	7D	★かれ ★かの	ヒ	彼女、彼 (かのジョ、かれ)
195	経	7E		★ケイ	経理課 (ケイリカ)
196	済	7E		★ザイ	経済学 (ケイザイガク)
197	門	7E		★モン	専門 (センモン)
198	系	7E		★ケイ	系列、工学系 (ケイレツ、コウガクケイ)
199	忙	8A	★いそが(しい)	ボウ	忙しい、多忙 (いそが、タボウ)
200	研	8A	と(ぐ)	★ケン	研究する (ケンキュウ)
201	究	8A		★キュウ	究明する (キュウメイ)
202	室	8A		★シツ	会議室で会う (カイギシツ、あ)
203	元	8A	もと	★ゲン	お元気ですか (ゲンキ)
204	品	8B	★しな	★ヒン	新しい製品、品物 (あたら、セイヒン、しなもの)
205	器	8B	うつわ	★キ	オフィス機器 (キキ)
206	販	8B		★ハン	販売する (ハンバイ)
207	売	8B	★う(る)	★バイ	売る、売買 (う、バイバイ)
208	安	8C	★やす(い)	アン	安い、安心する (やす、アンシン)
8	大	8C	おお(きい)	ダイ／★タイ	大量に作る (タイリョウ、つく)
209	量	8C		★リョウ	分量を計る (ブンリョウ、はか)
210	産	8C	う(まれる)	★サン	生産する (セイサン)
211	費	8C	つい(やす)	★ヒ	費用がかかる (ヒヨウ)
212	説	9A	と(く)	★セツ	小説を読む (ショウセツ、よ)

213	明	9A	★あか(るい) あき(らか)	★メイ	説明する
214	開	9A	ひら(く) あ(く)	★カイ	開く、開発する
215	発	9A		★ハツ	発明、発見、出発する
216	速	9A	はや(い)	★ソク	速い、速度を上げる
217	合	9B	★あ(う)	ゴウ	合う、試合、合成する
218	自	9B	みずか(ら)	★ジ	自分
219	動	9B	★うご(く)	★ドウ	自動車、動く
210	的	9B	まと	★テキ	日本的
211	答	9B	★こた(える)	トウ	質問に答える
185	場	9C	★ば	ジョウ	場合
212	無	9C		★ム	無料サービス
213	消	9C	★け(す)	★ショウ	消す、消化する
214	費	9C	つい(やす)	★ヒ	消費する
165	者	9C	もの	★シャ	生産者、消費者ガイド
215	価	10A	あたい	★カ	評価する
216	格	10A		★カク	価格を引き下げる
217	台	10A		★ダイ	車を一台買う
218	別	10A		★ベツ	別に、特別
219	全	10A	すべ(て) まった(く)	★ゼン	全部
114	少	10B	すく(ない) ★すこ(し)	ショウ	少し
220	問	10B	★と(う)	モン	問い合わせる
221	知	10B	★し(る)	チ／ヂ(ジ)	知っている、ご存知ですか
222	割	10B	★わりわ(る)	カツ	一割、分割する
223	直	10C	なお(す)	★チョク	直接、こしょうを直す
224	商	10C	あきな(い)	★ショウ	商品を売る、商事
225	問	10C	と(う)	★モン	問題がある
226	題	10C		★ダイ	題、問題がある
227	乗	10C	★の(る)	ジョウ	乗り気だ、バスに乗る
228	文	10C		★ブン	英文を書く
69	書	10C	か(く)	★ショ	文書で送る
229	届	11A	★とど(く)		ファックスが届く

Appendix A: Kanji Index 241

6	下	11A	した ★さ(げる)	カゲ	価格を下げる
55	子	11A	こ	★シ	電子、男子、女子
230	質	11B		★シツ	質問する、性質を調べる
231	法	11B		★ホウ	方法、法学
232	向	11B	む(く)	★コウ	左の方向
233	画	11C		★カク ガ	企画、映画を見る
234	遅	11C	★おく(れる) おそ(い)	チ	クラスに遅れる、遅い、遅刻
235	裁	11C	さば(く)	★サイ	決裁する、裁判

Kanji Summary

1	山	11	学	21	六	31	火	41	何	51	姉	61	行	71	高
2	日	12	生	22	七	32	水	42	分	52	妹	62	来	72	校
3	田	13	先	23	八	33	木	43	半	53	男	63	帰	73	出
4	人	14	私	24	九	34	金	44	今	54	女	64	食	74	会
5	上	15	川	25	十	35	土	45	家	55	子	65	飲	75	買
6	下	16	一	26	百	36	曜	46	族	56	目	66	見	76	専
7	中	17	二	27	千	37	年	47	父	57	口	67	聞	77	攻
8	大	18	三	28	万	38	時	48	母	58	耳	68	読	78	社
9	小	19	四	29	円	39	間	49	兄	59	足	69	書	79	思
10	本	20	五	30	月	40	週	50	弟	60	手	70	話	80	電

81	面	91	果	101	言	111	聞	121	議	131	前	141	談	151	記
82	力	92	英	102	提	112	様	122	席	132	持	142	集	152	紙
83	企	93	日	103	営	113	申	123	急	133	通	143	計	153	池
84	業	94	課	104	海	114	少	124	番	134	決	144	表	154	数
85	語	95	員	105	外	115	々	125	号	135	取	145	算	155	字
86	好	96	君	106	村	116	朝	126	伝	136	引	146	座	156	意
87	度	97	使	107	気	117	工	127	用	137	方	147	待	157	味
88	結	98	仕	108	部	118	失	128	件	138	論	148	窓	158	代
89	名	99	事	109	長	119	礼	129	同	139	相	149	客	159	便
90	所	100	毎	110	新	120	係	130	午	140	値	150	作	160	利

161	料	171	定	181	製	191	介	201	究	211	費	211	答	221	知
162	国	172	入	182	造	192	状	202	室	212	説	212	無	222	割
163	信	173	悪	183	世	193	性	203	元	213	明	213	消	223	直
164	機	174	心	184	市	194	彼	204	品	214	開	214	費	224	商
165	械	175	配	185	場	195	経	205	器	215	発	215	価	225	問
166	者	176	速	186	拡	196	済	206	販	216	速	216	格	226	題
167	忘	177	連	187	張	197	門	207	売	217	合	217	台	227	乗
168	暗	178	接	188	考	198	系	208	安	218	自	218	別	228	文
169	証	179	待	189	願	199	忙	209	量	219	動	219	全	229	届
170	予	180	頼	190	紹	200	研	210	産	210	的	220	問	230	質

231	法
232	向
233	画
234	遅
235	裁

Appendix B: Japanese-English Glossary

あ

あ (interj)　oh!, 2.d.conv
ああ (interj)　oh!, ahh! , 1.a.conv
ああいった (prenom)　that kind of [shared experience; = あんな], 1.c.add
アイコーでんき (アイコー電気) (n)　Aiko Electric (company name), 8.c.4
あいさつ (挨拶) (n)　greeting, 6.b.4, 6.gr.4
あいだ (間) (n)　while; during [S 間"while S (throughout)"; S 間に"while S"], 4.b.conv
あいたい (会いたい) (v: aw/u) [たい-form of あう] want to meet, 7.d.2
あいてがわ (相手側) (n)　the other side/party, 4.d.conv
あいにく (adv)　unfortunately, 3.com.2, 5.g.conv
アイビーエム (IBM) (n)　IBM, 1.gr.6
あう (会う) (v: aw/u)　to meet, see, 3.c.1
あう (合う) (v: aw/u)　to match, be compatible, 9.b.conv
あえたら (会えたら) (v: aw/u) [COND of あう] if one meet, 7.b.1
あえる (会える) (v: aw/u) [POT of あう] can meet, 7.gr.8
あお (青) (n)　blue color, 5.gr.7
あおい (青い) (い-adj)　blue, 6.gr.6
あおき (青木) (n)　Aoki [family name], 2.a.conv
あか (赤) (n)　red color, 5.gr.7
あか (赤) ちゃん (n) baby, 6.b.3
あかい (赤い) (い-adj)　red, 6.gr.6
あがる (上がる) (vi: agar/u) (something) goes up, rises [vt: あげる], 6.c.3, 11.c.2
あかるい (明るい) (い-adj) bright, 6.gr.9
あきこ (明子) (n)　Akiko [woman's name], 2.com.1
あきスペース (空きスペース) (n)　free space, 5.gr.6
あきはばら (秋葉原) (n)　Akihabara [electronics town in Tokyo], 4.d.2
あく (開く) (vi: ak/u)　(something) opens, is open [vt: あける], 6.a.conv, 6.a.1
アクション (n)　action, 9.lc
あけてみる (開けてみる) (phr)　try and open; open and see, 6.gr.1
あけといて (開けといて) (v: ake/ru) [Contraction of あけておいて] keep (something) open; open in advance, 6.a.conv
あける (開ける) (vt: ake/ru) to open (something) [大きくあける "open wide"] [vi: あく], 6.a.1
あげる (上げる) (vt: age/ru)　to give (to others) [V てあげる "to give (others) a favor of V-ing"],10.c.1
あげる (上げる) (vt: age/ru)　to raise, lift, 4.e.conv
あさ (朝) (n)　morning, 5.gr.5
あさって (明後日) (n)　the day after tomorrow, 1.gr.4
あさひ (朝日) (n)　morning sun; Asahi [last name], 3.c.conv
あさひしんぶん (朝日新聞) (n)　Asahi Newspaper, 9.a.3
あさひでんき (朝日電気) (n)　Asahi Electric [company name], 1.lc
アジア (n)　Asia, 1.b.2
あした (明日) (n)　tomorrow, 1.a.2

あしたじゅう (明日中) (phr)　all day tomorrow, 11.b.2
あす (明日) (n)　tomorrow (= あした), 4.e.conv
あそばせる (遊ばせる) (v: asob/u) [CAUS of あそぶ] to make/let (someone) play , 9.a.1
あそばれる (遊ばれる) (v: asob/u) [↑ of あそぶ] to play; [ADV-PASS of あそぶ] to be played, 8.b.1
あそぶ (遊ぶ) (v: asob/u)　to play; to be idle, 9.gr.2
あそべる (遊べる) (v: asob/u) [POT of あそぶ] can play, 8.b.1
あたたかい (暖かい) (い-adj)　warm [of weather], 7.e.1
あたま (頭) (n)　head [頭がいたい "to have a headache"], 1.gr.6
あたらしい (新しい) (い-adj)　new, 6.a.6
あたりまえ (当たり前) (n)　natural thing; obvious thing, 4.a.5
あちら (pro)　that place over there (far away), 9.c.1
あつい (熱い) (い-adj)　hot, 1.c.3
あつかい (扱い) (n)　handling, treatment, 5.e.conv
あつかう (扱う) (v: atsukaw/u)　to deal with, 8.b.conv
あつかったら (暑かったら) (い-adj) [COND of あつい] if it's hot, 7.e.3
あつく (厚く) (い-adj) [く-form of あつい] deeply, 7.rw.1
あつい (暑い) (い-adj)　hot, 5.c.1, 7.d.conv
あつそう (暑そう) (phr) [Stem of あつい + そう] looks hot, 8.a.1
あったら (v: ar/u) [COND of ある] if ... exist; if ... have, 2.a.conv
あってほしい (会ってほしい) (phr) [て-form of あう + ほしい] want (other person) to meet, 7.d.2
あってみよう (会ってみよう) (phr) [て-form of あう + VOL of みる] I will meet, 7.e.conv
あつまる (集まる) (v: atsumar/u)　to gather, assemble, meet, 4.e.conv
あてさき (宛先) (n)　to, destination of mail, 4.rw2
あと (n)　after [あとで "some time after; later"], 4.b.conv, 6.b.conv
あとで (phr)　after [X のあとで "after X"], 2.a.2, 6.b.1
アドバイス (n)　advice, 6.lc
アトランタ (n)　Atlanta, 2.a.3
あに (兄) (n)　older brother ↓, 1.c.3
アニメ (n)　animation; animated cartoon, 11.a.3
あね (姉) (n)　older sister ↓, 1.c.3
あの (interj)　umm... [hesitation noise to get someone's attention], 1.b.1, 5.b.conv
あのう (interj)　umm... [hesitation noise to get someone's attention], 5.b.conv
あのかた (あの方) (phr)　that person; he, 2.e.1
あのように (phr)　in that way; like that, 10.c.2
アパート (n)　apartment, 10.a.1
アフターサービス (n)　customer service; after care [after + service; word coined by Japanese], 9.c.conv
あぶない (危ない) (い-adj)　dangerous, 8.b.1
あぶらえ (油絵) (n)　oil painting, 10.gr.4
アポイントメント (n)　appointment, 6.gr.4
アマチュアむせん (アマチュア無線) (n)　ham/amateur radio, 1.rw

あまり (adv) (not) very much; (not) very often [followed by NEG], 1.d.conv
あめ (雨) (n) rain, 1.b.3
アメリカ (n) America, 1.a.conv
アメリカしゃ (アメリカ車) (n) American car, 1.b.5
アメリカじん (アメリカ人) (n) American (person), 1.b.6
あらう (洗う) (v: araw/u) to wash, 2.a.2
あり (v: ar/u) [V-stem of ある] there is/are; to have, 1.b.conv
ありがたい (い-adj) grateful, 7.c.conv
ありがとう (phr) Thank you., 1.e.conv
ありがとうございました (phr) Thank you very much (for what you did)., 1.e.conv
ありましたら (v: ar/u) [POL あったら] if there is; if you have, 2.a.2
ある (v: ar/u) there is/are [inanimate things]; to have. [V てある "(something) is V-ed deliberately"], 1.b.conv, 1.b.1, 2.c.conv, 2.c.1
あるきかた (歩き方) (n) the way of walking, 5.gr.8
あるく (歩く) (v: aruk/u) to walk, 7.gr.4
アルトロンしゃ (アルトロン社) (n) Ultron [company name], 9.a.conv
アルバイト (n) part-time job, 1.rw
あわせてある (合わせて〜) (v: aw/u) [CAUS of あって + ある] match deliberately, 9.b.conv
あわせる (合わせる) (v: aw/u) [CAUS of あう] to make/let (something/someone) match, be compatible, 9.b.conv
あんしょうばんごう (暗証番号) (n) security code, person identification number, 5.c.conv
あんないじょう (案内状) (n) invitation card, 6.c.4
あんない (案内) する (n/v) to guide, usher; guidance, invitation, 9.1c
あんなに (phr) that (much); that way, 6.b.conv
あんなふうに (phr) in that way; like that, 10.c.2
あんまり (adv) [alternate form of あまり] (not) very..., 1.b.1

い

いい (い-adj) good, nice; OK, 1.b.conv
いいえ (interj) No [disagreement]; Don't mention it., 1.d.conv
いいかた (言い方) (n) the way of speaking, 5.gr.8
Eメール (n) Email, 4.gr.10
いう (言う) (v: iw/u) to say; [〜ていう or 〜という "is called"], 1.a.1
いうばかり (言うばかり) (phr) All one does is say., 9.c.2
いえ (家) (n) house, 1.com.4
いえ, いえいえ (interj) No/No, no., 1.d.conv, 6.c.conv
いえる (言える) (v: iw/u) [POT of いう] can say, 1.b.6
いか (以下) (n) below, (equal to or) less [いかのとおり "as follows"], 6.rw
いかが (qw) how?; how about? [POL of どう] [いかがですか "How about...?"], 2.a.2
いかがなもの (qw) What kind of thing? How about it?, 10.b.conv
いかさせる (行かせる) (v: ik/u) [CAUS of いく] to make/let (someone) go, 9.a.1
いかされる (活かされる) (v: ikas/u) [PASS of いかす] to be made use of; [↑ of いかす] to make use of, 8.b.1
いかしたい (活かしたい) (v: ikas/u) [たい-form of いかす] want to make the most of, 4.d.2
いかす (活かす) (v: ikas/u) to make the most of, 1.b.3, 8.b.1

いかせる (活かせる) (v: ikas/u) [POT of いかす] can make the most of, 1.b.conv
いかれます (行かれます) (v: ik/u) [↑ of いく] (someone) goes; [ADV-PASS of いく] (someone) goes, 8.c.5
いかれる (行かれる) (v: ik/u) [↑ of いく] (someone) goes; [ADV-PASS of いく] (someone) goes, 8.b.1
いきたい (行きたい) (v: ik/u) [たい-form of いく] want to go, 1.b.4
いきたがって (行きたがって) (v: ik/u) [いきたい + suffix がる] (someone) shows signs of wanting to go, 6.a.conv
いきたくなさそう (行きたくなさそう) (phr) [く-form of いきたい + Stem of ない + さそう] appear not wanting to go, 9.a.1
いく (行く) (v: ik/u) to go, 1.a.1, 1.gr.2, 6.a.1
いくら (qw) how much, 9.c.2
いくらか (phr) somewhat; for some price, 6.a.3
いくらきいても (いくら聞いても) (phr) no matter how much I ask, 11.b.2
いくらたかくても (いくら高くても) (phr) no matter how expensive, 11.b.2
いけば (行けば) (v: ik/u) [PROV of いく] if/provided one goes, 7.c.2
いける (行ける) (v: ik/u) [POT of いく] can go, 1.b.5
いければ (行ければ) (v: ik/u) [PROV of いける] if/provided that we can go, 11.b.2
いけん (意見) (n) opinion, 5.gr.4
いこう (以降) (n) after [time], 3.rw2
いしい (石井) (n) Ishii [family name], 1.gr.7
いしの (石野) (n) Ishino [family name], 10.c.conv
いじょう (以上) (n) above; That's all.; [number + いじょう "equal to or more"], 1.rw, 10.gr.1
いす (椅子) (n) chair, 2.gr.4, 5.c.conv
いそがしい (忙しい) (い-adj) busy, 2.gr.6, 3.d.conv, 6.a.3
いそがせる (急がせる) (v: isog/u) [CAUS of いそぐ] to make/let (someone) hurry, 9.a.1
いそがれる (急がれる) (v: isog/u) [↑ of いそぐ] (someone) hurries; [ADV-PASS of いそぐ] (someone) hurries, 8.b.1
いそぎ (急ぎ) (n) in a hurry, 3.gr.3
いそぐ (急ぐ) (v: isog/u) to hurry, 1.b.5, 2.c.2, 3.d.1
いそげば (急げば) (v: isog/u) [PROV of いそぐ] if/provided one hurries, 7.c.2
いそげる (急げる) (v: isog/u) [POT of いそぐ] can hurry, 1.b.5
いたい (痛い) (い-adj) painful, 1.gr.6, 7.c.2
いたして (v: itas/u) [て-form of いたす] do [↓ of して], 5.g.conv
いたします (v: itas/u) [POL of いたす] to do [↓ of する], 1.b.2
いただかなくても (v: itadak/u) [て-form of いただかない + も] even if one does not receive [↓ of もらわなくても], 5.b.1
いただかれる (v: itadak/u) [PASS of いただく] to be received; [↑ of いただく] to receive, 8.c.5
いただきたい (v: itadak/u) [たい-form of いただく] want to receive [↓ of もらいたい], 3.f.conv
いただく (v: itadak/u) to receive; to eat; to drink [↓ of もらう], 3.f.4, 3.f.5, 4.a.3
いただける (v: itadak/u) [POT of いただく] can receive [↓ of もらえる], [お時間いただけませんか "May I have your time?"], 5.f.2, 5.gr.12, 8.b.conv
いただければ (v: itadak/u) [PROV of もらえる] if/provided that we can receive [いただければとおもいます "We hope you give me..."] [↓ of もらえれば], 7.c.conv, 11.b.3

いたる (至る) (v: itar/u) to reach; to arrive at, 10.rw.1
いちおう (一応) (adv) just in case, 4.a.conv
いちぞん (一存) (n) one's own decision, 4.d.conv
いちだい (一台) (num) one unit (of machines), 10.a.conv
いちど (一度) (n) once, one time, 1.d.conv
いちにち (一日) (num) one day, 5.e.1
いちにちじゅう (一日中) (n) all day long, 7.e.1
いちねん (一年) (num) one year, 3.gr.1
いちねんかん (一年間) (num) one year, 9.a.1
いちばん (一番) (adv) the most; the first; the best; number one, 9.a.conv
いちらんばらい (一覧払い) (n) payment at sight, 11.b.conv
いつ (qw) when, 2.c.conv
いつか (phr) some time; some day, 6.a.3
いっか (一課) (n) Section #1, 3.a.conv
いつきても (いつ来ても) (phr) no matter when I come, 11.b.2
いっきゅう (一級) (n) first class, 1.rw
いっきょく (一曲) (num) one song, 7.b.3
いっしき (一式) (n) a complete set, 9.rw.1
いっしゅうかん (一週間) (num) one week, 5.e.conv
いっしょ (一緒) (n) together [いっしょに V "V together"], 4.gr.5, 7.e.conv
いっしょけんめい (一所懸命) (n) one's best, 2.lc
いっしょに (一緒に) (phr) together, 6.c.conv
いっしょの (一緒の) (phr) the same; together, 8.a.conv
いったら (言ったら) (v: iw/u) [COND of いう] if one says, 2.a.2
いったら (行ったら) (v: ik/u) [COND of いく] if one goes, 2.a.2
いっておく (言っておく) (phr) [て-form of いう + おく] to say it in advance, 4.e.conv
いってくる (行ってくる) (phr) go and come back, 6.gr.1
いってくる (言ってくる) (phr) [て-form of いう + くる] (someone) to speak from a distant place, come over saying; 11.a.conv
いってみたい (行ってみたい) (phr) [て-form of いく + みたい] want to go and see; want to try and go, 6.b.2
いつでも (phr) whenever, 4.gr.5
いつでんわをかけても (いつ電話をかけても) (phr) no matter when I call, 11.b.2
いっとく (言っとく) (phr) [contraction of いっておく] to say (it) in advance, 4.a.4, 4.a.5
いっぱい (n) full; a great deal [今週いっぱい "throughout this week"], 7.gr.3
いっぱい (一杯) (num) one cup, 5.gr.6, 6.b.4
いっぱく (一泊) (num) one night (stay), 10.a.1
いっぱん (一般) (n) general, 5.rw.1
いっぱんしょく (一般職) (n) clerical post, 2.a.4
いつも (n) always, 6.a.3
いな (否) (n) not, 5.rw.1
いない (以内) (n) within, inside, 9.lc
いなか (田舎) (n) countryside; rural area, 10.gr.4
いま (今) (n) emergent, 1.c.2
いまでは (今では) (phr) by now, 8.c.conv
いみ (意味) (n) meaning, interpretation [意味がない "not meaningful"], 5.a.add, 11.b.2
いもうと (妹) さん (n) younger sister [お = ↑], 1.c.2
いや (interj) No., 6.c.conv
いや (嫌) (な-adj) dislike, uncomfortable, 10.lc
いやあ (interj) well; oh; wow, 7.d.conv
いやいや (interj) No, no., 8.a.conv

いらして (v: irasshar/u) [= いらっしゃって; て-form of いらっしゃる] come; go; is/stay, 4.a.3
いらっしゃいませ (v: irasshar/u) Welcome!, 5.a.conv
いらっしゃいません (v: irasshar/u) [POL ↑ of いない] not stay; not to be; there isn't/aren't [animate]; not come; not go, 6.a.3
いらっしゃる (v: irasshar/u) [↑ of いる] to come; to go; to be [animate], 1.a.2
いられる (v: i/ru) [POT of いる] can be; can stay, 1.b.5
いる (v: i/ru) to be; to stay [animate], 1.a.1
いる (要る) (v: ir/u) to need, be necessary, 4.c.conv
いるかね (phr) Is he/she there, I wonder? [very blunt], 3.d.4
いれましょう (入れましょう) (v: ire/ru) [VOL of いれる] I will put it/pour in, 1.gr.2
いれる (入れる) (vt: ire/ru) to put in; to pour; to turn (a switch) on [vi: はいる], 4.e.1, 5.c.1, 6.a.1
いろいろ (な-adj) various, 2.lc, 3.f.4
いわせる (言わせる) (v: iw/u) [CAUS of いう] to make/let (someone) say, 9.a.1
いわないで (言わないで) (phr) [NEG REQ form of いう] Don't say it., 6.b.4
いわなくても (言わなくても) (phr) even if you don't say it, 6.b.conv
いわれたら (言われたら) (v: iw/u) if one is told, 10.gr.3
いわれる (言われる) (v: iw/u) [PASS of いう] to be said; [↑ of いう] to say, 8.b.1, 8.c.4
いん (印)、いんかん (印鑑) (n) signature seal, 1.e.2, 5.b.conv
インストールする (n/v) to install; installation, 7.b.3
インターテック (n) InterTech [company name], 3.com.1
インターネット (n) Internet, 1.a.2
インテリソフト (n) Intellisoft [company name], 8.lc
インテル (n) Intel [company name], 9.a.3
インフレ (n) inflation, 5.gr.6

う

うえだ (上田) (n) Ueda [family name; place name], 1.rw
ウェブ (n) the Web, 9.c.4
ウェブページ (n) Web page, 9.lc
ウォールストリートジャーナル (n) Wall Street Journal, 1.gr.8
うかがいたい (伺いたい) (v: ukagaw/u) [たい-form of うかがう] want to ask, visit ↓, 5.f.conv
うかがう (伺う) (v: ukagaw/u) [↓ of きく/いく] to ask; to go/visit, 5.f.conv
うかがった (伺った) (v: ukagaw/u) [↓ of きいた/いった] asked; visited, 7.a.1
うけ (受) (n) received by, 3.rw.1
うけたまわる (承る) (v: uketamawar/u) [↓ of きく] to listen to (something); accept (something), 3.f.conv
うけつけ (受付) (n) reception desk, 4.gr.3
うける (受ける) (v: uke/ru) take [an exam]; accept, 4.gr.7
うた (歌) (n) song; singing, 6.b.conv
うたう (歌う) (v: utaw/u) to sing, 1.d.1, 6.b.conv
うたれる (打たれる) (v: ut(s)/u) [PASS of うつ] to be hit; [↑ of うつ] to hit, 8.b.1
うたわないで (歌わないで) (phr) [NEG REQ of うたう] Don't sing., 6.b.4
うち (家) (n) home; house; inside; we/us, 1.a.1

うち (内) (n)　inside; range (of comparison); ↓ I, we, my company, home, self [うちの my, our], 1.b.2 2.d.conv
うちあわせ (打ち合わせ) (n)　preliminary consultation, 3.gr.3
うちのもの (うちの者) (phr)　our men, women [ingroup] ↓, 3.c.1
うつ (打つ) (v: ut(s)/u)　to hit; to type [ワープロをうつ], 3.gr.3
うまい (い-adj)　tasty; is good at, 6.c.conv
うまく (い-adj) [く-form of うまい] well; skillfully [うまくいく "(it) goes well"], 8.gr.7
うまれ (生まれ) (n)　birth, 1.e.2
うめぞの (梅園) (n)　Umezono [restaurant name], 6.c.2
うりあげ (売り上げ) (n)　[the amount of] sales, 4.e.conv
うりあげしゅうけいひょう (売上げ集計表) (n)　sales journal chart, 4.rw.1
うりあげだか (売り上げ高) (n)　annual sales total, 8.rw.1
うる (売る) (vt: ur/u) to sell [vi: うれる], 8.gr.2
うるさい (い-adj) noisy, 7.b.3
うれしい (嬉しい) (n)　is glad, 11.b.2
うれる (売れる) (v: ur/u) [POT of うる] can sell, 10.gr.3
うれる (売れる) (vi: ure/ru) (product) sells, is sold [vt: うる], 7.gr.1, 11.gr.2
うん (interj)　Yes [INFORMAL of はい; agreement]; A verbal sign that says "I'm listening.", 1.a.1
うんちん (運賃) (n)　fare; freight fee, 5.com.1, 11.b.conv
うんてんしゅ (運転手) (n)　driver, 9.a.1

え

え (interj)　oh?, 2.b.conv
エアコン (n)　air conditioner, 4.gr.6, 5.c.1, 7.e.3
えいが (映画) (n)　movie, 1.com.4
えいかいわ (英会話) (n)　English conversation, 3.gr.7
えいぎょう (営業) する (n/v) to run business; sales, operation, 2.d.conv, 7.gr.2
えいぎょうぶ (営業部) (n)　sales division, 2.e.conv
えいご (英語) (n)　English, 1.a.1
エイズ (n)　AIDS, 11.gr.4
えいぶん (英文) (n)　English text, 9.a.1
えいよう (栄養) (n)　nutrition, 7.gr.2
ええ (interj)　umm... [hesitation noise], 1.d.conv
エーアイソフト (n)　AI Soft [company name], 8.lc
エーアイテック (n)　AI Tech [company name], 7.lc
Aしゃ (A社) (n)　Company A, 1.gr.2
えき (駅) (n)　station, 1.gr.8
エキスポ (n)　expo, 4.a.2
エキスポプラザ (n)　expo plaza, 9.rw.1
エコノミークラス (n)　economy class, 5.gr.7
エフオービー (n)　FOB (free on board), 11.b.conv
エラー (n)　error, 8.lc
えらぶ (選ぶ) (v: erab/u)　to choose; to select, 1.c.conv
エルシー (n)　L/C (letter of credit), 11.b.conv
エレクトロニクス (n)　electronics, 2.d.conv
えん (円) (n)　yen, 7.c.1
えんか (演歌) (n)　Japanese blues [song], 1.d.1
エンジニアリング (n)　engineering, 1.com.4
えんだか (円高) (n)　high yen; appreciation of the yen, 11.lc
えんだて (円建て) (n)　yen-based, 11.b.conv
えんりょ (遠慮) しないで (phr) [NEG REQ form of 遠慮する] Don't hold back., 6.b.4

えんりょ (遠慮) する (n/v)　to hold back, be reserved, 6.b.4, 6.gr.3

お

おいしい (い-adj)　delicious, tasty, 1.a.1, 1.b.1, 9.b.1
おいしそう (phr) [Stem of おいしい + そう] looks delicious, 8.a.1
おいそがしい (お忙しい) (い-adj)　busy [お = ↑], 2.a.2, 3.d.conv
おいそがしかったら (お忙しかったら) (い-adj) [COND of おいそがしい] if you are busy [お = ↑], 2.a.2
おいそぎ (お急ぎ) (n)　in a hurry [お = ↑], 3.d.conv, 3.f.5
おいでください (おいで下さい) (phr)　please come, 5.g.conv, 6.rw, 7.a.2
おいれする (お入れする) (v: ire/ru) [↓ of いれる] to put in, 4.e.1
おうかがいいたします (お伺いいたします) (v: ukagaw/u) [↓ of ききます／たずねます] to visit; go; ask, 7.c.conv
おうふく (往復) (n)　round trip, 5.com.1
おおい (多い) (い-adj)　many, numerous, 2.b.1
おおがたきかく (大型企画) (n)　large-scale project, 7.e.2
おおかった (多かった) (い-adj)　(were) many, numerous, 4.gr.3
おおきい (大きい) (い-adj)　large, 1.d.1, 6.b.3
おおくらしょうじ (大蔵商事) (n)　Okura Trading Company, 10.a.3
おおくりいただける (お送りいただける) (phr) [お + V-stem of おくる + POT of いただく] can receive someone's sending, 5.f.2, 6.c.2
おおげさ (大袈裟) (な-adj)　exaggeration, a big deal, 6.a.conv
おおごえ (大声) (n)　loud voice, 6.b.conv
おおさか (大阪) (n)　Osaka [a city in Japan], 4.a.conv
おおしえ (教え) (v: oshie/ru) [↑ stem of おしえます] to teach; to inform, 1.gr.3
おおしえする (お教えする) (v: oshie/ru) [↓ of おしえる] to teach, inform, 5.g.conv
オーストラリア (n)　Australia, 2.gr.7, 4.gr.6
おおた (太田) (n)　Ota [family name], 6.gr.2
おおたく (大田区) (n)　Ota Ward [of Tokyo], 1.rw
おおたに (大谷) (n)　Otani [family name], 3.f.conv
おおべやしゅぎ (大部屋主義) (n)　large-room-ism [work ethic emphasizing group cooperation in a large, partitionless room], 2.b.1
おおやまホテル (大山ホテル) (n)　Oyama Hotel, 10.a.3
おかあさん (お母さん) (n)　mother [お = ↑], 1.c.1
おかえり (お帰り) (n)　return [お + V-stem of かえる], 1.c.2
おかえり (お帰り) になる (v: kaer/u) [お + V-stem of かえる + に + なる] to return, go home [↑ of かえる], 7.e.3
おかけください (おかけ下さい) (v: kake/ru) [↑ request of かける] take (a seat), 2.d.conv
おかげさまで (phr)　I'm fine, thank you., 8.gr.8
おかげで (phr)　thanks to [S おかげで "thanks to the fact that S"; N のおかげで "thanks to N"], 11.c.conv
おかけになって (v: kake/ru) [↑ of かけて] sit down; to multiply; times [でんわをかける "to call"], 5.c.conv
おかしする (お貸しする) (v: kas/u) [↓ of かす] to lend, 5.g.1
おかだ (岡田) (n)　Okada [family name], 7.a.2
おかね (お金) (n)　money, 5.a.1, 5.d.conv
おがわ (小川) (n)　Ogawa (family name, 7.a.conv

おきめ（お決め）になる (v: kime/ru) to decide (on) [お= ↑], 5.c.conv
おきゃくさま（お客様）(n) guest, customer [お= ↑], 2.a.1, 5.b.conv
おきゃくさん（お客さん）(n) visitor, guest [お = ↑], 2.lc, 4.gr.3, 6.c.conv
おきる（起きる）(vi: oki/ru) (someone) wakes up, gets up [vt: おこす], 6.a.1
おく（置く）(v: ok/u) to put down; place [V ておく "V in advance for later use"], 4.a.conv
おくさま（奥様）／おくさん (n) wife ↑ [of someone else], 1.gr.5, 4.a.3
おくっていただきたい（送って～）(phr) [て-form of おくる + いただきたい] I want you to send it to me., 9.a.2
おくっていただけませんか（送って～）(phr) [て-form of おくる + いただけませんか] Couldnュt I receive your favor of sending it to me?, 9.a.2
おくってくる（送ってくる）(phr) [て-form of おくる + くる] to send (it) in, 11.a.1
おくってきたばかり（送って～）(phr) [て-form of おくる + きた + ばかり] (someone) has just sent (it) in, 11.a.2
おくらせていただきたい（送らせて～）(phr) [て-form of おくらせる + いただきたい] I want to take the liberty of sending it to you; I want to receive your favor of letting me send it to you., 9.a.2
おくらせていただきます（送らせて～）(phr) [て-form of おくらせる + いただきます] I'll take the liberty of sending it to you., 9.a.2
おくらせていただけませんか（送らせて～）(phr) [て-form of おくらせる + いただけませんか] Couldnュt I take the liberty of sending it to you? Could I receive your favor of letting me send it to you?, 9.a.2
おくらせてください（送らせて下さい）(phr) [て-form of おくらせる + ください] let me send it to you, 9.a.2
おくらせる（送らせる）(v: okur/u) [CAUS of おくる] to make/let (someone) send, 9.a.2
おくりたい（送りたい）(v: okur/u) [たい-form of おくる] want to send, 5.d.conv
おくりましょう（送り～）(v: okur/u) [VOL of おくります] let's send, 4.a.2
おくる（送る）(v: okur/u) to escort someone; to send something/someone [でんしメールをおくる "to send email"], 2.a.3, 3.e.conv, 3.e.add, 4.e.conv, 5.f.2
おくれる（遅れる）(v: okure/ru) to be late; to get delayed [= おそくなる], 2.c.2, 11.c.conv
おくろう（送ろう）(v: okur/u) [VOL of おくる] let's send, 4.a.2
おこさん（お子さん）(n) child(ren) [お = ↑], 3.b.1
おこし（お越し）(v: okos/u) [POL V-stem of こす] go/come over; cross; exceed ↑, 5.g.conv
おこす（起こす）(vt: okos/u) to wake up (someone) [vi: おきる], 6.a.1, 6.b.3
おこしください (phr) Please come over., 5.g.conv
おことづけ（お言付け）(n) message [お = ↑], 3.e.add
おこなう（行なう）(v: okonaw/u) to conduct; to carry out, 6.rw
おこのみやき（お好み焼き）(n) Japanese-style pancake, 10.gr.4
おさえる (v: osae/ru) hold down, control, 5.c.1
おさけ（お酒）(n) sake [Japanese rice wine], 2.gr.6, 6.b.conv

おさしつかえなければ (phr) [お + NEG PROV of さしつかえる "interfere"] provided that it does not interfere with you, 3.f.conv
おさそい（お誘い）(n) invitation, 6.gr.4
おさそいあわせのうえ（お誘い合わせの上）(phr) together, 6.rw
おさびしい（お淋しい）(い-adj) lonely [お = ↑], 11.lc
おしえられる（教えられる）(v: oshie/ru) [POT of おしえる] can teach; can inform, 1.b.5
おしえられる（教えられる）(v: oshie/ru) [PASS of おしえる] to be taught; to be told; [↑ of おしえる] to teach; to tell, 8.b.1
おしえる（教える）(v: oshie/ru) to teach, inform, tell, 1.gr.3, 2.c.conv, 2.c.1
おじかん（お時間）(n) your time [お = ↑], 5.gr.12
おじぎ（お辞儀）(n) bowing, 1.b.2, 2.a.4
おしごと（お仕事）(n) job; work [お = ↑], 1.c.1
おしはらい（お支払い）(v: shiharaw/u) [↑ V-stem of しはらう] pay, 5.d.conv
おじゃま（お邪魔）する↓ (n/v) to bother, interfere; interference, 7.a.1
おじょうず（お上手）(な-adj) skillful; is good at [お = ↑], 1.d.conv
おしらせ（お知らせ）(n) notice, 6.rw
おしらせいたします（お知らせ～）(v: shirase/ru) [↓ of しらせます] to notify, 1.e.conv
おす（押す）(v: os/u) to push, 2.gr.7
おすき（お好き）(な-adj) to like; to be fond of; favorite [お= ↑], 1.d.1
おすし（お寿司）(n) sushi [お = ↑], 2.c.3
おすまい（お住まい）(n) (other people's) home, house [お = ↑], 1.gr.1
おせわ（お世話）(n) care, help [お = ↑] [お世話になります "Thank you for your help." (Said before one is helped)], 2.a.conv
おせわになってばかり（お世話に～）(phr) All one does is to receive help., 9.c.2
おそい（遅い）(い-adj) late; slow, 8.c.4
おそく（遅く）(い-adj) [く form of おそい] late; slow [おそくなる "become late"], 3.gr.3, 5.g.1
おそくて（遅くて）(い-adj) [て-form of おそい] late; slow [おそくてもいい "OK even if it is late"], 5.b.1
おそくても（遅くても）(い-adj) [て-form of おそい + も] even if one is late/slow, 5.b.1
おそくなっても（遅くなっても）(phr) [く-form of おそい + なって + も] even if it gets late, 8.c.3
おそくまで（遅くまで）(phr) until late, 11.c.2
おそれいります（恐れ入ります）(v: osoreir/u) [POL of おそれいる] to be terribly sorry/intrusive; to be extremely grateful, 2.d.conv
おたく（お宅）(n) (other's) house/home [お = ↑], 2.a.1
おたくさま（お宅様）(n) you; your party [お = ↑], 2.a.1, 6.c.1
おだしする（お出しする）(vt: das/u) [↓ of だす] to put outside; to submit ↓, 6.gr.1
おだしになる（お出しになる）(vt: das/u) [↑ of だす] to put outside; to submit, 6.gr.1
おたのしみください（お楽しみ下さい）(phr) Please enjoy. ↑, 6.b.4
おちゃ（お茶）(n) Japanese tea, 2.b.conv

おちゃだし (お茶出し) (n)　tea serving, 2.b.conv
おつかい (お使い) (n)　use [お + V-stem of つかう], 1.c.2
おつかれ (お疲れ) (n)　fatigue [お = ↑], 3.d.3
おつかれさま (お疲れ様) (phr)　Thank you for your hard work! Good bye! [said to someone who is leaving after work], 4.b.conv
おつかれ (お疲れ) になる (phr) [お + V-stem of つかれる + に + なる] (someone) became tired [↑ of つかれる], 7.e.1
おつきあい (n)　going along with; socializing [お = ↑], 6.a.add
おつくり (お作り) (v: tsukur/u) [↑-POL V-stem of つくる] make; to cook, 1.b.1
おつくりになる (お作りになる) (v: tsukur/u) [↑-POL of つくる] to make; to cook, 5.a.conv
おっしゃいます (v: osshar/u) [POL ↑ of いう] to say, 2.e.1
おっしゃる (v: osshar/u) [↑ of いう] to say, 2.e.add, 4.c.conv
おつたえいただけませんか (お伝え～) (phr)　Couldnユt you inform (someone)? [Lit. "Couldnユt I receive your favor of informing...?"; つたえる "to inform"], 4.a.1
おつたえください (お伝え下さい) (phr) [↑ お + V-stem of つたえる + ください "Please V"] Please inform., 3.f.conv
おって (追って) (phr)　later, subsequently, 1.e.conv
おつとめ (お勤め) (n)　employment; job [お = ↑], 1.c.conv
おつとめさき (お勤め先) (n)　employer name [お = ↑], 5.rw.1
おつれする (お連れ～) (v: tsure/ru) [↓ of つれる] take/bring someone (somewhere), 6.c.conv
おてつだい (お手伝い) する (n/v) [↓ of てつだう] to help; to assist; assistance [おてつだいいたしましょうか "Shall I help you?"], 7.d.2, 7.lc
おでになる (お出になる) (vi: de/ru) [↑ of でる] to go out; to come out; to leave; to emerge [vt: おだしになる], 6.gr.1
おでんわいたします (お電話いたします) (n/v) [↓ of 電話します] to call; telephone, 3.c.conv
おでんわかわりました (お電話代わり～) (phr)　I switched the phone. [... speaking], 3.b.conv
おでんわです (お電話～) (phr)　You have a phone call; It's for you. [お = ↑], 3.b.add
おとうさん (お父さん) (n)　father [お = ↑], 1.c.1
おとうとさん (弟さん) (n)　younger brother [お = ↑], 1.c.2
おとおしする (お通しする) (v: toos/u) [↓ of とおす] to let someone in, 8.c.5, 8.lc
おとくい (お得意) (な-adj)　is good at (and likes it) [お = ↑], 1.d.conv
おところ (n)　address, 5.rw.1
おととい (一昨日) (n)　the day before yesterday, 1.gr.5
おとどけいん (お届け印) (n)　registered signature seal, 5.rw.1
おとりになる (お取り～) (v: tor/u) [↑ of とる] to take, 5.a.conv
おとりひき (お取引) (n)　business deal, transaction [お = ↑], 7.rw.1
おなか (お腹) (n)　stomach, abdomen, 7.c.2
おなじ (同じ) (n)　the same [can be used like an adjectival modifier: おなじほん "the same book"], 3.f.conv
おにいさん (お兄さん) (n)　older brother [お = ↑], 1.gr.2
おねえさん (お姉さん) (n)　older sister [お = ↑], 1.c.2
おねがい (お願い) (n)　request; wish, 2.c.conv
おねがいする (お願い～) (v: negaw/u) to request ↓, 1.a.conv, 5.b.1
おねがいできる (お願い～) (v: negaw/u) [POT of おねがいする] can request ↓, 5.b.1
おねがいできれば (お願い～) (phr) [PROV of おねがいできる] if/provided I can make a request [おねがいできれば(いい)とおもう "If I could make a request, wish."]., 11.b.conv
おのみになりませんか (お飲み～) (phr) [お + V-stem of のむ + に + なりません + か] Would you like to drink?, 7.d.2
おのみもの (お飲み物) (n)　drinks [お = ↑], 5.gr.7
おはなしできますでしょうか (お話し～) (phr)　Can I speak? [↓ POL], 7.a.3
おはなしになる (お話し～) (phr)　to speak [↑ of はなす], 4.d.2
おはようございます (phr)　Good morning! [POL of おはよう], 2.a.4
おひきたて (お引き立て) (n)　favor [お = ↑], 7.rw.1
おひさしぶり (お久しぶり) (n)　Long time, no see. [お = ↑]., 8.a.conv
おひとつ (お一つ) (num)　one [Japanese series] [お= ↑], 2.a.2
おひま (お暇) (な-adj)　idle; not busy [お= ↑], 6.a.3
おひらき (お開き) (n)　closing of an event [おひらきにする "close an event"], 6.b.4
おひる (お昼) (n)　lunch [= お昼ごはん]; noon, 3.f.5
オフィス (n)　office, 1.b.1
おふろ (お風呂) (n)　bathroom (to bathe in); bath, 2.gr.7
おべんとう (お弁当) (n)　box lunch, 8.gr.8
おぼえたい (覚えたい) (v: oboe/ru) [たい-form of おぼえる] want to memorize, 7.b.3
おぼえる (覚える) (v: oboe/ru)　to remember [おぼえている "remember"], 2.c.1
おまたせいたしました (お待たせ～) (v: mat(s)/u) [↓ CAUS of まつ] I kept you waiting., 3.d.conv, 7.b.conv, 7.b.conv
おまちいただける (お待ち～) (v: itadak/u) [お + V-stem + まつ + POT of いただく] (I) can receive someone's waiting, 5.f.2
おまちください[ませ] (お待ち下さい[ませ]) (phr)　Please wait. ↑, 3.b.conv, 7.b.conv, 9.gr.5
おまちする (お待ち～) (v: mat(s)/u)　to wait ↓, 2.gr.3, 4.b.1
おまちになる (お待ち～) (v: mat(s)/u)　to wait [↑ of まつ], 6.gr.1
おみえになる (お見え～) (v: mie/ru) [お + V-stem of みえる + になる] come (to see) [↑ of くる], 4.a.conv
おみやげ (お土産) (n)　souvenir, 7.gr.4
おむかえ (お迎え) (n)　receiving of someone; welcoming someone [お = ↑], 6.c.conv
おめにかかりたい (お目に～) (phr)　want to see/meet someone ↓, 4.lc
おめにかかる (お目に～) (phr)　to see/meet someone ↓, 4.a.conv
おもいまして (思い～) (v: omow/u) [POL て-form of おもう] think, 6.c.2
おもう (思う) (v: omow/u)　to think [おもう "I think"; おもっている "He/She thinks"], 1.a.1, 1.b.conv, 1.gr.6, 6.a.2
おもうかね (思うかね) (phr)　What do you think? [superior to subordinate; blunt prompting for a frank answer], 10.c.conv
おもえば (思えば) (v: omow/u) [PROV of おもう] if/provided one thinks, 7.c.2
おもえる (思える) (v: omow/u) [POT of おもう] can think, 1.b.5
おもしろい (い-adj)　interesting, 1.a.1, 3.gr.6

おもちいただければ (お持ち〜) (v: mot(s)/u; ga/o) [↓ POT PROV of もつ] if/provided you can bring, 7.c.conv
おもちになる (お持ち〜) (v: mot(s)/u) [お + V-stem of もつ + になる] to bring ↑, 4.b.conv
おもどりでしょう (お戻り〜) (phr) [お+V-stem of もどる + でしょう] is/has returned [↑ of もどるでしょう], 3.e.conv
おもに (主に) (adv) primarily, mainly, 8.b.conv
おもわせる (思わせる) (v: omow/u) [CAUS of おもう] to make/let (someone) think, 9.a.1
おやすみ (phr) Good night!; rest, 7.a.1
おやすみ (お休み) (n) rest, off duty [お = ↑], 3.f.5
およがせる (泳がせる) (v: oyog/u) [CAUS of およぐ] to make/let (someone) swim, 9.a.1
およがれる (泳がれる) (v: oyog/u) [↑ of およぐ] (someone) swims; [ADV-PASS of およぐ] (someone) swims, 8.b.1
およげる (泳げる) (v: oyog/u) [POT of およぐ] can swim, 8.b.1
およみする (お読みする) (v: yom/u) to read, pronounce ↓, 2.e.conv
およろこび (お慶び) (n) delight, joy, gladness [お = ↑] [およろこびもうしあげます "I congratulate you"], 7.rw.1
およろこびもうしあげます (お慶び申し上げます) (phr) I congratulate. ↓, 9.rw.1
おられます (v: or/u) [↑ of おります] is, stays [animate], 8.c.5
おられます (v: orare/ru) [↓ POL of いる] to stay; to be [animate], 3.a.conv
おられる (v: orare/ru) [↓ of いる] to stay; to be, 3.a.1
オリエンタルぼうえき (オリエンタル貿易) (n) Oriental Trading [company name], 11.lc
おりかえし (折り返し) (n) immediately (in response to something), 7.gr.4
おりまして (v: i/ru) [て-form of おります] is; stays, 8.b.conv
おります (v: or/u) [↓ of います] to be; to stay; there is/are [おせわになっております "Thank you for your/his/her/their help." Said while the help is provided.], 1.a.conv, 8.c.5
おりません (v: or/u) [↓ NEG of います] (someone) is not, hasn't, 3.e.conv, 6.a.3
おるす (お留守) (n) absence; not at home, 4.b.conv
おれい (お礼) (n) appreciation; courtesy; thanks [お = ↑], 4.a.5
おろしね (卸値) (n) wholesale price, 10.a.conv
おわかり (お分かり) (n) understanding [お + V-stem of わかる] [お = ↑], 1.c.2
おわったら (終わったら) (v: owar/u) [COND of おわる] if it is finished, if it ends, 2.gr.1, 7.c.1
おわってから (終わってから) (phr) [V てから "after V-ing"] after finishing, 9.c.2
おわり (終わり) (n) ending; end, 11.gr.4
おわりしだい (終わり次第) (phr) as soon as something is finished, 7.a.2
おわりそうだ (終わり〜) (phr) appear to end, 7.d.1
おわりそうにない (終わり〜) (phr) does not appear to end, 7.d.1
おわる (終わる) (v: owar/u) to finish, end, 2.a.3, 3.f.conv, 7.c.1
おんがく (音楽) (n) music, 1.lc
おんしゃ (御社) (n) your company [おん = ↑], 1.b.conv
おんど (温度) (n) temperature, 7.e.1
おんれい (御礼) (n) [おん = ↑] gratitude, 7.rw.1

か

か (p) question marker, 1.a.conv
が (con) but, however, 3.c.1
が (p) [subject marker]; [object marker of すき, きらい, etc.]; [object marker of pot-V], 1.a.conv
か (可) (n) possible, 5.rw.1
か (課) (n) section, 2.d.conv
カード (n) card, 5.f.2, 5.g.conv
かい (会) (n) meeting; society; club, 1.d.conv
かい (買い) (v: kaw/u) [V-stem of かいます] buy, 6.a.5
かいいれ (買い入れ) (n) purchase, 10.rw.1
かいがい (海外) (n) overseas, 2.d.conv
かいがいきんむ (海外勤務) (n) oversea job assignment, 9.a.1
かいぎ (会議) (n) conference, meeting, 1.b.6
かいぎしつ (会議室) (n) conference room, 7.gr.1
かいぎちゅう (会議中) (n) in the middle of a meeting, 3.d.conv
かいぎろく (会議録) (n) meeting log; minutes, 6.gr.2
かいけい (会計) (n) accounting, 4.e.2
がいこく (外国) (n) foreign country, 5.d.conv
がいこくきぎょう (外国企業) (n) foreign corporation, 7.e.2
がいこくじん (外国人) (n) foreigner, 7.d.2
かいし (開始) される (n/v) [PASS of 開始する] to be started; [↑ of 開始する], 11.c.3
かいし (開始) する (n/v) to start, begin, 11.c.3
かいしゃ (会社) (n) company, 1.b.add
かいしゃいん (会社員) (n) company employee, 1.c.add
かいしゃがいよう (会社概要) (n) company brochure, 7.rw.1
かいしゃほうもん (会社訪問) (n) visit to company, 1.a.conv
がいしゅつ (外出) する (n/v) to go out; going out, 3.gr.7
がいしゅつちゅう (外出中) (n) during one is out (of office), 3.com.2
かいじょう (会場) (n) place of the meeting, 6.c.2, 9.rw.1
がいじん (外人) (n) foreigner, 4.gr.3
かいたく (開拓) する (n/v) to pioneer, develop; cultivation, pioneering, 8.c.conv
かいちょう (会長) (n) chairman; president, 1.d.conv, 4.e.3
かいても (書いても) (v: kak/u) even if one writes, 5.b.conv
ガイド (n) guide, 8.b.conv
かいはつ (開発) される (n/v) [PASS of 開発する] to be developed;[↑ of 開発する] develop, 8.c.1, 9.a.conv
かいはつ (開発) する (n/v) to develop, development; 1.b.conv, 1.b.2
かいはつ (開発) なさる (n/v) [↑ of 開発する] to research; study, 1.b.2
かいひ (会費) (n) party fee; fee for an event, 6.rw
かいましょう (買いましょう) (v: kaw/u) [VOL of かいます] let's buy, 4.a.2
がいむしょう (外務省) (n) Ministry of Foreign Affairs, 3.lc
かいもの (買い物) (n) shopping [買い物をする "to shop"], 1.d.1
かいやく (解約) (n) closing of an account, 5.a.1
かいろ (回路) (n) circuit, 4.d.2
かいわ (会話) (n) conversation, 9.lc
かう (買う) (v: kaw/u) to buy, 1.b.5, 3.f.4, 7.c.1
かえす (返す) (v: kaes/u) to return (something), 5.gr.11
かえりしだい (帰り次第) (phr) as soon as one returns, 7.a.2, 10.c.2

かえりたいそうです (帰りたいそう～) (phr) [かえりたい + そうです] They say (someone) wants to return., 8.a.1
かえりたそうです (帰りたそう～) (phr) [V-stem of かえりたい + そうです] looks (someone) wants to return, 8.a.1
かえる (帰る) (v: kaer/u) to go home; to return; to leave for home, 1.gr.3, 2.d.1
かえる (買える) (v: kaw/u) [POT of かえる] can buy, 1.b.5
かえるわけにはいかない (帰る訳には～) (phr) can't really leave, 10.b.2
かえれる (帰れる) (v: kaer/u) [POT of かえる] can return; can go home; can leave for home, 1.b.5
かおう (買おう) (v: kaw/u) [VOL of かう] let's buy, 4.a.2
かかく (価格) (n)   price, 4.rw.1, 10.a.conv
かがく (科学) (n)   science, 5.gr.8
かがくてき (科学的) (な-adj) scientific [科学的に "scientifically"], 5.d.1
かかせる (書かせる) (v: kak/u) [CAUS of かく] to make/let (someone) write , 9.a.1
かかっている (phr) [て-form of かかる + いる] is locked, applied, etc. かぎがかかっている "it's locked", 6.c.4
かかってきた (phr) [て-form of かかる + きた] (phone call) came all the way in, 11.a.1
かかなくても (書かなくても) (v: kak/u) even if one does not write, 5.b.conv
かかりそうだ (phr) appear to take [time/money], 7.d.1
かかりちょう (係長) (n) subsection manager; chief, 2.a.add, 3.d.conv
かかりのもの (係りの者) (phr) person in charge, 5.f.conv
かかる (vi: kakar/u) to take [time/money]; [でんわがかかる "a phone call comes in"] [vt: かける], 2.c.1 , 5.e.conv, 5.e.1, 6.a.1
かかれる (書かれる) (v: kak/u) [PASS of かく] to be written; [↑ of かく] to write, 8.b.1
かき (下記) (n)   written below, 3.rw.1
かぎ (鍵) (n)   key; lock [かぎをかける "to lock"; かぎがかかる "(something) gets locked"], 6.c.4
かきかた (書き方) (n)   the way of writing; how to write, 5.f.1
かきなおす (書き直す) (v: kakinaos/u)   to rewrite, 8.gr.2
かきのとおり (下記の通り) (phr) as shown below, 9.rw.1
がく (額) (n)   amount of money, 5.lc
かく (書く) (v: kak/u) to write, 1.e.1, 4.e.1
かくい (各位) (n)   title for everyone, 9.rw.1
がくせい (学生) (n)   student, 1.com.4
かくだい (拡大) (n)   expansion, 7.rw.1
かくちょう (拡張) される(n/v) [PASS of 拡張する] to be expanded; [↑ of 拡張する] to expand, 8.c.1, 8.gr.3
かくちょう (拡張) する (n/v) to expand, 7.b.conv, 8.gr.3
かくちょう (拡張) できたら (n/v) [COND POT of 拡張する] if one can expand, 7.b.1
かくべつ (格別) (n) special; extraordinary; unusual, 7.rw.1
かくほう (書く方) (phr) writing (side), 8.c.3
がくれき (学歴) (n) educational history, 1.e.2
かけてある (phr) [て-form of かかる + ある] is deliberately locked, applied, etc. [かぎを／が かけてある "it's deliberately locked"], 6.c.4
かけよう (v: kake/ru) [VOL of かける] let's present (it) at the meeting, 11.a.conv

かける (掛ける) (vt: kake/ru) to sit down; to multiply; to take (time/money) [でんわをかける "to call"; かぎをかける "lock"] [vi: かかる], 1.a.conv, 2.d.conv, 6.a.1, 6.b.1, 6.c.4
かける (書ける) (v: kak/u) [POT of かく] can write, 1.b.5
かこう (書こう) (v: kak/u) [VOL of かく] (let's) write; I will write, 6.a.2, 6.a.3
かしこまりました (v: kashikomar/u) Certainly. I understand. [Idiom]; [かしこまる "is awed; sit straight"], 3.f.conv
かしょ (箇所) (ct) [counter for locations], 2.c.conv
ガス (n)   natural gas, 5.d.conv
かす (貸す) (v: kas/u) to lend, 6.gr.5
かすが (春日) (n)   Kasuga [family name], 3.lc
かぜ (風) (n)   wind, 8.b.1
かぜ (風邪) (n)   cold [illness; 風邪をひく "catch a cold"], 6.a.4
かぞく (家族) (n)   family, 1.e.2
ガソリン (n) gasoline, 5.c.1
かた (方) (n)   person ↑, 1.a.conv
かたい (堅い) (い-adj) rigid, stiff, bookish, hard, 6.b.conv
かたち (形) (n)   shape, form [どういった形で "in what concrete ways?"], 1.b.conv
～かたよびだし (～方呼び出し) (n) paged by (owner of the phone), 1.e.2
カタログ (n)   catalogue, 3.f.5
かちょう (課長) (n) section manager, 1.d.1
かつ (勝つ) (v: kat(s)/u) to win, 11.gr.4
がっか (学科) (n)   school subject, 1.e.2
かっきてき (画期的) (な-adj) epoch-making, 9.rw.1
かつじ (活字) (n)   typed text, 11.a.3
かったら (買ったら) (v: kaw/u) [COND of かう] if one buys, 2.gr.5
かっておかない (買っておかない) (v: kaw/u) [contraction of かっておかない] not buy something in advance, 4.a.5
かっとかない (買っとかない) (phr) [contraction of かっておかない] not buy in advance, 4.a.4
かっとく (買っとく) (phr) [contraction of かっておく] to buy (it) in advance, 4.a.4
かどうか (phr) whether or not [embedded Yes-No question: X かどうか "whether X or not..."], 2.c.1
かな (sp)   I wonder, 4.c.conv
かない (金井) (n)   Kanai [family name], 5.b.conv
かならず (必ず) (adv) absolutely [followed by AFF], 11.rw.1
かね (sp)   I wonder [blunt informal question; softer than V-plain か], 3.d.4, 10.c.conv
かねこ (金子) (n)   Kaneko [family name], 4.a.conv
かのう (可能) (な-adj) possible, 9.b.conv
かのうせい (可能性) (n) possibilities, 6.lc, 10.c.conv
かのじょ (彼女) (pro) she; her, 1.lc, 7.d.conv
カバー (n)   cover, 5.gr.7
かばん (n)   bag, 4.a.3
かぶ (株) (n)   stocks, 6.c.3
かぶしきがいしゃ (株式会社) (n) company, Inc. (Incorporated), 3.a.2
かみ (髪) (n)   hair, 5.lc
カメラ (n)   camera, 2.a.2
かもがわ (鴨川) (n) Kamogawa [restaurant name], 6.a.5
かもしれない (phr) possibly, 6.lc, 11.a.conv
かよう (火曜) (n)   Tuesday, 5.com.2
かようび (火曜日) (n) Tuesday, 3.f.1

から (con)　because, since, 1.b.6
から (p)　from [time, place, level]; since [time], 1.b.6
カラー (n)　color, 8.b.1
カラオケ (n)　karaoke (bar); sing-along machine [カラ "empty"; オケ a short form of "orchestra"], 1.d.1
カラオケバー (n)　karaoke bar, 6.a.conv
からだ (体) (n)　body, 4.c.2, 11.gr.4
かりられる (借りられる) (v: kari/ru) [POT of かりる] can borrow, rent, 2.gr.3
かりる (借りる) (v: kari/ru)　to borrow, rent, 1.b.1, 5.b.1
かれ (彼) (pro)　he; him, 5.1c, 6.a.6, 7.d.conv
がわ (側) (n)　side, 1.e.2
かわせ (為替) (n)　exchange (of money), 5.d.conv
かわせレート (為替レート) (n)　foreign exchange rate, 5.e.conv
かわだ (川田) (n)　Kawada [family name], 3.d.conv
かわり (代わり/変わり) (v: kawar/u) [V-stem of かわる] change; replace; switch, 3.com.1
かわる (代わる/変わる) (v: kawar/u)　to switch; change [X にかわって "in substitute of X"], 3.b.conv, 3.b.2 , 5.d.conv
かんがえ (考え) (n)　thought; thinking, 5.d.1
かんがえさせてください (考えさせて下さい) (phr) [て-form of かんがえる + させてください]let me think, 9.a.2
かんがえさせる (考えさせる) (v: kangae/ru) [CAUS of かんがえる] to make/let (someone) consider, 9.a.2
かんがえなおす (考え直す) (v: kangaenaos/u)　to reconsider, to think over, 7.gr.4
かんがえましょう (考えましょう) (v: kangae/ru) [VOL of かんがえます] let's think, 4.a.2
かんがえよう (考えよう) (v: kangae/ru) [VOL of かんがえる] let's think, 4.a.2
かんがえる (考える) (v: kangae/ru)　to consider [more deliberate thinking than おもう], 4.a.2, 7.b.conv
かんきょう (環境) (n)　environment, 6.com.1
かんげい (歓迎) (n)　welcome, 5.com.2
かんけい (関係) (n)　relationship; related to, 1.rw
かんげいかい (歓迎会) (n)　welcome party; reception, 6.a.conv
かんじ (漢字) (n)　kanji [Chinese symbols], 6.gr.3
かんじ (幹事) (n)　organizer [of an event], 6.rw.1
かんして (関して) (n/v) [て-form of 関する] is concerned [X に関して "regarding X"], 10.c.conv
かんしまして (関しまして) (n/v) [POL て-form of 関する] regarding, concerning [X に関しまして "regarding, concerning X"], 9.c.conv
かんじゃ (患者) (n)　patient, 11.gr.4
かんたん (簡単) (な-adj)　simple, easy [簡単に "simply, easily"], 1.a.conv, 10.gr.4
かんぱい (乾杯) (phr)　Cheers!, 6.b.4
かんばん (看板) (n)　billboard, 4.c.2, 8.b.1

き

き (気) (n)　mind, feelings, spirit, attention [気をつける "pay attention, be careful"; 気にする "worry"], 4.a.conv
き (記) (n)　notes, 9.rw.1, 11.c.3
きあん (起案) (n)　origin of the proposal, 11.c.3
きあんしゃ (起案者) (n)　originator of the proposal, 11.c.3
きあんび (起案日) (n)　date of originating the proposal, 11.c.3
キーシュ (n)　quiche, 10.gr.4

きいたり (聞いたり) (v: kik/u) [たり-form of きく] listen [きいたりする "do things like listening"], 4.gr.7
きいておく (聞いておく) (phr)　to ask for (something) in advance for later use, 4.a.conv
きいてみて (聞いてみて) (phr)　ask and see; try to ask, 6.b.2
キーボード (n)　keyboard, 10.gr.1
きいろい (黄色い) (い-adj)　yellow, 8.gr.8
きえてしまう (消えてしまう) (phr)　(something) disappears completely, 6.gr.1
きえる (消える) (vi: kie/ru)　(something) disappears, is turned off, goes out [でんきがきえている "lights are off"] [vt: けす], 6.a.1
きかい (機械) (n)　machine, 5.f.conv
きかいてき (機械的) (な-adj)　machine-like, mechanical [機械的に like machines], 5.d.1
きかく (企画) (n)　planning, 2.d.add
きかくあん (企画案) (n)　project plan, 6.c.4
きかくかいぎ (企画会議) (n)　planning meeting; project meeting, 11.a.conv
きかくしょ (企画書) (n)　planning report, 6.1c
きかん (期間) (n)　period, 11.c.3
きき (機器) (n)　machine equipment, 7.a.conv
ききたい (聞きたい) (phr)　want to listen, 3.gr.6
ききたがって (聞きたがって) (v: kik/u) [て-form of ききたがる] (other person) wants to ask, listen, 6.a.6
きぎょう (企業) (n)　enterprise; company, 1.c.conv
きく (聞く) (v: kik/u)　to ask, listen, hear, 1.gr.4, 2.a.conv, 2.c.1
きくち (菊池) (n)　Kikuchi [family name], 1.gr.7
きこえる (v: kikoe/ru)　(something) is heard, audible, 6.b.conv
きじ (記事) (n)　newspaper article, 7.d.2
きしだい (来次第) (phr)　as soon as (something/someone) comes, 7.gr.4
きしゃ (貴社) (n)　your company ↑, 7.rw.1
ぎじゅつ (技術) (n)　skills; technology, 1.rw
ぎじゅつてき (技術的) (な-adj)　technological, 7.e.conv
きせつ (季節) (n)　season, 9.rw.1
きたがわ (北川) (n)　Kitagawa [family name], 3.a.conv
きたしだい (来た次第) (phr)　it turned out that (someone) came, 10.c.2
きたら (来たら) (iv) [COND of くる] if one comes (here), 2.gr.2
きたる (来る) (phr)　upcoming, 9.rw.1, 11.c.3
きつい (い-adj)　hard; painful, 10.gr.3
きっさてん (喫茶店) (n)　cafe; coffee shop, 5.gr.6
きっぷ (切符) (n)　ticket, 2.gr.8, 3.gr.4, 4.a.4
きて (来て) (iv) [て-form of くる] come (here), 6.a.4
きにする (気にする) (phr)　worry; mind, 6.gr.3
きにゅう (記入) する (n/v)　to fill in; write-in, 5.1c
きにゅうらん (記入欄) (n)　box to fill in, 1.e.2
きのう (機能) (n)　function, 8.b.conv
きのう (昨日) (n)　yesterday, 1.a.1
きのした (木下) (n)　[family name] Kinoshita, 4.e.conv
きびしい (厳しい) (い-adj)　strict, hard, 2.c.3
きぶん (気分) (n)　feeling [気分がわるい "feel sick"; 気分がいい "feel good"], 1.gr.2
きぼう (希望) (n)　preference; wish, 1.e.2, 1.rw
きぼうしゃ (希望者) (n)　applicant; those who wish/request, 6.rw
きます (来ます) (v: iv) [POL of くる] to come (here), 2.c.1

きまりしだい (決まり次第) (phr)　as soon as something is decided, 7.a.2
きまる (決まる) (vi: kimar/u)　(something) is decided; comes to be decided [vt: きめる], 6.a.1, 10.c.2
きみ (君) (pro)　you [toward a peer or subordinate person], 2.a.conv, 4.e.conv
キム (n)　Kim [family name], 1.b.1
きむら (木村) (n)　Kimura [family name], 1.gr.7
きめられる (決められる) (v: kime/ru) [POT of きめる]　can decide, 3.gr.4, 4.d.conv
きめる (決める) (vt: kime/ru) to decide (on) (something) [vi: きまる], 3.gr.4, 4.c.conv, 6.a.1, 10.c.2
きもちがいい (気持ちがいい) (phr)　feel good, 9.lc
キャッシュ (n)　cash, 1.gr.8
キャッシュカード (n)　ATM card, 5.c.conv
キャラクター (n)　character (of anime), 5.rw.1
キャンセルする (n/v)　to cancel, 8.c.4
きゅうけい (休憩) (n)　break, rest, 10.b.conv
90ねんだい (90年代) (num)　90's, 5.gr.8
きゅうな (急な) (な-adj)　sudden, 7.rw2
きゅうよ (給与) (n)　wage, 11.c.3
きょう (今日) (n)　today, 1.d.conv
ぎょうかい (業界) (n)　business industry, 7.rw.1
きょうじゅう (今日中) (n)　within/throughout today, 7.gr.3
きょうしゅく (恐縮) する (n/v)　to feel obliged, terribly sorry; grateful, 2.e.add, 7.gr.4
きょうしゅく (恐縮) ながら(phr)　feel sorry, but [まことに恐縮ながら "feel truly sorry, but..."], 10.rw.1
きょうそう (競争) (n)　competition, 7.rw.1, 11.a.conv
きょうそうげきか (競争激化) (n)　increased competition, 10.rw.1
きょうと (京都) (n)　Kyoto [a city in Japan], 6.com.1
きょうみ (興味) (n)　interest [Xに興味がある "is interested in X"], 1.b.conv, 10.c.3
ぎょうむ (業務) (n)　work, job, task, duty, 11.c.3
きょうりょく (協力) する (n/v) to cooperate [Xと協力する "cooperate with X"]; cooperation, 7.e.2
きょか (許可) (n)　permission, 7.d.2
きょねん (去年) (n)　last year, 3.gr.1
きらい (嫌い) (な-adj)　to dislike; to hate, 1.d.add
きれい (な-adj)　pretty; clean, 1.b.1
きをつける (気をつける) (phr)　to be careful; to pay attention, 4.a.conv
きをわるくする (気を悪くする) (phr)　become upset; feels bad, 6.b.conv
きんがく (金額) (n)　amount of money, 5.rw.1
ぎんこう (銀行) (n)　bank, 1.c.1
ぎんこういん (銀行員) (n)　banker; teller, 5.lc
ぎんざ (銀座) (n)　Ginza [place name], 1.b.3
きんねん (近年) (n)　in recent years, 7.rw.1

く

グアム (n)　Guam, 10.gr.2
くうこう (空港) (n)　airport, 2.c.1
くぎ (釘) (n)　nail, 8.b.1
くじ (九時) (num)　nine o'clock, 11.a.3
くじまでかもしれない (九時まで〜) (phr)　possibly until 9 o'clock, 11.a.3
くすり (薬) (n)　medicine [薬をのむ "take medicine"], 3.f.4
ください (下さい) (v: kudasar/u) [POL IMP of くれる] give (to me); [POL request marker if preceded by a て-form verb: Vて下さい: "Please V."], 1.a.conv
くださいませんか (下さい〜) (n) [NEG of 下さいますか] not give me, 2.c.conv
くださる (下さる) (v: kudasar/u) to give (to me) ↑, 3.f.4, 4.e.1
くちコミ (口コミ) (n)　word of mouth [コミ = communication], 8.c.conv
くぼた (久保田) (n)　Kubota [family name], 5.f.conv
〜ぐらい (suf)　about [approximation of general quantity; どのぐらい "how long"], 2.gr.2
グリーン (n)　Green [family name]; green, 7.lc
くる (来る) (iv)　to come (here), 1.b.5, 6.a.3, 6.a.4
くるま (車) (n)　car, 1.b.1, 3.b.2
クレジットカード (n)　credit card, 8.c.3
くれば (来れば) (v/e) [PROV of くる] if/provided one comes, 7.c.2
くれる (くれる) (v: kure/ru)　to give (to me) [V てくれる "to give (me) a favor of V-ing"], 4.e.conv
くろい (黒い) (い-adj)　black, 5.gr.5
くろさわ (黒沢) (n)　Kurosawa [family name], 3.d.4
〜くん (suf)　[title used after one's peers or subordinates; often used with younger males], 2.a.conv

け

けいえい (経営) する (n/v)　to manage; management, business, 7.gr.10, 8.c.conv
けいえい (経営) ぶり (n)　the way of managing; the way of conducting business, 7.rw.1
けいかく (計画) (n)　plan, 11.c.3
けいき (景気) (n)　economic state, 7.c.1
けいぐ (敬具) (phr)　a closing remark in a letter, 7.rw.1
けいけん (経験) (n)　experience, 1.lc
けいざい (経済) (n)　economy, 1.b.2
けいざいがく (経済学) (n)　Economics, 1.gr.1, 7.e.conv
けいさんしょ (計算書) (n)　calculation sheet, 5.com.2
けいさん (計算) する (n/v)　to calculate/ calculation, 4.e.conv, 4.gr.9, 10.b.conv
けいたい (携帯) (n)　[short form of けいたいでんわ "cell phone"], 3.rw2
けいたいでんわ (携帯電話) (n)　cell phone, 2.gr.7
けいやくしょ (契約書) (n)　contract document, 10.c.4
けいやく (契約) する (n/v)　to have a contract; contract, 4.e.conv, 4.gr.9
けいやく (契約) にこぎつける (phr) make a contract (lit. "row up to a contract"), 7.gr.5, 11.c.2
けいり (経理) (n)　accounting, 4.e.2
けいりか (経理課) (n)　accounting section, 4.e.conv
ケーキ (n)　cake, 2.b.1
ケーブル (n)　cable, 9.lc
ゲームき (ゲーム機) (n) game machines, 9.b.3
けさ (今朝) (n)　this morning, 6.a.3
けしてしまう (消してしまう) (phr)　erase/turn off completely, 6.gr.1
けす (消す) (v: kes/u) to erase (something); to turn off (something), 5.gr.11, 6.a.1, 6.a.1
けずる (削る) (v: kezur/u) to reduce, shave off, 8.c.conv
けっか (結果) (n)　results, consequences, 1.e.conv
けっかんひん (欠陥品) (n)　defective products, 11.gr.3

けっきょく (結局) (n) eventually; at the end, 6.c.1
けっこう (結構) (な-adj) good, satisfactory [けっこうです: No, thank you], 3.c.1, 5.b.conv
けっこんしき (結婚式) (n) wedding ceremony, 9.gr.3
けっこん (結婚) する (n/v) to get married, 6.c.1
けっさい (決裁) する (n/v) to decide; decision, 11.a.3
けっさいび (決裁日) (n) date of final decision, 11.c.3
けっさんしょ (決算書) (n) balance sheet, 4.c.conv
けっさんほうこくしょ (決算報告書) (n) balance sheet, 4.b.conv
けっして (決して) (adv) never, not at all [always followed by a negative predicate], 8.b.conv
げつよう (月曜) (n) Monday, 5.com.2
げつようび (月曜日) (n) Monday, 5.gr.5
けつろん (結論) (n) conclusion [結論をだす "form a conclusion"], 4.d.conv, 5.gr.12
けど (con) but [informal of が], 2.b.conv
けん (件) (n) matter, incident [Xのけんで "regarding the matter of X"], 3.rw2, 4.d.conv, 7.a.3
けん (兼) (n) also; doubles as, 5.rw.1
げんか (原価) (n) original price; production cost, 4.e.conv
げんかけいさん (原価計算) (n) cost accounting, 4.rw.1
げんき (元気) (な-adj) energetic, healthy, fine [INFORMAL of お元気ですか] How are you?, 7.e.2
げんきじゃなさそう (元気じゃ〜) (phr) [Stem of 元気じゃない + さそう] looks (someone) is not healthy, 8.a.1
げんきそう (元気そう) (phr) [元気 + そう] appears healthy, 8.a.conv
げんきそうじゃない (元気そう〜) (phr) [NEG of 元気そうだ] does not look healthy/great, 8.a.1
げんきなだけ (元気なだけ) (phr) All he/she is being healthy, 9.b.1
けんきゅう (研究) いたします (n/v) [↓ of 研究する] to study, research, 1.b.1, 1.b.2
けんきゅうかいはつ (研究開発) (n) research and development, 4.e.2
けんきゅうしつ (研究室) (n) research laboratory, 8.a.conv
けんきゅう (研究) する (n/v) to research, study, 1.b.conv, 1.b.2
けんきゅう (研究) なさる／なさいます (n/v) [↑ of 研究する] to study, research; research 1.b.1, 1.b.2
けんこう (健康) (n) health, 1.e.2
げんざい (現在) (n) at present; currently, 1.e.2, 7.b.conv
げんしゅ (厳守) (n) to be adhered to, 11.rw.1
けんしゅう (研修) (n) training, 2.a.add
けんしゅうしゃいん (研修社員) (n) company trainee, 2.a.conv
げんじゅうしょ (現住所) (n) present address, 1.e.2
けんせつ (建設) する (n) to construct; construction, 11.gr.4
げんだい (現代) (n) modern; contemporary, 4.c.2
けんとう (検討) いたします (n/v) [↓ of 検討します] to consider; discuss, 10.rw.1
けんとう (検討) する (n/v) to investigate, examine, discuss; examination, consideration, discussion [まえむき(前向き)に検討する "discuss the matter with a positive attitude"], 4.rw2, 7.a.3, 10.c.3, 10.rw.1, 11.b.conv

こ

ご、ろくにち (五、六日) (num) five to six days, 11.b.1
ごあんない (ご案内) (n) invitation; notice; guide, 9.rw.1
ごいっしょ (ご一緒) する (n/v) [↓] to do (it) together, go [there] together, 9.gr.3
ごいんけんのうえ (ご引見の上) (phr) by taking in something to look; after looking at, 7.rw.1
こう (候) (n) season, 7.rw.1
ごう (号) (suf) editions, products, models [used for counting] [いちごう "the first"], 11.c.3
こういった (prenom) this kind of [=こんな], 1.c.add
こうえん (公園) (n) park, 7.gr.4
こうがく (高額) (な-adj) expensive, 8.c.conv
こうがくけい (工学系) (n) engineering field, 7.e.conv
ごうかく (合格) する (n/v) to pass [a test]; passing, 11.gr.2
こうかだいがく (工科大学) (n) Technology Institute, 1.a.conv
こうかんレート (交換レート) (n) exchange rate, 5.lc
こうぎょう (工業) (n) manufacturing; manufacturer, 3.c.conv
こうきょうじぎょう (公共事業) (n) public works, 10.a.2
こうきょうりょうきん (公共料金) (n) public utility fees, 5.d.conv
こうこう (高校) (n) high school, 1.rw
こうざ (口座) (n) account, 5.a.conv
こうじちゅう (工事中) (phr) under construction, 6.b.4
こうじょう (工場) (n) factory, 1.c.1
こうしょう (交渉) する (n/v) to negotiate; negotiation, 4.d.conv, 11.lc
こうせいのう (高性能) (n) high performance, 1.c.conv
こうちゃ (紅茶) (n) black tea, 1.gr.2
こうつうひ (交通費) (n) commuting cost, 11.c.3
こうにゅう (購入) する (n/v) to purchase; purchase, 11.c.conv, 11.gr.2
こうはい (後輩) (n) one's junior, 2.a.add
こうばい (購買) (n) purchase, 4.e.2
こうもくべつに (項目別に) (n) grouped by the category, 1.e.2
こうりね (小売値) (n) retail price, 10.b.conv
こうれい (恒例) (n) tradition; annual/usual event, 6.rw
コーヒー (n) coffee, 1.b.1
ゴールデンウィーク (n) golden week [a long holiday week between 4/29 through 5/4], 10.gr.2
こがいしゃ (子会社) (n) subsidiary company, 8.c.4
ごかいだく (ご快諾) (n) prompt approval [ご = ↑], 11.rw.1
ごかぞく (ご家族) (n) family [ご = ↑], 1.lc
こがた (小型) (n) small size, 1.b.add
こぎって (小切手) (n) (bank) check, 5.a.1
ごきにゅう (ご記入) (n) write-in [ご = ↑; 記入する "write down/fill in"], 5.b.conv
ごきぼう (ご希望) (n) desire, wish, request [ご = ↑], 7.rw.1
こくさい (国際) (n) international, 8.gr.7
こくさいかいぎ (国際会議) (n) international conference, 1.lc
こくさいかんけいろん (国際関係論) (n) [study/theory of] international relations, 1.gr.2
こくない (国内) (n) domestic; national, 2.d.add
ごくろうさん (ご苦労さん) (phr) Thanks for your hard work. [Greeting toward one's subordinates], 4.c.conv
ここ (pro) here, this place, 2.a.conv
ごご (午後) (n) p.m., 1.b.3
ごこうはい (ご高配) (n) kind consideration [ご高配たまわりますよう、おねがいします "We ask for your kind consideration"], 7.rw.1
ごこうらんください (ご高覧下さい) (phr) please look at ↑, 9.rw.1, 11.rw.1
こころづよい (心強い) (い-adj) feel encouraged, 11.b.2

こころより (心より) (phr)　sincerely [lit. "from the heart"], 10.rw.1
ございまして (v: gozar/u) [て-form of ございます] there is/are [inanimate], 4.a.conv
ございます (v: gozar/u) [courteous form of あります] there is/are [inanimate], 4.a.1, 5.d.conv, 10.a.2
こさせる (来させる) (v/e) [CAUS of くる] to make (someone) come, 9.a.1
ごさんかください (ご参加下さい) (n/v) [↑ of 参加して下さい] please participate, 9.rw.1
ごじ (五時) (num)　five o'clock, 1.c.2
ごじたく (ご自宅) (n)　home [ご = ↑], 5.rw.1
ごしつもん (ご質問) (n)　question [ご= ↑], 2.a.2
ごしぼう (ご志望) (n)　desire, aspiration [ご = ↑], 1.b.2
ごしゅっしん (ご出身) (n)　home town [ご = ↑], 1.d.2
ごしょうかい (ご紹介) (n)　introduction [ご = ↑], 7.a.1
ごしょうかいいただいた (ご紹介いただいた) (phr)　received a favor of being introduced, 7.a.1
ごしょうかい (ご紹介) いたします (n/v) [↓ of 紹介する] to introduce, 1.gr.8
こしょう (故障) する (n/v)　to break down, 9.c.conv
ごしょくぎょう (ご職業) (n)　profession [ご = ↑], 5.rw.1
ごしんき (ご新規) (n)　new account [ご = ↑], 5.a.conv
ごじんりょく (ご尽力) する (n)　help; effort [ご = ↑], 11.c.conv
コストダウンする (n/v)　to reduce cost; price reduction, 8.c.conv, 8.gr.3
ごせいえい (ご清栄) (n)　prosperity [ご = ↑] [ご清栄のことと~ "(speak of) your prosperity"; と is a quotative], 7.rw.1, 9.rw.1
ごせいしょう (ご清祥) (n)　prosperity [ご = ↑] [ますますご清祥のことと "that you are increasingly prosperous"], 11.rw.1
ごせつめい (ご説明) する (n/v)　explanation [ご = ↑], 9.a.conv
ごせつめい (ご説明) いたしましょうか (n/v)　Shall I explain? [ご = ↑], 7.d.2
ごせつめい (ご説明) させていただく (phr) [CAUS of する + いただく] let me explain; receive a favor of letting (me) explain, 9.a.conv
ごぜん (午前) (n)　a.m., 4.a.1
ごぜんさま (午前様) (n)　one who returns home in the morning [↑], 6.b.4
ごぜんちゅう (午前中) (n)　in the morning (during 'a.m.'), 1.b.3
こそ (p)　[emphatic marker], 2.a.conv
ごそうだん (ご相談) する (n/v)　consultation [ご = ↑], 7.a.conv
ごぞんじありません (ご存知ありません) (phr)　does not know [↑ of しらない], 5.gr.6
ごぞんじだ (ご存知だ) (n)　to know [↑ of しっている], 3.c.1, 6.com.1
ごぞんじです (ご存知です) (phr)　(someone) knows [↑ of しっている], 3.c.1
こたえ (答え) (n)　answer, 3.gr.4, 6.a.1
こたえる (答える) (v: kotae/ru)　to answer, reply, 9.b.conv
ごたようちゅう (ご多用中) (phr)　while you are busy [ご = ↑], 7.rw.1
ごたんとうしゃ (ご担当者) (n)　person(s) in charge [ご = ↑], 9.rw.1
ごちそう (ご馳走) する (n/v)　treat someone for dinner; feast [ご = ↑], 3.f.5

こちら (pro)　this way (toward me); this place here, 1.b.conv
こちらこそ (phr)　The same here., 2.a.conv
こっち (n)　this side (near me), 1.gr.4
ごていじ (ご提示) する (n/v)　to present; presentation [ご = ↑], 10.rw.1
ごてはい (ご手配) する (n/v)　to deliver; delivery [ご = ↑], 11.rw.1
こと (n)　fact; thing; matter, 2.a.conv
ことができる (phr)　be able to V, 9.b.conv
ことにする (phr)　make it a rule to..., 6.gr.4
ことになっている (phr)　is supposed that S, 6.c.conv
ことぶき (寿) (n)　happiness; luck, 2.c.3
こども (子供) (n)　child(ren), 9.a.1
ことわる (断る) (v: kotowar/u)　to refuse, reject, 10.b.2
ことわるわけにもいかなくて (断る訳にも～) (phr)　can't really even refuse, 10.b.2
このぐらい (phr)　this much, 10.b.conv
このごろ (この頃) (phr)　lately, these days, 7.com., 9.b.3
このたび (この度) (phr)　at this time; on this occasion, 7.rw.1
このつぎ (この次) (phr)　next time; next chance, 9.a.1
このような (phr)　this kind of; like this, 10.c.4
ごはいそう (ご配送) (n)　delivery [ご = ↑], 11.rw.1
こばやし (小林) (n)　Kobayashi [family name], 2.d.conv
ごはん (ご飯) (n)　meal, 1.b.2
コピーき (コピー機) (n)　copy machine, 5.b.1
コピーする (n/v)　to copy; copy, 1.e.1, 2.b.1, 2.c.4
こまる (困る) (v: komar/u)　to be in trouble, annoyed, 2.lc, 4.a.conv
こむ (混む) (v: kom/u)　to get crowded [こんでいる "is crowded"], 1.c.3
ごめいわく (ご迷惑) (n)　trouble; nuisance [ご = ↑; ごめいわくでなければ "if it's not too much trouble"], 3.d.conv
ごめんください (ごめん下さい) (phr)　Excuse me (for leaving)., 3.c.1
ごゆっくり (phr)　Take your time., 6.b.4
こよう (雇用) (n)　hiring, employment, 11.c.3
こよう (来よう) (v/e) [VOL of くる] let's come, 4.a.2, 6.a.2
ごようけん (ご用件) (n)　business, things to do [ご = ↑], 3.f.conv
ごよてい (ご予定) (n)　schedule; plan [ご = ↑], 3.gr.7
ごらいしゃ (ご来社) (n)　coming to our company [ご = ↑], 7.b.conv
こられたら (来られたら) (v/e) [↑ of きたら] if/when (someone) comes; [ADV-PASS of きたら] if/when (someone) comes, 8.c.5
こられる (来られる) (v/e) [↑ of くる] (someone) comes; [ADV-PASS of くる] (someone) comes, 8.b.1
こられる (来られる) (iv) [POT of くる] can come, 1.b.5
ごらんください (ご覧下さい) (phr)　Please take a look. [↑ of みてください], 8.b.conv
ごらんになりました (ご覧になりました) (phr)　looked, saw [↑ of みた], 9.c.4
ごらんになる (ご覧になる) (phr)　look at ↑, 7.a.3, 7.rw2
ごりかい (ご理解) (n)　understanding [ご = ↑], 10.rw.1
ごりゅうせいのこと (ご隆盛のこと) (phr)　the fact that you are prosperous ↑ [ますますご隆盛のこととおよろこびもうしあげます "I congratulate your increasing prosperity"], 10.rw.1

ごりょうしょうください (ご了承下さい) (n/v) [↑ of 了承して下さい] Please understand., 11.rw.1
ごりょうしん (ご両親) (n)　parents [ご = ↑], 1.gr.6
ゴルフ (n)　golf, 1.d.1
ゴルフクラブ (n)　golf club, 6.lc1, 7.c.1
ゴルフたいかい (ゴルフ大会) (n)　golf tournament, 7.c.2
ゴルフツアー (n)　golf tour, 5.com.2
これ (n)　card, 1.d.1
これから (phr)　from now (on), 2.lc, 4.a.conv
these (来れる) (iv) [POT of くる] can come, 1.b.5
ごれんらく (ご連絡) (n)　notification, contact, communication [ご = ↑], 3.f.conv
～ごろ (suf) [approximation for time; なんじごろ "about what time?"], 2.gr.5
こわされた (壊された) (v: kowas/u) [PASS of こわした] was broken, was damaged; [↑ of こわした] broke (something), 8.b.1
こわす (壊す) (vt: kowas/u) to break or damage (something) [vi: こわれる], 8.b.1, 8.c.1
こわれる (壊れる) (vi: koware/ru) to be broken; to become out of order [vt: こわす], 11.gr.4
こんかい (今回) (n)　this time, 10.c.conv
こんごとも (今後とも) (phr)　both the present and the future, 7.lc
こんしゅう (今週) (n)　this week, 6.gr.2
こんしゅうまつ (今週末) (n)　this weekend, 6.c.conv
こんど (今度) (n)　next time, 1.a.2
こんな (pre-n)　this kind of, 10.c.4
こんなふうな (phr)　this kind of; like this, 10.c.4
こんなんである (困難である) (な-adj)　difficult [である is a formal cop (=だ)], 10.rw.1
こんばん (今晩) (n)　this evening; tonight, 2.gr.7
コンビニ (n)　convenience store, 11.a.3
コンピュータ (n)　computer, 1.a.conv
コンピュータサイエンス (n)　computer science, 1.com.1
コンピュータショー (n)　computer show, 7.lc
コンファレンス (n)　conference, 6.gr.6
こんや (今夜) (n)　this evening, tonight, 7.b.3
こんしゅうちゅう (今週中) (n)　during this week, 6.gr.2

さ

サービス (n)　service, 9.c.conv
サービスセンター (n)　service center, 11.gr.1
さい (際) (n)　occasion, time [X のさい "at the time of X"], 7.c.conv
～さい (才／歳) (ct) [counter for age] years old, 1.e.2
サイエンス (n)　science, 1.a.conv
さいど (再度) (n)　one more time; again, 10.rw.1
ざいむ (財務) (n)　finance, 4.e.2
ざいむぶちょう (財務部長) (n)　finance division manager, 10.c.conv
さいようしゃ (採用者) (n)　employer, office, 1.e.2
サイン (n)　signature, 5.b.conv
さがす (探す) (v: sagas/u)　to search, look for, 1.lc
さかな (魚) (n)　fish, 2.gr.5
さがる (下がる) (vi: sagar/u) (something) gets lowered [vt: さげる], 11.gr.4
さかん (な-adj)　popular; flourishing, 4.d.1

さき (先) (n)　ahead [さきに "ahead of the time/place"]; previously, 2.gr.4, 4.c.conv, 7.d.1
さきだちまして (先立ちまして) (phr)　prior to, 9.rw.1
さきほど (先ほど) (n)　a while ago [formal of さっき], 3.c.conv
さぎょう (作業) (n)　(manual) work, task, 11.c.3
さく (割く) (v: sak/u)　to spare; divide [じかんをさく "spare time"], 8.a.conv
さくせい (作成) する (n/v)　to make, create; making, creation, 4.rw2
さくらい (桜井) (n)　Sakurai [family name], 2.e.conv
さけ (酒) (n)　sake [Japanese rice wine], 6.b.4
さげる (下げる) (vt: sage/ru) to lower, reduce [vi: さがる], 11.a.conv
さげるかもしれない (下げる～) (phr)　might lower (something), 11.a.3
さしあげる (差し上げる) (v: sashiage/ru) [↓ of あげる] to give, 3.f.4, 4.e.1
させる (v) [CAUS of する] to make/let (someone) do, 9.a.conv, 9.a.1
さっき (n)　a while ago, 4.e.1
さっきゅう (早急) (な-adj)　immediate [さっきゅうに "immediately"], 9.c.conv
さっきょく (作曲) する (n/v)　to compose music; music composition, 10.gr.4
ざっし (雑誌) (n)　magazine, 8.b.1
さっそく (早速) (n)　immediate; without delay, 2.b.conv
ざっと (adv)　roughly, 10.b.conv
さて (con)　by the way; incidentally, 7.rw.1
さむい (寒い) (い-adj)　cold, 6.gr.9
さむくなければ (寒く～) (い-adj) [PROV of する] if/provided it is not cold, 7.c.2
～さま (様) (suf)　Mr., Mrs., Miss, Ms. [↑ title used after names], 2.a.1
さようでございますか (左様で～) (phr) [FORMAL of そうですか] Is that so?, 7.b.conv
さらいしゅう (再来週) (n)　the week after next, 4.lc
サラリーマン (n)　salaried workers, 2.b.1
される (v) [PASS of する] to be done; [↑ of する] to do, 8.b.1
さんか (参加) する (n/v)　to participate; participation, 6.rw
さんかい (三階) (num)　third floor, 5.gr.3
さんがつ (三月) (num)　March, 3.gr.1
さんぎょう (産業) (n)　industry, 1.c.add
ざんぎょう (残業) する (n/v)　to work overtime; overtime work, 4.gr.3, 6.a.add, 9.c.1
ざんぎょうてあて (残業手当) (n)　overtime pay, 9.c.1
さんぎょうよう (産業用) (n)　use for industrial purposes, 8.b.1
～さん (suf)　Mr., Mrs., Miss, Ms. [title used after names], 1.a.1
さんじ (三時) (num)　three o'clock, 1.b.6
さんじゅっぷん (三十分) (num)　half an hour, 7.c.1
さんせい (賛成) する (n/v)　to agree, in favor; agreement [賛成のかた "those in favor"] 7.gr.3, 10.c.1
ざんねん (残念) (な-adj)　sorry; regrettable; unfortunate, 6.gr.2
サンプル (n)　sample, 6.com.3

し

し (con)　and (furthermore), 10.a.conv
じ (字) (n)　letter, character, 1.gr.6

ジェトロ (n)　JETRO (Japan External Trade Organization), 7.a.conv
じか (時下) (n)　at this time of the year, 9.rw.1
しがいきょくばん (市街局番) (n)　area code, 1.e.2
しかく (資格) (n)　qualification, 1.e.2
しかし (con)　however, but, 8.b.conv
しかたがない (仕方がない) (phr)　can't help it; nothing can be done about it, 11.lc
じかん (時間) (ct/n)　hours; time, 1.gr.4
じかんきゅう (時間給) (n)　hourly wage, 11.c.3
しきゅう (至急) (n)　urgently; immediately, 3.f.conv
じぎょうぶ (事業部) (n)　business division, 10.lc
しけん (試験) (n)　examination, 11.gr.2
じこ (事故) (n)　accident, 1.gr.8
じこしょうかいしょ (自己紹介書) (n)　self-introduction form, 1.e.2
じこしょうかい (自己紹介) する (n/v)　to introduce oneself, 1.a.conv
しごと (仕事) (n)　work, job, 1.b.5
しごとちゅう (仕事中) (n)　in the middle of work, 3.d.add
しじしていただければ (支持して〜) (n/v) [PROV of 支持していただける] if/provided that (someone) can support me/us ↓, 11.b.2
しじ (支持) する (n/v)　to support; support, 8.gr.7
じしょ (辞書) (n)　dictionary, 2.gr.2
しじょう (市場) (n)　market, 7.b.conv
しじょうせんゆうりつ (市場占有率) (n)　percentage of market share, 7.rw.1
しずか (静か) (な-adj)　quiet [静かにする "to be quite"], 4.gr.7
JISきかく (JIS規格) (n)　Japan Industrial Standard, 9.b.conv
システム (n)　system, 2.com.1, 8.b.1
システムソフト (n)　system software, 5.gr.6
したい (iv) [たい-form of する] want to do, 1.b.5
しだい (次第) (n)　turn of events [N 次第 "entirely depending on N"; V た次第 "it turned out that (someone) V-ed"; V-stem 次第 "as soon as V-ing"], 7.a.conv, 10.c.conv
したうけ (下請け) (n)　subcontracting [下請けにだす "submit to a subcontractor"], 4.gr.3
じたく (自宅) (n)　home residence, 5.f.2
しち、はちまい (七、八枚) (num)　seven to eight sheets, 11.b.1
しちがつ (七月) (num)　July, 2.gr.7
しつ (質) (n)　quality, 8.c.conv
じっし (実施) いたします (n/v) [↓ of 実施する] to enforce, carry out; enforcement, 9.rw.1
じっし (実施) する (n/v) to enforce, carry out; enforcement, 9.rw.1
しった (知った) (v: shir/u) [PAST of しる] came to know, 7.lc
しっています (知っています) (phr)　know, 3.gr.5
じつは (実は) (adv)　truthfully, actually, 6.com.4
じつは (実は) (adv)　truthfully; actually; to tell you the truth, 6.a.conv, 6.com.4, 7.a.conv
しつもん (質問) (n)　question, 2.a.2, 9.b.conv
しつれい (失礼) (な-adj)　impolite, rude, 2.e.conv
しつれいいたしました (失礼いたし〜) (n/v)　Excuse me. (I commit rudeness.), 3.a.conv
しつれいいたします (失礼いたし〜) (n/v) [POL ↓ of 失礼する] excuse me [Lit. "commit rudeness"], 1.e.conv
しつれい (失礼) します (n/v) [POL of 失礼する] Excuse me (for entering/leaving)., 1.a.conv
しつれい (失礼) する (n/v)　to commit an act of rudeness, 1.gr.2
して (iv) [て-form of する] do, 1.a.conv
しております (iv) [↓ of しています] is doing [role をしている "do [role], act as [role]"], 2.d.conv
しといて (iv) [contraction of しておいて] do something in advance, 4.a.4
じどうしゃ (自動車) (n)　automobile, 3.a.2
じどうてき (自動的) (な-adj)　automatic [じどうてきに automatically], 5.d.conv
じどうひきおとし (自動ひきおとし) (n)　automatic deduction (from a bank account), 5.d.conv
じどうひきおとしき (自動引き落とし機) (n)　cash machine, 5.lc
しとく (phr) [contraction of しておく] to do (it) in advance, 4.a.4
しない (iv) [NEG of する] not do, 5.b.1
しないで (iv) [NEG REQ form of する] Don't do., 6.b.4
しないほう (しない方) (phr)　not doing (side), 8.c.3
しなくても (iv) [NEG て-form of する + も] even if one does not do (it), 5.b.1
しなもの (品物) (phr)　goods, 6.gr.4, 11.b.2
じはつてき (自発的) (な-adj)　voluntary, spontaneous [じはつてきに "spontaneously, voluntarily"], 8.c.conv
しはらい (支払い) (n)　payment, 5.gr.8, 11.b.2
しはらう (支払う) (v: shiharaw/u)　pay, 5.gr.8
しばらく (phr) [INFORMAL of しばらくです] Long time, no see. [lit., It's been a while!], 5.c.conv
しぶい (渋い) (い-adj)　bitter, sober, quiet, subdued, tasteful, 6.b.conv
じふ (自負) する (n/v)　to take a pride, 8.c.conv
じぶん (自分) (n)　self, 10.gr.3
しぼう (志望) (n)　desire, aspiration, 1.b.2
しぼう (志望) いたします (n/v) [↓ of 志望する] to desire; to choose, 1.b.conv
しぼうする (志望する) (n/v)　to aspire, choose, desire; aspiration, 1.b.conv
しほんきん (資本金) (n)　capital, 8.rw.1
しまいたい (v: shimaw/u) [たい-form of しまう] want to V completely, 6.gr.3
しまう (v: shimaw/u)　to put away [V てしまう "V completely" or "end up V-ing (unexpectedly)"], 5.g.conv, 6.gr.3
しましょう (iv) [POL VOL of する] let's do it; we shall do it., 6.a.6
します (iv) [POL of する] to do [Xにする "decide on X; choose X"], 1.b.1
しまる (閉まる) (vi: shimar/u) (something) closes; is closed [vt: しめる], 6.a.1
じむしょ (事務所) (n)　company office, 2.b.2
しめい (氏名) (n)　name, 1.e.2
しめる (閉める) (vt: shime/ru) to close (something) [vi: しまる], 6.a.1
じゃ (phr)　is/are (not) [contraction of では: copula + は], 6.b.conv
じゃ (phr)　then, well, 2.b.conv
しゃいん (社員) (n)　company employee, 2.a.add, 4.e.3
しゃいんいちどう (社員一同) (n)　everyone in the company, 8.c.conv
しゃくん (社訓) (n)　company motto, 6.gr.4

しゃしん (写真) (n)　photograph [カメラで 写真をとる "take pictures with a camera"], 1.e.2
しゃちょう (社長) (n)　president [of a company], 1.a.1
じゃないか (phr) [plain-S じゃないか] isn't it?; don't you see? [blunt], 4.a.conv
じゃなくても (cop) [て-form of じゃない + も] even if it isn't/they aren't, 5.b.1
じゃなければ (cop) [PROV of じゃない] if it is not N, 7.c.2
しゃべる (v: shaber/u) to chat, 6.b.conv
しゃめい (社名) (n)　company name, 8.rw.1
しゃよう (社用) (n)　company business, 7.d.conv
シャワーをあびる (シャワーを浴びる) (phr)　to take a shower, 7.gr.1
しゅうけい (集計) (n)　sum; total, 4.e.conv
じゅうじつ (充実) (n)　substantiality, fullness, completion, 9.c.conv
じゅうしょ (住所) (n)　address, 1.com.2
しゅうしょく (就職) する (n/v)　to be employed; employment, 1.a.add
しゅうまつ (週末) (n)　weekend, 2.gr.7
じゅうらい (従来) (n)　existing, past, 9.a.conv
しゅくがかい (祝賀会) (n)　celebration party, 8.gr.7
しゅくじ (祝辞) (n)　a word of congratulations, 8.gr.7
しゅっしゃ (出社) する (n/v)　to go to the company, 6.b.4
しゅっしん (出身) (n)　place of one's upbringing, background, 2.lc, 7.e.conv
しゅっちょう (出張) する (n/v)　to go on a business trip; business trip, 4.a.4, 10.lc, 11.c.conv
しゅみ (趣味) (n)　hobby, 1.d.2
しゅようせいひん (主要製品) (n)　main products, 8.rw.1
しゅるい (種類) (n)　kind, type, 5.rw.1
じゅんび (準備) (n)　preparation, 9.c.2
ジョイントベンチャー (n)　joint venture, 10.c.2
しよう (v) [VOL of する] let's do; I will do, 4.a.2, 6.a.2
しょうか (消化) する (n/v)　to digest; digestion, 11.c.3
しょうかいじょう (紹介状) (n)　introduction letter, 3.f.5, 7.c.conv
しょうかい (紹介) する (n/v)　to introduce; introduction, 1.a.add, 1.e.1
しょうかいなさいます (紹介〜) (n/v) [POL ↑ of 紹介する] to introduce, 1.e.1
じょうきょう (状況) (n)　situation, 10.rw.1
しょうけん (証券) (n)　securities, 3.a.2
じょうけん (条件) (n)　conditions, terms, requirement, qualification, 4.c.conv
しょうけんかいしゃ (証券会社) (n)　securities company, 3.a.2
しょうじ (商事) (n)　trading (company), 3.a.2, 11.c.2
じょうし (上司) (n)　one's superior or supervisor, 2.a.add
しょうじかいしゃ (商事会社) (n)　trading company, 3.a.2
じょうしき (常識) (n)　common sense, 4.a.conv
しょうじき (正直) (な-adj)　honest [正直なところ "to be honest"], 8.b.conv
しょうしょう (少々) (adv)　[more formal of ちょっと] a little; somewhat, 3.b.conv
じょうず (上手) (な-adj)　skillful; is good at, 1.d.1
しょうせん (商戦) (n)　sales competition, 10.rw.1, 11.c.3
しょうたい (招待) する (n/v) to invite, 2.gr.8
じょうたい (状態) (n)　state, condition, 1.e.2
しょうち (承知) いたしました (n/v)　Certainly. [= かしこまりました], 3.d.conv
しょうち (承知) いたします (n/v)　accept [a request]; acknowledgement, 3.d.conv
しょうちし (承知) ました (n/v)　Certainly/I see. [=かしこまりました], 4.gr.6, 8.c.5
しようとしているところ (phr)　when (someone) is about to do..., 9.c.4
しょうにん (承認) する (n/v)　to approve; approval, 9.c.2
しょうばつ (賞罰) (n)　awards and charges [賞罰なし: awards & charges - none], 1.rw
しょうひしゃ (消費者) (n)　consumer, 8.b.conv
しょうひしゃガイド (消費者ガイド) (n)　consumer guide, 3.gr.2, 8.b.conv
しょうひん (商品) (n)　merchandise, 8.b.conv
じょうぶ (丈夫) (な-adj)　strong, sturdy, 11.b.2
しょうぶ (勝負) する (n/v)　to compete, fight; victory or defeat, 8.c.conv
しょうほう (商法) (n)　commerce, 5.b.1
じょうほうしょり (情報処理) (n)　information processing, 1.rw
じょうむとりしまりやく (常務取締役) (n)　managing director, 4.e.3
しょうわ (昭和) (n)　the Showa era (1926-1989), 1.rw
ショールーム (n)　showroom, 9.rw.1
しょか (初夏) (n)　early summer, 7.rw.1
しょくじ (食事) (n)　meal, 5.gr.3
しょくじつき (食事付き) (n)　including meals, 10.a.1
しょくしゅ (職種) (n)　job type, 11.c.3
しょくれき (職歴) (n)　employment history, 1.e.2
しょしゅうのこう (初秋の候) (phr)　early fall, 10.rw.1
じょせい (女性) (n)　female; woman, 6.rw, 7.d.conv
しょりそくど (処理速度) (n)　processing speed, 9.a.conv
しょりび (処理日) (n)　date of processing, 11.c.3
しょるい (書類) (n)　document, 3.e.2, 4.e.conv
ジョンソン (n)　Johnson [family name], 1.gr.7
しらいし (白石) (n)　Shiraishi [family name], 10.a.3
しらいしホテル (白石ホテル) (n)　Shiraishi Hotel, 10.a.3
しらせる (知らせる) (v: shirase/ru)　to notify, 1.e.conv
しらべさせる (調べさせる) (v: shirabe/ru) [CAUS of しらべる] to make/let (someone) check, 9.a.1
しらべる (調べる) (v: shirabe/ru)　to check, examine, 11.lc
しられて (知られて) (v: shir/u) [PASS of しって] is known, 8.b.1
しりたい (知りたい) (v: shir/u) [たい-form of しる] want to know, 6.com.1, 10.b.conv
しりたがる (知りたがる) (v: shir/u)　(others) want to get to know, 6.lc
しらない (知らない) (v: shir/u) [NEG of しっている] does not know, 3.gr.5
しりょう (資料) (n)　information materials, 7.a.3, 7.e.conv
しる (知る) (v: shir/u)　to get to know [しっている "know"], 2.c.1
じれい (辞令) (n)　company order, 11.lc
しろ (白) (n)　white color, 5.gr.7
しんがた (新型) (n)　new model, 1.b.add
しんかんせん (新幹線) (n)　Shinkansen bullet train, 1.gr.6
しんこうちゅう (進行中) (n)　in progress, 11.c.3
じんじ (人事) (n)　personnel, 4.e.2
しんじゅく (新宿) (n)　Shinjuku [a ward in Tokyo], 1.rw
しんじゅくえき (新宿駅) (n)　train station, 1.gr.6
しんしゅつ (進出) する (n/v)　to make inroads; advance, 9.c.conv

Appendix B: Japanese-English Glossary

しんじょうしょ (身上書) (n) personal disclosure form, 1.e.2
しんせい (申請) いたします (n/v) [↓ of 申請します] propose; apply, 11.c.3
しんせい (申請) する (n/v) to apply for, propose; application, 11.c.3
しんせいひん (新製品) (n) new product, 1.b.conv
シンセサイザー (n) synthesizer, 10.gr.4
しんとみホテル (シントミホテル) (n) Hotel Shintomi, 1.gr.6
しんにゅうしゃいん (新入社員) (n) newly hired employee, 2.b.conv
しんぱい (心配) する (な-adj/v) to worry; worry, 6.b.conv
しんぱい (心配) しないで (phr) Don't worry., 6.b.conv
しんばし (新橋) (n) Shinbashi [place name], 7.c.1
しんぶん (新聞) (n) newspaper, 1.b.2, 1.gr.5
しんぼく (親睦) (n) friendship; good will, 1.d.conv
シンポジウム (n) symposium, 8.gr.7

す

すいどう (水道) (n) water (line), 5.d.conv
ずいぶん (adv) very; very much; a lot [followed by an affirmative predicate], 8.c.conv
すいようび (水曜日) (n) Wednesday, 1.gr.4
すう (吸う) (v: suw/u) to smoke, 1.d.1
すうがく (数学) (n) mathematics, 1.rw
すうじ (数字) (n) number, digit, 5.c.conv
すうりょう (数量) (n) quantity, 11.rw.1
すき (好き) (な-adj) to like; to be fond of; favorite, 1.b.6
スキー (n) ski, 6.a.3
すぐ (adv) immediately, 1.b.6, 6.b.3
スクリーン (n) screen, 8.b.1
すぐれた (優れた) (v: sugure/ru) excellent [adjectival form], 7.rw.1
すぐれる (優れる) (v: sugure/ru) to excel (at) [Usu. in the form すぐれている "is excellent"], 1.c.conv
すこし (少し) (n) a little, 5.gr.11, 6.c.1
すしや (寿司屋) (n) sushi restaurant, 4.gr.3
すずき (鈴木) (n) Suzuki [family name], 1.gr.7
すずしい (涼しい) (い-adj) cool, 4.gr.6, 5.c.1, 7.d.conv
すすむ (進む) (v: susum/u) to advance; to go forward, 7.gr.4
スター (n) star, celebrity, 2.gr.1
ずっと (adv) continuously, throughout; by far, 4.b.1
すてる (捨てる) (v: sute/ru) to throw away; discard, 8.gr.2
すばらしい (素晴らしい) (い-adj) wonderful, terrific, 1.b.conv
すばらしかった (素晴らしかった) (い-adj) was wonderful, 4.d.2
スピーチ (n) speech, 1.d.1
スピード (n) speed, 8.1c
スペインご (スペイン語) (n) Spanish (language), 1.gr.4
スポーツ (n) sports, 1.com.1
スポーツカー (n) sports car, 10.a.1
スミス (n) Smith [family name], 1.gr.7
すみたい (住みたい) (v: sum/u) [たい-form of すむ] want to live, 10.gr.4
スミタこうぎょう (スミタ工業) (n) Sumita Manufacturing [company name], 6.gr.4
すみません (phr) I'm sorry.; Excuse me., 6.b.3
すむ (住む) (v: sum/u) to live; to reside, 1.d.1
する (iv) to do [Xにする "to decide on X; to choose X"; role をする "to act as X"], 1.b.3
するほう (する方) (phr) doing (side), 8.c.3
すれば (iv) [PROV of する] if/provided one does, 7.c.2
すんだら (住んだら) (v: sum/u) [COND of すむ] if one lives, 2.gr.1

せ

せいさくしょ (製作所) (n) manufacturing (plant), 3.f.conv
せいさん (生産) する (n/v) to produce; production, 8.c.conv, 8.gr.4
せいぞう (製造) する (n/v) to manufacture; manufacturing, 4.e.2, 7.a.conv
せいちょう (成長) する (n/v) to grow; growth, 3.gr.4
せいで (phr) due to [S せいで "due to the fact that S"; N の せいで "due to N"], 11.c.conv
せいど (制度) (n) (social) system; institution; convention, 11.gr.4
せいねんがっぴ (生年月日) (n) date of birth, 1.e.2
せいのう (性能) (n) capability [of machines], 11.gr.1
せいひん (製品) (n) product, 1.b.add
せいふく (制服) (n) uniform, 3.b.1
せいべつ (性別) (n) sex; gender, 5.rw.1
せいやく (製薬) (n) pharmaceutical [company], 3.a.2
せいやくかいしゃ (製薬会社) (n) pharmaceutical company, 3.a.2
せいりつ (成立) (n) completion; achievement, 11.a.conv
セールス (n) sales, 2.d.add
セールスウーマン (n) saleswoman, 7.e.conv
セールスマン (n) salesman, 10.b.1
せかいてき (世界的) (な-adj) world-wide; of the world [せかいてきに all over the world], 1.c.conv
せがたかい (背が高い) (い-adj) tall, 1.b.1
せき (席) (n) seat, 3.b.1
せきゆ (石油) (n) oil; petroleum, 5.c.1, 10.gr.1
セクション (n) section, 5.gr.7
せっかく (adv) go to the trouble of V-ing, 10.gr.2
せっきゃくちゅう (接客中) (n) in the middle of meeting a client, 3.d.add
せっきょくてき (積極的) (な-adj) positive, is willing, active, constructive, 10.c.3
せつぞく (接続) される (n/v) [PASS of 接続する] to be connected; [↑ of 接続する] to connect, 9.b.conv, 9.b.3
せつぞく (接続) する (n/v) to connect; connection, 9.b.3
せったい (接待) する (n/v) to receive a guest, entertain; reception, 6.c.conv, 7.e.1
せってい (設定) される (iv) [PASS of 設定する] is configured; is set up; [↑ of 設定する] to configure, 9.b.conv
せってい (設定) する (n/v) to configure; configuration, 9.b.conv
せつめい (説明) いたしましょうか (phr) [↓ POL VOL of 説明する + か] shall I explain, 7.d.2
せつめいかい (説明会) (n) meeting for explanation, exposition, etc., 9.rw.1
せつめいしょ (説明書) (n) user manual, explanation , 7.e.2
せつめい (説明) する (n/v) to explain; explanation, 7.d.2, 7.e.2
ぜひ (adv) by all means, 4.a.conv
ぜひとも (phr) by all means; please [= ぜひ], 7.rw.1
せまい (狭い) (い-adj) narrow, cramped, 1.c.3

セミナー (n) seminar, 2.gr.6, 3.gr.4, 5.b.1
ぜんかい (前回) (n) previous time, 10.rw.1
せんげつ (先月) (n) last month, 1.gr.5
せんこう (専攻) いたして (n/v) [↓ て-form of 専攻する] major (in), 1.e.1
せんこういたしました (専攻いたしました) (n/v) [POL ↓ of 専攻した] majored (in), 1.b.2
せんこう (専攻) する (n/v) to major (in); major, 1.a.conv, 1.a.1, 1.e.1
せんこう (専攻) なさって (n/v) [↑ of 専攻して] major (in), 1.e.1
せんじつ (先日) (n) the other day, 3.a.conv, 7.a.3
せんしゅう (先週) (n) last week, 11.c.conv
せんせい (先生) (n) teacher, 1.c.3
ぜんぜん (全然) (n) never [followed by NEG], 2.b.1
せんでん (宣伝)する (n/v) to advertise; advertizement [宣伝になる "become an advertisement"], 8.c.conv, 8.gr.3, 11.b.2
せんでんひ (宣伝費) (n) advertising cost, 8.c.conv
セントオーガスティン (n) St. Augustine, 1.lc
せんぱい (先輩) (n) one's senior, 2.a.conv
ぜんぶ (全部) (n) all; everything [ぜんぶで "in total"], 2.a.2
せんむ (専務) (n) senior managing director, 11.gr.4
せんむとりしまりやく (専務取締役) (n) senior managing director, 4.e.3
せんもん (専門) (n) specialty, 1.a.conv

そ

ぞ (sp) [particle for expressing a strong resolve], 11.a.conv
そう (pro) that way; like that, 1.a.conv
そういうことで (phr) being that kind of thing; OK then, 11.c.conv
そういった (prenom) that kind of [unshared experience; = そんな], 1.c.conv
そうか (phr) [PLAIN of そうですか] Is that right?, 3.c.1
そうがく (総額) (n) total amount of money, 6.gr.1
そうきん (送金) する (n/v) to send money; remittance; sending of money, 5.a.1, 5.e.1
そうごう (総合) (n) comprehensive, 5.rw.1
そうごうしょく (総合職) (n) general post, 2.a.4
そうしんしゃ (送信者) (n) sender, 4.rw2
そうだ (phr) appear [S そうだ "it appears that S"], 7.b.3
そうだな (interj) Let me see., 2.a.conv
そうだん (相談) しよう (n/v) [VOL of 相談する] (let's) consult; I will consult, 6.a.2
そうだん (相談) する (n/v) to consult; consultation, 4.e.conv
そうむ (総務) (n) general affairs, 4.e.2
そうりつ (創立) (n) establishment; year established, 8.rw.1
そくたつ (速達) (n) express mail, 5.com.1
そくとう (即答) する (n/v) to answer immediately; immediate answer, 4.d.conv
そこ (pro) there, that place (near you), 2.b.conv
そつぎょう (卒業) する (n/v) to graduate; graduation, 1.rw
そと (外) (n) outside, 9.a.1
ソニー (n) Sony [company name], 1.c.3
ソニーさん (n) Sony [lit. "Mr. Sony"], 1.b.2
その (prenom) that (near you), 1.b.conv
そのうえ (con) on top of that; furthermore, 8.c.conv
そのように (phr) in that way; like that, 10.c.4

そば (n) Japanese soba noodles, 6.lc
ソフト (n) software, 1.b.conv
それ (pro) that one (near you), 1.d.conv
それから (con) then; besides; since then, 1.d.conv
それで (con) given that; so; thus; therefore, 1.c.conv
それでは (con) well then, 1.a.conv
それと (con) in addition, 2.d.conv
それに (con) furthermore, on top of that, 10.b.conv
それまでに (phr) by that time, 4.e.conv
そろそろ (adv) slowly, 6.b.4
ぞんじております (存じて～) (phr) I know. [↓ of しています], 1.gr.8
ぞんじます (存じます) (v: zonji/ru) I think [ねがいたくぞんじます "would like to request"] ↓, 10.rw.1
そんな (pro) that kind of, 2.b.1
そんなふうに (phr) in that way; like that, 10.c.4

た

だ (cop) [PLAIN of です] is/are, 1.b.6
だい (台) (ct) unit [counter for machines], 10.a.conv
だい (題) (n) subject, 4.rw2
だい3ごう (第 3 号) (num) number three, 11.c.3
たいいくかん (体育館) (n) gymnasium, 1.gr.8
だいいち (第一) (num) number one; first, 9.c.conv
だいいっか (第一課) (n) Section #1, 2.rw
たいおう (対応) (n) coping, matching, 7.gr.4
たいかい (大会) (n) tournament, 7.c.2
だいがく (大学) (n) university, college, 1.a.conv
だいさんかいぎしつ (第三会議室) (n) the third conference room, 8.lc
だいじ (大事) (な-adj) important; precious, 6.gr.3
だいしきゅう (大至急) (n) extremely urgent(ly); immediate(ly); big hurry, 3.f.add
だいじこ (大事故) (n) big accident, 10.c.2
たい (対) して (n/v) [て-form of 対する] is toward; is contrasted (with) [X に対して "toward X"], 10.c.conv
たいしょう (大正) (n) the Taisho era (1912-1926), 5.rw.1
だいじょうぶ (大丈夫) (な-adj) OK; all right; safe, 2.c.conv
だいすう (台数) (n) the number of units (machines), 10.a.conv
だいすき (大好き) (な-adj) to like the best, 2.gr.5
たい (対) する (n/v) to go against; oppose, 11.b.3
たいそう (体操) (n) calisthenics, 6.gr.4
だいにかいぎしつ (第二会議室) (n) the second conference room, 8.lc
だいひょうとりしまりやく (代表取締役) (n) chief executive officer, 4.e.3
タイプ (n) type, 5.e.1
タイプいたします (n/v) [↓ of タイプする] to type, 9.gr.3
たいふう (台風) (n) typhoon, 4.c.2, 8.c.1
タイプする (n/v) to type, 1.gr.2
たいへん (大変) (な-adj) very much; extreme; overwhelming; rough; terrible [大変もうしわけない "terribly sorry"], 1.b.conv, 7.e.1
だいり (代理) (n) deputy, 4.e.3
だいりてん (代理店) (n) sales agency store, 10.c.3
たいりょう (大量) (n) mass, massive, 8.c.conv
たかい (高い) (い-adj) high, expensive, tall, 1.b.1

たかいだけ (高いだけ) (phr) All X is is being expensive, 9.b.1
たかくなくても (高くなくても) (い-adj) [NEG て-form of たかい + も] even if it is not high, expensive, tall, 5.b.1
たかければ (高ければ) (い-adj) [PROV of たかい] if/provided it is expensive, 7.c.2, 8.gr.4
たかそう (高そう) (phr) [Stem of たかい + そう] looks expensive, 8.a.1
たくさん (n) a lot; many [たくさんの N "a lot of N"], 4.gr.6, 6.gr.3, 8.b.1
タクシー (n) taxi, 4.gr.8
だけ (p) only, just [X だけでいい "Given X, it is OK."; V だけで、ほかになにもしない "All one does is V, and do nothing else."], 9.b.conv
ださせる (出させる) (v: das/u) [CAUS of だす] to make/let (someone) bring out/submit, 9.a.1
だしたばかり (出したばかり) (phr) has just put/introduced [to the market], 11.a.conv
だしてある (出してある) (phr) (something) is deliberately sent/taken out/submitted, 6.c.4
だしておく (出しておく) (phr) is submit/sent/taken out for later use, 6.c.4,
たしゃ (他社) (n) other companies, 8.c.conv
だす (出す) (vt: das/u) to put outside; to submit; turn in [でんしメールをだす "to send email"] [vi: でる], 2.b.conv, 3.e.1
たすかる (助かる) (v: tasukar/u) to be rescued, helped, 3.gr.3
たずさわりたい (携わりたい) (v: tazusawar/u) [たい-form of たずさわる] want to take part (in), 1.b.conv
たずさわる (携わる) (v: tazusawar/u) to engage in [X にたずさわる "engage in X"], 1.b.conv
だせなかったら (出せなかったら) (v: das/u) [COND POT of だす] if one can put outside/submit, 2.gr.1
だせる (出せる) (v: das/u) [POT of だす] can put outside [ちからをだす "realize one's capability"], 1.c.conv
だそう (出そう) (v: kas/u) [VOL of だす] let's submit, 4.a.2
ただいま (ただ今) (n) right now; [greeting] I'm home! I'm back!, 3.d.conv
ただしい (正しい) (い-adj) correct, 7.e.2
だった (cop) [PLAIN PAST of です] was, were, 1.b.1
だったら (cop) [COND of だ] if it is, 2.a.2
たなか (田中) (n) Tanaka [family name], 1.a.1
たなかしょうじ (田中商事) (n) Tanaka Trading [company name], 8.gr.2
たの (他の) (phr) other, 9.b.3
たのしみ (楽しみ) (n) joy [〜をたのしみにする "look forward to..."], 6.b.4
たのしむ (楽しむ) (v: tanoshim/u) enjoy, 6.b.4
たのまれる (頼まれる) (v: tanom/u) [PASS of たのむ] to be requested, asked; [↑ of たのむ] to ask, to request, 10.b.2, 10.lc
たのみたい (頼みたい) (v: tanom/u) [たい-form of たのむ] want to ask (for help), 8.c.4
たのむ (頼む) (v: tanom/u) to ask (someone) for (something), 3.e.2
たのんだら (頼んだら) (v: tanom/u) [COND of たのむ] if one asks (someone) for (something), 2.a.2
たばこ (煙草) (n) cigarette, 1.d.1
たべ (食べ) (v: tabe/ru) [Stem of たべます] eat, 6.a.5
たべさせる (食べさせる) (v: tabe/ru) [CAUS of たべる] to make/let (someone) eat, 9.a.1

たべてから (食べてから) (phr) [て-form of たべる + から] eat and...; after eating, 6.a.conv
たべてきたばかり (食べて来たばかり) (phr) have just come back after eating, 9.c.3
たべましょう (食べましょう) (v: tabe/ru) [POL VOL of たべる] let's eat; we shall eat., 4.a.2, 6.a.3
たべよう (食べよう) (v: tabe/ru) [VOL of たべる] let's eat, 4.a.2
たべようとする (食べようとする) (phr) [VOL of たべる + とする] try to eat it (without success), 6.c.3
たべられる (食べられる) (v: tabe/ru) [POT of たべられる] can eat, 1.b.5
たべられる (食べられる) (v: tabe/ru) [PASS of たべる] to be eaten, 8.b.1
たべる (食べる) (v: tabe/ru) to eat, 1.a.1, 1.b.3, 1.b.5
たべれば (食べれば) (v: tabe/ru) [PROV of たべる] if/provided one eats, 7.c.2
たべれる (食べれる) (v: tabe/ru) [POT of たべる] can eat, 1.b.5, 8.b.1
〜たほうがいい (〜た方がいい) (phr) had better ...; should, 4.a.5
たまには (adv) once in a while, 10.gr.2
たまわり (賜り) (v: tamawar/u) [V-stem of たまわる] receive; is granted [more polite than いただく], 7.rw.1
たまわります (賜ります) (v: tamawar/u) [POL of たまわる] to give (to me) ↑, 10.rw.1
たまわります (賜ります) (v: tamawar/u) [POL of たまわる] to receive; is granted [more polite than いただく] ↓, 7.rw.1
たむら (田村) (n) Tamura [family name], 1.gr.7
タムラしょうじ (タムラ商事) (n) Tamura Trading [company name], 8.gr.2
たむらでんき (田村電気) (n) Tamura Electric, 2.e.conv
ため (n) purpose; reason [N のため(に) "for the reason of N"; S ため(に) "in order that S", 4.c.2, 6.rw.1
だめ (な-adj) no good; useless, 6.b.4
ためしてみて (試してみて) (phr) [て-form of ためす + みて] try and see, 9.a.conv
ためす (試す) (v: tames/u) to try; to attempt (to use), 9.a.conv
だれ (誰) (qw) who, 1.com.4
だれか (誰か) (n) someone, 6.a.3
だれがしても (誰がしても) (phr) no matter who does it; whoever does it, 11.b.2
だれでも (誰でも) (phr) no matter who it is; whoever it is, 11.b.2
だれにも (誰にも) (phr) (not) to anyone, 6.gr.6
だれも (誰も) (phr) not anyone; no one [followed by a negative predicate], 6.a.3
だろう (cop) [PLAIN of でしょう] probably S, 2.c.conv
たろう (太郎) (n) Taro [male given name], 1.a.1
たんか (単価) (n) price per unit, 11.rw.1
だんごう (談合) (n) bid-rigging, 11.gr.4
だんじょ (男女) (n) men and women, 11.c.3
たんしんふにん (単身赴任) (n) one-person relocation (transfer to a distant work place), 11.lc
だんせい (男性) (n) male; man, 6.rw, 7.d.add
たんとう (担当) (n) (person in) charge, 10.a.3

ち

ち (地) (n) ground, earth, 8.c.conv
ちいさい (小さい) (い-adj) small, 1.c.3

チェック (n)　check, 5.a.1
ちえん (遅延) (n)　delay, 11.rw.1
ちか (地下) (n)　underground, basement, 5.gr.3, 6.rw
ちかい (近い) (い-adj)　close, near, 1.com.4
ちかいうちに (近いうちに) (phr)　in the near future, 7.b.conv
ちがう (違う) (v: chigaw/u)　to be wrong, be different, 4.lc, 6.c.2, 10.a.1
ちかてつ (地下鉄) (n)　subway, 1.c.3
ちから (力) (n)　power, strength, capability, 1.c.conv
チキン (n)　chicken, 5.gr.7
ちち (父) (n)　father ↓, 1.gr.1
ちっとも (adv)　(not) at all [followed by a negative predicate; = ぜんぜん], 9.b.1
ちなみに (con)　in this connection; in that regard, 8.b.conv
ちめいど (知名度) (n)　name recognition, 8.b.conv
ちゅう (中) (n)　middle [of], 4.a.conv
ちゅうい (注意) する (n/v)　to be careful; caution, 4.c.2
ちゅうきゅう (中級) (n)　intermediate; medium, 6.gr.7
ちゅうごくご (中国語) (n)　Chinese (language), 1.gr.4
ちゅうもん (注文) (n)　order, 4.b.conv
ちゅうもんうけつけ (注文受付) (n)　order taking, 11.c.3
ちゅうもんしょ (注文書) (n)　order form, 4.b.conv
ちゅうもん (注文) する (n/v)　to order; order, 6.gr.4, 10.a.conv
ちょうこうそく (超高速) (n)　super fast, 9.rw.1
ちょうこがた (超小型) (n)　ultra small, 1.b.conv
ちょうし (調子) (n)　condition, 11.gr.4
ちょくせつ (直接) (n)　direct, 10.c.conv
ちょっと (adv)　a little, 1.gr.2

つ

ついたばかり (着いたばかり) (phr)　have just arrived, 9.c.3
ついて (v: tsuk/u) [て-form of つく] stick; accompany; become attached, 2.a.conv
ついていた (v: tsuk/u) [て-form of つく + いた] was lucky, 8.c.4
つうきん (通勤) (n)　commuting to work, 1.lc
つうじる (通じる) (v: tsuuji/ru)　make oneself understood, 4.gr.3
つうしん (通信) (n)　telecommunication, 1.b.conv
つうしんいん (通信員) (n)　correspondent, 2.rw
つうちょう (通帳) (n)　passbook, 5.rw.1
つうやく (通訳) する (n/v)　to interpret, translate; interpretation, 1.d.1, 1.lc
つうろがわ (通路側) (n)　isle side, 3.gr.4
つかいかた (使い方) (n)　use, usage, method [the way of using], 5.f.conv
つかいたい (使いたい) (v: tsukaw/u) [たい-form of つかう] want to use, 1.b.4
つかいたがって (使いたがって) (v: tsukaw/u) [て-form of つかいたがる] (others) want to use, 6.a.6
つかう (使う) (v: tsukaw/u)　to use, employ, 1.b.4, 1.b.5, 2.b.conv
つかうことができる (使うこと〜) (phr)　is able to use, 9.b.2
つかえなければ (使えなければ) (v: tsukaw/u) [PROV of つかえない] if/provided that (someone) can't use it, 11.b.3
つかえば (使えば) (v: tsukaw/u) [PROV of つかう] if/provided one uses, 8.gr.1
つかえる (使える) (v: tsukaw/u) [POT of つかう] can use, 1.b.5
つかったばかり (使ったばかり) (phr)　have just used, 9.c.3
つかったら (使ったら) (v: tsukaw/u) [COND of つかう] if one uses, 2.a.2
つかれる (疲れる) (v: tsukare/ru)　to get tired, 2.gr.2, 10.gr.3
つかわれる (使われる) (v: tsukaw/u) [PASS of つかう] to be used; [↑ of つかう] to use, 8.b.1
つき (suf)　equipped; included [バストイレつき "equipped with a bathroom and a toilet"], 10.a.1
つき (月) (n)　month; the moon, 1.d.conv
つぎ (次) (n)　next, 1.a.conv
つきましては (phr)　regarding; thus/therefore/and so; based on the preceding, 7.b.conv, 9.rw.1, 11.c.3
つく (vi: tsuk/u) (something) is attached; [でんきがつく "light comes on"]; [light] comes on [ついている "(light) is on"] [vt: つける], 6.a.1
つく (着く) (vi: tsuk/u) to arrive; reach [ちにあしがつく "be firmly on the ground"], 2.c.4, 7.c.1, 8.c.conv
つくえ (机) (n)　desk, 2.b.conv
つくらせる (作らせる) (v: tsukur/u) [CAUS of つくる] to make/let (someone) make, 9.a.1
つくらなければ (作らなければ) (v: tsukur/u) [PROV of つくらない] if/provided one does not make, 7.c.2
つくられる (作られる) (v: tsukur/u) [PASS of つくる] is made; [↑ of つくる] to make, 8.b.1
つくりだす (作り出す) (v: tsukuridas/u)　to produce; to create [つくる "make" + だす "put outside"], 1.c.conv
つくる (作る) (v: tsukur/u)　to make; to cook, 1.b.1, 8.b.1
つくることができる (作る〜) (phr)　is able to make, 9.b.2
つくれる (作れる) (v: tsukur/u) [POT of つくる] can make, 1.b.5
つけましょう (v: tsuke/ru) [POL VOL of つける] let's attach, include, turn on, 10.a.conv
つけましょうか (v: tsuke/ru) [POL VOL of つける + か] shall I turn (it) on?, 7.e.3
つける (vt: tsuke/ru) to turn on; to put on, attach; [くすりをつける "apply medicine"; でんきをつける "turn on lights"] [vi: つく], 6.a.1, 6.c.4, 7.e.3, 10.a.conv
つごう (都合) (n)　schedule [つごうがいい "schedule is open; good timing"], 5.gr.5
つじ (辻) (n)　Tsuji [family name], 3.lc
つたえる (伝える) (v: tsutae/ru)　to communicate, 3.e.2, 10.c.conv
つづきがら (続柄) (n)　relationship (to applicant), 1.e.2
つづく (続く) (vi: tsuduk/u)　(something) continues/lasts; is continued [vt: つづける], 7.gr.3
つづける (続ける) (vt: tsuduke/ru)　to continue (something) [vi: つづく], 8.gr.3
って (p) [quotation marker; INFORMAL of と], 5.a.conv
つとめる (勤める) (v: tsutome/ru)　to work for [X につとめている "work for X"], 1.c.1
つなぐ (v: tsunag/u)　to connect, link, access [つないでいる "is connecting; have connected"], 4.c.2, 9.lc
つめたい (冷たい) (い-adj)　cold, 6.a.3
つもり (n)　intention [plain V つもりだ "intend to V"], 2.c.conv
つゆ (梅雨) (n)　rainy season [June through mid-July], 8.gr.8
つよい (強い) (い-adj)　strong; potent, 6.b.4
つらぬく (貫く) (v: tsuranuk/u)　to stick with, hold onto (idea or policy); to penetrate, 8.c.conv
つれて (連れて) (v: tsure/ru) [て-form of つれる] accompany [つれていく "take, accompany, escort"], 6.a.6

て

て (p) [quotation marker; INFORMAL of と] [なんていう "What do you say/is it called?"], 2.a.2
で (p) in, at [location of activities], 1.a.conv
で (cop) [て-form of だ/です] is/are; being, 1.b.conv
で (p) [instrument/means marker] by, by means of, by using, with, in, 1.c.conv
て (手) (n) hand; arm [手で "by hand"], 1.gr.5
ていあん (提案) (n) proposal, 10.c.1
ていきゅうび (定休日) (n) designated day for a business to close, 3.f.1
ていきよきん (定期預金) (n) fixed time account; time deposit account, 5.(title).
ていけい (提携) する (n/v) to cooperate [with other business]; [business] cooperation 4.d.1
ていコスト (低コスト) (n) low cost, 1.c.conv
ていしゅつ (提出) してある (phr) is submitted deliberately, 6.c.4
ていしゅつ (提出) しておく (phr) is submitted in advance, 6.c.4
ていしゅつ (提出) する (n/v) to submit; turn [= だす], 2.c.conv
ディスカウント (n) discount, 10.b.conv
ていねい (丁寧) (な-adj) meticulous, 8.c.4
ていねいに (丁寧に) (adv) meticulously; carefully, 10.gr.3
でいらっしゃいます (v: deirasshar/u) [↑ of copula です] to be, 3.b.conv
データコンプレッション (n) data compression, 1.a.conv
てがき (手書き) (n) hand writing, 5.b.1
でかける (出かける) (v: dekake/ru) to go out, 1.a.1, 6.b.4
てがみ (手紙) (n) letter, mail, 3.e.1
できそう (phr) [V-stem of できる + そう] looks it can be done, 8.a.1
できそうでした (phr) appeared able to do it, 7.d.1
できそうです (phr) appear able to do it, 7.d.1
できそうにない (phr) [V-stem of できる + そう + に + POL of ない] does not look it can be done, 7.d.1, 8.a.1
できたそうです (phr) they say (someone) was able to do it, 7.d.1
できたら (v: deki/ru) [COND of できる] if one can, 2.a.2
できないそうです (phr) they say (someone) can't do it, 7.d.1
できなかったら (v: deki/ru) [NEG COND of できる] if one cannot, 2.a.2
できなければ (v: deki/ru) [PROV of できない] if/provided that (someone) can't do it, 11.b.3
できなさそう (phr) [Stem of できない + さそう] looks it can't be done, 8.a.1
できますでしょうか (phr) [softer expression of できますか: "I wonder if I could..."]., 7.a.conv
できる (iv) [POT of する] can do; finish, 1.b.5, 1.gr.4, 2.a.2, 3.e.1
できるそうです (phr) they say (someone) can do it, 7.d.1
できれば (v: deki/ru) [PROV of できる] if/provided that one can do, 7.d.conv
テクニカル (n) technical, 8.1c
でございます (cop) [Courteous form of です] is/are, 3.a.1, 3.d.conv, 3.f.1
デザイン (n) design, 1.c.3, 5.rw.1
でしだい (出次第) (phr) as soon as (something) comes out, 7.gr.4
でしたら (cop) [POL COND of だ] if it is, 2.a.2
デジタルカメラ (n) digital camera, 9.gr.5
デジタルマシン (n) Digital Machine [company name], 7.a.conv
デジタルマシンしゃ (デジタルマシン社) (n) Digital Machine [company name], 10.c.conv
でして (cop) [polite て-form of です] is/are, 3.f.conv
でしょう (cop) [TENTATIVE of です] probably is/are; maybe, 1.a.1
です (cop) [POL of だ] is, are [い-adj だ Politeness marker], 1.a.conv
てすうりょう (手数料) (n) handling charge, 5.e.conv
テスト (n) test, exam, quiz, 2.a.3
でたくない (出たくない) (v: de/ru) not want to go/come out, 7.c.2
てつだう (手伝う) (v: tetsudaw/u) to help, assist, 7.d.2, 7.e.3, 7.1c
てつだってほしい (手伝ってほしい) (phr) [て-form of てつだう + ほしい] want (other person) to assist, 7.d.2
でなければ (cop) [NEG PROV of です] if it is not...; provided it is not..., 3.d.conv
テニス (n) tennis, 1.d.conv
テネシー (n) Tennessee, 1.d.2
での (phr) by means of [N1 での N2 "N2 by means of N1"], 7.e.2
では (con) then; well, 1.b.conv
では (cop+p) [X ではない "is not X"], 1.d.conv
デパート (n) department store, 1.gr.5
てまえみそ (手前味噌) (n) home-made miso (Japanese bean paste) [手前味噌ですが (idiom) "I don't mean to brag, but..."]., 8.b.conv
でも (con) but, 4.c.conv
でられそうだ (出られ～) (phr) appears able to go out, 7.d.1
でられそうにない (出られ～) (phr) not appear able to go/come out, 7.d.1
でられる (出られる) (vi: de/ru) [POT of でる] can go out; can come out; can leave; can emerge, 6.com.1
でる (出る) (vi: de/ru) to go out; come out, emerge; to leave, graduate [vt: だす], 1.b.6, 3.f.5, 6.a.1, 6.b.1
でることになっている (出ることになっている) (phr) it is decided/the rule that (something) will come out, 9.b.3
テレコム (n) telecommunication, 3.a.conv
テレビ (n) TV (set), 1.b.conv
テレビゲーム (n) video game, 9.c.2
てをむすぶ (手を結ぶ) (phr) cooperate, 10.c.3
てん (点) (n) point, aspect, fact [～という点で "with regard to the fact that..."], 1.c.conv
でんき (電気) (n) light, electricity; electric, 3.a.2
でんきこうがく (電気工学) (n) Electrical Engineering, 1.rw
でんきこうがくか (電気工学科) (n) Dept. of Electrical Engineering, 1.rw
でんきこうぎょう (電気工業) (n) electric equipment manufacturing; electric equipment company, 3.a.2
でんきさんぎょう (電気産業) (n) electric equipment industry; electric equipment company, 3.a.2
でんごん (伝言) (n) message, 3.e.add
でんし (電子) (n) electronic, 3.a.2
てんじかい (展示会) (n) exhibition, 3.com.3
でんしこうぎょう (電子工業) (n) electronic manufacturing; electronics company, 3.a.2

でんしさんぎょう (電子産業) (n) electronic industry; electronics company, 3.a.2
でんしメール (電子メール) (n) email, 1.gr.7
でんしゃ (電車) (n) (electric) train, 1.gr.8
でんしん (電信) (n) electronic transfer, 5.e.conv
でんしんあつかい (電信扱い) (n) electronic handling, 5.gr.9, 7.c.1
でんち (電池) (n) battery, 10.gr.1
てんぷしょるい (添付書類) (n) attachment; attached documents, 11.c.3
てんぷしりょう (添付資料) (n) attachment [てんぷする "to attach"], 9.rw.1
てんぷ (添付) する (n/v) to attach; attachment, 9.rw.1
てんぷら (n) tempura (deep fried fish and vegetables), 6.com.1
でんわ (電話) (n) telephone [電話をかける／する "to call"; 電話にでる "to answer the call"; 電話をとる "to pick up the receiver"; 電話がはいる "to have a phone call"; 電話がある "had a phone call"; 電話をかりる "to use (someone's) phone"; 電話をかけなおす "to call again"; 電話をかえす "to return a call"], 1.b.conv
でんわがあった (電話があった) (phr) You had a phone call., 3.b.add
でんわがはいっている (電話が入っている) (phr) You have a phone call., 3.b.add
でんわ (電話) したら (n/v) [COND of 電話する] if one calls, 2.a.2
でんわする (電話する) (n/v) to call; telephone [Xに電話する "call X"], 2.a.add, 3.a.add
でんわだい (電話代) (n) telephone charge, 5.d.conv
でんわちゅう (電話中) (n) is on the phone; is in the middle of a phone call, 3.d.add
でんわつき (電話付き) (n) attached with a phone, 10.a.1
でんわ (電話) なさる (n/v) [↑ of 電話する] to call, telephone, 3.e.2
でんわにでられない (電話に出られない) (phr) cannot come to the phone, 3.a.add
でんわにでる (電話に出る) (phr) answer a phone call, 3.a.add
でんわばんごう (電話番号) (n) phone number, 3.e.conv
でんわをかえす (電話を返す) (phr) return the phone call, 3.c.add
でんわをかけたところ (電話をかけた所) (phr) I have just called, 9.c.4
でんわをかけているところ (電話をかけている所) (phr) I am calling right now., 9.c.4
でんわをかけなおす (電話をかけ直す) (phr) call again, 3.c.add
でんわをかける (電話をかける) (phr) make a phone call; call, 3.a.add
でんわをかけるところ (電話をかける所) (phr) I'm about to call., 9.c.4
でんわをかりる (電話を借りる) (phr) use [someone's] phone, 3.b.add
でんわをとる (電話を取る) (phr) pick up the phone, 3.a.add

と

と (p) and [と combines nouns.], 2.b.1
と (con) [non-past S1 と、S2 "if/when S1, S2"] [けつろんからもうしますと "to state the conclusion first," "in a nutshell"], 4.d.conv, 7.c.conv
と (p) [quotation marker; FORMAL of って], 1.a.conv
ど (度) (ct) [counter for events or degrees] times; degrees, 1.d.conv
ドア (n) door, 6.a.1
といあわせる (問い合わせる) (v: toiawase/ru) to inquire, ask, 10.b.conv
ということだ (phr) said that..., 4.a.1
ということにしましょう (phr) Let's decide on what you call ...[X ということにする "make (it) so-called X"], 10.b.conv
というと (phr) if you say that, 8.c.4
というふうに (phr) [という + ふう + に] in such a way that..., to the effect that..., 10.c.conv
というより (phr) rather than saying that, 8.c.4
といたしましても (phr) [↓ of として + も ("also")] also as for; also as far as, 7.rw.1
ドイツ (n) Germany, 1.lc
ドイツしゃ (ドイツ車) (n) German car, 1.gr.5
トイレ (n) toilet, rest room, 4.gr.7
どう (qw) how?; how about? [どうですか "How about...?"], 2.a.2
とう (問う) (v: tow/u) to question, 11.c.3
どういう (qw) what kind of, 1.d.conv
どういった (prenom) what kind of, 1.b.conv
どうか (phr) in some way, 2.c.1, 6.a.3
どうき (動機) (n) motivation, 1.e.2
とうきょう (東京) (n) Tokyo [capital city of Japan], 1.gr.1
とうきょうこうぎょう (東京工業) (n) Tokyo Manufacturing [company name], 8.gr.5
とうきょうタイムス (東京タイムス) (n) Tokyo Times, 7.d.2
とうきょうテレコム (東京テレコム) (n) [company name] Tokyo Telecom, 4.b.conv
とうきょうと (東京都) (n) Tokyo Capital, 1.rw
どうこう (同行) する (n/v) to accompany, 6.c.conv
とうさい (搭載) してあり (phr) [て-form of とうさいする + V-stem of ある] is loaded with [deliberately], 9.a.conv
とうさい (搭載) する (n/v) to load; loading, 9.a.conv
とうざよきん (当座預金) (n) current checking account, 5.(title).
どうした (phr) [PLAIN of どうしましたか] What happened? [どうしたんですか], 1.gr.6
どうして (qw) How come? Why?, 1.b.6, 4.c.conv
どうしても (phr) no matter how I do it; however I do it, 11.b.2
とうしゃ (当社) (n) our company, 11.rw.1
どうしゃ (同社) (n) aforementioned company, 7.rw.1
とうしょ (当初) (n) initial, 10.rw.1
どうぞ (phr) please; Go ahead.; Here it is!, 1.a.conv
とうだい (東大) (n) the University of Tokyo, 3.gr.5
とうとう (adv) finally, 11.c.add
どうなっていますか (phr) How is it being done?, 9.c.conv
どうふう (同封) させていただく (n/v) [て-form of 同封させる + いただく] to take liberty of enclosing, 9.rw.1
どうふう (同封) する (n/v) to enclose in a letter, 9.rw.1
どうふうのうえ (同封の上) (phr) enclosed [～のうえ "on top of..." or "by means of..."], 7.rw.1
どうも (phr) Thanks!, Sorry., 1.e.conv
どうりょう (同僚) (n) one's colleague, 2.a.add
とおい (遠い) (い-adj) distant; remote, 1.gr.6
とおくて (遠くて) (い-adj) [て-form of とおい] is far; is distant, 1.gr.8

Appendix B: Japanese-English Glossary

とおす (通す) (vt: toos/u) to pass; to put through [めをとおす "browse"] [vi: とおる], 5.f.2, 6.a.1
とおっしゃると (phr) if you say that [↑ of というと], 8.c.4
トーマス (n) Thomas [first name], 2.a.conv
とおらないで (通らないで) (phr) [NEG REQ form of とおる] Don't go through; Don't pass; Don't cross., 6.b.4
とおり (通り) (n) the way; street [かきのとおり "as follows"]; [そのとおり "exactly; it's just the way"]; [おっしゃるとおり "as you say"], 3.rw.1, 8.c.conv, 11.b.3
とおる (通る) (vi: toor/u) (someone/something) passes through [vt:とおす], 6.a.1
とか (p) and/or [A とか B A and B and the like], 2.b.conv
とかい (都会) (n) urban area, 10.gr.4
とき (時) (n) time; occasion; when..., 3.f.5, 4.a.conv
とくい (得意) (な-adj) is good at (and likes it), 1.d.conv
とくに (特に) (adv) especially, 1.a.conv
どこ (qw) where, which place, 1.lc
どこか (n) somewhere, 6.a.3
どこでたべても (どこで食べても) (phr) no matter where I eat, 11.b.2
どこへおつれしても (どこへお連れしても) (phr) no matter where I take him/her, 11.b.2
どこも (phr) [+ affirmative predicate] everywhere; [+ negative predicate] nowhere, 6.a.3
ところ (所) (n) place; point in time/space [V-past + ところ "when (someone) V-ed"], 1.lc, 2.c.conv, 3.d.conv, 6.gr.7, 6.gr.9, 7.a.conv
ところで (con) incidentally; by the way, 1.c.conv
として (phr) as, for, 10.b.conv
としょかん (図書館) (n) library, 1.gr.6
とじる (閉じる) (v: toji/ru) to close, 5.a.1
とちゅう (途中) (n) middle of activity/operation/journey, 7.gr.8
どちら (qw) which place, which one, 1.gr.1
どちらか (phr) either one, 6.a.3
どちらさま (どちら様) (n) who; which party ↑, 3.b.conv
どちらでも (phr) either way; whichever, 11.b.conv
とっきじこう (特記事項) (n) special remarks, 11.rw.1
とつぜん (突然) (n) sudden, 7.rw.1
とっておきましょう (取っておきましょう) (phr) [て-form of とる + おきましょう] Let's set aside (for future use)., 10.b.1
とても (adv) very, 1.b.conv
とどうふけん (都道府県) (n) Tokyo-Hokkaido-Osaka/Kyoto-Prefecture, 1.e.2
とどく (届く) (v: todok/u) (something) reaches (destination), 11.a.conv
どなた (qw) who [POL of だれ], 6.a.3
どなたか (phr) someone ↑, 7.b.2
どなたも (phr) not anyone; no one [followed by a negative predicate] [↑], 6.a.3
となり (隣) (n) the next (side), neighbor, 7.b.3
との (phr) with [N1 との N2 "N2 with N1"], 7.e.2
どの (prenom) which, 1.a.conv
とのこと (phr) said that..., 3.rw2 , 4.a.1
どのぐらい (qw) how long; how much, 2.c.1
とまらないで (止まらないで) (v: tomar/u) [NEG REQ form of とまる] Don't stop., 6.gr.1
とまる (止まる) (vi: tomar/u) (something) stops; (someone) stays over [vt: とめる], 3.b.2, 6.a.1, 10.a.3

とめないで (止めないで) (v: tome/ru) [NEG REQ of とめる] Don't stop/park (something)., 1.gr.3
とめられる (止められる) (v: tome/ru) [POT of とめる] can stop (something), 1.b.5
とめる (止める) (vt: tome/ru) to stop, quit (something) [vi: とまる], 1.gr.3, 3.b.2, 5.gr.4, 6.a.1
～ども (suf) [↓ plural title], 2.a.1
ともだち (友達) (n) friend, 4.e.1
ともに (共に) (adv) both, together, 8.b.conv
どようび (土曜日) (n) Saturday, 2.gr.7
とらせる (取らせる) (v: tor/u) [CAUS of とる] to make/let (someone) take , 9.a.1
とらないで (取らないで) (phr) Don't take (it).; without taking [NEG of とる + で "without taking"; とらないで下さい "Please don't take it."], 6.gr.4
トラベラーズチェック (n) traveler's checks, 5.lc
とられる (取られる) (v: tor/u) [PASS of とる] to be taken; [↑ of とる] to take, 8.b.1
とり (取り) (v: tor/u) [V-stem of とる] take, 6.a.5
とりけす (取り消す) (v: torikes/u) to cancel, 11.rw.1
とりしまりやく (取締役) (n) director [of a company], 4.e.3
とりたい (取りたい) (v: tor/u) [たい-form of とる] want to take, 4.e.conv
とりひき (取り引き) (n) business dealing, transaction, trading, 4.c.conv
とりひきじょうけん (取り引き条件) (n) conditions for a business deal, 4.lc
ドリンク (n) drink, 7.gr.2
とる (取る) (v: tor/u) to take; to get; to occupy; [おとりになる ↑ "take"; とっておく "set (it) aside"], 1.e.1, 5.a.conv, , 6.gr.4, 7.b.3, 10.b.1
ドルだて (ドル建て) (n) dollar-based, 11.b.conv
どれか (phr) one of them; whichever one (of many), 6.a.3
とれる (取れる) (v: tor/u) [POT of とる] can take, 10.a.3
とわない (問わない) (v: tow/u) [NEG of とう] will not question, 11.c.3
とんでもない (phr) Heavens no!, 6.c.conv
どんな (qw) what kind of, 1.gr.1
どんなに (phr) no matter how (much), 11.b.2
どんなひとでも (どんな人でも) (phr) no matter what kind of person he/she is, 11.b.2

な

な (p) X な Y: X's Y; Y of X, 1.c.conv
な (sp) [particle for expressing blunt confirmation], 2.a.conv
ない (い-adj) [NEG of ある] there isn't/aren't [inanimate things]; don't have; negative suffix of verbs and adjectives, 2.c.1
なお (con) in addition, 9.rw.1
なおす (直す) (vt: naos/u) to fix, cure, repair, correct [vi: なおる], 6.a.1
なおる (直る) (vi: naor/u) (something) is repaired/healed; (someone) recovers [vt: なおす], 6.a.1
なか (中) (n) inside, middle, 9.a.3
ながい (長い) (い-adj) long, 1.com.1, 7.gr.3
なかじま (中島) (n) Nakajima [family name], 1.gr.6
なかったら (い-adj) [COND of ない] if there isn't/aren't [inanimate things]; if one doesn't have; negative COND suffix of verbs and adjectives, 2.gr.1

なかなか (adv)　considerably; pretty, 7.e.1, 7.gr.4
なかなかのもの (phr)　pretty good thing, 6.c.conv
なかやま (中山) (n)　Nakayama [family name], 1.a.conv
なくて (v: ar/u) [て-form of ない] there isn't/aren't; don't have, 5.b.1
なくても (v: ar/u) [て-form of ない + も] even if there isn't/aren't; even if one doesn't have, 5.b.1
なくなる (phr)　to run out; to disappear [く form of ない + なる], 4.a.4
なければ (い-adj) [PROV of ない] if there isn't; [V なければ "if it is not V-ed"; N じゃなければ "if it is not N"], 7.c.2
なごや (名古屋) (n)　Nagoya [a city in Japan], 6.gr.1
なさいます (v: nasar/u) [↑ POL of する] to do, 1.b.2
なさそう (phr) [Stem of ない + さそう] looks there is nothing, 8.a.1, 9.c.2
なさる (v: nasar/u) [↑ of する] to do, 1.b.2
なし (n)　none, 1.rw
なつ (夏) (n)　summer, 2.gr.6
なつお (夏男) (n)　Natsuo [male given name], 1.rw
なったら (v: nar/u) [COND of なる] if one/something has become, 2.gr.1
なっております (phr) [て-form of なる + おります] has become; it is done ↓, 9.a.conv
なつふく (夏服) (n)　summer uniform, 3.b.1
など (suf)　and so on; etc., 2.b.1
なに (何) (qw)　what, 2.c.1
なにか (何か) (n)　something, 6.a.conv
なにとぞ (何とぞ) (adv)　[FORMAL] please, 7.rw.1, 10.rw.1
なにも (何も) (phr)　not anything; nothing [followed by a negative predicate], 6.a.3
なにをしても (何をしても) (phr)　no matter what I do; whatever I do, 11.b.2
なので (con)　because, since, so [follows a noun/な-adj], 1.b.6
なら (cop) [PROV of だ] if/provided it is that... [S1 なら S2 "if it's that S1, S2"; N なら "if it's N"], 7.c.2, 7.e.conv
なられました (v: nar/u) [↑ of なりました] became; [ADV-PASS of なった] became, 11.c.2
なりそう (v: nar/u) [V-stem of なる + そう] appears to become, 7.d.conv
なりたい (v: nar/u) [たい-form of なる] want to become, 8.c.3
なる (v: nar/u)　to become, come to be [おせわになっています "Thank you for your/his/her/their help."], 1.gr.3, 6.c.1, 8.c.3
なるべく (adv)　as much as possible, 3.lc
なるほど (phr)　I see; That makes sense., 1.c.conv
なれば (v: nar/u) [PROV of なる] if/provided one/it becomes, 7.gr.1
なれる (v: nar/u) [POT of なる] can become, 1.b.5
なれる (慣れる) (v: nare/ru)　become used to; become accustomed to, 2.a.conv
なん (何) (qw)　what, 1.b.conv
なんか (suf)　and so on [informal form of など], 2.b.conv
なんじ (何時) (qw)　what time, 1.gr.2
〜なんだ (phr) [PLAIN of 〜なんです] it's that it's N [blunt; indicating explanation or inference], 4.gr.3, 7.b.3
なんだい (何台) (qw)　how many units of cars, machines, etc., 9.b.2
なんでしたら (何でしたら) (phr) [なん + POL of だったら] if it's what you may call it, 10.b.conv
なんでも (何でも) (phr)　anything; whatever it is, 11.b.2
なんとか (adv)　somehow [なんとかなる (idiom) "manage somehow"], 3.gr.2
なんにち (何日) (qw)　how many days, 4.gr.8
なんにも (何にも) (phr) nothing; whatever [followed by NEG], 6.lc
なんばん (何番) (qw)　what number, 5.gr.11
なんまい (何枚) (qw)　how many [sheets]?, 6.gr.2

に

に (p)　by [in a passive sentence], 8.b.1
に (p)　to, toward [destination marker; marks the place one arrives at or one chooses to have], 1.a.1
に、さんかしょ (二、三か所) (num)　two or three places, 2.c.conv
に、さんびゃくだい (二、三百台) (num)　200 to 300 units of machines/cars, 11.b.1
において (phr)　in, at, 7.rw.1
にかい (二回) (num)　twice, 9.b.3
にかい (二階) (num)　second floor, 5.gr.3
にがて (苦手) (な-adj)　is poor at (and dislikes it), 1.d.add
にきゅう (二級) (n)　second class, 1.rw
にし (西) (n)　Nishi [family name], 1.gr.7
にじかい (二次会) (n)　second party, 6.a.conv
にしもと (西本) (n)　Nishimoto [family name], 3.gr.5
にしやま (西山) (n)　Nishiyama [family name], 3.c.conv
にじゅうし、ごにん (二十四、五人) (num)　24 to 25 people, 11.b.1
にち (日) (ct)　[counter for days], 2.c.conv
にちじ (日時) (n)　date and time, 6.rw, 9.rw.1
にちべい (日米) (n)　Japan-U.S., 1.a.2
にちようび (日曜日) (n)　Sunday, 7.e.1
について (phr)　about; on, 1.a.conv
についての (phr)　about [N1 についての N2 "N2 about N1"], 7.e.2
につきまして (n)　about, regarding [POL of について], 7.a.3, 10.rw.1
にともない (に伴い) (phr)　along with; accompanying, 7.rw.1
にほん (二本) (num)　two long objects, 2.c.4
にほん (日本) (n)　Japan, 1.b.6
にほんエレクトロニクス (日本エレクトロニクス) (n)　Japan Electronics [company name], 11.a.conv
にほんけいざいしんぶん (日本経済新聞) (n)　Nikkei Journal (Japan Economy Newspaper), 8.b.1, 9.a.3
にほんご (日本語) (n)　Japanese language, 1.b.5
にほんしゃ (日本車) (n)　Japanese car, 1.gr.5
にほんしょく (日本食) (n)　Japanese food, 11.b.2
にほんじんてき (日本人的) (な-adj)　Japanese-like [日本人的に "in a Japanese way"], 5.d.1
にほんりょうり (日本料理) (n)　Japanese cooking, Japanese foods, 1.com.4
ニューエージ (n)　New Age, 10.gr.4
にゅうがく (入学) (n)　entrance/enrollment to school, 11.gr.2
にゅうきんでんぴょう (入金伝票) (n)　deposit slip, 5.rw.1
にゅうしゃ (入社) する (n/v) to enter a company (to be hired), 2.lc
ニュース (n)　news, 9.c.4
ニューヨーク (n)　New York, 1.a.1
によって (phr)　by; depending on, 8.b.1, 10.a.conv

による (phr) by [N1 による N2] N2 due to/thanks to N1, 8.c.conv
によると (phr) according to, 9.b.3
にわり (二割) (num) 20% [1割 = 10%], 10.b.conv
にんき (人気) (n) popularity, 1.gr.6, 9.b.conv

ね

ね (p) [confirmation/agreement-seeking particle], 1.c.conv
ねがいたく (願いたく) (v: negaw/u) [く-form of ねがいたい] want to request, 10.rw.1
ねさげ (値下げ) する (n/v) to reduce prices; discount, 6.a.6, 7.gr.4
ねだん (値段) (n) price, 7.gr.6, 8.c.conv
ねびき (値引き) する (n/v) to reduce prices; discount [= かかくのひきさげ], 4.d.conv, 4.gr.10, 10.a.conv
ねびき (値引き) させていただいております (phr) [て-form of CAUS of 値引きする + いただいて + おります] We are taking the liberty of reducing the price. ↓, 10.a.conv
ねびき (値引き) できる (n/v) to be able to discount; to be able to reduce the price, 10.a.2
ねまわし (根回し) (n) ground work to secure support/agreement [lit. "root-binding before transplanting a tree"], 4.d.conv, 9.gr.4, 11.a.conv
ねまわし (根回し) する (n/v) do the ground work or root binding work before a large tree is transplanted, 4.rw.1
ねむる (眠る) (v: nemur/u) to sleep, 2.c.4
ねられる (寝られる) (v: ne/ru) [POT of 寝る] can sleep, 7.b.3
ねる (寝る) (v: ne/ru) to sleep; to go to bed, 4.gr.7
〜ねん (年) (ct) year, 1.b.conv
ねんのため (念のため) (phr) to make sure, 11.rw.1
ねんまつ (年末) (n) year-end, 10.rw.1, 11.c.3
ねんれい (年齢) (n) age, 11.c.3

の

の (nom) (it's) that... [PLAIN ending of んです indicating explanation or inference], 2.b.conv
の (nom) one; -ing [marker to make a noun from a verb; テレビをみるのがすきです "I like watching TV."] V-ing, to V, 1.d.conv
の (p) X の Y: X's Y; Y of X, 1.a.conv
の (p) [subject marker in a clause modifier "ピザのおいしいレストラン "a restaurant where pizza tastes good"], 1.b.1
のうき (納期) (n) delivery date, 11.rw.1
のうちで (のうちで) (phr) among; within, 9.a.3
のうにゅう (納入) (n) shipping; delivery; payment of money, 11.rw.1
ノートパソコンぶもん (ノートパソコン部門) (n) notebook/laptop computer division, 7.rw.1
のこりもの (残り物) (n) leftover, 8.gr.8
のだしょうじ (野田商事) (n) Noda Trading Company, 5.com.3
のちほど (後ほど) (n) later, 3.f.conv
ので (con) because, since, so [more formal than から], 1.b.conv
のなかで (の中で) (phr) among; within, 9.a.3
のに (con) despite that, 6.a.conv, 7.b.1
のばしつつある (伸ばし〜) (phr) is expanding/extending [V つつある "is V-ing"; = のばしている], 7.rw.1
のびる (伸びる) (v: nobi/ru) (something) is extended, expanded, 8.gr.3

のべる (述べる) (v: nobe/ru) to state, mention, 8.gr.7
〜のほうから (〜の方から) (phr) from the direction of, 3.e.conv
のませる (飲ませる) (v: nom/u) [CAUS of のむ] to make/let (someone) drink, 9.a.1
のまれる (飲まれる) (v: nom/u) [PASS of のむ] to be drunken, 8.b.1
のみ (飲み) (v: nom/u) [V-stem of のむ] drink, 6.a.conv
のみたい (飲みたい) (v: nom/u) [たい-form of のむ] want to drink, 7.d.2
のみにいく (飲みに行く) (phr) to out for a drink, 9.c.2
のみほうだい (飲み放題) (n) unlimited drinking, 6.rw
のみましょう (飲みましょう) (v: nom/u) [POL VOL of のむ] let's drink; we shall drink., 2.gr.1
のむ (飲む) (v: nom/u) to drink, 1.b.1, 1.c.3
のむばかり (飲むばかり) (phr) All one does is drink., 9.c.2
のめば (飲めば) (v: nom/u) [PROV of のむ] if/provided one drinks, 7.c.2
のめる (飲める) (v: nom/u) [POT of のむ] can drink, 1.c.3
のもう (飲もう) (v: nom/u) [VOL of のむ] let's drink, 4.a.2
のような (phr) like [N1 のような N2 "N2 like N1"], 7.e.1
のように (phr) like [N のように "like N"], 7.e.1
のりき (乗り気) (n) willingness [X にのりきだ "is willing toward X"], 10.c.conv
のる (乗る) (v: nor/u) to ride; to take (transportation), 4.gr.7
のることができる (乗ることが〜) (phr) is able to ride, 9.b.2
のれる (乗れる) (v: nor/u) [POT of のる] can ride; can get on [a vehicle], 9.b.2
のんだばかり (飲んだばかり) (phr) have just drunk, 9.c.3
のんだら (飲んだら) (v: nom/u) [COND of のむ] if one drinks, 7.c.2
のんでばかり (飲んでばかり) (phr) drink only; [のんでばかりいる／のんでばかりだ "All one does is drink."], 9.c.2

は

は (p) [topic/contrast marker] [Xは "as for X", "X at least", "X in contrast", "speaking of X", "How about X?"], 1.a.conv
はあ (interj) yes, 7.e.conv
ばあい (場合) (n) case, time, occasion, 9.c.conv
パーティー (n) party, 7.b.3
ハードウェア (n) hardware, 1.rw
パートタイマー (n) part-time worker, 11.c.3
ハードディスク (n) hard disk, 5.gr.6
はい (interj) Yes [agreement]; A verbal sign that says "I'm listening," "Here it is", "Present!", etc., 1.a.conv
パイ (n) pie, 2.b.1
はいけい (拝啓) (n) Greeting! [an opening remark in a letter], 7.rw.1
はいけん (拝見) する (n/v) [↓ of みる] to look at, watch, 7.1c
はいしゃさん (歯医者さん) (n) dentist, 6.a.1
はいっても (入っても) (phr) [て-form of はいる + も] even if you enter, 8.a.1
ハイテク (n) high technology, 1.c.add
はいりたい (入りたい) (v: hair/u) [たい-form of はいる] want to enter, 1.1c
はいりょ (配慮) する (n/v) to be considerate; consideration, 7.rw2

はいる（入る）(vi: hair/u) to enter [おふろにはいる "take a bath"] [vt: いれる], 5.gr.5, 6.a.conv, 6.a.1
ばかり (n)　just, only [V たばかり "has just V-ed"], 9.c.conv
はかる（図る）(v: hakar/u)　to plan, scheme [じゅうじつをはかる "plan to complete"], 9.c.conv
はげしい（激しい）(い-adj)　severe; violent; heated, 7.rw.1
はこび（運び）(n)　plan; course of action [はこびとなりました "it turned out that (we will take) a course of action (that...)"], 9.rw.1
はじまる（始まる）(v:i hajimar/u) (something) begins [vt: はじめる], 3.f.3
はじめ（始め）(n)　beginning, 2.b.1
はじめて（初めて）(n)　first time, 2.lc
はじめておいてください（始めておいて下さい）(phr) [て-form of はじめる + て-form of おく + ください] please start (it) in advance; please go ahead and start, 9.c.1
はじめに（始めに）(adv)　at beginning, 10.rw2
はじめまして（初めまして）(phr)　How do you do?, 2.a.add
はじめる（始める）(vt: hajime/ru) to begin (something) [vi: はじまる], 4.d.1, 9.lc
ばしょ（場所）(n)　place, 4.lc, 5.b.1, 6.rw
はしらせる（走らせる）(v: hashir/u) [CAUS of はしる] make (it) run, operate, 9.b.conv
はずす (v: hazus/u)　to remove [せきをはずす "is not at one's seat; has stepped out"], 3.d.conv
パスする (n/v)　to pass, 9.b.2
バストイレ (n)　bath and toilet, 10.a.1
バストイレつき（バストイレ付き）(n)　attached with bath and toilet, 10.a.1
パスポート (n)　passport, 4.gr.10
パソコン (n)　personal computer, 8.c.3
はたらいていれば（働いて〜）(phr)　if/provided (someone) is working, 10.gr.3
はたらきたい（働きたい）(v: hatarak/u) [たい-form of はたらく] want to work, 1.gr.6
はたらく（働く）(v: hatarak/u)　to work; function [Xではたらいています "work at X"], 1.c.1
パチンコ (n)　pachinko pinball machine, 2.b.1
はつおん（発音）する (n/v)　to pronounce; pronunciation, 5.d.1
はつか（二十日）(num)　20th day of the month; 20 days, 4.gr.8
はっきり (adv)　clearly, 9.c.3
バックアップする (n/v) to back up; support, 11.c.1
はつげん（発言）する (n/v)　speak; remark, 5.gr.4
バッジ (n)　badge, 3.f.4
はっしんおん（発信音）(n)　dial tone, 3.e.add
はっそう（発送）(n)　shipping, 11.c.3
はってん（発展）(n)　expansion, growth, 7.rw2
はつばいする（発売する）(phr)　to start selling, 9.rw.1
はなさせる（話させる）(v: hanas/u) [CAUS of はなす] to make/let (someone) speak, 9.a.1
はなされる（話される）(v: hanas/u) [PASS of はなす] to be spoken; [↑ of はなす] to speak, 8.b.1
はなし（話）(n)　story, talk, 4.gr.3, 7.e.2
はなしあう（話し合う）(v: hanashiaw/u)　to discuss, 10.rw2
はなしかた（話し方）(n)　the way of speaking; how to speak, 5.f.1

はなしたくなさそう（話したく〜）(phr) [Stem of はなしたくない + さ + そう] looks (someone) does not want to speak, 8.a.1
はなしたそう（話したそう）(phr) [Stem of はなしたい + そう] looks (someone) wants to speak, 8.a.1
はなしちゅう（話し中）(n)　(phone is) busy, 3.d.conv
はなしにくい（話しにくい）(い-adj)　difficult to talk with, 9.a.3
はなしやすい（話しやすい）(い-adj)　easy to talk with, 9.a.3
はなす（話す）(v: hanas/u)　to speak; to talk, 1.a.2, 1.b.5
はなすことができる（話すこと〜）(phr)　is able to speak, 9.b.2
はなすほう（話す方）(phr)　speaking (side), 8.c.3
はなせば（話せば）(v: hanas/u) [PROV of はなす] if/provided one speaks, 7.c.2
はなせる（話せる）(v: hanas/u) [POT of はなす] can speak, 1.b.5, 1.b.6
はなそう（話そう）(v: hanas/u) [VOL of はなす] let's speak/talk, 1.d.conv
はなそうかい（話そう会）(n)　Let's-Speak Society, 1.d.conv
はは（母）(n)　mother ↓, 1.gr.6
はぶく（省く）(v: habuk/u)　to omit, save, curtail, reduce, economize, 10.b.conv
バブルけいざい（バブル経済）(n)　bubble economy, 5.gr.8
はま（浜）(n)　Hama [restaurant name]; beach, 2.gr.5
はやい（速い）(い-adj)　quick, fast, 1.c.3, 2.a.2, 9.a.conv
はやく（早く）(い-adj) [く-form of はやい] early, 3.lc
はやめ（早目）(n)　early, 4.gr.6, 7.d.2
はやめに（早めに）(adv)　somewhat early, somewhat soon, 7.d.2
はらいもどし（払い戻し）(n)　refund, 10.c.4
ハリス (n)　Harris [family name], 1.a.conv
はる（春）(n)　spring, 7.e.1
パルコ (n)　Parco [department store name], 3.f.5
はるこ（春子）(n)　Haruko [female given name], 1.rw
はれそう（晴れそう）(phr)　appears to be fair [of weather], 7.gr.3
はれる（晴れる）(v: hare/ru)　to become , 1.b.3
バレンタイン (n)　Valentine, 1.gr.5
ばん（晩）(n)　night; evening, 6.a.conv
はんこ (n)　signature seal, 5.b.1
ばんごう（番号）(n)　number, 11.c.3
ばんごうふだ（番号札）(n)　number tag, number card, 5.a.conv
はんたい（反対）(n)　opposite; opposed [反対のかた "those opposed"], 10.c.1
はんたいいけん（反対意見）(n)　opposing opinion, 10.gr.1
はんちょう（班長）(n)　foreman, 4.e.3
はんどうたい（半導体）(n)　semiconductor, 9.a.3
ハンドル (n)　steering wheel, 1.b.1
はんばい（販売）(n)　sales, 2.d.add, 4.d.conv
はんばいかいぎ（販売会議）(n)　sales meeting, 4.rw2
はんばいかかく（販売価格）(n)　sales price, 4.rw2
はんばいけいやく（販売契約）(n)　sales contract, 4.rw.1
はんばいこうしょう（販売交渉）(n)　sales negotiation, 4.rw.1
はんばい（販売）する (n/v)　to sell; sale, 4.d.1
はんばいていけい（販売提携）(n)　sales contract, 10.gr.1
はんばいぶ（販売部）(n)　sales division, 3.com.1, 11.c.3
パンフレット (n)　brochure, 3.f.5

ひ（日）(n)　day; sun, 2.c.conv
Bしゃ（B社）(n)　Company B, 8.c.3

ピーというおと (ピーという音) (n) beep, 3.e.add
ビーフ (n) beef, 5.gr.7
ビール (n) beer, 1.d.1
ひかえ (控え) (v: hikae/ru) [V-stem of ひかえる] to be located for immediate use; to be ready [もくぜんにひかえる "to face"], 10.rw.1
ひかんてき (悲観的) (な-adj) pessimistic [X に(たいして)悲観的 "is pessimistic about X"], 10.c.conv
ひきさげ (引下げ) (n) reduction, 4.rw.1, 10.rw.1
ひく (引く) (v: hik/u) to pull [かぜをひく "catch cold"]; to subtract; minus (-), 6.a.4, 6.gr.9
ひこうき (飛行機) (n) airplane, 1.gr.5
ひこうちゅう (飛行中) (n) the middle of flight; during flight, 2.gr.7
ピザ (n) pizza, 1.a.1
ビジネス (n) business, 2.com.1, 4.c.2
ひしょ (秘書) (n) secretary, 7.a.conv
ひだり (左) (n) left (side), 1.b.1
ひづけ (日付) (n) date, 4.rw2
ひっちゃく (必着) (n) must arrive, 11.rw.1
ヒットしょうひん (ヒット商品) (n) hit commercial product, 10.c.conv
ヒットする (n/v) to become a hit, 9.c.4
ひつよう (必要) (な-adj) necessary [必要なばあい "in case of necessity"], 4.c.conv
ビデオ (n) video, 6.gr.8
ひと (人) (n) person, 1.b.1
ひどい (phr) terrible, 9.c.4
ひとがいい (人がいい) (phr) good-natured, too trusting, naive, 3.gr.2
ひとこと (一言) (n) one word; in brief, 10.gr.4
ひとつ (一つ) (num) one [Japanese series up to 10], 2.a.2
ひとびと (人々) (n) people, 10.a.2
ひとまえ (人前) (n) in front of people; in public, 1.d.1
ひとり (一人) (num) one person, 6.com.2
ひま (暇) (な-adj) idle; not busy, 2.a.2
ひょう (表) (n) table; chart, 4.e.conv
びょういん (病院) (n) hospital, 2.a.2
ひょうか (評価) される (n/v) to be evaluated, 8.b.conv, 10.a.2
ひょうか (評価) する (n/v) to evaluate; evaluation, 7.rw.1, 8.b.conv
びょうき (病気) (n) illness, sickness [病気になる "to fall ill, become ill"], 1.b.1
ひょうじ (表示) (n) display, 9.b.conv
ひらがな (n) hiragana, 5.b.conv
ひらかれる (開かれる) (v: hirak/u) [PASS of ひらく] to be opened; [↑ of ひらく] to open, 8.c.5
ひらく (開く) (v: hirak/u) [vt/vi] to open, 5.a.conv
ひらしゃいん (平社員) (n) plain employee, 4.e.3
ビル (n) building, 1.gr.6
ひるごはん (昼ご飯) (n) lunch, 1.gr.8
ひるま (昼間) (n) daytime, 6.c.conv
ひろい (広い) (い-adj) wide, spacious, 1.c.3
ひんしつ (品質) (n) product quality, 7.gr.1, 8.b.conv
ひんめい (品名) (n) product name, 11.rw.1

ふ

ぶ (部) (n) division [of an organization], 2.d.add
ファーストクラス (n) first class, 2.c.3
ファイル (n) file, 6.gr.1
ファックス (n) fax machine; [ファックスをおくる "to send a fax"], 3.e.add
フィルム (n) film, 4.gr.6, 9.gr.5
ブース (n) booth, 3.com.3
ふうとう (封筒) (n) envelop, 1.lc
ふうに (phr) like; likely; appearance [N ふうに V "V in a N-like way"; 日本ふうにする "make it look like Japanese"], 10.c.2
ふうの (phr) like; likely; appearance [N1 ふうの N2 "N2-like N1"; 日本ふうのいえ "Japanese-like house"], 10.c.2
VTR (n) VCR, 9.gr.5
ふえる (増える) (vi: hue/ru) (something) increases [vt: ふやす], 4.d.1
フォード (n) Ford [family name], 3.com.1
ふか (不可) (n) impossible, 5.rw.1
ぶか (部下) (n) one's subordinate, 2.a.add
ふかめる (深める) (v: hukame/ru) to deepen, 1.d.conv
ふき (付記) する (n/v) to append a note to; a note, memo, 11.rw.1
ふく (副) (prefix) assistant; vice, 4.e.3
ふくしゃちょう (副社長) (n) vice president [of a company], 1.gr.8, 4.e.3
ふじゅうぶん (不十分) (な-adj) insufficient, 9.c.conv
ふせつこうじ (敷設工事) (n) installation construction, 3.rw2
ふぞくひん (付属品) (n) peripheral items/devices, 10.lc
ぶちょう (部長) (n) division manager, 1.d.1, 3.a.conv
ふつう (普通) (n) ordinary, normal, regular, 4.a.5, 5.b.conv
ふつうよきん (普通預金) (n) regular savings account, 5.b.conv
ぶっか (物価) (n) prices, 7.b.1
ふつかよい (二日酔い) (n) hangover, 6.b.4
ふったら (降ったら) (v: hur/u) [COND of ふる] if it rains, 7.c.2
ぶひんだい (部品代) (n) the cost of parts, 9.lc
ふべん (不便) (な-adj) inconvenient; useless, 1.gr.8
ふゆふく (冬服) (n) winter uniform, 3.b.1
ブラウン (n) Brown [family name], 1.b.6
ふらふらする (iv) to feel dizzy, 6.b.4
フランスご (フランス語) (n) French language, 1.gr.4
ふり (降り) (v: hur/u) [stem of ふる] fall (of rain/snow), 1.b.3
ふりこみ (振込) (n) deposit; fund transfer, 5.f.conv
プリンタ (n) printer, 1.gr.6
プリント (n) printout, 4.c.2
プリントする (n/v) to print, 4.c.2
プリントできる (n/v) [POT of プリントする] can print, 5.gr.5
ふる (降る) (v: hur/u) to fall (from the sky); to rain; to snow, 1.b.2
ふるい (古い) (い-adj) old [of things; not of people], 6.gr.7
ぶれいこう (無礼講) (n) no-law occasion where disrespectful words under the influence of alcohol will be overlooked and forgotten, 6.b
プレゼンテーション (n) presentation, 3.gr.2
プレゼント (n) present, gift, 1.gr.5
フレックスタイム (n) flex-time; flexible work hour arrangement, 7.com.
ふれば (降れば) (v: hur/u) [PROV of ふる] if/provided it rains, 7.c.2
プログラム (n) program, 7.b.3
プロジェクト (n) project, 4.c.conv

フロリダ (n)　Florida, 1.lc
〜ふん (分) (ct)　minutes [on the clock], 2.c.3
ぶんしょ (文書) (n)　document, 8.lc, 10.c.conv
ぶんや (分野) (n)　field; realm, 1.a.conv

へ

ヘアスタイル (n)　hair style, 10.gr.4
へいしゃ (弊社) (n)　our company ↓, 9.rw.1
へいせい (平成) (n)　the Heisei era (1989-), 1.rw
へいそ (平素) (n)　usual; routine, 7.rw.1
ベーカーせんむ (ベーカー専務) (n)　Senior Managing Director Baker, 3.f.4
ペーストする (n/v) to paste, 2.gr.7
ペーパー (n)　paper, 10.gr.2
へた (下手) (な-adj)　unskilled; is poor at, 1.d.add
べつ (別) (n)　separate; excluded; apart from, 10.a.conv
べつに (別に) (adv)　(not) particularly [べつに〜ない: not particularly...], 6.a.conv
へや (部屋) (n)　room, 4.gr.6, 10.a.3
へる (減る) (vi: her/u) (something) decreases [vt: へらす], 4.d.1
ペン (n)　pen, 2.gr.4
へん (辺) (suf)　vicinity [このへん "in this vicinity"], 5.gr.3
べんきょう (勉強) する (n/v)　to study; studying, 1.a.conv
べんきょうちゅう (勉強中) (n)　middle of studying, 1.d.conv
へんじ (返事) (n)　reply, 2.gr.2, 6.b.3
べんり (便利) (な-adj)　convenient; useful, 1.b.1

ほ

ほう (interj)　Oh, (I see.), 1.d.conv
ほう (方) (n)　way, direction, side [always preceded by a modifier; Xのほう "the side of X"; V たほうがいい "had better V"], 5.f.2
ぼうえき (貿易) (n)　trade, 1.a.2
ほうこう (方向) (n)　direction, 11.b.conv
ほうこく (報告) (n)　report, 4.(title)., 4.gr.9
ほうこくしょ (報告書) (n)　report document, 4.gr.3, 5.gr.5, 7.e.2
ほうこく (報告) する (n/v)　to report; a report, 4.gr.9, 7.e.2
ほうしん (方針) (n)　policy, principle, 8.c.conv
ぼうねんかい (忘年会) (n)　year-end party (Lit. "year-forgetting party"), 6.b.4
ほうほう (方法) (n)　method, 11.b.conv
ほうめん (方面) (n)　direction, way, sphere, field, issue, 1.b.conv, 7.e.conv
ボーナス (n)　bonus, 3.gr.2, 7.c.1
ボールペン (n)　ball-point pen, 5.gr.5
ほか (他) (n)　other; another, 10.gr.3
ほかに (他に) (phr)　besides, 11.c.3
ほかの (他の) (phr)　other, 9.gr.3
ぼく (pro)　I, me [male], 6.b.conv
ほくべい (北米) (n)　North America, 3.com.3
ポケベル (n)　pager [derived from "pocket bell"], 1.c.3
ほけん (保険) (n)　insurance, 10.gr.1
ほごしゃ (保護者) (n)　guardian, 1.e.2
ほさ (補佐) (n)　deputy, 4.e.3
ほしい (欲しい) (い-adj)　want [V てほしい "want (other) to V"], 3.rw2, 7.d.conv
ホスト (n)　host, 11.b.2
ほっかいどう (北海道) (n)　Hokkaido [place name], 1.gr.5
ホテル (n)　hotel, 1.b.1
ほど (p)　as much as, about, approximately [X ほど + NEG "not as much ... as X"], 8.b.conv
ほん (本) (n)　book, 1.a.1
〜ほん (本) (ct)　[counter for long cylindrical objects], 1.b.1
ほんじつ (本日) (n)　today, 1.e.conv, 11.c.conv
ほんしゃ (本社) (n)　main office, headquarter, 10.b.conv
ほんせいひん (本製品) (n)　this product, 9.rw.1
ほんせき (本籍) (n)　place of birth, 1.e.2
ほんとう (本当) (n)　truth [本当に "truly"; "really"; "indeed"], 4.gr.4
ほんにん (本人) (n)　self, applicant, 1.e.2
ほんぶちょう (本部長) (n)　(main) division manager, 11.c.3
ほんやく (翻訳) する (n/v)　to translate; translation, , 2.lc, 4.a.3, 5.g.1, 11.a.conv

ま

まあ (interj)　well, I guess, 2.a.conv
マーケットシェア (n)　market share, 9.a.3
マーケティング (n)　marketing, 7.lc
マージャン (n)　mahjong [Chinese game similar to a game of bridge], 2.b.1
マージン (n)　margin, 10.b.conv
マーティン (n)　Martin [family name], 2.lc
マイク・ジョーダン (n)　Mike Jordan [men's name], 2.com.
マイクロスター (n)　Microstar [product name], 8.b.conv
マイクロスター800 (n)　Microstar 800 (product name), 9.a.conv
マイクロプロセッサ (n)　microprocessor, 9.a.conv
マイコンソフト (n)　Myconsoft [company name], 2.gr.6
まいしゅう (毎週) (n)　every week, 3.f.1
まいとし (毎年) (n)　every year, 9.b.3
まいにち (毎日) (n)　everyday, 6.gr.4
まいにちしんぶん (毎日新聞) (n)　Mainichi Newspaper, 9.a.3
まいりましょう (参りましょう) (v: mair/u) [VOL of まいります] let's go!; I will come/go., 3.lc, 6.c.conv
まいります (参ります) (v: mair/u) [↓ of いく／くる] to come; to go [Used in polite form only], 4.a.1
まえ (前) (n)　front, previous, 3.gr.3
まえに (前に) (phr)　before; prior to [X のまえに "before X"], 10.rw2
まえもって (前もって) (phr)　beforehand, 8.gr.7
まける (負ける) (v: make/ru)　to lose, 11.b.2
まことに (誠に) (adv)　truly, 7.rw.1
まさつ (摩擦) (n)　friction [ぼうえき摩擦 "trade friction"], 7.com.
〜まして (phr) [POL て-form of V ます] V and..., 3.f.1
まじめ (真面目) (な-adj)　hard-working; serious-minded; straight, 6.lc
ますます (益々) (adv)　increasingly, more and more, 7.rw.1
また (n)　again, 3.c.conv
また (con)　in addition, also, 1.b.conv
まだ (adv)　still [with an affirmative predicate]; (not) yet [with a negative predicate], 3.e.conv
またせている (待たせている) (phr) [て-form of またせる + いる] keep (someone) waiting, 9.a.1
またせる (待たせる) (v: mat(s)/u) [CAUS of まつ] to make/let (someone) wait , 9.a.1

まだまだ (adv) [more emphatic than まだ] still [with an affirmative predicate]; (not) yet [with a negative predicate], 1.d.conv
またれる (待たれる) (v: mat(s)/u) [↑ of まつ] (someone) waits; [ADV-PASS of まつ] (someone) waits, 8.b.1
まち (町) (n) town, 1.b.1
まちがい (間違い) (n) error, 9.gr.5
まつ (待つ) (v: mat(s)/u) to wait, 1.b.5, 1.gr.2, 1.gr.4
まったく (adv) completely; utterly, 9.rw.1
まってほしい (待ってほしい) (phr) want (other person) to wait, 9.c.2
まってました (phr) We've been waiting for this!, 6.b.conv
まつばかり (待つばかり) (phr) All that is left to do is wait., 9.c.2
まで (p) until [time]; as far as [place]; until V, 1.gr.4, 2.a.conv
までに (p) by [time], 2.c.conv
まてば (待てば) (v: mat(s)/u) [PROV of まつ] if/provided one waits, 7.c.2
まてる (待てる) (v: mat(s)/u) [POT of まつ] can wait, 1.b.5
まど (窓) (n) window, 6.a.1
まとう (待とう) (v: mat(s)/u) [VOL of まつ] let's wait, 4.a.2
まどぐち (窓口) (n) (teller) window, 5.a.conv
まとめてかく (まとめて書く) (n) write in summary, 1.e.2
まにあう (間に合う) (v: maniaw/u) to be in time (for); on time, 2.c.conv
マニュアル (n) manual, 2.gr.4
マネジメント (n) management, 1.com.4
マルチメディア (n) multimedia, 3.a.conv
まわす (回す) (vt: mawas/u) to reroute, rotate, pass, spin [vi: まわる], 2.b.conv
まわり (周り) (n) surrounding; people/things around something, 2.a.conv
まわる (回る) (vi: mawar/u) to go around, run in circle [vt: まわす], 2.b.add
まん (満) (n) full (age), 1.e.2

み

み (見) (v: mi/ru) [V-stem of みる] look; watch; view, 6.a.5
ミーティング (n) meeting, 1.a.2
みえる (見える) (v: mie/ru) come; arrive ↑; (something) can be seen; is visible, 3.gr.1, 6.b.3
みかた (見方) (n) the way of seeing; how to see, 5.f.1
みぎ (右) (n) right (side), 2.gr.7
みこみ (見込み) (n) prospect, 1.rw
みさせる (見させる) (v: mi/ru) [CAUS of みる] to make/let (someone) see, 9.a.1
ミシェル (n) Michelle [given name], 7.1c
みじかい (短い) (い-adj) short (in length), 5.b.1
みじかくて (短くて) (い-adj) [て-form of みじかい] short (in length), 5.b.1
みじかくても (短かくても) (い-adj) [て-form of みじかい + も] even if it is short, 5.b.1
みせ (店) (n) shop, store, 1.b.1
みせる (見せる) (v: mise/ru) to show, 1.e.1, 3.f.4
みたそうです (見たそうです) (phr) [V-stem of みたい + そうです] looks (someone) wants to see it., 8.a.1
みたそうです (見たそうです) (phr) [みた + そうです] They say (someone) saw it., 8.a.1
みため (見た目) (n) appearance, 5.b.1
みたらい (御手洗) (n) Mitarai [family name], 2.e.1
みち (道) (n) road, street, direction (to somewhere), 6.b.4
みっか (三日) (num) the third day of the month; three days, 5.e.conv
みつける (見つける) (v: mitsuke/ru) to find, 4.gr.10
みつもり (見積もり) (n) estimate, 4.c.conv
みつもりしょ (見積り書) (n) estimate (document), 4.b.conv
みなみプロダクション (南プロダクション) (n) Minami Production [company name], 3.d.4
みましょう (見ましょう) (v: mi/ru) [VOL of みます] let's see, 4.a.2
みよう (見よう) (v: mi/ru) [VOL of みる] let's see, 4.a.2
ミラー (n) Miller [family name], 1.gr.5
みられる (見られる) (v: mi/ru) [POT of みる] can watch; can look; can see, 1.b.5
みられる (見られる) (v: mi/ru) [PASS of みる] to be seen, 8.b.1
みる (v: mi/ru) try V-ing; V and see [V てみる "try to V" or "V and see"], 6.gr.5
みる (見る) (v: mi/ru) to look, watch, see, 1.b.5, 5.f.conv, 6.a.3
みれる (見れる) (v: mi/ru) [POT of みる] can watch; can see; can look, 1.b.5, 8.b.1
みんな (n) everybody [INF of みなさん], 6.b.conv

む

むかえ (迎え) (v: mukae/ru) [V-stem of むかえる] welcome; see [someone at a place] [むかえにいく "go to see someone"], 3.gr.3, 6.a.5
むけて (向けて) (v: muke/ru) toward, 11.c.3
むこう (向こう) (n) over there, place beyond, the other side, 3.gr.4
むずかしい (難しい) (い-adj) difficult, hard, 1.gr.8, 7.c.1
むずかしくなさそう (難しく〜) (phr) [Stem of むずかしくない + さそう] looks it's not difficult, 8.a.1
むずかしければ (難しければ) (い-adj) [PROV of むずかしい] if/provided it is difficult, 7.c.2
むすめ (娘) (n) daughter ↓, 4.e.1
むり (無理) しない (n/v) not overexert; don't do the impossible, 11.b.2
むり (無理) しないで (phr) [NEG REQ form of 無理する] Don't overexert., 6.b.4
むり (無理) する (な-adj/v) to overexert; impossible[無理をいう "make an unreasonable request"], 3.f.5 6.b.4, 6.gr.3, 11.b.2
むり (無理) なようなので (phr) [無理な + ような + ので] because it seems it is impossible, 11.b.2
むりょう (無料) (n) no charge, free, 9.c.conv

め

め (目) (n) eye [お目にかかる "to see ↓"; 目をとおす "to browse through"], 4.b.conv; 目がわる (悪) くなる "become nearsighted", 6.gr.9
めい (名) (ct) [formal counter for people], 11.c.3
めいし (名刺) (n) business cards, 2.d.add
めいじ (明治) (n) the Meiji era (1868-1912), 5.rw.1
メール (n) email, 2.gr.2, 6.b.3
メールアドレス (n) email address, 1.gr.1
めがね (眼鏡) (n) glasses, 1.gr.8
メガバイト (ct) megabyte, 7.b.3

メキシコ (n)　Mexico, 8.gr.2
めしあがってください (召し上がって下さる) (phr)　Please eat. [↑ of たべてください], 11.b.2
めしあがる (召し上がる) (v: meshiagar/u)　to eat, drink ↑, 11.b.2
メッセージ (n)　message, 3.e.add
メモリー (n)　memory, 4.d.2
メモリーチップ (n)　memory chip, 1.b.2, 9.gr.5
メリット (n)　merit, 8.lc
めをとおす (目を通す) (phr)　glance through, 3.gr.2
めん (面) (n)　aspect; face, 7.e.conv
めんかい (面会) (n)　face-to-face meeting, 7.a.add
めんきょ (免許) (n)　license, 1.e.2
めんぜいひん (免税品) (n)　duty-free items, 7.c.1
めんせつ (面接) する (n/v)　to interview, 1.a.add

も

も (p)　also, too, as well, 1.b.conv
もう (adv)　already [with an affirmative predicate]; (not) any more/longer [with a negative predicate], 3.e.conv
もういちど (もう一度) (phr)　once again, 5.gr.5
もういっぱい (もう一杯) (phr)　one more cup, 6.b.4
もうしあげたくぞんじます (申し上げたく存じます) (phr)　I would like to say, 7.rw.1
もうしあげられない (申し上げられない) (v: moushiage/ru) [↓ POT of いう] can't say, 9.c.3
もうしあげられる (申し上げられる) (v) [POT of もうしあげる] can say ↓, 9.c.3
もうしあげる (申し上げる) (v: moushiage/ru) [↓ of いう] say (it) humbly, 11.c.conv
もうしこみしょ (申込書) (n)　application form, 5.rw.1
もうしつたえます (申し伝えます) (v: moushitsutae/ru) [↓ of いいつたえる] to communicate, 3.f.conv
もうしつたえる (申し伝える) (v: moushitsutae/ru) [↓ of つたえる] to tell; to inform, 3.e.conv
もうしばらく (phr)　a while longer, 9.a.1
もうします (申します) (v: mous/u) [POL ↓ of いう] to say; [～ともうします] is called, 1.a.conv
もうしわけ (申し訳) (n)　excuse, 3.c.conv
もうしわけありません (申し訳ありません) (phr)　I'm sorry; Excuse me., 7.a.1
もうしわけありませんでした (申し訳ありませんでした) (phr)　I'm sorry (to have V-ed), 7.a.1
もうしわけございません (申し訳ございません) (phr)　I'm sorry., 3.c.conv
もうすぐ (adv)　soon, 4.a.4
もうすこし (もう少し) (adv)　a little more, 4.gr.5, 6.c.1
もくぜん (目前) (n)　in front of one's eyes; right before, 10.rw.1
もくようび (木曜日) (n)　Thursday, 1.gr.4
もし (phr)　if; suppose, 3.f.conv
もしもし (interj)　Hello [on the telephone], 3.a.conv
もたせる (持たせる) (v: mot(s)/u) [CAUS of もつ] to make/let (someone) hold, 9.a.1
もたれる (持たれる) (v: mot(s)/u) [PASS of もつ] to be held; [↑ of もつ] to hold, 8.b.1
もちろん (adv)　of course, 9.b.conv
もつ (持つ) (v: mot(s)/u)　to hold; to have [もっていく "bring"],, 2.a.2

もっと (adv)　more [もっといい "better"], 4.d.conv
モットー (n)　motto, slogan, 9.c.conv
モデム (n)　modem, 4.c.2, 9.lc
もてる (持てる) (v: mot(s)/u) [POT of もつ] can hold, 8.b.1
もと (n)　origin, 7.e.conv
もどる (戻る) (vi: modor/u) to go back [vt: もどす], 1.b.6, 3.e.conv
モニター (n)　monitor, 10.gr.1
モニターつき (n)　with a monitor, 10.a.conv
モネ (n)　Monet, 10.gr.4
もの (n)　matter [non-past adjective/non-past V + ものだ "it's a matter of natural consequence..."], 11.b.conv
もの (者) (n)　person ↓, 3.c.1, 7.d.conv
もの (物) (n)　thing, object, matter, 3.c.1
もらいたい (v: moraw/u) [たい-form of もらう] want to receive, 4.d.conv, 7.d.2
もらいたがって (v: moraw/u) [て-form of もらいたがる] (other person) wants to receive, 6.a.6
もらう (v: moraw/u)　to receive [V てもらう "receive a favor of V-ing"], 4.a.conv
もらえない (v: moraw/u) [NEG POT of もらう] cannot receive, 6.c.conv
もらえません (v: moraw/u) [NEG POT of もらいます] can't receive, 5.f.2
もらえる (v: moraw/u) [POT of もらう] can receive, 5.f.2
もらわれる (v: moraw/u) [PASS of もらう] to be received (by); [↑ of もらう] to receive, 8.c.5
もり (森) (n)　Mori [family name], 3.a.conv
もりもと (森本) (n)　Morimoto [family name], 6.gr.1
もんだい (問題) (n)　problem, 10.c.conv

や

や (p)　and [や combines nouns. A や B "A and B, and things like that"], 2.b.1
やくそく (約束) (n)　promise, appointment, 7.a.add
やさしくなさそう (phr) [Stem of やさしくない + そう] looks it's not easy/gentle, 8.a.1
やさしそう (phr) [Stem of やさしい + そう] looks easy/gentle, 8.a.1
やさしそうじゃない (phr) [NEG of やさしそうだ] does not look easy/gentle, 8.a.1
やしろ (八代) (n)　Yashiro [place name], 3.gr.3
やすい (安い) (い-adj)　cheap, 1.c.3
やすくなりそう (安く～) (phr) [く-form of やすい + なりそう] it looks it may become cheap, 11.a.conv
やすみ (休み) (n)　vacation; day off, 2.b.1
やすみたい (休みたい) (v: yasum/u) [たい-form of やすむ] want to rest, 6.a.3
やすむ (休む) (v: yasum/u)　to rest; to take a day off, 1.c.3
やすめば (休めば) (v: yasum/u) [PROV of やすむ] if/provided one rests, 7.c.2
やちん (家賃) (n)　rent, 1.gr.8
やっと (adv)　finally, at long last, 11.c.conv
やっぱり (adv)　after all, as expected, on second thought, 8.c.4, 11.a.conv
やまかわ (山川) (n)　Yamakawa [family name], 1.b.6
やまだ (山田) (n)　Yamada [family name], 1.gr.1
やまとでんし (ヤマト電子) (n)　Yamato Electronics [company name], 11.a.conv
やまなか (山中) (n)　Yamanaka [family name], 1.d.1

やまばと (山鳩) (n)　dove, 1.lc
やまばとたっきゅうびん (やまばと宅急便) (n)　Yamabato Delivery Service, 1.lc
やまもと (山本) (n)　Yamamoto [family name], 3.c.conv
やまもとでんき (山本電気) (n)　Yamamoto Electric [company name], 2.d.2
やめたい (止めたい) (v: yame/ru) [たい-form of やめる] want to quit, 1.gr.4
やめる (止める) (v: yame/ru)　to quit; to stop, 1.d.1
やらせていただきます (phr) [て-form of やらせる + いただきます] I'll take the liberty of doing it; I will receive your favor of letting me do it., 9.a.2
やらなくて (v: yar/u) [NEG て-form of やる] not do; not give, 6.gr.2
やる (v: yar/u) [INF of する] to do, 4.gr.3, 5.d.conv, 6.gr.2
やる (v: yar/u) [INF of あげる] to give [V てやる "to give down to (others) a favor of V-ing"], 4.e.1

ゆ

ユーエス・リース (n)　US Lease [company name], 7.gr.4
ユーザーマニュアル (n)　user's manual, 10.gr.3
ゆうしょく (夕食) (n)　supper, dinner, 6.a.conv
ゆうじん (友人) (n)　friend, 7.d.conv
ユースホステル (n)　youth hostel, 10.a.1
ゆうびんきょく (郵便局) (n)　post office, 5.gr.3
ゆうびんばんごう (郵便番号) (n)　zip code, 1.e.2
ゆうべ (夕べ) (n)　last night; last evening, 1.gr.6
ゆうめい (有名) (な-adj)　famous, 1.lc
ユーロ (ct)　Euro, 5.lc
ゆしゅつ (輸出) する (n/v)　to export; exportation [日本への輸出 "export to Japan"], 3.gr.4, 4.d.1, 5.c.1, 7.c.1
ゆしゅつぎょうむ (輸出業務) (n)　export business, operation, 7.rw.1
ゆにゅう (輸入) する (n/v)　to import; importation, 4.d.1
ゆにゅうりょう (輸入量) (n)　the amount of import, 10.gr.1

よ

よ (sp) [assertion marker], 2.c.conv
よい (良い) (い-adj)　good, nice [more formal than いい], 11.b.conv
よう (な-adj)　the way [V よう(に)いう "to tell (someone) to V"], 3.e.conv
よう (要) (n)　necessary, 5.rw.1
よういん (要員) (n)　required personnel, 11.c.3
ようけん (用件) (n)　business, things to do, 3.f.conv
ようし (用紙) (n)　form, 5.b.conv
ようじ (用事) (n)　errand, 1.gr.8
ようす (様子) (n)　situation; condition [ようすをみる "observe" or "wait and see"], 9.c.1
ようだ (phr)　seem [S ようだ "it seems that S"; N のようだ "it seems to be N/it is like N"; な-adj なようだ "it seems な-adj"], 7.e.1
ような (phr)　like [S ような N "like N that S"], 7.e.1
ように (phr)　in such a way [V1 ように V2: V2 in the manner of V1; V2 so that V1; V2 in such a way that V1]; [V ようにいう／つたえる／もうしつたえる "tell/inform (someone) to V"], 3.e.2, 6.b.3
ように (phr)　such that [V1 ようになる "it becomes such that V1"], 9.b.3

よかったら (い-adj) [COND of いい] if it is good, 2.a.2
よきん (預金) する (n/v)　deposit money; money in a bank account, 5.b.conv, 5.lc
よく (い-adj) [く form of いい] good, well, often [よくわからない "do not understand well"], 1.gr.2
よくなさそう (良くなさそう) (phr) [Stem of よくない + さそう] looks it's not good, 8.a.1
よこがわアメリカ (n)　Yokogawa America [company name], 8.b.1
よこはま (横浜) (n)　Yokohama [a port city south of Tokyo], 3.f.4
よさ (良さ) (n)　goodness; merit, 7.c.1
よさそう (良さそう) (phr)　[Stem of よい + さそう] looks good, 8.a.1
よし (phr)　All right., 11.a.conv
よしだ (吉田) (n)　Yoshida [family name], 1.d.1
よそう (予想) される (n/v) [PASS of 予想する] to be predicted; [↑ of 予想する] to predict, 10.rw.1
よっか (四日) (num)　the fourth day of the month; four days, 5.e.conv
よてい (予定) (n)　schedule; plan, 3.f.conv
よばせる (呼ばせる) (v: yob/u) [CAUS of よぶ] to make/let (someone) call , 9.a.1
よばれる (呼ばれる) (v: yob/u) [PASS of よぶ] to be called; [↑ of よぶ] to call, 8.b.1
よぶ (呼ぶ) (v: yob/u)　to call; to summon, 1.b.5, 5.lc
よべば (呼べば) (v: yob/u) [PROV of よぶ] if/provided one calls, summons, 7.c.2
よべる (呼べる) (v: yob/u) [POT of よぶ] can call; can summon, 1.b.5
よませる (読ませる) (v: yom/u) [CAUS of よむ] to make/let (someone) read , 9.a.1
よまれる (読まれる) (v: yom/u) [PASS of よむ] to be read; [↑ of よむ] reads, 8.b.1
よみうりしんぶん (読売新聞) (n)　Yomiuri Shinbun [newspaper], 8.gr.2
よみたい (読みたい) (v: yom/u) [たい-form of よむ] want to read, 1.b.4
よむ (読む) (v: yom/u)　to read, 1.b.5, 1.gr.2, 8.b.1
よめる (読める) (v: yom/u) [POT of よむ] can read, 1.b.5, 6.b.2
よめるようになっている (読める〜) (phr)　(something) is made in such a way that you can read, 9.b.3
よやくしておく (予約しておく) (phr) [て-form of よやくする + おく] to reserve (a seat/hotel) in advance, 4.a.4, 6.a.conv
よやく (予約) する (n/v)　to reserve (a seta/hotel), reservation, 3.gr.3, 4.a.4, 8.c.4
より (p)　from [= から], 9.rw.1
より (p)　than [Xより〜 "more 〜 than X"], 8.c.conv
よる (v: yor/u)　to depend; is due to; is thanks to, 8.c.conv
よろこぶ (喜ぶ) (v: yorokob/u)　to feel glad [よろこんでする "do it gladly"], 1.lc, 9.a.2
よろしい (い-adj) [FORMAL of いい] is good; is nice, 3.f.5, 4.d.conv
よろしく (phr)　Nice to meet you!; [Request phrase], 1.a.conv
よろしくおねがいします (よろしくお願いします) (phr)　I wish for your best regard; I hope you will look after me., 2.a.conv
よろしければ (い-adj) [PROV of よろしい] if/provided it is good/OK, 7.gr.2
よわい (弱い) (い-adj)　weak, 4.c.2, 5.lc

よんけた（四桁）(n) four digits, 5.c.conv
よんだり（読んだり）(v: yom/u) [たり-form of よむ] read [よんだりする "do things like reading"], 4.gr.7

ら

らいがっき（来学期）(n) next [academic] term, 6.gr.7
らいげつ（来月）(n) next month, 3.b.1
らいしゅう（来週）(n) next week, 3.gr.4
らいしゅうちゅう（来週中）(n) during next week, 5.gr.11
らいにち（来日）する (n/v) to come to Japan; a visit to Japan, 7.d.conv
らいねん（来年）(n) next year, 4.gr.6
らく（楽）(な-adj) comfortable; easy, 2.c.3
ラケットボール (n) racket ball, 1.gr.8
らっかんてき（楽観的）(な-adj) optimistic, 10.c.add
ラッシュ (n) rush hour, 1.d.1
ラップトップ (n) laptop computer, 6.a.6
らん（欄）(n) column or box (to fill in), 5.c.conv

り

りし（利子）(n) interest [of a bank account], 5.b.1
りっぱ（立派）(な-adj) splendid; wonderful, 9.a.conv
りゆう（理由）(n) reason, 1.b.conv
りゅうがく（留学）する (n/v) to study abroad, 10.c.3
りょうがえ（両替え）(n) exchange of money, 5.1c
りょうこう（良好）(な-adj) good, 1.rw
りょうしん（両親）(n) parents ↓, 1.com., 6.com.
りょうてい（料亭）(n) Japanese-style restaurant, 6.c.conv
りょうり（料理）(n) cuisine, cooking, 1.b.1
りょかん（旅館）(n) Japanese-style inn, 3.gr.3
りょこう（旅行）(n) travel; trip, 10.gr.2
りれきしょ（履歴書）(n) resume, 1.e.2
りんぎしょ（稟議書）(n) group decision form, 11.a.conv
りんぎばんごう（稟議番号）(n) group decision number, 11.c.3
りんじ（臨時）(n) temporary, 11.c.3

る

ルイス (n) Lewis [family name], 7.a.conv
るすちゅう（留守中）(n) in the middle of absence; while one is away, 3.d.add
るすでん（留守電）(n) answering machine [short form of 留守電でんわ]; [留守電にメッセージをのこす "to leave a message on the answering machine"], 3.e.add
るすばんでんわ（留守番電話）(n) answering machine; [留守番電話にメッセージをのこす "to leave a message on the answering machine"], 3.e.add

れ

れいの（例の）(phr) that, so-called, 4.c.conv
レーザー (n) laser, 4.d.1
レーザープリンタ (n) laser printer, 4.c.2
れきし（歴史）(n) history, 1.b.conv
レストラン (n) restaurant, 1.b.1
レッスン (n) lesson, 3.gr.7
レポート (n) report, 2.c.conv
れんしゅう（練習）する (n/v) to practice, 6.gr.4, 6.gr.9, 8.gr.7
レンタカー (n) rented car, 9.gr.5
れんらく（連絡）する (n/v) to contact; communication, 3.f.conv, 5.f.2, 6.rw
れんらく（連絡）いたします (n/v) [↓ POL of 連絡する] to contact, 5.f.2
れんらくさき（連絡先）(n) mailing address, 1.e.2
れんらくようのでんわ（連絡用の電話）(n) intercom

ろ

ローマじ（ローマ字）(n) Roman letters, 6.gr.3
ろくじ（六時）(num) six o'clock, 7.c.1
ロス (n) Los (Angeles), 10.gr.2
ロスアンジェルス (n) Los Angeles, 5.com.1
ロビー (n) lobby, 1.gr.2
ロベルト・ノートン (n) [ロベルト is more often pronounced as ロバート] Robert Norton, 2.com.1
ロボティックスジャパン (n) Robotics Japan, 9.c.4
ロボット (n) robot, 1.gr.6
ろんぶん（論文）(n) report, thesis, essay article, 2.c.add

わ

わ (sp) [feminine sentence-end marker], 2.c.conv
ワードプロセシング (n) word-processing, 6.b.3
ワープロ (n) word processor, 1.d.1
ワールドコンピュータ (n) World Computer [company name], 1.c.conv
ワールドテック (n) World Tech (company name), 1.gr.1
ワールドテレコム (n) World Telecom [company name], 1.com.
わがしゃ（我が社）(n) our company, 1.b.conv
わかもの（若者）(n) young person/people, 1.gr.6
わからなかったら (v: wakar/u) [COND of わからない] if (someone) understands, 2.b.conv
わからなければ（分から〜）(v: wakar/u) [PROV of わからない] if/provided one does not understand, 7.c.2
わかりそうだ（分かり〜）(phr) appears to understand, 7.d.1
わかりそうにない（分かり〜）(phr) not appear to understand, 7.d.1
わかる (v: wakar/u) to understand, 1.a.conv, 1.c.3, 2.a.conv, 2.c.1
わかれば (v: wakar/u) [PROV of わかる] if/provided one understands, 7.c.2
わけ（訳）(n) reason, sense, situation, case [V わけにはいかない "can't really V"; V わけにもいかない "can't really even V" (fewer alternatives)], 10.b.conv
わざわざ (adv) intentionally, 10.b.conv
わしょく（和食）(n) Japanese food, 1.com.4
わすれる（忘れる）(v: wasure/ru) to forget, 2.c.1, 5.g.conv, 6.gr.9
わたくし（私）(pro) I, me [formal], 2.a.1
わたくしども（私ども）(pro) we, us ↓, 2.a.1, 5.d.conv
わたし（私）(pro) I, me, 1.a.conv
わたしたち（私達）(pro) we, us [たち is a plural suffix for people], 6.c.1
わりびき（割り引き）(n) discount, 4.c.1
わるい（悪い）(い-adj) bad, 1.gr.2, 8.b.conv

を

を (p) [object marker], 1.a.conv

ん

んで (con) so, therefore [=ので], 10.b.conv

〜んです (phr) It's that... [sentence ending indicating explanation or inference], 1.a.1

Appendix C: English-Japanese Glossary

a little　ちょっと, すこし（少し）しょうしょう（少々）(adv) 1.gr.2, 3.b.conv, 5.gr.11, 6.c.1
a little more　もうすこし（もう少し）(adv) 4.gr.5, 6.c.1
a lot; many　たくさん (n) 4.gr.6, 6.gr.3, 8.b.1
a while ago　さっき, さきほど（先ほど）(n) 3.c.conv, 4.e.1
a while longer　もうしばらく (phr) 9.a.1
a.m.　ごぜん（午前）(n) 4.a.1
able to V　～することができる (phr) 9.b.conv
about　についての (phr) 7.e.2
about, approximately　～ぐらい (suf) [どのぐらい "how long"] 2.gr.2
about, regarding, on　について, につきまして (n) 1.a.conv, 7.a.3, 10.rw.1
above; That's all.; equal to or more　いじょう（以上）(n) 1.rw, 10.gr.1
absence; not at home　おるす（お留守）(n) 4.b.conv
absolutely　かならず（必ず）(adv) [followed affirmative] 11.rw.1
accept [a request]　しょうち（承知）いたします↓ (n/v) 3.d.conv
accident　じこ（事故）(n) 1.gr.8
accompany　どうこう（同行）する (n/v) つれていく（連れて行く）(v) 6.a.6, 6.c.conv
according to　によると (phr) 9.b.3
account　こうざ（口座）(n) 5.a.conv
accounting　かいけい（会計), けいり（経理）(n) 4.e.2
accounting section　けいりか（経理課）(n) 4.e.conv
accustomed to　なれる（慣れる）(v) 2.a.conv
action　アクション (n) 9.lc
address　じゅうしょ（住所), おところ (n) 1.com.2, 5.rw.1
adherence　げんしゅ（厳守）(n) 11.rw.1
advance, make inroads, advancement　しんしゅつ（進出）する (n/v) 9.c.conv
advance, go forward　すすむ（進む）(v) 7.gr.4
advertise, advertisement　せんでん（宣伝）する (n/v) 8.c.conv, 8.gr.3, 11.b.2
advertising cost　せんでんひ（宣伝費）(n) 8.c.conv
advice　アドバイス (n) 6.lc
aforementioned company　どうしゃ（同社）(n) 7.rw.1
after　いこう（以降）(n) [time] 3.rw.2
after　あと, あとで (phr) 2.a.2, 4.b.conv, 6.b.conv, 6.b.1
after all, as expected　やっぱり (adv) 8.c.4, 11.a.conv
after looking at　ごいんけんのうえ（ご引見の上）(phr) 7.rw.1
again　また (n) 3.c.conv
age　ねんれい（年齢）(n) 11.c.3
agree, agreement　さんせい（賛成）する (n/v) 7.gr.3, 10.c.1
ahead; previously　さき（先）(n) 2.gr.4, 4.c.conv, 7.d.1
AIDS　エイズ (n) 11.gr.4
air conditioner　エアコン (n) 4.gr.6, 5.c.1, 7.e.3
airplane　ひこうき（飛行機）(n) 1.gr.5
airport　くうこう（空港）(n) 2.c.1
all day long　いちにちじゅう（一日中）(n) 7.e.1
all day tomorrow　あしたじゅう（明日中）(phr) 11.b.2

All right.　OK.　よし (phr) 11.a.conv
all; everything　ぜんぶ（全部）(n) [全部で "in total"] 2.a.2
along with; accompanying　にともない（に伴い）(phr) 7.rw.1
already; (not) any more/longer　もう (adv) 3.e.conv
also　また (con) 1.b.conv
also as for; also as far as　といたしましても↓ (phr) [= としても] 7.rw.1
also, too, as well　も (p) 1.b.conv
also; doubles as　けん（兼）(n) 5.rw.1
always　いつも (n) 6.a.3
America　アメリカ (n) 1.a.conv
American (person)　アメリカじん（アメリカ人）(n) 1.b.6
American car　アメリカしゃ（アメリカ車）(n) 1.b.5
among; within　のなかで（の中で), のうちで (phr) 9.a.3
amount of import　ゆにゅうりょう（輸入量）(n) 10.gr.1
amount of money　きんがく（金額), がく（額）(n) 5.rw.1, 5.lc
and　と (p) [と combines nouns.] 2.b.1
and　や (p) [や combines nouns.　A や B "A and B, and so on"] 2.b.1
and (furthermore)　し (con) 10.a.conv
and so on, etc.　など, なんか (suf) 2.b.conv, 2.b.1
and/or　とか (p) [A とか B "A and B and the like"] 2.b.conv
animation; animated cartoon　アニメ (n) 11.a.3
annoyed, in trouble　こまる (v) [こまっている "is in trouble"] 2.lc, 4.a.conv
annual sales total　うりあげだか（売り上げ高）(n) 8.rw.1
answer　こたえ（答え）(n) 3.gr.4, 6.a.1
answer a phone call　でんわにでる（電話に出る）(phr) 3.a.add
answer immediately, immediate reply　そくとう（即答）する (n/v) 4.d.conv
answer, reply　こたえる（答える）(v) 9.b.conv
answering machine　るすでん（留守電) or るすばんでんわ（留守番電話）(n) 3.e.add
anything; whatever it is　なんでも（何でも）(phr) 11.b.2
apartment　アパート (n) 10.a.1
appear　そうだ (phr) [S そうだ "it appears that S"] 7.b.3
appear able to do it　できそうだ (phr) 7.d.1
appear to end　おわりそうだ（終わりそうだ）(phr) 7.d.1
appear to take [time/money]　かかりそうだ (phr) 7.d.1
appear unable to do it　できそうにない (phr) 7.d.1
appearance　みため（見た目）(n) 5.b.1
appear able to go out　でられそうだ（出られそうだ）(phr) 7.d.1
appear healthy/great　げんきそう（元気そう）(phr) 8.a.conv
appear to be fair [of weather]　はれそう（晴れそう）(phr) 7.gr.3
appear to become　なりそう (v) 7.d.conv
appear to understand　わかりそうだ（分かりそうだ）(phr) 7.d.1
append a note to, additional remark　ふき（付記）する (n/v) 11.rw.1
applicant; those who wish/request　きぼうしゃ（希望者）(n) 6.rw
application form　もうしこみしょ（申込書）(n) 5.rw.1
apply for, propose　しんせい（申請）する (n/v) 11.c.3
appointment　アポイントメント (n) 6.gr.4
appreciation; courtesy; thanks　[お]れい（礼）(n) [お = ↑] 4.a.5

approve, approval　しょうにん（承認）する（n/v）9.c.2
area code　しがいきょくばん（市街局番）(n) 1.e.2
arrangement　ごてはい（ご手配）(n) [ご = ↑] 11.rw.1
arrive; reach　つく（着く）(v) 2.c.4, 7.c.1, 8.c.conv
as expected　やっぱり (adv) 8.c.4, 11.a.conv
as far as　まで (p) 1.gr.4, 2.a.conv
as follows, equal to or below/less　いか（以下）(n) 6.rw.
as much as possible　なるべく (adv) 3.lc
as much as, about, approximately　ほど (p) 8.b.conv
as shown below　かきのとおり（下記の通り）(phr) 9.rw.1
as soon as (something) comes out　でしだい（出次第）(phr) 7.gr.4
as soon as (someone) comes　きしだい（来次第）(phr) 7.gr.4
as soon as one returns　かえりしだい（帰り次第）(phr) 7.a.2, 10.c.2
as soon as something is decided　きまりしだい（決まり次第）(phr) 7.a.2
as soon as something is finished　おわりしだい（終わり次第）(phr) 7.a.2
as, for　として (phr) 10.b.conv
Asahi Newspaper　あさひしんぶん（朝日新聞）(n) 9.a.3
Asia　アジア (n) 1.b.2
ask and see; try to ask　きいてみる（聞いてみる）(phr) 6.b.2
ask for (something) in advance　きいておく（聞いておく）(phr) 4.a.conv
ask, request　たのむ（頼む）(v) 3.e.2
ask; go; visit　うかがう↓（伺う）(v) [= きく／いく] 5.f.conv, 7.a.1
ask; listen; hear　きく（聞く）(v) 1.gr.4, 2.a.conv, 2.c.1, 4.gr.7
aspect; face　めん（面）(n) 7.e.conv
assemble　あつまる（集まる）(vi) 4.e.conv [vt: あつめる]
assist, help, assistance　てつだう（手伝う）(v), おてつだい（お手伝い）する↓ (n/v) 7.d.2, 7.e.3, 7.lc
assistant; vice　ふく（副）(prefix) 4.e.3
at　において (phr) 7.rw.1
at beginning　はじめに（始めに）(adv) 10.rw.2
at present; currently　げんざい（現在）(n) 1.e.2, 7.b.conv
at this time of the year　じか（時下）(n) 9.rw.1
at this time; on this occasion　このたび（この度）(phr) 7.rw.1
at [location of activities]　で (p) 1.a.conv
Atlanta　アトランタ (n) 2.a.3
ATM card　キャッシュカード (n) 5.c.conv
attach (to a letter), attachment　てんぷ（添付）する (n/v) 9.rw.1
attach, include, turn on　つける, い（入）れる (vt) [vi: つく, はいる] 5.c.1, 10.a.conv
attached with a phone　でんわつき（電話付き）(n) 10.a.1
attached with bath and toilet　バストイレつき（付き）(n) 10.a.1
attached, included　つく (vi) 6.a.1, 8.c.conv
attachment; attached documents　てんぷしりょう（添付資料）, てんぷしょるい（添付書類）(n) 9.rw.1, 11.c.3
Australia　オーストラリア (n) 2.gr.7, 4.gr.6
automatic　じどうてき（自動的）(な-adj) [自動的に automatically] 5.d.conv
automatic deduction (from a bank account)　じどうひきおとし（自動ひきおとし）(n) 5.d.conv
automobile　じどうしゃ（自動車）(n) 3.a.2
awards and charges　しょうばつ（賞罰）(n) 1.rw

B

baby　あか（赤）ちゃん (n) 6.b.3
back up　バックアップする (n/v) 11.c.1
bad　わるい（悪い）(い-adj) 1.gr.2, 8.b.conv
badge　バッジ (n) 3.f.4
bag　かばん (n) 4.a.3
balance sheet　けっさんほうこくしょ（決算報告書）, けっさんしょ（決算書）(n) 4.b.conv, 4.c.conv
ball-point pen　ボールペン (n) 5.gr.5
bank　ぎんこう（銀行）(n) 1.c.1
bank check　こぎって（小切手）(n) 5.a.1
banker　ぎんこういん（銀行員）(n) 5.lc
bath and toilet　バストイレ (n) 10.a.1
bathroom (to bathe in)　おふろ（お風呂）(n) 2.gr.7
battery　でんち（電池）(n) 10.gr.1
be　でいらっしゃいます↑ (cop) [= です] 3.b.conv
be (located)　いる, いらっしゃる↑, おります↓ (v) [animate] 1.a.conv, 1.a.1, 1.a.2, 4.a.3
be able to take　とれる（取れる）(v) [POT of とる] 10.a.3
be asked (to do something)　たのまれる（頼まれる）(v) [PASS of たのむ] 10.b.2
be broken, be damaged　こわされる（壊される）(vt) [PASS of こわす] 8.b.1
be careful　きをつける（気をつける）(phr) 4.a.conv
be considerate, consideration　はいりょ（配慮）する (n/v) 7.rw.2
be developed　かいはつ（開発）される (n/v) [PASS of 開発する] 9.a.conv
be done　される (v) [PASS of する] 8.b.1
be formed (as in laws)　せいりつ（成立）する (n/v) 11.a.conv
be in time (for)　まにあう（間に合う）(v) 2.c.conv
because, since, so　から, ので, なので (con) 1.b.6, 1.b.conv
become　なる (v) 1.gr.3, 6.c.1, 11.c.2
become a hit　ヒットする (v) 9.c.4
become decided　きまる（決まる）(vi) [vt: きめる] 6.a.1, 10.c.2
become used to　なれる（慣れる）(v) 2.a.conv
beef　ビーフ (n) 5.gr.7
beep　ピーというおと（ピーという音）(n) 3.e.add
beer　ビール (n) 1.d.1
before　まえに（前に）(phr) 10.rw.2
beforehand　まえもって（前もって）(phr) 8.gr.7
begin　はじまる（始まる）(vi) [vt: はじめる] 3.f.3
begin (something)　はじめる（始める）(vt) [vi: はじまる] 4.d.1, 9.lc
beginning　はじめ（始め）(n) 2.b.1
being that kind of thing; OK then　そういうことで (phr) 11.c.conv
besides　ほかに（他に）(phr) 11.c.3
bid-rigging　だんごう（談合）(n) 11.gr.4
big accident　だいじこ（大事故）(n) 10.c.2
billboard　かんばん（看板）(n) 4.c.2, 8.b.1
birth　うまれ（生まれ）(n) 1.e.2
bitter　しぶい（渋い）(い-adj) 6.b.conv
black　くろい（黒い）(い-adj) 5.gr.5
black tea　こうちゃ（紅茶）(n) 1.gr.2
blue　あおい（青い）(い-adj) 6.gr.6
blue color　あお（青）(n) 5.gr.7
body　からだ（体）(n) 4.c.2, 11.gr.4
bonus　ボーナス (n) 3.gr.2, 7.c.1
book　ほん（本）(n) 1.a.1

booth ブース (n) 3.com.3
borrow かりる (借りる) (v) 1.b.1, 5.b.1
both the present and the future こんごとも (今後とも) (phr) 7.lc
bother, interference [お]じゃま (邪魔) する↓ (n/v) [お = ↑] 7.a.1
bowing おじぎ (お辞儀) (n) 1.b.2, 2.a.4
box lunch おべんとう (お弁当) (n) 8.gr.8
box to fill in きにゅうらん (記入欄) (n) 1.e.2
break down, out of order こしょう (故障) する (n/v) 9.c.conv
break or damage (something) こわす (壊す) (vt) [vi: こわれる] 8.b.1, 8.c.1
break, rest きゅうけい (休憩) (n) 10.b.conv
break; become out of order こわれる (壊れる) (vi) [vt: こわす] 11.gr.4
bright あかるい (明るい) (い-adj) 6.r.9
bring おもち (お持ち) になる↑ (v) 4.b.conv
brochure パンフレット (n) 3.f.5
browse めをとおす (目を通す) (phr) 4.b.conv
bubble economy バブルけいざい (バブル経済) (n) 5.gr.8
building ビル (n) 1.gr.6
business ビジネス (n) 2.com.1, 4.c.2
business cards めいし (名刺) (n) 2.d.add
business deal, transaction [お]とりひき (取引) (n) [お = ↑] 7.rw.1
business dealing, transaction, trading とりひき (取り引き) (n) 4.c.conv
business division じぎょうぶ (事業部) (n) 10.lc
business industry ぎょうかい (業界) (n) 7.rw.1
business trip しゅっちょう (出張) (n) 10.lc, 11.c.conv
business, things to do [ご]ようけん (用件) (n) [ご = ↑] 3.f.conv
busy [お]いそがしい (忙しい) (い-adj) [お = ↑] 2.a.2, 2.gr.6, 3.d.conv, 6.a.3
but けど, が (con) [が is more formal than けど] 2.b.conv, 3.c.1
but, however でも (con) 4.c.conv
buy かう (買う) (v) 1.b.5, 3.f.4, 6.a.5, 7.c.1
buy (it) in advance かっとく (買っとく) (phr) [contraction of かっておく] 4.a.4, 4.a.5
by, due to に, による (phr) 8.b.1, 8.c.conv
by all means ぜひ, ぜひとも (adv) 4.a.conv, 7.rw.1
by far ずっと (adv) 4.b.1
by means of での (phr) 7.e.2
by now いまでは (今では) (phr) 8.c.conv
by taking in something to look ごいんけんのうえ (ご引見の上) (phr) 7.rw.1
by that time それまでに (phr) 4.e.conv
by the way ところで, さて (con) 1.c.conv, 7.rw.1
by [time] までに (p) 2.c.conv
by, by means of, by using, with, in で (p) 1.c.conv

C

cable ケーブル (n) 9.lc
cafe きっさてん (喫茶店) (n) 5.gr.6
cake ケーキ (n) 2.b.1
calculate, calculation けいさん (計算) する (n/v) 4.e.conv, 4.gr.9, 10.b.conv
calculation sheet けいさんしょ (計算書) (n) 5.com.2

calisthenics たいそう (体操) (n) 6.gr.4
call よぶ (呼ぶ) (v) 1.b.5, 5.lc, 8.b.1
call again でんわをかけなおす (電話をかけ直す) (phr) 3.c.add
call [telephone] でんわ (電話) する, 電話なさる↑, お電話いたします↓ (n/v) 2.a.add, 3.a.add, 3.c.conv, 3.e.2
came to know しった (知った) (v) [PAST of しる] 7.lc
camera カメラ (n) 2.a.2
can put outside だせる (出せる) (vt) [POT of だす] 1.c.conv
can request おねがい (お願い) できる (n/v) [POT of おねがいする] 5.b.1
can say いえる (言える), もうしあげられる↓ (申し上げられる) (v) [POT of いう／もうしあげる] 1.b.6, 9.c.3
can decide きめられる (決められる) (v) [POT of きめる] 4.d.conv
can swim およげる (泳げる) (v) [POT of およぐ] 8.b.1
can become なれる (v) [POT of なる] 1.b.5
can come こられる (来られる), これる (来れる) (v) [POT of くる] 1.b.5
can be seen, be visible みえる (見える) (v) 3.gr.1, 6.b.3
can't really leave かえるわけにはいかない (帰る訳にはいかない) (phr) 10.b.2
can't really even refuse ことわるわけにもいかない (断る訳にもいかない) (phr) 10.b.2
can't help it しかたがない (仕方がない) (phr) 11.lc
cancel とりけす (取り消す) (v), キャンセルする (n/v) 8.c.4, 11.rw.1
capability [of machines] せいのう (性能) (n) 11.gr.1
capital しほんきん (資本金) (n) 8.rw.1
car くるま (車) (n) 1.b.1, 3.b.2
card カード (n) 5.f.2, 5.g.conv
care おせわ (お世話) (n) [お = ↑] [お世話になる "be cared for"] 2.a.conv, 8.c.3
careful きをつける (気をつける) (phr), ちゅうい (注意) する (n/v) 4.a.conv, 4.c.2
carry out おこなう (行なう) (v) 6.rw
case, time, occasion ばあい (場合) (n) 9.c.conv
cash キャッシュ (n) 1.gr.8
cash machine じどうひきおとしき (自動引き落とし機) (n) 5.lc
catalogue カタログ (n) 3.f.5
caution ちゅうい (注意) する (n/v) 4.c.2
celebration party しゅくがかい (祝賀会) (n) 8.gr.7
cell phone けいたいでんわ (携帯電話), けいたい (携帯) (n) 2.gr.7, 3.rw.2
Certainly./I see. しょうち (承知) しました, 承知いたしました↓ (n/v), かしこまりました (v) 3.d.conv, 3.f.conv, 4.gr.6, 8.c.5
chair いす (椅子) (n) 2.gr.4, 5.c.conv
chairman かいちょう (会長) (n) 1.d.conv, 4.e.3
change, substitute かわり (代わり/変わり) (v) [V-stem of かわる] 3.com.1
character (of anime) キャラクター (n) 5.rw.1
chat しゃべる (v) [COLLOQ of はなす] 6.b.conv
cheap やすい (安い) (い-adj) 1.c.3
check チェック (n) 5.a.1
check, examine しらべる (調べる) (v) 11.lc
Cheers! かんぱい (乾杯) (phr) 6.b.4
chicken チキン (n) 5.gr.7
chief executive officer だいひょうとりしまりやく (代表取締役) (n) 4.e.3

child(ren) こども (子供), おこさん↑ (お子さん) (n) [お = ↑] 3.b.1, 9.a.1
Chinese (language) ちゅうごくご (中国語) (n) 1.gr.4
choose えらぶ (選ぶ) (v) 1.c.conv
cigarette たばこ (煙草) (n) 1.d.1
circuit かいろ (回路) (n) 4.d.2
clearly はっきり (adv) 9.c.3
clerical post いっぱんしょく (一般職) (n) 2.a.4
close とじる (閉じる) (v) 5.a.1
close, (something) closes しまる (閉まる) (vi) [vt: しめる] 6.a.1
close (something) しめる (閉める) (vt) [vi: しまる] 6.a.1
closing of an account かいやく (解約) (n) 5.a.1
closing of an event おひらき (お開き) (n) [おひらきにする "close an event"] 6.b.4
closing remark in a letter けいぐ (敬具) (phr) 7.rw.1
coffee コーヒー (n) 1.b.1
coffee shop きっさてん (喫茶店) (n) 5.gr.6
cold つめたい (冷たい) (い-adj) 6.a.3; さむい (寒い) (い-adj) 6.gr.9
cold [illness] かぜ (風邪) (n) [風邪をひく "catch a cold"] 6.a.4, 6.gr.9
color カラー (n) 8.b.1
column or box (to fill in) らん (欄) (n) 5.c.conv
come (to see) みえる (見える), おみえ (お見え) になる↑ (vi) [= くる] 3.gr.1, 4.a.conv, 6.b.3
come (here) くる (来る), いらっしゃる↑, まいります↓ (参ります) (v) 1.a.2, 1.b.5, 2.c.1, 4.a.1, 4.a.3, 6.a.4
come over おこし (お越し) (v) [POL V-stem of こす] [↑] [おこし下さい = おいで下さい] 5.g.conv
come to Japan, a visit to Japan らいにち (来日) する (n/v) 7.d.conv
comes こられる (来られる) (v) [ADV PASS or ↑ PASS] 8.b.1
comes on, a light comes on つく (vi) [vt: つける] 6.a.1, 8.c.conv
comfortable らく (楽) (な-adj) 2.c.3
coming to our company ごらいしゃ (ご来社) (n) [ご = ↑] 7.b.conv
commerce しょうほう (商法) (n) 5.b.1
commit an act of rudeness しつれい (失礼) する (n/v) 1.gr.2
common sense じょうしき (常識) (n) 4.a.conv
communicate つたえる (伝える) (vt) 3.e.2, 10.c.conv
communicate orally もうしつたえる↓ (申し伝える) (v) [= いいつたえる] 3.f.conv
commuting cost こうつうひ (交通費) (n) 11.c.3
commuting to work つうきん (通勤) (n) 1.lc
company かいしゃ (会社) (n) 1.b.add
company brochure かいしゃがいよう (会社概要) (n) 7.rw.1
company business しゃよう (社用) (n) 7.d.conv
company employee かいしゃいん (会社員), しゃいん (社員) (n) 1.c.add, 2.a.add, 4.e.3
company motto しゃくん (社訓) (n) 6.gr.4
company name しゃめい (社名) (n) 8.rw.1
company order じれい (辞令) (n) 11.lc
company trainee けんしゅうしゃいん (研修社員) (n) 2.a.conv
company, Inc. かぶしきがいしゃ (株式会社) (n) 3.a.2
victory or defeat, match, fight しょうぶ (勝負) する (n/v) 8.c.conv
compete, competition きょうそう (競争) する (n/v) 7.rw.1, 11.a.conv

complete set いっしき (一式) (n) 9.rw.1
completely まったく (adv) 9.rw.1
compose music, composition さっきょく (作曲) する (n/v) 10.gr.4
comprehensive, synthesize そうごう (総合) する (n/v) 5.rw.1
computer コンピュータ (n) 1.a.conv
computer science コンピュータサイエンス (n) 1.com.1
computer show コンピュータショー (n) 7.lc
conclude けつろん (結論) をだす (phr) form a conclusion, 5.gr.12
conclusion けつろん (結論) (n) 4.d.conv
condition ちょうし (調子) (n) 11.gr.4
conditions じょうけん (条件) (n) 4.c.conv
conditions for a business deal とりひきじょうけん (取り引き条件) (n) 4.lc
conference かいぎ (会議), コンファレンス (n) 1.b.6, 6.gr.6
conference room かいぎしつ (会議室) (n) 7.gr.1
configure, configuration せってい (設定) する (n/v) 9.b.conv
congratulatory address しゅくじ (祝辞) (n) 8.gr.7
connect, connection せつぞく (接続) する (n/v), つなぐ (v) 4.c.2, 9.b.conv, 9.b.3, 9.lc
consider かんがえる (考える) (v) [deliberate thinking] 4.a.2, 7.b.conv
considerably なかなか (adv) 7.e.1, 7.gr.4
construct, construction けんせつ (建設) する (n/v) 11.gr.4
consult, consultation そうだん (相談) する, [ご]相談 (n/v) [ご = ↑] 4.e.conv, 6.a.2, 7.a.conv
consumer しょうひしゃ (消費者) (n) 8.b.conv
consumer guide しょうひしゃガイド (消費者ガイド) (n) 3.gr.2, 8.b.conv
contact, notification れんらく (連絡) する, 連絡いたします↓ (n/v) 3.f.conv, 5.f.2, 6.rw
continue (something) つづける (続ける) (vt) 8.gr.3
continuously ずっと (adv) 4.b.1
contract けいやく (契約) する (n/v) 4.e.conv
contract document けいやくしょ (契約書) (n) 10.c.4
contrasted (with), against たい (対) して (n/v) 10.c.conv
convenience store コンビニ (n) 11.a.3
convenient べんり (便利) (な-adj) 1.b.1
conversation かいわ (会話) (n) 9.lc
cooking, cuisine りょうり (料理) (n) 1.b.1
cool すずしい (涼しい) (い-adj) 4.gr.6, 5.c.1, 7.d.conv
cooperate, cooperation きょうりょく (協力) する (n/v), てをむすぶ (手を結ぶ) (phr) 7.e.2, 10.c.3
cooperate (with other business) ていけい (提携) する (n/v) 4.d.1
coping たいおう (対応) (n) 7.gr.4
copy コピーする (n/v) 1.e.1, 2.b.1, 2.c.4
copy machine コピーき (コピー機) (n) 5.b.1
correct ただしい (正しい) (い-adj) 7.e.2
correct なおす (直す) (vt) [vi: なおる] 6.a.1
correspondent つうしんいん (通信員) (n) 2.rw
cost accounting げんかけいさん (原価計算) (n) 4.rw.1
cost down; price reduction コストダウン (n) 8.c.conv
cost of parts ぶひんだい (部品代) (n) 9.lc
countryside; rural area いなか (田舎) (n) 10.gr.4
cover カバー (n) 5.gr.7
credit card クレジットカード (n) 8.c.3
cure なおす (直す) (vt) [vi: なおる] 6.a.1

current checking account とうざよきん (当座預金) (n) 5.(title).
customer おきゃくさま (お客様) (n) [お = ↑] 2.a.1, 5.b.conv
customer service アフターサービス (n) 9.c.conv

D

dangerous あぶない (危ない) (い-adj) 8.b.1
data compression データコンプレッション (n) 1.a.conv
date ひづけ (日付) (n) 4.rw.2
date and time にちじ (日時) (n) 6.rw, 9.rw.1
date of birth せいねんがっぴ (生年月日) (n) 1.e.2
date of final decision けっさいび (決裁日) (n) 11.c.3
date of originating the proposal きあんび (起案日) (n) 11.c.3
date of processing しょりび (処理日) (n) 11.c.3
daughter むすめ (娘) (n) [↓] 4.e.1
day ひ (日) (n) 2.c.conv
days にち (日) (ct) [counter for days] 2.c.conv
daytime ひるま (昼間) (n) 6.c.conv
deal with あつかう (扱う) (v) 8.b.conv
decide (on) おきめ (お決め) になる↑ (vt) [= きめる] 5.c.conv
decide (on) (something) きめる (決める) (vt) [vi: きまる] 3.gr.4, 4.c.conv, 6.a.1, 10.c.2
decide, decision けっさい (決裁) する (n/v) 11.a.3
decreases へる (減る) (vi) [vt: へらす] 4.d.1
deepen ふかめる (深める) (vt) 1.d.conv
deeply あつく (厚く) (い-adj) 7.rw.1
defective products けっかんひん (欠陥品) (n) 11.gr.3
delay ちえん (遅延) (n) 11.rw.1
delicious, tasty おいしい (い-adj) 1.a.1, 1.b.1
delight [お]よろこび (慶び) (n) [お = ↑] [およろこびもうしあげます "I congratulate you"] 7.rw.1
deliver, delivery [ご]はいそう (配送) する (n/v) [ご = ↑] 11.rw.1
delivery date のうき (納期) (n) 11.rw.1
dentist はいしゃさん (歯医者さん) (n) 6.a.1
department store デパート (n) 1.gr.5
depending on によって (phr) 8.b.1, 10.a.conv
deposit ふりこみ (振込) (n) 5.f.conv
deposit money, deposit よきん (預金) する (n/v) 5.lc
deposit slip にゅうきんでんぴょう (入金伝票) (n) 5.rw.1
Dept. of Electrical Engineering でんきこうがくか (電気工学科) (n) 1.rw
deputy だいり (代理), ほさ (補佐) (n) 4.e.3
design デザイン (n) 1.c.3, 5.rw.1
designated day for a business to close ていきゅうび (定休日) (n) 3.f.1
desire, choose, choice, [ご]しぼう (志望) する (n/v) [ご = ↑] 1.b.conv, 1.b.2
desire, wish, request [ご]きぼう (希望) する (n/v) [ご = ↑] 7.rw.1
desk つくえ (机) (n) 2.b.conv
despite that のに (con) 6.a.conv
develop, development かいはつ (開発) する, 開発なさる↑, 開発いたします↓ (n/v) 1.b.conv, 1.b.2, 8.c.1
dial tone はっしんおん (発信音) (n) 3.e.add
dictionary じしょ (辞書) (n) 2.gr.2
different ちがう (違う) (v) 4.lc
difficult to talk with はなしにくい (話しにくい) (い-adj) 9.a.3

difficult, hard むずかしい (難しい), こんなんだ (困難だ) (い-adj; な-adj) 1.gr.8, 7.c.1, 10.rw.1
digestion, completion しょうか (消化) (n) 11.c.3
digital camera デジタルカメラ (n) 9.gr.5
direct ちょくせつ (直接) (n) 10.c.conv
direction ほうこう (方向) (n) 11.b.conv
direction, field ほうめん (方面) (n) 1.b.conv, 7.e.conv
director [of a company] とりしまりやく (取締役) (n) 4.e.3
disappear きえる (消える) (vi) [でんきがきえている "lights are off"] [vt: けす] 6.a.1
disappears completely きえてしまう (消えてしまう) (phr) 6.gr.1
discount ディスカウント, わりびき (割り引き) (n) 4.c.1, 10.b.conv
discuss はなしあう (話し合う) (v) 10.rw.2
discuss and examine, investigation けんとう (検討) する, 検討いたします↓ (n/v) 4.rw.2, 7.a.3, 10.rw.1, 11.b.conv
dislike きらい (嫌い) (な-adj) 1.d.add
display ひょうじ (表示) する (n/v) 9.b.conv
distant とおい (遠い) (い-adj) 1.gr.6, 1.gr.8
division manager ぶちょう (部長) (n) 1.d.1, 3.a.conv
division [of an organization] ぶ (部) (n) 2.d.add
do する/やる, なさる↑, いたします↓ (v) 1.a.conv, 1.b.1, 1.b.2, 1.b.3, 4.gr.3, 5.d.conv, 5.g.conv
do (it) in advance しとく (phr) [contraction of しておく] 4.a.4
do (it) together, together [ご]いっしょ (一緒) する (n/v) [↓] 9.gr.3
do something in advance しといて (v) [contraction of しておいて] 4.a.4
do the ground work ねまわし (根回し) する (n/v) [root binding work before a large tree is transplanted] 4.rw.1
document ぶんしょ (文書), しょるい (書類) (n) 3.e.2, 4.e.conv, 8.lc, 10.c.conv
does not appear to end おわりそうにない (終わりそうにない) (phr) 7.d.1
do not know しりません (知りません), ごぞんじありません↑ (ご存知ありません) (v) 3.gr.5, 5.gr.6
does not look easy/gentle やさしそうじゃない (phr) [NEG of やさしそうだ] 8.a.1
does not look it can be done できそうにない* (phr) [V-stem of できる + そう + に + ない] 8.a.1
dollar-based ドルだて (ドル建て) (n) 11.b.conv
domestic; national こくない (国内) (n) 2.d.add
Don't do. しないで (phr) [NEG REQ form of する] 6.b.4
Don't hold back. えんりょ (遠慮) しないで (phr) [NEG REQ form of 遠慮する] 6.b.4
Don't overexert. むり (無理) しないで (phr) [NEG REQ form of 無理する] 6.b.4
Don't worry. しんぱい (心配) しないで (phr) 6.b.conv
door ドア (n) 6.a.1
dove やまばと (山鳩) (n) 1.lc
drink のむ (飲む), めしあがる↑ (召し上がる) (v) 1.b.1, 1.c.3, 6.a.conv, 8.b.1, 11.b.2
drinks ドリンク, [お]のみもの (飲み物) (n) [お = ↑] 5.gr.7, 7.gr.2
driver うんてんしゅ (運転手) (n) 9.a.1
due to, by による (v) 8.c.conv; せいで (phr) 11.c.conv
during next week らいしゅうちゅう (来週中) (n) 5.gr.11
during one is out (of office) がいしゅつちゅう (外出中) (n) 3.com.2

during this week こんんしゅうちゅう (今週中) (n) 6.gr.2
duty-free items めんぜいひん (免税品) (n) 7.c.1

E

early はやく (早く), はやめ (早目) (い-adj; n) [く-form of はやい] 3.lc, 4.gr.6, 7.d.2
early fall しょしゅうのこう (初秋の候) (phr) 10.rw.1
early summer しょか (初夏) (n) 7.rw.1
easily かんたんに (簡単に) (adv) 10.gr.4
easy to talk with はなしやすい (話しやすい) (い-adj) 9.a.3
eat たべる (食べる), めしあがる↑ (召し上がる) (v) 1.a.1, 1.b.3, 1.b.5, 6.a.5, 8.b.1, 11.b.2
economic state けいき (景気) (n) 7.c.1
Economics けいざいがく (経済学) (n) 1.gr.1, 7.e.conv
economy けいざい (経済) (n) 1.b.2
economy class エコノミークラス (n) 5.gr.7
editions ごう (号) (suf) [used for counting] [いちごう "the first"] 11.c.3
educational history がくれき (学歴) (n) 1.e.2
effort, make efforts [ご]じんりょく (尽力) する (n/v) [ご = ↑] 11.c.conv
either one どちらか (phr) 6.a.3
either way どちらでも (phr) 11.b.conv
electric equipment industry でんきさんぎょう (電気産業) (n) 3.a.2
electric equipment manufacturing でんきこうぎょう (電気工業) (n) 3.a.2
electric train でんしゃ (電車) (n) 1.gr.8
Electrical Engineering でんきこうがく (電気工学) (n) 1.rw
electronic でんし (電子) (n) 3.a.2
electronic handling でんしんあつかい (電信扱い) (n) 5.gr.9, 7.c.1
electronic industry でんしさんぎょう (電子産業) (n) 3.a.2
electronic manufacturing でんしこうぎょう (電子工業) (n) 3.a.2
electronic transfer でんしん (電信) (n) 5.e.conv
electronics エレクトロニクス (n) 2.d.conv
email メール, でんしメール (電子メール), Eメール (n) 1.gr.7, 2.gr.2, 4.gr.10, 6.b.3
email address メールアドレス (n) 1.gr.1
emergent いま (今) (n) 1.c.2
employer さいようしゃ (採用者) (n) 1.e.2
employer name おつとめさき (お勤め先) (n) [お = ↑] 5.rw.1
employment しゅうしょく (就職) (n) 1.a.add
employment history しょくれき (職歴) (n) 1.e.2
enclose in a letter どうふう (同封) する (n/v) 9.rw.1
end おわり (終わり) (n) 11.gr.4
energetic げんき (元気) (な-adj) 7.e.2
enforce, enforcement じっし (実施) する (n/v) 9.rw.1
engage in たずさわる (携わる) (v) [X にたずさわる "engage in X"] 1.b.conv
engineering エンジニアリング (n) 1.com.4
engineering field こうがくけい (工学系) (n) 7.e.conv
English えいご (英語) (n) 1.a.1
English conversation えいかいわ (英会話) (n) 3.gr.7
English text えいぶん (英文) (n) 9.a.1
enjoy たのしむ (楽しむ) (v) 6.b.4
enrollment to school にゅうがく (入学) (n) 11.gr.2
enter はいる (入る) (vi) [vt: いれる] 5.gr.5, 6.a.conv, 6.a.1

enter a company (be hired) にゅうしゃ (入社) する (n/v) 2.lc
enterprise きぎょう (企業) (n) 1.c.conv
envelop ふうとう (封筒) (n) 1.lc
environment かんきょう (環境) (n) 6.com.1
epoch-making かっきてき (画期的) (な-adj) 9.rw.1
equipped つき (suf) [バストイレつき "equipped with a bathroom and a toilet"] 10.a.1
erase けす (消す) (vt) 5.gr.11, 6.a.1, 6.a.1
erase completely けしてしまう (消してしまう) (phr) 6.gr.1
errand ようじ (用事) (n) 1.gr.8
error エラー, まちがい (間違い) (n) 8.lc, 9.gr.5
escort someone; send something/someone おくる (送る) (v) 2.a.3, 3.e.conv, 3.e.add, 4.e.conv, 5.f.2
especially とくに (特に) (adv) 1.a.conv
establishment そうりつ (創立) (n) 8.rw.1
estimate みつもり (見積もり) (n) 4.c.conv
estimate (document) みつもりしょ (見積り書) (n) 4.b.conv
Euro ユーロ (ct) 5.lc
evaluate, evaluation ひょうか (評価) する (n/v) 7.rw.1, 8.b.conv, 10.a.2
even if there isn't/aren't なくても (v) [て-form of ない + も] 5.b.1
even if it isn't/they aren't じゃなくても (cop) [て-form of じゃない + も] 5.b.1
even if one does not do (it) しなくても (v) [NEG て-form of する + も] 5.b.1
eventually けっきょく (結局) (n) 6.c.1
every week まいしゅう (毎週) (n) 3.f.1
every year まいとし (毎年) (n) 9.b.3
everybody みんな (n) [colloquial form of みなさん] 6.b.conv
everyday まいにち (毎日) (n) 6.gr.4
everyone in the company しゃいんいちどう (社員一同) (n) 8.c.conv
everywhere; nowhere どこも (phr) 6.a.3
exaggeration おおげさ (大袈裟) (な-adj) 6.a.conv
examination しけん (試験) (n) 11.gr.2
excel (at) すぐれる (優れる) (v) 1.c.conv
excellent すぐれた (優れた) (v) [adjectival form] 7.rw.1
exchange (of foreign money) かわせ (為替) (n) 5.d.conv
exchange of money りょうがえ (両替え) する (n/v) 5.lc
exchange rate こうかんレート (交換〜), かわせレート (為替〜) (n) 5.lc
excuse もうしわけ (申し訳) (n) 3.c.conv
Excuse me (for what I'm about to do). しつれい (失礼) します, 失礼いたします↓ (n/v) 1.a.conv, 1.e.conv
Excuse me (for entering/leaving). ごめんください (ごめん下さい) (phr) 3.c.1
Excuse me (for what I did). しつれい (失礼) いたしました (v) 3.a.conv
exhibition てんじかい (展示会) (n) 3.com.3
existing じゅうらい (従来) (n) 9.a.conv
expand, expansion かくちょう (拡張) する, かくだい (拡大) する (n/v) 7.b.conv, 7.rw.1, 8.gr.3
expensive たかい (高い), こうがく (高額) (い-adj; な-adj) 1.b.1, 8.c.conv
experience けいけん (経験) (n) 1.lc
explain, explanation [ご]せつめい (説明) する (n/v) [ご = ↑] 7.d.2, 7.e.2, 9.a.conv

explanation, user manual; direction　せつめいしょ（説明書）(n) 7.e.2
expo　エキスポ (n) 4.a.2
expo plaza　エキスポプラザ (n) 9.rw.1
export　ゆしゅつ（輸出）する (n/v) 3.gr.4, 4.d.1, 5.c.1, 7.c.1
export business　ゆしゅつぎょうむ（輸出業務）(n) 7.rw.1
express mail　そくたつ（速達）(n) 5.com.1
extend/expand　のびる（伸びる）(v) 8.gr.3
extremely grateful　おそれいります（恐れ入ります）(v) 2.d.conv
extremely grateful, sorry　きょうしゅく（恐縮）する (n/v) 2.e.add, 7.gr.4
eye　め（目）(n) 4.b.conv

F

face-to-face meeting　めんかい（面会）(n) 7.a.add
fact　こと (n) 2.a.conv
factory　こうじょう（工場）(n) 1.c.1
family　[ご]かぞく（家族）(n) [ご = ↑] 1.lc
famous　ゆうめい（有名）(な-adj) 1.lc
far　とおい（遠い）(い-adj) 1.gr.8
fare　うんちん（運賃）(n) 5.com.1, 11.b.conv
father　おとうさん（お父さん）, ちち（父）(n) [お = ↑] 1.c.1, 1.gr.1
fatigue　おつかれ（お疲れ）(n) [お = ↑] 3.d.3
favor　おひきたて（お引き立て）(n) [お = ↑] 7.rw.1
fax machine　ファックス (n) 3.e.add
feast　ごちそう（ご馳走）(n) 3.f.5
feel bad　きをわるくする（気を悪くする）(phr) 6.b.conv
feel dizzy　ふらふらする (v) 6.b.4
feel encouraged　こころづよい（心強い）(い-adj) 11.b.2
feel glad　よろこぶ（喜ぶ）(v) 1.lc
feel good　きもちがいい（気持ちがいい）(phr) 9.lc
feel sorry, but　きょうしゅくながら（恐縮ながら）(phr) 10.rw.1
feeling　きぶん（気分）(n) 1.gr.2
female　じょせい（女性）(n) 6.rw., 7.d.conv
field　ぶんや（分野）(n) 1.a.conv; ほうめん（方面）(n) 1.b.conv, 7.e.conv
file　ファイル (n) 6.gr.1
fill in　きにゅう（記入）する (n/v) 5.lc
film　フィルム (n) 4.gr.6, 9.gr.5
finally　やっと (adv) 11.c.conv; とうとう (adv) 11.c.add
finance　ざいむ（財務）(n) 4.e.2
finance division manager　ざいむぶちょう（財務部長）(n) 10.c.conv
find　みつける（見つける）(v) 4.gr.10
finish　おわる（終わる）(v) 2.a.3, 3.f.conv, 7.c.1
first class (of planes, trains, etc.)　ファーストクラス (n) 2.c.3
first, best, number one　いちばん（一番）(adv) 9.a.conv
first time　はじめて（初めて）(n) 2.lc
first level　いっきゅう（一級）(n) 1.rw.
fish　さかな（魚）(n) 2.gr.5
five to six days　ご、ろくにち（五、六日）(num) 11.b.1
fix　なおす（直す）(vt) [vi: なおる] 6.a.1
fixed time account; time deposit account　ていきよきん（定期預金）(n) 5.(title).
flex-time　フレックスタイム (n) 7.com.
Florida　フロリダ (n) 1.lc
FOB (free on board)　エフオービー (n) 11.b.conv

foreign corporation　がいこくきぎょう（外国企業）(n) 7.e.2
foreign country　がいこく（外国）(n) 5.d.conv
foreign exchange rate　かわせレート（為替レート）(n) 5.e.conv
foreigner　がいじん（外人）, がいこくじん（外国人）(n) 4.gr.3, 7.d.2
foreman　はんちょう（班長）(n) 4.e.3
forget　わすれる（忘れる）(v) 2.c.1, 5.g.conv, 6.gr.9
form　ようし（用紙）(n) 5.b.conv
four digits　よんけた（四桁）(n) 5.c.conv
fourth day of the month; four days　よっか（四日）(num) 5.e.conv
free (of charge)　むりょう（無料）(n) 9.c.conv
free space　あきスペース（空きスペース）(n) 5.gr.6
freight fee　うんちん（運賃）(n) 5.com.1, 11.b.conv
French language　フランスご（フランス語）(n) 1.gr.4
friction　まさつ（摩擦）(n) 7.com.
friend　ともだち（友達）, ゆうじん（友人）(n) 4.e.1, 7.d.conv
friendship　しんぼく（親睦）(n) 1.d.conv
from　より (p) [= から] 9.rw.1
from now (on)　これから (phr) 2.lc, 4.a.conv
from the direction of　〜のほうから（〜の方から）(phr) 3.e.conv
from [time, place, level]　から (p) 1.b.6
front (side); previous　まえ（前）(n) 3.gr.3
full (age)　まん（満）(n) 1.e.2
full, fully　いっぱい (n) 7.gr.3
function　きのう（機能）(n) 8.b.conv
furthermore　そのうえ (con) 8.c.conv; それに (con) 10.b.conv

G

game machines　ゲームき（ゲーム機）(n) 9.b.3
gasoline　ガソリン (n) 5.c.1
gather　あつまる（集まる）(v) 4.e.conv
general　いっぱん（一般）(n) 5.rw.1
general affairs　そうむ（総務）(n) 4.e.2
general post　そうごうしょく（総合職）(n) 2.a.4
German car　ドイツしゃ（ドイツ車）(n) 1.gr.5
Germany　ドイツ (n) 1.lc
get a job　しゅうしょく（就職）する (n/v) 1.a.add
get crowded　こむ（混む）(v) [こんでいる "is crowded"] 1.c.3
get married　けっこん（結婚）する (n/v) 6.c.1
get tired　つかれる（疲れる）(v) 2.gr.2, 7.e.1, 10.gr.3
get to know　しる（知る）(v) [しっている "know"] 2.c.1
give　さしあげる↓（差し上げる）(v) [= あげる] 3.f.4, 4.e.1
give (to me)　くださる↑（下さる）(v) 3.f.4, 4.e.1
give (to me)　たまわる↓（賜る）(v) 10.rw.1
give (to me)　くれる（くれる）(v) [V てくれる "give (me) a favor of V-ing"] 4.e.conv
give (to me) please　ください（下さい）(v) [V てください: "Please V."] 1.a.conv
give (to others)　あげる（上げる）(v) [V てあげる "give (others) a favor of V-ing"] 4.e.conv
give (to others)　やる (v) [V てやる "to give (down) to (others) a favor of V-ing"] 4.e.1, 6.gr.2
glad, happy　うれしい（嬉しい）(n) 11.b.2
gladly　よろこんで（喜んで）(v) [て-form of よろこぶ] 9.a.2
glance through　めをとおす（目を通す）(phr) 3.gr.2
glasses　めがね（眼鏡）(n) 1.gr.8

go いく (行く), いらっしゃる↑, まいります↓ (参ります) (v) 1.a.1, 1.a.2, 1.gr.2, 4.a.1, 4.a.3, 6.a.1
go and come back いってくる (行ってくる) (phr) 6.gr.1
go around まわる (回る) (vi) [vt: まわす] 2.b.add
go back もどる (戻る) (vi) [vt: もどす] 1.b.6, 3.e.conv
go home かえる (帰る) (v) 1.gr.3
go on a business trip しゅっちょう (出張) する (v) 4.a.4
go out for a drink のみにいく (飲みに行く) (phr) 9.c.2
go out; emerge でる (出る), おで (お出) になる↑ (vi) [= でる] [vt: だす／おだしになる] 1.b.6, 3.f.5, 6.a.1, 6.gr.1
go out でかける (出かける) (v), がいしゅつ (外出) する (n/v) 1.a.1, 3.gr.7, 6.b.4
go over おこし (お越し) (v) [POL V-stem of こす] [↑] 5.g.conv
go to the company しゅっしゃ (出社) する (n/v) 6.b.4
go to the trouble of V-ing せっかく (adv) 10.gr.2
go up, rise あがる (上がる) (vi) 6.c.3, 11.c.2
going along with [お]つきあい (n) [お = ↑] 6.a.add
golden week ゴールデンウィーク (n) [a long holiday week between 4/29 through 5/4] 10.gr.2
golf ゴルフ (n) 1.d.1
golf club ゴルフクラブ (n) 6.lc1, 7.c.1
golf tour ゴルフツアー (n) 5.com.2
golf tournament ゴルフたいかい (ゴルフ大会) (n) 7.c.2
good りょうこう (良好) (な-adj) 1.rw.
good いい, よい (良い), よろしい (い-adj) [よい／よろしい = more formal than いい] 1.b.conv, 1.gr.2, 3.f.5, 4.d.conv, 11.b.conv
good; satisfactory けっこう (結構) (な-adj) [けっこうです: No, thank you] 3.c.1, 5.b.conv
good at (and likes it) [お]とくい (得意) (な-adj) [お = ↑] 1.d.conv
Good morning! おはようございます (phr) [POL of おはよう] 2.a.4
Good night! おやすみ (phr) 7.a.1
good will しんぼく (親睦) (n) 1.d.conv
good-natured ひとがいい (人がいい) (phr) 3.gr.2
goodness よさ (良さ) (n) 7.c.1
goods しなもの (品物) (phr) 6.gr.4, 11.b.2
graduation そつぎょう (卒業) (n) 1.rw
grateful ありがたい (い-adj) 7.c.conv
gratitude おんれい (御礼) (n) [おん = ↑] 7.rw.1
greeting あいさつ (挨拶) (n) 6.b.4, 6.gr.4
Greeting! [an opening remark in a letter] はいけい (拝啓) (n) 7.rw.1
ground ち (地) (n) 8.c.conv
ground work to secure support/agreement ねまわし (根回し) (n) [lit. "root-binding before transplanting a tree"] 4.d.conv, 9.gr.4, 11.a.conv
group decision form りんぎしょ (稟議書) (n) 11.a.conv
group decision number りんぎばんごう (稟議番号) (n) 11.c.3
grouped by the category こうもくべつに (項目別に) (n) 1.e.2
grow, growth せいちょう (成長) する (v) 3.gr.4
Guam グアム (n) 10.gr.2
guardian ほごしゃ (保護者) (n) 1.e.2
guest おきゃくさま (お客様) (n) [お = ↑] 2.a.1, 5.b.conv
guide ガイド (n) 8.b.conv
gymnasium たいいくかん (体育館) (n) 1.gr.8

had better 〜たほうがいい (〜た方がいい) (phr) 4.a.5
hair かみ (髪) (n) 5.lc
hair style ヘアスタイル (n) 10.gr.4
half an hour さんじゅっぷん (三十分) (num) 7.c.1
ham/amateur radio アマチュアむせん (アマチュア無線) (n) 1.rw.
hand て (手) (n) [手で "by hand"] 1.gr.5
hand writing てがき (手書き) (n) 5.b.1
handling あつかい (扱い) (n) 5.e.conv
handling charge てすうりょう (手数料) (n) 5.e.conv
hang (it) on かける (v) [でんわをかける "call"] 6.b.1
hangover ふつかよい (二日酔い) (n) 6.b.4
hard きつい (い-adj) 10.gr.3
hard disk ハードディスク (n) 5.gr.6
hard-working まじめ (真面目) (な-adj) 6.lc
hardware ハードウェア (n) 1.rw.
has become なっております↓ (phr) 9.a.conv
has just sent (it) in おくってきたばかり (送ってきたばかり) (phr) 11.a.2
has just submitted だしたばかり (出したばかり) (phr) 11.a.conv
hate いや (嫌) (な-adj) 10.lc
have a contract けいやく (契約) する (n/v) 4.gr.9
have a phone call でんわがある (電話がある), でんわがはいっている (電話が入っている) (phr) 3.b.add
have just arrived ついたばかり (着いたばかり) (phr) 9.c.3
have just come back after eating たべてきたばかり (食べて来たばかり) (phr) 9.c.3
have just drunk のんだばかり (飲んだばかり) (phr) 9.c.3
have just used つかったばかり (使ったばかり) (phr) 9.c.3
he; him かれ (彼) (pro) 5.lc, 6.a.6, 7.d.conv
head あたま (頭) (n) [あたまがいたい "to have a headache"] 1.gr.6
health けんこう (健康) (n) 1.e.2
healthy げんき (元気) (な-adj) 7.e.2
Heavens no! とんでもない (phr) 6.c.conv
Heisei era へいせい (平成) (n) [1989-present] 1.rw.
Hello [on the telephone] もしもし (interj) 3.a.conv
help てつだう (手伝う) (v), おてつだい (お手伝い) する↓ (n/v) 7.d.2, 7.e.3, 7.lc
helped おせわになる (phr) 8.c.3
here, this place ここ (pro) 2.a.conv
high たかい (高い) (い-adj) 1.b.1
high performance こうせいのう (高性能) (n) 1.c.conv
high school こうこう (高校) (n) 1.rw.
high technology ハイテク (n) 1.c.add
high yen; appreciation of the yen えんだか (円高) (n) 11.lc
hiragana ひらがな (n) 5.b.conv
hiring こよう (雇用) (n) 11.c.3
history れきし (歴史) (n) 1.b.conv
hit うつ (打つ) (v) [ワープロをうつ] 3.gr.3, 8.b.1
hit commercial product ヒットしょうひん (ヒット商品) (n) 10.c.conv
hobby しゅみ (趣味) (n) 1.d.2
Hokkaido ほっかいどう (北海道) (n) 1.gr.5
hold back, reservation えんりょ (遠慮) する (n/v) 6.b.4, 6.gr.3
hold, carry, have もつ (持つ) (v) [もっていく "bring"] 2.a.2, 8.b.1

hold down おさえる (v) 5.c.1
holiday おやすみ (phr) 7.a.1
home [ご]じたく (自宅) (n) [ご = ↑] 5.rw.1
home residence じたく (自宅) (n) 5.f.2
home town [ご]しゅっしん (出身) (n) [ご = ↑] 1.d.2
home, house [お]すまい (住まい) (n) [お = ↑] 1.gr.1
home-made miso (Japanese bean paste) [てまえみそですが (idiom) "I don't mean to brag, but..."]. てまえみそ (手前味噌) (n) 8.b.conv
home; house; inside; we/us うち (家) (n) 1.a.1
honest しょうじき (正直) (な-adj) [しょうじきなところ "to be honest"] 8.b.conv
hospital びょういん (病院) (n) 2.a.2
host ホスト (n) 11.b.2
hot あつい (熱い) (い-adj) 1.c.3
hot [of weather] あつい (暑い) (い-adj) 5.c.1, 7.d.conv
hotel ホテル (n) 1.b.1
hourly wage じかんきゅう (時間給) (n) 11.c.3
hours; time じかん (時間) [お時間 your time] (ct/n) 1.gr.4
house いえ (家) (n) 1.com.4
house/home おたく (お宅) (n) [お = ↑] 2.a.1
How come? Why? どうして (qw) 1.b.6, 4.c.conv
How do you do? はじめまして (初めまして) (phr) 2.a.add
How is it being done? どうなっていますか (phr) 9.c.conv
how long; how much どのぐらい (qw) 2.c.1
how many days なんにち (何日) (qw) 4.gr.8
how many units of cars, machines, etc. なんだい (何台) (qw) 9.b.2
how many [sheets]? なんまい (何枚) (qw) 6.gr.2
how much いくら (qw) 9.c.2
how?; how about? どう, いかが (qw) 2.a.2
however, but しかし (con) 8.b.conv
hurry いそぐ (急ぐ) (v) 1.b.5, 2.c.2, 3.d.1

I

I congratulate. およろこびもうしあげます↓ (お慶び申し上げます) (phr) 9.rw.1
I kept you waiting. おまたせいたしました↓ (お待たせいたしました) (v) 3.d.conv, 7.b.conv, 7.b.conv
I know. ぞんじております↓ (存じております) (phr) [= しっています] 1.gr.8
I see; That makes sense. なるほど (phr) 1.c.conv
I switched the phone. [... speaking] おでんわかわりました (お電話代わりました) (phr) 3.b.conv
I will meet あってみよう (会ってみよう) (phr) 7.e.conv
I will wait (for you) おまち (お待ち) する↓ (v) [= まちます] 2.gr.3
I wish for your best regard. よろしくおねがいします (よろしくお願いします) (phr) 2.a.conv
I wonder かな, かね (sp) [かね = blunt informal question] 3.d.4, 4.c.conv, 10.c.conv
I wonder if I could... できますでしょうか (phr) [softer than できますか] 7.a.conv
I would like to say もうしあげたくぞんじます (申し上げたく存じます) (phr) 7.rw.1
I'll take the liberty of doing it. やらせていただきます (phr) 9.a.2
I'll take the liberty of sending it to you. おくらせていただきます (送らせていただきます) (phr) 9.a.2
I'm about to call. でんわをかけるところ (電話をかける所) (phr) 9.c.4
I'm fine, thank you. おかげさまで (phr) 8.gr.8
I'm sorry (for what I did). もうしわけありませんでした (申し訳ありませんでした) (phr) 7.a.1
I'm sorry; I have no excuse. すみません, もうしわけ (申し訳) ありません; もうしわけ (申し訳) ございません (phr) 3.c.conv; 6.b.3, 7.a.1
I, me わたし (私), わたくし (私) (pro) [わたくし = more formal] 1.a.conv, 2.a.1; ぼく (pro) [male] 6.b.conv
idle; not busy [お]ひま (暇) (な-adj) 2.a.2, 6.a.3
if ... exist; if ... have あったら (v) 2.a.conv
if it is だったら, でしたら (cop) 2.a.2
if it's what you may call it なんでしたら (何でしたら) (phr) 10.b.conv
if one can できたら (v) 2.a.2
if there is; if you have ありましたら (v) 2.a.2
if there isn't/aren't なかったら (い-adj) 2.gr.1
if you say that というと (と言うと), とおっしゃると↑ (phr) 8.c.4
if/provided I can make a request おねがいできれば (お願いできれば) (phr) 11.b.conv
if/provided it is good/OK よろしければ (い-adj) 7.gr.2
if/provided it is not N じゃなければ (cop) 7.c.2
if/provided it is not... でなければ (cop) 3.d.conv
if/provided it is that... なら (cop) 7.c.2, 7.e.conv
if/provided one comes くれば (来れば) (v) 7.c.2
if/provided one does すれば (v) 7.c.2
if/provided one thinks おもえば (思えば) (v) 7.c.2
if/provided that one can do できれば (v) 7.d.conv
if/provided there isn't なければ (い-adj) 7.c.2
if/when(ever) と (con) 4.d.conv, 7.c.conv
if; suppose もし (phr) 3.f.conv
illness びょうき (病気) (n) 1.b.1
immediate さっきゅう (早急) (な-adj) 9.c.conv
immediate answer そくとう (即答) (n) 4.d.conv
immediately すぐ, さっそく (早速) (adv) 1.b.6, 2.b.conv, 6.b.3
immediately (in response to something) おりかえし (折り返し) (n) 7.gr.4
impolite, rude しつれい (失礼) (な-adj) 2.e.conv
import ゆにゅう (輸入) する (n/v) 4.d.1
important; precious だいじ (大事) (な-adj) 6.gr.3
impossible; unsatisfactory ふか (不可) (n) 5.rw.1
impossible むり (無理) (な-adj) 3.f.5, 11.b.2
in において (phr) 7.rw.1
in a hurry [お]いそぎ (急ぎ) (n) [お = ↑] 3.d.conv, 3.f.5, 3.gr.3
in addition なお, それと (con) v, 9.rw.1
in favor さんせい (賛成) (n) 10.c.1
in front of one's eyes もくぜん (目前) (n) 10.rw.1
in front of people ひとまえ (人前) (n) 1.d.1
in progress しんこうちゅう (進行中) (n) 11.c.3
in recent years きんねん (近年) (n) 7.rw.1
in some way どうか (phr) 2.c.1, 6.a.3
in such a way ように (phr) 3.e.conv, 6.b.3
in such a way that..., to the effect that... というふうに (phr) 10.c.conv
in that regard ちなみに (con) 8.b.conv

Appendix C: English-Japanese Glossary

in that way あのように, あんなふうに (phr) 10.c.2; そのように, そんなふうに (phr) 10.c.4
in the middle of a meeting かいぎちゅう (会議中) (n) 3.d.conv
in the middle of absence るすちゅう (留守中) (n) 3.d.add
in the middle of meeting a client せっきゃくちゅう (接客中) (n) 3.d.add
in the middle of work しごとちゅう (仕事中) (n) 3.d.add
in the morning (during 'a.m.') ごぜんちゅう (午前中) (n) 1.b.3
in the near future ちかいうちに (近いうちに) (phr) 7.b.conv
in this connection ちなみに (con) 8.b.conv
in trouble こまる (v) 4.a.conv
in [location of activities] で (p) 1.a.conv
incidentally, by the way ところで (con) 1.c.conv; さて (con) 7.rw.1
included つき (suf) [バストイレつき "equipped with a bathroom and a toilet"] 10.a.1
including meals しょくじつき (食事付き) (n) 10.a.1
inconvenient ふべん (不便) (な-adj) 1.gr.8
increased competition きょうそうげきか (競争激化) (n) 10.rw.1
increases ふえる (増える) (vi) [vt: ふやす] 4.d.1
increasingly ますます (益々) (adv) 7.rw.1
industry さんぎょう (産業) (n) 1.c.add
inflation インフレ (n) 5.gr.6
information materials しりょう (資料) (n) 7.a.3, 7.e.conv
information processing じょうほうしょり (情報処理) (n) 1.rw
initial とうしょ (当初) (n) 10.rw.1
inquire といあわせる (問い合わせる) (v) 10.b.conv
inside なか (中) (n) 9.a.3
inside; range (of comparison); I, we うち (内) (n) 2.d.conv
install インストールする (n/v) 7.b.3
installation construction ふせつこうじ (敷設工事) (n) 3.rw.2
insufficient ふじゅうぶん (不十分) (な-adj) 9.c.conv
insurance ほけん (保険) (n) 10.gr.1
intention, plan つもり (n) 2.c.conv
intentionally わざわざ (adv) 10.b.conv
intercom れんらくようのでんわ (連絡用の電話) (n) 5.f.conv
interest きょうみ (興味) (n) 1.b.conv
interest [of a bank account] りし (利子) (n) 5.b.1
interested (in) きょうみがある (興味がある) (phr) 10.c.3
interesting おもしろい (い-adj) 1.a.1, 3.gr.6
interfere [お]じゃま (邪魔) する (n/v) [↓] 7.a.1
intermediate ちゅうきゅう (中級) (n) 6.gr.7
international こくさい (国際) (n) 8.gr.7
international conference こくさいかいぎ (国際会議) (n) 1.lc
international relations (study/theory of) こくさいかんけいろん (国際関係論) (n) 1.gr.2
Internet インターネット (n) 1.a.2
interpret, interpreting つうやく (通訳) する (n/v) 1.d.1, 1.lc
interview めんせつ (面接)する (n/v) 1.a.add
introduce, introduction [ご]しょうかいする (紹介する), 紹介なさいます↑, 紹介いたします↓ (v) [ご = ↑] 1.a.add, 1.e.1, 1.gr.8, 7.a.1
introduce oneself じこしょうかい (自己紹介)する (n/v) 1.a.conv
introduction letter しょうかいじょう (紹介状) (n) 3.f.5, 7.c.conv
invitation おさそい (お誘い) (n) 6.gr.4
invitation; guide ごあんない (ご案内) (n) 9.rw.1
invitation card あんないじょう (案内状) (n) 6.c.4
invite しょうたい (招待) する (n/v) 2.gr.8

is able to make つくることができる (作ることができる) (phr) 9.b.2
is able to ride のることができる (乗ることができる) (phr) 9.b.2
is able to speak はなすことができる (話すことができる) (phr) 9.b.2
is able to use つかうことができる (使うことができる) (phr) 9.b.2
is evaluated ひょうか (評価) される (n/v) [PASS of ひょうかする] 8.b.conv
is expanding/extending のばしつつある (伸ばしつつある) (phr) [V つつある "is V-ing"; = のばしている] 7.rw.1
Is he/she there, I wonder? いるかね (phr) [blunt, masculine] 3.d.4
is heard きこえる (v) 6.b.conv
is not, hasn't おりません↓ (v) 3.e.conv, 6.a.3
is not; are not じゃありません (cop) 1.d.1
is on the phone でんわちゅう (電話中) (n) 3.d.add
is poor at (and dislikes it) にがて (苦手) (な-adj) 1.d.add
is supposed that S ことになっている (phr) 6.c.conv
Is that right? そうか (phr) [PLAIN of そうですか] 3.c.1
is, are だ, です, でございます (cop) 1.a.conv, 1.b.6, 3.a.1, 3.d.conv
is, stays [animate] おられます (v) [↑ PASS of おります] 8.c.5
is/are (not) じゃ (phr) [contraction of では: copula + は] 6.b.conv
is/are... and でして, でございまして、 (cop) [polite て-form of です] 3.f.conv, 3.f.1
is/are; being で (cop) [て-form of だ/です] 1.b.conv
is/has returned おもどりでしょう (お戻りでしょう) (phr) 3.e.conv
isle side つうろがわ (通路側) (n) 3.gr.4
isn't it?; don't you see? じゃないか (phr) [blunt] 4.a.conv
isn't/aren't じゃない (cop) 2.c.conv
(it's) that... の (nom) [PLAIN form of んです] 2.b.conv
it is done なっております↓ (phr) 9.a.conv
it looks it may become cheap やすくなりそう (安くなりそう) (phr) 11.a.conv
it's that it's N 〜なんだ (phr) [PLAIN of 〜なんです] 4.gr.3, 7.b.3
It's that... 〜んです (phr) [sentence ending indicating explanation or inference] 1.a.1

J

Japan にほん (日本) (n) 1.b.6
Japan Economy Newspaper にほんけいざいしんぶん (日本経済新聞) (n) 9.a.3
Japan Industrial Standard JISきかく (JIS規格) (n) 9.b.conv
Japan-U.S. にちべい (日米) (n) 1.a.2
Japanese blues [song] えんか (演歌) (n) 1.d.1
Japanese car にほんしゃ (日本車) (n) 1.gr.5
Japanese cooking, Japanese foods にほんりょうり (日本料理), にほんしょく (日本食), わしょく (和食) (n) 1.com.4, 11.b.2
Japanese language にほんご (日本語) (n) 1.b.5
Japanese soba noodles そば (n) 6.lc
Japanese tea おちゃ (お茶) (n) 2.b.conv
Japanese-like にほんじんてき (日本人的) (な-adj) 5.d.1
Japanese-style inn りょかん (旅館) (n) 3.gr.3
Japanese-style pancake おこのみやき (お好み焼き) (n) 10.gr.4
Japanese-style restaurant りょうてい (料亭) (n) 6.c.conv

JETRO (Japan External Trade Organization) ジェトロ (n) 7.a.conv
job, work おつとめ (勤め) (n) [お = ↑] 1.c.conv; [お]しごと (仕事) (n) [お = ↑] 1.c.1
job type しょくしゅ (職種) (n) 11.c.3
joint venture ジョイントベンチャー (n) 10.c.2
joy [お]よろこび (慶び) (n) [お = ↑] 7.rw.1
joy たのしみ (楽しみ) (n) 6.b.4
July しちがつ (七月) (num) 2.gr.7
just in case いちおう (一応) (adv) 4.a.conv
just, only ばかり (n) [V-past ばかり "has just V-ed"] 9.c.conv

K

kanji かんじ (漢字) (n) 6.gr.3
karaoke bar カラオケバー (n) 6.a.conv
karaoke; sing-along machine カラオケ (n) [カラ "empty"; オケ a short form of "orchestra"] 1.d.1
keep (someone) waiting またせている (待たせている) (phr) [て-form of またせる + いる] 9.a.1
keep (something) open for later use あけといて (開けといて) (v) [Contraction of あけておいて] 6.a.conv
key かぎ (鍵) (n) [かぎをかける "to lock"; かぎがかかる "(something) gets locked"] 6.c.4
keyboard キーボード (n) 10.gr.1
kind consideration ごこうはい (ご高配) (n) 7.rw.1
kind, type しゅるい (種類) (n) 5.rw.1
know しっています (知っています), ごぞんじだ↑ (ご存知だ) (phr) 3.c.1, 3.gr.5, 6.com.1
known しられている (知られている) (v) 8.b.1
Kyoto [a city in Japan] きょうと (京都) (n) 6.com.1

L

L/C (letter of credit) エルシー (n) 11.b.conv
laptop computer ラップトップ (n) 6.a.6
large おおきい (大きい) (い-adj) 1.d.1, 6.b.3
large-room-ism おおべやしゅぎ (大部屋主義) (n) 2.b.1
large-scale project おおがたきかく (大型企画) (n) 7.e.2
laser レーザー (n) 4.d.1
laser printer レーザープリンタ (n) 4.c.2
last つづく (続く) (v) 7.gr.3
last month せんげつ (先月) (n) 1.gr.5
last night ゆうべ (夕べ) (n) 1.gr.6
last week せんしゅう (先週) (n) 11.c.conv
last year きょねん (去年) (n) 3.gr.1
late; become late おくれる (遅れる) (v) [= おそくなる] 1.gr.8, 2.c.2, 11.c.conv
late; slow おそい (遅い) (い-adj) [おそくなる "become late"] 3.gr.3, 5.b.1, 5.g.1, 8.c.4
lately, these days このごろ (この頃) (phr) 7.com., 9.b.3
later のちほど (後ほど) (n) 3.f.conv
later, subsequently おって (追って) (phr) 1.e.conv
leave でる (出る), おで (お出) になる↑ (vi) [= でる] [vt: だす／おだしになる↑] 1.b.6, 3.f.5, 6.a.1, 6.gr.1
left (side) ひだり (左) (n) 1.b.1
leftover のこりもの (残り物) (n) 8.gr.8
lend かす (貸す), お貸しする↓ (v) 5.g.1, 6.gr.5
lesson レッスン (n) 3.gr.7

let me explain [ご]せつめい (説明) させていただきます (phr) 9.a.conv
Let me see. そうだな (interj) 2.a.conv
let me think かんがえさせてください (考えさせて下さい) (phr) 9.a.2
let someone in おとおしする↓ (お通しする) (v) [= とおす] 8.c.5, 8.lc
Let's decide on what you call ... ～ということにしましょう (phr) 10.b.conv
let's do it; we shall do it. しよう, しましょう (v) 4.a.2, 6.a.2, 6.a.6
let's go!; I will come/go. まいりましょう (参りましょう) (v) 3.lc, 6.c.conv
let's present (it) at the meeting かけよう (v) 11.a.conv
let's speak/talk はなそう (話そう) (v) 1.d.conv
Let's-Speak Society はなそうかい (話そう会) (n) 1.d.conv
letter, character じ (字) (n) 1.gr.6
letter, mail てがみ (手紙) (n) 3.e.1
library としょかん (図書館) (n) 1.gr.6
license めんきょ (免許) (n) 1.e.2
light, electricity; electric でんき (電気) (n) 3.a.2
like のような, のように, ような (phr) 7.e.1
like that あのように, あんなふうに (phr) 10.c.2; そのように, そんなふうに (phr) 10.c.4
like the best だいすき (大好き) (な-adj) 2.gr.5
like; be fond of; favorite [お]すき (好き) (な-adj) [お = ↑] 1.b.6, 1.d.1
like; likely; appearance ふうの, ふうに (phr) 10.c.2
listen (something); accept (something) うけたまわる↓ (承る) (v) [= きく] 3.f.conv
live; reside すむ (住む) (v) 1.d.1
load とうさい (搭載) する (n/v) 9.a.conv
lobby ロビー (n) 1.gr.2
located for immediate use; be ready ひかえ (控え) (v) [V-stem of ひかえる] 10.rw.1
locations かしょ (箇所) (ct) [counter for locations] 2.c.conv
lock かぎ (鍵) (n) 6.c.4
locked, applied, etc. かかっている (phr) 6.c.4
lonely [お]さびしい (淋しい) (い-adj) [お = ↑] 11.lc
long ながい (長い) (い-adj) 1.com.1, 7.gr.3
Long time, no see. [お]ひさしぶり (久しぶり), しばらく (n) [お = ↑] 5.c.conv, 8.a.conv
look forward to たのしみ (楽しみ) にする (phr) 6.b.4
look healthy げんき (元気) そうだ (phr) 8.a.1
look, watch, see みる (見る), ごらん (ご覧) になる↑ (v), はいけん (拝見) する↓ (n/v) 1.b.5, 5.f.conv, 6.a.3, 6.a.5, 7.a.3, 7.rw.2, 7.lc, 9.c.4
looks good よさそう (良さそう) (phr) 8.a.1
looks it can be done できそう (phr) 8.a.1
looks it can't be done できなさそう (phr) 8.a.1
looks it's not good よくなさそう (良くなさそう) (phr) 8.a.1
looks there is nothing なさそう (phr) 8.a.1, 9.c.2
Los Angeles ロスアンジェルス or ロス (n) 5.com.1, 10.gr.2
lose まける (負ける) (v) 11.b.2
loud voice おおごえ (大声) (n) 6.b.conv
low cost ていコスト (低コスト) (n) 1.c.conv
lower さがる (下がる) (vi) [vt: さげる] 11.a.conv, 11.gr.4
lower the price ねびき (値引き) する, ねさげ (値下げ) する (n/v) 4.d.conv, 7.gr.4, 10.a.2
lower, reduce さげる (下げる) (vt) [vi: さがる] 11.a.conv

luck ことぶき (寿) (n) 2.c.3
lucky ついている (v) 8.c.4
lunch ひるごはん (昼ご飯) (n) 1.gr.8
lunch; noon おひる (お昼) (n) 3.f.5

M

machine きかい (機械) (n) 5.f.conv
machine equipment きき (機器) (n) 7.a.conv
machine-like きかいてき (機械的), (な-adj) 5.d.1
machine/car counter だい (ct) 11.b.1
make/let (it) run, operate はしらせる (走らせる) (v) 9.b.conv
make/let (someone) come こさせる (来させる) (v) 9.a.1
make/let (something/someone) match, be compatible あわせる (合わせる) (v) 9.b.conv
magazine ざっし (雑誌) (n) 8.b.1
mahjong [Chinese game similar to a game of bridge] マージャン (n) 2.b.1
mailing address れんらくさき (連絡先) (n) 1.e.2
main division manager ほんぶちょう (本部長) (n) 11.c.3
main office, headquarter ほんしゃ (本社) (n) 10.b.conv
main products しゅようせいひん (主要製品) (n) 8.rw.1
Mainichi Newspaper まいにちしんぶん (毎日新聞) (n) 9.a.3
major (in college) せんこう (専攻) (n) 1.a.1
major (in) せんこう (専攻) する, 専攻なさる↑, 専攻いたします↓ (v) 1.a.conv, 1.b.2, 1.e.1
make a contract けいやく (契約) する, 契約にこぎつける (v) 7.gr.5, 11.c.2
make a phone call; call でんわ (電話) をかける (phr) 3.a.add
make it a rule to... ことにする (phr) 6.gr.4
make oneself understood つうじる (通じる) (v) 4.gr.3
make sure ねんのため (念のため) (phr) 11.rw.1
make the most of いかす (活かす) (v) 1.b.3, 8.b.1
make, create つくる (作る) (v), さくせい (作成) する (n/v) 1.b.1, 4.rw.2
make/let (someone) do させる (v) [CAUS of する] 9.a.conv, 9.a.1
make; cook つくる (作る), お作りになる↑ (v) 1.b.1, 5.a.conv, 8.b.1
male; man だんせい (男性) (n) 6.rw., 7.d.add
manage (business), management けいえい (経営) する (n/v) 7.gr.10
management けいえい (経営), マネジメント (n) 1.com.4, 8.c.conv
managing director じょうむとりしまりやく (常務取締役) (n) 4.e.3
manual マニュアル (n) 2.gr.4
manufacturing せいぞう (製造) (n) 4.e.2, 7.a.conv
manufacturing (plant) せいさくしょ (製作所) (n) 3.f.conv
manufacturing; manufacturer こうぎょう (工業) (n) 3.c.conv
many, numerous おおい (多い) (い-adj) 2.b.1, 4.gr.3
March さんがつ (三月) (num) 3.gr.1
margin マージン (n) 10.b.conv
market しじょう (市場) (n) 7.b.conv
market share マーケットシェア (n) 9.a.3
marketing マーケティング (n) 7.lc
married, marriage けっこん (結婚) する (n/v) 6.c.1
mass, massive たいりょう (大量) (n) 8.c.conv
match あわせる (合わせる) (v) 9.b.conv
match deliberately あわせてある (合わせてある) (v) 9.b.conv

match, be compatible あう (合う) (v) 9.b.conv
match, cope たいおうする (対応する) (v) 7.gr.4
mathematics すうがく (数学) (n) 1.rw.
matter, fact こと (n) 2.a.conv
matter, thing もの (n) 11.b.conv
matter, incident けん (件) (n) 3.rw.2, 4.d.conv, 7.a.3
meal ごはん (ご飯), しょくじ (食事) (n) 1.b.2, 5.gr.3
meaning, interpretation いみ (意味) (n) 5.a.add
mechanical きかいてき (機械的), (な-adj) 5.d.1
medicine くすり (薬) (n) 3.f.4
meet あつまる (集まる) (vi) 4.e.conv
meet, see あう (会う) (v) 3.c.1
meeting ミーティング (n) 1.a.2
meeting for explanation, exposition, etc. せつめいかい (説明会) (n) 9.rw.1
meeting log; minutes かいぎろく (会議録) (n) 6.gr.2
meeting; society; club かい (会) (n) 1.d.conv
megabyte メガバイト (ct) 7.b.3
Meiji era めいじ (明治) (n) [1868-1912] 5.rw.1
memory メモリー (n) 4.d.2
memory chip メモリーチップ (n) 1.b.2, 9.gr.5
men and women だんじょ (男女) (n) 11.c.3
merchandise しょうひん (商品) (n) 8.b.conv
merit メリット (n) 8.lc
message メッセージ, でんごん (伝言), [お]ことづけ (言付け) (n) [お = ↑] 3.e.add
method ほうほう (方法) (n) 11.b.conv
meticulous ていねい (丁寧) (な-adj) 8.c.4
meticulously; carefully ていねいに (丁寧に) (adv) 10.gr.3
Mexico メキシコ (n) 8.gr.2
microprocessor マイクロプロセッサ (n) 9.a.conv
middle of activity/operation/journey とちゅう (途中) (n) 7.gr.8
middle of flight; during flight ひこうちゅう (飛行中) (n) 2.gr.7
middle of studying べんきょうちゅう (勉強中) (n) 1.d.conv
middle [of] ちゅう (中) (n) 4.a.conv
might lower (something) さげる (下げる) かもしれない (phr) 11.a.3
mind, feelings, spirit, attention き (気) (n) 4.a.conv
Ministry of Foreign Affairs がいむしょう (外務省) (n) 3.lc
minutes [on the clock] 〜ふん (分) (ct) 2.c.3
mistake エラー, まちがい (間違い) (n) 8.lc, 9.gr.5
modem モデム (n) 4.c.2, 9.lc
modern; contemporary げんだい (現代) (n) 4.c.2
Monday げつよう[び] (月曜[日]) (n) 5.gr.5, 5.com.2
money おかね (お金) (n) 5.a.1, 5.d.conv
money in a bank account よきん (預金) (n) 5.b.conv
monitor モニター (n) 10.gr.1
month; the moon つき (月) (n) 1.d.conv
more もっと (adv) [もっといい "better"] 4.d.conv
morning あさ (朝) (n) 5.gr.5
morning sun; Asahi [last name] あさひ (朝日) (n) 3.c.conv
mother [お]かあさん↑ (お母さん), はは (母)↓ (n) [お = ↑] 1.c.1, 1.gr.6
(not) at all ちっとも (adv) [followed by NEG; = ぜんぜん] 9.b.1
motivation どうき (動機) (n) 1.e.2
motto, slogan モットー (n) 9.c.conv
movie えいが (映画) (n) 1.com.4

Mr., Mrs., Miss, Ms. ～さま (様) (suf) [↑ title used after names] 2.a.1
Mr., Mrs., Miss, Ms. ～さん (suf) [title used after names] 1.a.1
multimedia マルチメディア (n) 3.a.conv
multiply かける (v) 1.a.conv, 2.d.conv, 6.a.1, 6.c.4
music おんがく (音楽) (n) 1.lc
must arrive ひっちゃく (必着) (n) 11.rw.1
my company, home, self うち (内) (n) 1.b.2

N

Nagoya [a city in Japan] なごや (名古屋) (n) 6.gr.1
nail くぎ (釘) (n) 8.b.1
naive ひと (人) がいい (phr) 3.gr.2
name しめい (氏名) (n) 1.e.2
name recognition ちめいど (知名度) (n) 8.b.conv
narrow, cramped せまい (狭い) (い-adj) 1.c.3
natural gas ガス (n) 5.d.conv
natural thing; obvious thing あたりまえ (当たり前) (n) 4.a.5
near ちかい (近い) (い-adj) 1.com.4
nearsighted め (目) がわる (悪) い (phr) 6.gr.9
necessary よう (要) (n) [written text only] 5.rw.1
need, be necessary いる (要る) (v)、ひつよう (必要) (な-adj) 4.c.conv
negotiate, negotiation こうしょう (交渉) する (n/v) 4.d.conv, 11.lc
never ぜんぜん (全然) (n) [followed by NEG] 2.b.1
never, not at all けっして (決して) (adv) [followed by NEG] 8.b.conv
new あたらしい (新しい) (い-adj) 6.a.6
new account [ご]しんき (新規) (n) [ご= ↑] 5.a.conv
New Age ニューエージ (n) 10.gr.4
new model しんがた (新型) (n) 1.b.add
new product しんせいひん (新製品) (n) 1.b.conv
New York ニューヨーク (n) 1.a.1
newly hired employee しんにゅうしゃいん (新入社員) (n) 2.b.conv
news ニュース (n) 9.c.4
newspaper しんぶん (新聞) (n) 1.b.2, 1.gr.5
newspaper article きじ (記事) (n) 7.d.2
next つぎ (次) (n) 1.a.conv
next (side), neighbor となり (隣) (n) 7.b.3
next month らいげつ (来月) (n) 3.b.1
next time こんど (今度) (n) 1.a.2
next time; next chance このつぎ (この次) (phr) 9.a.1
next week らいしゅう (来週) (n) 3.gr.4
next year らいねん (来年) (n) 4.gr.6
next [academic] term らいがっき (来学期) (n) 6.gr.7
Nice to meet you! よろしく (phr) [Request phrase] 1.a.conv
night; evening ばん (晩) (n) 6.a.conv
Nikkei Journal (Japan Economic Newspaper) にほんけいざいしんぶん (日本経済新聞) (n) 8.b.1
nine o'clock くじ (九時) (num) 11.a.3
ninety's 90ねんだい (90年代) (num) 5.gr.8
no good; useless だめ (な-adj) 6.b.4
no-law occasion ぶれいこう (無礼講) (n) 6.b
no matter how (much) どんなに (phr) 11.b.2
no matter how I do it; however I do it どうしても (phr) 11.b.2

no matter who it is; whoever it is だれでも (誰でも) (phr) 11.b.2
No, no. いえいえ、いやいや (interj) 6.c.conv, 8.a.conv
No. いいえ、いえ、いや (interj) 1.d.conv, 6.c.conv
noisy うるさい (い-adj) 7.b.3
none なし (n) 1.rw.
noon; lunch おひる (お昼) (n) 3.f.5
North America ほくべい (北米) (n) , 3.com.3
not いな (否) (n) 5.rw.1
not anyone; no one だれも (誰も), どなたも ↑ (phr) [followed by NEG] 6.a.3
not anything; nothing なにも (何も) (phr) [followed by NEG] 6.a.3
not busy ひま (暇) (な-adj) 2.a.2
not buy in advance かっとかない (買っとかない) (phr) [contraction of かっておかない] 4.a.4
not do しない (v) [NEG of する] 5.b.1
not do; not give やらない (v) [NEG of やる] 6.gr.2
not doing (side) しないほう (しない方) (phr) 8.c.3
not meaningful いみがない (意味がない) (phr) 11.b.2
(not) particularly べつに (別に) (adv) 6.a.conv
not stay; not to be; there isn't/aren't [animate]; not come; not go いらっしゃいません↑ (v) [= いない] 6.a.3
(not) to anyone だれにも (誰にも) (phr) 6.gr.6
(not) very much; (not) very often あんまり、あまり (adv) [followed by NEG] 1.b.1, 1.d.conv
(not) yet まだ (adv) 3.e.conv
notebook/laptop computer division ノートパソコンぶもん (ノートパソコン部門) (n) 7.rw.1
notes き (記) (n) 9.rw.1, 11.c.3
nothing; whatever なんにも (何にも) (phr) [followed by NEG] 6.lc
notice おしらせ (お知らせ) (n) 6.rw.
notification, contact, communication [ご]れんらく (連絡) (n) [ご= ↑] 3.f.conv
notify しらせる (知らせる)、おしらせいたします↓ (お知らせいたします) (v) 1.e.conv
number ばんごう (番号) (n) 11.c.3
number of units (machines) だいすう (台数) (n) 10.a.convs
number one; first だいいち (第一) (num) 9.c.conv
number tag, number card ばんごうふだ (番号札) (n) 5.a.conv
number three だい3ごう (第 3 号) (num) 11.c.3
number, digit すうじ (数字) (n) 5.c.conv
nutrition えいよう (栄養) (n) 7.gr.2

O

obliged, feel terribly sorry きょうしゅく (恐縮) する (n/v) 2.e.add, 7.gr.4
occasion, time さい (際) (n) [X のさい "at the time of X"] 7.c.conv
of course もちろん (adv) 9.b.conv
office オフィス、じむしょ (事務所) (n) 1.b.1, 2.b.2
oh! あ (interj) 2.d.conv
oh!, uhh! ああ (interj) 1.a.conv
Oh, (I see.) ほう (interj) 1.d.conv
oh? え (interj) 2.b.conv
oil painting あぶらえ (油絵) (n) 10.gr.4
oil; petroleum せきゆ (石油) (n) 5.c.1, 10.gr.1

OK; all right; safe　だいじょうぶ（大丈夫）(な-adj) 2.c.conv
old [of things; not of people]　ふるい（古い）(い-adj) 6.gr.7
older brother　おにいさん↑（お兄さん），あに↓（兄）(n) 1.c.3, 1.gr.2
older sister　おねえさん↑（お姉さん），あね↓（姉）(n) 1.c.2, 1.c.3
omit　はぶく（省く）(v) 10.b.conv
on second thought　やっぱり (adv) 8.c.4, 11.a.conv
on top of that　そのうえ (con) 8.c.conv
once again　もういちど（もう一度）(phr) 5.gr.5
once in a while　たまには (adv) 10.gr.2
once, one time　いちど（一度）(n) 1.d.conv
one [お]ひとつ（一つ）(num) [Japanese series up to 10; お= ↑] 2.a.2
one cup　いっぱい（一杯）(num) 5.gr.6, 6.b.4
one day　いちにち（一日）(num) 5.e.1
one more cup　もういっぱい（もう一杯）(phr) 6.b.4
one more time; again　さいど（再度）(n) 10.rw.1
one night (stay)　いっぱく（一泊）(num) 10.a.1
one of them; whichever one (of many)　どれか (phr) 6.a.3
one person　ひとり（一人）(num) 6.com.2
one song　いっきょく（一曲）(num) 7.b.3
one unit (of machines)　いちだい（一台）(num) 10.a.conv
one week　いっしゅうかん（一週間）(num) 5.e.conv
one who returns home in the morning　ごぜんさま（午前様）(n) 6.b.4
one word; in brief　ひとこと（一言）(n) 10.gr.4
one year　いちねん（一年）(num) 3.gr.1; いちねんかん（一年間）(num) 9.a.1
one's best　いっしょけんめい（一所懸命）(n) 2.lc
one's colleague　どうりょう（同僚）(n) 2.a.add
one's junior　こうはい（後輩）(n) 2.a.add
one's own decision　いちぞん（一存）(n) 4.d.conv
one's senior　せんぱい（先輩）(n) 2.a.conv
one's subordinate　ぶか（部下）(n) 2.a.add
one's superior or supervisor　じょうし（上司）(n) 2.a.add
one-person relocation (transfer to a distant work place)　たんしんふにん（単身赴任）(n) 11.lc
one; V-ing　の (nom) 1.d.conv
only, just　だけ (p) 9.b.conv
open　ひらく（開く）(vt/vi) 5.a.conv, 8.c.5
open (something)　あける（開ける）(vt) [vi: あく] 6.a.1
open, is open　あく（開く）(vi) [vt: あける] 6.a.1, 6.a.conv
opinion　いけん（意見）(n) 5.gr.4
oppose, vs.　たい（対）する (n/v) 11.b.3
opposing opinion　はんたいいけん（反対意見）(n) 10.gr.1
opposite; opposed　はんたい（反対）(n) 10.c.1
optimistic　らっかんてき（楽観的）(な-adj) 10.c.add
order　ちゅうもん（注文）する (n/v) 4.b.conv; 6.gr.4, 10.a.conv
order form　ちゅうもんしょ（注文書）(n) 4.b.conv
order taking　ちゅうもんうけつけ（注文受付）(n) 11.c.3
ordinary, normal, regular　ふつう（普通）(n) 4.a.5, 5.b.conv
organizer [of an event],　かんじ（幹事）(n) 6.rw.1
origin　もと (n) 7.e.conv
origin of the proposal　きあん（起案）(n) 11.c.3
original price; production cost　げんか（原価）(n) 4.e.conv
originator of the proposal　きあんしゃ（起案者）(n) 11.c.3
Osaka [a city in Japan]　おおさか（大阪）(n) 4.a.conv

Ota Ward [of Tokyo]　おおたく（大田区）(n) 1.rw.
other　ほかの（他の），たの（他の）(phr) 9.b.3, 9.gr.3
other companies　たしゃ（他社）(n) 8.c.conv
other; another　ほか（他）(n) 10.gr.3
our company　わがしゃ（我が社），とうしゃ（当社），へいしゃ↓（弊社）(n) 1.b.conv, 9.rw.1, 11.rw.1
our men and women　うちのもの↓（うちの者）(phr) 3.c.1
outside　そと（外）(n) 9.a.1
over there, place beyond, the other side　むこう（向こう）(n) 3.gr.4
overexert; do the impossible　むり（無理）する (n/v) 6.b.4, 6.gr.3, 11.b.2
overseas job assignment　かいがいきんむ（海外勤務）(n) 9.a.1
overseas　かいがい（海外）(n) 2.d.conv
overtime pay　ざんぎょうてあて（残業手当）(n) 9.c.1
overtime work　ざんぎょう（残業）(n) 6.a.add

P

p.m.　ごご（午後）(n) 1.b.3
pachinko pinball machine　パチンコ (n) 2.b.1
paged by (owner of the phone)　～かたよびだし（～方呼び出し）(n) 1.e.2
pager　ポケベル (n) 1.c.3
painful　いたい（痛い），きつい (い-adj) 1.gr.6, 7.c.2, 10.gr.3
paper　ペーパー (n) 10.gr.2
parents　[ご]りょうしん（両親）(n) [ご = ↑], 1.gr.6
park　こうえん（公園）(n) 7.gr.4
part-time job　アルバイト (n) 1.rw.
part-time worker　パートタイマー (n) 11.c.3
participation　さんか（参加）(n) 6.rw.
party　パーティー (n) 7.b.3
party fee; fee for an event　かいひ（会費）(n) 6.rw.
pass through　とおる（通る）(vi) [vt: とおす] 6.a.1
pass [a test]　パスする (v) 9.b.2; ごうかく（合格）する (n/v) 11.gr.2
pass; put through　とおす（通す）(vt) [vi: とおる] 5.f.2, 6.a.1
passbook　つうちょう（通帳）(n) 5.rw.1
passport　パスポート (n) 4.gr.10
paste　ペーストする (v) 2.gr.7
patient　かんじゃ（患者）(n) 11.gr.4
pay　しはらう（支払う）(v) 5.gr.8
pay attention　きをつける（気をつける）(phr) 4.a.conv
payment　[お]しはらい（支払い）(v) [お = ↑] 5.d.conv, 5.gr.8, 11.b.conv
payment at sight　いちらんばらい（一覧払い）(n) 11.b.conv
payment method　しはらいほうほう（支払い方法）(n) 5.g.1
pen　ペン (n) 2.gr.4
people　ひとびと（人々）(n) 10.a.2
people　めい（名）(ct) [formal counter for people] 11.c.3
percentage of market share　しじょうせんゆうりつ（市場占有率）(n) 7.rw.1
period　きかん（期間）(n) 11.c.3
peripheral items/devices　ふぞくひん（付属品）(n) 10.lc
permission　きょか（許可）(n) 7.d.2
person　ひと（人），かた↑（方），もの↓（者）(n) 1.a.conv, 1.b.1, 3.c.1, 7.d.conv

person in charge かかりのもの (係りの者) (phr) 5.f.conv; [ご]たんとうしゃ (担当者) (n) [ご = ↑] 9.rw.1; たんとう (担当) (n) 10.a.3
personal computer パソコン (n) 8.c.3
personal disclosure form しんじょうしょ (身上書) (n) 1.e.2
personnel じんじ (人事) (n) 4.e.2
pessimistic ひかんてき (悲観的) (な-adj) 10.c.conv
pharmaceutical company せいやくかいしゃ (製薬会社) (n) 3.a.2
pharmaceutical [company] せいやく (製薬) (n) 3.a.2
phone call came all the way in かかってきた (phr) 11.a.1
phone is busy はなしちゅう (話し中) (n) 3.d.conv
phone number でんわばんごう (電話番号) (n) 3.e.conv
photograph しゃしん (写真) (n) 1.e.2
pick up the phone でんわをとる (電話を取る) (phr) 3.a.add
pie パイ (n) 2.b.1
pioneer, develop かいたく (開拓) する (n/v) 8.c.conv
pizza ピザ (n) 1.a.1
place ばしょ (場所), ところ (所) (n) 4.lc, 5.b.1, 6.gr.9, 6.rw
place of birth ほんせき (本籍) (n) 1.e.2
place of one's upbringing, background しゅっしん (出身) (n) 2.lc, 7.e.conv
place of the meeting かいじょう (会場) (n) 6.c.2, 9.rw.1
place; point in time/space ところ (所) (n) 1.lc, 2.c.conv, 3.d.conv, 6.gr.7, 7.a.conv
plain employee ひらしゃいん (平社員) (n) 4.e.3
plan けいかく (計画) (n) 11.c.3
plan, scheme はかる (図る) (v) 9.c.conv
plan; course of action はこび (運び) (n) 9.rw.1
planning きかく (企画) (n) 2.d.add
planning meeting; project meeting きかくかいぎ (企画会議) (n) 11.a.conv
planning report きかくしょ (企画書) (n) 6.lc
play; be idle あそぶ (遊ぶ) (v) 8.b.1, 9.gr.2
please なにとぞ (何とぞ) (adv) [FORMAL] 7.rw.1, 10.rw.1
please come おいでください↑ (おいで下さい) (phr) 5.g.conv, 6.rw., 7.a.2
Please eat. めしあがってください↑ (召し上がって下さい) (phr) [= たべてください] 11.b.2
Please enjoy. おたのしみください↑ (お楽しみ下さい) (phr) 6.b.4
Please inform. おつたえください↑ (お伝え下さい) (phr) 3.f.conv
please look at ごこうらんください↑ (ご高覧下さい) (phr) 9.rw.1, 11.rw.1
please participate ごさんかください↑ (ご参加下さい) (v) [= さんかする] 9.rw.1
please start (it) in advance はじめておいてください (始めておいて下さい) (phr) 9.c.1
Please take a look. ごらんください↑ (ご覧下さい) (phr) [= みてください] 8.b.conv
Please understand. ごりょうしょうください↑ (ご了承下さい) (v) [= 了承してください] 11.rw.1
Please wait. おまちください (ませ)↑ (お待ち下さい(ませ)) (phr) 3.b.conv, 7.b.conv, 9.gr.5
please; Go ahead.; Here it is! どうぞ (phr) 1.a.conv
point, aspect, fact てん (点) (n) 1.c.conv
policy, principle ほうしん (方針) (n) 8.c.conv
popular; flourishing さかん (な-adj) 4.d.1

popularity にんき (人気) (n) 1.gr.6, 9.b.conv
positive, forward-looking まえむき (前向き) (n) 10.c.3
positive, is willing, active, constructive せっきょくてき (積極的) (な-adj) 10.c.3
possibilities かのうせい (可能性) (n) 6.lc, 10.c.conv
possible か (可) (n) 5.rw.1; かのう (可能) (な-adj) 9.b.conv
possibly かもしれない (phr) 6.lc, 11.a.conv
post office ゆうびんきょく (郵便局) (n) 5.gr.3
power, strength, capability ちから (力) (n) 1.c.conv
practice れんしゅう (練習) する (n/v) 6.gr.4, 6.gr.9, 8.gr.7
predict よそう (予想) する (n/v) 10.rw.1
preference; wish きぼう (希望) (n) 1.e.2, 1.rw.
preliminary consultation うちあわせ (打ち合わせ) (n) 3.gr.3
preparation じゅんび (準備) (n) 9.c.2
present address げんじゅうしょ (現住所) (n) 1.e.2
present, gift プレゼント (n) 1.gr.5
present, presentation [ご]ていじ (提示) する (n/v) [ご = ↑] 10.rw.1
presentation プレゼンテーション (n) 3.gr.2
president かいちょう (会長) (n) 1.d.conv, 4.e.3
president [of a company] しゃちょう (社長) (n) 1.a.1
pretty good thing なかなかのもの (phr) 6.c.conv
pretty; clean きれい (な-adj) 1.b.1
previous time ぜんかい (前回) (n) 10.rw.1
price かかく (価格), ねだん (値段) (n) 4.rw.1, 7.gr.6, 8.c.conv, 10.a.conv
price per unit たんか (単価) (n) 11.rw.1
price reduction, discount ねびき (値引き), ねさげ (値下げ) (n) [= かかくのひきさげ] 4.gr.10, 6.a.6, 10.a.conv
prices ぶっか (物価) (n) prices, 7.b.1
primarily, mainly おもに (主に) (adv) 8.b.conv
print プリントする (v) 4.c.2
printer プリンタ (n) 1.gr.6
printout プリント (n) 4.c.2
prior to まえに (phr) 10.rw.2
prior to; ahead さきだちまして (先立ちまして) (phr) 9.rw.1
probably is/are; maybe でしょう, だろう (cop) [TENTATIVE of です／だ] 1.a.1, 2.c.conv
problem もんだい (問題) (n) 10.c.conv
processing speed しょりそくど (処理速度) (n) 9.a.conv
produce, create, production つくりだす (作り出す) (v) 1.c.conv; せいさん (生産) する (n/v) 8.gr.4
product せいひん (製品) (n) 1.b.add
product name ひんめい (品名) (n) 11.rw.1
product quality ひんしつ (品質) (n) 7.gr.1, 8.b.conv
production せいさん (生産) (n) 8.c.conv
profession [ご]しょくぎょう (職業) (n) [ご = ↑] 5.rw.1
program プログラム (n) 7.b.3
progress はってん (発展) (n) 7.rw.2
project プロジェクト (n) 4.c.conv
project plan きかくあん (企画案) (n) 6.c.4
promise, appointment やくそく (約束) (n) 7.a.add
prompt approval [ご]かいだく (快諾) (n) [ご = ↑] 11.rw.1
pronounce, pronunciation はつおん (発音) する (n/v) 5.d.1
propose, proposal ていあん (提案) する (n/v) 10.c.1
propose; apply しんせい (申請) いたします↓ (v) 11.c.3
prospect みこみ (見込み) (n) 1.rw.

prosperity, prosperous ごせいえい (ご清栄), ごせいしょう (ご清祥), ごりゅうせい (ご隆盛) (n) [ご = ↑] 7.rw.1, 9.rw.1, 10.rw.1, 11.rw.1
provided that it does not interfere with you おさしつかえなければ (phr) 3.f.conv
public utility fees こうきょうりょうきん (公共料金) (n) 5.d.conv
public works こうきょうじぎょう (公共事業) (n) 10.a.2
pull; subtract; minus (-) ひく (引く) (v) [かぜをひく "catch cold"] 6.a.4
purchase, buy こうにゅう (購入) する (n/v) 11.c.conv, 11.gr.2
purchase かいいれ (買い入れ), こうばい (購買) (n) 4.e.2, 10.rw.1
purpose ため (n) [N のため(に) "for the reason of N"; S ため(に) "in order that S", 4.c.2
push おして (押して) (v) [て-form of おす] 2.gr.7
put away しまう (v) [V-てしまう "V completely"] 5.g.conv, 6.gr.3
put down; place おく (v) [V ておく "V in advance for later use"] 4.a.conv
put in; pour いれる (入れる), おいれする↓ (お入れする) (vt) [vi: はいる] 4.e.1, 6.a.1
put outside; submit だす (出す), おだしする↓ (お出しする), おだしになる↑ (お出しになる) (vt) [vi: でる] 2.b.conv, 3.e.1, 6.gr.1

Q

qualification しかく (資格) (n) 1.e.2
quality しつ (質) (n) 8.c.conv
quantity すうりょう (数量) (n) 11.rw.1
question [ご]しつもん (質問) (n) [ご= ↑] 2.a.2, 9.b.conv
question, ask とう (問う) (v) 11.c.3
question marker か (p) 1.a.conv
quiche キーシュ (n) 10.gr.4
quick(ly), fast はやく (速く) (い-adj) 2.a.2, 9.a.conv
quick, fast はやい (速い) (い-adj) 1.c.3
quiet しずか (静か) (な-adj) 4.gr.7
quit; stop やめる (止める) (v) 1.d.1

R

racket ball ラケットボール (n) 1.gr.8
rain あめ (雨) (n) 1.b.3
rain or snow ふる (降る) (v) 1.b.2, 1.b.3
rainy season つゆ (梅雨) (n) [June through mid-July] 8.gr.8
raise; lift あげる (上げる) (v) 4.e.conv, 10.c.1
rather than saying that というより (phr) 8.c.4
reach; arrive at いたる (至る) (v) 10.rw.1
reaches (destination) とどく (届く) (v) 11.a.conv
read, pronounce よむ (読む), お読みする↓ (v) 1.b.5, 1.gr.2, 2.e.conv, 4.gr.7, 8.b.1
realm ぶんや (分野) (n) 1.a.conv
reason ため (n) [N のため(に) "for the reason of N"; S ため(に) "in order that S", 4.c.2
reason, sense, situation, case わけ (訳), りゆう (理由) (n) 1.b.conv, 10.b.conv
receive もらう (v) [V てもらう "receive a favor of V-ing"] 4.a.conv
receive a favor of being introduced ごしょうかいいただく↓ (ご紹介いただく) (phr) 7.a.1
receive a guest, entertain, reception せったい (接待) する (n/v) 6.c.conv, 7.e.1
receive; eat; drink いただく↓ (v) [= もらう] 3.f.4, 3.f.5, 4.a.3
receive; is granted たまわります↓ (賜ります) (v) 7.rw.1
received by うけ (受) (n) 3.rw.1
receiving of someone; welcoming someone [お]むかえ (迎え) (n) [お = ↑] 6.c.conv
reception desk うけつけ (受付) (n) 4.gr.3
reconsider, think over かんがえなおす (考え直す) (v) 7.gr.4
recover, healed なおる (直る) (vi) [vt: なおす] 6.a.1
red あかい (赤い) (い-adj) 6.gr.6
red color あか (赤) (n) 5.gr.7
reduce cost, cost down コストダウンする (n/v) 8.gr.3
reduce the price ねびき (値引き) する, ねさげ (値下げ) する (n/v) 4.d.conv, 7.gr.4, 10.a.2
reduced; shaved off けずった (削った) (v) [PAST of けずる] 8.c.conv
reduction ひきさげ (引下げ) (n) 4.rw.1, 10.rw.1
refund はらいもどし (払い戻し) (n) 10.c.4
refuse, reject ことわる (断る) (v) 10.b.2
regarding, concerning かんして (関して), 関しまして (v) 9.c.conv, 10.c.conv
regarding; thus/therefore/and so; based on the preceding つきましては (phr) 7.b.conv, 9.rw.1, 11.c.3
registered signature seal おとどけいん (お届け出印) (n) 5.rw.1
regular savings account ふつうよきん (普通預金) (n) 5.b.conv
relationship (to applicant) つづきがら (続柄) (n) 1.e.2
relationship; related to かんけい (関係) (n) 1.rw.
remember おぼえる (覚える) (v) [おぼえている "remember"] 2.c.1
remittance; sending of money そうきん (送金) (n) 5.a.1
remove はずす (v) [せきをはずす "is not at one's seat; has stepped out"] 3.d.conv
rent, borrow かりる (借りる) (v) 1.b.1, 5.b.1
rent やちん (家賃) (n) 1.gr.8
rented car レンタカー (n) 9.gr.5
repair なおす (直す) (vt) [vi: なおる] 6.a.1
replace かわる (代わる) (v) 3.b.conv, 5.d.conv
replacement かわり (代わり/変わり) (v) 3.com.1
reply へんじ (返事) (n) 2.gr.2, 6.b.3
report ほうこく (報告), レポート (n) 2.c.conv, 4.(title)., 4.gr.9; ほうこく (報告) する (n/v) 4.gr.9, 7.e.2
report document ほうこくしょ (報告書) (n) 4.gr.3, 5.gr.5, 7.e.2
report, thesis, essay article ろんぶん (論文) (n) 2.c.add
request, wish おねがい (お願い) する (n/v) 1.a.conv, 2.c.conv, 5.b.1
required personnel よういん (要員) (n) 11.c.3
reroute, rotate, pass, spin まわす (回す) (vt) [vi: まわる] 2.b.conv
rescued, helped たすかる (助かる) (vi) 3.gr.3
research and development けんきゅうかいはつ (研究開発) (n) 4.e.2
research laboratory けんきゅうしつ (研究室) (n) 8.a.conv
research; study けんきゅう (研究) する, 研究なさる↑, 研究いたします↓ (v) 1.b.conv, 1.b.1, 1.b.2
reserve (a seat/hotel) reservation よやく (予約) する (n/v) 3.gr.3, 4.a.4, 8.c.4

reserve (a seat/hotel) in advance　よやく（予約）しておく (phr) 4.a.4, 6.a.conv
rest, off duty　[お]やすみ（休み）(n) [お = ↑] 3.f.5
rest; take a day off　やすむ（休む）(v) 1.c.3
restaurant　レストラン (n) 1.b.1
results, consequences　けっか（結果）(n) 1.e.conv
resume　りれきしょ（履歴書）(n) 1.e.2
retail price　こうりね（小売値）(n) 10.b.conv
return; go home　かえる（帰る）(v) 1.gr.3
return　おかえり（お帰り）, おかえりになる↑（お帰りになる）(n) 1.c.2, 2.d.1, 7.e.3
return (something)　かえす（返す）(v) 5.gr.11
return the phone call　でんわをかえす（電話を返す）(phr) 3.c.add
rewrite　かきなおす（書き直す）(v) 8.gr.2
ride; take (transportation)　のる（乗る）(v) 4.gr.7
right (side)　みぎ（右）(n) 2.gr.7
right now; [greeting] I'm home! I'm back!　ただいま（ただ今）(n) 3.d.conv
rigid, stiff, bookish, hard　かたい（堅い）(い-adj) 6.b.conv
road, street, direction (to somewhere)　みち（道）(n) 6.b.4
robot　ロボット (n) 1.gr.6
Roman letters　ローマじ（ローマ字）(n) 6.gr.3
room　へや（部屋）(n) 4.gr.6, 10.a.3
roughly　ざっと (adv) 10.b.conv
round trip　おうふく（往復）(n) 5.com.1
run business; open for business　えいぎょう（営業）する (n/v) 7.gr.2
run out; disappear　なくなる (phr) [く form of ない + なる] 4.a.4
rush hour　ラッシュ (n) 1.d.1

S

said that...　〜とのこと (phr) 3.rw.2, 4.a.1; 〜ということだ (phr) 4.a.1
sake [Japanese rice wine]　[お]さけ（酒）(n) [お = ↑] 2.gr.6, 6.b.conv, 6.b.4
salaried workers　サラリーマン (n) 2.b.1
sales　えいぎょう（営業）, はんばい（販売）, セールス (n) 2.d.conv, 2.d.add, 4.d.conv
sales (the amount of)　うりあげ（売り上げ）(n) 4.e.conv
sales agency store　だいりてん（代理店）(n) 10.c.3
sales competition　しょうせん（商戦）(n) 10.rw.1, 11.c.3
sales contract　はんばいけいやく（販売契約）(n) 4.rw.1
sales cooperation　はんばいていけい（販売提携）(n) 10.gr.1
sales division　えいぎょうぶ（営業部）, はんばいぶ（販売部）(n) 2.e.conv, 3.com.1, 11.c.3
sales journal chart　うりあげしゅうけいひょう（売上げ集計表）(n) 4.rw.1
sales meeting　はんばいかいぎ（販売会議）(n) 4.rw.2
sales negotiation　はんばいこうしょう（販売交渉）(n) 4.rw.1
sales price　はんばいかかく（販売価格）(n) 4.rw.2
salesman　セールスマン (n) 10.b.1
saleswoman　セールスウーマン (n) 7.e.conv
same　おなじ（同じ）(n) 3.f.conv
same; together　いっしょの（一緒の）(phr) 8.a.conv
sample　サンプル (n) 6.com.3
satisfactory　けっこう（結構）(な-adj) 3.c.1, 5.b.conv

Saturday　どようび（土曜日）(n) 2.gr.7
say　おっしゃる↑ (v) [= いう] 2.e.add, 2.e.1, 4.c.conv
say (it) humbly　もうしあげる↓（申し上げる）(v) [= いう] 11.c.conv
say (it) in advance　いっとく（言っとく）, いっておく（言っておく）(phr) 4.a.4, 4.a.5, 4.e.conv
(say) that　と, って, て (p) [quotation marker] 1.a.conv, 2.a.2, 5.a.conv
say; is called　いう（言う）, もうします↓（申します）(v) 1.a.conv, 1.a.1, 8.b.1, 8.c.4
schedule; plan　よてい（予定）(n) 3.f.conv; つごう（都合）(n) 5.gr.5
schedule; plan　[ご]よてい（予定）(n) [ご = ↑] 3.gr.7
school subject　がっか（学科）(n) 1.e.2
science　かがく（科学）, サイエンス (n) 1.a.conv, 5.gr.8
scientific　かがくてき（科学的）(な-adj) 5.d.1
screen　スクリーン (n) 8.b.1
search, look for　さがす（探す）(v) 1.lc
season　こう（候）(n) [written expression] 7.rw.1; きせつ（季節）(n) 9.rw.1
seat　せき（席）(n) 3.b.1
second class　にきゅう（二級）(n) 1.rw.
second conference room　だいにかいぎしつ（第二会議室）(n) 8.lc
second floor　にかい（二階）(num) 5.gr.3
second party　にじかい（二次会）(n) 6.a.conv
secretary　ひしょ（秘書）(n) 7.a.conv
section　か（課）, セクション (n) 2.d.conv, 5.gr.7
Section #1　だいいっか（第一課）, いっか（一課）(n) 2.rw, 3.a.conv
section manager　かちょう（課長）(n) 1.d.1
securities　しょうけん（証券）(n) 3.a.2
securities company　しょうけんかいしゃ（証券会社）(n) 3.a.2
security code, person identification number　あんしょうばんごう（暗証番号）(n) 5.c.conv
see, look, watch　みる（見る）(v) 8.b.1
see/meet someone　おめにかかる↓（お目にかかる）(phr) 4.a.conv
seem　ようだ (phr) 7.e.1
select　えらぶ（選ぶ）(v) 1.c.conv
self　じぶん（自分）(n) 10.gr.3
self, applicant　ほんにん（本人）(n) 1.e.2
self-introduction form　じこしょうかいしょ（自己紹介書）(n) 1.e.2
sell　うる（売る）(v), はんばい（販売）する (n/v) [vi: うれる] 4.d.1, 8.gr.2
sell, sold　うれる（売れる）(vi) [vt: うる] 7.gr.1, 11.gr.2
semiconductor　はんどうたい（半導体）(n) 9.a.3
seminar　セミナー (n) 2.gr.6, 3.gr.4, 5.b.1
send (it) in　おくってくる（送ってくる）(phr) [て-form of おくる + くる] 11.a.1
send money, remittance　そうきん（送金）する (n/v) 5.e.1
sender　そうしんしゃ（送信者）(n) 4.rw.2
senior managing director　せんむとりしまりやく（専務取締役）(n) 4.e.3; せんむ（専務）(n) 11.gr.4
separate; excluded; apart from　べつ（別）(n) 10.a.conv
serious-minded　まじめ（真面目）(な-adj) 6.lc
service　サービス (n) 9.c.conv
service center　サービスセンター (n) 11.gr.1

seven to eight sheets しち、はちまい（七、八枚）(num) 11.b.1
severe; violent; heated はげしい（激しい）(い-adj) 7.rw.1
sex; gender せいべつ（性別）(n) 5.rw.1
Shall I explain? [ご]せつめい（説明）いたしましょうか (phr) 7.d.2
shall I turn (it) on? つけましょうか (v) [POL VOL of つける + か] 7.e.3
shape, form かたち（形）(n) 1.b.conv
she; her かのじょ（彼女）(pro) 1.lc, 7.d.conv
Shinbashi [place name] しんばし（新橋）(n) 7.c.1
Shinjuku [a ward in Tokyo] しんじゅく（新宿）(n) 1.rw.
Shinkansen bullet train しんかんせん（新幹線）(n) 1.gr.6
shipping はっそう（発送）(n) 11.c.3
shipping; delivery; payment of money のうにゅう（納入）(n) 11.rw.1
shop, store みせ（店）(n) 1.b.1
shopping かいもの（買い物）(n) 1.d.1
short (in length) みじかい（短い）(い-adj) 5.b.1
show みせる（見せる）(v) 1.e.1, 3.f.4
Showa era しょうわ（昭和）(n) [1926-1989] 1.rw.
showroom ショールーム (n) 9.rw.1
shows signs of wanting to go いきたがって（行きたがって）(v) 6.a.conv
sickness びょうき（病気）(n) 1.b.1
side がわ（側）(n) 1.e.2
signature サイン (n) 5.b.conv
signature seal はんこ、いん（印）、いんかん（印鑑）(n) 1.e.2, 5.b.conv, 5.b.1
simple, easy かんたん（簡単）(な-adj) 1.a.conv
simply かんたんに（簡単に）(adv) 10.gr.4
sincerely こころより（心より）(phr) 10.rw.1
sing うたう（歌う）(v) 1.d.1, 6.b.conv
sit down かける、おかけになる↑ (v) 1.a.conv, 5.c.conv
situation じょうきょう（状況）(n) 10.rw.1
situation; condition ようす（様子）(n) 9.c.1
six o'clock ろくじ（六時）(num) 7.c.1
ski スキー (n) 6.a.3
skillful; is good at [お]じょうず（上手）(な-adj) [お = ↑] 1.d.conv, 1.d.1
skills; technology ぎじゅつ（技術）(n) 1.rw.
sleep ねむる（眠る）(v) 2.c.4
sleep; go bed ねる（寝る）(v) 4.gr.7
slowly そろそろ (adv) 6.b.4
small ちいさい（小さい）(い-adj) 1.c.3
small size こがた（小型）(n) 1.b.add
smoke すう（吸う）(v) 1.d.1
so それで (con) 1.c.conv
so, therefore んで (con) [= ので] 10.b.conv
social system; institution; convention せいど（制度）(n) 11.gr.4
socializing [お]つきあい (n) [お = ↑] 6.a.add
software ソフト (n) 1.b.conv
some time; some day いつか (phr) 6.a.3
somehow なんとか (adv) 3.gr.2
someone だれか（誰か）、どなたか↑ (n) 6.a.3, 7.b.2
something なにか（何か）(n) 6.a.conv
somewhat early, somewhat soon はやめに（早めに）(adv) 7.d.2
somewhat; for some price いくらか (phr) 6.a.3
somewhere どこか (n) 6.a.3

song; singing うた（歌）(n) 6.b.conv
soon もうすぐ (adv) 4.a.4
sorry; regrettable; unfortunate ざんねん（残念.）(な-adj) 6.gr.2
souvenir おみやげ（お土産）(n) 7.gr.4
Spanish (language) スペインご（スペイン語）(n) 1.gr.4
spare; divide さく（割く）(v) [じかんをさく "spare time"] 8.a.conv
speak from a distant place いってくる（言ってくる）(phr) 11.a.conv
speak; remark はつげん（発言）する (n/v) 5.gr.4
speak; talk はなす（話す）、おはなしになる↑（お話しになる）(v) 1.a.2, 1.b.5, 4.d.2, 8.b.1
special remarks とっきじこう（特記事項）(n) 11.rw.1
special; extraordinary; unusual かくべつ（格別）(n) 7.rw.1
specialty せんもん（専門）(n) 1.a.conv
speech スピーチ (n) 1.d.1
speed スピード (n) 8.lc
splendid; wonderful りっぱ（立派）(な-adj) 9.a.conv
sports スポーツ (n) 1.com.1
sports car スポーツカー (n) 10.a.1
spring はる（春）(n) 7.e.1
star, celebrity スター (n) 2.gr.1
start selling はつばい（発売）する (n/v) 9.rw.1
start, beginning かいし（開始）する (n/v) 11.c.3
state, condition じょうたい（状態）(n) 1.e.2
state, mention のべる（述べる）(v) 8.gr.7
station えき（駅）(n) 1.gr.8
stay いる、おります (v) [animate] 1.a.1, 1.a.conv
stay over とまる（泊まる）(v) 10.a.3
stay; be おられます↓ (v) [= いる] 3.a.1, 3.a.conv
stay; be; there is/are [animate]; come; go いらっしゃいます↑ (v) [= いる] 1.a.2
steering wheel ハンドル (n) 1.b.1
stick with; hold on(idea or policy); penetrate つらぬく（貫く）(v) 8.c.conv
stick; accompany; become attached つく (v) 2.a.conv
still まだ (adv) 3.e.conv
still; (not) yet まだまだ (adv) [more emphatic than まだ], 1.d.conv
stocks かぶ（株）(n) 6.c.3
stomach, abdomen おなか（お腹）(n) 7.c.2
stop (something) とめる（止める）(vt) [vi: とまる] 1.gr.3, 3.b.2, 5.gr.4, 6.a.1
stop; stay over とまる（止まる）(vi) [vt: とめる] 3.b.2, 6.a.1
story, talk はなし（話）(n) 4.gr.3, 7.e.2
strict, hard きびしい（厳しい）(い-adj) 2.c.3
strong, sturdy じょうぶ（丈夫）(な-adj) 11.b.2
strong; potent つよい（強い）(い-adj) 6.b.4
student がくせい（学生）(n) 1.com.4
study べんきょう（勉強）する (n/v) 1.a.conv
study abroad りゅうがく（留学）する (n/v) 10.c.3
subcontracting したうけ（下請け）(n) 4.gr.3
subdued tastefully しぶい（渋い）(い-adj) 6.b.conv
subject だい（題）(n) 4.rw.2
submit; turn ていしゅつ（提出）する (n/v) [= だす] 2.c.conv
subsection manager; chief かかりちょう（係長）(n) 2.a.add, 3.d.conv
subsidiary company こがいしゃ（子会社）(n) 8.c.4

substantiality, fullness, completion じゅうじつ (充実) (n) 9.c.conv
subway ちかてつ (地下鉄) (n) 1.c.3
such that ように (phr) 9.b.3
sudden(ly) きゅうな (急な), とつぜん (突然) (な-adj; n) 7.rw.1, 7.rw.2
sum; total しゅうけい (集計) (n) 4.e.conv
summer なつ (夏) (n) 2.gr.6
summer uniform なつふく (夏服) (n) 3.b.1
summon よぶ (呼ぶ) (v) 1.b.5, 5.1c, 8.b.1
Sunday にちようび (日曜日) (n) 7.e.1
sunny はれる (晴れる) (v) 1.b.3
super fast ちょうこうそく (超高速) (n) 9.rw.1
supper, dinner ゆうしょく (夕食) (n) 6.a.conv
support バックアップする, しじ (支持) する (n/v) 8.gr.7, 11.c.1
surrounding; people/things around something まわり (周り) (n) 2.a.conv
sushi [お]すし (寿司) (n) [お = ↑] 2.c.3
sushi restaurant すしや (寿司屋) (n) 4.gr.3
swims およがれる (泳がれる) (v) [ADV PASS or ↑ PASS] 8.b.1
switch かわり (代わり/変わり) (v) [V-stem of かわる] 3.com.1
switch; change かわる (代わる/変わる) (v) 3.b.2
symposium シンポジウム (n) 8.gr.7
synthesizer シンセサイザー (n) 10.gr.4
system システム (n) 2.com.1, 8.b.1
system software システムソフト (n) 5.gr.6

T

table; chart ひょう (表) (n) 4.e.conv
Taisho era たいしょう (大正) (n) [1912-1926] 5.rw.1
take (a seat) おかけください↑ (おかけ下さい↑) (v) 2.d.conv
take (time/money) intentionally かける (vt) [vi: かかる] 1.a.conv, 2.d.conv, 6.a.1, 6.c.4
take a pride じふ (自負) する (v) 8.c.conv
take a shower シャワーをあびる (浴びる) (phr) 7.gr.1
take the liberty of ... ～させていただいております↑ (phr) 10.a.conv
Take your time. ごゆっくり (phr) 6.b.4
take [an exam]; accept うける (受ける) (v) 4.gr.7
take [time/money] かかる (vi) [vt: かける] 2.c.1, 5.e.conv, 5.e.1, 6.a.1
take/bring someone おつれ (お連れ) する↑ (n/v) 6.c.conv
take; get; occupy とる (取る) (v) 1.e.1, 5.a.conv, 6.a.5, 7.b.3, 8.b.1, 10.b.1
tall せがたかい (背が高い) (い-adj) 1.b.1
task, (manual) work さぎょう (作業) (n) 11.c.3
tasty; is good at うまい (い-adj) 6.c.conv
taxi タクシー (n) 4.gr.8
tea serving おちゃだし (お茶出し) (n) 2.b.conv
teach; inform おしえる (教える), お教えする↑ (v) 1.gr.3, 2.c.1, 2.c.conv, 5.g.conv, 8.b.1
teacher せんせい (先生) (n) 1.c.3
technical テクニカル (n) 8.1c
technological ぎじゅつてき (技術的) (な-adj) 7.e.conv
Technology Institute こうかだいがく (工科大学) (n) 1.a.conv

telecommunication テレコム, つうしん (通信) (n) 1.b.conv, 3.a.conv
telephone でんわ (電話) (n) 1.b.conv
telephone charge でんわだい (電話代) (n) 5.d.conv
tell/inform (someone) to V ように (phr) 3.e.2
tell; inform もうしつたえる↓ (申し伝える) (v) [= つたえる] 3.e.conv
teller window まどぐち (窓口) (n) 5.a.conv
temperature おんど (温度) (n) 7.e.1
temporary りんじ (臨時) (n) 11.c.3
tempura (deep fried fish and vegetables) てんぷら (n) 6.com.1
ten percent いちわり (一割) (num) 10.b.conv
Tennessee テネシー (n) 1.d.2
tennis テニス (n) 1.d.conv
terrible ひどい (phr) 9.c.4
terribly sorry おそれいります (恐れ入ります) (v) 2.d.conv
test, exam, quiz テスト (n) 2.a.3
than より (p) [Xより～ "more ～ than X"] 8.c.conv
Thank you for your hard work! Good bye! おつかれさま (お疲れ様) (phr) 4.b.conv
Thank you very much (for what you did). ありがとうございました (phr) 1.e.conv
Thank you. ありがとう (phr) 1.e.conv
Thanks for your hard work. ごくろうさん (ご苦労さん) (phr) 4.c.conv
thanks to おかげで (phr) 11.c.conv
Thanks!, Sorry. どうも (phr) 1.e.conv
that (much); that way あんなに (phr) 6.b.conv
that (near you) その (prenom) 1.b.conv
That is right. さようでございます (左様でございます) (phr) [= そうです] 7.b.conv
that kind of そんな (pro) 2.b.1
that kind of ああいった (prenom) [shared experience; = あんな] 1.c.add
that kind of そういった (prenom) [unshared experience; = そんな] 1.c.conv
that one (near you) それ (pro) 1.d.conv
that person; he あのかた (あの方) (phr) 2.e.1
that place over there (far away) あちら (pro) 9.c.1
that way; like that そう (pro) 1.a.conv
that, so-called れいの (例の) (phr) 4.c.conv
the day after tomorrow あさって (明後日) (n) 1.gr.4
the day before yesterday おととい (一昨日) (n) 1.gr.5
the other day せんじつ (先日) (n) 3.a.conv, 7.a.3
the other side/party あいてがわ (相手側) (n) 4.d.conv
The same here. こちらこそ (phr) 2.a.conv
then, well じゃ (phr) 2.b.conv
then; besides; since then それから (con) 1.d.conv
then; well では (con) 1.b.conv
there is/are ございます (v) [= あります] 4.a.conv, 4.a.1, 5.d.conv, 10.a.2
there is/are; to have ある (v) 1.b.conv, 1.b.1, 2.c.conv
there isn't/aren't; don't have ない, ありません (い-adj) 2.c.1, 5.b.1
there, that place (near you) そこ (pro) 2.b.conv
therefore それで (con) 1.c.conv
thing, object, matter もの (物) (n) 3.c.1
think おもう (思う) (v) 1.a.1, 1.b.conv, 1.gr.6, 6.a.2, 6.c.2

think ぞんじます↓ (存じます) (v) [ねがいたくぞんじます "would like to request"] 10.rw.1
third conference room だいさんかいぎしつ (第三会議室) (n) 8.lc
third day of the month; three days みっか (三日) (num) 5.e.conv
third floor さんかい (三階) (num) 5.gr.3
this evening, tonight こんや (今夜), こんばん (今晩) (n) 2.gr.7, 7.b.3
this kind of; like this こんな, こういった, このような, こんなふうな (pre-n) 1.c.add, 10.c.4
this morning けさ (今朝) (n) 6.a.3
this much このぐらい (phr) 10.b.conv
this product ほんせいひん (本製品) (n) 9.rw.1
this side (near me) こっち (n) 1.gr.4
this time こんかい (今回) (n) 10.c.conv
this way (toward me); this place here こちら (pro) 1.b.conv
this week こんしゅう (今週) (n) 6.gr.2
this weekend こんしゅうまつ (今週末) (n) 6.c.conv
thought; thinking かんがえ (考え) (n) 5.d.1
three o'clock さんじ (三時) (num) 1.b.6
throw away; discard すてる (捨てる) (v) 8.gr.2
Thursday もくようび (木曜日) (n) 1.gr.4
thus それで (con) 1.c.conv
ticket きっぷ (切符) (n) 2.gr,8, 3.gr.4, 4.a.4
till まで (p) 1.gr.4, 2.a.conv
time; occasion; when... とき (時) (n) 3.f.5, 4.a.conv
times; degrees ど (度) (ct) 1.d.conv
title for everyone かくい (各位) (n) 9.rw.1
to, destination of mail あてさき (宛先) (n) 4.rw.2
to, toward に (p) [destination marker; marks the place one arrives at or one chooses have] 1.a.1
today きょう (今日), ほんじつ (本日) (n) 1.d.conv, 1.e.conv, 11.c.conv
together ともに (共に), いっしょに (一緒に) (adv) 4.gr.5, 6.c.conv, 7.e.conv, 8.b.conv
together (with your friends) おさそいあわせのうえ (お誘い合わせの上) (phr) 6.rw
toilet, rest room トイレ (n) 4.gr.7
Tokyo Capital とうきょうと (東京都) (n) 1.rw
Tokyo [capital of Japan] とうきょう (東京) (n) 1.gr.1
Tokyo-Hokkaido-Osaka/Kyoto-Prefecture とどうふけん (都道府県) (n) 1.e.2
tomorrow あした (明日), あす (明日) (n) 1.a.2, 4.e.conv
total amount of money そうがく (総額) (n) 6.gr.1
tour あんない (案内) する (v) 9.lc
tournament たいかい (大会) (n) 7.c.2
toward たい (対) して (n/v), むけて (向けて) (v) 10.c.conv, 11.c.3
town まち (町) (n) 1.b.1
trade ぼうえき (貿易) (n) 1.a.2
trading company しょうじ (商事), しょうじかいしゃ (商事会社)(n) 3.a.2, 11.c.2
tradition; annual/usual event こうれい (恒例) (n) 6.rw
train station しんじゅくえき (新宿駅) (n) 1.gr.6
training けんしゅう (研修) (n) 2.a.add
translate, translation ほんやくする (翻訳する) (v) 2.lc, 4.a.3, 5.g.1, 11.a.conv
travel; trip りょこう (旅行) する (n/v) 10.gr.2

traveler's checks トラベラーズチェック (n) 5.lc
treat someone for dinner ごちそう (ご馳走) する (n/v) 3.f.5
treatment あつかい (扱い) (n) 5.e.conv
trouble; nuisance [ご]めいわく (迷惑) (n) [ご = ↑] 3.d.conv
truly まことに (誠に) (adv) 7.rw.1
truth ほんとう (本当) (n) 4.gr.4
truthfully; actually; to tell you the truth じつは (実は) (adv) 6.a.conv, 6.com.4, 7.a.conv
try and open; open and see あけてみる (開けてみる) (phr) 6.gr.1
try and see ためしてみて (試してみて) (phr) 9.a.conv
try to V (without success) しようとする (phr) 6.c.3
try V-ing; V and see してみる (v) 6.b.2, 6.gr.5
try; attempt (to use) ためす (試す) (v) 9.a.conv
Tuesday かよう[び] (火曜[日]) (n) 3.f.1, 5.com.2
turn of events しだい (次第) (n) 7.a.conv, 10.c.conv
turn off けす (消す) (vt) 5.gr.11, 6.a.1, 6.a.1
turn off completely けしてしまう (消してしまう) (phr) 6.gr.1
turn on; put on つける (vt) [vi: つく] 6.a.1, 6.c.4, 7.e.3
TV (set) テレビ (n) 1.b.conv
twentieth day of the month; twenty days はつか (二十日) (num) 4.gr.8
twice にかい (二回) (num) 9.b.3
two long objects にほん (二本) (num) 2.c.4
two or three places に、さんかしょ (二、三か所) (num) 2.c.conv
type タイプする, タイプいたします↓ (v) 1.gr.2, 9.gr.3
type タイプ (n) 5.e.1
typed text かつじ (活字) (n) 11.a.3
typhoon たいふう (台風) (n) 4.c.2, 8.c.1

U

umm... あの, あのう, ええ (interj) [hesitation noise] 1.b.1, 1.d.conv, 5.b.conv
under construction こうじちゅう (工事中) (phr) 6.b.4
underground, basement ちか (地下) (n) 5.gr.3, 6.rw
understand わかる (分かる) (v) 1.a.conv, 1.c.3, 1.c.2, 2.c.1
understanding, comprehension [ご]りかい (理解) (n) [ご = ↑] 10.rw.1
unfortunately あいにく (adv) 3.com.2, 5.g.conv
uniform せいふく (制服) (n) 3.b.1
unit [counter for long cylindrical objects] 〜ほん (本) (ct) 1.b.1
unit [counter for machines] だい (台) (ct) 10.a.conv
University of Tokyo とうだい (東大) (n) 3.gr.5
university, college だいがく (大学) (n) 1.a.conv
unlimited drinking のみほうだい (飲み放題) (n) 6.rw
unskilled; is poor at へた (下手) (な-adj) 1.d.add
until まで (p) 1.gr.4, 2.a.conv
until late おそくまで (遅くまで) (phr) 11.c.2
upcoming きたる (来る) (phr) 9.rw.1, 11.c.3
upset きをわるくする (気を悪くする) (phr) 6.b.conv
urban area とかい (都会) (n) 10.gr.4
urgently だいしきゅう (大至急) (n) 3.f.add
urgently; immediately しきゅう (至急) (n) 3.f.conv
use つかう (使う) (v) 1.b.5, 2.b.conv, 8.b.1
use for industrial purposes さんぎょうよう (産業用) (n) 8.b.1
use [someone's] phone でんわをかりる (電話を借りる) (phr) 3.b.add
use; employ つかいます (使います) (v) [POL of つかう] 1.b.4

user's manual ユーザーマニュアル (n) 10.gr.3
usual; routine へいそ (平素) (n) 7.rw.1

V

vacation; day off やすみ (休み) (n) 2.b.1
Valentine バレンタイン (n) 1.gr.5
various いろいろ (な-adj) 2.lc, 3.f.4
VCR VTR (n) 9.gr.5
very とても (adv) 1.b.conv
very much; extreme; overwhelming; rough; terrible たいへん (大変) (な-adj) 1.b.conv
very; very much; a lot ずいぶん (adv) [followed by AFF] 8.c.conv
vice president [of a company] ふくしゃちょう (副社長) (n) 1.gr.8, 4.e.3
vicinity へん (辺) (suf) [このへん "in this vicinity"] 5.gr.3
video ビデオ (n) 6.gr.8
video game テレビゲーム (n) 9.c.2
visible みえる (見える) (v) 3.gr.1, 6.b.3
visit to company かいしゃほうもん (会社訪問) (n) 1.a.conv
visit; go; ask おうかがい (お伺い) いたします↓ (v) [= うかがう] 7.c.conv
visitor, guest おきゃくさん (お客さん) (n) [お = ↑] 2.lc, 4.gr.3, 6.c.conv
voluntary, spontaneous じはつてき (自発的) (な-adj) 8.c.conv

W

wage きゅうよ (給与) (n) 11.c.3
wait まつ (待つ), お待ちになる↑, お待ちする↓ (v) 1.b.5, 1.gr.2, 1.gr.4, 4.b.1, 6.gr.1
wait またれる (待たれる) (v) [ADV PASS or ↑ PASS] 8.b.1
wake up (someone) おこす (起こす) (vt) [vi: おきる] 6.a.1
wakes up, gets up おきる (起きる) (vi) [vt: おこす] 6.a.1
walk あるく (歩く) (v) 7.gr.4
Wall Street Journal ウォールストリートジャーナル (n) 1.gr.8
want ほしい (欲しい) (い-adj) 3.rw.2, 7.d.conv
want (other person) to meet あってほしい (会ってほしい) (phr) 7.d.2
want to ask, visit うかがいたい↓ (伺いたい) (v) 5.f.conv
want to become なりたい (v) 8.c.3
want to do したい (v) 1.b.5
want to go and see; want to try and go いってみたい (行ってみたい) (phr) 6.b.2
want to know しりたい (知りたい) (v) 6.com.1, 10.b.conv
want to make the most of いかしたい (活かしたい) (v) 4.d.2
want to receive もらいたい, いただきたい↓ (v) 3.f.conv, 4.d.conv, 7.d.2
want to request ねがいたい (願いたい) (v) 10.rw.1
want to see/meet someone おめにかかりたい↓ (お目にかかりたい) (phr) 4.lc
want to take part (in) たずさわりたい (携わりたい) (v) 1.b.conv
wants to ask, listen ききたがる (聞きたがる) (v) [third-person form] 6.a.6
wants to get to know しりたがる (知りたがる) (v)) [third-person form] 6.lc
warm [of weather] あたたかい (暖かい) (い-adj) 7.e.1
was, were だった (cop) 1.b.1

wash あらう (洗う) (v) 2.a.2
water (line) すいどう (水道) (n) 5.d.conv
way of managing; the way of conducting business けいえいぶり (経営ぶり) (n) 7.rw.1
way of seeing; how to see みかた (見方) (n) 5.f.1
way of speaking いいかた (言い方) (n) 5.gr.8
way of speaking; how to speak はなしかた (話し方) (n) 5.f.1
way of using, usage, method つかいかた (使い方) (n) 5.f.conv
way of walking あるきかた (歩き方) (n) 5.gr.8
way of writing; how to write かきかた (書き方) (n) 5.f.1
way, direction, side ほう (方) (n) 5.f.2
way; street とおり (通り) (n) 3.rw.1, 8.c.conv, 11.b.3
We've been waiting for this! まってました (phr) 6.b.conv
we, us わたしたち (私達) (pro) [たち = plural suffix for people] 6.c.1; わたくしども↓ (私ども) (pro) 2.a.1, 5.d.conv
weak よわい (弱い) (い-adj) 4.c.2, 5.lc
Web (WWW) ウェブ (n) 9.c.4
Web page ウェブページ (n) 9.lc
wedding ceremony けっこんしき (結婚式) (n) 9.gr.3
Wednesday すいようび (水曜日) (n) 1.gr.4
week after next さらいしゅう (再来週) (n) 4.lc
weekend しゅうまつ (週末) (n) 2.gr.7
welcome かんげい (歓迎) (n) 5.com.2
welcome party; reception かんげいかい (歓迎会) (n) 6.a.conv
Welcome! いらっしゃいませ (v) 5.a.conv
welcome; go to see [someone] むかえる (迎える) (v) 3.gr.3, 6.a.5
well いい (い-adj) 1.b.conv, 1.gr.2
well, I guess まあ (interj) 2.a.conv
well then それでは (con) 1.a.conv
well; oh; wow いやあ (interj) 7.d.conv
well; skillfully うまく (い-adj) 8.gr.7
what なん (何), なに (何) (qw) 1.b.conv, 2.c.1
What do you think? どうおもうかね (思うかね) (phr) [superior to subordinate] 10.c.conv
What happened? どうしたの, どうしましたか, どうしたんですか (phr) 1.gr.6
what kind of どんな, どういう, どういった (qw) 1.b.conv, 1.d.conv, 1.gr.1
What kind of thing? How about it? いかがなもの (qw) 10.b.conv
what number なんばん (何番) (qw) 5.gr.11
what time なんじ (何時) (qw) 1.gr.2
when いつ (qw) 2.c.conv
when (someone) is about to do... しようとしているところ (phr) 9.c.4
whenever いつでも (phr) 4.gr.5
where, which place どこ (qw) 1.lc
whether or not かどうか (phr) 2.c.1
which どの (prenom) 1.a.conv
which place, which one どちら (qw) 1.gr.1
whichever どちらでも (phr) 11.b.conv
while you are busy [ご]たようちゅう (多用中) (phr) [ご = ↑] 7.rw.1
while; during あいだ (間) (n) 4.b.conv
white color しろ (白) (n) 5.gr.7
who だれ (誰), どなた↑ (qw) 1.com.4, 6.a.3
who; which party どちらさま↑ (どちら様) (n) 3.b.conv

Appendix C: English-Japanese Glossary

wholesale price おろしね (卸値) (n) 10.a.conv
Why don't you give me? くださいませんか↑ (下さいませんか) (n) 2.c.conv
wide, spacious ひろい (広い) (い-adj) 1.c.3
wife [of someone else] おくさま↑ (奥様), おくさん↑ (奥さん) (n) 1.gr.5, 4.a.3
will not question とわない (問わない) (v) 11.c.3
willingness のりき (乗り気) (n) 10.c.conv
win かつ (勝つ) (v) 11.gr.4
wind かぜ (風) (n) 8.b.1
window まど (窓) (n) 6.a.1
winter uniform ふゆふく (冬服) (n) 3.b.1
with, together with との (phr) 7.e.2
with a monitor モニターつき (n) 10.a.conv
within, inside いない (以内) (n) 9.1c
within/throughout today きょうじゅう (今日中) (n) 7.gr.3
without taking とらないで (取らないで) (phr) 6.gr.4
woman じょせい (女性) (n) 6.rw., 7.d.conv
wonderful, terrific すばらしい (素晴らしい) (い-adj) 1.b.conv, 4.d.2
word of mouth くちコミ (口コミ) (n) [コミ = communication] 8.c.conv
word processor ワープロ (n) 1.d.1
word-processing ワードプロセシング (n) 6.b.3
work, job [お]つとめ (勤め), しごと (仕事) (n) [お =] 1.b.5, 1.c.conv
work for つとめる (勤める) (v) 1.c.1, 1.e.1
work overtime ざんぎょう (残業) する (n/v) 4.gr.3, 9.c.1
work, job, task, duty ぎょうむ (業務) (n) 11.c.3
work; function はたらく (働く) (v) 1.c.1
world-wide; of the world せかいてき (世界的) (な-adj) 1.c.conv
worrisome; is concerned しんぱい (心配) (な-adj) 6.b.conv
worry; mind きにする (気にする) (phr) 4.a.conv, 6.gr.3
Would you like to drink? おのみ (お飲み) になりませんか↑ (phr) 7.d.2
write かく (書く) (v) 1.e.1, 4.e.1, 8.b.1

write in summary まとめてかく (まとめて書く) (n) 1.e.2
write-in [ご]きにゅう (記入) する (n/v) [ご = ↑] 5.b.conv
written below かき (下記) (n) 3.rw.1
wrong; be different ちがう (違う) (v) 4.1c, 6.c.2, 10.a.1

Y

year ～ねん (年) (ct) 1.b.conv
year-end ねんまつ (年末) (n) 10.rw.1, 11.c.3
year-end party ぼうねんかい (忘年会) (n) 6.b.4
years old さい (歳／才) (ct) 1.e.2, 11.c.3
yellow きいろい (黄色い) (い-adj) 8.gr.8
yen えん (円) (n) 7.c.1
yen-based えんだて (円建て) (n) 11.b.conv
Yes はい, はあ, うん (interj) [うん = INF] 1.a.conv, 1.a.1, 7.e.conv
yesterday きのう (昨日) (n) 1.a.1
Yokohama よこはま (横浜) (n) [a port city south of Tokyo] 3.f.4
Yomiuri Shinbun [newspaper] よみうりしんぶん (読売新聞) (n) 8.gr.2
you きみ (君) (pro) 2.a.conv, 4.e.conv
You have a phone call; It's for you. [お]でんわ (電話) です (phr) 3.b.add
you; your party おたくさま (お宅様) (n) [お =] 2.a.1, 6.c.1
young person/people わかもの (若者) (n) 1.gr.6
younger brother おとうと↓ (弟), 弟さん↑ (n) 1.c.2
younger sister いもうと↓ (妹), 妹さん↑ (n) 1.c.2
your company おんしゃ (御社), きしゃ (貴社) (n) [おん = ↑] 1.b.conv, 7.rw.1
youth hostel ユースホステル (n) 10.a.1

Z

zip code ゆうびんばんごう (郵便番号) (n) 1.e.2

Appendix D: Grammar Index (English Headers/Alphabetical Order)

A - B - C

a thing called X, [X って(いうの)], 5.a.1
about N, regarding N, [N について], 1.a.2; [N1 についての N2 "N2 about N1"], 7.e.2
about to V; have just V-ed; in the middle of V-ing, [V-nonpast ところ／V-past ところ／V ているところ], 9.c.4
adverbial form, [X てきに "in X-like way", e.g., じどうてきに "automatically"], 5.d.1
advice, [S ものだ "it is the rule that S"], 4.a.5; [S のがじょうしきだ, "It is the common sense that S"], 4.a.5; [S のがあたりまえだ "It is the norm that S"], 4.a.5
after N; after V-ing, [N のあと(で)／V たあと(で)], 6.b.1
after V-ing, [V てから], 6.a.4
appears to V, [V-stem + そうだ], 7.d.1
approximate numbers, [二、三 "two or three"], 11.b.1
approximation for time, [ごろ], 2.gr.5
as N; in the capacity of N, [N として], 10.b.1
as soon as having V-ed, [V-stem + しだい], 7.a.2
assertion marker, [S よ], 2.c.conv
because S, [S ので, N なので, S から], 1.b.6
become, [X が Y になる "X becomes Y"], 5.c.1
blunt confirmation, [な], 2.a.conv
by S, [V までに], 2.c.4
by N; X by N, [N によって／N による], 8.c.1
Can/Could I receive your favor of V-ing?, [V てもらえる／いただける], 5.f.2
can't really V, [V わけにはいかない], 10.b.2
can't really even V, [わけにもいかない], 10.b.2
causative, [V(さ)せる "make/let someone V"], 9.a.1
clause modifier, [clause + noun], 1.b.1
comparative, [X は Y より／X のほう "X is more ... than Y; the side of X"], 8.c.3
conditional, [V/A/N たら "if..."], 2.a.2
confirmation marker, [X ね], 1.c.conv
Could I (humbly) receive your favor of V-ing?, [お V いただける], 5.f.2
く-form of A, [A く], 1.c.3

D - E - F

て-forms, [V て], 1.b.3; [A くて], 1.c.3; [N で], 1.c.3
depending on N, [N しだい], 10.c.2; [N によって], 10.a.2
do something in advance for subsequent use or for the time being, [V ておく], 4.a.4
does not appear to V, [V-stem そうにない], 7.d.1
due to X, [X のせいで], 11.c.1
during N, [N のあいだ(に)], 4.b.1
embedded question, [S か, X か Y か, S かどうか], 2.c.1
emphatic marker, [N こそ], 2.a.conv
feminine marker, [S わ], 2.c.conv
finally (favorable outcome), [やっと], 11.c.2
finally, [とうとう], 11.c.2
furthermore, [S1 し, S2], 10.a.3

G - H - I

give (to me); give (me) the favor of V-ing, [くれる／V てくれる], 4.e.1
give (to others); give the favor of V-ing, [あげる／V てあげる], 4.e.1
go to V; go for V-ing, [V-stem に行く], 6.a.5
have V-ed completely; V unintentionally, [V てしまう], 5.g.1
honorific of いう, [おっしゃいます], 4.c.1
honorific request, [お V 下さい], 2.d.1
honorific verb, お V です, 1.c.2
honorific passive, 8.c.5
honorific of N する, [N なさる], 1.b.2
honorific of います, [おられます "stay/is located"], 3.a.1
honorific verb, [お V になります], 3.c.1
honorific of くれる, [下さる／V て下さる "give (to me) / V (for me)"], 3.f.4
honorific of しっている, [ごぞんじです, "know"], 3.c.1
honorific of 言う, [おっしゃいます "say/pronounce"], 2.e.1
honorific verb, [お V です、お V でございます、お V でいらっしゃいます], 3.d.1
honorific of います, [いらっしゃいます "stay/is located"], 3.a.1
honorific of いる／来る／行く, [いらっしゃる], 4.a.1
honorific of です, [でいらっしゃいます], 3.b.1
how to V; a way of V-ing, [V-stem かた], 5.f.1
humble of 読む, [X とお読みする "is pronounced as X"], 2.e.1
humble of あげる, [さしあげる／V てさしあげる "give (to others) / V (for others)"], 3.f.4
humble of V ている, [V ております, "is V-ing/has V-ed"], 1.a.1
humble of N する, [N いたします], 1.b.2
humble of もらう, [いただく／V ていただく "receive / receive (other's favor of V-ing)"], 3.f.5
humble of 行く／来る, [まいります "come, go"], 4.a.1
humble of 言う, [もうします "say/pronounce"], 1.a.1, 2.e.1
humble of いる, [おります "is located"], 1.a.1
humble verb (for other's benefit), [お V します、お N します], 1.e.1
I wonder if S, [S かと思う／かんがえる], 6.c.2
I heard that S, [S + そうだ], 7.b.3
I think it would be nice if..., [conditional + (いい)と思う], 7.b.1
If it is all right with you, [おさしつかえなければ], 3.f.2
if/when S1, S2, [non-past-S1 と, S2], 7.c.1
if it's that S1, then S2, [S1 なら, S2], 7.e.3
in X-like way; X-ly, [X てきに, adverbial form], 5.d.1
in order to V; for the purpose of V-ing, [V-stem に; V のに; V ために], 4.c.2
in X-like way, [X ふうに V "V in X-like way"], 10.c.4
in order to V; for the purpose of V-ing, [する (の) に], 8.c.2
in case S, [S ばあい], 9.c.1
in such a way, [S ようになっている "it's made in such a way that S"], 9.b.3
including N; N is attached, [N つき], 10.a.1
intend to V, [V つもりだ], 2.c.2
intransitive verb, [e.g., X がかわる "X changes, is switched"], 3.b.2

is already going to V / has already V-ed / is already V-ing, [もう + AFF], 3.e.1
is still going to V / is still V-ing, [まだ + AFF], 3.e.1
is not going to V any more / is not V-ing any more, [もう + NEG], 3.e.1
it turns out that S; it is decided that S, [S ことになる], 6.c.1
it does not appear to be Adj/N, [Adj/N じゃなさそうだ], 8.a.1
it seems S; it seems like N/な-adj, [S ようだ／N のようだ／な-adj なようだ], 7.e.1
it appears Adj, [Adj そうだ], 8.a.1
it's that..., [S んです, N なんです], 1.c

J - K - L

just V-ed, [V-past ばかり], 9.c.3
know, [しっています], 3.c.1
like, [N がすき, V のがすき], 1.d.1
like N, [N1 ふうの N2 "N1-like N2"], 10.c.4
listing elements, [X など／なんか], 2.b.1

M - N - O

make X Y; decide on Y, [X を Y にする／なさる], 5.c.1
make/let (someone) V, [causative V て + あげる／くれる／もらう], 9.a.2
mostly, for the most part/time, [N ばかり／V てばかり／V-nonpast ばかり], 9.c.2
N that has just V-ed, [V-past ばかりの N], 11.a.2
NEG request, "Don't V"; "without V-ing", [V ないで], 6.b.4
no matter what/when/who...[wh + gerund + も], 11.b.2
nominalization of N する, [N (particle)の N], 4.d.1
nothing, no one, never, etc., [wh + も + NEG], 6.a.3
object marker, [N を], 1.a.conv
object marker of すき, きらい, etc., [X が], 1.a.conv
only/just; nothing else but, [S だけ/な-adj なだけ], 9.b.1
other person wants to V, [V たがっている], 6.a.6

P - Q - R

passive, [V(ら)れる], 8.b.1
permission not to V, [V なくてもいい "one doesn't have to V, it is all right even if one does not V"], 5.b.1
permission to V, [V てもいい "one may V; it is all right to V], 5.b.1
personal title, [name + くん/さま], 2.a.1
phone call from X, [X から電話です], 3.d.4
plain volitional of V, [V よう "let's V; I/we shall V"], 4.a.2
plan of N, [N のよていだ], 3.f.3
plan to V, [V よていだ], 3.f.3
play the role of X; work as X, [role をしている], 2.d.3
polite copula gerund/polite ます gerund, [N でして／V まして], 3.f.1
polite conditional, [でしたら], 5.e.conv
polite of です, [でございます], 3.b.1
polite question/request, [V ますでしょうか], 7.a.3
possibly X, [X かもしれない], 11.a.3
potential verb, [e.g., 食べられる, いける], 1.b.5
potential, [V ことができる "be able to V; is possible to V"], 9.b.2
probably S/N, [S だろう/N だろうと思う], 2.c.3

provided S; if S, [provisional (V ば)], 7.c.2
provisional of potential verbs [できれば "if/provided that X can V"], 11.b.3
provisional [ごめいわくでなければ "provided/if not too intrusive"], 3.d.2
rather than saying that...; (What do you mean) if you say..., [というより／というと], 8.c.4
receives the favor of V-ing; V for (the speaker), [もらう/V てもらう], 4.a.3
reporting, [S とのこと／S ということ], 4.a.1

S - T - U

sample-listing, [X や Y], 2.b.1
someone's N; N from someone, etc., [wh + かの + N], 7.b.2
something, someone, someday, etc., [wh + か], 6.a.3
strong resolve, [S ぞ], 11.a.conv
subject marker, [が], 1.a.conv
subject marker in a clause modifier, [N の], 1.b.1
takes (time/money) for V-ing, [V-plain のに (time/money) がかかる], 5.e.1
takes (time/money) for N, [N に (time/money) がかかる], 5.e.1
tell (someone) to V, [V よう(に) 言う／つたえる／もうしつたえる], 3.e.2
thanks to X, [X のおかげで], 11.c.1
that S, [S こと], 4.d.2
the most/number one... among, [の中で／のうちで一番], 9.a.3
things like X, [X とか], 2.b.1
think of V-ing, [しようと思う／思っている], 6.a.2
this kind of N; N like this, [こんなふうな N], 10.c.4
to the effect that X, [X というふうに], 10.c.4
topic/contrast marker, [N は], 1.a.conv
toward N/against N, [N にたいして], 10.c.1
transitive verb, [e.g., X をかわる "switch X"], 3.b.2
transitive verbs vs. intransitive verbs, 6.a.1
transitive verb, [かえる "change X"], 3.b.2
try to V; V and see, [V てみる／V-plain-present ようにする], 6.b.2, 6.b.3
try to V (without success), [V-volitional ようとする], 6.c.3
until S, [S まで], 2.a.3

V - W - X

V and see, try to V [V てみる／V-plain ようにする], 6.b.2, 6.b.3
V toward me/us, [V てくる], 11.a.1
V-ed deliberately, [V てある], 6.c.4
V-stem, [e.g., のみ], 1.b.3
V2 in the manner of V1; V2 so that V1; V2 in such a way that V1, [V1 ように V2], 6.b.3
want (others) to V, [V て + ほしい], 7.d.2
want to V, [V たい], 1.b.4
When S1, (this led to) S2, [S1 ところ, S2 しだいです], 7.a.1
while N, [N のところ], 3.d.3; [V ているあいだ(に)], 4.b.1
while S, [S ところ], 3.d.3
willing toward X, [X にのりきだ], 10.c.3
with regard to N, [N にかんして], 10.c.1
work for [place], [place につとめる], 1.c.1
work at [place], [place ではたらく], 1.c.1
X-like, [X てきな], 5.d.1

Appendix E: Grammar Index (English Headers/Appearance Order)

Chapter 1

subject marker, [が], 1.a.conv
topic/contrast marker, [N は], 1.a.conv
object marker, [N を], 1.a.conv
confirmation marker, [X ね], 1.c.conv
object marker of 好き, きらい, etc., [X が], 1.a.conv
humble of 言う, [もうします "say"], 1.a.1
humble of いる, [おります "is located"], 1.a.1
humble of V ている, [V ております, "is V-ing/has V-ed"], 1.a.1
about N, regarding N, [N について], 1.a.2
clause modifier, [clause + noun], 1.b.1
subject marker in a clause modifier, [N の], 1.b.1
humble of N する, [N いたします], 1.b.2
honorific of N する, [N なさる], 1.b.2
て-form of V, [V て], 1.b.3
V-stem, [e.g., 飲み], 1.b.3
want to V, [V たい], 1.b.4
potential verb, [e.g., たべられる, いける], 1.b.5
because S, [S ので, N なので, S から], 1.b.6
work for [place], [place につとめる], 1.c.1
work at [place], [place ではたらく], 1.c.1
honorific verb, お V です, 1.c.2
て-form of A, [A くて], 1.c.3
く-form of A, [A く], 1.c.3
て-form of N, [N で], 1.c.3
like, [N が好き, V のが好き], 1.d.1
humble verb (for other's benefit), [お V します, お N します], 1.e.1
it's that..., [S んです, N なんです], 1.c

Chapter 2

blunt confirmation, [な], 2.a.conv
emphatic marker, [N こそ], 2.a.conv
personal title, [name + くん/さま], 2.a.1
conditional, [V/A/N たら "if..."], 2.a.2
until S, [S まで], 2.a.3
listing elements, [X など/なんか], 2.b.1
things like X, [X とか], 2.b.1
sample-listing, [X や Y], 2.b.1
assertion marker, [S よ], 2.c.conv
feminine marker, [S わ], 2.c.conv
embedded question, [S か, X か Y か, S かどうか], 2.c.1
intend to V, [V つもりだ], 2.c.2
probably S/N, [S だろう/N だろうと思う], 2.c.3
by S, [V までに], 2.c.4
honorific request, [お V 下さい], 2.d.1
play the role of X; work as X, [role をしている], 2.d.3
humble of 読む, [X とおよみする "is pronounced as X"], 2.e.1
honorific of 言う, [おっしゃいます "say/pronounce"], 2.e.1
humble of 言う, [もうします "to say/pronounce"], 2.e.1
approximation for time, [ごろ], 2.gr.5

Chapter 3

honorific of います, [おられます "stay/is located"], 3.a.1
honorific of います, [いらっしゃいます "stay/is located"], 3.a.1
honorific of です, [でいらっしゃいます], 3.b.1
polite of です, [でございます], 3.b.1
transitive verb, [e.g., X をかわる "switch X"], 3.b.2
intransitive verb, [e.g., X がかわる "X changes, is switched"], 3.b.2
transitive verb, [かえる "change X"], 3.b.2
honorific verb, [お V になります], 3.c.1
know, [しっています], 3.c.1
honorific of しっている, [ごぞんじです, "know"], 3.c.1
honorific verb, [お V です, お V でございます, お V でいらっしゃいます], 3.d.1
provisional [ごめいわくでなければ "provided/if not too intrusive"], 3.d.2
while S, [S ところ], 3.d.3
while N, [N のところ], 3.d.3
phone call from X, [X から電話です], 3.d.4
is already going to V / has already V-ed / is already V-ing, [もう + AFF], 3.e.1
is not going to V any more / is not V-ing any more, [もう + NEG], 3.e.1
is still going to V / is still V-ing, [まだ + AFF], 3.e.1
tell (someone) to V, [Vよう(に) 言う／つたえる／もうしつたえる], 3.e.2
polite copula gerund/polite ます gerund, [N でして／V まして], 3.f.1
If it is all right with you, [おさしつかえなければ], 3.f.2
plan to V, [V よていだ], 3.f.3
plan of N, [N のよていだ], 3.f.3
humble of あげる, [さしあげる／V てさしあげる "give (to others) / V (for others)"], 3.f.4
honorific of くれる, [下さる／V て下さる "give (to me) / V (for me)"], 3.f.4
humble of もらう, [いただく／V ていただく "receive / receive (other's favor of V-ing)"], 3.f.5

Chapter 4

reporting, [S とのこと／S ということ], 4.a.1
humble of 行く／来る, [まいります／いらっしゃいます], 4.a.1
honorific of いる／来る／行く, [いらっしゃる], 4.a.1
plain volitional of V, [V よう "let's V; I/we shall V"], 4.a.2
receives the favor of V-ing; V for (the speaker), [もらう/V てもらう], 4.a.3
do something in advance for subsequent use or for the time being, [V ておく], 4.a.4
advice, [S ものだ "it is the rule that S"], 4.a.5; [S のがあたりまえだ "It is the norm that S"], 4.a.5; [S のがじょうしきだ, "It is the common sense that S"], 4.a.5
during N, [N のあいだ(に)], 4.b.1

Chapter 5 (continued from previous)

while N, [V ているあいだ(に)], 4.b.1
in order to V; for the purpose of V-ing, [V-stem に + いく; V-plain-present ために or のに], 4.c.2
honorific of 言う, [おっしゃいます], 4.c.1
nominalization of N する, [N (particle)の N], 4.d.1
that S, [S こと], 4.d.2
give (to others); give the favor of V-ing, [あげる／V てあげる], 4.e.1
give (to me); give (me) the favor of V-ing, [くれる／V てくれる], 4.e.1

Chapter 5

a thing called X, [X って(いうの)], 5.a.1
permission to V, [V てもいい "one may V; it is all right to V"], 5.b.1
permission not to V, [V なくてもいい "one doesn't have to V, it is all right even if one does not V"], 5.b.1
make X Y; decide on Y, [X を Y にする／なさる], 5.c.1
become, [X が Y になる "X becomes Y"], 5.c.1
adverbial form; in X-like way; X-ly, [X てきに "in X-like way"], 5.d.1
X-like, [X てきな], 5.d.1
polite conditional, [でしたら], 5.e.conv
takes (time/money) for N, [N に (time/money) がかかる], 5.e.1
takes (time/money) for V-ing, [V-plain のに (time/money) がかかる], 5.e.1
how to V; a way of V-ing, [V-stem かた], 5.f.1
Can/Could I receive your favor of V-ing?, [V てもらえる／いただける], 5.f.2
Could I (humbly) receive your favor of V-ing?, [お V いただける], 5.f.2
have V-ed completely; have V-ed without my intention, [V てしまう], 5.g.1

Chapter 6

transitive verbs vs. intransitive verbs, 6.a.1
think of V-ing, [しようと思う／思っている], 6.a.2, 6.c.3
something, someone, someday, etc., [wh + か], 6.a.3
nothing, no one, never, etc., [wh + も + NEG], 6.a.3
after V-ing, [V てから], 6.a.4
go to V; go for V-ing, [V-stem に行く], 6.a.5
other person wants to V, [V たがっている], 6.a.6
after N; after V-ing, [N のあと(で)／V たあと(で)], 6.b.1
try to V; V and see, [V てみる／V ようにする], 6.b.2, 6.b.3
V2 in the manner of V1; V2 so that V1; V2 in such a way that V1, [V1 ように V2], 6.b.3
NEG request, "Don't V"; "without V-ing", [V ないで], 6.b.4
it turns out that S; it is decided that S, [S ことになる], 6.c.1
I wonder if S, [S かと思う／かんがえる], 6.c.2
try to V (without success), [V-volitional ようとする], 6.c.3
V-ed deliberately, [V てある], 6.c.4

Chapter 7

When S1, (this led to) S2, [S1 ところ、S2 しだいです], 7.a.1
as soon as having V-ed, [V-stem + しだい], 7.a.2
polite question/request, [V ますでしょうか], 7.a.3
I think it would be nice if..., [conditional + (いい)とおもう], 7.b.1
someone's N; N from someone, etc., [wh + かの + N], 7.b.2
I heard that S, [S + そうだ], 7.b.3
if/when S1, S2, [non-past-S1 と、S2], 7.c.1
provided S; if S, [provisional (V ば)], 7.c.2
appears to V, [V-stem + そうだ], 7.d.1
does not appear to V, [V-stem そうにない], 7.d.1
want (others) to V, [V て + ほしい], 7.d.2
it seems S; it seems like N/な-adj, [S ようだ／N のようだ／な-adj なようだ], 7.e.1
about, [N1 についての N2 "N2 about N1"], 7.e.2
if it's that S1, then S2, [S1 なら、S2], 7.e.3

Chapter 8

it appears Adj, [Adj そうだ], 8.a.1
it does not appear to be Adj/N, [Adj／N じゃなさそうだ], 8.a.1
passive, [V(ら)れる], 8.b.1
by N; X by N, [N によって／N による], 8.c.1
in order to V; for the purpose of V-ing, [する (の) に], 8.c.2
comparative, [X は Y より／X のほう "X is more ... than Y; the side of X"], 8.c.3
rather than saying that...; (What do you mean) if you say..., [というより／というと], 8.c.4
honorific passive, 8.c.5

Chapter 9

causative, [V(さ)せる "make/let someone V"], 9.a.1
make/let (someone) V, [causative V て + あげる／くれる／もらう], 9.a.2
the most/number one... among, [の中で／のうちで一番], 9.a.3
only/just; nothing else but, [S だけ/な-adj なだけ], 9.b.1
potential, [V ことができる "be able to V; is possible to V"], 9.b.2
in such a way, [S ようになっている "it's made in such a way that S"], 9.b.3
in case S, [S ばあい], 9.c.1
mostly, for the most part/time, [N ばかり／V てばかり／V-nonpast ばかり], 9.c.2
just V-ed, [V-past ばかり], 9.c.3
about to V; have just V-ed; in the middle of V-ing, [V-nonpast ところ／V-past ところ／V ているところ], 9.c.4

Chapter 10

including N; N is attached, [N つき], 10.a.1
depending on N, [N によって], 10.a.2; [N しだい], 10.c.2
furthermore, [S1 し、S2], 10.a.3
as N; in the capacity of N, [N として], 10.b.1
can't really V, [V わけにはいかない], 10.b.2
can't really even V, [わけにもいかない], 10.b.2
with regard to N, [N にかんして], 10.c.1
toward N/against N, [N にたいして], 10.c.1
willing toward X, [X にのりきだ], 10.c.3
this kind of N; N like this, [こんなふうな N], 10.c.4
in X-like way, [X ふうに V "V in X-like way"], 10.c.4
to the effect that X, [X というふうに], 10.c.4
like N, [N1 ふうの N2 "N1-like N2"], 10.c.4

Chapter 11

strong resolve, [S ぞ], 11.a.conv
V toward me/us, [V てくる], 11.a.1
N that has just V-ed, [V-past ばかりの N], 11.a.2
possibly X, [X かもしれない], 11.a.3
approximate numbers, [に、さん "two or three"], 11.b.1
no matter what/when/who...[wh + gerund + も], 11.b.2
provisional of potential verbs [できれば "if/provided that X can V"], 11.b.3
thanks to X, [X のおかげで], 11.c.1
due to X, [X のせいで], 11.c.1
finally (favorable outcome), [やっと], 11.c.2
finally, [とうとう], 11.c.2

Appendix F: Grammar Index (Japanese Headers/あいうえお Order)

あ - お

あげる／V てあげる, [give (to others); give the favor of V-ing], 4.e.1

あと, [N のあと(で)／V たあと(で) "after N; after V-ing"], 6.b.1

いただく／V ていただく, [humble of もらう] receive / receive (other's favor of V-ing), 3.f.5

いつ〜ても, [wh + gerund + も, "no matter when; whenever"], 11.b.2

いつか, [wh + か, "someday"], 6.a.3

いつかの, [wh + かの + N, "N of someday"], 7.b.2

いつも〜ない, [wh + も + NEG, "at no time"], 6.a.3

いらっしゃいます, [honorific of います "stay/is located"], 3.a.1

いらっしゃる, [honorific of いる／来る／行く], 4.a.1

お N します, [humble verb (for other's benefit)], 1.e.1

お V いただける, [Lit. Could I (humbly) receive your favor of V-ing?], 5.f.2

お V 下さい, [honorific request], 2.d.1

お V します, [humble verb (for other's benefit)], 1.e.1

お V でいらっしゃいます, [honorific verb], 3.d.1

お V でございます, [honorific verb], 3.d.1

お V です, [honorific verb], 3.d.1

お V です, [honorific verbs], 1.c.2

お V になります, [honorific verb], 3.c.1

おかげで, [X のおかげで "thanks to X"], 11.c.1

おさしつかえなければ, [If it is all right with you], 3.f.2

おっしゃいます, [honorific of いう "to say/pronounce"], 2.e.1

おっしゃいます, [honorific of いう], 4.c.1

お読みする, [humble of 読む: X とお読みする "is pronounced as X"], 2.e.1

おられます, [honorific of います "stay/is located"], 3.a.1

おります, [humble of いる], 1.a.1

か - こ

が, [object marker of 好き, きらい, potential V, etc.], 1.a.conv

が, [subject marker], 1.a.conv

かえる, [transitive verb, "change X"], 3.b.2

かと思う／かんがえる, [S かと思う／かんがえる "I wonder if S"], 6.c.2

かもしれない, [possibly X], 11.a.3 かわる, [transitive verb, "change X", intransitive verb, "X changes"], 3.b.2

く, [A く, く-form of A], 1.c.3

下さる／V て下さる, [honorific of くれる "give (to me) / V (for me)"], 3.f.4

くて, [A くて, て-form of A], 1.c.3

くれる／V てくれる, [give (to me); give (me) the favor of V-ing], 4.e.1

くん, さま, [personal title: name + くん/さま], 2.a.1

こそ, [emphatic marker], 2.a.conv

ごぞんじです, [honorific of しっている "know"], 3.c.1

こと, [S こと "that S"], 4.d.2

ことができる, [potential: V ことができる "be able to V; is possible to V"], 9.b.2

ことになる, [S ことになる "it turns out that S; it is decided that S"], 6.c.1

ごめいわくでなければ, [provisional "provided/if not too intrusive"], 3.d.2

ごろ, [approximation for time], 2.gr.5

こんなふうな N, [this kind of N; N like this], 10.c.4

さ - そ

さしあげる／V てさしあげる, [humble of あげる "give (to others) / V (for others)"], 3.f.4

しだい [V-stem + しだい "as soon as having V-ed"], 7.a.2

しっています, [know], 3.c.1

している, [role をしている "play the role of X; work as X"], 2.d.3

じゃなさそうだ, [Adj／N じゃなさそうだ "it does not appear to be Adj/N"], 8.a.1

しようと思う／思っている, [think of V-ing], 6.a.2

しようとする, [try to V (without success)], 6.c.3

する (の) に, [in order to V; for the purpose of V-ing], 8.c.2

する／なさる, [X を Y にする／なさる, "make X Y; decide on Y"], 5.c.1

せいで, [X のせいで "due to X"], 11.c.1

ぞ, [strong resolve], 11.a.conv

そうだ, [Adj そうだ "it appears Adj"], 8.a.1

そうだ, [S + そうだ "I heard that S"], 7.b.3

そうだ, [V-stem + そうだ "appears to V"], 7.d.1

そうにない, [V-stem そうにない "does not appear to V"], 7.d.1

た - と

たがっている, [V たがっている "(other person) wants to V"], 6.a.6

だけ, [S だけ/な-adj なだけ "only/just S; nothing else but N"], 9.b.1

ため(に), [V-plain-present ため(に): "for the purpose of V-ing"], 4.c.2

たら, [conditional: V/A/N たら "if..."], 2.a.2

だれ〜ても, [wh + gerund + も, "no matter who; whoever"], 11.b.2

だれか, [wh + か, "someone"], 6.a.3

だれかの, [wh + かの + N, "someone's N"], 7.b.2

だれも〜ない, [wh + も + NEG, "no one"], 6.a.3

だろう(と思う), [probably], 2.c.3

つとめる, [place につとめる "work for (place)"], 1.c.1

つもり, [V つもりだ "intend to V"], 2.c.2 でいらっしゃいます, [honorific of です], 3.b.1

できれば, [provisional of potential verbs "if/provided that X can V"], 11.b.3

でございます, [polite of です], 3.b.1

でしたら, [polite conditional], 5.e.conv

てきな, [X てきな, "X-like"], 5.d.1

てきに, [X てきに, adverbial form "in X-like way"], 5.d.1

でんわです, [X から電話です "X is on the phone"], 3.d.4

って(いう), [X って(いうの), "a thing called X"], 5.a.1
というふうに, [X というふうに, "to the effect that X"], 10.c.4
というより／というと, [rather than saying that...; What do you mean if you say...], 8.c.4
とうとう, [finally], 11.c.2
とか, [X とか "things like X"], 2.b.1
どこ(に／で)も～ない, [wh + も + NEG, "nowhere"], 6.a.3
どこ～ても, [wh + gerund + も, "no matter where; wherever"], 11.b.2
どこか, [wh + か, "somewhere"], 6.a.3
どこかの, [wh + かの + N, "N of somewhere"], 7.b.2
ところ, [S ところ "while S"; N のところ "while N"], 3.d.3
ところ／しだい, [S1 ところ、S2 しだいです "When S1, (this led to) S2"], 7.a.1

な－の

な, [blunt confirmation], 2.a.conv
など／なんか, [X など／なんか "X and so on"], 2.b.1
なに～ても, [wh + gerund + も, "no matter what; whatever"], 11.b.2
なにか, [wh + か, "something"], 6.a.3
なにかの, [wh + かの + N, "N of something"], 7.b.2
なにも～ない, [wh + も + NEG, "nothing"], 6.a.3
なら, [S1 なら, S2 "if it's that S1, then S2"], 7.e.3
なる, [X が Y になる, "X becomes Y"], 5.c.1
二、三, [approximate numbers], 11.b.1
についての, [N1 についての N2 "N2 about N1"], 7.e.2
ね, [confirmation marker], 1.c.conv
の, [subject marker in a clause modifier], 1.b.1
のが好き, [V のが好き, "like to V"], 1.d.1
の中で／のうちで一番, [the most... among ...], 9.a.3
のりき, [X にのりきだ, "is willing toward X"], 10.c.3

は－ほ

は, [topic/contrast marker], 1.a.conv
ばあい, [S ばあい "in case S"], 9.c.1
はたらく, [place ではたらく "work at (place)"], 1.c.1
ふうに, [X ふうに V "V in X-like way"], 10.c.4

ま－も

まいります／いらっしゃいます, [humble of 行く／来る], 4.a.1
まして, [V まして, て-form of V ます], 3.f.1
ますでしょうか, [V ますでしょうか, polite question/request], 7.a.3
まだ + NEG, [is still not going to V / has not V-ed yet], 3.e.1
まで, [S まで "until S"], 2.a.3
までに, [S までに "by S"], 2.c.4
もう + AFF, [is already going to V / has already V-ed / is already V-ing], 3.e.1
もう + NEG, [is not going to V any more / is not V-ing any more], 3.e.1
もうします, [humble of 言う "to say/pronounce"], 2.e.1
もうします, [humble of 言う], 1.a.1
もらう/V てもらう, [receives the favor of V-ing; V for (the speaker)], 4.a.3

や－よ

や, [sample-listing: X や Y], 2.b.1
やっと, [finally (favorable outcome)], 11.c.2 よ, [assertion marker], 2.c.conv
よう, [V よう, plain volitional of V "let's V; I/we shall V"], 4.a.2
ようだ, [S ようだ／N のようだ／な-adj なようだ "it seems S; it seems like N/な-adj"], 7.e.1
ように [V1 ように V2 "V2 in the manner of V1; V2 so that V1; V2 in such a way that V1"／V-plain ようにする "try to V"], 6.b.3
ように [Vよう(に) 言う／つたえる／もうしつたえる "tell (someone) to V"], 3.e.2
ようになっている, [S ようになっている "it's made in such a way that S"], 9.b.3
よてい [V よていだ "plan to V"], 3.f.3
より／のほう, [comparative: X は Y より／X のほう "X is more ... than Y; the side of X"], 8.c.3

わ－ん

わ, [feminine marker], 2.c.conv
わけにはいかない, [can't really V], 10.b.2
わけにもいかない, [can't really even V], 10.b.2
を, [object marker], 1.a.conv
んです, [S んです, N なんです "It's that..."], 1.c

Appendix G: Grammar Index (Japanese Headers/Appearance Order)

Chapter 1

が, [subject marker], 1.a.conv
は, [topic/contrast marker], 1.a.conv
を, [object marker], 1.a.conv
ね, [confirmation marker], 1.c.conv
が, [object marker of 好き, きらい, potential V, etc.], 1.a.conv
もうします, [humble of 言う], 1.a.1
おります, [humble of いる], 1.a.1
V ております, [humble of V ている], 1.a.1
N について, about N, regarding N, 1.a.2
の, [subject marker in a clause modifier], 1.b.1
N いたします, [humble of N する], 1.b.2
N なさる, [honorific of N する], 1.b.2
V て, [て-form of V], 1.b.3
V たい, want to V, 1.b.4
V(ら)れる, [potential verb], 1.b.5
S ので, 1.b.6
S から, 1.b.6
N なので, 1.b.6
つとめる, [place につとめる "work for (place)"], 1.c.1
はたらく, [place ではたらく "work at (place)"], 1.c.1
お V です, [honorific verbs], 1.c.2
A くて, [て-form of A], 1.c.3
A く, [く-form of A], 1.c.3
N で, [て-form of N], 1.c.3
N が好き, like N, 1.d.1
V のが好き, like to V, 1.d.1
お V します, [humble verb (for other's benefit)], 1.e.1
お N します, [humble verb (for other's benefit)], 1.e.1
んです, [S んです, N なんです "It's that..."], 1.c

Chapter 2

な, [blunt confirmation], 2.a.conv
こそ, [emphatic marker], 2.a.conv
くん, さま, [personal title: name + くん/さま], 2.a.1
たら, [conditional: V/A/N たら "if..."], 2.a.2
まで, [S まで "until S"], 2.a.3
など/なんか, [X など/なんか "X and so on"], 2.b.1
とか, [X とか "things like X"], 2.b.1
や, [sample-listing: X や Y], 2.b.1
よ, [assertion marker], 2.c.conv
わ, [feminine marker], 2.c.conv
S か, X か Y か, S かどうか, [embedded question], 2.c.1
つもり, [V つもりだ "intend to V"], 2.c.2
だろう(とおもう), [probably], 2.c.3
V までに, [by S], 2.c.4
お V 下さい, [honorific request], 2.d.1
している, [role をしている "play the role of X; work as X"], 2.d.3
およみする, [humble of よむ: X とおよみする "is pronounced as X"], 2.e.1
おっしゃいます, [honorific of 言う "to say/pronounce"], 2.e.1
もうします, [humble of 言う "to say/pronounce"], 2.e.1
ごろ, [approximation for time], 2.gr.5

Chapter 3

おられます, [honorific of います "stay/is located"], 3.a.1
いらっしゃいます, [honorific of います "stay/is located"], 3.a.1
でいらっしゃいます, [honorific of です], 3.b.1
でございます, [polite of です], 3.b.1
かわる, [transitive verb, "change X", intransitive verb, "X changes"], 3.b.2
かえる, [transitive verb, "change X"], 3.b.2
お V になります, [honorific verb], 3.c.1
しっています, [know], 3.c.1
ごぞんじです, [honorific of しっている "know"], 3.c.1
お V です, [honorific verb], 3.d.1
お V でございます, [honorific verb], 3.d.1
お V でいらっしゃいます, [honorific verb], 3.d.1
ごめいわくでなければ, [provisional "provided/if not too intrusive"], 3.d.2
ところ, [S ところ "while S"; N のところ "while N"], 3.d.3
電話です, [X から電話です "X is on the phone"], 3.d.4
もう + AFF, [is already going to V / has already V-ed / is already V-ing], 3.e.1
もう + NEG, [is not going to V any more / is not V-ing any more], 3.e.1
まだ + NEG, [is still not going to V / has not V-ed yet], 3.e.1
ように [V よう(に) 言う／つたえる／もうしつたえる "tell (someone) to V"], 3.e.2
N でして, polite copula gerund, 3.f.1
V まして, polite ます gerund, 3.f.1
おさしつかえなければ, [If it is all right with you], 3.f.2
よてい [V よていだ "plan to V"], 3.f.3
N のよていだ, [N is the plan], 3.f.3
さしあげる／V てさしあげる, [humble of あげる "give (to others) / V (for others)"], 3.f.4
下さる／V て下さる, [honorific of くれる "give (to me) / V (for me)"], 3.f.4
いただく／V ていただく, [humble of もらう] receive / receive (other's favor of V-ing), 3.f.5

Chapter 4

S とのこと／S ということ, [reporting], 4.a.1
まいります／いらっしゃいます, [humble of いく／くる], 4.a.1
いらっしゃる, [honorific of いる／くる／いく], 4.a.1
V よう, [plain volitional of V "let's V; I/we shall V"], 4.a.2
もらう/V てもらう, [receives the favor of V-ing; V for (the speaker)], 4.a.3

V ておく, [do something in advance for subsequent use or for the time being], 4.a.4
S ものだ, [It is the rule that S], 4.a.5
S のがあたりまえだ, [advice, "It is the norm that S"], 4.a.5
S のがじょうしきだ, [advice, "It is the common sense that S"], 4.a.5
N のあいだ(に), during N, 4.b.1
V ているあいだ(に), while N, 4.b.1
V-stem に; V のに; V ために, [in order to V; for the purpose of V-ing], 4.c.2
おっしゃいます, [honorific of いう], 4.c.1
N (particle)の N, [nominalization of N する], 4.d.1
こと, [S こと "that S"], 4.d.2
あげる／V てあげる, [give (to others); give the favor of V-ing], 4.e.1
くれる／V てくれる, [give (to me); give (me) the favor of V-ing], 4.e.1

Chapter 5

X って(いうの), a thing called X, 5.a.1
V てもいい, [permission to V: "one may V; it is all right to V"], 5.b.1
V なくてもいい, [permission not to V: "one doesn't have to V, it is all right even if one does not V"], 5.b.1
X を Y にする／なさる, [make X Y; decide on Y], 5.c.1
X が Y になる, [X becomes Y], 5.c.1
X てきに, [adverbial form "in X-like way"], 5.d.1
X てきな, [X-like], 5.d.1
でしたら, [polite conditional], 5.e.conv
N に (time/money) がかかる, [takes (time/money) for N], 5.e.1
V-plain のに (time/money) がかかる, [takes (time/money) for V-ing], 5.e.1
V-stem かた, [how to V; a way of V-ing], 5.f.1
V てもらえる／いただける, [Lit. Can/Could I receive your favor of V-ing?], 5.f.2
お V いただける, [Lit. Could I (humbly) receive your favor of V-ing?], 5.f.2
V てしまう, [have V-ed completely; have V-ed without my intention], 5.g.1

Chapter 6

しようと思う／思っている, [think of V-ing], 6.a.2, 6.c.3
wh + か, [something, someone, someday, etc.], 6.a.3
wh + も + NEG, [nothing, no one, never, etc.], 6.a.3
V てから, [after V-ing], 6.a.4
V-stem に行く, [go to V; go for V-ing], 6.a.5
たがっている, [V たがっている "(other person) wants to V"], 6.a.6
あと, [N のあと(で)／V たあと(で) "after N; after V-ing"], 6.b.1
V てみる, [try to V; V and see], 6.b.2
ように [V1 ように V2 "V2 in the manner of V1; V2 so that V1; V2 in such a way that V1"／V ようにする "try to V"], 6.b.3
V ないで, [NEG request, "Don't V"; "without V-ing"], 6.b.4
ことになる, [S ことになる "it turns out that S; it is decided that S"], 6.c.1

かと思う／かんがえる, [S かと思う／かんがえる "I wonder if S"], 6.c.2
しようとする, [try to V (without success)], 6.c.3
V てある, [V-ed deliberately], 6.c.4

Chapter 7

ところ／しだい, [S1 ところ、S2 しだいです "When S1, (this led to) S2"], 7.a.1
しだい [V-stem + しだい "as soon as having V-ed"], 7.a.2
V ますでしょうか, [polite question/request], 7.a.3
conditional + (いい)と思う, [I think it would be nice if...], 7.b.1
wh + かの + N, [someone's N; N from someone, etc.], 7.b.2
そうだ, [S + そうだ "I heard that S"], 7.b.3
non-past-S1 と、S2, [if/when S1, S2], 7.c.1
provisional (V ば), [provided S; if S], 7.c.2
そうだ, [V-stem + そうだ "appears to V"], 7.d.1
そうにない, [V-stem そうにない "does not appear to V"], 7.d.1
V て + ほしい, [want (others) to V], 7.d.2
ようだ, [S ようだ／N のようだ／な-adj なようだ "it seems S; it seems like N/な-adj"], 7.e.1
についての, [N1 についての N2 "N2 about N1"], 7.e.2
なら, [S1 なら、S2 "if it's that S1, then S2"], 7.e.3

Chapter 8

そうだ, [Adj そうだ "it appears Adj"], 8.a.1
じゃなさそうだ, [Adj／N じゃなさそうだ "it does not appear to be Adj/N"], 8.a.1
V(ら)れる, [passive], 8.b.1
N によって／N による, [by N; X by N], 8.c.1
する (の) に, [in order to V; for the purpose of V-ing], 8.c.2
より／のほう, [comparative: X は Y より／X のほう "X is more ... than Y; the side of X"], 8.c.3
というより／というと, [rather than saying that...; What do you mean if you say...], 8.c.4

Chapter 9

V(さ)せる, [causative, "make/let someone V"], 9.a.1
causative V て + あげる／くれる／もらう, [please make/let (someone) V], 9.a.2
の中で／のうちで一番, [the most... among ...], 9.a.3
だけ, [S だけ／な-adj なだけ "only/just S; nothing else but N"], 9.b.1
ことができる, [potential: V ことができる "be able to V; is possible to V"], 9.b.2
ようになっている, [S ようになっている "it's made in such a way that S"], 9.b.3
ばあい, [S ばあい "in case S"], 9.c.1
N ばかり／V てばかり／V-nonpast ばかり, [mostly N/V, N/V for the most part/time], 9.c.2
V-past ばかり, just V-ed, 9.c.3
V-nonpast ところ／V-past ところ／V ているところ, [is about to V; have just V-ed; in the middle of V-ing], 9.c.4

Chapter 10

N つき, [including N; N is attached], 10.a.1
N によって, [depending on N], 10.a.2
S1 し、S2, [S1 and (furthermore) S2], 10.a.3
N として, [as N; in the capacity of N], 10.b.1
わけにはいかない, [can't really V], 10.b.2
わけにもいかない, [can't really even V], 10.b.2
N にかんして, [with regard to N], 10.c.1
N にたいして, [toward N/against N], 10.c.1
N しだい, [depending on N], 10.c.2
X にのりきだ, [is willing toward X], 10.c.3
こんなふうな N, [this kind of N; N like this], 10.c.4
ふうに, [X ふうに V "V in X-like way"], 10.c.4
X というふうに, [to the effect that X], 10.c.4
N1 ふうの N2, [N1-like N2], 10.c.4

Chapter 11

ぞ, [strong resolve], 11.a.conv
V てくる, [V toward me/us], 11.a.1
V-past ばかりの N, [N that has just V-ed], 11.a.2
かもしれない, [possibly X], 11.a.3
二, 三, [approximate numbers], 11.b.1
wh + gerund + も, [no matter what/when/who...], 11.b.2
できれば, [provisional of potential verbs "if/provided that X can V"], 11.b.3
おかげで, [X のおかげで "thanks to X"], 11.c.1
せいで, [X のせいで "due to X"], 11.c.1
やっと, [finally (favorable outcome)], 11.c.2
とうとう, [finally], 11.c.2